FROM
EMANCIPATION
TO CATASTROPHE

THE RISE AND HOLOCAUST
OF HUNGARIAN JEWRY

T D Kramer

University Press of America, ® Inc.
Lanham • New York • Oxford

Copyright © 2000 by
University Press of America,® Inc.

4720 Boston Way
Lanham, Maryland 20706

12 Hid's Copse Rd.
Cumnor Hill, Oxford OX2 9JJ

Library of Congress Cataloging-in-Publication Data

Kramer, T. D.
From Emancipation to catastrophe : the rise and Holocaust of
Hungarian Jewry / T. D. Kramer.
p.   cm.
Includes bibiographical references and index.
1.   Jews—Hungary—History—19th century. 2. Jews—Hungary—
History—20th century. 3. Holocaust, Jewish (1939-1945)—Hungary. 4.
Antisemitism—Hungary—History. 5. Jews—Legal status, laws, etc.—Hungary. 6.
Hungary—Ethnic relations. I. Title
DS135.H9K73 2000   305.892' 40439—dc21   00—041753 CIP

ISBn 0-7618-1759-X (cloth: alk. ppr)

♾™ The paper used in this publication meets the minimum
requirements of American National Standard for Information
Sciences—Permanence of Paper for Printed Library Materials,
ANSI Z39.48—1984

Dedicated

To my parents, Yolanda and Jozsef
To my maternal aunt, Gizella
To my father's extended family, including his sister
and six brothers, who perished in the Hungarian Holocaust

CONTENTS

FIGURES & MAPS

ACKNOWLEDGEMENTS

As expected in endeavours of this nature, numerous individuals made significant contributions to the following research. Notable were those activists and eyewitnesses who, despite advanced years and sometimes uncertain health, extended their patience, goodwill and energy to the writer in an exemplary manner. Although many are named in the text, all deserve recognition for their wartime efforts. Especially deserving heartfelt gratitude are Dr Gyorgy Gergely, numerous Halutz activists (many still living their ideology on Israeli *kibbutzim*), and Arthur Stern. Without their co-operation and encouragement, the following study would not have been possible.

Deep appreciation, for advice and support beyond the call of duty, must also be extended to steadfast friends, relatives, archivists, publishing consultants and scholars — in the latter category, particularly Professors Alan Crown, Carole Adams, Yehuda Bauer, Shlomo Aronson and, of course, Randolph Braham, the doyen of Hungarian Holocaust scholars. Their unstinting commitment, good humour and generosity of time and spirit provided the foundation upon which this book is based.

Recognition should also be allocated to the system that granted the writer an Australian Government Post-graduate Research Award (APRA), the catalyst facilitating the PhD that, in turn, generated the basis for this book. Federal Treasurers may be interested to learn that an income staggering along the poverty line is — despite rumours to the contrary — a useful adjunct in keeping the mind focused on midnight oil. Finally, thanks are in order to Mr Charles Schlacks Jr, publisher of *The Soviet and Post-Soviet Review*, for permission to republish those portions of "The Kallay Interregnum" which first appeared in the *Review*.

T D Kramer
The University of Sydney
May 2000

ABBREVIATIONS

━━━◆◆◆▭▭▭▭▭▭▭▭▭▭▭▭▭▭▭▭▭▭▭◆◆◆━━━

AJC	American Jewish Congress
AJDC	American Jewish Joint Distribution Committee (often, the Joint)
CZA	Central Zionist Archives, Jerusalem
ET	Eichmann Trial
GGA	Gyorgy Gergely Archive
GGPA	Gyorgy Gergely Private Archive
HCNL	Hebrew Committee for National Liberation (The Bergson Group, USA)
HJJ	Hungarian Jewish Journal (*Magyar Zsidok Lapja*)
IRC	International Red Cross (sometimes ICRC)
IRD	Israel (Palestine) Rescue Delegation in Istanbul
JA	Jewish Agency for Palestine
JC	Jewish Council (*Zsido Tanacs*; *Judenrat*)
JLS	Jewish Labour Service (*Munkaszolgalat*)
JMB	Jewish Museum of Budapest
JMBA	Jewish Museum of Budapest Archives
KEOKH	Central Secretariat for the National Control of Foreigners (*Kulfoldieket Ellenorzo Orszagos Kozponti Hatosag*)
MA	Moreshet Archive
MIEFHOE	National Association of Hungarian Jewish Students (*Magyar Izraelita Egyetemi es Foiskolai Hallgatok Orszagos Egyesulete*)
MIPI	Hungarian Jewish Welfare Bureau (*Magyar Izraelitak Partfogo Irodaja*)
MoRS	Moratorium on Reality Syndrome
NAP	National Antisemitic Party
NBJWV	National Bureau of Jewish War Veterans (*Orszagos Izraelita Irodak Hadviseltek Bizottsaga*)
NG	Nürnberg Government (documents related to Nazi ministries)
NOT	National Council of People's Tribunals, the post-War Court of Appeal (*Nepbirosagok Orszagos Tanacsa*)
OMIKE	National Hungarian Jewish Cultural Society (*Orszagos Magyar Izraelita Kozmuvelodesi Egyesulet*)

OMZSA National Hungarian Jewish Assistance Campaign (*Orszagos Magyar Zsido Segito Akcio*)
ORRC Orthodox Rabbis' Rescue Committee of USA and Canada
PC Presidential Council (the JC's executive committee — Stern, Peto, Wilhelm)
PP People's Party
PRO Public Record Office, London
RAF Royal Air Force (UK)
RSHA Reich Security Head Office
SD SS security and intelligence division
USAF United States Air Force
WG Working Group (*Pracovna Skupina*, Bratislava)
WJC World Jewish Congress
WRB War Refugee Board (USA)
YA Yivo Archives, New York
YVA Yad Vashem Archives, Jerusalem

PREFACE

As indicated by its title, the following study examines the pressures upon, and the reactions of, Hungarian Jewry during the period 1848–1945. Particular attention is allocated to the Holocaust process, which was inaugurated in Hungary by the Antisemitic White Terror of 1919. In order to analyse the dilemmas and options confronting Hungarian Jewish leaders, and to comprehend their consequent responses during this epoch, the book appraises the "Jewish Question" in Hungary in broad historical context. This approach is essential to understanding why, for example, Hungary was the first European country after World War I to introduce Antisemitic legislation (the *Numerus Clausus* of 1920) yet was one of the last countries in the Nazi domain to deport her Jewish citizens.

No single volume can wholly engage, much less accomplish, such monumental objectives. Consequently, some significant matters — particularly the situation of provincial Jews, and the well-traversed courage of Raoul Wallenberg — are mentioned *en passant*, research focusing on Jewish leaders and the situation in Budapest. This choice is justified on the basis that the hierarchical Jewish leadership was concentrated in the capital, with policy flowing from Budapest to the subordinate provinces. Furthermore, in contradistinction to the fate of Budapest's Jewish community, the German Occupation of 19 March 1944 sealed the destiny of Hungary's provincial Jews in a swift and virtually unopposed manner.

As with most studies of this kind undertaken in Australia, considerable difficulties were generated by the paucity of locally available sources, the complete absence of local scholarship concerning the Hungarian Jewish community, language barriers, isolation and the tyranny of distance. Fortunately, most such problems were resolved through the time, energy and goodwill of numerous dedicated individuals and authorities throughout the world. In a small minority of cases, however, co-operation was sadly lacking — particularly from the International Red Cross in Geneva and, to a lesser extent, the Hungarian National Archives in Budapest. Needless to say, this attitude by two important repositories exacerbated difficulties arising from the wartime destruction of much critical primary material (especially the Neolog and Orthodox archives in Budapest), and the passing of many important eyewitnesses to the tragedy.

Apart from the monumental work of Professor Randolph Braham, and the valuable contributions of the late Dr Asher Cohen, original research on the Hungarian Holocaust is scarce in the English language, and of variable utility. Doubtless, a major cause is the small (and sadly declining) number of Holocaust historians with a working knowledge of the Hungarian language living in English-speaking countries. This barrier has seriously inhibited direct discussion with critical primary sources, the many non-English speaking eyewitnesses to the *Endlösung* in Hungary. Apart from interviews with such people and with recognised authorities, research for the thesis was conducted at pertinent archives throughout the world. These included (alphabetically): Central Zionist Archives (Jerusalem), Columbia University, The Hebrew University of Jerusalem (Oral Documentation Centre), Hungarian National Archives (Budapest), Jewish Museum of Budapest, Lochamei Ha'Gettaot, Moreshet (Givat Haviva), Public Record Office (London), The University of Sydney (Archive of Australian Judaica), US War Refugee Board Archives (Franklin D Roosevelt Library, New York), Wiesenthal Centre (Los Angeles), Yad Vashem, Yale University (Fortunoff Archive), YIVO (New York) and Zefat Holocaust Museum Archive (Israel). Grateful mention must also be accorded Arthur Stern and — particularly — Dr Gyorgy Gergely for unfettered access to their private files. In line with increasingly popular contemporary English practice, accents in the text are provided for German but not Hungarian words.

As appropriate, the credibility of sources is assessed throughout the book. During this process, considerable — though judicious — emphasis is accorded oral testimony, both as a valuable adjunct to documentation and, in the absence of written evidence, as a means of elucidating otherwise unfillable gaps in existing knowledge. The multifaceted and wide-ranging testimonies, affidavits, correspondence and documents of the prominent contemporary activist and leader Dr Gyorgy Gergely are an especially valuable primary resource in this regard. With little doubt, the hitherto unresearched Gergely archives — a record encompassing over 250,000 words — constitute the most comprehensive and valuable eyewitness chronicle of the Hungarian *Shoah* by a Jewish leader of the Holocaust epoch.

As final points: the doctoral dissertation that generated this book was submitted for examination on 15 May 1994[1] — fifty years to the day since mass deportation of Hungarian Jews to Auschwitz commenced; and, to the best of the writer's knowledge, there has been no other PhD, specifically on the Holocaust in Hungary, awarded in the English language.[2]

Preface: Notes

1. To be pedantic, as 15 May 1994 fell on Sunday, the thesis was submitted to the examiners on the closest prior working day — Friday 13 May.

2. This information is based on personal discussion with scholars and authorities throughout the world, and from computer searches of databases containing millions of postgraduate theses. Of the two discovered theses related to the Holocaust in Hungary, both of which are listed in the Bibliography, about half of Robert Rozett's 1987 PhD is concerned with Slovakia, whilst Bernard Klein's dissertation (*circa* 1956) was not submitted at the doctoral level.

*"The hand of fate shall also seize Hungarian Jewry.
And the later this occurs, and the stronger this Jewry becomes,
the more cruel and hard shall be the blow, which shall be delivered
with greater savagery. There is no escape."*

*Theodor Herzl to Erno Mezei, Hungarian MP
10 March 1903*

CHAPTER I

30 B.C.E. to 1918

HISTORICAL PERSPECTIVE
THE "JEWISH QUESTION" IN HUNGARY

The fate of Hungarian Jewry during the Holocaust is a particularly bitter[1] and controversial[2] chapter in the most tragic epoch of Jewish history. To comprehend why the large mass of Hungarian Jews felt they were residing in an island sanctuary, insulated from the destiny of their European co-religionists,[3] we must delve into their history as well as the collective psyches that their historical context generated. Though necessarily brief, this exposition is critical to the comprehensive understanding and evaluation of subsequent chapters.

The initial arrival of Jews in the land that is now called Hungary is a matter of some conjecture, even though the Jewish Museum of Budapest contains concrete evidence as to the antiquity of Jewish settlement — in particular, a third century CE (AD) Jewish gravestone excavated in Esztergom, central northern Hungary. Taken in conjunction with the 30 BCE observation of the famous Greek traveller Strabo, who noted that Jews "are already in every town [of the Roman Empire] and it is difficult to find a place where they have not settled",[4] it is probable that Jews reached the present territory of Hungary around a millennium[5] before the Magyar equestrian brigands.[6] Arriving at the end of the ninth century, it was this ferocious invasion that formed the basis of what the English-speaking world came to call Hungarians.[7]

The first law specifically restricting the rights of Jews in Hungary was promulgated in the Christian era, by the Synod of Szabolcs in 1092.[8] In subsequent centuries, the policy of rulers oscillated between two diametrically opposed poles: a theologically inspired "righteousness", as manifest in the mid-fourteenth century expulsion by the religious militant Lajos the Great (1342–1382),[9] and the exigencies of economic necessity, as indicated by Lajos' recall of the expelled in 1364. This bi-polar antagonism, between the proponents of a multifaceted hostility and what may be termed the pragmatic advocates of Jewish security[10] — generally motivated by a concern for the private and/or public exchequer — was a significant factor that commenced impinging on Hungarian Jewry in the Medieval era. Whilst oscillating in intensity, this duality, though not unique to Hungary, remained an abiding characteristic of that country through to the Holocaust epoch, and continues to exist at the time of writing.

Figure 1.1 **Ancient Jewish Tablets displayed in the stairwell of the Jewish Museum of Budapest. The third century B.C.E. limestone gravestone (left) was excavated in Esztergom, central northern Hungary.** (Photo: TDK, 1991)

Prior to the Age of Enlightenment, widespread legal restrictions and the prohibition on urban residence severely constricted Hungarian Jewry's social and financial activities. The Edict of Tolerance, proclaimed in 1782 by the Hapsburg Emperor Joseph II (1780–90),[11] was the first institutional attempt in post-Enlightenment Europe to formalise the security and status of Jews.[12] By granting permission to reside in towns, the Edict not only transformed the socio-economic status of Hungary's 83,000 Jews[13] but was the stimulus generating a radical realignment of their demographic and communal structure.[14] Yet despite its general thrust, not all forms of discrimination were abolished. In particular, the "Tolerance Tax" was maintained as a unique imposition on Jewry.[15]

Notwithstanding the immense authority of the Emperor, these changes generated considerable opposition from those elements of society scandalised by what they perceived as the attempted integration of Jews into the social fabric.[16] The advent of Francis I (1792–1835) led to a reaction, with sundry restrictions being reimposed; however, the main thrust of the Edict was not revoked.[17] This was in spite of widespread theological hostility being reinforced by the economically motivated antagonism of middle class residents in the Royal "Free Cities", who feared the significant inroads made by entrepreneurial Jews into what were formerly their prerogatives and monopolies.

During the Reform Period (1830–48), the "Jewish Question" became a subject of considerable public controversy and discussion, involving both parliament and the media of the day.[18] The Jews' allies, primarily the great landowners who valued their commercial enterprise and economic utility, and the liberal gentry[19] who approved of progressive ideology, were able to negate the thrust of the theological and fiscal reactionaries.[20] These allies were later joined by many Hungarian nationalists, who considered Jews favourably because of the ready Jewish propensity to adopt the Hungarian language — in stark contrast to the predominantly Swabian (German-speaking) urban middle class.[21] Janos succinctly summarises the respective attitudes and relevant ethos thus:

> "The Jewish people show daily and glorious examples of quick adaptation to the Magyar nation."[22] This eagerness compared favourably with the reluctance and traditional isolation of certain elements of the German bourgeoisie. Thus, the "real Jews," one radical journalist argued in 1848, were not the new immigrants from Poland, but the *Spiessburger* who had come from Wurttemberg and Saxony centuries before, and during all this time had not "taken the trouble" to learn the language of the "sweet motherland."[23] Confronted with the choice between a Jewish and a German bourgeoisie, most of the liberals had no hesitation to opt for the former. "Watch your way, cousin!" a popular pamphlet fulminated during the anti-Jewish riots of the German bourgeoisie in 1848, "If the nation has to choose between the two of you, it will damn well know what to do and, before long, will send you packing back to Germany." The rest of the pamphlet is a single flow of abuse, showing how philosemitism could serve as a vehicle for expressing anti-German sentiment. The author, Ignatius Benedek, called the burghers "uneducated Swabian louts, murderers, bloodsuckers, hyenas, who attempt to murder the honor of the reborn fatherland in its very cradle,....godless heathens they, who harass the poor Jew in his life, and would deny him rest even in his grave."[24]

Janos utilises poetic licence in his use of the term "philosemitism". Despite its egalitarian overtones,[25] much of the support for Jews was conditional,[26] based on what might be termed the *quid pro quo* of enlightened self-interest rather than an appreciation of the culture and philosophy of Judaism. Even such prominent supporters as Lajos Kossuth[27] argued that to gain full acceptance, Jews would have to reform their religion by abandoning their distinct particularities, especially those aspects of their faith that non-Jews perceived as contradicting the vested interests of a progressive state. Furthermore, as Janos states in his following paragraph,[28] Jews were advised[29] to renounce participation in politics and government administration, areas that were to remain the prerogatives of the declining gentry class.[30] Consequently, support for Jewry during this era may be more appropriately characterised as basically consisting of the liberals' anti-Antisemitism indirectly aided by the apathy of the conservatives to the "Jewish Question" issue.

Yet despite these significant caveats, it was this period that witnessed the genesis of the great symbiotic relationship between the Jews and "Hungarianism" as represented by the Magyar ruling class. As will be seen, it was the Jews' fervent, abiding, yet basically naive faith in the continuing coherence of this symbiosis, and consequently of the integrity of the Hungarian state, that was a central catalyst generating the devastating consequences for Hungarian Jewry during the tragic months of 1944.

This relationship was further consolidated by one of the most profound events in Hungarian history, the Revolution of 1848.[31] Representing Hungary's greatest attempt at achieving its "manifest destiny" via a bid for independence, during the initial phase of the uprising the revolutionary leadership attempted to re-orientate the country's ideology, administration, society and economy to enlightened and progressive standards.[32]

This re-orientation was enthusiastically supported by a large majority of the country's Jews, who proved their loyalty by flocking to the banner of independence.[33] Hundreds of Jewish volunteers won promotions, medals and citations from the revolutionary hierarchy, and as reward, Jewish Majors were entrusted with the command of important forts and regions.[34] Nassi states that the Hungarian Medical Corps "was a Jewish unit",[35] although Handler is more restrained, merely noting that "Jewish army doctors worked valiantly".[36] In addition, continues Nassi, Jews held posts as directors of ministries, distinguished themselves as spies, administrators, and organisers of the munitions industry of besieged Hungary, as well as being responsible for the avoidance of economic collapse. Moreover, Jewish communities donated huge amounts for the purchase of medical necessities, war material etc, and Jewish merchants were a critical factor in providing supplies and ensuring their orderly distribution.[37] Nassi succinctly assesses the situation thus: "The Austrian chief, General Haynau, was correct in declaring that the Hungarian Revolution would not have stood up [sic] without the participation of the Jews."[38]

But critically, additional to the efforts described above, in their intense enthusiasm and loyalty Jews progressed a quantum leap beyond the mere provision of men and material. Large and increasing proportions also aligned their ideology and identity with the Hungarian cause. Representative of this sector's attitude was the proclamation issued by the Jewish Leadership of Hungary and Transylvania on 17 March 1848, just two days after the outbreak of the Revolution. Their statement translates as follows:

> We are Hungarians and not Jews, not a separate nation, because we are only distinct when we pray to the Almighty in our houses of worship and express our deepest indebtedness for the benevolence bestowed on our homeland and ourselves; in every other respect we are exclusively patriots, exclusively Hungarian.[39]

The Austrian authorities, combining their inherent Antisemitism with a recognition of the Jews' manifold contributions to the uprising, resolved to impose particular retribution not only on individual Jews but also on their community as a whole. Consequently, when on 14 February 1849 the Commander of the Imperial Forces, Prince Alfred Windischgratz, issued a Proclamation against subversive activity, one-third of his statement was directed at Jews, viz:

> Finally the Buda, Pest and particularly the O-Buda Jewish communities are warned against associating with Kossuth supporters and the rebellious forces; especially as spies, suppliers of goods and the propagators of false and left-wing views that cause fear and insecurity. Any Jew caught in the above activity will be immediately and severely punished under military jurisdiction, and the Jewish community to which he belongs will be fined 20,000 pengo forints.[40]

Yet despite their outstanding contribution to the independence movement, full Jewish emancipation was only proclaimed by the Kossuth government as one of its last acts, on 28 July 1849, when defeat by the Austrian-Russian coalition had become an inevitability. And even this granting of legal equality was conditional on the Jewish community convening a rabbinical assembly and developing a reformed Judaism. Katz places this caveat in historical perspective thus:

> Other governments in granting emancipation had entertained the expectation of a concomitant reform of Judaism, and Napoleon had even threatened revocation in order to force the rabbis to act. But the direct link between emancipation and reform is unique to the Hungarian revolution and clearly reflects Kossuth's radical and ultimately self-defeating views.[41]

Once again, even *in extremis*, the Hungarian bi-polar attitude towards the Jews survived — diminished, but still a force that could not be ignored. Even the most democratically inclined Hungarians were prepared to accept the Jews as "innate" Magyars only on the basis that they abandoned their "other" particularities.

The final defeat of the revolutionary remnants, on 5 October 1849 at Komarom, permitted a counter-reaction by the Austrian victors.[42] With regard to Jews, the authoritarian military regime of Baron Julius Haynau (1786–1853)[43] not only reverted to legal and economic discrimination,[44] but also imposed a collective penalty of 2,300,000 guilders, which subsequent economic circumstance caused to be reduced to 1,000,000.[45] Yet despite the comprehensive Austrian victory, Jews generally maintained their intense loyalty to the Hungarian cause. This adherence was intellectually facilitated and ideologically bolstered by the endeavours of various "progressive" Rabbis, particularly Lipot Lov (1811–1875), arguably the most distinguished and influential Hungarian rabbi of the mid-nineteenth century.[46]

Liberal Jewish intellectuals, having accepted Kossuth's Hungarian nationalism — a strident ideology that subsumed conflicting religious and ethnic particularities — recognised that some Orthodox (fundamentalist) Jewish rituals provided an obvious impediment to Jews being accepted within the fold of Kossuth's national amalgamation.[47] An ardent supporter of both Jewish emancipation and Hungarian nationalism, in 1844 Rabbi Lov instituted the radical departure of delivering his sermons in Hungarian.[48] Subsequently, whilst serving as an army chaplain in the revolutionary forces, his stirring anti-Hapsburg invective resulted in the Austrian Commander Haynau sentencing him to three months' gaol in the Ujepulet prison.[49]

Handler succinctly summarises Rabbi Lov's contribution to the intellectual fervour of Hungarian Jewry thus:

> An enthusiastic and indefatigable exponent of Magyarisation, Low argued that the Diaspora had terminated the national identity of Jews[50]...[furthermore he] removed a major obstacle in the path of assimilation by declaring that Jewish Messianic expectations were exclusively religious in nature and that Jews were distinguishable from the peoples they lived among only in their belief and practice of their faith, thus rebutting the frequently expressed charge of the Jews' inherent inassimilability and questionable loyalty as citizens.[51]

Despite severe antagonism from the Orthodox, this response was quickly adopted by the "enlightened-progressive" sector of the rabbinate. Significantly, it also generated a potent ideological catalyst — as well as a powerful spiritual justification — for the development of the "assimilationist" Neolog sector of Hungarian Jewry, the segment that was to dominate the Jewish community in Trianon (post-World War I) Hungary.

[It should be noted that this spiritual and communal turmoil was not unique to Hungarian Jews, being but a specific aspect of the intellectual conflict that evolved within European Jewry towards the latter portion of the eighteenth century. Although an exposition of this philosophical fervour is beyond the scope of this book, the Jewish emancipationist-enlightenment movement, the *Haskalah*, is generally considered to have been formalised by Moses Mendelssohn, eminent leader of the reformist elements of German Jewry. Contemporaneous to, and in sympathy with, the ideals of progress and open-mindedness that broadly characterised the general Enlightenment attitude in Europe, the *Haskalah* was confined to the then minority "assimilationist" section of West and Central European Jewry. As one of the prime foci of this grouping was the desire to achieve a position of acceptance by the wider non-Jewish society, it should be emphasised that the *Haskalah* was based on theological, philosophical and social assumptions and objectives that differed significantly from some of those motivating the non-Jewish Enlightenment movement.[52]]

The Orthodox leadership in Hungary, aware that secularist tendencies had caused the erosion of traditional Judaism amongst even the observant sections of French and German Jewry, sought to reinforce the status quo within Hungarian Jewry. Consequently, the 1865 Rabbinical Assembly at Nagymihaly not only prohibited any amendments to synagogue ritual but also forbade adherents from either studying languages or partaking of secular education.[53] Clearly, the Orthodox aim was to ensure the continuation of Judaism's "Other" traits via a self-imposed seclusion from society in general. The Neolog-Orthodox enmity, which had its genesis in the turmoil of the revolutionary era, generated a deep and abiding rupture within the Jewish community. Institutionalised over succeeding decades via the development of two separate and distinct communal bureaucracies (see below), this conflict became such an inherent characteristic of Hungarian Jewry that even the cumulative threat of Hitler, the Third Reich, Hungarian Fascism and Hungary's alignment with the virulently Antisemitic and patently expansionist Nazi Germany was insufficient stimulus to cause its extinction.

THE EMANCIPATION ERA: 1867–1918[54]

The "Golden Age" of Hungarian Jewry

The unexpectedly swift and decisive victory by Prussia over the incompetently commanded Austrian army at the Battle of Koniggratz (July 1866) led to a soul-searching reappraisal of policy by the Hapsburg monarchy. The Emperor Franz Jozsef I (1830–1916), influenced by the imperatives of *real-politik*, reluctantly concluded that the survival of his domains depended upon a fundamental restructuring of the Empire.[55] Consequently in 1867 the previously sacrosanct principle of *Reichseinheit*[56] was replaced by a painstakingly negotiated Compromise, the *Ausgleich*,[57] under which the Empire was effectively transformed into a constitutional "Dual Monarchy" of two regions: the Austrian west and the Hungarian east. The head of the Hapsburg dynasty became *in perpetuum* the Emperor of Austria and King of Hungary,[58] but with the exception of common Ministers for Foreign Affairs and War — who administered their portfolios as if regulating a unitary state — each half of the Empire became independent of its partner although, naturally, consulting on matters of mutual concern.[59] Thus, by abrogating the political passions of 1848, Hungary achieved the status of an integral political entity with a high degree of internal autonomy.[60]

The design of the *Ausgleich* ensured the erection in Hungary of a paradoxical and inherently unstable political edifice, its constitutional facade masking a neo-feudal structure that lacked the reinforcement of neo-absolutist foundations. Yet despite these inherent contradictions, the construction proved its durability by surviving the cataclysm of defeat in World War I, the collapse of its monarchist progenitors and the savage territorial dismemberment imposed on a prostrate Hungary by the 1920 Treaty of Trianon. The ramshackle erection was maintained with almost mystic devotion by the Hungarian establishment until the whole edifice was contemptuously razed by a tragi-comic *coup de grace,* the German inspired, organised and conducted *putsch* of 15 October 1944 (see Chapter IV).

Contemporaneous with the political restructuring was a concerted effort to modernise the administrative, judicial, educational and religious apparatus of the new Hungarian entity.[61] Unlike national minorities, the Jewish community was far from neglected in this process. Infused with the *laissez-faire* mercantile principles of the industrial revolution, and recognising the general unwillingness of educated Magyars to become "sullied" in the entrepreneurial arts, the government turned to the Jews — the most accomplished, innovative and loyal element of the population — as proxy for a largely nonexistent indigenous, commercially oriented middle class, arguably the foremost stimulus and catalyst in generating national growth and development.[62]

Consequently, in December 1867 the Hungarian parliament virtually completed the process of institutional emancipation by approving a Bill sponsored by the Minister of Education and Religious Affairs,[63] Baron Jozsef Eotvos (1813–71), that annulled almost all remaining anti-Jewish statutes. By this stroke individual Jews were elevated to a position of civil and political equality with individual Christians,[64] even though the Bill — maintaining the venerable Hungarian duality towards "Magyars of the Israelite Faith" — denied the Jewish faith recognition as one of the *Religiones Receptae* (Accepted Religions) and thus excluded the community from

8 *From Emancipation to Catastrophe*

incorporation into the sanctum of the nation's constitution. Consequences of this exclusion included the loss of ex-officio representation in the Upper House of Parliament, and the non-acceptance of Christian conversions — that is, the state refused to recognise the conversion of Christians *to* Judaism.[65]

The Jewish Congress of 1868–69

In an attempt to prevent newfound freedoms and equalities from exacerbating internecine conflicts, and to formulate the community's position vis-à-vis the national constitution, educational developments and organisational reform, in 1867 progressive elements of Hungarian Jewry persuaded Baron Eotvos to convene a general Jewish Congress to which delegates from all sections of the community would be invited.[66]

Such a proposal was not a new conception, having originated with the early generation of reformers in the mid-1820s. Whilst sundry initiatives had been attempted in the interim[67] — all of which failed — they invariably advocated three far-reaching changes to the institutional structure of the community: the establishment of a central authority operating under some form of governmental jurisdiction; the reorganisation of education by the development of a network of Jewish primary schools providing modern curricula; and the establishment of a central rabbinical seminary, thus removing the training and ordination of the rabbinate from the traditional *Yeshivot* (Orthodox) system.[68]

These modernist initiatives further aggravated tensions in the community over issues involving theological principle and practice.[69] The principal responses of the religious fundamentalists — conferences of Orthodox Rabbis (1864, Nyiregyhaza; 1865, Nagymihaly; 1866, Michalowitz[70]) and the formation of a political grouping, *Shomre Hadath* (Guardians of the Faith)[71] — were attempts to consolidate the existing system via the reinforcement of established custom, thus pre-empting what the traditionalists interpreted as the reformers' push towards communal secularisation and the erosion of rabbinic authority.[72]

The aspirations of the Guardian group were formalised in their statute of 14 September 1867, one objective of which was, paradoxically, to increase knowledge of the Hungarian language amongst the Orthodox, an aim dictated by the necessities of *real-politik*.[73] Anti-reformist activity was further magnified by the founding of a weekly journal *Magyar Zsido*[74] (Hungarian Jew), an Orthodox publication appearing in Hungarian even though the majority of that segment was unfamiliar with the national vernacular. Of equal importance was the contemporary affiliation of the anti-modernists with rampant Hungarianism, elements of intense patriotism becoming embedded in their secular attitudes.

Without presenting evidence or references, Katzburg designates these re-alignments on language and nationalism as akin to a public relations exercise, a means of improving the Orthodox image in non-Jewish circles.[75] At first glance, because of their non-worldly stereotype, this scepticism appears justified. However there is little doubt that the Orthodox leadership, feeling increasingly threatened by the growing momentum of the modernist ethos within the country in general and the urban Jewish community in particular, recognised their need to achieve new levels of sophistication and appeal in their campaigns. Alignment with Magyar patriotism and language was a logical, populist and fortifying strategy, transgressing no laws of *Halachah*,[76] and in concert with analogous tendencies developing within urban

Orthodox communities throughout much of western and central Europe. Equally indisputable is that by the turn of the century the majority of Orthodox, along with the large majority of their progressive co-religionists, had become convinced Hungarian chauvinists.[77]

Regardless of motivation, the primary significance of the anti-reformists' new *modus operandi* was that it was the first instance of a traditionalist Jewish group utilising modern political methods to propagate its views. Such bizarre alloying of disparate phenomena generated external attention, the London *Jewish Chronicle*'s editorial of 12 June 1868, "Jewish Orthodoxy and Reform in Hungary", being quite devoid of Katzburg's scepticism:

> For the first time the ultra-orthodox party, such as is altogether unknown in the west, admits a nationality, a patriotism due to the land of birth...they admit the propriety of considering the Magyar tongue the national language...
>
> Jewish orthodoxy does not hesitate to emerge from the conventional shelter of the synagogue and the *Beth Hamidrash* and to appear in the light of day — the light of public discussion and intellectual combat.
>
> It is undeniable that the steps taken by the orthodox party in effect tend to ally them with modern civilisation.[78]

Leader of the progressives following the Compromise of 1867 was Dr Ignac Hirschler (1832–91), President of the Jewish Community of Pest, an eminent, affluent, progressive stronghold that considered itself the *de facto* agent — and aspired to become the *de jure* embodiment — of Hungarian Jewry. As the paramount communal leader, and a trusted friend of Baron Eotvos, Hirschler lobbied the Minister to call a national Jewish Congress, and consequently submitted to Eotvos a list of thirty-six Jewish leaders who would plan such a convention. Accepting Hirschler's arguments, Eotvos and representatives of Hungary's Jewish leadership met on 16 February 1868 for preliminary discussions regarding the forthcoming assembly.[79]

Conscious of the divisive undercurrents within the community, and as a concession to the Orthodox, Hirschler had attempted to avoid discussion of religious issues by excluding Rabbis from the delegation.[80] Notwithstanding this precaution, on the second day of deliberations six Orthodox delegates appealed to Eotvos for permission to negotiate as a caucus separate from the progressives. The Minister refused the request on the basis that Hungarian law recognised only a single Jewish faith — that is, a unitary, non-segmented creed. Disregarding this rebuff the Orthodox delegates continued to act in concert, consistently disputing the opinions and decisions of the large non-orthodox majority.[81]

Undaunted by this persistent dissidence, the majority of delegates at these preliminary discussions approved a three-point programme for consideration by the forthcoming national Congress, setting an agenda in close alignment with modernist inclination. A central authority presiding over Hungarian Jewry was proposed, this body to then institute a network of communal schools, and a national academy for the training of rabbis and teachers. As expected, Orthodox delegates dissented, particularly to the principle of centralisation, fearing that non-Orthodox members of the proposed central authority would obtain some input into and/or influence over Orthodox communities and practices. As such, the Orthodox supported the maintenance of communal autonomy through retention of the decentralised status quo.

Eotvos, realising his invidious situation, adjudicated by attempting a compromise. Although consenting to the establishment of separate religious secretariats, he refused non-theological matters being similarly delineated between two distinct, ideologically based jurisdictions. The government's hope was to institute a Jewish command authority, a single negotiating power analogous in function to the hierarchy of a Christian denomination: it did not favour the prospect of negotiating future agreements involving Jewry with two divergent bodies often in potentially irreconcilable conflict.

The Minister's wish to broker a single community was not fulfilled, both parties conducting large-scale energetic campaigns on behalf of their respective candidates standing for election to the national Jewish Congress. The Orthodox, led by prominent clergy and the *Shomre Hadath* (see above), mounted vigorous opposition to the Congress' proposed agenda. This campaign contributed substantially to the development of Orthodoxy's abiding and inflexible antagonism to any attempt to impose administrative centralisation onto Hungarian Jewry.[82] The ballot, held on 18 November 1868 under the supervision of state authorities, resulted in the election of 220 delegates — 126 progressive and 94 Orthodox, the former winning the popular vote 57.5 percent to 42.5 percent.

Baron Eotvos opened the Congress — held in Pest from 14 December 1868 to 23 February 1869[83] — with an address meant to pacify and reassure the disaffected traditionalist minority. The Minister declared that the aim of the government-sponsored Congress was the establishment of a structure for the autonomous administration of Hungarian Jewry, and that its franchise did not incorporate authority in matters of religious principle or practice.[84] Yet despite this attempt to define, isolate and insulate contentious issues from discussions concerning civil administration, secular and religious matters became fearfully entwined during the deliberations, to such an extent that on 5 February 1869 forty-eight delegates walked out of the conference, never to return.[85] They departed protesting against what they regarded as modernist domination and declared their refusal to accept the Congress' pronouncements. The Orthodox resolve, and this active defiance of government authority — walking out of the Congress was, *inter alia*, walking out on the government — generated genuine attempts in the final resolutions to moderate divisiveness and placate the disaffected minority.[86] Consequently, the Charter adopted by the Congress, whilst planning a comprehensive restructuring of Hungarian Jewry's civil administration, was less centralising and monolithic than initially envisaged by the progressives or feared by their opponents.

However centralism and modernisation still remained the prime foci of the Charter. A hierarchical civic administration was imposed on Hungarian Jewry; lay leaders were given responsibility for non-religious administration, including the employment of Rabbis; a National School Foundation, controlled by communal presidents, was instituted; and mandatory affiliation was introduced, with no Jew being permitted to remain detached from the jurisdiction of a local Jewish community of his or her choice.[87]

The leaders of the Congress' progressive majority, wary of Orthodox intransigence, attempted to expedite government ratification of the approved Charter, fully realising that such assent would implement state-supported (that is, compulsory) modernist-orientated obligations on all of Hungarian Jewry. In countermeasure, the Orthodox petitioned the Emperor and, at their audience of April

1869, requested that Royal Sanction be denied the Congress statutes. The modernist Charter, however, was approved by Parliament in June 1869, after the Emperor had dismissed the Orthodox appeal on the basis that authority for such internal matters resided exlusively with the Hungarian Minister.[88]

Undeterred by these setbacks, and still adamant in their opposition, the Orthodox proceeded to petition the Hungarian Lower House. Arguing that the coercion inflicted on their communities by the Charter violated their freedom of conscience, they further declared that the irreconcilable differences between themselves and their progressive opponents proved the existence of two distinct Jewish denominations.[89] On 18 March 1870 the Lower House upheld the petition, pronouncing that the loss of religious freedom by the Orthodox nullified the Charter's validity. In accordance with this edict, on 5 November 1871 an Imperial Decree approved a rival communal statute, this time pertaining to Orthodox adherents.[90]

For assorted reasons, a number of communities declined to accept either of the competing Charters and resolved to maintain their existing, separate *modus operandi*. This minority, called the *Status Quo Ante*,[91] evolved to constitute the smallest of the three formal segments of Hungarian Jewry. Due to the absence of a central secretariat, each individual Status Quo community continued to liaise directly with the appropriate government departments.

Paradoxically, the government-progressive attempt to fuse the disparate community into a single, coherent, modern administrative entity resulted in the formal rupture of Hungarian Jewry into three distinct groupings[92] — the Orthodox (religious fundamentalist), the Neolog (mildly progressive)[93] and the Status Quo. Post-Congress activities ensured that the fissures expanded into an unbridgeable schism, even smallish Jewish communities not infrequently maintaining two or sometimes three denominations. The question of whether an administratively unified Jewry would have been better endowed to prepare for, and survive, the Nazi cataclysm will be addressed in the following chapters.

Despite the above traumas, the Congress produced several highly significant resolutions that were translated into permanent features of Hungary's Jewish infrastructure. On 2 March 1871 the National Bureau of Magyar Israelites was established to integrate the activities of its adhering (progressive) communities, and on 4 October 1877 the National Rabbinical Institute was inaugurated. In addition, some of Hungarian Jewry's most important cultural and social welfare organisations were formed within a decade of these deliberations.[94] Furthermore, with the benefit of tragic hindsight, it is clear that the ability of the Nazis to identify and deport the large mass of Hungarian Jewry with speed and ease was greatly facilitated by the introduction of mandatory affiliation (see above), *inter alia* a governmentally authorised religious registration of the Jewish populace.[95]

It is pertinent to note that the Orthodox leadership's chosen stratagies generated the apparent paradox of religious traditionalists being the first to utilise non-traditional methods in defending their religious interests. Katz succinctly summarises the effects of these Orthodox endeavours on the Orthodox community: "The act of quasidefiance of the governmentally supported assembly was portrayed as a heroic stance and converted into a veritable myth, serving as a shining ideal for the succeeding generations."[96]

It appears that this successful application of progressive political methods resulted in Orthodox leaders considering activist and innovative secular strategies as a positive virtue. Hungarian Orthodox propensity towards considering non-theological innovation as an appropriate and effective political tool, and not as a threat to identity and way of life, developed in this epoch and became inculcated into the consciousness, and administrative approach, of successive generations of Orthodox leaders. In contrast, the modernist, secularly progressive Neologs, being the dominant grouping and generally having the sympathetic ear of post-Emancipation governments, seem to have developed a culture of working "passively" through authorised procedures and established channels.[97] As with their Orthodox opponents, this particular political culture, nurtured and reinforced over the long, formative "Golden Age" of 1868–1918, eventually became ingrained into the psychological and administrative ethos of successive generations of Neolog leaders. Consequently they not only failed to develop a positive consciousness towards innovative (non-authorised) strategies but, even in times of considerable duress, were unable to depart significantly from the usual procedures, tried and proven in their period of greatest achievement and influence.

The Emancipation era thus provides a significant insight into the disparate responses of Hungarian Jewry's dual pillars, the Orthodox and the Neolog, during the post-Monarchist era. Additionally, it also contributes a historical perspective on the hitherto neglected conundrum of why the closest and most significant Jewish co-operation during the Holocaust era in Hungary occurred between the Orthodox and the Zionists, characterised as bitter ideological enemies, and not between the somewhat less divided Orthodox-Neolog or Neolog-Zionist combinations.[98] There is little doubt that the Neolog's ingrained "passive" (authorised channels) leadership ethos was one of the most significant factors that effectively precluded them from either initiating or co-operating in unconventional endeavours during the period of the Hungarian *Shoah*.[99] Conversely, as will be seen, the sharing of compatible activist attitudes by the Orthodox and the Zionists was arguably the major factor that enabled these groups to eventually overcome their apparently unbridgeable ideological hostilities.

Contemporary evaluations of the Congress generally concur with subsequent assessments that the venture failed to achieve its stated goals.[100] Instead of fostering unity via the resolution of divisive issues, Hungarian Jewry became saddled with the additional burden of both factions hardening their respective positions. However, with the benefit of historical perspective, it is fair to state that there was very little prospect of the basically irreconcilable elements uniting under a single banner. *Post-factum* examination reveals that despite the deep polarisation and formal rupture discussed above, both segments of Jewry ultimately achieved meaningful results for their respective branches. The Neolog obtained their much-desired modernisation and restructuring — not for the whole of Hungarian Jewry as initially proposed, but certainly for those communities deciding to accept the Congress Charter. Conversely, the Orthodox retained control over their cherished particularities via parliament's eventual approval of their rival statutes. Consequently, Hungarian Jewish life became formally organised into two separate, internally coherent public bodies,[101] both self-governing within the confines of state sanction. Furthermore, the introduction of mandatory affiliation ensured that every Jew residing in Hungary had state-imposed legal and financial obligations to the Jewish denomination of his or her choice.

The government, though not involved in the actual Congress, played a highly significant catalytic role in some critical aspects of the proceedings. To reiterate: preliminary discussions were convened by the Minister; election of delegates was conducted under government auspices; the rival Charters were subject to government approval; and the implementation of decisions was at the pleasure of Parliament. Thus did Hungarian Jewry achieve "emancipation", not via genuine autonomy but within the framework of a politically ratified quasi-independence. For lurking in the background, and recognised by all parties, was the formal, real and constant factor of polarised Jewry ultimately having to obtain government acceptance for its proposed actions. But because of the basically benign and supportive nature of successive "Golden Age" (Dual Monarchy) governments, it was the Emancipation Era that reconciled Hungarian Jewry to the concept of direct political intervention into its affairs. There is little doubt that this reconciliation was one of the major factors facilitating Jewish acquiescence to the Antisemitic impositions of the post-1918 Trianon years. As will be seen, state intrusion remained a constant factor in Hungary's Jewish policy through to the twentieth century, intensifying after World War I and reaching a crescendo during the Holocaust epoch. [Ideologically reinforced during the postwar Communist regimes, it continues — albeit in much abbreviated and largely beneficial form — at the time of writing.]

The Spectre of Antisemitism

Despite comprehensive support by the state, quietude regarding the emancipation of Hungarian Jewry proved to be a transient phenomenon. As elsewhere in Europe where Jewish emancipation was concomitant with the displacement of vested interests and socio-economic privileges, elements soon emerged to campaign against what they claimed was the corruptive and avaricious influence of the Jews. In the main, these Judeophobes were based in those strata of Hungarian society adversely affected by disruptions resulting from the advancement of liberalism and capitalism, both developments being viewed by the agitators as Jewish-induced, alien and hostile phenomena. Despite the diversity of their often conflicting ideologies, these established interest groups, particularly *déclassé* gentry, skilled artisans, Swabians (ethnic Germans) and sections of the Catholic church, were united in their attempts to reignite financial ("Jewish economic dominance and exploitation") and/or religious ("Christ-killers") prejudices against the Jews. Consequently, to substantial numbers of those who accepted these fulminations, the threat posed by the highly assimilated Hungarian-Jewish plutocrat and the impoverished Orthodox pedlar from Galicia merged to become the bi-polar elements of a unitary Jewish menace.

In Hungary the spokesperson for these disgruntled groupings was a hitherto obscure backbench member of the governing Liberal Party, Gyozo Istoczy (1842–1915), lawyer, public servant, and a parliamentary representative from 1872 to 1895.[102] On 8 April 1875, barely seven years after the Emancipation gained legislative approval, Istoczy confronted the government with three parliamentary questions that, once again, publicly exposed the anti-Jewish undercurrent endemic in sections of Hungarian society. Attempting to capitalise on the hardship and social discontent generated by the financial turmoil of 1873,[103] Istoczy challenged the government to ban the immigration of Jews, reverse its policy on

Jewish equality and not hinder the development of a "self-defence movement" against this "aggressive caste".[104]

These questions, far from being a genuine request for information or elucidation of government policy, were a blatant attempt by Istoczy to elevate his political profile and generate publicity for his ideological position.[105] In particular, as was well known at the time, anti-immigration legislation was contemplated by the government prior to the granting of emancipation, but had been abandoned — not on the basis of egalitarian principles, but because of technical difficulties.[106] Prime Minister Bela Wenckheim (1811–79), ignoring Istoczy's provocation, dismissed his questions as ill-timed, inopportune, and contrary to the principles enshrined in the national constitution.[107]

Istoczy's attitude towards the Jews was based on his perception of Judaism being an ancient caste, closed and homogeneous. Religion was only one element in its multifaceted agenda, the ultimate, inveterate aim of which was nothing less than world domination. The apparent split between progressive and traditionalist elements was a facade designed to lure the unsuspecting victims into a sense of false security. Jewish assimilation and intermarriage was a ruse designed to further the caste's perennial aspirations, an intrigue aimed at penetrating the hierarchy of the host nation. According to Istoczy's conspiracy theory, which has overtones of Francois Hell's "state within a state" diatribe,[108] the assimilated, intermarried and apostates were an advance guard of infiltrators, a "fifth column" preparing the way for the caste's ultimate domination of its gullible and naive host. Accordingly, the progressive-traditionalist schism was a mere division of responsibility, the Orthodox function being to maintain the centrality of the creed, thus sustaining the Judaic nucleus for future generations. Additionally, the Orthodox provided a reservoir for replenishing the zeal of assimilated emissaries, the parasites returning from their missions in the outside world.[109] Despite this theoretical basis,[110] Istoczy initially avoided advocating the abandonment of Jewish emancipation, considering it an untenable objective due to prevailing government attitudes and the advances already secured by the Jews. Again, his solution to the "Jewish Question" was the organisation of society in its own defence — hence the import of his third parliamentary question mentioned above.

During the 1878 Congress of Berlin, Istoczy took advantage of public focus on questions of ethnic self-determination to advocate in parliament that if a Congress participant proposed the establishment of a Jewish state as part of the overall resolution of the Balkan and Near Eastern problem, then the Hungarian government should support such a proposal. The derision generated by his address forced Istoczy to retract, claiming his speech to be merely another attempt at drawing attention to the "Jewish Question" in general.

Istoczy's allegations of an international Jewish conspiracy were given superficial credence when the Jewish Community of Berlin, in association with the Alliance Israelite Universelle of France and the Zion Society of Bucharest, appealed to the chairman of the Berlin Congress, the German Chancellor Otto von Bismarck, to propose a clause in the settlement granting equal rights to Roumanian Jews. Stimulated by this intervention, civil equality for members of all religions in the Balkans was incorporated in a special paragraph of the peace treaty.[111] Istoczy's allegations and prestige were enhanced by the publication in Germany of Wilhelm Marr's influential and best-selling pamphlet of February 1879, *The Victory of*

Judaism over Germandom. A notorious Jew-hater,[112] coiner of the term "Anti-semite", founder of the *Antisemiten-Liga* in 1879 and pioneer in the utilisation of "scientific" Jew-hatred as political propaganda, Marr (1818–1904) wrote in the above tract: "Who derived the real benefit at the Congress of Berlin from the spilled blood of the Orient? Jewry. The Alliance Israelite Universelle was first in line. Rumania was forced to open officially its doors and gates to destructive Semitism."[113]

Despite the disparagement generated by his parliamentary address of 1878, Istoczy devoted considerable time and energy, in numerous arenas, attempting to propagate his jaundice on the "Jewish Question". Professor Macartney states that in 1880 alone "a Deputy named Istoczy founded no less than 78 specifically anti-Semitic organisations..."[114] Significant amongst these was the Federation of Non-Jewish Hungarians, an organisation soliciting the support of all those who, irrespective of origin or ideological affiliation, sought protection from "Jewish exploitation".[115] Also of importance was his monthly publication *12 Ropirat* (12 Tracts). Founded in October 1880, it remained the mouthpiece of the Antisemitic movement until its demise in 1892.[116]

In an epoch incorporating lavish tensions generated by ethnic chauvinism and rapid socio-economic transformation, not surprisingly, the assiduous nurturing of noxious seeds eventually cultivated grievous fruit. The first substantive manifestation of this growth occurred in early February 1881, when Jews enrolled at the University of Pest were attacked by Antisemitic elements in the student body.[117] Although firmly reprimanded by the University Rector, and proscribed by the Minister of the Interior from holding a public meeting to publicise their alleged afflictions, the Antisemitic students were undeterred from issuing a proclamation demanding the reduction of Jewish numbers at the University.[118] Moreover, in furtherance of their cause, on 10 February an Antisemitic student delegation called on their mentor, Istoczy, and presented him with a petition conveying the support of several hundred of their *confrères*.[119]

Recognising this as an opportunity for consolidating his constituency and elevating his political profile, on 3 March Istoczy interceded in parliament to support his student disciples. Criticising the government's prohibition of their meeting and supporting their scheme to restrict Jewish matriculation, he continued by denouncing Jewish control of the press and proceeded to deliver his usual lengthy, defamatory tirade against "Jewish exploiters and parasites", concluding with a typical exhortation: "For we shall triumph and the future shall be ours!"

A succinct overview of one of Istoczy's most offensive parliamentary speeches of this period is presented thus by Professor Katz:

> He referred to the examples of bygone centuries when similar circumstances led up to "the mass extermination of the Jews." Though unlikely to occur as long as the Jewish domination continued, it could well take place in case of "a great political upheaval or a social convulsion that would engulf the society of several states." No moral considerations would impede such a solution; in Istoczy's view it would be nothing but the exercise of the nations' right to defend themselves.[120]

Katz comments: "These are shocking assertions, especially in historical retro-spect, since we cannot fail to view them as foreshadowing the mentality that made Nazi atrocities possible."[121]

Recognising the limitations that emancipation had imposed upon their ability to resolve the "Jewish Problem" to their satisfaction, the overt Hungarian Antisemites then presented to parliament a series of petitions opposing Jewish equality. Organised via a series of public meetings held in rural districts, the Antisemites' strategy was to isolate, then erode and finally outflank the influence of the liberal metropolis. Not coincidentally, the first of these petitions, presented to parliament in the autumn of 1881, was organised by priests in Istoczy's own electorate. In a rebuff to their cause, however, in February 1882 the government's Petitions Committee displayed solidarity with Hungarian Jewry and decisively rejected the petition as contravening one of the nation's chief legislative accomplishments.[122]

This Antisemitic campaign was synchronous with the outbreak of anti-Jewish rioting in several districts of northern Hungary. Erupting in the spring of 1881, and contemporaneous with the first major pogroms in Russia following the assassination of Tsar Alexander II, these events were described by Venetianer thus: *"fenyes nappal veresre vertek zsidokat, hazakba betortek, uzleteket fosztogattak"* (Jews were beaten in broad daylight until bloodied, their houses ransacked and businesses looted) — actions that influenced the whole of the *Felvidek* (northern) region.[123]

By 1882 Istoczy's insistent agitation had coalesced a grouping of five like-minded parliamentary supporters. Of most influence were three members of the opposition Independence Party — Gyula Verhovay (1848–1906), publisher and fervent anti-*Ausgleich* jingoist whose activities earned him national renown as the "little Kossuth"; Geza Onody, of the straitened nobility, Istoczy's rural consultant; and Ivan Simonyi (1836–1904), Istoczy's most fervent disciple, a man with a reputation for vicious, unyielding Antisemitism.[124]

The mood of rural Hungary, upon which the above agitators preyed and where they generated their greatest impact, is evocatively portrayed by Professor Handler thus:

> In the intellectually suppressed, illiterate world of the countryside, in which Christian beliefs remained inextricably fused with pagan traditions, the peasants' spiritual tranquillity, guarded and promoted by the Church, was at times shattered. The economic and intellectual backwaters of Hungary, far beneath the deceptively glittering facade of progress-oriented Budapest, eagerly absorbed the inflammatory speeches and writings of Istoczy and his collaborators. Thus the ever-smoldering fire of popular superstition, the age-old fear of witches and sorcerers, especially the one disguised as a traveling student who could raise storms, and the unmitigated contempt for the avaricious "Christ-killer" Jews converged with the modern tenets of political anti-Semitism and formed a new synthesis. The fire that the anti-Semites had started in the political arena was about to set the whole of Hungary ablaze.[125]

The conflagration referred to concerns the infamous episode known as "The Blood Libel of Tiszaeszlar", one of the most notorious manifestations of the ritual-slaughter canard since medieval times.[126] As the trial affected Hungary almost to the same extent that the Dreyfus case destabilised France, a brief résumé is unavoidable.[127]

The disappearance on 1 April 1882 of a fourteen-year-old domestic servant, Eszter Solymosi, from the village of Tiszaeszlar[128] generated a fervour and passion that was to achieve worldwide notoriety. As the girl vanished three days before the Jewish festival of *Pesach* (the Passover), Istoczy's parliamentary colleague Geza

Onody — who, coincidentally, lived in Tiszaeszlar — commenced propagating the fabrication that Jews murdered the young girl so as to utilise her blood in the baking of *matzo*, the unleavened bread used throughout the *Pesach* period.[129] In this slander Onody was supported by two prominent local dignitaries, the mayor and a Catholic priest. Adding fuel to the fire, on 20 May the latter wrote an article in the Budapest Catholic newspaper *Magyar Allam* (Magyar State) in which he referred to the "virtual certainty" that Jews had commited ritual murder in Tiszaeszlar.[130]

The investigation of the girl's disappearance, carried out by state officials who were sympathetic to the accusation, involved acts of brutality and gross contraventions of natural justice.[131] By the use of physical force and subterfuge, the investigators succeeded in coercing a fourteen-year-old Jewish youth, Moric Scharf, to admit that he had witnessed his father and other Jews murder the missing girl in the local synagogue, drain her blood and collect it in a bowl.

Both the investigation and the subsequent trial aroused enormous publicity and controversy. Istoczy and his cohorts, seizing their opportunity, intensified their vicious Antisemitic propaganda; the parliament, in particular, was the scene of frenzied mass debates on the subject. This agitation was indirectly aided by decisions of the state prosecutor-general and the Liberal Prime Minister Kalman Tisza,[132] both of whom, whilst basically sympathetic to the Jewish victims,[133] avoided intervening in the judicial process because of concerns about the possible political consequences of such an interference.

The protracted trial of the accused, held in the nearby county seat of Nyiregyhaza during the summer months of 1883, eventually produced a favourable result for the accused, all fifteen defendants being exonerated in full. The acquittal resulted largely from the efforts of Karoly Eotvos, a noted lawyer, author, politician, and Liberal member of the national parliament. His brilliant analyses discredited the charges to such an extent that, in its final summary, the prosecution advocated the acquittal of the accused.[134]

Despite the defendants' unqualified acquittal, anti-Jewish agitation continued unabated. Notwithstanding the collective sigh of relief by liberal elements, Antisemitic propagandists neither accepted the falsity of their accusations nor withdrew the stigmas their allegations had imposed on Hungarian Jewry as a whole. Istoczy's *12 Ropirat* labelled the verdict a moral defeat for the Jews; *Fuggetlenseg* (Independence), published by Istoczy's *confrère* Verhovay, remained convinced of the defendants' guilt; and the Budapest Catholic newspaper *Magyar Allam*, whilst reluctantly accepting the verdict, commented menacingly: "Unfortunately, Hungary has reached the point where its prosperity is unconditionally dependent on compromise and transaction with Jewish interests." The *Magyar Korona* (Magyar Crown) perhaps best summarised the turmoil and confusion in the public mind by asking "Where is Eszter Solymosi? Who killed Eszter Solymosi?".[135] The foreign press generally reacted by denouncing the Hungarian Antisemites; some even suggested bringing charges against those attempting to pervert the course of justice.[136]

Contemporaneous with this continuing turmoil, protracted eruptions of violent Jew-hatred raged out of control in both Budapest and non-metropolitan areas. In response, the authorities proclaimed states of emergency and employed the army to defend Jewish lives and property. Riots that flared in Budapest on 7 August were promptly answered by the government ordering the police and the militia to restore order. Despite these forceful measures, it was not until 12 August that the metropolitan disturbances were finally quelled.[137]

The endorsements of the acquittal by the Court of Appeal, in December 1883, and then the Supreme Court, in April 1884, scarcely affected the intensity or distribution of Antisemitic virulence.[138] Recognising the extended outbreak of Jew-hatred as a political opportunity, on 6 October 1883, after months of preliminary groundwork, Istoczy and his cohorts formed the National Antisemitic Party (henceforth NAP).

By this time Istoczy had become a conspicuous political personality, his fame/notoriety having been enhanced within Hungary via his victory over the Liberal government's attempt to prosecute him for an article appearing in his journal *12 Ropirat*.[139] His presence on the international stage, via his participation at the first international conference of Antisemites, held in Dresden in September 1882, also helped to elevate his profile in the electorate. Besides Istoczy, who presented his "Manifesto to the Governments and Nations of Christian States Endangered by Judaism",[140] two other members of the Hungarian parliament also attended the Dresden convention, all three eventually playing important roles at the gathering. One of these members, Ivan Simonyi, delivered a speech, "Antisemitism and the Laws of Human Society", and was appointed one of the congressional chairmen.[141]

Istoczy's new political grouping, realising the electoral limitations of a single-issue agenda, attempted to broaden its appeal by advocating an extensive restructuring of the nation's economic, financial and agricultural base. Yet despite this considerable widening of political horizons, six of the twelve founding principles of the NAP still promoted an attack on Jews or Jewish influence.[142]

Unfortunately for the Antisemitic cause, the enthusiasm generated by the formation of the NAP was soon dampened by a sensational scandal. Following a series of disclosures that appeared in the liberal press, a police raid on Gyula Verhovay's newspaper *Fuggetlenseg* (Independence) led to charges of major embezzlement being laid against Verhovay and his brother Lajos. Creating uproar, and considerable embarrassment to the Antisemitic movement, the subsequent trial dragged on for two years. However, this tumult was soon overshadowed by another furore, this time generated by the government's controversial attempt to introduce civil marriage between Christians and Jews. The spectre of Tiszaeszlar was resurrected, with Istoczy railing against "paid philosemites" and thundering that no Christian parent of a missing child could be certain that the child will not "...in a few days fall victim to the fanatical Jews who exceed the cannibals in ritualistic madness...For in spite of the acquittals, deep down in their heart, everyone is convinced that the unfortunate Eszter Solymosi found her tragic fate in the synagogue of Tiszaeszlar."[143]

After five days of tempestuous debate, the Lower House passed the civil marriage measure only to have it rejected by a narrow majority of six in the conservative Upper House. Utilising this setback to the government's policy of facilitating Jewish integration into the social fabric, the Antisemites laid claim to having been instrumental in the government's defeat; the Christian soul of Hungary had been saved by the heroic efforts of the NAP.

The national elections, held in 1884, proved to be the zenith of virulent Antisemitism in Dualist Hungary, seeing the return of seventeen NAP members in a House of 274 and the defeat of their arch opponent, Karoly Eotvos.[144] The subsequent decline in the party's fortunes originated in the disputes between the supporters of the *Ausgleich*, including Istoczy, and those representatives holding a contrary view. Such disagreements eventually led to a split in the NAP's ranks, with Istoczy and two others seceding from the group. This breach was the beginning of the party's demise. Gradually its political influence declined and, piecemeal, NAP parliamentary deputies either retired or were defeated at elections. Hungarian Jewry was, basically, to remain physically unmolested for three decades, until the upheavals following the military debacle of 1918.

However, it should not be thought that the NAP's modest success in the 1884 elections was a true indication of the extent of contemporary Hungarian Antisemitism. Influenced by centuries of ingrained religious prejudice, not inconsequential numbers of impoverished peasants, like their exploited industrial counterparts, harboured an enduring penchant for blaming their afflictions on the alleged avarice and financial manipulations of the Jews, whether of the poor rural Orthodox shopkeeper class or the converted Budapest plutocrat variety. This deep and abiding consciousness in the populace was largely blocked from parliamentary expression by the nation's highly restrictive franchise system, only about six percent of the potential electorate being permitted to vote. Combined with the government's blatant electoral chicanery, intimidation and ruthless use of state resources for political purposes, this oligarchical franchise negated the possibility of the national parliament being representative of national opinion.[145] Clearly, the true barometer of Jew-hatred was the extent and intensity of Antisemitic activity. Unlike NAP numbers in parliament, Antisemitism in Hungary was rarely a marginal phenomenon.

The Tiszaeszlar case, however, marked a turning point in the history of Hungarian Antisemitism. Despite the frenzy generated by the blood-libel fabrication, the real issue at question was the moral integrity of Jews and Judaism. Henceforth Jew-hatred based on medieval superstitions and religious bigotry was to be largely superseded by the prejudice and chauvinism developed from racial Darwinism, arguably the epitome of nineteenth-century intellectual perversions.[146] In Hungary, such a coterie of what might be termed "intellectual Antisemites" was augmented by those elements in the country whose socio-economic position was being eroded by the growth of liberalism and *laissez-faire* capitalism, both developments being viewed by Judeophobes as Jewish-induced phenomena alien to the natural order in general and the Magyar spirit in particular.[147]

The standard-bearer of Antisemitism during the last quarter century of Dualist Hungary was the Catholic People's Party. Founded in 1894 by a coalition of clergy and latifundia aristocrats, the Party's aim was to draw rural smallholders and artisans into upholding the status quo. Led largely by the "village intelligentsia" of priests and elementary school teachers, its greatest influence occurred in the early years of the twentieth century. Holding thirty-four seats in the 1906 lower House, the People's Party (henceforth PP), like its predecessor the NAP, became the target of governmental and bureaucratic attack. Once again an assault by the political establishment on a newly emerging competitor was successful and the PP, like the NAP, gradually declined in significance.[148] Political Antisemitism in the Golden Age of Hungarian Jewry had run its institutional course.

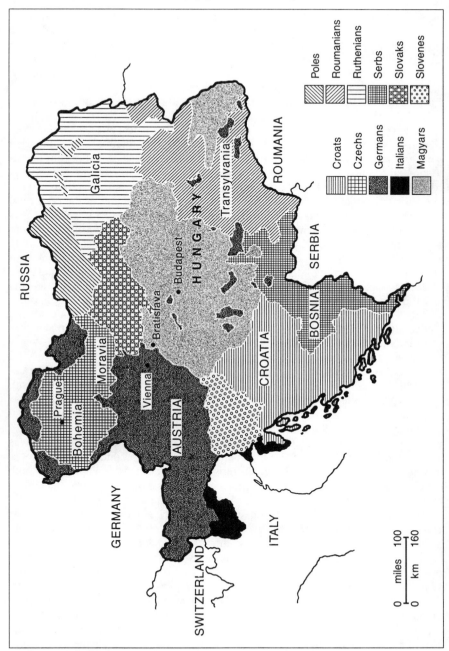

Map 1.1 **Ethnic Distribution in the Austro-Hungarian Empire.**
Based on the census of 1910, the map indicates the major ethnic group in various regions.

The Minorities Question

As previously mentioned, the emancipation of Hungarian Jews instigated a rapid and profound realignment in the self-perception of the "Magyars of the Israelite Faith". In increasing proportions, and with increasing intensity, both sectors of Hungarian Jewry, but especially the Neolog, identified with the ethnic Magyar rulers of Dualist Hungary.[149] In particular, the predominant personal manifestation of this realignment, the replacement of Yiddish, German and other national vernaculars with Magyar as the mother tongue, rose sharply amongst Hungarian Jews — from 58.5 percent in 1880 to 77.8 percent in 1910, an increase of one-third in just over a generation.[150] In marked contrast, despite the intensity of the government's Magyarisation policy (see below), in 1910 over three-quarters of Hungary's non-Magyar population was still ignorant of the Hungarian idiom.[151]

From the second half of Kalman Tisza's premiership (1875–90), Magyar attitudes to the subordinate minorities became increasingly chauvinistic and repressive.[152] Even the facade of ethnic recognition incorporated in the Nationality Law of 1868 was abrogated in practice, with the minorities becoming subjected to a ruthless and concerted Magyarisation. In line with this policy the Hungarian educational system, especially in the villages and high schools, was refashioned in an attempt to thoroughly inculcate ethnic minorities into the predominant Magyar ethos.[153] Safeguarding its hegemony from attack, the government resorted to its usual policy of corruption and intimidation to deny non-Magyars effective parliamentary representation.[154]

Hungarian Jews were not uninvolved bystanders in the government's policy of ethnic repression. The mainly Jewish-owned "liberal", middle class press not only gave unqualified support to this policy but, not infrequently, saw fit to advocate an intensification of the Magyarisation campaign.[155] In this they were echoing the views of their co-religionists, especially those in Budapest, whose "most noticeable feature was their Magyar hyperpatriotism."[156] Thus Hungarian Jewry of this era became characterised as totally loyal, stridently chauvinist, composing Magyar songs and verse, and founding new factories for the benefit of the "fatherland". Even in those provinces where the minorities outnumbered their Magyar rulers, most Jews maintained their intense identification with Magyar ethnicity. In minority villages, Jewish shopkeepers and medical practitioners were often the sole speakers of the Magyar vernacular, hence becoming inherently associated with — and the *de facto* representatives of — the policies of ethnic repression. The general non-Magyar attitude towards Jews in rural areas was reinforced in those, not infrequent, provincial localities where Jewish schools were the sole providers of instruction in the Magyar language.[157]

The symbiosis between Hungarian Jewry and the Magyar establishment brought benefits to both parties. As previously indicated, after emancipation removed restrictions on their business and professional advancement, Jewish enterprise — and consequently Hungary's economic and social infrastructure — developed at an unprecedented rate. Government support and gratitude, indicated via the effective repression of overt Antisemitism and the passing of legislation facilitating Jewish socio-economic integration, was conspicuously reinforced by the "veritable flood of new Jewish ennoblements and other glitter."[158] From emancipation to the fall of the Hapsburgs, over 300 titles were awarded to prominent

Hungarian Jews. These awards constituted 20 percent of total ennoblements and encompassed a very wide spectrum of endeavour — including academia, agriculture, commerce, finance, industry, the military, politics and the professions.[159] One authority estimates that by 1918 about one in every 500 Hungarian Jew had some form of title.[160] Little wonder that the politically successful Antisemitic Lord Mayor of Vienna, Carl Lueger — whom Wistrich calls "the first political role-model for the young Adolph Hitler" — denounced Hungary with the contemptuous epitaph "Judeo-Magyars" and derided its capital with his sneering sobriquet "Judapest".[161]

Besides acting as a surrogate for a well-nigh nonexistent entrepreneurially orientated Christian-Magyar bourgeoisie, Jews provided the Magyar establishment with a politically critical element lacking in the ethnically heterogeneous kingdom: Hungarian Jews provided the Magyar hegemonists with political legitimacy. As the 910,000 Jews counted by the census of 1910 comprised about five percent of the population, and as the Magyars numbered about 49 percent, a combination of the two groups produced a narrow majority of 54 percent[162] — hardly required considering the government's muscular gerrymandering, but critical from the point of view of providing government policies with political legitimacy. *Ergo*, even by their own far from unbiased assessment,[163] without Jews the Magyars would have constituted a minority in *Magyarorszag*, the Land of the Magyars, as Hungary is termed by its inhabitants. Consequently, from both the hegemonist and ethnic minority points of view, this loyal, entrepreneurial, Jewish five percent not only largely designed, manufactured and directed the engine of Hungarian economic development, but also provided the ethnic Magyar establishment with a politically critical element — apparent political legitimacy in the Kingdom of Hungary.

The epitome of empathy between Jews and Magyars occurred in 1895 when, by Law XLII, the Jewish faith was accorded the status of a *Religion Recepta*, thus eliminating the remaining vestiges of institutional discrimination against organised Jewry. Despite the vehement opposition of the Catholic Church, and the Law being rejected twice by the clerically influenced Upper House, the government steadfastly supported the Bill from its parliamentary introduction (April 1893) until its tortuous acceptance by the Upper House (May 1895), when that chamber's president cast the tie-breaking vote.[164]

By this Act Hungarian Jewry finally achieved full, institutional equality with the other received religions of the nation,[165] viz: the Jewish faith became incorporated into the national constitution, Jewish leaders were appointed ex-officio members of the Upper House, reciprocity of conversions was legally recognised, Jewish chaplains were appointed to the military forces, and the state subsidised Jewish schools. Furthermore, to reinforce the government's liberal credentials regarding matters of personal faith, and as an additional factor facilitating Jewish integration into the social fabric, the parliament concurrently passed legislation permitting civil marriage and the free practice of religion.[166]

The Hungarian millennium celebrations of 1896, described by Professor Macartney as akin to an "orgy of self-congratulation",[167] drew an enthusiasm from Hungarian Jewry unsurpassed by any other group in the nation. The Jewish participation, however, celebrated not only a significant Hungarian milestone but the self-perception that Magyars of the Israelite Faith had finally been accorded the principled, unqualified equality to which they had so long aspired. Unlike their French and German co-religionists, Hungarian Jews now considered themselves not merely contributors to the national weal but full partners with the Magyars in the creation of a new, unitary nation.[168] The fervent passion of Hungarian Jewry for Magyarorszag was exemplified by the prolific poet, author and translator, Rabbi Arnold Kiss, who unabashedly proclaimed: "We are prepared to die for our country, die to the last man!"[169] [Some observers of this era of Hungarian history occasionally permit such hyperenthusiasm to infect their better judgement. A notable example is the prominent authority who maintains: "In fact, never in their history did Jews achieve more personal dignity than precisely in this period..."[170] — arguably the most breathtaking generalisation ever inflicted upon Jewish historiography.]

Misguided by this sincerely held passion, Hungarian Jewry misinterpreted the formal apparatus of legal, institutional equality as the equivalent of full and unqualified acceptance. In reality an unofficial, unwritten but widely accepted undercurrent within the establishment — Janos calling this overtone an "informal social contract"[171] — ensured that Jewish progress was effectively confined to strictly delineated sectors of the Hungarian state. Consequently, whilst economic and religious emancipation ensured liberation from a medieval-type pariah status, Jews remained emphatically blocked from a commensurate advancement in fields such as the public service, the police and the regular military forces.[172] Hungarian Jewry, in effect, retained significant neo-feudal elements in its social topography. It remained a highly visible, non-integrated social entity, patently distinguishable from other groups within Hungary by its brilliant cultural and economic achieve-ments yet transparently dependent on the continuing goodwill and tolerance of its Magyar establishment patron. It was the removal of this patronage following the debacle of 1918 that sanctioned the reactivation of Hungary's endemic, though at that stage largely covert, Judeophobia.

The potential for such hostility, via a redirection of Magyar chauvinism, was not entirely lost on a perceptive, mainly younger element within the Jewish intelligent-sia. This minority's conception of the true relationship between Jews and Magyars, can be found in the works of the mid-nineteenth century poet Salamon Rosenzweig, who wrote prophetically:

> If you knew all that, you'd comprehend that which saddens my soul,
> The object of my love is my mother,
> But she loves me not.[173]

Writing in 1903, a native son, Theodor Herzl, was to extend the argument: "The hand of fate shall also seize Hungarian Jewry. And the later this occurs, and the stronger this Jewry becomes, the more cruel and hard shall be the blow, which shall be delivered with greater savagery. There is no escape."[174]

Socio-Economic Aspects of Hungarian Jewry

Whilst an enunciation of the economic history of Hungary's Jews is well beyond the scope of this book, it is pertinent to note that there is considerable overlap, if not consensus, regarding the substantial role of Jews in Hungary's economic develop-ment. One end of this spectrum of opinion is occupied by authorities such as Professor Randolph Braham, who refers to Jewish participation in the Hungarian economy as being a "major" rather than a dominant phenomenon,[175] and Professor Jacob Katz, who places the totality of Jewish contribution to Hungary in context by stating: "Their [respective] contribution to the development of their country was greater than that of any other European Jewish community."[176] Andrew Janos and Professor Macartney typify the opposite end of the spectrum, the end that could be broadly termed "The School of Jewish Dominance". The former characterises twenty or so of the grandest Jewish families — his "interlocking clans" — as operating much like the Japanese *Zaibatsu*,[177] whilst the latter comments:

> ...it is hard to see how, without the Jews, Hungary could ever have accomplished the transition from a "feudal" to a modern capitalist economy... The capitalist development of modern Hungary, in so far as it had been carried out by "domestic" forces at all, had been almost entirely of their [the Jews'] making, and the results of it were concentrated chiefly in their hands.[178]

The vital statistics of the 1910 census seem to confirm the second portion of Macartney's assessment, with figures revealing that Jews comprised 85 percent of self-employed persons in finance and banking, and 42 percent of their employees; with regard to self-employed traders, the figures are 54 percent and 62 percent respectively. Additionally, Macartney states that most of the *higher* branches of banking, finance and industry (above the artisan level) were owned and staffed by Jews, and then remarks — certainly gratuitously, possibly disdainfully — that a large portion of the profits from these endeavours "went into Jewish pockets".[179] In keeping with his sometimes supercilious manner, Macartney fails to acknowledge that in 1887, 62.2 percent of businessmen paying the highest rate of tax were Jews;[180] that it was Jewish bankers, using their own capital and their international connections, who reversed Hungary's traditional role as a nett importer of investment funds, thus setting the nation on the road to economic independence;[181] and that it was these bankers who guided Budapest to become, by 1900, the largest European financial centre east of Vienna.[182] Furthermore, Jews made profound contributions to most facets of Budapest's spectacular socio-economic development, Jewish input helping to make this city not only the sixth largest in Europe[183] but also the fastest-growing European capital in the nineteenth century.[184]

Jewish association with agriculture tended towards large-scale farming. Whilst these rural involvements were generally of more modest proportion than their urban co-religionists' economic endeavours, they were still substantially greater than the Jewish percentage in the population would indicate. In 1910, 73.2 percent of all large-scale agricultural tenants were Jewish.[185] Furthermore, even though not permitted to own land prior to emancipation, by the turn of the century Jews held twenty percent of all latifundia property with an area greater than 1,000 *hold* (570 hectares),[186] their holdings escalating in the years 1884–94 from 1.75 million *hold* (1.0 million hectares) to 2.62 million *hold* (1.5 million hectares) — a 50 percent increase in a single decade. From around this period it became an almost social obligation for members of the financial aristocracy to acquire a country estate.[187] At the other end of the scale, with subsistence to intermediate-scale agriculture, that is involving farms of less than 100 *hold*,[188] Jewish involvement was negligible. Belying their ghetto stereotype, Jewish success in rural endeavour is indicated by the fact that between 1892 and 1912 Jewish farmers won 20 percent of all prizes awarded in agricultural shows.[189]

In essence, irrespective of the term used to describe their degree of involvement, by the turn of the century Jews had made themselves indispensable in most if not all areas of the Hungarian economy.[190] A similar situation, it can be argued, was developing with regard to the affluent, middle class professions. In the legal profession, for example, during the last decade of the century the total number of practitioners increased by 7.2 percent, whilst in the same period the number of Jewish lawyers escalated by 68.6 percent.[191] The children of the newly Magyarised Jews flocked to the universities and institutes of higher learning with such enthusiasm, and in such numbers, that by the turn of the century Jews constituted 42 percent of journalists, 45 percent of lawyers, 49 percent of registered medical practitioners[192] and 37 percent of engineers.[193] In 1903–04 Jews comprised 30 percent of all university enrolments. These achievements were based on a massive expansion of Jewish involvement in secular secondary education, their numbers escalating from 5.5 percent of enrolments in 1853–54 to 23.6 percent in 1903–04.[194] However, in contrast to the popular stereotype of Jewish focus on the traditional *bourgeois* professions, in the latter year Jews formed 20 percent of pupils at Hungary's 170 classical high schools (*gimnaziumok*) but 38 percent at the country's 32 technical high schools (*realiskolak*).[195]

The above description of Jewish fiscal endeavours should not be taken as a complete economic characterisation of Hungarian Jewry. Some historians of the period neglect to mention that 35 percent of Hungary's Jews were manual labourers, most of whom were burdened with the same grinding poverty that afflicted their non-Jewish counterparts. Yet despite this fact, in country areas and villages of this era, the terms "Jew" and "shopkeeper" became synonymous,[196] this stereotyping doubtless being reinforced by the presence in Hungary of 18,000 Jewish tavern-keepers,[197] two-thirds of whom were self-employed.[198]

Despite Hungarian Jewry's fervour regarding their ancient relationship with the Magyars, it is estimated that after the Turkish withdrawal of 1699, a mere 4,000 Jews remained in Hungary, 90 percent of whom resided along the Austrian-Moravian border. Immigration and internal dispersion were to reduce this proportion progressively until by 1910 it had declined to 36 percent.[199] The *Conscriptio Judaeorum* of 1735–38 showed Jewish numbers had risen modestly, to 12,000, one percent of the population, possibly largely due to an influx from Bohemia–Moravia.[200] But henceforth two major migrations were to produce profound increases.[201]

Later censi indicate that between 1787 and 1825 the Jewish population expanded from 81,000 to 185,000, an increase from 1.3 to 2.1 percent of total inhabitants.[202] It was at this stage that the spectacular escalation in absolute numbers commenced. By the beginning of the *Ausgleich* era in 1869 the Jewish population in Hungary numbered 542,000 (4.0 percent of the total), this growth continuing unimpeded until the end of the Hapsburg reign.

The census of 1910 counted 910,000 Hungarians of the Israelite Faith, 5 percent of "Hungary proper" inhabitants,[203] a 68 percent growth in somewhat under two generations. Immediately prior to World War I, the Hapsburg Empire contained the second-largest concentration of Jews in the world — 2.26 million compared with the Tsar's 6.95 million.[204]

This last phase of Jewish migration into Hungary, commencing from about the second decade of the nineteenth century, was dominated by immigrants of Polish origin[205] — notably, impoverished Jews attempting to escape a life of grinding poverty in Galicia.[206] Marton estimates that in 1941 50 percent of Hungarian Jews were descended from this Polish influx. Between 1787 and 1910 the total population of Hungary increased by 125 percent, whist the number of Hungarian Jews leapt over tenfold.[207]

The progressive Neolog sector of Hungarian Jewry was largely based in the affluent strata of Jewish society. Generally of Bohemian-Moravian origin,[208] this layer had little intercourse with the bottom levels of the Jewish social spectrum, the unskilled working class of mainly Polish lineage, whom a good many Neolog tended to disparage as benighted *Ostjuden* and an impediment to Jewish integration and acceptance within Magyarorszag. What was to become the guiding light of Hungarian Jewish acculturation, the Jewish Community of Pest, was formally incorporated as a *kehilah* in 1800.[209] By 1840 the community had grown to 10,000,[210] and in 1859 its growing, affluent membership consecrated a magnificent 3,000 seat Moorish Revival synagogue in Dohany Street, an architectural treasure that achieved world renown, served as the design inspiration for the Central Synagogue in New York[211] and remains, to this day, the largest synagogue in Europe.[212]

Jewish numbers in the capital continued to escalate, leaping fourfold to 40,000 by 1869.[213] Contemporaneous with this growth was a concerted, accelerating movement of Jews from rural areas: in the sixty years from 1830 to 1890 the percentage of Hungarian Jews living in urban localities doubled from 32 to 64 percent.[214] The growth of the Budapest *kehilah* was particularly influenced by this movement, the Jewish population of the city soaring from 70,000 in 1880 to 167,000 at the turn of the century, almost one in four of the capital's 700,000 inhabitants.[215] The rapid expansion continued; at the end of the next decade this number had increased by a further 22 percent, Budapest in 1910 containing 204,000 Jews.[216] At the turn of the century, Hungarian Jewry consisted of approximately 2,200 communities, of which 541 were substantial *kehilot* — 315 Orthodox, 160 Neolog and 66 Status Quo.[217]

Despite — or perhaps because of — Hungarian Jewry's fervent Magyarisation, during the early phase of the People's Party an ominous change in mood started appearing within *déclassé* Magyar gentry, the lesser nobility who had sought refuge in government employment after their traditional way of life had been disrupted by economic change and vicissitude. These gentry-bureaucrats increasingly abandoned their self-description "gentlemanly middle class" (*uri kozeposztaly*) in favour of the inherently chauvinistic appellation of — from a Jewish point of view — "Christian middle class".[218] This alteration in self-conception, by one of the pillars of the Magyar establishment, marked the first significant overt departure — albeit at this stage merely psychological — from the emancipation principle of socio-economic integration irrespective of religious adherence. Henceforth, although in theory all accepted religions continued to be treated as constitutional equals, in the reality of Dualist Hungary some religions became increasingly more equal than others.

Notwithstanding such ominous straws in the ideological wind, Hungarian Jewry's nexus with its surrounding society remained stronger than that of their co-religionists in any other European country.[219] Although this led to some conversion, largely concentrated amongst the intellectual, financial and political elite, Professor Deak is palpably erroneous in claiming that "a good many" Jews converted each year to Christianity.[220] The fallacy of this position is clear from statistics: Hungarian Jewish converts total a mere 10,000 during the *whole* of the nineteenth century.[221] This low conversion rate amongst Jews as a whole can be attributed to several factors, arguably one of the most important being the rigidly hierarchical nature of Hungarian society.

As a general rule, conversion led to alienation from the Jewish community without a commensurate acceptance in the wider Christian sphere, the apostate becoming burdened in both communities with the derisive designation "converted Jew". Although some of the Jewish elite abandoned their religious identity, generally in an attempt to curry favour with paramount Christian circles, others were clearly unabashed in drawing attention to their heritage. In particular, twenty-three of the twenty-nine Jewish nobles created between 1887 and 1896 were members of the Pest Jewish community.[222]

As with conversion, mixed marriage, although increasing from 2.7 percent at the turn of the century to 4.3 percent in 1908, was statistically — at least by current Diaspora standards — a strictly marginal phenomenon.[223] Not surprisingly, both Orthodox and Neolog hierarchies opposed such abandonment of religious identity; not only for theological reasons, but also to reject the notion that Jewishness was somehow an impediment to integration and loyalty to the nation.

Jewish contribution to Hungarian cultural attainment is described by Professor Macartney as "hardly smaller" than their role in the country's economic development, viz: "a very great number of the nation's most boasted achievements in learning, science, literature and the arts were the work of Jews."[224] However, in his sometimes somewhat dubious manner when referring to Jews, Macartney qualifies his assessment of Jewish endeavour by characterising the Jews' contributions to Hungary's cultural vibrancy and international reputation as "their infiltration of the national life".[225]

Zionism

Despite two of the most eminent Zionist pioneers, Theodor Herzl (1860–1904) and Max Nordau (1849–1923), being born in Budapest, the chauvinism of Magyars of the Israelite Faith precluded a powerful manifestation of Zionism in the country.[226] Hungarian Jews vehemently opposed a policy that, *inter alia*, advocated a changed status for the country's Jews. To this great majority, it appeared that Zionists were attempting to exchange the security and benefits accorded state-supported Jewry for the doubtful privilege of becoming either the pioneering white colonisers of a small, impoverished country ruled by a despotic Moslem regime or, alternatively — should Zionism fail — another ethnic minority dominated by the authoritarian, chauvinist Magyars. Such a change in status threatened not only Jews' continuing socio-economic integration; their hard-won position, in Prime Minister Kalman Tisza's 1882 words, "as the most industrious and constructive segment of the Hungarian population";[227] their security of living in a society where supportive governments reinforced Jewish emancipation by promptly and effectively suppressing Antisemitic outbreaks; their reputation as staunch patriots; and, not least, it threatened them with the prospect of being subjected to the sort of socio-cultural repression with which the Magyars ruled "their" disloyal, intransigent minorities in Magyarorszag. In addition, on theological grounds the Orthodox strongly opposed any concept of a secular-induced *Aliya*.[228]

This vehement opposition by the overwhelming majority to the very concept of Zionism remained a constant within Hungarian Jewry until the end of the Second World War. Rabinowicz succinctly summarises the rancour and turmoil that developed from this cleavage in self-conception: "The struggle of Hungarian assimilationism against Zionism was fought with a bitterness that probably surpassed that found in any other land."[229] A not surprising situation in light of the fact that Hungarian Jewry, not unreasonably, given its circumstances, considered it had a great vested interest in maintaining its status quo, an interest arguably greater than that of any other European Jewry. Thus, although Zionist organisations were established in several Hungarian cities in 1897,[230] under the influence of established Jewry the Hungarian government refused until 1927 to approve the statutes of the 1903-inaugurated Hungarian Zionist Organisation.[231]

Yet despite the fierce hostility of their co-religionists, Hungarian Zionists, energised by the holding of the Mizrachi[232] movement's first world conference at Pozsony (Bratislava, Slovakian; Pressburg, German) in August 1904, commenced constructing an infrastructure early in the century. Included in this network were student and sporting organisations, and several publishing ventures.[233] The secession of the most successful body, the religiously inclined Mizrachi, from the National Organisation at the tenth Hungarian Zionist Conference held at Kassa in 1910 inaugurated a period of decline, with several groups subsequently becoming moribund and then defunct.[234] During World War I, apart from publication of the periodical *Zsido Szemle* (Jewish Review), Zionist activity in Hungary became practically nonexistent.[235] Despite British hopes, the Balfour Declaration of 1917 did not sway Hungary's Jews from loyalty to the Hapsburg cause.

Jews in Politics

Taking cognisance of, and concurring with, Prime Minister Banffy's 1882 declaration that "being a unified national state, Hungary cannot tolerate political parties on the basis of nationality",[236] Hungarian Jewish leaders as a matter of policy opposed the formation of a specifically Jewish political party. In the absence of such a Jewish national electoral grouping, Hungarian Jews involved in the political process had to widen their horizons and engage in activity beyond the confines of their religious community.

Despite the Jewish establishment being a pillar of the aristocrat-plutocrat-gentry oligarchy that controlled *Ausgleich* Hungary, Jews featured prominently — if not predominantly — as vanguards of the Left in the progressive sectors of art, theatre, literature and politics. With regard to politics, this assessment is clearly supported by Janos' examination of Left radical elites for the period 1900–19. Although based on somewhat tenuous assumptions, Janos' analysis indicates that on the average, Jews constituted 45 percent of the membership of such groups, with another 18 percent of such participants being "possibly Jewish".[237] In the centre of the political spectrum, Vilmos Vazsonyi, who did more than any other individual Jew to secure the Jewish religion's "received" status, founded the urban-based Democratic Party, fought Zionism all his life,[238] and became the Minister of Justice during the Great War.[239]

In an attempt to inhibit Jewish participation in politics outside the boundaries of oligarchic sanction, and to consolidate his hold on power, Prime Minister Istvan Tisza's first premiership, 1903–05, saw a determined effort by the government to cultivate a still closer alignment between upwardly mobile Jews and the ruling party. Under the influence of this policy, the number of parliamentary deputies with Jewish parentage increased from twenty-six to eighty-four, the latter figure representing 22 percent of all MPs, that is, some four and a half times the Jewish proportion of the population. During this period, there were from six to eight Ministers, nine Secretaries of State, a Lord Mayor of Budapest and sixteen members of the Upper House who were of Jewish origin.[240] However, to place these figures in some perspective, it should be noted that in Budapest, although Jews comprised about one-quarter of the populace, the oligarchical franchise — based on highly restricted financial and educational criteria[241] — meant that about half the electorate was Jewish. *Ergo* it can be reasoned that, relative to their proportion of this debased franchise, Jews were — if anything — under-represented in parliament.

Another aspect of the campaign to court Jews was the intensification of the previously mentioned policy of granting Jewish ennoblements, 105 alone being awarded during Tisza's second premiership of June 1913–June 1917. Notwithstanding these policies of encouraging further Jewish upward social mobility, a "tacit but firm expectation", combined with the subliminal but nonetheless forceful pressures exerted by the establishment, appear to have ensured that the majority of aforementioned MPs eventually converted to Christianity.[242]

The Great War

The history of the Austro-Hungarian Empire after the assassination of the Crown Prince, Archduke Franz Ferdinand (by a Bosnian extremist in Sarajevo on 28 June 1914), is too well documented to warrant repetition in this book. However, suffice it to say that the Emperor's sole adviser to counsel against war was the Hungarian Prime Minister, Count Istvan Tisza,[243] who feared defeat via the possibility of a widespread conflict involving Britain, France and Russia. Paradoxically, he also feared victory — due to the prospects of a successful war undermining Magyar hegemony through the incorporation of additional Slavs, and possibly Roumanians, into the Kingdom's fragile polyglot domain.[244] During the period of conflict Hungary mobilised 3.6 million citizens, constituting 17.5 percent of her population. Of this number over half were either killed (660,000), wounded (740,000), or taken prisoner (730,000).[245] As in the revolution of 1848, Hungarian Jews were enthusiastic in rallying to the flag, with Jewish officers receiving 154 medals of the three highest orders and 656 decorations of the fourth (Great Silver) rank. During the 1914–18 conflagration over 10,000 Hungarian Jews fell defending the country's cherished "thousand year frontier".[246]

Yet despite these Jewish heroes and fallen; despite displays of conspicuous patriotism by Hungarian Jewry's leaders, Rabbis[247] and members;[248] despite the Heir Apparent Karl and the Archdukes Jozsef and Franz Peter publicly praising the Jewish contributions to the War effort; despite the Imperial General Staff unanimously praising the "uncommon distinction" with which heroic Jews had served in the War's bloodiest campaigns, including the "bitter and terrible fighting in the Carpathians";[249] despite the majority of military surgeons being Jewish; despite Jewish industrialists being commended for their role in the War economy; and despite the millions of crowns contributed, individually and collectively, by Hungarian Jews, an intensifying Antisemitism permeated Hungarian society.[250] The abiding Hungarian Judeophobia was re-energising, with Antisemitic movements

K.U.K. INF. REG.
№ 32.
BUDAPESTI.
HÁZIEZRED.
1917. BEN.
ISTENTISZTELET
A KÁRPÁTOKBAN.
SÁMUEL F.

Figure 1.2 *Istentisztelet* **(Divine Worship)**
Religious service for Jewish members of a Budapest regiment in the
Carpathian Mountains, 1917. (Source: JMB, 89.107)

collecting ten million crowns for their purposes.[251] The pressures and prejudices generated by a devastating conflict were relentlessly pushing the pendulum of Antisemitism from the covert to the overt phase of activity.

Without justification, a growing tide of propaganda accused collective Jewry of conspiring against the War effort, of undermining morale, of shirking military duty, of profiteering[252] and, above all, of controlling and subverting the nation's vital economic, cultural and political apparatus.[253] These allegations were part of a widespread Magyar conviction that the "non-warlike" minorities in Magyarorszag, by focusing on their own ethnic particularities and/or business acumen, debased the venerated principles of honour, sacrifice, courage and faith in a time of great national peril. Consequently, although Budapest generally suffered less privation than most other European capitals,[254] the War nevertheless caused immense bitterness, frustration and hostility in the Magyars, feelings which often found expression in heightened convictions of their superiority vis-à-vis the minorities.[255]

With regard to Jews, this attitude was reinforced by two synchronous manifestations. Firstly, the substantial Jewish involvement in the economy, particularly by high-profile plutocrats, exposed Hungarian Jewry as a whole to criticism regarding war-induced shortages, inflation and profiteering. Additionally, the flood of non-acculturated, ultra-Orthodox Jews fleeing the Russian invasions of Galicia and the Carpathians, created consternation in ethnic-Magyar areas, particularly Budapest. Such previously unknown concentrations of Chassidic, patently foreign, "ethnic" Jews generated anxiety, hostility, and — not infrequently — vilification from an increasingly war-weary populace yearning for a return to normalcy. The scapegoat syndrome, via a chauvinistic focus on the bi-polar Jewish "threat" — profiteering plutocrat and parasitic Chassid — was off and running.[256]

Chapter I: Notes

1. On 11 July 1944, Sir Winston Churchill wrote to his Foreign Minister, Anthony Eden, regarding the implementation of the Final Solution in Hungary: "There is no doubt that this is probably the greatest and most horrible crime ever committed in the whole history of the world..." (Prime Minister's Personal Minute, M 818/4, Top Secret, Premier papers, 4/51/10, folio 1331; cited Gilbert 1984:277)

2. Braham (1985:vii) states: "Perhaps no other chapter in the Holocaust has elicited as many agonising questions and given rise to so many heated debates as the destruction of Hungarian Jewry."

3. An authority assesses the attitude of Hungarian Jews as "almost oblivious to the systematic destruction of the Jewish communities in Nazi dominated Europe". (Braham 1985:vii)

4. Marton 1966:4.

5. The *Enclopaedia Judaica* (henceforth *En J*) states that "the Jewish community of Komarno [Komarom, Hungarian] was considered one of the oldest in the Danube region...it is possible that Jews went there with the Roman legions." (*En J* 10, 1174, "Komarno")

6. The Magyar pillages were so violent and extensive that congregations throughout much of Christendom recited the prayer "De sagittis Hungarorum libera nos Domina" (From the arrows of Hungarians, save us O Lord). (Makkai 1973:27) It is piquant to note Martin Gilbert's statement (1985:25) that the Jewish Kingdom of Kazaria "gave military aid to the Magyars in their conquest of Hungary". Handler (1985:4) gives a slightly different version: "Three Judaized Khazar tribes, known as Kabars, who had left their Crimean homeland in the aftermath of a civil war, joined the Magyars as allies and fought valiantly alongside them. Amiable relations, however, could not survive the Hungarians' conversion to Christianity..."

Handler continues his narrative (1985:8): "That the Kabars were no mere tagalongs is a matter of record. For some time after the conquest the Magyars even spoke the Khazar language in addition to their own." Makkai (1973:17) is even more specific in emphasising the importance of the Khazar involvement. Relying on Arabic and Byzantine sources he states: "The Khazar *conquerors* appointed chiefs to head the Hungarian tribes..." (Emphasis added)

7. Although contemporary idiom equates the terms "Magyar" and "Hungarian", it is vital to note that until the Treaty of Trianon (1920), "Magyar" generally indicated an ethnic group and "Hungary" a political entity. In post-Trianon Hungary the two terms lost this delineation. For an exposition of the critical significance to Hungarian Jewry of this change in Hungarian self-conception, see the following chapters.

8. Christianity, being based on the principle of universality, provided a viable method of eroding clan and tribal allegiances. King Istvan I (997-1038) entrenched Christianity in Hungary primarily as a means of consolidating his reign. His formal coronation, to which the Pope sent the crown, is traditionally considered to have occurred on Christmas Day 1,000 CE. For details concerning the political usage of Christianity during this period see Makkai 1990:15-22.

9. Katzburg 1984:5; Marton 1966:12; Katzburg 1985:5.

10. The most important protective regulation relating to Jews in medieval Hungary was the charter issued in 1251 by King Bela IV (1235-70). Cancelling the restrictions of the Synod of Szabolcs, and motivated by the devastating Mongol invasion of 1241-42, the charter — known as the Golden Bull of Hungarian Jewry — adopted a benevolent attitude towards Jewish commercial activities and confirmed the Jews' position in the Hungarian social hierarchy. (Marton 1966:9-10)

11. The Austrian Hapsburg dynasty had ruled Hungary since the Ottoman withdrawal. This situation was formalised in 1699 by the Treaty of Karlowitz. (Pamlenyi 1973:577)

12. Applying to Vienna, lower Austria, Moravia and Hungary, the Edict enabled Jews in these regions to consider themselves as permanent residents. By 1815 this situation had extended to the whole of western and central Europe. (Katz 1980:52)

13. Laszlo 1966:68.

14. For detailed demographics of the earlier era, see "*Conscipto Judeorum* of 1735-38" in Marton 1966:30-39. For a more general view over a broader period see Laszlo 1966:64-117.

15. *En J* 8, 1089; Katzberg 1966:138. Introduced by Maria Theresa in 1744, the tax was imposed on Jews for being permitted to reside in the country. As it was the obligation of the Jews themselves to collect the revenue, the tax had the paradoxical effect of strengthening the community's infrastructure. Originally levied at the rate of 20,000 guilders per annum, by the beginning of the nineteenth century the annual imposition had escalated to 160,000 guilders.

16. For the arguments propagated by the proponents of continued Jewish isolation, see Katz 1980:53-62.

17. Katz 1978:164.

18. In 1839, by large majorities, both chambers of the Hungarian parliament passed legislation that abolished the Tolerance Tax and granted virtual equal rights to Jews. The legislation was vetoed by the Crown following insistent campaigning by the cities. (Janos 1982:82-3) The tax was finally abolished on 24 June 1846 when Emperor Ferdinand V accepted the Jewish offer of 1,200,000 guilders as an abrogation payment. [Isidor Singer (Ed.) *The Jewish Encyclopedia*. New York: Funk and Wagnalls Company, 1904:6, 500]

19. This progressive gentry class, consisting of the moderately affluent, poorer and landless of the lesser nobility, emerged in this period and coalesced into the "historic middle class" — the grouping that came to dominate Hungarian administration up to the end of World War II.

20. Janos 1982:80.

21. Some nationalists, particularly the Vienna-born Count Istvan Szechenyi, believed that Jewish acculturation was a mere facade. This element maintained that Jews were too deeply committed to the "German spirit", which nationalists considered the main obstacle to the development of Hungarian nationhood. (Katz 1980:232-5, especially 234.)

22. Written by Charles Zay, contained in Bela Bernstein, *A magyar szabadsagharc es a zsidok* (The Hungarian War of Independence and the Jews). Budapest: Franklin 1898:22; cited Janos 1982:81.

23. Jeno Zsoldos (ed.), *1848-1849 a magyar zsidosag eleteben* (1848-49 in the life of Hungarian Jewry). Budapest: Neuwald 1948:23; cited Janos 1982:81.

24. Ibid; cited Janos 1982:81-82. In many cultures the word "cockroach" is used as a derogatory epithet. It is therefore interesting to observe that the Hungarian term for cockroach is *svabbogar*, ie: Swabe bug. Note that the Hungarian alphabet does not contain the letter "w".

25. Typified by the great Hungarian poet Sandor Petofi in his verse "The poets of the Nineteenth Century":

When from the cornucopia of plenty
All can equally partake,
When all can equally sit
At the table of justice,
When the sunshine of the spirit
Sparkles on the window of every home:
Only then shall we say,
Let's stop now, Caanan has come!
(Quoted Barany 1990:207)

26. A foremost exception being the great liberal statesman Baron Jozsef Eotvos (1813-71). His book *The Emancipation of the Jews* (1840) urged complete and unqualified equality for Jews. Despite this philosophy Eotvos was not free of the Hungarian bi-polar ethos towards the Jews, being of the personal opinion that assimilation was the preferred eventual solution to the "Jewish Question". (Katzburg 1984:9) For a Jewish interpretation of his literary endeavours, religious philosophy and political accomplishments see Dr Bernat Heller "Eotvos Jozsef *baro*" (Baron Jozsef Eotvos), in Jozsef Banoczi (ed.), *Az Izr. Magyar Irodalmi Tarsulat XXXVI Evkonyv 1913* (Thirty-sixth Yearbook of the Hungarian Jewish Literary Society, 1913). Budapest 1913:7-55.

27. Representative of Kossuth's attitude of this period was his proclamation of May 1844: "The Jews in our country must be regarded as a group living in the midst of the people of our land who differ from the rest only in religion. It would then follow that the Jews in our country constitute a religious denomination... But Moses was not only the founder of a religion, he was a maker of civil laws as well... Thus the Jews cannot be emancipated because their religion is a political institution that is based on theocratic foundations, which cannot be harmonised politically with the existing system of government." (Cited Handler 1980:11) For an exposition of Kossuth's philosophy, as well as that of his opponents, see Barany 1990:174-208 and Katz 1980:230-244.

28. Janos 1982:82.

29. Via an "easily discernible undercurrent". (Ibid)

30. Kossuth himself belonged to this class. (Barta 1975:231)

31. For a detailed chronology of this era see Deak 1990:209-34, Barta 1973:241-84, and Janos 1982:69-91.

32. Deak 1990:209.

33. Jews comprised 20,000 of the rebel army's 180,000 troops, ie: 11 percent (Vida 1939:23). Although demographic figures in this period are matters of some conjecture, it is clear that the above percentage is well in excess of the Jewish proportion of the population. For comprehensive Hungarian Jewish demographic statistics, see Ujvari 1929:552-564.

34. Despite the egalitarian motivation of the revolutionary militia, only those of noble descent could rise above the rank of Major. (Nassi 1986:198)

35. Ibid.

36. Handler 1985:5.

37. Ibid.

38. Nassi 1986:198.

39. Vida 1939:63. Unless otherwise indicated, translations from Hungarian to English are by the writer.

40. Archive of the Jewish Museum of Budapest [henceforth JMBA], serial number 68.65. Translation by Elenora David, Sydney.

41. Katz 1980:236.

42. Deak 1990:233-4. The Hungarians and the Austrians each lost about 50,000 troops; the Russians lost some 11,550 — 550 in battle and 11,000 to cholera. (Ibid)

43. Handler 1980:15.

44. Important examples being the Jewish Oath and the prohibition on acquiring real estate. (*En J* 8, 1090)

45. Ibid. In 1856 this latter sum was reimbursed as an educational and welfare fund.

46. Vida 1939:21; Katzburg 1984:10.

47. Katz 1980:236.

48. *En J* 11, 444.

49. Vida 1939:21.

50. Handler 1980:13.

51. Handler 1985:5.

52. It is poignant to note the *En J* summary of Mendelssohn's attitude towards the establishment of a Jewish state in Palestine: "He assumed that the realization of the project could only take place through a generalized European war, otherwise it would certainly be held up by one of the powers." (*En J* 11, 1335) For an exposition of the philosophy of the non-Jewish Enlightenment, see Berlin:1961.

53. Katz 1977:48.

54. Some historians propose that the "Golden Age" extended from 1867 to the start of World War I. However, as Emancipation was promulgated and nurtured by the Dual Monarchy regime, it is appropriate to consider the era to have extended to the cessation of hostilities in 1918. Certainly the Great War, especially its latter phases, witnessed Hungarian Jewry under increasing social and economic pressures, but it was only with the collapse of the Monarchy and the consequent ascendancy of the White Counter-revolutionary Junta that a clear and decisive break with the policy of institutional equality was inaugurated. Thus, whilst it is germane to consider World War I as forming a transitional phase, this interregnum is more appropriately characterised as constituting the end of the Emancipation period rather than the beginning of the Antisemitic epoch.

55. Hanak 1973a:316.

56. *Reichseinheit*: absolutist centralism and territorial unity under Austrian domination.

57. Despite the fierce opposition of the Hungarian nationalists — principally the exiled Kossuth and his supporters — on 29 May, after a series of acrimonious debates, the Hungarian legislature ratified the Compromise (Law XII of 1867) by the substantial majority of 209 pro, 89 against, with 83 abstentions. (Janos 1982:90; Somogyi 1990:251-52) Demands for equal consideration by representatives of five restive minorities now governed from Budapest — the Slovaks, Serbs, Roumanians, Ruthenians and Germans — were answered by the Nationality Act 1868. Whilst generating a liberal facade via, for example, permitting the use of minority vernaculars in certain situations, the Act denied non-Magyars separate ethnic rights and political institutions, refusing even to acknowledge the existence of national minorities. Despite these fundamental omissions, Magyar public opinion, in its

fervent desire for a unitary nation-state, decided that the Bill granted too many concessions to the non-Magyar population. (Frank 1990:254-5; Hanak 1973b:324)

58. For a recent account of Hungarian attitudes towards the Monarch and his regime see Andras Gero *Ferenc Jozsef, a magyarok kiralya* (Franz Jozsef, King of the Hungarians). Hungary: Novotrade RT, 1988.

59. Crankshaw 1981:240. Most importantly, Hungary obtained a separate constitution and legislature and Magyar became the official language of education and administration. Monetary linkage remained via a joint customs union and Hungary's contribution to the Imperial exchequer, both of these financial agreements being subject to renegotiation every ten years. (Handler 1980:1)

60. Hanak 1973b:324. This situation permitted the latifundia class to consolidate their position at the expense of three restive elements — the rising middle class, the impoverished peasants and the disaffected national minorities. (Hanak 1973a:319)

61. The reformers realised that a modern, progressive state could not be developed with the 1867 literacy rates, ie: 41 percent for males, and 24 percent for females, over the age of six. So in 1868, despite the hostility of Catholic clergy and their supporters, an Education Reform Bill received parliamentary approval. A state system of education was introduced, religious schools became subject to state supervision and inspection, and the state designated certain subjects as mandatory in both systems. (Frank 1990:258)

62. Handler 1980:4.

63. Some authorities retain Eotvos' original title — "Minister of Cults and Public Instruction" — which today conveys an archaic and/or inappropriate connotation.

64. Handler 1980:16.

65. Katzburg 1966:142-43.

66. Katzburg 1984:10.

67. Because of the increasingly virulent socio-theological turmoil that was to embroil Hungarian Jewry in the following decades, it is poignant to note that during the Revolution, on 5 July 1848, a general Jewish conference at Pest decided to petition parliament for emancipation and stipulated that no concessions were possible regarding matters of faith, even if the legislators insisted on reform as a condition for the granting of equality. (*The Jewish Encyclopedia* 1904:6, 501)

68. Katzburg 1966:5.

69. On occasion the government attempted to resolve such conflicts, most forcefully on 20 October 1852, when five small independent congregations based on the radical reform principles advocated by the *Genossenschaft fur Reform im Judenthume* of Berlin were ordered to disband, the members being required to rejoin their original congregations. (Handler 1980:192, n27) *The Jewish Encyclopedia* (1904:6, 502), however, is of the opinion that the dissolution was an example of the then government's general policy of suppressing the advocates of change. Irrespective of the government's prime motivation, state intervention in the religious affairs of the community was clearly possible.

70. The Michalowitz assembly issued a noted *Psak Beth Din* (Rabbinical Judgement) that prohibited nine modernist proposals for reforming (some proponents called it "civilising") synagogue practice, in particular banning sermons in the vernacular, ie: in languages other than Yiddish. Despite approval by sixty-seven Rabbis, the Judgement had the unintended consequence of producing a split in Orthodox ranks, some highly respected Rabbis refusing to endorse them primarily because, in their view, the *Psak* would generate unfavourable impressions in non-Jewish circles. (Katzburg 1969:6-7)

71. Katzburg 1969:10.

72. Handler 1980:17.

73. Katzburg 1969:10.

74. Published from 10 November 1867 to 1 September 1870. (Katzburg 1969:28, n25)

75. Katzburg 1969:11.

76. The fundamental code of traditional Jewish conduct.

77. See Braham 1981:1-12.

78. This contradiction of his position — by a primary source — was cited by Katzburg himself (1969:11 and 28, n27). For additional details regarding the traditionalists' secular political activities see McCagg Jr 1989:136-37. After considering the 1910 census, McCagg Jr (p190) concludes: "These figures tell clearly that it was not only the Neolog of Budapest who Magyarised themselves. The Orthodoxy of the peripheral regions, despite their antipathy to Neolog ways, opted decisively against the developing nationalities", ie: became aligned with the Magyarist cause by adopting the Magyar language.

79. Handler 1980:17-18; Katzburg 1969:12.

80. Dr Hirschler's motivation as stated in his private correspondence with Rabbi Lov. (Handler 1980:18)

81. Ibid.

82. Ibid.

83. Conducted under the presidency of Dr Ignac Hirschler, the Congress administered 33 plenary meetings and 107 committee sessions, the latter consisting of 25 delegates — 14 progressive and 11 Orthodox. (Katzburg 1969:15-16)

84. Katzburg 1984:10.

85. Handler 1980:19. A minority of thirty-five Orthodox delegates decided to remain in attendance. Named the "Cultured Orthodox", they attempted to recognise modern circumstance from within the prism of traditional belief. (Handler 1980:193, n37)

86. Of the 220 original delegates, only 116 attended the final voting sessions, of whom 103 supported the proposed statutes. (Katzburg 1969:31, n36) On this basis, despite the overwhelming vote in favour (103 to 13), the community charter was approved by only a minority of the Congress, being supported by just 103 of the original 220 elected representatives.

87. For a synopsis of the statutes, see Katzburg 1969:16-19.

88. Katzburg 1969:18.

89. In this supplication the Orthodox requested the (Liberal) government to preserve their separate identity, an apparently paradoxical request as Liberal opinion favoured a unitary state. However, because of constant controversies between Catholics and Protestants, the issue of religious freedom was a prime concern of the Liberals, a grouping whose philosophy rejected compulsion in questions of theology.

90. Handler 1980:19.

91. Often abbreviated to the obvious "Status Quo".

92. In keeping with the heterogeneous nature of the Austro-Hungarian Empire, the Jewish situation in Hungary was far from representative of the condition pertaining to Jews in other regions of the Hapsburg domain. The facade of religious unity was maintained in Vienna "but the price was the wholesale abandonment of control... Because the Hungarian state legally acknowledged the disunity of the Jews, the Pest Neologs could make their own decisions in a way the Viennese [progressives] could not..." Furthermore, "no Jewish organisation spoke at all for Jewish Galicia or for the Jews of Bukovina, where total disunity prevailed." (McCagg 1989:250-51)

93. The specifically Central European term "Neolog" was applied by the Orthodox to their progressive opponents at about the time of the Congress in question. (Katzburg 1990: 45, n5)

94. Including institutes for orphans, handicapped and aged members of the community. (Handler 1980:19)

95. It should be emphasised that individual Jews had the right to affiliate with the synagogue of their choice. In turn, each *kehilah* had the obligation to provide its governing secretariat with details of its affiliates, the respective secretariat thence conveying these details to the appropriate state authority. The Status Quo communities, lacking a central

secretariat, operated on the basis that each individual community provided its details directly to the government.

96. Katz 1990:19.

97. During the Emancipation period there was scant need for Neolog leaders to jeopardise their reputation or position by attempting procedures out of keeping with the behavioural format expected of a governmentally sanctioned authority. As one historian has summarised, the Neolog "had much better contacts in the government than the Orthodox did, and the tides of the times worked for them. The more modern education spread among the nation's Jews, and the more the 'little Jews' flocked to dynamic, capitalistic, metropolitan Budapest, the more the Neolog community's membership grew." (McCagg Jr 1989b:251)

98. In broad terms, the Orthodox and the Zionists were characterised as being separated by rival religious *and* political ideologies, whereas the Orthodox-Neolog and the Neolog-Zionist schisms were singular in nature, being based on religion and politics respectively.

99. This is not to suggest that the Neolog leadership collaborated with the Antisemites in *any* sense.

100. Katzburg 1969:21 and 32, n40.

101. Lacking a central secretariat, each Status Quo community operated independently, but still within the framework as specified by the state. Although the schism between the Orthodox, Neolog and Status Quo involved fundamental differences in religious philosophy, each faction continued accepting its rivals as being unequivocally Jewish.

102. Katzburg 1985:10, n1.

103. The crash of 1873 was sufficiently severe to cause the near bankruptcy of the state. Fiscal penury was only averted by securing a loan of 150 million gulden from a consortium of foreign financiers, including the Jewish House of Rothschild. (Hanak 1973b: 332-33)

104. Nathaniel Katzburg, *Anti-Semitism in Hungary.* (Tel-Aviv: Dvir, 1969), 25-28; cited in Katz 1980:237. Referring to the above questions Katz (Ibid) comments: "One has to keep the persistence of Jewish Orthodoxy in mind in order to understand the anti-Semitic reaction that first appeared in Hungary as early as 1875..." By suggesting that Orthodox particularity was primarily responsible for the generation of Antisemitism, Prof. Katz not only seems to blame a distinct section of Jewry for the existence of Jew-hatred but ignores the thesis, which I believe is more than amply validated by the Holocaust, that Jewish assimilation and economic competition are more virulent generators of Antisemitism than is the maintenance of a distinctive Jewish identity. On p. 322 of his above work, Katz universalises his argument by writing: "I regard the very presence of the unique Jewish community among the other nations as the stimulus to the animosity directed at them." Once again Prof. Katz is demonstrably wrong. Numerous examples of Antisemitism could be cited in countries that are effectively *Judenrein,* contemporary instances being Poland and Malaysia.

105. For Istoczy's political agenda see Venetianer 1922: 314-18, 324-5, 340.

106. As the substantive flow originated in Bohemia, Moravia and Galicia, and as these lands were fellow members of the Hapsburg domain, the "immigrants" were technically not foreigners. (Katz 1980:238)

107. Katz 1980:240.

108. Written in 1779 as an apologia to defend those, including himself, who had forged documents in attempting to prove nonexistent repayments to Jewish creditors, Hell indicted Jewry for maintaining a state-like authority over its membership. Later he extended his thesis to criticise Jews for retaining this monolithic cohesion despite having been accepted into the French commonwealth. (Katz 1980:108-09) Similar arguments were expounded in Austria in the 1840s by a destitute aristocrat, Count Ferdinand Schnirnding. (Katz 1980:225-26)

109. Katz 1980:239-40.

110. A member of the lower gentry, a class whose economic position was declining due to the advancements facilitated by Jewish capital and enterprise, Istoczy had some "unpleasant experiences" with Jewish litigants in his home county in Western Hungary. (Ibid) The *En J*

states that his committing an irregularity forced his resignation from the bench. His claim that "the Jews" had "framed him" seems to be the origin of his "persecution mania...and pathological hatred of Jews". (*En J* 9, 1099, "Istoczy, Gyozo")

111. Mendes-Flohr and Reinharz 1980:273, n8. Regarding Jews, this commitment to equality in the Balkan successor states was observed more in the omission than in the application.

112. The *En J* (11, 1015, "Marr, Wilhelm") states: "There is no proof for the often repeated assertion that he was of Jewish origin." Anthony Quinton ("Idealists Against the Jews" *The New York Review of Books,* 7 November 1991, 38) concurs but claims that Marr's first three wives were Jewish. For an elaboration of the ideologies and endeavours of Marr and his German and Austrian Antisemitic *confrères* see Wistrich 1991:54-65, Katz 1980:245-72, and Carsten 1967:22-41. An assortment of important racial and political Antisemitic tracts can be found in Mendes-Flohr and Reinharz 1980:252-300.

113. Mendes-Flohr and Reinharz 1980:272.

114. Macartney 1971:712.

115. Despite its avowed agenda, the Federation, in a token gesture towards the liberalism of the age, retained a facade of humanitarian impartiality — it permitted converted Jews to clamber from their pariah status by accepting such converts as members, albeit in undisclosed form. (Katz 1980:274) Once again the age-old Hungarian duality towards Jews had survived, even in this most unlikely crevice. The significance of this survival is the clear indication that Hungarian Antisemitism, by permitting individual redemption from collective Jewish iniquity, had yet to metamorphose into a virulent, unyielding racism in which all Jews, irrespective of their religion, were automatically and irrevocably confined to the innermost circle of damnation and persecution.

116. Handler 1980:32.

117. Katz 1980:274.

118. Venetianer 1922:342-43. At this time 36 percent of medical and 26 percent of law students were Jews (Katz 1980:274), respectively some seven and five times the Jewish percentage of the Hungarian population.

119. Katz 1980:274.

120. Katz 1980:241. The relevant minister responded to this speech by dismissing it as "a mere literary exercise", whilst the Speaker chastised Istoczy for being unparliamentary and contrary to good taste.

121. Ibid.

122. Handler 1980:34.

123. Venetianer 1922:342, who alludes to Russian influence in the disturbances by adding that the ringleaders of these pogroms were pan-Slav extremists.

124. Handler 1980:31.

125. Handler 1980:34, 35.

126. Emerging in the second century CE, the outrageous accusations of ritual murder and desecration of the host were originally directed against the early Christians. These canards were resurrected by European Christians of the twelfth and thirteenth centuries, but only to be redirected against the Jews. It is pertinent to note that Jew-hatred became so widespread and deep-seated that it persisted even in those European states that were officially *Judenrein*, for example England and France of the sixteenth and seventeenth centuries. In these places "Jewish wickedness was taken for granted and continued to serve as a criterion for the acme of evil." (Leperer 1991:12)

127. Lucas 1988:188.

128. At this time Tiszaeszlar, approximate population 2,700, contained about twenty-five Jewish families of the Chassidic persuasion. (*En J* 15, 1155, "Tiszaeszlar"; Katz 1980:276)

129. Venetianer 1922:346. Commemorating their liberation from slavery in ancient Egypt, Jews eat unleavened bread throughout the eight days of the *Pesach* Festival.

130. Handler 1980:52.

131. For a precis of the investigators' malicious *modus operandi*, see Handler 1980: 52-54.

132. The Prime Minister made numerous speeches supporting the Jews (Handler 1980:111); however, Tisza retained the services of his Justice Minister, Tivadar Pauler, who believed that a "few uncivilised Jews employed Christian blood for their religious worship". (*En J* 15, 1155, "Tiszaeszlar")

133. Also supportive of the Jewish position was the long-exiled but still influential Kossuth, who wrote: "As a man of the nineteenth century, I am ashamed by this anti-Semitic agitation, as a Hungarian it embarrassed me, as a patriot I condemn it." (Frank 1990:264)

134. Ibid. For a succinct overview of Eotvos' concluding address see Handler 1980:164-66. Karoly Eotvos' account of the case can be found in his book *A Nagy Per* (The Great Trial). Budapest: Szepirodalmi Konyvkiado, repr. 1968.

135. Handler 1980:173.

136. *The New York Times,* however, was ambivalent. On 6 August 1883, after condemning the affair as "a case conducted with great barbarity", it continued by praising the authorities for preventing an Antisemitic crusade that "...would have swept the Hebrews out of all Central and eastern Europe, where, as a race, they are hated with a hatred such as Americans and Englishmen cannot conceive..." (Handler 1980:174-75)

137. Handler 1980:176-77.

138. Handler 1980:179-80. For a lucid summary of the Appeal Court's judgement, see Handler 1980:180-81. The supremacy of Antisemitic mythology and prejudice over the reality of court judgements is confirmed by the research of a Hungarian journalist, Ivan Sandor. Interviewing variously aged residents of Tiszaeszlar in 1973, Sandor found that only a minority of those interviewed had any knowledge of the blood libel allegation. However, with the exception of the last two Jewish residents of the town, all those claiming knowledge of the case either stated that the girl was ritually slaughtered by Jews or else repeated popular Antisemitic myths and calumnies. Apart from the two Jews, not one person interviewed knew the verdict of the trial. It should be noted that collective consciousness and memory may well have been influenced by the popular folk song:
Eszter Solymosi went to the store for thread,
The rascal Jews lured her into the temple.
The rascal Jews lured her into the temple,
Her red blood flowed into a pot there. (Handler 1980: 183-85)

139. Handler 1980: 109-10.

140. The Austrian government saw fit to ban distribution of Istoczy's tract. (Katz 1980:226)

141. Divided by philosophical, political and economic ideology, the convention proved to be an ineffectual affair. Despite the formation of the *Alliance Antijuive Universelle* at Dresden, a subsequent gathering at Chemnitz, in 1883, proved equally ineffective. (Katz 1980:279)

142. The six Antisemitic principles have been summarised thus: "1. loosening and counterbalancing the powerful Jewish controls on Hungary's political, economic and cultural life; 2. revision of the penal code to prevent the repetition of unjust verdicts, like the one that had ended the trial of the Tiszaeszlar Jews in Nyiregyhaza; 3. a new law, regulating the issuance of permits for the sale of alcoholic beverages, that would prevent Jews from owning taverns; 4. the transfer of Jewish registry offices from community to state jurisdiction; 5. the nullification of the law permitting marriages between Jews and Christians; 6. the termination of the influx of foreign Jews into Hungary." [Judit Kubinszky *Politikai Antiszemitizmus*

40 *From Emancipation to Catastrophe*

Magyarorszagon, 1875-1890 (Political Antisemitism in Hungary, 1875-1890). Budapest: Kossuth Konyvkiado, 1976; cited Handler 1980:177-78.]

143. Quoted Handler 1980:179.

144. *En J* 15, 1155, "Tiszaeszlar".

145. In discussing the Liberal government's electoral *modus operandi,* Hanak (1973b:340) states: "Lawlessness became the unwritten law of electioneering, abuses became the usual practice, and corruption was elevated to a political principle."

146. The use of Charles Darwin's name in no sense implies that the great biologist and natural philosopher had any sympathy for the views of racial or religious bigots.

147. Particularly notable in upsetting rural socio-economic equilibrium was the seemingly inexorable decline in agricultural commodity prices, especially grain. Outmoded methods, high land rents and repeated natural disasters made Hungarian farming particularly vulnerable to the huge quantities of cheap, mainly North American, grain that flooded onto the European market from about 1880. Hungary's prolonged rural crisis, instigated by dramatic improvements in North American farming and transportation technology, resulted in the penury of small and dwarfholding peasants as well as the bankruptcy of the majority of the landowning rural gentry. The latter sought, and often found, alternative employment in the military, bureaucracy and public life. (Hanak 1973b:350) Whilst relinquishing their previous *modus vivendi,* these *déclassé* gentry clung tenaciously to the symbols and pretensions of their former status. Ominously for the Jews, many of them blamed their decline on the machinations of "foreign" elements.

148. Janos 1982:146-48. This decline was in marked contrast to the fortunes of the PP's Austrian counterpart, the Christian Social Movement, which continued to have success — even when confronted with the Emperor's undisguised hostility.

149. The manner and extent to which some Orthodox Jewish communities were influenced by the Magyarist enthusiasms of this era is indicated by Noach Valley. Writing of these Jews' descendants, who now reside in New York, Rabbi Valley states: "Some Jews who live in the Williamsburg section of Brooklyn contend that Moses spoke not Yiddish — but Hungarian — and that, therefore, God originally gave the Torah to Moses in the Hungarian language! It was only later on, according to their view, that the Torah was translated into Hebrew." (Noach Valley, "President's Message", Jewish Vegetarians of North America *Newsletter,* Volume VIII, no. 2, Summer 1991, 5)

150. Statistics indicate that Jewish migrants in Hungary also participated significantly in this great cultural metamorphosis. (See McCagg Jr. 1989b:246)

151. Janos 1982:127. The exceptions to this cultural dogmatism were the German and Slovak minorities. In Hungarian statistics of this era, nationality was allocated according to the native language of the individual, not by religion, ethnic affiliation or the individual's personal choice of identity. (Lucas 1988:n125)

152. For a discussion of the minority question of this era see Macartney 1971:721-39.

153. Frank 1990:255.

154. Janos 1982:126.

155. The Jewish press not only aroused nationalist chauvinism against Austria but also "took the crudest jingoistic attitude in the national [minority] struggles and was a chief obstacle to a reasonable compromise among the rival nations." (Cited Braham 1981:10)

156. Professor S.M. Dubnow, cited Braham 1981:34, n26. McCagg Jr concurs, and summarises the influence of the Budapest Neolog leadership thus: "And in sum the patriotic atmosphere sustained by the Neolog Jewish congregational leadership seems to have played a vital role in making credible the euphoric Magyar nationalism of the period." (McCagg Jr 1989a:192)

157. Janos 1982:117-18. Christian children also attended these Jewish schools. (Cohen 1939:3)

158. The Pest Neolog community was particularly prominent in the symbiotic

relationship, with twenty-three of the twenty-nine Jewish nobles created between 1887 and 1896 belonging to that congregation. (McCagg Jr 1989a:191)

159. Handler 1982:4.

160. Patai 1985:165.

161. Wistrich 1991:63. Elected in 1897 on the Christian-Social Party's specifically Antisemitic platform, Dr Lueger held office until his death in 1910.

162. Braham 1981:5. Note that these figures refer to "Hungary proper" — they exclude the Hungarian-controlled region of Croatia–Slavonia. The following (rounded) statistics denote the absolute numbers and percentages of the various religious denominations residing in "Hungary proper" in 1900: Roman Catholic 8,200,000 (49%); Greek Catholic 1,850,000 (11%); Reformed Church 2,450,000 (14.5%); Evangelical 1,250,000 (7.5%); Greek Oriental 2,200,000 (13%); Unitarians 70,000 (0.5%); Jews 850,000 (5%). (De Vargha 1911:32) Macartney (1971:710), in his "reprinted with corrections edition", mistakenly claims that Jews in 1900 formed 8.49 percent of the population. Prof. Macartney, the generally acknowledged doyen of Anglo-Saxon historians of the Danubian basin, is also incorrect when he writes: "...in 1906, the Jewish community in Hungary split into two great bodies, the Neologs [sic] and the Orthodox..." (Macartney 1971:711) As previously shown, the great split occurred as a result of the Jewish Congress of 1868-69.

163. Indications of the bias prevalent in Hungarian statisticians can be liberally collected from the writings of Julius De Vargha, Director of the Central Statistical Office of the Kingdom of Hungary. Writing in 1911, Dr De Vargha unabashedly proclaimed: "In Hungary it is the Magyars who, numerically, and in point of wealth and culture, are destined to lead the way: in ethnical development too they form the centre of gravity. In respect of culture, the Magyar race is superior to the nationalities not only in point of elementary education but in higher culture too. By the side of the wealthy and brilliant literature of the Magyars, those of the nationalities (with the one exception of the German) are completely overshadowed. It is a mere waste of energy to work in the service of the latter..." (De Vargha 1911:22)

164. Katzburg 1966·143; Handler 1982:4. By sweet coincidence the Bill was drafted by Baron Lorand Eotvos, Minister for Education and Religious Affairs, whose father Jozsef was not only instrumental in the emancipatory legislation of 1867 but also held the same ministry as his son. (Handler 1980:21)

165. Hungary's accepted (established) religions thus became the Catholic (Roman, Greek and Armenian), Calvinist, Lutheran, Unitarian, Orthodox (Serbian and Roumanian) and Israelite. The Moslem religion was added to the list in 1908, after the annexation of Bosnia. (Macartney 1971:699, n1)

166. Katzburg 1966:143.

167. Macartney 1971:706.

168. Katz 1977:47.

169. Handler 1985:3.

170. Istvan Deak, "Fun City", *The New York Review of Books*, 16 March 1989, 24.

171. Janos 1982:113.

172. With the (obvious) exceptions of the medical and legal corps.

173. Quoted Handler 1980:187.

174. Quoted Mendelsohn 1983:94.

175. Braham 1981:9.

176. Katz 1977:49.

177. Janos 1982:114. *Zaibatsu*: Japanese term for structured, powerful cartels.

178. Macartney 1971:710–11.

179. Macartney 1971:710. One never becomes quite immune to Macartney's sometimes insidious references to Jews and their activities. See also ibid pp 710 and 711, n2.

180. Janos 1982:113.

181. Katzburg 1966:146.

182. Lucas 1988:93.

183. Jeszenszky 1990:274.

184. Mendes-Flohr and Reinharz 1980:532, "Budapest".

185. Janos 1982:115.

186. Veghazi 1969:74. Latifundia property constituted well under 1 percent of the total number of agricultural holdings, but involved about 30 percent of aggregate farming area (De Vargha 1911:43). In 1904 an Antisemitic author claimed that Jews held no less than 37.5 percent of Hungary's arable land. (Patai 1985:166)

187. Lucas 1988:94.

188. These types of holding constituted 99 percent of all farms. (De Vargha 1911:43)

189. Veghazi 1969:74-75.

190. Handler 1982:22.

191. Braham 1981:9.

192. Macartney 1971:710.

193. Janos 1982:177, n81.

194. Janos 1982:17, table 25.

195. Venetianer 1922:468-69. See ibid 453-85 for extensive demographic, educational and professional statistics on Hungary's Jews. For general information on the Hungarian educational system of this period, see De Vargha 1911:31-43.

196. Berend 1985:32.

197. As previously mentioned, the NAP blamed Jews for Hungary's serious alcohol problem and advocated prohibiting them from tavern ownership. This was in spite of the fact that Jews constituted only 18,000 of Hungary's 58,000 publicans (*Korcsmaros*). (Venetianer 1922:483)

198. Veghazi 1969:76.

199. Marton 1966:38-40.

200. Marton 1966:32. Marton attributes this migration largely to a proclamation by Charles III who, in 1726, decreed that in Bohemia–Moravia only one male member of a Jewish family was to be permitted to marry. (Marton 1966:44)

201. Comprehensive demographic statistics can be found in Ujvari 1929:552-64, "*Magyarorszag Zsidosaga*" (Hungarian Jewry) and Laszlo 1966:61-136, "Hungarian Jewry: Settlement and Demography, 1735-1910".

202. Katzburg 1966:166.

203. Ibid.

204. Jewish Publication Society of America *American Jewish Yearbook 1918-19* (Philadelphia: 1918), 339.

205. Marton (1966:42) argues that this Polish migration reached its peak in 1825, that there was no significant further immigration, and that the subsequent spectacular population growth was "almost exclusively the result of the very high natural increase". Laszlo (1966:61-62) demonstrates that this view is clearly erroneous.

206. Marton 1966:45, who continues by mentioning that almost the sole occupation of these destitute Galician Jews was the distilling of spirits, they having been forced from all other types of enterprise.

207. Laszlo 1966:70.

208. Katzburg 1966:149.

209. Braham 1981:86.

210. Katzburg 1966:139.

211. Oscar Israelowitz *Guide to Jewish New York City* (New York: Israelowitz Publishing, 1990), 64-66.

212. *En J* 4, 1451, fig. 2.

213. Katzburg 1966:139.

214. Braham 1981:76.

215. Macartney 1971:704.

216. Mendes-Flohr and Reinharz 1980:532. This compares with the Jewish populations of Warsaw, 306,000; Vienna 175,000; and Berlin, 144,000; constituting 39 percent, 9 percent and 4 percent of the respective capitals' inhabitants. (Ibid)

217. Of the approximately 1,650 miniature (non-substantial) communities, the Orthodox outnumbered the Neolog by the ratio of over four to one. (Katz 1990:19)

218. Lucas 1988:89.

219. Katz 1977:50.

220. Istvan Deak, "Fun City", *The New York Review of Books*, 16 March 1989, 24.

221. Mendes-Flohr and Reinharz 1980:539. When considering the intensity of conversion, it should be noted that these 10,000 converts must not be considered as a percentage of the some 900,000 Jews living in Hungary at the turn of the century but as a percentage of Jews who lived in Hungary during the *whole* of the nineteenth century.

222. McCagg Jr 1989a:191.

223. Mendes-Flohr and Reinharz 1980:538. These figures refer to Hungary as a whole. The rate for Budapest at the turn of the century was 7 percent.

224. Macartney 1971:711. See also Balla 1969:85-136, "The Jews in Hungary: A Cultural Overview".

225. Macartney 1971:711.

226. Herzl's article "A Solution to the Jewish Question", published in the January 1896 issue of *The Jewish Chronicle*, can be found in Mendes-Flor and Reinharz 1980:422-29.

227. Janos 1982:115.

228. *Aliya*: traditional Jewish term for describing a return to the land of Israel.

229. Rabinowicz 1971:25.

230. Braham 1971:523.

231. Rabinowicz 1971:113, n28.

232. Mizrachi, the religious sector of the Zionist movement, was founded in Vilna in 1902. The movement's motto expresses its aims and philosophy, *viz*: "The Land of Israel, for the People of Israel, according to the *Torah* [Law] of Israel." (*En J* 12, 175, "Mizrachi")

233. The first three Professors at the Hebrew University of Jerusalem were Hungarian — the Professors of Chemistry, Talmud and Palestinology. For a brief outline of the history of Hungarian Jews in Israel, see Farkas 1971:522-23.

234. McCagg Jr. 1989a:194.

235. Braham 1971:524.

236. Lucas 1988:126-27. Prime Minister Kalman Tisza (1875-90) advised the minorities to "Be silent and pay". A successor, Kalman Szell (1899-1903), declared: "The Magyars have conquered this country for the Magyars and not for others. The supremacy and the hegemony of the Magyars is fully justified." These and similar sentiments from other Hungarian Prime Ministers can be found in Kann 1977, 1:390, n79.

237. Janos 1982:177, table 24. Janos assumes that a person's given name, family name or combination thereof can determine whether that person is an actual or a "possible" Jew.

238. McCagg Jr. 1989a:193-94.

239. Macartney 1971:823, wherein he calls Vazsonyi "a professing Jew".

240. Janos 1982:178-79.

241. Deak 1989:23.

242. Janos 1982:179-80, who states that at least three-quarters of these MPs converted to Christianity.

243. This was Istvan Tisza's second term as PM. His first term encompassed the period November 1903-June 1905, his second premiership being June 1913-June 1917. (Vardy 1969:2, 399)

244. Macartney 1971:807.

245. Deak 1989:11.

246. Vida 1939:49-50.

247. The National Rabbinical Association encouraged enlistment and called upon Jewish communities to pray for victory. (Handler 1982:5)

248. Two hundred and fifty Hungarian Jewish families contributed five or more sons to the defence of their country. (Vida 1939:50) Included in this category were the writer's paternal uncles from Komarom, in western Hungary. All five of my father's older brothers rallied to the colours, two of them becoming officers. All survived, only to perish in the Holocaust, as did my father's other two siblings.

249. Crankshaw 1981:417.

250. Handler 1982:5.

251. Ibid.

252. As is usual in conditions of general scarcity and privation, corruption, inflation and the black market became endemic during the War years. (Hanak 1973b:409)

253. Handler 1982:6.

254. Lucas 1988:209.

255. Deak 1985:47.

256. From the commencement of the War, the Tsarist generals commanded that "Jewish subversives" be cleared from military zones. By some estimates these orders, and the War in general, created refugees of 400,000 Jews — half the Jewish population of Galicia. Prior to the Russian capitulation of 1917, opposing armies invaded eastern Galicia on not less than six occasions. After the cessation of hostilities, Budapest, Prague and Vienna all attempted to repatriate their Jewish Galician refugees. (McCagg Jr 1989a:203-04)

CHAPTER II

1919 TO 19 MARCH 1944

FROM GENESIS TO EXODUS
THE HOLOCAUST PROCESS IN
POLITICAL CONTEXT

The military debacle of the Central Powers in late 1918 generated the most serious geopolitical situation to confront Hungary since that nation's devastating defeat in 1526 by the Ottoman Turks. The ceasefires signed by Hapsburg forces in early November 1918 signified the implosion of the old regime. In Hungary, the resulting vacuum was quickly filled by an enthusiastically received but fragile liberal-socialist coalition, led by the progressive Count Mihaly Karolyi, which included several Jewish ministers.[1] Despite the proclamation on 16 November 1918 of an initially popular Hungarian People's Republic, the government's cohesion quickly degenerated, being destabilised by a combination of factors, including the Allies' intractable and vindictive peace proposals,[2] the incessant agitation of the extreme Left, the country's postwar economic impoverishment and a peasant rebellion that erupted in early November. Notwithstanding Karolyi's attempts at socio-economic amelioration — particularly land reform (beginning with his own vast estate), the arrest of prominent agitators, the introduction of democratic rights, and the eight-hour day — social turmoil and the outrage generated by the Allies' unabating intransigence led to the resignation of his government.

The coalition was swiftly replaced by an initially popular regime led by Bela Kun (1886-1939?),[3] an ex-Russian POW of Jewish origin who, radicalised by the Bolsheviks during his captivity, had returned and formed the Communist Party of Hungary on 24 November 1918. In keeping with its predominant ideology, the new administration promptly embarked on a series of radical measures aimed at rapidly transforming Hungary into a doctrinaire socialist society. The government intro-duced equal pay for women; assumed control over bank deposits, jewellery, medium to large estates, cultural activities, schools, and larger apartments; and nationalised all but small enterprises.[4]

Kun considered his regime (21 March–1 August 1919) as the harbinger of revolution throughout central Europe. The Allies, attempting to maintain a *cordon sanitaire* around Lenin's experiment, considered Kun's newly proclaimed Hungar-ian Soviet Republic as threatening their policy of containing the Russian

Revolution. Consequently on 28 March, a week after Kun's assumption of authority, not only did the Allies impose an economic blockade on Hungary but, in April, condoned, if not instigated, Czechoslovak and Roumanian invasions of the country.[5] Furthermore, in June, when the incursion faltered in the north, French Premier Clemenceau threatened a general intervention by the Allied powers, all of whom were hostile to the prospect of a second Soviet regime — this time strategically located in central Europe. The Kun government's inevitable capitulation to this intimidation alienated nationalist sentiment, and so marked the beginning of the regime's end. Confronted with seemingly insoluble military, political, social and economic obstacles to its continuation, on 1 August 1919 Kun's badly divided ministry of 133 days resigned. Three days later the Roumanian army marched into Budapest. Occupying the city until mid-November they then departed — with a considerable portion of Hungary's rolling stock and treasure,[6] thus exacerbating the country's impoverishment. Shortly thereafter, on 16 November 1919, the White "national army" of 12,000, led by their commander Admiral Miklos Horthy — riding the proverbial hero's prancing white steed — marched into Budapest.

The Hungarian Soviet's demise terminated the epoch now known as the Red Terror. During this period, which claimed about 600 lives,[7] a strategy that may be termed largely selective violence was adopted in attempting to subjugate the Soviet's real and supposed enemies. Hungarian Jewry, being ideologically committed to the old regime and being more affluent than the population as a whole, was particularly adversely affected by the introduction of the sweeping socialist protocol. Not surprisingly therefore, the large majority of Jews strongly opposed the practice and theory of Kun's regime. Tragically, however, as about two-thirds of the Soviet's Commissars were of Jewish origin,[8] in a considerable proportion of public opinion Hungarian Jewry became intimately identified, if not synonymous, with the Communist dictatorship.

Jewish prominence in the Soviet hierarchy became a matter of open discussion and public opposition, to such an extent that the regime's leadership was forced to confront the issue. At the Congress of Soviets in June 1919, Kun noted that Antisemitism was emerging even in the Soviet, that he himself had been subject to Antisemitic vituperation and that although not ashamed of his Jewish birth, he was no longer a Jew but a Communist.[9]

This secular philosophy was held by the large majority of the many "nominal" Jews active in Left-radical movements of this era. Emanating mainly from the intellectual stratum of society, amongst whom Jews were a substantial percentage,[10] these Jewish political activists generally had scant regard for, or connection with, their Jewish heritage. Almost totally alienated from the institutional community, they acted neither as identifiable Jews nor in the Jewish interest. Furthermore, their alienation and adopted ideology often engendered an overt animus towards their co-religionists' socio-economic and political interests. Yet despite this open hostility of the "Jewish" Left towards the philosophy and aspirations of institutional Jewry, and despite Hungarian Jewry's official rejection of Bolshevik ideology,[11] the public perception of collective Jewry being the temporal and spiritual rectors of Hungarian communism became so firmly embedded in public consciousness that it became a *sine qua non* of even serious political discussion until — at least — the end of World War II. Writing as early as May 1919, the noted

Figure 2.1 *Minden A Mienk!* (Everything is Ours!)
**Antisemitic cartoon of 1919 portraying a Jewish commissar ("Nepbizto[s]")
scurrying with his loot whilst an incapacitated war veteran watches helplessly.**

British historian R.W. Seton-Watson prophesied: "Personally, I do not think that anything on earth can stop the anti-Semitic movement in Hungary, but sheer massacre at least can be stopped."[12]

The White Terror

As in Russia, the accession of a Bolshevik regime galvanised the opponents of Communism into militant counter-action. In Hungary this "White" reaction was initially divided between two paramilitary groupings, one based at Szeged in southern Hungary, the other in Vienna. Unfortunately for Kun's regime, the nation-wide turmoil generated by a catastrophic World War, foreign intervention, economic collapse and social upheaval masked the reality of the White counter-revolution being overtly supported by Hungary's enemies, the victorious and apparently vindictive Entente. Thus, whilst the Reds were portrayed in anti-Communist propaganda as foreign-dominated internationalist conspirators, Kun's regime, with considerable irony, was engaged in a debilitating struggle to retain the country's traditional territory.

The Szeged and Vienna coteries, whilst both vehemently opposing the Soviet regime, differed in some important respects. The latter was the less extreme of the two groups. Led by the great landowner Count Istvan Bethlen, and including Count Pal Teleki — both future Prime Ministers — the Vienna assemblage consisted largely, but not exclusively, of the traditional gentry-aristocratic coalition that had been so prominent in Dualist Hungary. In marked contrast, the Szeged cohort, involving those of humbler social origin, advocated a more forthright, dynamic

Figure 2.2 *Feherterror* (**The White Terror**)
Sketches of the White Militia in action. (Source: Pamlenyi and Szekely 1967:II, 366-67)

counter-revolutionary policy than their Vienna *confrères'* anti-revolutionary strategy of a conservative-dominated status quo. Consisting mainly of professional military officers, public servants, *déclassé* gentry and other disgruntled or dispossessed elements, the Szeged grouping synthesised a doctrinaire ideology which they proclaimed as the *Szegedi Gondolat* (The Szeged Concept). Advocating a centralised, authoritarian state based on a vague amalgam of virulent nationalism, chauvinism, Antisemitism, anti-Communism and territorial revisionism, the *Gondolat* enunciated a simplistic propaganda crusade against the perceived corrupters of the counter-revolution's deeply cherished, semi-mythical, age-old Christian Hungary. In the near future the supporters of this proclamation were to often boast of themselves as the precursors of Fascism and Nazism.[13]

The two groups, unifying their militias in mid-year under the command of Admiral Miklos Horthy — last Commander-in-Chief of the Hapsburg navy and *Aide-de-Camp* to the Emperor — launched a campaign of indiscriminate terror against whomever they saw fit to declare as enemies. Notwithstanding the fundamental incompatibility of Judaism and atheistic Communism, the fervent patriotism of Hungarian Jewry, the significant Jewish role in anti-Bolshevik activity,[14] the substantial financial support of the Szeged Jewish Community,[15] and the presence of two Jews in the Szeged hierarchy,[16] the White Terror dwarfed in magnitude and intensity the violence perpetrated on Hungary's Jews by the Red's equivalent campaign. Berend and Ranki summarise this violent and bloody period thus: "There were an exceptionally large number of Jewish victims of the bloodbath. Unbridled anti-Semitism combined with the counter-revolutionary terror led to a string of pogroms reminiscent of the Middle Ages."[17] Thousands of real and alleged enemies — Jews plus Communists, Socialists, unionists, democrats and sundry suspected "traitors" — were butchered in cold blood.

The White policy of "national purification and regeneration" was based on a strategy of massacring the "alien Judeo-Bolshevik" hierarchy and terrorising into acquiescence or flight their "cadres" conspiring within the Hungarian body politic.[18] At the termination of their national crusade, the Whites had murdered 5–6,000 of their alleged enemies, many if not most of the victims being innocent Jews.[19] To add additional dimensions of intimidation and terror, these atrocities were often committed in public.[20] Furthermore, to reinforce the cleansing process, during the first three months of the counter-revolution alone over 70,000 "suspects" were either imprisoned or interned in newly created concentration camps.[21] Despite recognition that a Jewish appeal to Hungary's enemies would expose the community to charges of collective disloyalty if not traitorous conduct, Jewish suffering became so intense that 100,000 members of the Budapest community petitioned the Paris Peace Conference, appealing for their lives and the restoration of order via the return to the capital of the loathed Roumanian troops.[22]

Realising the potentially disastrous consequences of xenophobe-generated terror for Hungary's international reputation, and for her position at the Paris Peace Conference, less extreme White leaders organised a delegation of notables, led by Count Bethlen, to solicit Horthy to restrain the Antisemitism of his officers.[23] This concern was reinforced by Count Albert Apponyi, chief of the Hungarian delegation at the Paris peace negotiations, and his Prime Minister who, in March 1920, admonished the Lower House: "The hatred of the Jews, and the antipathy felt towards the Jews, are not worth as much as the territorial integrity of Hungary."[24]

Such apprehensions about foreign repercussions appeared to be justified. The outspoken protests of international labour organisations were augmented in 1920 by two British investigations of the Hungarian situation. Unfortunately, however, the conclusions reached by these two contemporary enquiries were almost diametrically opposed. The British parliamentary White Paper, entitled "Alleged Existence of 'White Terror' in Hungary", heavily biased towards British policy of nurturing anti-Bolshevik regimes in central Europe, admitted acts of violence but denied the existence of a White Terror. Professor Katzburg explains the basis of this fundamental distortion thus: "An examination of the Foreign Office documents proves that the [British representatives'] despatches printed in the White Paper had been meticulously [ie: selectively] edited before publication."[25] The moral and factual bankruptcy of the White Paper was revealed in May 1920 by the other British document, the result of a Trades Union Congress–Labour Party delegation led by Lt. Col. Josiah Wedgwood MP.[26] Entitled "The White Terror in Hungary: Report of the British Joint Labour Delegation to Hungary", this enquiry confirmed the existence of a systematic White Terror, noted with concern Horthy's policy of protecting the perpetrators, determined that most of the victims were Jews, and deprecated the conclusions and implications of the British Government's White Paper.[27]

Yet despite their trials and tribulations, Hungarian Jewry retained an intense loyalty to Magyarorszag. This affinity was particularly evident in the attempt to mobilise world Jewry to help maintain Hungary's territorial integrity and, consequently, the country's "civilising mission" in Central Europe. Furthermore, after a period of uncertainty, in an overt display of affection for their "fatherland", the Neolog leadership, having concluded that the Terror was but a transient phenomenon, determined to emphasise their patriotism by avoiding public criticism of the Antisemitic horrors. In marked contradistinction, the small Hungarian Zionist grouping firmly rejected the Neolog policy of passivity and attempted to alleviate the horrors by vigorously soliciting the support of international Jewry. The Neolog leadership, in a sequel to past clashes and a precursor to future conflicts, promptly characterised the Zionist campaign as "betraying the Magyar fatherland".[28] Once again confrontation between what may be termed an "activist" (Zionist) as opposed to a "passivist" (Neolog) Jewish ideology had embroiled Hungarian Jewry in a vituperative and debilitating internecine imbroglio.

Notwithstanding the official Neolog attitude, the public concerns of the British Board of (Jewish) Deputies,[29] the French *Alliance Israelite Universelle*, the British Labour Party, international trade union movements, the Federation of Hungarian Jews in America[30] and the American Jewish Committee were arguably influential in eventually moderating the virulence of the White campaign. In particular, Louis Marshall, president of the Committee, wrote to the US Secretary of State on 21 May 1920 and left no doubt as to the stance expected from the USA and the Allies:

> I am quite sure that at this time, when the fate of Hungary is dependent upon the action of the Great Powers and the attitude of the Supreme Council [of the Paris Peace Conference], when she is seeking to rehabilitate herself and expects to be relieved from the obligations which she is about to assume under the Treaty of Peace, an indication from the Great Powers or from the Supreme Council that these anti-Semitic demonstrations must cease, will not be disregarded.[31]

There is little doubt that the British and US governments' subsequent interventions on behalf of Hungarian Jews resulted largely from the activities of UK and US Jewry. In particular, on 26 May 1920, just five days after Marshall's communication, the US representative in Hungary received instructions to "informally make it clear that American sympathy for Hungary will depend largely on fair treatment given [to] minorities in Hungary by Hungarian officials".[32] These and other intercessions arguably strengthened the position of the less extreme White elements; at all events, by early 1921 a distinct diminution in the distribution and intensity of Antisemitic activity had become discernible. Henceforth, until the country's entry into World War II, Hungarian Antisemitism focused on the attempted erosion, rather than the arbitrary physical violation, of Jewish equality.

In important respects, however, the White Terror inaugurated (and Horthy's subsequent career legitimised) a generally accepted overt antipathy towards the Jews, a pervasive psycho-social and political ethos that, in the not too distant future, was progressively boosted by the increasing Nazi successes in Germany. There is little doubt that Horthy and his cohorts' successful postwar stereotyping of Hungarian Jewry as the "alien Judeo-Bolshevik cancer", and their conditioning of the populace to the formerly marginal — if not entirely foreign — attitude that systematic physical brutality was a legitimate means of solving the "Jewish problem", significantly facilitated Hungary's intimate involvement with the Jewish catastrophe of 1944. In substantial respects, for Hungarian Jewry, the White Terror was the genesis of the Holocaust.

The Treaty of Trianon

Although utilising the secret ballot, the nation-wide election of 25–26 January 1920, called by the White junta at the behest of the Entente, was conducted in an atmosphere of turmoil, intimidation and terror. Without the participation of the Left — the Socialists boycotted the poll and the Communists were banned — the Right won a substantial victory. Subsequently, on 1 March 1920, the resulting parliament was induced to proclaim overwhelmingly the White Commander-in-Chief, Admiral Miklos Horthy (1868–1957), as Regent of the Kingdom of Hungary.[33] In the best traditions of comic operetta, a land-locked country proclaimed an Admiral as its leader, that leader representing a Royal dynasty which had been deposed from the nation's henceforth vacant throne.[34]

Thus did Horthy ascend the pinnacle of institutional power. The generalissimo (*Legfelsobb Hadur*), and now Head of State, acquired the authority to appoint and dismiss Prime Ministers, veto Acts of Parliament, and convoke or prorogue the legislature. Although lacking the Royal prerogative of creating nobles, Horthy compensated for this deficiency by gaining the right to appoint members to the Upper House, and by instituting his "Order of Heroes", the *Vitez rend*. Pledging allegiance to Horthy himself,[35] the *Vitez* was an exclusively Christian paramilitary corps[36] whose decorations were often publicly utilised to recognise and reward examples of conspicuous White zealotry. By these awards, which included a plot of land,[37] the State and its supreme authority, Horthy, further legitimised the concept and practice of the White Terror, particularly the brutal and bloody pogroms. Despite the convulsions and tribulations endemic to Europe throughout much of the interwar era, Horthy — whom some authorities typically but misguidedly dismiss as a "political neophyte of mediocre abilities"[38] — managed to consolidate

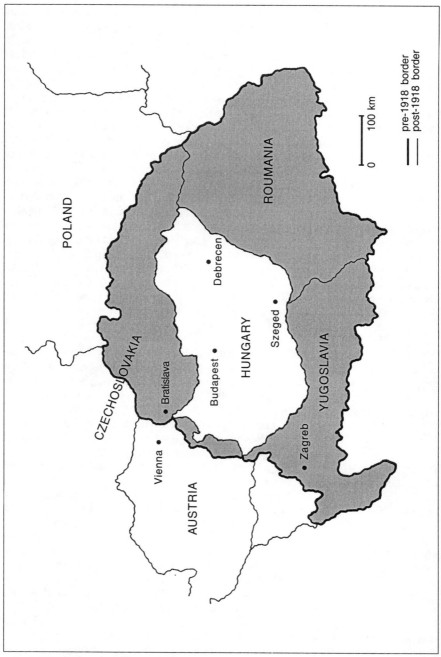

Map 2.1 **Hapsburg and Trianon Hungary.**
The shaded area indicates territory taken from Hungary by the Treaty of Trianon.

his power to such an extent that he became the embodiment of institutional authority in Hungary, a *sine qua non* which even Germany was forced to acknowledge — until his attempted *volte-face* in October 1944 (see below).

In early June 1920, at the Trianon Palace in Versailles, Hungary was officially mutilated and declared to be at peace.[39] One authority describes Budapest's response thus:

> On a bright sunny day, June 4 1920, street life in Budapest came to a standstill. Shops were closed. The trolley cars stopped. Black flags flew. The church bells rang...Hungary's dismemberment was without precedent in European history, save perhaps for the second partition of Poland...It was a day of national mourning.[40]

Of all the treaties imposed on the vanquished at Paris, Hungary's proved to be the most Draconian.[41] Her losses were staggering: two-thirds of her territory, three-fifths of her total population, one-third of ethnic Magyars and enormous losses in commodities, agricultural resources plus commercial and industrial infrastructure.[42] Trianon transformed Hungary from a country of 280,000 sq km containing 18 million people to a residual of 93,000 sq km with fewer than 8 million inhabitants. Three million ethnic Magyars became foreigners, citizens of newly created Czechoslovakia, Yugoslavia and the enlarged Roumania. Next to Austria, Hungary became the most homogeneous of the successor states, with nine out of ten Trianon Hungarians being ethnic Magyars.[43] The largest remaining minority were now the Swabes (ethnic Germans) who comprised a mere 6.9 percent of the populace.[44] The country as a whole rose against Trianon, the "almost demoniac violence" of Hungary's immutable interwar irredentism being expressed by the unceasing, passionate refrain *"Nem, Nem, Soha!"* (No, No, Never!).[45]

The *Numerus Clausus* of 1920

The loss of huge, formerly Magyar-dominated, territory to the newly created (successor) states resulted in a surge of about 350,000 embittered ethnic Magyar refugees — public servants, gentry, military officers, intellectuals and professionals — to the now diminutive Hungary.[46] Although motivated by sundry factors, including patriotic attachment and the loss of traditional entitlements, the majority of this migration resulted from the understandable policy of the successor state bureaucracies replacing ethnic Magyars with their own nationals. This influx, the country's dire economic circumstances, and the loss of territory and people to govern, generated soaring unemployment amongst administrators and university graduates in Trianon Hungary, especially in Budapest. Simultaneously, to Magyar chauvinist perceptions, Hungarian Jewry remained safely ensconced in its dominance of the professions, finance, commerce, industry and the arts. On the basis of this conception, on 22 September 1920 the government of Count Pal Teleki (formed 19 July 1920) introduced the *Numerus Clausus* Act, the first significant piece of anti-Jewish legislation enacted in postwar Europe.[47] Stipulating that the admission of Jews to institutes of higher learning be limited to 6 percent — the Jewish proportion of the population[48] — the *Numerus Clausus* was the first breach in the constitutional equality granted Hungarian Jews by the Emancipation of 1867.

As the threat to Magyar hegemony, and the Magyar character of the state, disappeared with the ethnic minorities, Hungarian Jews were no longer needed to ensure a Magyar majority in the now almost ethnically homogeneous Hungary.

Thus it was that Hungarian Jewry became politically bereft in the White Terror, an isolation reinforced by the popularity of the regime's rhetoric and legislation. The government's response to unemployment was both simple and simplistic: extrude Jews from the economy, the resulting vacancies generating an inevitable movement of Christians into Jewish-dominated fields of endeavour. By this populist tactic of pre-empting — if not expropriating — Jewish enterprise, the regime was able to successfully mask its refusal to countenance meaningful socio-economic reforms. Furthermore, Hungarian Jewry thus became enmeshed in the chauvinist's double bind: prosperity was to be achieved at the expense of the Jews but, if prosperity failed to eventuate, internal and international Jewish machinations against Hungary would be exposed to all.

The most conspicuous success of the Act occurred in the Ludovika Military Academy where, in 1925, a situation of *Numerus Nullius* prevailed.[49] In general, however, over time many Jewish (civilian) matriculants were able to circumvent the intent — if not the spirit — of the Act. Significant numbers enrolled in foreign universities, officials not infrequently accepted gratuities, and the administration of quotas was often haphazard. Furthermore, the appointment of the pragmatically inclined Prime Minister Count Istvan Bethlen (see below) moderated government attitudes. Thus in 1925, when the High Court cast doubt on the legality of the Act, the Minister of Education ordered its provisions to be "quietly ignored".[50] As a result of these factors, Jewish matriculants increased from the strictly enforced quota of 5.9 percent in 1920–21 to 14.1 percent in 1931–32.[51] This latter figure, although only half the prewar level of 28.4 percent, was still almost triple the Jewish proportion of the population.

Because rigid application of the Act had a relatively short duration, the proportion of Jews in most professions declined but slightly. For the period 1920 to 1930, Jews in the legal profession decreased from 57.0 percent to 55.7 percent, with reductions for medicine and journalism from 47.8 percent to 40.2 percent, and 39.5 percent to 36.1 percent respectively.[52] The most significant influence of the *Numerus Clausus* was in the further radicalisation of society, particularly institutes of higher learning.[53] Acting as a militant advance guard for chauvinist (Hungarist) ideology, these organisations became maelstroms of Antisemitic agitation. In particular, medical students, influenced by the pernicious mythology of Eugenics, conducted protracted campaigns of attempting to humiliate and intimidate their Jewish colleagues.

Although overt Judeophobia was a familiar feature in Hungarian tertiary institutes throughout the Horthy epoch, the abrogation of Bethlen's largely pragmatic policies by his successors (see below) led to academia's Antisemitic campaigns increasing in intensity and distribution. Following the example of their newly empowered German mentors, student agitation became particularly wide-spread in 1933, occurring in all universities and peaking from mid-November to late December. Physical confrontations with Jewish students were not uncommon, particularly at places such as Szeged University, where Jewish students refused to be segregated onto "ghetto benches". The anti-Jewish campaigns of 1933, failing to enforce the provisions of *Numerus Clausus*, were thus repeated in 1935.[54] The fact that these confrontations were organised and not spontaneous actually benefited Jewish students, sympathisers being able to issue warnings as to the times and places of proposed demonstrations.

Reinforcing the official *Numerus Clausus* legacy of the 1920s, the physically intimidatory, "unofficial" *Numerus Clausus* of the Antisemitic student organisations in the 1930s contributed substantially to further reducing Jewish enrolments.[55] From a level of 14.3 percent in 1932–33, total Jewish student numbers in universities fell to 8.3 percent in 1936–37. For all institutes of higher learning, the relevant figures are 12.0 percent and 7.3 percent respectively. The total of Jewish matriculants entering universities declined even more dramatically, numbers being slashed from 14.1 percent of all new enrolments in 1931–32 to 6.1 percent in 1936–37 and 4.6 percent in 1937–38.[56] For prospective Jewish tertiary students of this period, street muscle obviously had greater deterrent value than government fiat.

In responding to institutional Antisemitism as expressed in the *Numerus Clausus*, Hungarian Jewry decided to continue its policy of patriotic fervour — if not obsequious devotion — to the "Fatherland". Such attitudes were forcefully and typically expressed by Vilmos Vazsonyi (1868–1926), former Minister of Justice and foremost leader of Hungarian Jewry.[57] At the annual general meeting of the Pest Jewish Community in October 1924, Vazsonyi voiced Jewry's official opposition to an international appeal for the enforcement of the Minorities Protection Treaty, an appendage to the Trianon agreement imposed upon Hungary. "The Peace Treaty of Trianon," proclaimed Vazsonyi, "which deprived [the Hungarians] of their rights, cannot be the source of our rights."[58] Expanding on his theme, and simultaneously reinforcing official Jewry's anti-Zionist credentials, he concluded: "We do not invoke the Treaty [because] we do not consider ourselves a national minority, seeking the protection of Geneva."[59]

Like Hungarian Jewry as a whole, Vazsonyi considered the Antisemitism of the era to be a transient phenomenon — somewhat akin to the Tiszaeszlar imbroglio — with the blanket charge of a Judeo-Bolshevik conspiracy being a cankerous canard transmitted by the fever of the times, a tragic infection of the body politic, but able to be medicated by rational discussion, greater efforts in public education and continuing expressions of patriotic fervour.

Typical of the public relations campaigns conducted by official Jewish leaders were the proclamations of Dr Sandor Lederer, President of the Pest Jewish Community. In the *Zsido Evkonyv* (Jewish Yearbook) of 1927–28, after chastising Hungarian Jews for hardly knowing their own thousand-year history ("*A magyar zsidok alig ismerik sajat ezereves tortenetuket*") — this complaint thereby absolving the ignorance of the Magyars regarding Jewish contributions to Magyarorszag — Lederer states:

> The worthy study of Hungarian history will show that we Hungarian Jews have been in this our fatherland for over 1,000 years. Not on a piecemeal basis, drifting in as occasional immigrants, but as conquerors, descendants of the armies of Arpad, with ancient rights. The fact that in the flow of time we have been treated as aliens and pariahs, people undeserving of rights, in no way lessens our commitment to our fatherland or our current entitlement to these rights.[60]

Of similar vein was the article in the same publication by the Jewish MP Dr Bela Fabian. Entitled "*Az egyenlo jog — legfobb nemzeti erdek*"[61] (Equal rights — the prime national interest), Fabian lambasted the White Terror's Antisemitic panacea,[62] appealed to Hungarian chivalry as exemplified by Kossuth and Petofi, declared Jewish equal rights as the most important of Hungarian considerations, and proclaimed that it was "a matter of life-or-death for Hungary to appear before the peoples of the world as the home of classical freedoms".

In such a public relations manner was the campaign conducted against the principle and practice of *Numerus Clausus*. Of particular concern to Hungarian Jewry was the fact that, for the first time in Hungarian history, Jews had been classified by the state as a "race" or nationality, and not a religious community. Foreshadowing the ominous thrust of Hitler's Nuremburg Laws, this classification also applied to baptised Jews and their descendants.[63] For the first time since the Emancipation of 1867, Jews were once again officially classified as aliens, an "other" able to be legally distinguished — and hence treated differently — from the "normal" (innate) citizens of the nation. By this action the State, in effect, sanctified the Antisemitism endemic in large sections of Hungarian society. Importantly, by providing Judeophobia with constitutional legitimacy, it substantially eroded the impropriety attached to such prejudice.

Notwithstanding Hungarian Jewry's refusal to accept assistance from their international co-religionists, British and French Jewry, in particular, were greatly concerned at the precedent set by the Horthy regime. As such, The British Board of Deputies and the French *Alliance Israelite Universelle* submitted petitions to the League of Nations in November 1921 and January 1925. During the petitions' consideration in 1925, these Jewish organisations argued before the League that the *Numerus Clausus* violated article 58 of the Trianon Treaty. Further action was pre-empted by Hungary presenting assurances regarding the transient nature of the Act. After further pressure, in February 1928 the Act was liberalised, but not revoked.[64]

Yet despite (or perhaps because of) this largely foreign-induced success, Hungarian Jewry, understandably succumbing to their nation's pervasive chauvinism, patriotism and revisionism, recognised the need to defuse accusations of an International Jewish Conspiracy against Hungary. The tactic adopted was to publicly repudiate their co-religionists in the reviled Entente for interference in what Hungarian Jewry officially proclaimed was a purely internal matter. Accordingly, in 1930 for example, whilst addressing a memorandum to the *Alliance Israelite Universelle*, Hungarian Jewish leaders admonished: "The foreign Jews can do most for Hungarian Jewry by co-operating in the improvement of the situation of all of Hungary and by seeing to it that the severe injustice that befell Hungary by being truncated at Trianon is remedied."[65] In effect, through tranquillity and tempest Hungarian Jewry's paramount — if not solitary — defence mechanism remained public and private proclamations that the community was more Hungarian than the Hungarians.

The Bethlen Consolidation: 1921–31

Continuing social turmoil, dire economic circumstances and international disapproval forced a general reappraisal of government policy. To accommodate and implement the newly acknowledged demands of *real-politik*, in April 1921 Horthy appointed as Prime Minister his friend and confidant Count Istvan Bethlen (1874–1947). A dispossessed Transylvanian landowner, ardent nationalist, politician, Privy Councillor, and prominent leader of the White coalition's "moderate" Vienna faction, Bethlen saw his prime task as stabilising the socio-economic situation under the leadership of the country's "historic classes".

Consequently, to restore stability and consolidate the authority of the ruling oligarchy, Bethlen initiated a minor land reform programme,[66] reintroduced a restrictive franchise (30 percent), an open (non-secret) ballot in non-urban electorates (1922),[67] obtained a $50,000,000 loan from the League of Nations (July 1924), reformed the currency (1925), and negated the prospects of electoral change by forcing the socialists to accept an amnesty that effectively truncated their political *modus operandi*.[68] To consolidate these policies, and to reinforce both political stability and his leadership, Bethlen gradually emasculated the government's radical Szeged wing.[69]

Rejecting the concept of White Terror for philosophical as well as cogent pragmatic reasons,[70] the government now attempted to attain its goals via financial inducement rather than through arbitrary power, physical coercion or economic expropriation. Bethlen, considered an aristocratic Anglophile, instituted policies that may be classified as neo-corporate — a pragmatic *Etatism* in which the authority of the state was paramount but not all-consuming, public opinion attaining limited but significant input into the processes of policy formulation.[71] In the political arena, for example, whilst rural constituencies were invariably and unashamedly manipulated into providing the government with its parliamentary majority,[72] voting in urban areas adhered largely to acknowledged democratic practice.[73] The legislature thus provided a forum for meaningful if limited exchange, as well as opportunities for the exposure of incompetence, corruption and arbitrary behaviour. Furthermore, with the restoration of the Upper House in 1926, diversity was augmented by the appointment to that chamber of representatives of various interest groups — professional associations, industrial and commercial chambers, aristocrats, and the recognised religious denominations, including Jewry. This diversity was reflected and reinforced by the tenor of Hungary's press. Even in 1921, on the heels of the White Terror, of twenty-nine major newspapers fourteen were described as "thoroughly inappropriate", "democratic" or "Jewish"; only seven could be classified as "Christian" or "national" in spirit.[74]

In economic policy Bethlen's prime aim was the reassurance of local and foreign investors. Accordingly, tariffs were substantially increased (1924), subsidies introduced, and capital was safeguarded against the agitation of both the Left and the ultra-Right. To Bethlen, who considered that economic progress was largely correlated with industrial development, the goodwill of international capital was of paramount consideration, to be nurtured as a matter of national priority. As such, Bethlen considered that the national interest necessitated a mutually advantageous accommodation with the country's financial and entrepreneurial class, that is local investors who were consulted by international capital and represented their interests in Hungary. The fact that these local investors were largely Jewish meant that, for reasons of national weal, the Szeged Ultras had to be politically neutralised. Thus it was that as early as 1919, two years before his appointment as premier, Bethlen approached Horthy regarding the consequences of the White Terror (see above). The Prime Minister's policy ensured that by 1922, despite bombing outrages at Jewish functions in 1923 and 1925, Jews could once again summon the police and expect protection for life and property. Furthermore, in 1926, using methods employed so successfully by Prime Minister Tisza after Tiszaeszlar (see Chapter I), Bethlen eliminated most of the virulent Antisemites from parliament.[75]

To Jewish perceptions, the Bethlen political steamroller, following Tisza's forty-year-old precedent, appeared to be successfully restoring Hungarian Jewry and the Magyar establishment's mutually beneficial symbiosis. To reinforce this perception, in November 1925 Bethlen acknowledged in parliament that *Numerus Clausus* provided a "legitimate grievance" for Hungarian Jewry, described the Act as "a purely ephemeral phenomenon", and assured a speedy return to the spirit of Emancipation which, he promised, would "in no way be abridged".[76] It was in accordance with this pledge that the principle of ex-officio Jewish representation on political bodies was restored, firstly to the Upper House in 1926 and then, in 1929, to municipal and provincial councils.[77]

Although Jewish equality thus appeared to be re-emerging on a fairly broad front, in effect the age-old Hungarian duality towards the Jews retained a not inconspicuous presence. As a matter of policy, apart from token appointments, Jews were no longer recruited into either the public service or the government political apparatus. Consequently, in the decade after World War I the number of Jews employed in county bureaucracies declined from 4.5 to 0.7 percent, in the judiciary from 5.0 to 1.7 percent and in the ministries from 4.9 to 1.5 percent. Furthermore, in marked contrast to the 1903–05 government of Istvan Tisza, which contained eighty-four Jewish deputies and six to eight Jewish Ministers, Bethlen's backbench contained but a handful of Jewish members and only a solitary Jew in the Cabinet.[78] The overt and covert forms of discrimination, whilst reduced in both intensity and distribution, remained obvious indicators of Hungarian Jewry's inherently "other" — if no longer alien — status.

Yet notwithstanding these clear indicators of inequity and iniquity, Hungarian Jewry could be fairly well satisfied at the end of the 1920s. The rabid perpetrators of White Terror were largely dispossessed of authority, and the state, once again, guarded Jewish life and limb; reaffirmed as the nation's foremost entrepreneurs, Jews were once again acknowledged by the establishment — albeit grudgingly — as economic stalwarts and the power structure's prime financial pivot;[79] and the *Numerus Clausus*, Jewry's greatest institutional threat since the Emancipation, whilst still extant, was visibly and rapidly eroding. Importantly, from historical perspective, the Jewish strategy of maintaining absolute loyalty to Hungary and the Hungarian Establishment was once again vindicated. This policy, lovingly nurtured in the six decades since Emancipation, had, to the understandable perceptions of Hungarian Jewry, delivered the community from the greatest threat since medieval times. Whilst acknowledging the need for further improvement, Hungarian Jewry, considering itself once again cocooned within a pragmatic Establishment, faced the future with confidence in its ability to weather any foreseeable menace on the horizon.[80]

Resurgence of the Right

The Great Depression struck Hungary in 1930–31, a year later than most industrialised nations. The results, as elsewhere, were highly traumatic, but especially so for such a relatively poor, largely underdeveloped country. Whilst struggling to recover from the grossly debilitating effects of World War I, adding to instability was the fact that Hungary had yet to attain the social cohesion generated by a consensus regarding the distribution and exercise of power within its society.

Agricultural prices were shattered and, critical to the welfare of the Hungarian economy, agricultural exports collapsed. The peasantry fell into debt, 600,000 agricultural workers became redundant and, in the period 1928–32, industrial unemployment rose from 5 to 36 percent whilst industrial output crashed between 40 to 80 percent.[81] Unemployed tertiary graduates, forming a sizeable group, were not infrequently engaged in clearing snow from streets and attending soup kitchens. In 1930, for example, 46 percent of recent medical graduates were either unemployed or working in a non-medical domain.[82] Social discontent erupted in September 1930, with a huge demonstration in Budapest and hunger marches in the provinces.

The replacement of Bethlen's ministry in August 1931 with the conservative Cabinet of Count Gyula Karolyi[83] — appointed to restore law, order and strong government — failed to stem the tide of discontent. The campaigns of the tolerated Left were more than matched by the greater, more vigorous agitation of the Radical Right, these antagonisms further polarising society. In concession to this growing right-wing virulence, on 29 September 1932 Horthy appointed as Prime Minister his intimate White comrade-in-arms, the notorious right-wing radical Gyula Gombos (1886–1936), founder of secret ultra-patriotic associations and Minister of Defence during the periods 1919–20 and 1929–32.[84] Calling himself a National Socialist in 1919 — years before Hitler adopted that term[85] — Gombos was instrumental in founding the radical Right, rabidly Antisemitic *Fajvedo Part* (Party of Racial Defence) in 1923,[86] and in 1925 took a leading role in organising the World Antisemitic Congress in Budapest[87]. Succumbing to Bethlen's seduction, however, the *Fajvedo* Party was liquidated, with Gombos being co-opted into the Defence Ministry, becoming Under Secretary in 1928 and then Minister in 1929. It was this latter tenure, which lasted until his appointment as Prime Minister, that enabled Gombos to commence appointing and promoting many of his avowed supporters to positions of authority in the now expanding army. The radicalisation of the officer corps was arguably Gombos' most important and enduring contribution towards advancing the cause of the Hungarian radical Right.

Despite his hardline past, by accepting the premiership Gombos was manoeuvred into a considerable restriction of his political latitude. As a condition of appointment, Miklos Horthy, the allegedly "hapless intermediary between opposing factions at home and abroad",[88] obtained pledges from Gombos to refrain from altering existing political institutions, from calling new elections prior to the expiry of the then parliamentary term, and from introducing Antisemitic legislation.[89] Furthermore, in case being saddled with a basically Bethlenite parliament was insufficient restraint on his authority, the Regent forced Gombos to appoint members of the establishment Horthy Right[90] to the key portfolios of Foreign Affairs, Agriculture and the Interior[91]. As a final precaution, the former Prime Minister, Count Istvan Bethlen, remained active behind the scenes, using his considerable prestige, influence and following to ensure that Gombos failed to realise any significant element of his radical agenda.[92] Henceforth, rival groups headed by the Prime Minister and his predecessor "waged an embittered and dingdong struggle for power", a conflict that was only terminated by Gombos' death in 1936.[93]

Belying his reputation for inflexibility, Gombos surprised many by genuflecting towards the demands of *real-politik* and presenting his Ministry as one advocating national development rather than the fundamental restructuring of society. The contentious conundrum of land reform was postponed until economic buoyancy was regained and, critical to the reassurance of Hungarian Jewry, a rapprochement was negotiated with the community. In this "compact" the government apparently gave Jewry's paramount leaders, Samuel Stern (Neolog) and Eugene Szabo (Orthodox), certain assurances in return for Jewry's commitment to support the government's economic endeavours.[94]

As an attempted, formal exculpation of his rabid Antisemitism, and as a means of reassuring Jewish investors, on 11 October 1932, less than two weeks after his elevation to the premiership, Gombos stated in parliament:

> To Jewry I say openly and honestly, I revised my viewpoint. That part of Jewry which recognizes that it has a common fate with our nation, I wish to consider my brothers as much as my Hungarian brethren. I saw in the War Jewish heroes. I know Jews who have the golden medal and I know that they fought courageously. I know leading Jews who pray with me for the Hungarian fate and I know that that part of Jewry which does not want or cannot fit into the nation's social life, the Jews themselves will be the first to condemn...[95]

The credibility of this statement was enhanced by knowledge that even in the virulent phase of his Judeophobia Gombos had admitted certain "acceptable" Jews — albeit invariably wealthy — into his Antisemitic movement and secret societies.[96]

Yet despite his apparent newfound moderation, Gombos retained many elements of his previously unconstrained authoritarian enthusiasms. In particular, in June 1933 he was the first foreign premier to visit the newly installed German Chancellor, Adolph Hitler.[97] Having thus reinforced his Fascist credentials, he set about reconstructing the Army's General Staff, the public service and the government's political apparatus by utilising the technique of favouring his supporters with promotions and appointments.[98] Moreover, he surreptitiously and otherwise encouraged and supported radical Right students in their "unofficial" *Numerus Clausus* campaign against their Jewish colleagues.[99] To add practical effect, in 1933 a government campaign to find positions for unemployed graduates omitted Jews from the list of potential employees.[100] Yet contemporaneous with these discriminations, Gombos attempted to maintain an aura of reason, understanding and sympathy for the situation of Hungarian Jewry. Klein summarises this dichotomy thus:

> The Right-Radicals spared no efforts to reject charges of Antisemitism and defended their policies through such devices as making a distinction between two kinds of Jews: the loyal, native, assimilated Hungarian Jew and the foreign, destructive, east-European Jew, who possessed a ghetto personality. The first group they claimed to respect; the latter they wanted to expel for the benefit of the Jews themselves.[101]

The zenith of Gombos' influence followed the brutally manipulated election of 1935,[102] the resulting House containing a government majority (170 to 74 seats[103]) largely sympathetic to his radical agenda. Emboldened by this victory, his penchant for forthright exposition returned, with not infrequent public and private declarations supporting radical Right practice and principle. In particular, in September 1935 he signed a secret memorandum with Göring to the effect that within two years Hungary would be a politically monolithic state modelled on the Third Reich. Gombos' ambition was thwarted due to his developing a severe kidney disorder.[104]

Notwithstanding his questionable effectiveness in re-orienting Hungary's internal policies, Gombos had undoubted success in discarding Bethlen's cautious, tentatively pro-Western approach to foreign affairs. By expounding the notion that Hungary's greatest chance of a favourable territorial revision lay in supporting Hitler's attempted destruction of the postwar border arrangements, Gombos was able to commence redirecting his country's foreign policy into an alignment with the Third Reich. As a bonus for the PM, this realignment appeared to generate favourable financial consequences for Hungary. Stimulated by the politically inspired economic compact of February 1934, in the next four years Germany's trade with Hungary doubled.[105] By the outbreak of hostilities in 1939, Germany provided over half of Hungary's foreign trade (imports *and* exports). Quite simply, the Reich bestrode the Magyar economy like a colossus and thus became a prime determinant of Hungarian prosperity.[106]

Gombos' domestic policies as Premier can be summarised as opportunistic, an expedient straddling of fundamental incompatibilities. With the advent and support of Nazi Germany, it is doubtful whether his ultimate strategy — if he had survived — would have deviated significantly from his original radical intentions. Nevertheless, irrespective of hypothetical considerations, the important implication for the perceptions of Hungarian Jewry was that, yet again, its abiding symbiosis with the Magyar Establishment had managed to substantially refract — if not totally reflect — an avowed threat to its traditional socio-economic *modus operandi*.

Gombos' death in October 1936 led to the installation of Kalman Daranyi as Prime Minister. Considered by the Establishment to be a loyal supporter of the Bethlenite line of political pragmatism, Horthy appointed the ideologically flexible Daranyi in an attempt to inhibit the political momentum of radical Right forces both within and outside of the government. Recognising this expectation, the new Prime Minister quickly neutralised the government's radical MPs by restructuring his predecessor's political apparatus. To reinforce the official abandonment of ideological zealotry, Horthy, in a broadcast to the nation, proclaimed that land reform was impossible to accomplish since there was insufficient arable land to distribute. Consequently, declared the Regent, Hungary's future prosperity was to be assured not by policies advocating a redistribution of income and assets, but by those promoting economic growth and development.[107]

Daranyi's declared policy of maintaining the status quo further alienated large sections of the socio-economically dispossessed, as well as those aligned with the splintered but growing radical Right. The influence and self-confidence of the latter groups was given tremendous impetus by the growth of German power, particularly after the *Anschluss* with Austria in March 1938. For the first time since the immediate postwar years, the Hungarian Establishment became perturbed at the direction of political developments, especially as the country now shared a common border with the Third Reich. Thus it was that the Horthyists decided to simultaneously pre-empt and repress the rapidly growing rabid ideologues to the Right of the government.

The Hungarian ultra-Right

Emerging from the chaos and catastrophe of World War I, the White counter-revolutionaries were the physical precursors and ideological mentors of the Hungarian ultra-Right. In particular, two of the most prominent White leaders, Regent Horthy and future Prime Minister Gyula Gombos, were closely associated with the embryonic Nazi movement in Germany, both being implicated in Hitler's attempted *putsch* in Munich in November 1923.[108]

Fiscal necessity, and the Establishment's need to regain political control, meant a reversal of government policy. Ideological purity became subordinate to both economic pragmatism and the resolute determination to maintain the status quo in most matters of internal policy. The growing radical sectors of society, favouring a comprehensive redesign of the country's socio-economic and political structures, became increasingly alienated by this progressive drift from the substance to what they dismissed as an intermittent facade of activist policies. These disgruntled and largely dispossessed elements, blocked from involvement with the Left by the memory of the Kun epoch; the truncation of socialist and union activity; the reality of police repression; the primacy of Hungary's pervasive, virulent chauvinism; and the perception of the Left being the puppet of an international Judeo-Bolshevik conspiracy; were also frustrated by the continuing failure of the government's incessant, passionate propaganda campaign for territorial revision. Of future significance, radical Right alienation was reinforced by what zealots considered to be the government's merely tokenist Antisemitism.

Such disaffections generated not infrequent attempts to form political parties advocating a more intense and comprehensive pro-Fascist policy.[109] Also of continually growing significance was the fact that with the death of Gombos, the enormous resources and authority of the Third Reich — no longer inhibited by the Göring–Gombos memorandum[110] — focused upon ensuring that the predominant factors in the Hungarian political equation became German-oriented Fascism in general and pro-Nazism in particular. Despite this assistance, Hungary, in sharp contradistinction to Italy, Spain and Germany, lacked an ultra-Right leader with sufficient charisma, vision, aptitude and mass support to impose his personal and political hegemony on the country's continually squabbling radical Right.[111] These internecine antagonisms remained a constant throughout the whole of the Horthy era until, maddened by the Regent's tragi-comic blunders of October 1944 (see below), the German occupiers were, in effect, forced to anoint the *Nyilas* (Arrow Cross) commander, Ferenc Szalasi, as Leader of the Nation.

Typical of the early ultra-Right parties, the *Nemzeti Szocialista Magyar Munkaspart* (Hungarian National Socialist Worker's Party) was founded in 1931. Adopting the "scythe cross" as its symbol,[112] this group preached land reform and social justice, thus appealing to landless peasants and impoverished workers who, in an untrammelled electoral system — arguably — would have been drawn towards supporting the Left of the political spectrum. Sharing much of the ultra-Right's ebullience, party members described themselves as the "Fateful Death Reapers of the Jewish Swine and their hirelings".[113] In 1933 a breakaway faction, the United National Socialist Party, became the first group to openly use the swastika in Hungary. Largely replicating the German Nazi programme — including the *SS*, Storm Troopers, and a Hitler *Jugend*-type youth movement — the party leader, Count Fidel Palffy, was to become a member of Szalasi's junta after the dramatic events of 15 October 1944 (see below).

The use of the swastika by a rival National Socialist Party — formed in 1934 by the substantial landowner and eccentric Count Sandor Festetics — alarmed the government into banning the use of foreign political emblems. As a result, Festetics replaced the German Nazi icon with a symbol composed of intersecting double-headed arrows. After being purloined by Szalasi, it was this symbol that ultimately became the generic emblem of the Hungarian ultra-Right.[114]

The imbroglio regarding symbols was symptomatic of the fundamental paradox confronting the Hungarian radical Right during the 1930s. Despite its chauvinism, xenophobia and Antisemitism, and despite its intense irredentist crusade for a reborn greater Magyarorszag, many Hungarians viewed much of the domestic ultra-Right as a foreign manifestation, that is, a German intrusion into the nation's body politic. This perception generated tension within the extremists' far from homogeneous ranks, particularly between Magyar hegemonists (admiring the Nazis but largely paranoid at the prospect of German expansionism) and the Aryan supremacists who idealised the Third Reich, idolised its leader, and operated under the principle of *"Magyar-nemet sorskozosseg"* (Hungarian-German common destiny).[115]

Although never successfully overcoming this schism, the *Nyilas* (Arrow Cross) Party leader Ferenc Szalasi (born 1897 in Transylvania of mixed Armenian and non-Magyar parentage,[116] executed as a War Criminal in Budapest, 1946) was to become the Hungarian extreme Right's foremost protagonist and only genuinely popular leader. Formally commencing his Fascist career in 1930 by joining a clandestine racialist organisation, the Hungarian Life Association, Szalasi's 1933 tract, "Plan for the Building of the Hungarian State", outlined his concept of a fascist, Hungarist nation.[117] After resigning as a Major from the Army General Staff in March 1935, Szalasi founded the Party of National Will (*Nemzet Akaratanak Partja*) which, in October 1937, amalgamated with several other Fascist groups to form the Hungarian National Socialist Party.

Gradually the Hungarian ultra-Right coalesced into two broad categories. One, a middle-class amalgam (both employed and otherwise) of middle management, non-Jewish professionals, the military, public servants, and refugees from the lost territories, all collectively envious of, and engaged in fierce economic competition with, the Jewish *bourgeoisie*; the other, largely lower-class dispossessed who espoused a more intense ardour for comprehensive national restructuring. The fundamental difference between these two groups was that the former was paranoid about slipping down, whereas the latter was obsessive about clawing its way up, the socio-economic hierarchy.[118] Apart from irredentism, the great common denominator between the two groups was their consensus that resolution of the "Jewish Question" in Hungary was the *sine qua non* for solving all the country's ailments.

Notwithstanding Hungary being perhaps the only feudal regime remaining in postwar Europe[119] — Hungarian agriculture generating abject misery for the bulk of the rural populace, who either possessed no land or whose holdings were below subsistence level — and despite the ultra-Right advocating radical socio-economic and land reform,[120] in 1937 only 8 percent of the 20,000 *Nyilas* Party members were of the peasant class.[121] In marked contrast, a leading Party official contemporaneously estimated that 17 percent of members were army officers, some of very senior rank, 12 percent were professionals or self-employed, with the lower middle classes and the intelligentsia being strongly represented in the balance.[122] By the end of 1940, the Party had attracted a membership of 116,000.[123]

The general election of May 1939 was disastrous for the moderate Left

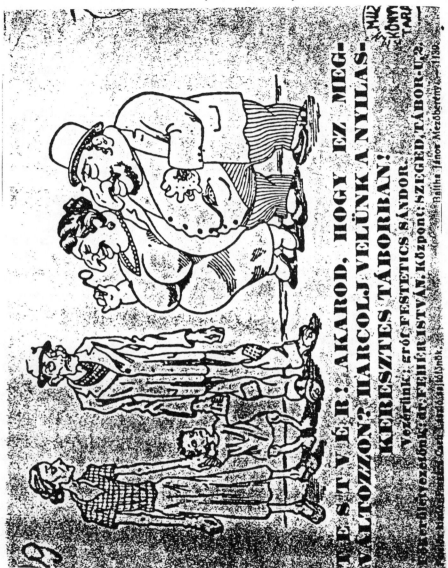

Figure 2.3 *Testver!* (Brother!)
Antisemitic poster by Count Sandor Festetics' Arrow Cross Party. The cartoon depicts a conspicuously wealthy, grotesquely bloated Jewish couple encountering an emaciated, poverty-stricken non-Jewish family. The Jewish woman sneers at the child whilst her companion retains his aloof composure, the wretched family presenting themselves for inspection with desolate stare (mother) and averted gaze (father). The poster's message translates as follows: "Brother! Do you want this to change? Fight with us in the Arrow-Cross. Leader: Count Sandor Festetics." (Source: Photo 11, album 57, YVA Photography Collection; n.d.)

and Centre alignments. And notwithstanding the government's usual best endeavours at intimidation and harassment of political opponents, the *Nyilas* forces scored sweeping gains. Despite standing in less than half the electorates,[124] ultra-Right forces amassed some 25 percent of the total vote and returned fifty deputies. Of this number, the *Nyilas* Party, benefiting from German moral and financial support, won thirty-one seats, mainly in economically deprived electorates.[125] In Budapest, the ultra-Right vote increased from 2 percent in 1935 to 31 percent in 1939.[126]

Claiming a dubious 50.5 percent of the total vote,[127] the 183 government members elected formed 70 percent of the new House.[128] Despite this apparently impregnable majority, the Horthy Right constituted a mere one-third of government deputies, the balance being either uncommitted opportunists or outright Fascist sympathisers.[129] Thus it was that the election of May 1939 thrust another paradox upon paradox-ridden Hungary. The result, in effect, produced a "minority government" of the Horthy Right which, *inter alia*, became the official opposition to the pro-Fascist majority in parliament. As shall be seen, this paradox was to have substantial repercussions for Hungarian Jewry.

Thus, despite regaling the populace with the bread of Jewish expropriation and the psychic circus of increasingly successful irredentism (see below), as in much of Eastern and South-eastern Europe — particularly Poland and Roumania — government attempts to undermine the extreme Right by adopting Fascist policies were unsuccessful, the Establishment being unable to regain control of the political agenda. The Horthyists' failure in the May 1939 elections, combined with the growing momentum of the ultra-Right, generated a de facto compact between the government and its extremist political enemies. The Horthy Right, in effect, acquiesced in the ultras generating the parameters of Hungary's political discussion whilst, in return, the *Nyilas*, in effect, acquiesced in the government setting the *perimeters* within which the *Nyilas*-generated *parameters* could operate.[130] Notwithstanding the mutual hostility and suspicion — if not fear and loathing — between these antagonists, this system remained the basic *modus operandi* of Hungarian politics until the German Occupation of March 1944, when the perimeters were subverted and a much more rabid set of Antisemitic parameters introduced (see below).

As a final point regarding paradox, it is piquant to note that, prior to the outbreak of hostilities, the abiding Hungarian bi-polar ambivalence towards the Jews was occasionally manifest in ultra-Right circles, even at the highest echelons — albeit from convoluted motivations. Szalasi advocated the solution to the "Jewish Question" within terms of a partial mass emigration of Jews from Hungary,[131] whilst a rival National Socialist pioneer, Count Sandor Festetics, publicly supported the Zionist movement[132] and was expelled from his own party for refusing to dismiss the Jewish bailiffs, managers and accountants employed on his vast estate[133].

INSTITUTIONAL ANTISEMITISM 1938–44

As previously discussed, the rise of the ultra-Right generated disquiet within the Hungarian Establishment, particularly after an attempted right-wing coup in March 1937.[134] This concern was substantially magnified by the German-Austrian *Anschluss* of March 1938, Hitler's triumph presenting the ruling circle with an unwelcomed *fait accompli* — a common frontier with the Third Reich. In response to their anxieties, in 1937 the government embarked upon a series of measures aimed at both pre-empting and suppressing the extremists to their Right. Apart from neutralising the government's own radical Right wing, in mid-April 1937, the month after the attempted coup, the Minister of the Interior dissolved Szalasi's Party of National Will and arrested its leadership. Although released after ten days, in August 1938 Szalasi was re-arrested, sentenced to three years' hard labour and only released in September 1940, probably due to German pressure.[135]

The First Jewish Law

As a means of defusing the ultra-Right's incessant clamour for greater military spending and the radical solution of the "Jewish Question", on 5 March 1938 Prime Minister Daranyi announced two new policy initiatives — a massive rearmament, and the government's intention to resolve the Jewish issue in a legal manner. It was this speech — delivered in the town of Gyor and thus passing into the vernacular as "The Gyor Programme" — that led to the adoption of what became known as the First Jewish Law.[136] Daranyi's pronouncement generated several major, interdependent political effects that were to traumatise Hungarian Jewry. It thrust the "Jewish Question" into the forefront of government policy, projecting the position and endeavours of Hungarian Jewry into a crucial issue worthy of serious national consideration, added legitimacy to the ultra-Right's relentless Antisemitic agitation, and aligned Hungary with the vanguard of those countries attempting to ingratiate themselves with the Reich by officially adopting Germany's institutional Judeophobia.

The PM's introduction of formal discrimination against the Jews was justified thus: "Such an arrangement, which will enable the Christian society to acquire its proper place in industry, commerce, credit, and the other fields of the economy, is also in the best interests of Jewry, for it can ease considerably the [danger of] anti-Semitism and, consequently, the spread of extremist and intolerant movements."[137]

Following the Gyor pronouncement, the "Jewish Question" in Hungary became something akin to a national obsession.[138] This development was viewed with some favour by the politically significant latifundia class, whose highly privileged position, and unyielding opposition to social reform, was obscured by the furore surrounding the Jews. But enveloping all was the emotion generated by Pavlovian expectations of a general upward socio-economic mobility, an expectation based on the anticipated expropriation of Jewish assets and income. However when, subsequent to the *Anschluss*, Daranyi attempted a rapprochement with Szalasi, Horthy replaced him as PM on 8 May 1938 with the financial expert and reputed Anglophile, Bela Imredy (1891–1946).[139]

A month after Daranyi's Gyor pronouncement, the government introduced into the Lower House a Bill innocuously entitled "For a More Effective Safeguard of Equilibrium in Social and Economic Life".[140] Despite spirited objections from the remaining democratic elements in society[141] and a strange, transient coterie of parliamentary bedfellows — including liberal aristocrats, social democrats, Jews and the ultra-Right, the latter deputies deprecating the legislation for being insufficiently discriminatory[142] — both chambers passed the Bill by large majorities. The official Christian representatives in the Upper House also supported the Bill, only quibbling about minor details and the position of "Jews of the Christian Confession" (ie: converts), their advocacy further legitimising the concept of institutional Antisemitism.[143] By this Bill, which has come to be known as the First Jewish Law, Jews were defined to include those who had converted to Christianity after 1 August 1919.[144]

A forerunner of future Antisemitic legislation, the First Jewish Law, unlike its successors, in effect targeted the employee and professional classes and was based largely on socio-economic considerations; importantly, unlike the Nazi's 1935 Nuremberg statutes,[145] it lacked a virulently racialist basis[146]. The Law's clear intent was the introduction of an economic *Numerus Clausus*, with Jewish involvement in commerce, industry, the arts and the professions ultimately being reduced to 20 percent of total participants in each category. This aim was to be achieved by reviving the medieval concept of the trade guild, now officially termed a Chamber, with only accredited members being permitted to practise in a Chamber's particular field of endeavour. The Law obliged a Chamber to limit Jews to 20 percent of its total membership and, until this threshold was achieved, Jews could not exceed 5 percent of that Chamber's annual new admissions.[147]

Anticipations were that the Law's provisions would be achieved within five years, and that by the end of this period a total of 50,000 Jews (including dependants) would be affected.[148] The government argued that a 20 percent quota was fair and equitable on the basis that Jews constituted no more than 6 percent of the country's population. In attempting to mollify objections regarding the dangerous legal precedent set by the legislation, Prime Minister Daranyi gave repeated assurances that the Bill would terminate the question of discrimination and that no further Jewish Laws would be submitted to parliament.[149]

In customary manner, Hungarian Jewry responded to this threat by once again emphasising its distinctive contributions to Hungary in both peace and war, its unshakeable loyalty to the Magyar cause, and the iniquities and inequities inherent in the proposals. As with the *Numerus Clausus*, foreign Jewry was not invited to assist their Hungarian co-religionists and, on this occasion, there is no evidence to suggest that attempted interventions had any effect.[150] Yet despite campaigning against the legislation, with some justification Jewish leaders tended to consider the Law as inevitable, mild in the prevailing context of Eastern and Central European Antisemitism, and — importantly though incorrectly — as neutralising the much more virulent demands of the domestic ultra-Right. There is evidence from Mr H. Bruce (League of Nations Commissioner, British financial adviser to the Hungarian National Bank, and confidant of the Bank's president, Bela Imredy) that "serious, prominent" Jews (unfortunately unnamed) took what may well be a unique initiative in the annals of modern Antisemitism. According to Bruce's correspondence of 8 April 1938 to the British Legation in Budapest,[151] these Jews secretly advocated the introduction of mild anti-Jewish measures in order to pre-empt the extremists' rabid Antisemitic policies and thus allow the government to regain political control over the "Jewish Question".[152]

(It is important to note that because of the hierarchical nature of Hungarian Jewry, the terms "serious" and "prominent" were often contemporary code words used to indicate wealth, position and influence in Jewish elite circles. Even if the unnamed prominent individuals were not in formal leadership positions, they would almost certainly have had ready access to official Jewish leaders who, as members of the same largely homogeneous elite, shared the same social circle, vested interests and ideology. Consequently such persons, even if acting alone, can be considered as representing a significant proportion of their class' thinking.)

Confirming Bruce's credibility in this matter was the *Note*, of 26 April 1938, from the Governor of the Bank of England, The Right Honourable Montagu Norman, to the Foreign Minister, Lord Halifax. Based on information received orally from the Hungarian National Bank, of which, Norman states, "my friend and opposite number, Imredy, is President", the Governor informed the Foreign Minister:

> At the bottom of all this *crise de confiance* are, only too naturally, the Jews. ...many of the more far-sighted, on the principle of half a loaf being better than no bread, actually solicited the sacrifices imposed upon them by the economic programme and even by the anti-Jewish Law...[153]

Possibly reinforcing Bruce's credibility is the testimony of Tibor Eckhardt, a leader of the Smallholders Party. According to Eckhardt, the First Jewish Law was, in effect, drafted by the American Minister in Hungary and Samu Stern (President of the Pest Neolog community and foremost leader of Hungarian Jewry),[154] the two men attempting to reconcile the government's political requirements with Jewry's basic interests.

By adopting this attitude, such Jews were in effect stating their willingness to trade Hungarian Jewry's cherished and hard-won — albeit tottering — institutional co-existence, inaugurated in 1867 by the Law of Emancipation, for a nebulous tolerance.[155] That is, such individuals advocated the acceptance of a mild and hopefully transient discrimination in an attempt to pre-empt almost certain persecution of unforeseeable severity, but probably to be based on the extreme German model. Considering the contemporary European context, even with the benefit of hindsight it is difficult for an unmolested armchair theorist, safely ensconced in the certitudes of a liberal democracy, to denounce the appropriateness of this proposal. In any event, it would be patently absurd to consider such advocacy as constituting either the substance or spirit of a collaboration with pro-Nazi elements.

Notwithstanding the above, the Jewish leadership's analysis of the "relatively mild" First Jewish Law's utility for the community appeared to be confirmed shortly after the legislation's parliamentary approval. Prime Minister Imredy not only declared his intention to defend ancient constitutional liberties (code for, *inter alia*, henceforth maintaining Jewry's then status), and reiterated Daranyi's pledge not to reopen the "Jewish Question",[156] but also vigorously attacked the ultra-Right[157]. Prohibiting state employees and the military from membership of political parties, the government, as previously mentioned, targeted the *Nyilas* commandant Ferenc Szalasi, pursuing him with charges of subversion until, in August 1938, the Arrow Cross supremo was sentenced to three years' hard labour.[158] To further allay Jewish apprehension, in a major address at Kaposvar on 4 September 1938, Imredy declared the adequacy of existing discrimination and re-emphasised that no additional anti-Jewish measures would be introduced.[159]

Unfortunately for the Horthy Right, the sentencing of Szalasi, the ultra-Right's foremost and only genuinely popular leader, proved to be counterproductive. The imprisonment not only failed to inhibit the *Nyilas*, but actually incensed the movement. Through incarceration Szalasi became anointed with the aura of heroic defiance, if not personal martyrdom.[160] Moreover, the November 1938 conflagration of *Kristallnacht* electrified the ultra-Right, the zealots considering the German

Feuersbrunst as a testament — if not yet to be duplicated, then at least to behold as a flaming ideological icon.

With the benefit of hindsight, it can be stated that the First Jewish Law was Hungarian Jewry's greatest defeat in the three generations since the 1867 Law of Emancipation. In contradistinction to the *Numerus Clausus*, the 1938 Bill commenced an inexorable socio-economic decline into eventual impoverishment, extreme psychological and physical brutalisation, until the final *coup de grace*, a swift, ferocious deportation to Auschwitz. Any assessment — whether direct or indirect, anecdotal or objective — will indicate a significant (albeit partial) recovery from the depths of the *Numerus Clausus* period. There was to be no recovery from the introduction of the First Jewish Law.

In summary, it is valid to conclude that, even in the short term, the Jewish initiative regarding mild discrimination — and credible testimony strongly indicates that such initiative not only occurred but was transmitted to the highest government circles — produced little political benefit for the community. And, unfortunately, even this small advantage could not be consolidated. As shall be seen, Imredy's duplicity; the Third Reich's foreign triumphs, her domination of Hungary's international trade, the massive moral and financial subsidisation of her Hungarian supporters; and the ultra-Right's incessant, aggressive and increasingly popular campaign of claiming to represent the "Spirit of the Times"; all these factors prevented the Horthyists from regaining effective control of either domestic politics, foreign policy or the Antisemitic agenda.

Finally, if the above initiative of a few elite Jews is deemed to have legitimised institutional discrimination, it should also be acknowledged that basically all that was, in effect, being advocated was what current progressive thinking would describe as affirmative action on behalf of the less affluent sections of society. A surely not unreasonable proposition given the dictates of *real-politik*, especially since Jewry's relative affluence could be utilised to alleviate the anticipated hardship of a small portion (estimated at 50,000) of the Jewish community.

The First Vienna Award

Despite elements of not inconsiderable reservation, especially by the Horthyists, Hungary aligned itself with Germany over the Munich Crisis.[161] As a consequence, in November 1938 Hitler rewarded Magyarorszag with that portion of Slovakia where Magyars constituted a majority of the populace. The actual details of the territorial transfer were decided in early November 1938 by arbitration negotiations in Vienna between the German and Italian Foreign Ministers, von Ribbentrop and Ciano respectively. Their agreement, known as the First Vienna Award, transferred to Hungarian control a band of southern Slovakia and western Subcarpathian Ruthenia encompassing a total of 4,600 square miles (11,900 sq km) and 1,100,000 people, of whom some 68,000 were Jews, largely of the Orthodox persuasion.[162]

The regaining of this area, known as the Felvidek (Upper Province), was a major factor reinforcing Hungary's near-obsession with foreign policy, relations with the Third Reich, irredentism, and the "Jewish Question". Foremost amongst those affected was the reputedly Anglophile Prime Minister Imredy who, already profoundly impressed by Hitler's *Anschluss* (March 1938) and Czechoslovak accomplishments (September 1938), abandoned his caution in external affairs, joined the anti-Comintern Pact in January 1939, and rapidly re-oriented both foreign and internal policies in favour of the Third Reich. Like several of his successors as PM — but unlike any of his predecessors — Imredy was to be executed in 1946 as a Nazi collaborator and war criminal.

The most significant party political transfer resulting from the First Vienna Award was the relocation of the corrupt and unprincipled politician Andor Jaross from the Prague to the Budapest parliament.[163] A virulent Antisemite, anti-Communist, Hungarian chauvinist, and fervent disciple of ultra-Right principles, after the German Occupation of March 1944 Jaross was appointed Interior Minister, the portfolio most closely involved with deporting Hungary's Jews to Auschwitz.

The Second Jewish Law

Seizing the opportunity, Imredy gave impetus to his ideological realignment — a realignment considered "one of the most startling turnabouts of Hungarian history"[164] — by taking advantage of the national euphoria generated by the Axis-brokered irredenta. Emboldened by the exultation, he commenced recasting his cabinet, the military and the upper bureaucracy by removing Horthyists and replacing them with Germanophiles. At the same time, abandoning the conciliatory attitude expressed two months earlier at Kaposvar, Imredy started proclaiming the necessity for a more comprehensive and rigorous anti-Jewish programme than instituted by the First Jewish Law. He justified this *volte-face* by contending that re-acquisition of the Felvidek had not only increased the proportion of Jews in Hungary, but that the increasing virulence of Judeophobia elsewhere in Europe had also exposed the country to further infiltration by Jewish refugees escaping from much harsher foreign Antisemitic legislation.[165] Confronted with these threats the government had a duty, according to Imredy, "to re-establish in the press and in economic life [the] leadership of Christian elements and the Christian spirit which the country needed and to which it was entitled."[166]

The fruit of Imredy's desire, the Second Jewish Law, was presented to parliament on 23 December 1938 and, eschewing the euphemisms inherent in the Bill's predecessor, was realistically entitled "Concerning the Restriction of the Participation of the Jews in Public and Economic Life". The Second Jewish Law introduced the "legal" foundation for the Holocaust of Hungarian Jews: the often inhuman Labour Service Units into which male Jews were conscripted during hostilities, and the horrendous measures taken against Jewry during the German Occupation.

The avowed objective of the Second Jewish Law was to truncate Jewish participation in Hungary's cultural, financial and business sectors to a level corresponding with Jewry's percentage of the population. This, in effect, meant a severe reduction from the First Jewish Law's economic *Numerus Clausus* level of 20 percent to a drastic new threshold of 6 percent. Moreover, to ensure the Law's unambiguous interpretation and implementation, "Jewishness" was redefined from a religious to a racial classification.[167]

Regarding civil liberties, the legislation banned Jews from acquiring citizenship by due process (marriage, naturalisation, adoption), severely limited their political rights, and prohibited them from government employment, the purchase of land, and influential positions in the media.[168] The franchise, and the right to stand for elected office, was henceforth restricted to Jews with documentary evidence that either they or their antecedents had been born and domiciled in Hungary since 1867, this provision reducing Jewish suffrage in Budapest by some 45 percent — from 75,000 to 42,000 eligible voters.[169] Furthermore, the Interior Minister obtained the power to denaturalise any Hungarian who had obtained citizenship after 1 July 1914. Clearly, the thrust of this provision was aimed at Jews residing in the newly regained region of Felvidek. The prospect for these largely unassimilated, largely impoverished, largely Orthodox *Ostjuden* was the cold comfort of citizenship at the pleasure of the Minister's pen. An unprecedented consequence of the Second Jewish Law was that by November 1939, over 50,000 Hungarian Jews had applied to emigrate.[170] The vast majority of applicants not only lacked permission to transfer their capital overseas but — with Palestine, the USA and the rest of the world effectively closed to Jewish refugees — they also lacked countries willing to provide them with visas.

In a very real and direct sense, by this legislation Hungary signalled its adherence to the "political correctness" then prevailing in central and eastern Europe. By this philosophy, countries introducing repressive Antisemitism hoped to pre-empt their domestic ultra-Right, placate the Reich, force a substantial number of their own Jews to emigrate, and, not the least, erect a barrier against the growing mass of desperate, dispossessed European Jewish refugees generated by "the spirit of the times".[171] As such, the Second Jewish Law was motivated by internal considerations and by the hope of pre-empting an exacerbation of the "Jewish Problem", an exacerbation resulting from the potential influx (both legal and otherwise) of alien Jewish "parasites and exploiters" into what many *Magyars* considered to be a Jewish oasis, the overly benevolent and chivalrous Hungary.

Unlike its predecessor, the Second Jewish Law was designed to fundamentally restructure the Jewish community's socio-economic situation. According to government hopes, this restructuring would supplant Jewish dominance by reverting the nation's business and culture to Christian control.[172] To prevent the consequent Jewish unemployed becoming a permanent burden on the exchequer, for the first time a Hungarian government instituted a policy officially encouraging the emigration of Jews.

In response to the threats posed by this legislation, Hungarian Jewry invoked its abiding policy of attempting to influence both government and public opinion — its traditional and hitherto successful method of redressing grievances. Once again Jewish leaders organised legal protests to the government and issued petitions, pamphlets and the usual obsequious, highly emotive appeals to public opinion for justice, equality, brotherhood, humanitarian principles, traditional *Magyar* chivalry, and — above all — recognition of Jewry's eternal, unshakeable loyalty to the Hungarian cause. The tone of the Jewish campaign is exemplified by the petition of 12 January 1939, viz:

Is this what Hungarian Jewry deserved? The mutilation of our civic rights, the limitation of our private rights, the restriction on our livelihood, the ostracism of our youth? Is this what was deserved by the Hungarian Jewish community, whose only wish in the course of centuries-old history was to keep its religion and remain Hungarian and only Hungarian? Let the battlefields of the War for independence, the marshes of Volhynia, and the Karst rocks speak out on behalf of justice for us; in the trenches no one asked who was of which religion...Just as in the course of the millennial blows of fate, neither fire nor water nor scaffolds or stakes, nor galleon benches or handcuffs could deter us, so with the same determination we will cling to our Hungarian homeland, whose language is our language, whose history is our life. Just as our coreligionists, even after centuries of exile, have preserved the old Spanish language, the culture and love for their old homeland, so shall we keep vigil for our legitimation and for the Hungarian resurrection.[173]

The sixty-three page booklet *ITELJETEK! Nehany Kiragadott Lap A Magyar-Zsido Eletkozosseg Konyvebol* (JUDGE FOR YOURSELF! Scrapbook of Hungarian-Jewish Co-existence), *vide* Chapter I, was also a product of this campaign. The very last entry in the booklet was a proclamation by Hungarian Jewish leaders on 17 March 1848, two days after the country commenced its revolutionary attempt to emerge from Austrian control. The entry translates as follows:

> We are Hungarians and not Jews, not a separate nation, because we are only distinct when we pray to the Almighty in our houses of worship and express our deepest indebtedness for the benevolence bestowed on our homeland and ourselves, in every other respect we are exclusively patriots, exclusively Hungarian.[174]

To reinforce the 1939 campaign's major theme of Jewry's ceaseless, fervent loyalty, in a comment at the end of this statement the contemporary leadership proclaimed "*Ezt valljuk ma is, — 1939 tavaszan.*" (This is still our belief, — in the Spring of 1939.) Possibly the most high-profile action against the legislation's iniquities was the silent protest of some Jewish reserve officers. Dressed in mourning, and wearing numerous decorations, the officers appeared in the public gallery of the Lower House during the relevant parliamentary debate. Their protest caused a sensation.[175]

With the proposed introduction of the Second Jewish Law, the community's leadership, deeply concerned at the implications of the impending legislation, broke with its tenacious isolationism and approached British Jewry for assistance. After several rebuttals, a more forceful approach in April 1939 requested the formation of a British committee, composed of prominent Jews and non-Jews, to lobby on behalf of Hungarian Jewry, and to raise funds for community members determined to emigrate.[176]

Samu Stern and Dr Sandor Eppler, respectively president and general-secretary of the Pest Neolog Community, arrived in London in May 1939 to request assistance for the 250,000 Jews whom they claimed the Second Jewish Law would eventually impoverish.[177] Their mission should be considered successful within its necessarily limited terms of reference, being constricted by the realities of Hungarian Jewry's geopolitical situation and the obviously greater immediate needs of other European Jews. By this historic initiative, Hungarian Jewry overcame substantial impediments to emerge from a hitherto steadfast political isolationism. Moreover, Stern and Eppler convinced their British counterparts to establish a high-profile committee in London to politically support, and financially assist, Hungarian Jewry. Aware that this achievement might be branded by Magyar Antisemites as yet another international Jewish conspiracy, and sensitive to the political position of the Hungarian government, Stern subsequently announced that the latter's consent would be obtained prior to the implementation of any British aid programme.

Unfortunately for Hungarian Jews, the deteriorating international situation, allied with the greater and more urgent demands of other Central and eastern European Jewries, ensured that only relatively marginal assistance reached the

Hungarian community.[178] To compound difficulties, in an apparent major blow, the Chairman of the Evian Conference's Intergovernmental Committee on Refugee Resettlement refused Stern and Eppler's request to include Hungarian Jews on the Committee's agenda. Relying on a strictly technical interpretation of the Committee's charter, the Chairman announced that he "could make no observations on any matter concerning Hungarian Jews".[179] Tragically, such intransigence was to become an almost constant refrain by official non-Axis sources when confronted with pleas from threatened European Jews — even during the height of the Holocaust (see Chapter VI).

Except for the brief Kun and White Terror periods, all post-Emancipation governments prior to the Second Jewish Law supported the nation's neo-feudal *troika* of power elites. It will be recalled that before 1867, Hungary had a basically bi-polar division of spoils: power flowed from the state and privilege resided with the latifundia and the Church. As previously discussed, to this structure the Emancipation of 1867 had *inter alia* grafted a third, fundamentally irreconcilable, paradoxical element — the upwardly mobile, economically progressive Jewish elite. As has been shown, in the absence of a substantial Christian Magyar entrepreneurial class, Jews had, almost by default and with government encouragement, come to largely appropriate the role of managing finance, commerce and industry, and of acting as intermediaries between Hungary and the world economy.

The Second Jewish Law was thus no less than an unabashed attempt to transform the tri-faceted Hungarian hierarchy back to its pre-Emancipation format, an attempt to restructure the edifice from a tri-polar to a basically bi-polar Christian monopoly. Yet despite these harsh measures, Hungarian Jewry could take some comfort from the government's rejection of ultra-Right demands that Jews be eliminated from the nation's social fabric. Jewish endeavour was still to be permitted, albeit within a highly delineated, tightly constricted format. Moreover, as a token gesture towards equity, nine categories of Jews, each of strictly minor magnitude, received exemptions from the Law's provisions.[180] Notwithstanding government intentions, a facade system of "Aryanising" Jewish enterprises quickly developed. By this process Christian "partners" — largely of the silent or token variety, but invariably with impeccable non-Jewish credentials — were appointed as company directors. This not infrequent shuffling of corporate paperwork legally converted many Jewish enterprises to Aryan status. Much to the chagrin of the ultra-Right, properly "converted" companies remained under the ownership and control of the original Jewish proprietors.[181] Consequently, significant elements of the community's entrepreneurial sector — especially medium and large corporations — remained unaffected by the provisions of the Second Jewish Law, except for the often substantial cost of hiring Christian straw men.

[Because many of the largest industrial facilities in the country remained under effective Jewish control until the German Occupation of March 1944, Jewish firms — involuntarily and with tragic paradox — provided a substantial portion of Hungary's material contribution to the Reich's war effort. However, it should be clearly understood that under no circumstances can this tragic irony be interpreted as Jewish collaboration — or even alignment — with either domestic or foreign Nazidom.]

Thus, although much of the *bourgeoisie* became financially constrained — some individuals severely so — the main burden of the law fell on the lower socio-economic strata of Jewry, substantial portions of whom were discharged from the workforce and quickly reduced to near penury.[182] But even in these blue-collar sectors, the economic boom resulting from Hungary's rapid rearmament programme generated a labour shortage that alleviated much of the financial pressure on the Jewish working class.[183]

With exquisite poetic justice, Imredy was not permitted to luxuriate in the Judeophobic and Felvidek-driven euphoria, being unable to refute a politically inspired accusation of possessing a Jewish great-grandfather. Contemporary Magyar hypersensitivity regarding the "Jewish Question" is indicated by the fact that Imredy's ancestor in question, Jozsef Heller, had been born in 1807 and baptised at the age of seven.[184] In February 1939 the Regent, scandalised by the allegation and increasingly apprehensive at the government's lurch towards pro-Nazi attitudes, was also disenchanted with Imredy's inability or unwillingness to curb the destabilising influence of ultra-Right agitation.[185] Utilising Imredy's antecedent problem, the PM was dismissed by Horthy and replaced by Count Pal Teleki, the Regent's former Vienna-based White *confrère*. The complex and multifaceted Teleki (1879–committed suicide April 1941, see below), formerly Prime Minister (July 1920–April 1921) during the *Numerus Clausus* enactment, was a staunch Bethlenite, traditional conservative, moderate reformer, devout Catholic, dedicated chauvinist, declared Anglophile, and a steadfast proponent of "scientific, civilised" Antisemitism.[186]

In contrast to the vulgar and fanatical vilification of the ultra-Right, Teleki adhered to the "genteel" school of Judeophobia, which held that Jews had come to exercise too powerful an influence in the nation. From a dynamic entrepreneurial supplement envisaged at Emancipation, the well-nigh closed caste of Hungarian Jewry had, according to this view, rapidly transmogrified into the country's dominant economic powerbase. The purpose of Jewish policy, according to Teleki, was to ensure that the nation regained control of its socio-economic destiny from this inherently foreign element in a legal and orderly manner.

Formerly a renowned Professor of Geography at the University of Budapest, Teleki's "scholarly, scientific" approach to the "Jewish Question" is exemplified in a letter he wrote to London on 13 February 1939, three days before his appointment as PM:

> The Jews are not all of the same origin, but their groups in Eastern and western Europe, and anywhere else developed and lived for long-long [sic] centuries in absolute seclusion, not intermarrying with the people, in the midst of which they were living. In consequence they form biological groups which are distinct from the surrounding people... You can in eight or nine cases out of ten recognize the Jew. This proves that they form what we call a race. But the biological race and the blood is not so important. What is important is much more the ideological age-old seclusion, their own code and the whole ideology and behaviour in all the forms and actions of life which are thoroughly different from those of all the European peoples.[187]

Notwithstanding Teleki's generally moderate facade towards the "Jewish Question", and despite some significant opposition — particularly from the Upper House — the new PM's support ensured that in May 1939 the parliament approved virtually *in toto* the Imredy-inspired Second Jewish Law. The only concessions granted related to Christian Jews, such indulgence being demanded by Church deputies. In particular, the ecclesiastical representatives' participation in the debate was a clear indication of their future attitudes vis-à-vis the coming Jewish catastrophe. The (Catholic) Prince Primate of Hungary, Jusztinian Cardinal Seredi, declared in the Upper House: "I wish to emphasise...that I do not defend here the Jews or Israelites, but first I raise my voice for the sake of such [Jewish] Christians, and especially for the sake of my [Jewish] Catholic adherents, who had no share in the excesses of the Jews", continued by attacking "bad" Jews who "because of their excesses sinned against Hungary", and proclaimed that it was a matter of legitimate national self-defence "to drive the Jews back".[188]

For all practical purposes, the Cardinal's concern resided solely with protecting Jews of the Christian Confession, particularly Catholics, and in advancing the prospects of further Jewish conversions to Christianity.[189] In this attitude he was following the lead of his spiritual rectors, the Pontiffs Pius XI and Pius XII, who expressed kindred attitudes upon the *Duce's* introduction of Antisemitic legislation in Italy.[190] Whether acting independently or in collusion, the head of the Calvinist Church in Hungary, Bishop Laszlo Ravasz, echoed sentiments similar to those of his Catholic colleague.[191] By adopting this attitude, the leaders of Hungary's two major Christian denominations not only reinforced the legitimacy of institutional discrimination, thus providing Antisemitism with another powerful impetus, but also helped to erode further the moral disrepute still surrounding Judeophobia in the shrinking non-Fascist sector of Hungarian society.

Horthy took particular interest in the Second Jewish Law, discussing it with the German ambassador on 21 February 1939, a week after the appointment of Count Teleki as PM. The ambassador reported Horthy's attitude thus:

> ...he himself is a convinced anti-Semite, nevertheless it is clear to him that it is very dangerous in Hungary to take measures against the Jews too hastily and too radically. They occupy an extraordinary mighty position in Hungarian economic life, and in many fields they cannot yet be replaced by Hungarians. We cannot kill the cow that we want to milk. Hungary cannot block its sources of income, especially at a time when means are required for the rearmament which has become urgently necessary in view of the political situation. But in spite of the difficulties referred to, the Jewish problem must be solved.[192]

It is pertinent to note that despite the extraordinary pressures exerted on Horthy over the next six years, the Regent maintained the above ambivalence towards Hungarian Jewry even, as discussed below, at the risk of vituperative personal confrontations with Hitler. Whilst expressing contempt for the unassimilated, "parasitic", Orthodox *Ostjuden*, and ultimately abandoning them to Eichmann and his fanatical Hungarian collaborators, as shall be seen, Horthy remained convinced to the end that the assimilated Jewish *bourgeoisie* was indispensable to the Hungary that he led.

The Outbreak of Hostilities

Despite being a confessed Anglophile, in foreign affairs the new PM attempted the increasingly difficult if not impossible task of reconciling German objectives with Hungary's national interests. Like his predecessors, Teleki perceived the latter to include trade, economics and the satiation of Hungarian lust for territorial re-acquisition. Notwithstanding his wish to avoid compromising either Hungary's independence or her relationship with the Western powers, the Anglo-French strategy of appeasement generated an almost total Hungarian consensus that successful irredentism could be achieved most effectively via an alignment with the German-orchestrated "New Order" in Europe.

This opinion was reinforced by two salient factors: firstly, the 19 September 1938 refusal by the British PM, Neville Chamberlain, to support Hungary's claim for the Magyar-inhabited portion of Slovakia;[193] secondly, Anglo-French appeasement which, *inter alia*, prompted Hitler to focus his (prewar) expansion plans towards the Soviet Union's natural sphere of influence, Eastern and South-eastern Europe. A reduction of Soviet influence, even at the cost of a corresponding increase in German power, was an appetising prospect to substantial sections of perennially paranoid and virulently anti-Communist Hungary.

Having obtained prior German permission, on 15 March 1939 Teleki contributed to the irredenta-driven euphoria by militarily occupying the remaining portion of Subcarpathian Ruthenia. Formerly controlled by *Ausgleich* Hungary, this region encompassed 12,000 sq km and contained 670,000 people, of whom only 63,000 were considered to be Hungarians — the majority of the latter group being Jews.[194] According to the census of 1930 the occupied area contained a total of 103,000 Jews, the majority of whom were unassimilated, Yiddish-speaking, Orthodox and financially bereft.[195]

The Second World War commenced on 1 September 1939 without Hungarian participation. Deeply suspicious of the Nazi-Soviet Pact, and of Hitler's inglorious attitude towards Hungary's erstwhile friend Poland,[196] Teleki not only refused the *Wehrmacht* permission for transit rights across Hungarian territory, but also admitted the 140,000 Polish refugees who flooded across the Hungarian border subsequent to the German *Blitzkrieg*. Composed largely of military personnel, by June 1940 most had left Hungary and enlisted in the Allied forces.[197] At the end of 1943, of the 15,000 refugees who remained, some 3,000 were Jews, maintained chiefly by the Hungarian Jewish community.[198]

The Second Vienna Award

Roumania's June 1940 transfer to the USSR of Bessarabia and portions of Bukovina stimulated Hungary to seek similar concessions in Roumanian-control-led Transylvania. Concerned at the potential threat to Roumanian oilfields, the Germans, as in the Hungary–Czechoslovak dispute, offered to mediate between the two contestants. The resulting arbitration, again held in Vienna and involving the German and Italian Foreign Ministers, was announced on 30 August 1940. By this treaty, known as the Second Vienna Award, Hungary regained 43,000 sq km of North-Eastern Transylvania, an area containing 2.5 million people, of whom some 160,000 were Jews.[199]

Having fully occupied the awarded territory by mid-September, the newly installed authorities quickly enforced Hungary's anti-Jewish legislation in the newly regained region.[200]

As a result of the Second Vienna Award, the 21,000 Jews residing in the Transylvanian city of Nagyvarad — about 25 percent of the population — became the largest urban concentration of Jews outside Budapest.[201] Amongst the most important consequences of this territorial transfer for Hungarian Jewry was the relocation to Budapest of Transylvanian Zionist leaders, particularly Rezso Kasztner and Erno Marton (see below).

Like its predecessor, the Second Vienna Award generated a flood of nationalist exuberance, as well as a tide of gratitude towards the Reich. Recognising the portents, Teleki released Szalasi from prison in mid-September[202] and, in early October, announced his intention of adopting German "suggestions" for the introduction of new, more intense discriminatory legislation against the Jews. Yet despite this compliance with the cacophony demanding comprehensive Antisemitic legislation devoid of loopholes, Teleki attempted to maintain a token humane balance by arguing that resolution of the "Jewish Question" should be postponed until the postwar emergence of a new European order.[203] But once again a Hungarian PM's attempt to appease the ultras failed. Led by an embittered Bela Imredy and his ideological *confrères* Andor Jaross and the former Chief of Staff, Lieutenant-General Jeno Ratz, the extreme Right wing of the government seceded in mid-October to form the blatantly pro-Nazi *Magyar Megujulas Partja* (Party of Hungarian Renewal).[204] Although handicapped by consisting of only twenty MPs, the confidence and financial support of the Reich quickly enabled the group to acquire respectability and influence.[205]

The Delvidek, Teleki's Suicide and the War

As a means of proclaiming loyalty and gratitude towards Germany, on 20 November 1940 Teleki signed the Tripartite Pact, thus formally aligning Hungary's destiny with that of the Axis powers.[206] Reinforced by this alliance, the Nazi concept of the total expulsion of Jews from the nation's social fabric gained rapid and widespread acceptance — and respectability — especially within the government and senior bureaucracy. During his Tripartite Pact discussions with Hitler, Teleki referred to the banishing of Jews from Europe and, given this lead, subsequent Hungarian governments were to invoke mass expulsion as the eventual solution to the "Jewish Question" in Hungary.[207] One of the determinants facilitating the Holocaust, the legitimacy of expelling Jews, was thus firmly positioned; given official sanction, it grew rapidly in the nation's consciousness, and developed a dynamic of its own.

But notwithstanding this adherence to the Reich, Teleki still sought to maintain rapport with the West. In line with this attitude, and despite Hungarian claims to Magyar-inhabited regions of Yugoslavia, in mid-December 1940 Hungary signed the "Treaty of Peace and Eternal Friendship" with Yugoslavia, the sole remaining member of the pro-Western Little Entente.[208] After a complex series of dramatic manoeuvres that resulted in Hungary unilaterally abrogating this concordat, on 3 April 1941 Count Teleki committed suicide — possibly the last time a nation's premier took his life for reasons of a treaty violation.[209]

Less than a week after the German invasion of Yugoslavia, on 11 April 1941, Hungary commenced military operations against its "Treaty of Peace and Eternal Friendship" co-signatory.[210] As reward for this perfidy, Hungary regained the Bacska and the Baranya Triangle in north-west Yugoslavia, a Magyar-inhabited region of 11,600 sq km. Known collectively as the Delvidek (the Southern Region), the area contained about one million people, of whom some 14,000 were Jewish.[211] Delvidek, the final act of Trianon revision, brought the total territory regained by Horthy's Hungary to some 80,000 sq km, these regions containing five and a quarter million people. The now fifteen million inhabitants of Hungary were distributed over an area of some 170,000 sq km.[212] All of these gains were lost after the Axis collapse.

Teleki's successor, Laszlo Bardossy (born 1890–executed as a war criminal in

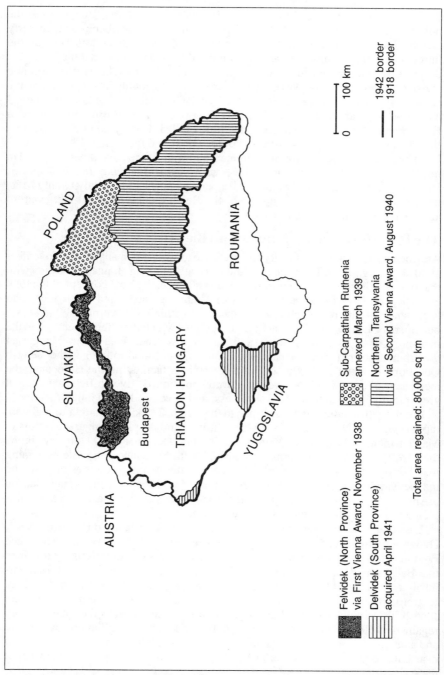

Map 2.2 **Trianon Hungary, 1920–45. The shaded areas indicate regained territory.**

Budapest, 1946) served as PM from April 1941 to March 1942. A typical right-wing, *bourgeois*, interwar politician of anti-Communist, revisionist, chauvinist and Judeophobic sensibilities, his premiership was to initiate and consolidate a sequence of events that led to the total destruction of the very system he was attempting to expand and reinforce. Under his tutelage, Hungary invaded Yugoslavia and Russia (27 June 1941), committed the 200,000-strong Second Hungarian Army plus some 50,000 Jewish Labour Service conscripts to the Eastern Front,[213] declared war on the UK and the USA (December 1941), and became a satellite in ever tighter orbit around the German sun.

Race Protection: The Third Jewish Law

Infatuated with the euphoria surrounding the Delvidek reacquisition, Bardossy, like his predecessor Teleki, expressed his gratitude and loyalty to the Reich by, amongst other manifestations, tightening the screws on the Jewish community. In mid-April, the new government adopted a decree degrading service conditions for Jewish Labour Brigade conscripts (see below).[214] Then, on 2 August 1941, the parliament passed the Race Protection (*Fajvedelmi*) or Third Jewish Law. Without even mentioning the word Jew in its seemingly inoffensive title ("On the Complement and Modification of the Law of Marriage"), this legislation finally introduced into Hungary the major tenets of Germany's virulent Nuremburg Protocols of September 1935.[215]

Despite its title, the legislation's motivation was clearly stated: "There is no doubt about the failure of the experiment in [Jewish] assimilation. We now want to exchange this for disassimilation."[216] In an effort to placate both German and domestic pressure, the Third Jewish Law eclipsed previous attempts to identify, and hence isolate, Hungarian Jewry by classifying as a Jew any person with at least two Jewish grandparents.[217] The singular thrust of the law was social engineering — the physical and psychological segregation of Jewry via the creation of an apartheid system that prohibited both marriage and extra-marital relations between Jews and non-Jews, the latter "crime" attracting a penalty of three years' imprisonment.[218]

There is thus a clear progression in the aims of Hungary's three Antisemitic laws introduced in the period 1938–41. From financial oligopolists (First Law, 1938), through economic and ethnic opponents (Second Law, 1939), the Third Law demonised Jews as "racial" enemies, ethnic polluters, and sexual predators. In less than a generation (1918 to 1941), Hungarian Jewry had been pushed from a constitutionally equal partnership generating national progress and development, to the status of a noxious socio-economic pariah — a canker corrupting the nation's heritage, birthright and security. But still, unlike regions of Nazi hegemony, even under the Third Jewish Law Hungarian Jewish citizens retained freedom of domicile and movement, and remained unencumbered by either discriminatory insignia or the terror of arbitrary arrest and summary deportation. The rampant pro-German euphoria created by the cavalcade of Hitler's seemingly endless, inevitable triumphs,[219] when coupled with knowledge of the anguished Jewish circumstance elsewhere in Europe, ensured that these "concessional liberties" appeared not insignificant to either Hungarian Jews or the domestic ultra-Right.

Jewish hopes for amelioration were raised by the Christian Churches' uniform opposition to the Bill in the Upper House, especially after the Calvinist representative, Bishop Laszlo Ravasz, tabled a petition of protest signed by all of Hungary's

Calvinist bishops.[220] Unfortunately for Hungarian Jewry, once again the Christian denominations were concerned solely with protecting the status of their converted Jewish congregants, ie: the "Jewish Christians" (see Chapter III), and not with a principled opposition to racism and/or institutional discrimination.[221] But by helping to persuade the Upper House to modify the Bill in favour of "Jewish Christians", the Churches' pressure prevented many Hungarians — including not a few members of the aristocracy and political establishment — from being classified as Jews. Paradoxically, this legislation was in keeping (although for totally different reasons) with the attitude of all three sectors of institutional Jewry, Neolog, Status Quo and Orthodox rejecting equally the concept of mixed marriage.

Being concerned with social engineering, the Law caused but slight tightening to the financial constraints previously imposed on Jews.[222] With seeming inevitability, however, once more government legislation gave major impetus to Antisemitism, this time by adding a humiliating "racial" segregation to the financial discriminations imposed upon the now officially outcast Jewish minority. Once again the ultra-Right were presented with an inglorious opportunity to propagate their political and ideological venom against Jews.

Devoid of meaningful options for independent action, and reliant on the graces of the Horthyist establishment for succour and protection, Jewry's usual pleas for decency, humanity and brotherhood fell on ears deafened by the Antisemitic cacophony of the times — a tumult inspired and amplified by the triumphant Reich, then at the zenith of its prestige and influence in Horthy's Hungary. Thus, whilst the first two Jewish Laws classified Jews as fiscal miscreants, it was the Third Jewish Law that branded collective Jewry as sexual predators and racial polluters, leading many Hungarians to conclude that *all* Jews were inherently unworthy of any place in Hungarian life.

Religious Disestablishment

Paradoxically, Judaism's constitutional status as one of Hungary's *Religiones Receptae* (Established Religions, see Chapter I) was unaffected by the three Jewish Laws. To correct this anomaly, on 17 December 1941 the government introduced a Bill entitled "On the Regulation of the Status of the Israelite Religious Community". This legislation, by changing Judaism's status from "Established" to "Recognised", eliminated the state's considerable subsidies to the community's comprehensive educational and welfare system.[223]

As this proposal did not affect Christian Jews, Church deputies in the Upper House approved the legislation's objectives — especially as one of the Bill's provisions prohibited Christian conversion to Judaism. Consequently, in June 1942 the Bill passed the Upper House without debate. Although the Law did not directly affect individual Jews, the cessation of state subsidies severely aggravated the economic difficulties of the community's institutions; in particular, many Jewish schools were forced to close.[224]

Expropriation of Jewish Estates

Despite both Baron Daniel Banffy, Minister of Agriculture from December 1940 to March 1944, and PM Kallay opposing National Socialism and the Nazis,[225] unrelenting pressure by the ultra-Right forced the government to intensify regulations discriminating against Jewish landowners.[226] The resulting Bill, dated

May 1942 and entitled "Agricultural and Horticultural Real Estates of Jews", was based on the premise that "...the value of land cannot be measured solely in economic terms, because not only seeds strike roots in the land but it also nurtures souls."[227] Not unexpectedly, the legislation encountered only desultory parliamentary opposition; but once again, the Ultras rejected the law as being of inadequate severity.[228]

By this legislation, promulgated in September 1942, individual Jews and Jewish-controlled companies were prohibited from acquiring agricultural holdings. Existing Jewish rural properties were confiscated although, to maintain a semblance of justice and humanity, partial compensation was promised and a small number of holdings were exempt from the Act.[229] A consequence of the law causing general astonishment was the revelation that the overwhelming majority of rural properties held by Jews fell into the small-estate category, a disclosure invalidating the popular notion that all Jewish landowners were plutocrats.[230]

Although the law impacted severely on those caught in its provisions — generally small-scale proprietors, and those unable or unwilling to "Aryanise" their land-holdings — because of the relatively modest numbers affected, the financial impost on Hungarian Jewry as a whole was not profound. Rather, the significance of the legislation was psychological and political; another tenet of Emancipation, the right to own and trade freely in land, had been revoked. Notwithstanding Kallay's intentions (see below), the institutional degradation of Jewry — albeit in fits and starts and with sputtering momentum — was still on course.

The Kamenets–Podolsk Carnage

Another quantum boost to the Judeophobia prevalent in Hungarian society occurred with Hungary's declaration of war against what was termed Judeo-Bolshevik Russia. As during the Great War, soon Jews were once again blamed for war-related hardships, particularly profiteering, general shortages and the black market. Numerous supplementary regulations were thus gazetted to close loop-holes in Antisemitic legislation, and to intensify the socio-economic pressures upon Hungarian Jewry.[231] Especially difficult was the plight of alien and refugee Jews residing in Hungary, the latter category embracing about 15,000 people.[232]

From 1930, all aliens residing in the country — even those born in Hungary but lacking citizenship because of alien parentage — were controlled by a special department within the Hungarian police, the *Kulfoldieket Ellenorzo Orszagos Kozponti Hatosag* (Central Secretariat for the National Control of Foreigners), the oppressive, efficient and feared KEOKH.[233] Despite opposition from the moderately inclined Minister of the Interior, Ferenc Keresztes-Fischer, in July 1941 KEOKH, with the approval of both Horthy and Bardossy, commenced the registration, internment and (often brutal) deportation of alien Jews in freight trains to recently "liberated" eastern Galicia. Placed under German control at the Polish border, by late August some 20,000 people had been deported and "resettled" in daunting conditions at Kamenets–Podolsk and environs.[234] On 27–28 August the large majority of these people, plus the remaining indigenous Jews in the area, were massacred by the *SS*, their Ukrainian collaborators, and — possibly — a platoon of Hungarian sappers.[235]

Regardless of the possible *Honvedseg* involvement in this particular carnage, many Hungarian military personnel witnessed atrocities committed against Jews, particularly by Germany's notorious *Einsatzgruppen* brigades in the Ukraine.[236] Furthermore, not only were such observations by Hungarian soldiers conveyed home in private correspondence, but eyewitness accounts of these atrocities by *Honvedseg* officers appeared in the US press.[237] Braham states that the carnage at Kamenets–Podolsk was the first five-figure massacre in the *Endlösung*.[238] When the survivors returned to Hungary and presented their testimonies, the humane Minister of the Interior, Ferenc Keresztes-Fischer, immediately banned further deportations. Apart from this saving grace, it should be noted that, at the time of the Kamenets–Podolsk massacres, the Hungarian political hierarchy were probably unaware of the Reich's *Endlösung* programme.[239]

The Delvidek Massacres

Hungarian military operations against partisans in the Delvidek (the Hungarian-occupied region of Yugoslavia), degenerated into full-scale massacres of the guerrillas' alleged civilian supporters. Occurring in January 1942, mainly at Ujvidek (Novi Sad) and environs, these atrocities resulted in the deaths of about 5,000 people. The victims included some 700 Jews, almost the entire Jewish population of the region.[240]

Reactions in Hungary to the massacres were such that demands for an investigation could not be stifled. After several protracted inquiries, in mid-December 1943 the trial of fifteen leading officers — including three generals — finally commenced in Budapest. The defence plea of obeying orders was rejected by the court, and in January 1944 five defendants were sentenced to death[241] and eight other ringleaders received gaol sentences ranging from ten to fifteen years.[242] Unfortunately, this arguably unprecedented act of ethical fortitude by an Axis satellite reassured many Hungarian Jews as to Hungary's inherent decency, ultimate regard for due legal process, and independence from German control — attitudes that, in hindsight, can be seen as a grasping at straws. The court's verdict, taken in conjunction with other aspects of the Kallay government's policies (see below), reinforced Hungarian Jewry's faith in the continuing relevance and viability of their long-established and much cherished symbiosis with the country's Establishment. Tragic consequences would flow from Jewish trust in government protection come what, at that stage, was still considered by the overwhelming majority of Hungarians as inconceivable — a German occupation of the country.

The Kallay Interregnum

Horthy's irritation at Bardossy's independence of action, combined with the Regent's increasing concern at the PM's growing collusion with the ultra-Right[243] — particularly his unilateral declarations of war against the USSR and the USA, his bid to exclude three Horthyist ministers from Cabinet, and his attempts to induce another anti-Jewish law — saw the appointment of a new Prime Minister, the pro-Horthyist Miklos Kallay (1887–1967), on 7 March 1942. Despite the seemingly invincible Reich vociferously advocating Bardossy's appointment to the Foreign Ministry, as an indication of Horthy and his new PM's independence from German control, Kallay doubled as Foreign Minister (until late July 1943) with the former PM being excluded altogether from the new cabinet.[244] Although beyond the scope of this book to analyse wartime relations between Hungary and Germany, it is pertinent to note that, as shall be seen, the extent to which Hungary was a master of its own destiny, particularly with respect to the "Jewish Question", was determined largely by this relationship.[245]

Kallay's policies have been characterised by the term *hintapolitika* — the politics of the pendulum. In 1942, numerous speeches and proposals indicated his adherence to the pro-German policies of his predecessor. Despite the absence of "German methods" vis-à-vis the "Jewish Question", Kallay's rhetoric, his legislation expropriating Jewish estates, and the continuing commitment of Hungarian forces (and Jewish Labour Service conscripts) to the Eastern Front (see below), generated German confidence in the PM and his policies. In particular, the German Minister in Budapest, Dietrich von Jagow, assessing Kallay's first few months in office, reported to von Ribbentrop in June 1942 that the PM had adopted a "sharper" position on the "Jewish Question" than any previous Hungarian premier, and that his loyalty to the cause of the Reich was beyond doubt.[246] Even towards the end of 1942, the German ambassador considered Kallay to be one of the Reich's most stalwart supporters.[247]

Having gained a substantial measure of German confidence, the PM set about maximising his country's manoeuvrability in both foreign and domestic affairs. When assessing Kallay's premiership, it must be realised that the Hungarian PM laboured from a position of considerable, and chronic, weakness. Retaining the confidence of only a minority of the Cabinet and back bench,[248] faced with a military high command dominated by pro-German attitudes (twenty-one of the twenty-nine top officers were Swabians, ie: ethnic Germans[249]), confronted with a surging domestic tide of anti-Communist and pro-German sentiment, Kallay's political lifeline was the support and confidence of his confidant and ideological *confrère*, Admiral Horthy.

Basing his actions on the Regent's unwavering goodwill, Miklos Kallay instituted a political regimen aimed at attempting to ensure that Hungary remained free from either Nazi or Soviet domination.[250] Whilst doubtless grateful for the Reich's assistance in the partial rectification of the Trianon Treaty's territorial excisions, the Hungarian PM introduced a cautious strategy of gradual extrication from the Axis alliance, masked by what may be termed a minimalist implementation of German demands. Of particular note, it should be acknowledged that neither Kallay nor Horthy was tardy in emphasising to Germany what they maintained were the fundamental differences between the Jewish situations in Hungary and the Reich. In his memoirs, Kallay states that even at his first discussion with Hitler (April 1942), after stressing the critical Jewish involvement in Hungary's war industries,[251] and the far greater percentage of Jews in his country's population,[252] he argued that "the elimination of the Jews from our national life without throwing it out of gear could only be a gradual process, and it could under no circumstances be achieved by force."[253] Upon his return to Hungary, Kallay, to placate Germany and thus restore equilibrium to the external equation, announced that "a final settlement of the Jewish problem could only come after the War, when the only solution would be to expel the 800,000 Jews".[254]

Although admitting in his memoirs the fearful nature of this statement, Kallay justified the announcement by claiming it provided sanctuary and security for Hungarian Jewry until the cessation of hostilities, and that, prior to its declaration, he had discussed it "with the official leader of the Jews".[255] But what Kallay's memoir fails to acknowledge is his pronouncement's official legitimisation of the

Nazis' policy of mass deportation, an *imprimatur* in no way affected by any secret assurances that may have been provided to the "official leader of the Jews". Even though the PM's overall non-Nazi strategy was apparent at the time — an obviousness that enraged the domestic ultra-Right, was welcomed by Horthy, and helped reinforce Hungarian Jewry's tragic sense of false security — Kallay's statement would have provided naught but political succour to Hungarian Judeophobes.

Gradually the Germans lost confidence in the PM's willingness to implement the attitudes outlined in his public rhetoric. Accordingly, a co-ordinated campaign, spreading ever more widely and of increasing intensity, was instituted by the Reich and domestic pro-Nazi elements in an attempt to induce Kallay to implement "German methods" — *pace* the infamous Wannsee Conference of January 1942 — vis-à-vis the "Jewish Question" in Hungary;[256] "German methods" as implemented by the Reich's acolytes in Croatia, Slovakia, Roumania *et cetera*. Early 1943 was, however, a critical turning point in the European balance of power. The wholesale destruction of the Second Hungarian Army at Voronezh (January),[257] combined with the German capitulation at Stalingrad (February), shook confidence in the invincibility of German arms and led to a growing pessimism regarding the eventual result of the conflict, an attitude subsequently reinforced by, amongst other factors, the downfall of Mussolini in July 1943.

Utilising these military reversals, and the consequent pessimism, as a window of opportunity, Kallay — with Horthy's knowledge and support — initiated a series of contacts with the Western powers via emissaries dispatched to neutral countries. Of particular significance were the negotiations for Hungary's "honourable extrication" from the Axis alliance conducted with Sir Hugh Knatchbull-Hugessen, British Ambassador in Ankara.[258]

These discussions were consummated on 9 September 1943, on a British vessel in the Sea of Marmara, when Hungary and Great Britain concluded a secret provisional armistice by which Hungary was to progressively reduce its economic and military contributions to the Axis war effort. By this agreement Hungary was spared aerial bombardment whilst, in turn, Allied aircraft were permitted to roam Hungarian airspace unmolested.[259] Kallay summarises this epoch thus:

> ...we were the first country within the German sphere — even Italy came after us — to notify the West officially through diplomatic channels of our withdrawal from collaboration with Germany. Our action was taken before we had been subjected to any pressure from the other side, been invaded or threatened with invasion, or otherwise been reduced to having no other choice. It was a spontaneous gesture and made of our own free will.[260] (Emphasis in the original)

The Germans, being fully informed of Hungarian manoeuvrings via their secret service, and concerned at von Jagow's disturbing telegram to von Ribbentrop (who was informed that "the local political situation becomes continually more un-friendly", with Jews regaining their influence and anti-Jewish laws remaining unenforced[261]), responded by inviting Horthy — sans Kallay — for discussions with Hitler. The meeting, occurring on 17–18 April 1943 at Schloss Klessheim near Salzburg, and now known as the First Schloss Klessheim Conference, deteriorated into a belligerent confrontation generating considerable animosity between the two leaders.[262]

During these discussions not only did the Regent refute Hitler's savage onslaughts on the Kallay government,[263] and reject repeated demands that he dismiss what the Germans contemptuously described as his defeatist PM, but, with regard to the "Jewish Question" in Hungary, Horthy defended Kallay's policy by declaring that he could not permit the economic expropriation of Jews to be followed by their physical annihilation.[264] Horthy's argument was rejected by von Ribbentrop, who stated that there were but two options for dealing with Jews — deportation to concentration camps or death. Hitler, in an extremely revealing intervention — one of the very few cases in which the *Führer* is officially minuted as referring to the mass destruction of Jews — asserted that in Poland non-productive Jews would be shot and those who could not work should perish. Reinforcing his argument, the German dictator fulminated that Jews were akin to TB bacilli and "peoples which did not protect themselves from Jews were doomed".[265]

The German assessment of the conference has been summarised by Göbbels, who confided to his diary: "The Jewish question is being solved least satisfactorily by the Hungarians. The Hungarian state is permeated with Jews, and the *Führer* did not succeed during his talks with Horthy in convincing the latter of the necessity of more stringent measures."[266] Even by Göbbels' assessment, the Austrian Corporal failed to intimidate the patrician Hungarian Admiral.

Horthy's detailed response can be gauged from his subsequent correspondence to Hitler. His letter of 7 May 1943[267] once again refuted German charges against Kallay's policies and defended his Prime Minister in a purposeful and courageous manner — even to the extent of stating unequivocally: "I should like to declare that Herr von Kallay always informs me in full detail of both his home and foreign political activities, and that he enjoys my full confidence."[268] With Horthy apparently having neutralised German attempts to interfere in Hungary's domestic affairs, Kallay in mid-1943, doubtless considering his delicate political position to be of lesser moment than Germany's continually deteriorating military situation, intensified his search for an exit from the Axis alliance. Accordingly, in mid-August 1943 the Horthy coterie formulated a protocol under which Hungary would be prepared to conclude a separate peace with the Allies.[269] Founded on a strongly anticipated Western landing in the Balkans,[270] and on the fantasy of Hungary negotiating as an equal partner with the Allies, the protocol had no basis in reality, no chance of being either accepted by the Allies — particularly the Soviets — or condoned by the Germans.

Horthy and his upper-class, neo-feudal coterie, a group whose political consciousness was nurtured largely in the halcyon days of the Austro-Hungarian Empire, appeared to behave as if the Empire's historical aura generated a corresponding contemporary reality. Unfortunately for their arrogance, their allies, and — above all — the trapped and defenceless Jews, diplomatic formalities were to be scant substitutes for cold steel, raw power and the strategic deployment thereof. And so it was that the charade could not last. Guided by *SS* General Edmund Veesenmayer's April and December 1943 reports on the situation in "defeatist" Hungary,[271] on 12 March 1944 an enraged Hitler signed the order to implement Operation Margarethe I, a previously devised formula for the "restricted occupation" of Hungary. Horthy, once again summoned to Schloss Klessheim, departed Budapest on 17 March — characteristically, without leaving any sort of contingency plans in his wake. Upon being presented with the inevitable, an ultimatum regarding the acceptance of German Occupation, Horthy capitulated. Physically isolated and bereft of contingencies, with a nod of his patrician head Admiral Miklos Horthy, Regent to the Crown of St Stephen, formalised the death throes of both historic Hungary and Hungarian Jewry. On 19 March 1944 the *Wehrmacht* occupied the country; except for a solitary garrison, the *Honvedseg* offered no resistance.[272]

Assessment: The Kallay Interregnum

Miklos Kallay's premiership remains, to this day, a matter of continuing high contention. Rarely has such a comprehensively documented period in Hungarian history generated such great — and heated — polarisation amongst noted authorities, the spectrum of opinion encompassing forthrightly derogatory, deter- minedly equivocal, and effusively supportive attitudes. The first position is typified by Professor Bela Vago who, after denigrating Kallay's memoirs as an example of "apologetic emigre literature", writes:

> [Kallay] became the captive of anti-Jewish demagoguery from the time when he assumed office to his downfall...he also contributed to the establishment and maintenance of that psychosis which identified the Jews as a criminal and harmful foreign body... The active participation or the passivity of the bulk of the Hungarian people was the direct consequence of the systematic hate campaign that raged during the Kallay period.
>
> To summarize: ...with his ambiguous, weak, cowardly, and vacillating attitude towards Germany he made concessions to the anti-Semitic course, which through legal measures and psychological effects, prepared the ground for the destruction of Hungarian Jewry.[273]

In abrupt contrast, at the opposite end of the spectrum of opinion are attitudes such as those represented by Professor Andrew Handler, attitudes refuting the entire thrust of Vago's argument, viz:

> Hungary's inherent anti-Semitism had been nurtured, even if not on the crude scale of the irredentist's demagoguery, by the conservative aristocracy led by Horthy and Bethlen, and by their middle-class disciples...
>
> The Kallay government remained remarkably resistant to the boisterous demands of the Hungarists and Hitler's stern warnings. In view of the dangerous proximity of Nazi Germany, Kallay's two-year-long (1942–44) political tour de force was one of the miracles in Hungary's modern history...
>
> The Jewish community reacted with determination to the narrow yet lifesaving political vacuum created by the Kallay government...[which] expended much effort to assist...the Jews whose livelihood had been destroyed by Aryanisation.[274]

The centrist position on Kallay, as exemplified by Professor Randolph Braham, treats the PM as a political "curate's egg". Although recognising Kallay's continuing and "increasingly frantic search" for disentanglement from the Reich's murderous embrace,[275] and acknowledging the PM's anti-Nazi measures — including the attempted elimination of pro-Nazi influence from the foreign service, recognition of the Badoglio (post-Mussolini) government, partial relaxation of censorship, pursuit of the Delvidek war criminals, and his continuing attempts to physically protect Hungarian Jewry[276] — Braham comments:

> Though eager to maintain an independent course and to avoid any occupation, his frequently equivocal and opportunistic position, his understandable mortal fear of

Russia and Communism, his failure to consider realistically the political and military ties that bound the Grand Alliance during the War, his and his representatives' ostentatious way of conducting 'secret' negotiations, and his failure to take any precautionary military measures at home brought about first the German and then the Soviet occupation...the Kallay government failed to take decisive military countermeasures and continued to pursue what many historians judge to have been a "cowardly, weak, and ambiguous course".[277]

One of the crucial points in assessing Kallay's premiership, and one that has been either insufficiently acknowledged or even ignored by his detractors, is that by late 1943 "Hungary was, for all practical purposes, a neutral country".[278] Allied aircraft roamed Hungarian airspace unmolested[279] and, in turn, refrained from aerial bombardment; from mid-1943, apart from neutral countries, Hungary was the only European state devoid of German forces, either as an army of occupation or as "comrades-in-arms";[280] *Honvedseg* units were detached from frontline activity after the military debacles of early 1943;[281] and Hungary was negotiating independently with the Allies in an "increasingly brazen" manner.[282] The general relationship between Germany and Hungary in this period has been summarised by Juhasz thus: "Apart from economic issues, there were hardly any German demands to which the Hungarian government did not react with reserve, arguments, reluctance or refusal."[283] One may interpose that all these factors reinforced Hungarian Jewry's perception that they were sheltering securely behind a government determinedly resisting German hegemony.

The above facts refute Vago's contention that Kallay's policy towards Germany was "ambiguous, weak, cowardly". Certainly the geopolitical-military imperatives of *real-politik* ensured an understandable prudence vis-à-vis the Reich during Kallay's first year of tenure. Yet with the decline in Nazi military supremacy, Kallay felt sufficiently emboldened to increase the pressure on Germany, especially for the withdrawal of Hungarian forces from the Ukraine. In fact Braham suggests that in February 1944 Kallay's "virtual ultimatum" to Field Marshal Wilhelm Keitel, Hitler's chief military adviser, regarding such withdrawal was the immediate issue triggering the German Occupation of Hungary.[284] It should be noted that in this contention Braham contradicts his criticism of Kallay, on the previous page of this reference, where he writes that the PM failed to plan against the possibility of a German Occupation and, in particular, was negligent in permitting the remnant of the Second Hungarian Army to remain in the Ukraine.[285] It is difficult to envisage any stronger, more determined option available to Kallay in relation to the Germans than the presentation of a "virtual ultimatum". Although such critics condemn the PM's failure to undertake contingency planning so as to thwart a possible German military intervention in Hungary, no critic has yet suggested a realistic scheme for preventing the type of armed occupation that occurred on 19 March 1944.

Braham refers to his judgement of Kallay being "cowardly, weak and ambiguous" — in contrast to Vago's judgement of Kallay being "ambiguous, weak, cowardly" (see above) — as being based on the opinions of Hungarian historians published in the Budapest of 1961.[286] As that year was within Hungary's Stalinist epoch, one questions whether opinions published at that time and place could have been anything but derogatory to anti-Communists, or to the anti-Communist position enunciated by Kallay.

As has been shown, even during the height of German military prowess, Kallay not infrequently pursued policies that were little if anything short of a courageous defiance of the Reich; policies that dispassionate observers may reasonably criticise as foolhardy rather than cowardly, weak and ambiguous. The confidential report of 31 July 1942 by Franz Jung, SOEG representative in Budapest,[287] serves to illustrate this point:

> In the talk between Barany (Hungarian National Bank) and [German Minister Dr Karl] Clodius, B. pointed out explicitly that an elimination of Jewry and Jewish capital from the Hungarian economy had to be viewed as an impossibility and that the Hungarian National Bank had to stand or fall on this question. So long as there was an independent Hungarian government, no responsible Hungarian political figure could act upon German initiative to bring about the complete elimination of Jewish capital. For the independence of Hungarian currency it was vital to maintain further Hungarian exports to countries free of German influence, and if need be to throttle such exports to Germany. Dr Clodius then threatened to block transit (of Hungarian goods through German-dominated territory).[288]

This is a far from unique example of Kallay's government acting with determination and courage in the face of German pressure, from the highest level, to resolve the "Jewish Question" in Hungary. As important instances not previously mentioned: in early June 1942 Martin Luther, State under-Secretary and head of the German section of the German Foreign Office, "suggested" to the Hungarian government that their Jews be physically marked with the Yellow Star and thence deported to the East. Kallay's rejection of this "suggestion" led to a series of increasingly strident German interventions regarding such proposals.[289] For example, on 15 January 1943 Luther rebuked Dome Sztojay, Hungary's (pro-Nazi) Ambassador to the Reich, warning the emissary that, irrespective of the War, Hitler was resolutely intent upon the removal of all Jews from Europe and that the Reich could not tolerate Hungary sheltering one million Jews "without action".[290] In spite of these pressures, the PM not only deflected German thrusts but also staunchly championed the rights of the relative handful of Hungary's Jewish citizens residing in German-occupied territories.[291]

These exchanges were part of a concerted effort, initiated in October 1942 by Foreign Minister von Ribbentrop and his deputies, Weizsacker and Luther, to compel Hungary to introduce the Yellow Star, totally eliminate Jews from the nation's social fabric, and deport the community to the East. In response, Sztojay — who ingratiated himself to the Reich to such an extent that he was appointed PM upon the German Occupation — felt obliged to warn Luther during their discussions that Kallay was not prepared to expose Jews to "misery or worse after their evacuation".[292] Kallay reinforced this response by adopting a position that was anything but ambiguous, weak or cowardly, viz: the "Jewish Question" in Hungary was an internal matter and any further pressure would be viewed as German intervention in Hungarian affairs.[293] Despite this forthright position, German coercion regarding the "Jewish Question" continued unabated, especially in the months following the Schloss Klessheim conference,[294] with Jews invariably being characterised by the Reich as "a more dangerous and greater enemy than any other adversary".[295] At the end of April 1943, Sztojay reported that "the German attitude to the Jewish question has stiffened and reached the gravest severity" and implored his government to institute policies that would avoid the necessity for the Reich to take "actual measures" against Hungary.[296] Kallay's position, however, was immovable: as confirmed by the German ambassador, von Jagow, the PM continued to advocate a "humanitarian", postwar solution to the "Jewish Question", a solution that would be compatible with Hungary's "Christian culture and character".[297]

None of the above should be interpreted as indicating that the Hungarian PM was a philosemite. Like his predecessor and ideological *confrère* Pal Teleki, but in marked contrast to the ultra-Right's fanatical ideologues, Kallay belonged to the "genteel, civilised, scholarly" segment of the Antisemitic spectrum. His position was clearly indicated on 19 March 1942, in his maiden speech to the parliament as Prime Minister, viz:

> When the nobles' privileges were abolished, there ought to have started a healthy blending, a seeping up of elements from below, while the dead debris of the upper strata vanished where it fell. But at that moment an impermeable stratum intruded, pushed itself in between the lower strata of the population and those above.
>
> The Jews were this impermeable stratum. In this respect, the Jewish problem, too, is a social problem. The fact that so few of the Hungarian peasantry, acknowledged by all of us to be gifted and even brilliant [sic], reached the higher social strata is mainly owing to the fact that this impermeable stratum prevented healthy social capillarization.[298]

To summarise: during Miklos Kallay's premiership, negotiations between Hungary and the Reich were consistently utilised by Germany to either cajole, incite or intimidate its Axis partner into a radicalisation of the latter's attitude towards Jews, a radicalisation aimed at the adoption of "German methods" to resolve the "Jewish Problem" in Hungary. In an attempt to alleviate what even his critics acknowledge were great domestic and external pressures,[299] Kallay adopted a policy of largely marginal concessions to German and ultra-Right demands. Consequently, although the PM issued a series of anti-Jewish proclamations, introduced financially oriented Antisemitic legislation, and permitted the transfer of tens of thousands of Jewish Labour Service conscripts abroad,[300] he was successful in deflecting, reducing or avoiding the general thrust of German and domestic Judeophobia.

During Kallay's tenure, Hungarian Jewish citizens retained freedom of domicile and movement; remained unencumbered by discriminatory insignia (the Yellow Star), the terror of arbitrary arrest and summary deportation; retained a presence in the Upper House of parliament; and continued to enjoy, in general, a relatively acceptable standard of living.[301] Particularly galling to Germany and her domestic acolytes was the continuing operation of the *Magyar Cionista Szovetseg* (Hungarian Zionist Association)[302] and the maintenance of steady, albeit modest, emigration to Palestine.[303] In short, Kallay's policy of resisting German encroachment and coercion was so successful that uninformed commentators, confusing cause and effect, have concluded in the following vein: "Until the end of 1943 there was probably less German interference in internal affairs in Hungary than in any other Axis country, Bulgaria, Italy and Spain included."[304]

Needless to say, considering the pressures under which the PM operated, there were negative — probably unavoidable — aspects to his premiership. Whilst Kallay's dissimulation was a necessary tactic in his overall anti-Nazi strategy, unfortunately for Hungarian Jewry his Antisemitic declarations and legislation, and his tolerance of the ultra-Right's virulent Judeophobia, reinforced *pre-existing* public opinion as to the legitimacy of anti-Jewish propaganda, and thus further heightened expectations regarding the solution of the "Jewish Problem" in Hungary. Yet when considered in context — especially with regard to the *real-politik* of his situation — Kallay's premiership, although falling short of Professor Handler's enthusiastic characterisation as a miraculous *tour de force* (see above), is certainly worthy of consideration as a remarkable endeavour. Quite simply, Miklos Kallay was so successful in maintaining Hungarian independence and, *inter alia*, safeguarding the country's Jews, that Hungarian Jewry — as mentioned in the first paragraph of this book — fell into the trap of considering itself to be residing in an island sanctuary; an island sanctuary isolated and insulated from the fate of their co-religionists elsewhere in the Reich's domain.

Chapter II: Notes

1. Hajdu and Nagy 1990:297.
2. Karolyi's initial popularity was based on the naive belief that his pro-Entente sympathies would elicit lenient treatment from the victorious Allies. (Nagy 1988:180)
3. After fleeing Hungary, Kun obtained refuge in the Soviet Union only to be purged as a Trotskyist in 1937. Probably executed by Stalin shortly before World War II, he was "rehabilitated" in the mid-1950s. (Katzburg 1981:34; Braham 1981:14)
4. Nagy 1973:436; Hajdu and Nagy 1990:304.
5. Nagy 1973:441.
6. Hajdu and Nagy 1990:311.
7. Braham 1981:35, n36.
8. Braham 1981:35, n34; Handler 1982:6; Katzburg 1981:34-35.
9. Katzburg 1981:35.
10. Deak 1985:46.
11. In particular, on 28 August 1919 the Pest Neolog Community leadership expressed its elation over the collapse of the "senseless and brutal" Kun Dictatorship, adding that for every Jewish Communist there were 1,000 loyal Jewish Magyar citizens. [Ujvari 1929:220-21, *"Ellenforradalom"* (Counter-revolution)]
12. Cited Katzburg 1981:35.
13. Braham 1981:18.
14. Handler 1982:7.
15. Handler 1980:186. Some wealthy Viennese Jews also contributed to the Vienna group.
16. Katzburg 1981:38, n10.
17. Berend and Ranki 1973:456.
18. For an evocative description of White atrocities, see a precis of the mid-September 1919 telegram by US Major Albert Halstead, in Katzburg 1981:39-40.
19. Katzburg 1981:41. From August 1919 to May 1920, pogroms occurred in some fifty locations.
20. Braham 1981:19.
21. Berend and Ranki 1973:456. The term "concentration camp" is from this reference.
22. Don 1990:148, n10.
23. Janos 1982:224. It is not clear whether the delegation argued for a complete cessation or for a mere moderation of the Terror.
24. Braham 1981:19.
25. Nathanial Katzburg "The British Foreign Office and the White Terror in Hungary in 1920" (Hebrew), in *Annual of Bar-Ilan University*, Bar-Ilan, vol. 7-8 (1970); cited Katzburg 1981:56.
26. Katzburg 1966:154.

27. Katzburg 1981:57.

28. Katzburg 1981:48-49, who notes that subsequently anti-Zionist reports appeared in the Budapest press.

29. On 26 August 1920 the Board wrote to the Foreign Office, expressed dissatisfaction with both the White Paper and the attitude of the British Government, and stated: "The truth is that all over the country, they [the Jews] have been the victims of great barbarities, and there is nothing to show that the authorities, whether civil or military, have made any serious effort to punish the perpetrators of these crimes or even to discourage them. Some of these barbarities, as reported by credible witnesses, reach a degree of bestiality and horror for which it would be difficult to find a parallel..." (Foreign Office 371/3558, 206720; cited Katzburg 1981:55) In a comment on the communique A.W.A. Leeper, of the Foreign Office, noted: "I dare say a good deal of this is true." (Foreign Office 371/3549 204354; quoted Katzburg 1981:55, n37)

30. On 16 June 1920 the Federation wrote to the US State Department to protest against the persecution of Hungarian Jewry. For the covering letter, see Katzburg 1975:73.

31. For Marshall's full letter see Katzburg 1975:74.

32. Quoted Katzburg 1981:58-59.

33. Chiefly via the stationing of armed officers in the parliament during the vote. (Nagy 1988:192)

34. The parliamentary vote was 131-7. Horthy showed his true Monarchist sympathies in 1921, twice chasing the last Emperor, Karl IV, out of Hungary when that hapless young Monarch attempted to regain his throne. For Horthy's version of these events, see his *Memoirs* 1956:116-27. Karl died on 1 April 1922, in exile on the Isle of Madeira. (Braham 1981:24)

35. Nagy 1988:193.

36. Jewish heroes, irrespective of the rank of their award, were excluded from membership of the *Vitez*. (Nagy-Talavera 1970:87)

37. Nagy 1988:193.

38. Handler 1982:12; Deak 1989:12.

39. The Hungarians themselves generated this reference to the partition by calling their post-Trianon country "*Csonka Magyarorszag*", mutilated or rump Hungary.

40. Lucas 1989:212.

41. Lendvai 1972:303; Handler 1985:19. The territory granted to Roumania from pre-Trianon Hungary was greater than that remaining to Hungary after the treaty. (Deak 1992:43)

42. Hungary's forfeiture included 89 percent of its iron production, 84 percent of its forests, 62 percent of its railway track, 46 percent of its food processing industry (Hajdu and Nagy 1990:314) and 43 percent of its arable land (Braham 1981:37, n56). Hajdu and Nagy continue by stating: "Practically all industrial raw materials and machines had to be imported."

43. Unless otherwise stated, from this point the term "Hungary" will be taken to mean "Trianon Hungary".

44. Half of the three million foreign Magyars lived in the Slovak and Roumanian regions adjacent to Hungary's borders. All figures in this paragraph of text are from Hajdu and Nagy 1990:314.

45. Taylor 1963:365.

46. Deak 1989:22.

47. Braham 1981:30.

48. The Act maintained a facade of objectivity by stipulating that the admission of students of different nationalities be in keeping with the proportion of such nationalities in the country. In effect, however, the thrust of the law was aimed specifically against the Jewish community. (Mendelsohn 1983:105)

49. Laszlo 1969:156. The following figures relate to universities and colleges for academic year 1925: (Faculty, No. of Jewish Students, Percent of Student Population):

Philosophy 129, 10.7%; Law 477, 11.2%; Medicine 481, 14.2%; Pharmacy 21, 6.5%; Economics 152, 10.7%; Chemical Engineering 13, 6.5%; Architecture 24, 8.0%; Mechanical Engineering 113, 8.8%; Other Engineering 40, 10.9%; Vet. Science 9, 3.1%; Agriculture 13, 0.3%; Mining and Forestry 0, 0.0%.

Additionally, 1,223 Hungarian citizens enrolled at foreign universities in 1925. Doubtless most of these were excluded from Hungarian institutes of higher learning because of their Jewish religion. (Ibid)

50. Janos 1982:226.

51. Klein 1966:87.

52. Except as indicated, all figures in this paragraph are from Janos 1982:226.

53. Braham 1981:30.

54. Klein 1982:113.

55. A favourite tactic was to intimidate Jewish students into not attending lectures, such absences leading to expulsions due to excessive non-attendance. (Klein 1966:84-85)

56. Klein 1982:121.

57. For a contemporary Jewish MP's assessment, see Vazsonyi's obituary by Pal Sandor in *Zsido Evkonyv* 1927:218-20.

58. Quoted Braham 1981:31.

59. Quoted Katzburg 1974:116.

60. Lederer 1927:238. Arpad seized power in 904 CE and died *circa* 907.

61. Fabian 1927:141-42.

62. Fabian (1927:141) wrote: "*A feher forradalom jelszava: a zsido. Kik az okai a haboru elvesztesenek?* A zsidok! *Kik csinaltak a forradalmakat?* A zsidok! *Kik az okai a mai helyzetnek?* A zsidok!*" (Motto of the White Revolution: *the Jew*. Who caused the War to be lost? *The Jews!* Who made the revolution? *The Jews!* Who caused the current situation? *The Jews!*)

63. Katzburg 1966:156. This clause was included to prevent the law being evaded by conversion.

64. Klein 1966:84, n25.

65. Quoted Braham 1981:43.

66. Of the country's arable land, less than 6 percent (948,000 out of 16,600,000 *holds*) was distributed amongst 411,000 peasant families. (Deak 1989:23)

67. Janos 1982:212.

68. The socialists obtained the right to organise workers and engage in collective bargaining but, in return, were limited to activities in urban areas and prohibited from engaging in political strikes. Trade unions were prohibited from unionising public employees or agricultural labourers. (Deak 1989:23)

69. See Braham 1981:39-44.

70. The main pragmatic reasons being international disapproval, the need for foreign investment and the possibility of the ultra-Right turning on the latifundia. Bethlen was a firm believer in the dictum that "the ways of the rabble were unpredictable".

71. According to Bethlen, "Real democracy grants a leading role to the educated and cultured element. Any political system that tries to negate this principle does not deserve the democratic label, for it merely engenders demagoguery and mob rule." (Quoted Janos 1982:210, n16)

72. Commonly included in the manipulation process were the tapping of telephones, the harassment of political activists, and the arrest of candidates. (Nagy 1973b:174)

73. Janos 1982:213.

74. Janos 1982:216. Freedom of the press was formally restored in December 1921. (Deak 1989:23)

75. Janos 1982:225.
76. Janos 1982:226.
77. Katzburg 1981:84.
78. Janos 1982:227.
79. Macartney 1954:xv.
80. Klein 1966:80.
81. Nagy 1988:197-98; Deak 1989:25.
82. Kovacs 1994:87.
83. Distant relation, and opponent, of Hungary's first president, Count Mihaly Karolyi. (Nagy 1988:198)
84. Like his radical Right competitors, Gombos appealed to the deep-rooted Hungarist mentality that venerated a hazy but allegedly glorious past. The most extreme early postwar xenophobes, the Turanians, worshiped an ancient Magyar War Lord, Hadur; considered that the Magyars' ancestors were ancient Persians, Hittites, Egyptians and Sumerians; and believed that Jesus Christ himself had been a Turanian. (Carsten 1970:175)
85. Nagy-Talavera 1970:52.
86. Carsten 1967:172.
87. Nagy-Talavera 1970:72.
88. Handler 1982:13.
89. Macartney 1957:I, 103.
90. Many authorities classify the Hungarian political Right of this era into three basic groupings: the Conservative-Liberal Right, the Radical Right and the pro-Nazi Right. Because of the often nebulous delineation between the latter two categories, it is appropriate to refer to these by the generic term "ultra-Right". Furthermore, the term "Conservative-Liberal" is both confusing and misleading. Consequently, from this juncture, the more meaningful "Horthy Right" will be used instead. Macartney, *inter alia*, supports this proposition when he writes that although Bethlen's group "described their own political tenets by the word 'Conservative-Liberal'...the foreign observer would have described the creed of the group, quite simply, as conservatism in a rather extreme sense." (Macartney 1954:xi)
91. Janos 1982:287.
92. Macartney 1954:xx.
93. Macartney 1954:xvi.
94. Janos 1982:288, n103.
95. Quoted Klein 1966:83.
96. Braham 1981:44.
97. Gombos' ideological affinity to, and known connections with, the German ultra-Right was one of the factors favouring his appointment as Prime Minister. It was hoped that this nexus would enable Hungarian agricultural exports to revive via Gombos obtaining access to the large German market. (Ranki 1984:265)
98. Macartney 1954:xx.
99. Klein 1966:86. For greater detail regarding this struggle see Klein 1982:113-24.
100. Klein 1966:89.
101. Klein 1966:90.
102. Nagy-Talavera 1970:98.
103. Braham 1981:52.
104. Braham 1981:53.
105. Macartney and Palmer 1962:315.
106. Janos 1982:301, n131.
107. Janos 1982:290.
108. Szinai and Szucs 1965:26-28; Carsten 1967:172-73.
109. Littlejohn (1985:101) states that of the "bewilderingly large" number of Hungarian

pro-Nazi parties during the interwar era, there were never fewer than ten at any given time.

110. In June 1933, Hitler promised Gombos not to incite either the Swabians or ultra-Right against him in return for Hungary supporting German policy in Roumania and Yugoslavia. (Nagy-Talavera 1970:101)

111. Nagy-Talavera 1970:110; Klein 1966:93.

112. Party leader Zoltan Boszormeny adopted the brown shirt, Storm Troopers and the salutation "*Heil* Boszormeny". Despite the party's 20,000 members, Gombos successfully prevented him from standing for parliament. (Nagy-Talavera 1970:108-09)

113. Carsten 1967:174.

114. Littlejohn 1985:102.

115. As its name implies, Szalasi's Hungarist movement advocated Magyar hegemonist policies. Major competitors Bela Imredy and Laszlo Baky (see below) were Aryan supremacists. (Janos 1982:275-76)

116. Nagy-Talavera 1970:114.

117. For a somewhat naive assessment of Szalasi's ideology, see Nagy-Talavera 1970:114-22.

118. Initially, another significant difference was that the former group tended to seek inspiration from Italian fascism, whilst the latter emulated the German Nazi model.

119. Carsten 1967:172.

120. Carsten 1967:175.

121. With little doubt, the low peasant membership of the *Nyilas* Party reflected the government's iron grip on rural politicking, the authorities invariably repressing anti-government activity in the provinces.

122. Carsten 1967:177.

123. Deak 1989:28.

124. Nagy-Talavera 1970:153, n4.

125. Nagy-Talavera 1970:153.

126. Janos 1982:270-71.

127. Janos 1982:297.

128. Braham 1981:185, n58.

129. Nagy-Talavera 1970:152.

130. The most important factor beyond the *Nyilas'* perimeter was the possibility of a parliamentary majority. Additionally, their organs of propaganda were censored and, on occasion, even banned.

131. Janos 1982:273, n85; Nagy-Talavera 1970:119.

132. The example of Count Festetics may have been the inspiration for Rabbi Bela Berend's solitary campaign during the German Occupation. Berend's attempt to "Zionise Antisemitism" is discussed below.

133. Klein 1966:92, Janos 1982:230.

134. Braham 1981:66.

135. Braham 1981:190, n99.

136. In March 1937 Bela Imredy, head of the National Bank of Hungary, submitted a memorandum to the PM advocating the introduction of such legislation. (Katzburg 1981:97)

137. Cited Braham 1981:121.

138. Mendelsohn 1983:122; Katzburg 1966:158; Braham 1981:121.

139. Deak 1989:29-30. Imredy's reputation as an Anglophile was largely, if not exclusively, based on his excellent financial connections in the City of London. (Janos 1982:291)

140. Katzburg 1981:100. Mendelsohn (1983:116) states this to be the first such piece of legislation passed in East Central Europe.

141. These elements included 100 leading members of the cultural establishment and twenty-four retired generals. (Janos 1982:290)

142. Katzburg 1981:102.

143. For a precis of the attitudes of Church leaders — Cardinal Jusztinian Seredi (Catholic), Bishop Sandor Raffay (Lutheran), and Bishop Laszlo Ravasz (Calvinist) — see Braham 1981:123-24.

144. Cohen 1939:5.

145. For the Nuremberg Laws of September 1935, officially called the "Law for the Protection of German Blood and German Honour", see Arad *et al* 1987:78-79. For contemporary commentaries, see pp 80-88.

146. Janos 1982:290.

147. Cohen 1939:5. Jewish war veterans and their families — amongst other numerically small categories — were exempted from the quota.

148. Braham 1981:126.

149. Janos 1982:291.

150. Katzburg 1981:106-13.

151. Regarding the proposed anti-Jewish legislation, Bruce wrote: "In view of the strong and ever-growing anti-Semitic feeling in this country, the Bill is an absolute necessity if violent and far more radical anti-Jewish measures are to be avoided... Serious Jews have themselves advocated some such measures that they may know where they stand and be sure that reasonable restriction shall not degenerate into persecution." (Public Record Office, London [henceforth PRO]: FO371/22375 R3978, p 106-07) In his preamble Bruce stated: "I myself have had prominent Jews come to me and beg me to explain to Imredy that they would welcome a law restricting Jewish employment if only they knew that that would be the end, as it is fully intended that it should be. The Jews are wise enough to know that half a loaf is better than no bread." (PRO: FO371/22375 R3978, p 105) Adding to Bruce's credibility is the 10 March 1938 correspondence of the US Minister in Budapest, John F. Montgomery, to his Secretary of State, viz: "Thus far, I have heard nothing but praise of the Government's action in this regard [ie: the First Jewish Law], from Jews and Gentiles alike, and I feel that the Government has met a situation fraught with danger by sanity and wisdom." (US National Archives, Washington: 864.4016/111; cited Katzburg 1981:262)

152. Indicating the controversial nature of Bruce's reports, a Foreign Office official, Mr A. Noble, rejoined sharply to Bruce's opinion thus: "I am not altogether convinced by Mr Bruce's apologia... It may be true that the law under consideration is better than the iniquitous system in force in Germany, but that does not make it anything but a wicked law." (PRO: FO 371/22375 R3978/126/21, p 103)

153. PRO: FO 371/22374 R4496/99/21, p 4. Norman adds that these solicitations included the desire that such a development would be simultaneous with firm government action against the ultra-Right.

154. Katzburg 1981:100, who adds: "I have found no evidence to corroborate this particular point."

155. The delineation between coexistence and tolerance has been succinctly summarised by Prof. Bernard Lewis, viz: "Tolerance means that a dominant group, whether defined by faith or race or other criteria, allows to members of other groups some — but rarely if ever all — of the rights and privileges enjoyed by its own members. Coexistence means equality between the different groups composing a political society as an inherent natural right of all of them — to grant it is no merit, to withhold or limit it is an offence." (Bernard Lewis, "Muslims, Christians and Jews", *New York Review of Books*, 26 March 1992, p 47)

156. Janos 1982:291.

157. During the late 1930s hundreds of *Nyilas* activists, including members of the leadership, were tried, convicted and imprisoned for subversive activities. Others sought refuge in Germany. (Janos 1982:270)

158. Szalasi's subversion arose from a *Nyilas* campaign accusing the Regent's consort of having Jewish antecedents, a charge considered by many as not without foundation.

159. Braham 1981:147.
160. Carsten 1967:178.
161. Revolving around German claims on Czechoslovakia, the crisis was "resolved" by the agreement signed in Munich on 30 September 1938.
162. Braham 1981:132. Population figures are from the census of 1941.
163. Nagy-Talavera 1970:148, n2.
164. Janos 1982:291-92.
165. Cohen 1939:8.
166. Imredy's speech to the government party, 15 November 1938; cited Katzburg 1981:116-17.
167. Deak 1989:30; Braham 1981:154; Katzburg 1981:139-42. With minor exceptions, a Jew was defined as an individual with one parent, or two grandparents, who were Jews, ie: belonged to a synagogue.
168. Cohen 1939:10. Jewish teachers, and public notaries, retained their positions until 1 January 1943.
169. Katzburg 1981:158 and 158, n1.
170. Cohen 1939:10-11.
171. For convoluted reasons, Poland was arguably the most assiduous nation in attempting to facilitate Jewish emigration. The Polish government not only supported Zionist demands for an increase in the Palestine immigrant quota, but also provided the *Irgun* and the *Haganah* (underground Jewish militias operating in Palestine) with training facilities. Of the 400,000 Jews who emigrated from Poland in the interwar period, somewhat over 65,000 found refuge in Palestine. (Gutman and Krakowski 1986:23)
172. Katzburg 1981:119.
173. Quoted Braham 1981:149-50.
174. Vida 1939:63.
175. Cohen 1939:9.
176. See Katzburg 1981:142-49.
177. For a summary of the Stern-Eppler discussions with a leader of British Jewry, and the latter's attitudes, see Neville Laski's letter of 15 June 1939 to Gerald Rufus, the Marquis of Reading. (C11/12/45, Historical Archives, British Board of Jewish Deputies, London; quoted Katzburg 1981:278-81) During this trip the delegation also visited Paris, but the French discussions proved to lack significance.
178. As a matter of principle, Jewish relief agencies rightly allocated priority to those Jewish communities living under direct Nazi control. (Gutman and Krakowski 1986:22)
179. Quoted Katzburg 1981:149.
180. See Cohen 1939:9-10. Exempted categories included war heroes and invalids, families of the fallen, Privy Councillors, university Professors, and Olympic champions.
181. Handler 1982:20; Kovacs 1994:115. Imredy, for one, was particularly bitter about the role of hirelings in facilitating the evasion of anti-Jewish legislation. (Katzburg 1981:162)
182. Mendelsohn 1983:122; Kovacs 1994:116. See also Samu Stern's presidential address of August 1941 to the Pest Neolog community. Stern's forthright and courageous statement was highly critical of the iniquities generated by the First and Second Jewish Laws. (Katzburg 1981:165-66)
183. Varadi 1985:414.
184. Cohen 1939:9. The accusation, initially made by political opponents led by Bethlen, was subsequently confirmed by a senior police officer.
185. It should be noted that the *Nyilas* were not beyond indulging in terrorism. For example, in February 1939 party members threw grenades at congregants leaving Hungary's largest synagogue, the Neolog's Dohany Street establishment. Twenty-two people were wounded; several died. (Braham 1981:153)
186. Mendelsohn 1983:271, n89; Braham 1981:140.

187. Letter to John Keyser of London, 13 February 1939; *Soviet Jewish Affairs*, London, no. 2, November 1971:109; cited Katzburg 1985:7. Compare this attitude with Teleki's statement at the Peace negotiations in 1919, viz: "The overwhelming majority of the Hungarian Jews have completely assimilated to the Hungarians. They gave us excellent Hungarian writers, artists and scientists. Because of their assimilation to the Hungarian national soul and spirit one must recognise that, from a social point of view, the Hungarian Jews are not Jews any more but Hungarians." (Nagy-Talavera 1970:66) Subsequently, Teleki claimed that this statement had been motivated by expediency. (Ibid, n2)

188. Cited Katzburg 1981:137.

189. Braham 1981:153.

190. Zuccotti 1987:51. Most Italian Antisemitic laws were effected on 17 November 1938, about a month before Imredy introduced the Second Jewish Law into parliament. Zuccotti (1987:40) comments: "In fact, Italian anti-Semitism had no ideological base, but was the product of mindless and cynical opportunism."

191. Katzburg 1981:137.

192. Quoted Katzburg 1981:127.

193. Deak 1989:30. See also Chamberlain's diplomatic apologia of 28 October 1938 in response to Horthy's request for British support. (Szinai and Szucs 1965:109-12)

194. Deak 1989:31. The majority of people in this region are ethnically akin to the Ukrainians.

195. Braham 1966b:224. The strength of Jewish tradition in this region is clearly indicated by the fact that less than 1 percent of the Jewish population chose a non-Jewish marriage partner. (Braham 1966b:225)

196. Macartney 1954:xxiv. Poland was the only neighbour with whom Hungary had not fought a war in the modern era.

197. Macartney 1957:368.

198. Braham 1981:186, n65.

199. Braham 1981:167.

200. Nagy 1988:224.

201. Braham 1981:168-69. Nagyvarad is now the Roumanian city of Oradea-Mare.

202. Nagy-Talavera 1970:165.

203. Macartney 1957:I, 458.

204. Nagy-Talavera 1970:166.

205. Braham 1981:175.

206. Formalised on 27 September 1940, the Tripartite Pact was a treaty binding Germany, Italy and Japan. During this period, "although with less whirling of arms, Hungary was running after Germany as determinedly as her neighbours". (Macartney and Palmer 1962:432)

207. Katzburg 1988b:347.

208. Nagy-Talavera 1970:167. Largely organised and supported by France, the interwar group known as the Little Entente consisted of Czechoslovakia, Roumania and Yugoslavia.

209. For Teleki's suicide *Note* to Horthy, see Szinai and Szucs 1965:174-75.

210. Berend and Ranki 1973:515.

211. Braham 1981:180.

212. Deak 1989:32-33.

213. Janos 1982:303, n141.

214. Braham 1981:192-93.

215. The government stated that the Bill aimed "to protect the purity of the blood and the spirit of those who belong to the community of the Magyar Race [*Magyar Fajkozosseg*]." (Cited Katzburg 1981:172-73)

216. Quoted Braham 1981:194.

217. Katzburg 1981:174.

218. Katzburg 1981:181, n70.

219. Hungary's official press of this period has been described as so fawningly pro-German that "the most haunted fantasy of man could conceive [of] nothing more degraded". (Macartney and Lawson 1962:432).

220. Braham 1981:195.

221. For Christian leaders' pronouncements in the Upper House, see Katzburg 1981:176-77.

222. Katzburg 1981:180.

223. Katzburg 1981:187.

224. Katzburg 1981:189-90.

225. Kallay 1954:294.

226. In his postwar memoirs, Kallay (1954:69) justified the legislation by claiming that "such measures could assume the character of economic adjustment and could be regarded by the fair-thinking section of Hungarian Jewry as their contribution to the War sacrifices of the nation".

227. Preamble to the Bill; quoted Katzburg 1981:195.

228. Several deputies, particularly in the Upper House, objected to the dangerous precedent that confiscation of rural property might set vis-à-vis any future land reform programme.

229. Properties owned by war heroes and invalids were exempted. Compensation was in the form of non-negotiable bonds redeemable after thirty years. (Katzburg 1981:198)

230. At this time, Jewish farm holdings consisted of 11,000 small estates of less than five *holds*; 423 medium estates of less than 500 *holds*; and fifty-four large estates. The aggregate holdings in each category were 24,000; 227,000; and 200,000 *holds* respectively. NB: one *hold* equals 0.57 hectares equals 1.42 acres. (Katzburg 1981:199, and 199 n47)

231. Braham 1981:199.

232. Braham 1981:218, n22.

233. Cohen 1986:18 and 25.

234. Rothkirchen 1966:xvii. Estimates of numbers range from 12,000 to 30,000. (Nagy-Talavera 1970:175)

235. See "Report USSR No. 80", 11 September 1941, Einsatzgruppe C to Berlin; in Yitzhak Arad, Shmuel Krakowski and Shmuel Spector (eds), *The Einsatzgruppen Reports* (New York: Holocaust Library and Yad Vashem, 1989) 128-29; Katzburg 1966:161. About 2,000 deportees survived the massacre.

236. The *Einsatzgruppen* were mobile killing units ordered to exterminate all Jews in conquered Soviet territory. In total, the four *Einsatzgruppen* divisions butchered about 1,500,000 Jews. (Morse 1968:304)

237. Morse 1968:305. Lipstadt states that in 1941, *The New York Times* reported the machine-gunning of "masses of Jews deported from Hungary to Galicia". [See Deborah Lipstadt, "Through the Looking Glass. Press Responses to Genocide" in *Social Education*, Vol. 55, No. 2 (February 1991), 116-120.]

238. Braham 1981:206.

239. Ibid.

240. Nagy-Talavera 1970:178.

241. Janos 1982:306, n151.

242. The dilemma generated by this verdict was resolved with typical Hungarian pragmatism — or duplicity. The principal defendants were permitted to escape to Germany, apparently without Prime Minister Kallay's knowledge. (Ibid)

243. In particular, Kallay (1954:8) states that Bardossy had suggested deporting the Jews.

244. Braham 1981:249, n1.

245. For a precis of Hungarian-German diplomatic relations 1940-44, see Browning 1978:127-33.

246. Vago 1969:189.

247. Vago 1969:207, n11.

248. The day after his appointment, Kallay was warned by the leaders of the government party that unless he implemented pro-German policies, and made concessions to public opinion on the "Jewish Question", he would lose rank and file support and be unable to govern effectively. Kallay states in his memoirs that it was this meeting that decided, as a compromise, to expropriate Jewish rural estates. (Kallay 1954:68-70)

249. Braham 1981:245.

250. As an example: to mask the attempted rapprochement with the West, Kallay publicly emphasised his anti-Communist ideology and anti-Russian policies. (Kallay 1954:14) Despite the latter, after the January 1943 destruction of the Second Hungarian Army on the Eastern Front, he refused to permit any further Hungarian troops to be committed to the front lines.

251. By this stage, 80 percent of Hungarian industry was "in the service" of Germany. (Braham 1981:235)

252. On a per capita basis, Hungary had about six times as many Jews as Germany, ie: 800,000 out of 14,000,000 versus 600,000 out of 60,000,000 respectively. (Handler 1982:21)

253. Kallay 1954:91.

254. Kallay 1954:99.

255. Ibid. Whilst unnamed, the official leader in question was, in all probability, Samu Stern. Janos (1982:302, n135) notes references which maintain that Kallay's version is corroborated by declarations of Stern and the wealthy, prominent converted Jewish industrialist Ferenc Chorin.

256. Braham 1981:229.

257. The Hungarians lost an estimated 140,000 of their 200,000 troops and about 40,000 of their 50,000 Jewish Labour Service conscripts. (Braham 1977:37) However, it should be clearly understood that whilst the Hungarian troops were killed as a result of enemy action, the majority of Labour Service fatalities resulted from Axis-inflicted atrocities.

258. Kallay 1954:373. Facilitating these negotiations was London's favourable reaction to Budapest's "dedication to maintain the parliamentary system and continue with its 'humanitarian treatment of the Jews' ". (Report of the Hungarian Minister in Lisbon, 11 February 1943; cited Vago 1969:195)

259. Kallay 1954:390. For the armistice agreement between Hungary and the UK, see Kallay 1954:373-74.

260. Kallay 1954:375-76.

261. Vago 1969:195.

262. Szinai and Szucs 1965:248.

263. Amongst German accusations were charges that Hungary was sabotaging the War effort. (Vago 1969:197) For Horthy's response, see his *Note* of 7 May 1943 to Hitler, in Szinai and Szucs 1965:249-55.

264. See *"Notes* on the conversation between the *Führer* and the Hungarian Regent Horthy at *Schloss* Klessheim, 17 April 1943", Nuremberg *Staatsarchiv* NG-5,628; in Levai 1961:53-54.

265. Ibid.

266. *The Goebbels Diaries, 1942-1943.* Louis M. Lochner (ed.) Garden City, NY: Double Day, 1948, p.357; cited Patai 1985:82.

267. For Horthy's response, see Szinai and Szucs 1965:249-55.

268. Ibid, page 250.

269. The protocol proposed that Hungary would basically retain its current regime,

receive guarantees regarding its future frontiers, and remain unoccupied by the Red Army. (Braham 1981:246)

270. See "Memorandum of Chief-of-Staff Col. General Ferenc Szombathelyi on the Military Situation", 12 February 1943, in Szinai and Szucs 1965:214.

271. For Veesenmayer's two reports, see Levai 1961:58-64.

272. Janos 1982:309.

273. Vago 1969:205-06.

274. Handler 1982:18-20.

275. Braham 1981:248.

276. Braham 1981:262-63.

277. Braham 1981:248.

278. Deak 1989:37.

279. Nagy-Talavera 1970:188.

280. Juhasz 1984:214.

281. Hungarian troops remained behind the front lines to act as an occupation and anti-partisan force.

282. Janos 1982:308.

283. Juhasz 1984:213-14.

284. Braham 1981:366.

285. Braham 1981:365. On page 362, Braham admits that after Voronezh (January 1943) the Hungarian government insisted ever more vocally "that the remnant of their armed forces be returned from Russia...".

286. See Braham 1981:254, n88 for references.

287. SOEG: *Südosteuropa — Gesellschaft e. V. Vienna* — an organisation engaged in economic intelligence operations in south eastern Europe. (Hilberg 1972:187)

288. Hilberg 1972:188.

289. Vago 1969:189-90.

290. Nuernberg Document NG 1798, in Mendelsohn and Detwiler 1982:206.

291. Braham 1977b:190.

292. Minutes of discussion between Martin Luther and Sztojay, 6 October 1942. Nuernberg Document NG 1800, p 6, in Mendelsohn and Detwiler 1982:201-04.

293. Vago 1969:192.

294. Vago 1969:198.

295. Report by Dome Sztojay regarding his discussions with the German Foreign Minister, 28 April 1943, ie: ten days after the Schloss Klessheim negotiations between Horthy and Hitler, in Levai 1961:57.

296. Levai 1961:55-57.

297. Vago 1969:198.

298. Kallay 1954:82. Despite Kallay's concern for facilitating the upward social mobility of the "gifted, even brilliant" Hungarian peasantry, an observer, who departed Hungary in July 1943, reported that at that time a Jewish tenant was still managing Kallay's estate in Nagy-Kallo. (CZA — S25/9285.)

299. Braham 1977b:188. On page 192 Braham describes the German pressure on Hungary as "relentless".

300. For Kallay's attempts to protect the Jewish Labour Service from the Germans, see Braham 1977b:197.

301. Nagy-Talavera 1970:183.

302. Braham 1981:25, n84.

303. Braham 1977b:197.

304. Seton-Watson 1962:197 (NB: the third edition of this work.) If only Seton-Watson had inserted the word "effective" between "less" and "German"...

CHAPTER III

HUNGARIAN JEWRY
1919 TO 1944

As has been seen, the debacle of World War I precipitated a dramatic and fundamental transformation in Magyar self-conception. During the *Ausgleich* era it had been largely acceptable in polyglot, Dualist Hungary for minorities — especially the Jews — to adopt Hungarian national identity and still maintain their religious proclivities. However Trianon nationalism, now rooted in an overwhelmingly homogeneous society motivated by the chauvinistic Antisemitism of the country's guiding ideology, the *Szegedi Gondolat* (see Chapter II), rejected the prewar supra-ethnic model of nationhood and, with this rejection, consciously abandoned the previously state-supported concept of religious tolerance. In essence, Hungarian nationalism had metamorphosed from a mobile, "open" form based on voluntary allegiance to a "closed" format based on a pre-ordained, immutable ethnicity that refused to tolerate intranational diversity. Henceforth, contrary to the steadfast, fervent hopes of a traumatised Jewish community, the concept of the Hungarian political state was largely superseded by that of a Hungarian nationhood based on "race".

Demographic Factors

Not unexpectedly, the economic and social oppression of Hungarian Jewry was contemporaneous with an upsurge in the rate of Jewish conversions to Christianity. By correlating the figures in Table 3.1 with the discussion in Chapter II, it is evident that the number of Jews formally accepting Christianity was directly related to the intensity of the socio-economic pressure applied to Hungarian Jewry, viz:

Year	Annual Conversions	Year	Annual Conversions
1919	7,146	1934	1,128
1920	1,925	1935	1,261
1921*	821	1936	1,647
1922*	499	1937	1,598
1923*	458	1938	8,584
1924*	433		

Table 3.1 **Conversions from Judaism to Christianity in Trianon Hungary (selected years).** [Sources: *Magyar Statisztikai Szemle* (Hungarian Statistical Review), 17, (October 1939), pp 1,113-1,120; those years marked *, Laszlo 1969:154–55.]

During 1938–39 some 14,000 Jews converted — a number Mendelsohn calls unparalleled in eastern Europe[1] — even though it was widely understood that a formal change in religious affiliation did not result in exemption from the racialist provisions of anti-Jewish legislation.

The aggregate effect on Hungarian Jewry of interwar circumstance — including the loss and subsequent readjustment of territory, conversion, intermarriage, emigration etc, (see below) — was revealed by the census of March–April 1941. Reduced by the Treaty of Trianon to a population of 470,000 in 1920,[2] the census recorded Hungary and its newly regained territories as containing 100,000 "Christian" Jews[3] plus 724,000 "unambiguous" Jews. Overwhelmingly, Hungarian Jews lived in medium to large settlements,[4] their numbers being distributed as follows:

Location	"Christian" Jews	Jews	Total	Ratio "Converts" to Jews
Budapest	62,000	184,000	246,000	0.34
Provinces	27,000	216,000	243,000	0.12
Trianon Hung.	89,000	400,000	489,000	0.22
Regained Areas	10,000	324,000	334,000	0.03
Total	99,000	724,000	823,000	0.14

Table 3.2 **Distribution of Hungarians Classified as Jews, April 1941.**
(Source: *Hungarian Jewry Before and After the Persecutions*. Budapest: Hungarian Section of the World Jewish Congress, 1949, p 2.)

These figures indicate clearly the minor diminution of Jewish identity in the provinces, the near-absolute adherence to Judaism by the Jewish populace in the regained territories, and that conversion was a phenomenon concentrated largely in the Neolog bastion of Budapest.

[Because converts were officially considered as remaining "racially" Jewish, and generally accorded treatment akin to that imposed on "unambiguous" Jews, for the sake of this discussion it is appropriate to consider converts as a subset of the Jewish community rather than as an element of the wider, Christian society. Accordingly, subsequent to the Third Jewish Law, Hungarian Jews — as opposed to Hungarian Jewry — were divided into four distinct segments, viz: Neolog, Orthodox, Status Quo and Christian. Consequently, Christian Jew is a more appropriate description for converts than Jewish Christian. As such, the description "Jews of the Christian Confession" would be more appropriately expressed as "Christians of the Jewish Race".]

The *Zsido Lexikon* (Jewish Lexicon), published in 1929, contains lists of prominent Hungarian Jews. Of fifty-one listed economists, twenty-five were converts to Christianity; of thirteen mathematicians, seven were converts; and, amongst writers and artists, rates of conversion were likewise substantial. Notwithstanding these losses, one authority has summarised the impact of apostasy thus:

> ...it is clear that conversion drained away a major part of the economic and intellectual elite of Hungarian Jewry. Nevertheless, the share of the Jews in the economic, intellectual, and cultural life of Hungary until World War II was so great that even this outflow from the community could not diminish it substantially.[5]

In mid-1942, the Protestant churches established the *Jo Pasztor Misszio* (Good Shepherd Mission) to reinforce Protestant Jews' newfound identity, facilitate their applications for social welfare, and — directly or otherwise — advance the prospects of further conversions to the Protestant confessions.[6] Likewise, Catholic Jews were organised into the *Szent Kereszt Egyesulet* (Holy Cross Society), for the same reasons.

It should be noted that the formal repudiation of Judaism was not the only factor contributing to the absolute decline of the Jewish population.[7] Apart from deaths exceeding births every year from 1927, a total of some 25–30,000 Jews emigrated from Hungary during the interwar period.[8] According to the German Foreign Office, about 16,000 of these departures occurred in the three-year period between the census of March 1941 and the Occupation of March 1944.[9] With the benefit of hindsight, an apologist for the Horthyist regime could conceivably argue that this latter figure indicates an officially sanctioned escape rate of about 100 Jews per week.[10]

During the decade 1920–30, Hungary's Jewish population declined by 6.1 percent whilst the total population increased by 8.7 percent, these variations equalling 29,000 and 700,000 people respectively. In the following decade, Jewish numbers in the Trianon region declined by another 40,000.[11] Generally, the Jewish birthrate in Trianon Hungary was significantly lower than that of the population as a whole. In 1935 the former was only 70 percent of the latter, whilst in 1939, as a result of the First Jewish Law, Jewish fecundity plunged by one-third compared to its previous level.[12] Moreover, the rate of ex-nuptial births amongst Jews was substantially below the national average; for example, of the 19,000 illegitimate births in 1925, a mere 204 (1 percent) were born to Jewish mothers.[13]

The low Jewish birth rate was reflected in the contemporary distribution of Jewish school pupils. Although unbiased comparison requires such statistics to be adjusted for socio-economic factors, in 1925, whilst 29,000 Jewish children comprised 18 percent of the secondary school population, 37,000 of their younger co-religionists constituted a mere 3.4 percent of primary school enrolments.[14]

With regard to intermarriage, the real rate is difficult to ascertain with any degree of accuracy. Official statistics indicate a peak of 14.2 percent in 1937 and thence a significant reduction, with numbers dropping to 9.9 percent in 1939[15] under the impact of institutional Antisemitism. Note that because many Jews entering into a mixed marriage converted prior to the ceremony, such unions had not always been classified as mixed. A contemporary source indicates that for marriages in Budapest during the period 1931–35, about 20 percent of Jewish grooms and 16 percent of Jewish brides married a non-Jewish partner.[16] For Hungary as a whole, all that can be stated with confidence is that the bulk of mixed unions occurred in the Neolog sector — especially in urban centres — and that the offspring of these marriages were generally baptised and/or raised outside the Jewish fold.

Socio-Economic Aspects

As previously discussed (see Chapter II), the enforcement of Hungary's three (anti)Jewish Laws varied with respect to speed, distribution and intensity of implementation. As a general rule, the Public Service was faster and more thorough than private enterprise in expelling Jewish employees.[17] State power in the public sector, Jewish prominence in free enterprise, and the lack of suitable non-Jewish

Figure 3.1 **Jewish wedding celebration in Budapest, 5 January 1941.**
A clear indication of the standard of living still enjoyed by many of
Budapest's upper *bourgeois* **Jews several years after the introduction of**
the First and Second Jewish laws. Note the bride's father in Hungarian
officer's uniform. The gentleman with the glasses and moustache in the
centre is Leo Stern (no relation to Samu). In 1942, Leo and his brother
Herman were foundation members of the Orthodox and then, in
November 1943, of the combined Zionist-Orthodox *Va'adat Ezra ve'Hazalah*
(Underground Jewish Relief and Rescue Committee).

replacements in the private sector were the most important factors generating this dichotomy.

Contemporaneous with the introduction of the *Numerus Clausus* in 1920, Hungarian Jewry (5 percent of the population) provided some 50 percent of the nation's lawyers, 46 percent of medical practitioners, 41 percent of veterinarians, 39 percent of engineers and chemists, 34 percent of journalists and newspaper editors, 25 percent of singers and musicians, 23 percent of actors, 17 percent of painters and sculptors, 12 percent of judges and district attorneys, 9 percent of high school teachers, 6 percent of MPs, 5 percent of university professors and civil servants, but only 1.6 percent of military officers and 2.9 percent of rank and file troops.

Regarding agriculture, in addition to owning 20 percent of large and 11 percent of medium agricultural estates, Jews constituted 26 percent of the owners or tenants of small estates. In the realms of commerce and industry, the Jewish community provided 54 percent of self-employed merchants, 47 percent of white collar and 33 percent of blue collar employees in commerce, 39 percent of white collar but only 8 percent of blue collar industrial workers, and 12 percent of self-employed tradesmen. Jews owned 12 percent of the mines and 41 percent of large and medium-sized industrial enterprises.[18]

As the situation of Jewish university students was discussed in Chapter II, suffice it to note that, under the influence of the *Numerus Clausus*, by 1925 about half of Hungarian Jewry's 2,400 tertiary students were studying at foreign institutes of higher learning.[19] A decade later, the *Hungarian Statistical Yearbook of 1935* stated that Jews constituted 51 percent of factory owners and 42 percent of managers. In the same year, the *Stock Exchange Year Book* reported that of the 336 board members controlling the twenty largest industrial enterprises in Hungary, 235 (ie: 70 percent) were Jews.[20]

Considering the higher than average rates of conversion amongst the upper socio-economic levels of Hungarian Jewry,[21] had Christian Jews been included in these figures, the recorded percentages may well have been significantly higher. Regarding the ethnicity of top echelon Hungarians (the "multipositional elite"), Lengyel's research on the ethnic origins of those directing enterprises, banks and employers' organisations found that, in 1937, Jews constituted a plurality in each category, viz: 45, 37 and 45 percent respectively.[22]

On the other hand, Jews filled only 16 percent of positions in the public sector elite,[23] substantially lower than in private enterprise but a figure still representing over three times Jewry's proportion of the nation's population.

In the Budapest of 1935, Jewish employment was heavily concentrated in the fields of commerce and industry. These sectors provided work for 45,600 and 40,200 respectively, figures representing 41 and 36 percent of the capital's Jewish workforce of 112,500. Jews filled 45 percent of commercial positions but, despite the closeness of the above figures, of Budapest's industrial workforce only 17 percent were Jewish, half of whom were engaged in blue-collar endeavour. The liberal professions and the public service respectively provided a livelihood for 7.2 and 1.7 percent of Budapest's Jewish breadwinners, such individuals comprising a widely divergent 32 percent and 4.4 percent of their respective occupational categories.[24]

As previously mentioned, the economically oriented Second Jewish Law of 1939 was implemented in an inconsistent manner. By the time of its approval, unemployment generated by the Depression had not only been largely overcome, but the government's Keynesian pump-priming resulted in the economic boom of 1939.[25] Demand exceeded the supply of labour, goods and services, and inflation was, once again, a factor of major consideration.[26] Consequently, despite the Antisemitic legislation, the Jewish contribution to private enterprise, management and the professions retained its economic importance, and came to be recognised as such by the "pragmatic" elements in the country. The opinion of these elements was often articulated by Horthy who, in October 1940, wrote to Prime Minister Teleki thus:

> As regards to the Jewish problem, I have been an anti-Semite through all my life...(however) it is impossible, in a year or two, to eliminate the Jews, who have everything in their hands, and replace them by incompetent, mostly unworthy big-mouthed elements, for we would become bankrupt. This requires a generation at least. I have perhaps been the first to loudly profess anti-Semitism, yet I cannot look with indifference at inhumanity, senseless humiliations, *when we still need them*. In addition, I consider for example the Arrow-Cross men to be by far more dangerous and worthless for my country than I do the Jew. The latter is tied to this country from interest, and is more faithful to his adopted country than the Arrow-Cross man, who...want to play the country into the hands of the Germans.[27] (Emphasis added)

The government's realignment towards pragmatism ensured that, much to the chagrin of the Germans and the domestic radical Right, Jewish enterprises of significance, in effect, largely avoided the provisions of Antisemitic legislation. Consequently, in 1941 over 91 percent of Jewish industrialists operating in 1939 still controlled their businesses,[28] the authorities either condoning the often fictitious "Christianisation" of many enterprises[29] or else failing to implement the provisions of the relevant Act. As particularly noteworthy examples, the enormous Manfred Weiss industrial conglomerate continued operations well-nigh undisturbed, as did Hungary's premier textile establishment, the Goldberger textile works.[30] The latter remained under the control of Leo Goldberger — prominent member of the Jewish elite, member of the Upper House Finance Committee (along with four fellow members of the Jewish hierarchy),[31] confidant of Admiral Horthy, and, according to his son-in-law Dr Gyorgy Gergely, one of Hungary's most hated plutocrats.[32] Like the Manfred Weiss conglomerate, the Goldberger corporation continued its production and investment programme until the German Occupation of March 1944.[33]

Jewish rural land-holdings, which had been subject to partial sequestration by the Second Jewish Law (1939) and total expropriation via Law XII of 1942, were treated in a manner similar to industrial holdings. Although some smaller properties were registered and appropriated, the majority of large estates were left intact. An Antisemite, Karl Schickert, complained that by late 1943 only 149,000 of the 610,000 acres (some 24 percent) held by Jews had been redistributed.[34]

Despite considerable fears expressed for the welfare of Hungarian Jewry's wage-earning sector,[35] and notwithstanding that tens of thousands of individuals did in fact become temporarily unemployed, labour shortages — caused by the economic boom and the War — alleviated conditions and removed the prospect of penury from many. The greatest economic hardship resulting from the anti-

Jewish laws fell upon the lower *bourgeoisie* and the petty entrepreneurs. Especially affected were small shopkeepers dependant on government licensing laws regulating the state's tobacco and alcohol monopolies. Also harshly affected were middle and lower echelon public servants, media workers and career soldiers. Notwithstanding Hungary's involvement in the War, by May 1942 only 129 Jewish officers remained on active duty, the majority of whom served at Army Corps Headquarters.[36]

This non-uniform implementation of institutional Judeophobia had the (perhaps) paradoxical effect of producing a regressive distribution of income and assets within Hungarian Jewry. The upper hierarchy maintained, and often increased, their proportion of wealth whilst the lower ranks suffered a diminution that could vary considerably depending on an individual's occupation, location, expertise and length of employment. Consequently, it is unproductive — as well as potentially highly misleading — to utilise the gross economic effects of the anti-Jewish protocols to calculate a (theoretical) mean impact on an individual or average family. Notwithstanding this caveat, it is interesting to note that an opinion published in Budapest in 1941 estimated that, as a result of government assault, Jewish wealth had diminished by 1.5 billion Pengo, a sum equivalent to a marginal 4.2 percent of national wealth and a relatively modest 18.75 percent of Jewish capital.[37] On the basis of this estimate, prior to the First Jewish Law of 1938, Jews controlled some 28 percent of national assets. By the time of the Third Jewish Law in 1941, this level had fallen to about 22 percent, a figure far exceeding the Jewish proportion of the population, but hardly the stranglehold alleged by the ultra-Right.

Jews and Politics

As previously discussed, the interwar epoch in Hungary can be delineated into three distinct phases, viz: the Revolution and counter-Revolution; the period of socio-economic consolidation; the economic depression and the rise of the radical Right. Although varying in virulence, a constant throughout these phases was the controversy generated by the position, function and — in the growing circles of the radical Right — the continuing presence in Hungary of that country's Jewish populace. During the Kun regime, the plutocratic Jew often served to symbolise the exploitative capitalism that the initially popular revolution had pledged to smash. Thus, many supporting the Revolution came to consider Jews responsible for the poverty and subjugation of the working class, and — in association with their international co-religionists — to be the local agents of a supranational conspiracy of Jewish plutocrats whose ultimate aim was world domination. Kun's mortal enemies, the White counter-revolutionaries, also believed in Jewry's subversion on behalf of an international financial conspiracy. However, via a process of bizarre and convoluted conceptualisation, the Whites also claimed — without the hint of a blush — that Jews were simultaneously attempting to deliver Hungary into the iron fist of Judeo-Bolshevism. Consequently, for both wings of the political spectrum, the abstract Jew became firmly entrenched as the symbol of subversion, exploitation and repression. Furthermore, the xenophobia directed against the ethnic minorities in the Dualist era was, in homogeneous Trianon Hungary, redirected at the Jews. This chauvinist campaign was energised by the additional dimensions of religious prejudice and economic envy, elements largely absent from the prewar offensive against the non-Magyar Christian minorities.

Prior to World War I, it was largely prominent young progressives of Jewish origin who scrutinised the Hungarian system and found it sadly wanting. The pogroms of the White Terror taught them, and the entire Jewish community, the consequences of attacking the status quo and, *inter alia*, challenging the Magyar Establishment's hegemony. So successful was the lesson that, during the entire Trianon epoch, Jewish leaders never felt the need to issue a single warning regarding anti-government agitation.[38] Maintenance of the community's low profile in radical politics, allied with emotive protestations regarding Jewry's munificent contribution, and inherent loyalty, to Magyarorszag, represented the community's unsuccessful attempt to transmute the eventual almost unanimous national consensus regarding Jews: that Jews were not only prime fermenters of Bolshevik revolution, but had an intrinsic collective proclivity towards Communism.

The leaders of Hungarian Jewry, unlike their *confrères* in some other European countries (notably Poland), rejected the concept of a specifically Jewish political party as a means of combating Antisemitism and of advancing the interests and welfare of their community. Noting the continuation of Hungarian Jewry's post-Emancipation political legacy — propounded pithily by Prime Minister Banffy in 1882, viz: "Being a unified national state, Hungary cannot tolerate political parties on the basis of nationality."[39] — some observers, for example Vago, mistakenly conclude that Trianon Hungary also remained without Jewish parties.[40] Although technically correct in the sense that Jewish lists or a Jewish-named party never eventuated, Jewish-affiliation parties existed in all but name. Vago himself concedes the point when he writes of the "great number" of Jews prominent in the leadership of the Social Democratic Party and its organs.[41] Furthermore, during the interwar period Hungary's small liberal parties were Jewish in the very real sense that Jews provided their principal source of finance and support.[42] In particular, Janos Vazsonyi's Progressive Party was commonly labelled "Jewish".[43] Moreover, being active in or closely associated with Jewish causes, the handful of Jewish MPs often acted as a de facto political caucus[44] — representatives of Hungarian Jewry in the corridors of power, and valuable conduits from the community to the government and its agencies.[45]

Some historians condemn the leadership of Hungarian Jewry for failing to develop a formally Jewish political party.[46] Such critics fail to acknowledge the reasonable facsimile thereof outlined above. They also fail to recognise that, with little doubt, such a grouping had the potential to split Jewry into even more mutually antagonistic segments; to force the community into mutually debilitating competition with its (admittedly weak) politically moderate non-Jewish allies; and to expose the community to chauvinist allegations of debasing Hungarian public life via the formation of an ethnically based, foreign-dominated, non-Magyar political grouping. The history of specifically Jewish parties in Hungary's immediate neighbours, Slovakia and Roumania, is an instructive — though not conclusive — source of comparison.[47] In Roumania, the Jewish party only achieved parliamentary representation for a short period in the early 1930s, and had but marginal influence on the government's Jewish agenda. In Czechoslovakia, although a Jewish party had been established contemporaneously with the formation of the country, and although in the 1920s Jewish parties attracted the vote of half the Jewish electors, Jewish political groupings also remained of marginal influence.[48] To compound Czechoslovak Jewry's problems, Jewish parties were opposed by the Orthodox, especially in Slovakia and Subcarpathian Ruthenia.[49]

In a very real sense, the formal absence of Jewish political parties in Hungary almost certainly inhibited intracommunal antagonism and conflict. This absence hence acted as a factor tending to consolidate the community. Unlike Roumania, where the Jewish vote was spread over sundry Jewish lists,[50] the Hungarian Jewish vote was, in effect, split in two. From an analysis of the 1935 elections, Vago concluded that, notwithstanding Budapest being a Socialist stronghold, the majority of Budapest's Jewish voters generally supported the *bourgeois* progressives whilst only a minority voted Socialist.[51]

Despite this clear progressive preference, because of limited participation in communal politics throughout the hierarchical Trianon epoch, Hungarian Jewry — like the Hungarian nation — remained directed by a largely upper-class, affluent leadership firmly welded to the strongly conservative, anti-Communist and nationalist protocol propagated by the country's establishment. As previous discussion has indicated, and as later discussion will confirm, circumstances were such that the Jewish leadership never had a realistic, viable alternative to either maintaining this position or continuing to support the Horthyist regime.

Reigning above the ebb and flow of party strife, it was Horthy, not parliament, who was the *sine qua non* of a Prime Minister's continuing authority. As Nicholas Kallay has written in his memoirs, by 1942 Horthy had become so entrenched and powerful that he had achieved a well-nigh overwhelming authority within Hungary.[52] His was an authority that the Germans themselves were continually forced to concede and respect — even after the Occupation of March 1944. With the Left largely neutralised and/or repressed, the Centre confined to urban areas, and the radical Right increasingly hostile to the very continuation of a Jewish presence in Hungary, the community's affiliation with the Horthyists generated the not inconsiderable benefit of a quasi-alliance with the political faction embodying the very essence of Trianon Hungary, a grouping led by Miklos Horthy, the dominant factor in national politics.

Hungarian Jewry's leadership thus based the community's future on an alignment with the only powerful, neo-pragmatic political grouping in the country. Even without the benefit of hindsight, such a strategy appears — in principle — beyond meaningful reproach. Those who criticise Hungarian Jewish leaders for adopting this course have yet to formulate an alternative, equally powerful political option available to the community, as well as a substitute for the sometimes intimate relationship between Horthy and his coterie of "court Jews". Paradoxically, despite aligning with a non-democratic, disruptive Magyar revisionism, through its consistent and powerful support for pragmatic elements in the regime, Trianon Jewry retained its prewar position as the nation's most important outward-looking, entrepreneurial and democratising segment.

Like their co-religionists in the "motherland" from which they were now separated, "Magyars of the Israelite Faith" residing in the "lost territories" also retained their allegiance to the cause of a Hungarian restoration. This affiliation was recognised and rewarded by the non-Jewish Magyar revisionists in the successor states. In particular, for almost two decades, the Hungarian Party in Transylvania — an autocratic group led largely by reactionary aristocrats and gentry — accepted Transylvania's "Hungarian Jews" as members and permitted them to attain leading positions in the party hierarchy.[53] Similarly, the Magyar-speaking Jews of Slovakia — especially the Neolog elements — maintained their allegiance to proto-

Figure 3.2 **Cultivating the Horthy legend.**
Top: **Riding the hero's proverbial white steed, Horthy leads the victorious White militia into Budapest; 16 November 1919.**
Middle: **Horthy, brandishing sword, ordains "warriors" into the ranks of his paramilitary *Vitezi rend* (Order of Heroes); Budapest, *circa* early 1920s.**
Bottom: **"The Spirit of the Times." Horthy and *confrère*; Kiel, 1938.**

authoritarian, expansionist Hungary rather than supporting democratic, non-expansionist Czechoslovakia.[54] To this limited extent, yet still with tragic paradox, "Magyars of the Israelite Faith", irrespective of their country of residence, supported the subversion and overthrow of their most powerful source of protection, the system of peace treaties conceived at Versailles.

Communal Structure

As previously discussed, subsequent to the Emancipation of 1867 Hungarian Jewry formally divided into three distinct segments — the Orthodox, Neolog and Status Quo "denominations". The Treaty of Trianon (1920), by transferring to the successor states many provincial areas of heavy Orthodox concentration, not only halved Hungary's Jewish population from 930,000 to 470,000 but also caused a radical shift in the intracommunal balance of power.[55] Resulting from these transfers, in 1920 the Neolog became the clearly paramount denomination. With some 300,000 adherents to the Orthodox's 130,000, the former represented about 65 percent of the Jewish population versus 30 percent for the latter. The marginal Status Quo grouping attracted 22,000 adherents, 5 percent of the total.[56] By transferring a large portion of the mostly unassimilated, Yiddish-speaking Orthodox to the successor states, Trianon had acted as a consolidating factor for Hungarian Jewry. The division within the community was henceforth based on a denominational delineation, rather than on language and theology, as had been the case prewar.

Although Neolog members now outnumbered Orthodox adherents by a ratio of over two to one, the situation was reversed with respect to the number of affiliating congregations. In this regard, the Orthodox maintained 452 *kehilot* to the Neolog's 263 and the Status Quo's fifty-two, the three denominations employing 314, 176, and 41 Rabbis respectively.[57] Not unexpectedly, Neolog strongholds were the large, progressive, sophisticated urban conglomerations (especially Budapest) whilst, conversely, Orthodox bastions were confined largely to rural regions (especially the East and North-East), and the smaller, less afluent, socially conservative non-metropolitan centres.

Unsettled by this progressive-conservative divide, Hungarian Jewry in the interwar years adopted a largely introspective stance. By consensus, each of the three denominations considered their official prerogatives confined to matters of religion, education, culture, welfare and inter/intra-denominational matters. Hungarian Jewry's only consistent extracommunal political activity during the interwar period involved its liaison with the Ministry of Education and Religious Affairs, the government agency monitoring each community's compliance with its legal obligations.[58]

Although Orthodoxy remained content with its status and constitution, the Neolog leaders, like their *Ausgleich* predecessors, continually sought to improve and modernise their statutes. Thus, because unification of Hungarian Jewry had proven to be a chimera for over half a century, and because the Neolog constitution had remained unrevised since 1869,[59] on 4 March 1935 the government convened a council of 210 Neolog delegates, the National Assembly of Neolog Jewry — in effect, a Jewish Congress without minority (Orthodox) participation. Consent for the Assembly was obtained through Samu Stern's close nexus with the government, particularly Prime Minister Gombos and Regent

Horthy, both of whom issued supportive statements to mark the occasion.[60]

The Assembly's main aim was to reform religious education, the Rabbinate, the structure of small congregations, and — of particular significance — communal taxation. A reform protocol, known as the Complementary Regulations, was approved overwhelmingly, the sole dissenter being the President of the Buda Neolog Community — the oldest Jewish congregation in Hungary, and unrelenting rival to the now much more populous, prosperous and powerful Pest Neolog *kehilah*. Because of this solitary objection, the paramount segment of Hungarian Jewry was prevented from instituting an overwhelmingly endorsed reform programme. Except for this opposition, Gombos would have ratified what has been called "the greatest accomplishment of Hungarian Jewry in communal legislation in modern times".[61] Despite lengthy negotiations with the authorities, Gombos' death, Buda's unrelenting opposition, and institutional Antisemitism prevented the Regulations receiving government ratification.

As discussed in Chapter I, during the Emancipation era Orthodoxy's tenacious, uncompromising insistence on the formal retention of communal autonomy ensured that the President of the *Magyarorszagi Izraelitak Orszagos Irodaja* (National Bureau of Hungarian Israelites) was little more than a figurehead, a conduit for communicating government decisions to regional presidents. As such, the Neolog's *Orszagos Iroda* (National Bureau) initially lacked either *de jure* authority or de facto sanction over its constituent organisations. Despite this regimen, through a combination of convenience and practice the National Bureau gradually accumulated influence until it eventually achieved the status of Jewry's de facto — though not *de jure* — central authority. As previously mentioned (see Chapter I), the government favoured negotiating with a single, supreme administrative body rather than attempting to attain consensus with a gaggle of disparate, often competing, sometimes intransigent jurisdictions. The National Bureau thus eventually became Hungarian Jewry's chief consultant to the government as well as the community's de facto representative, situations legitimised by years of co-operation and consultation between the Bureau and the agencies of state.

Notwithstanding this growth in the authority and influence of the National Bureau, generations of competition for the leadership of Hungarian Jewry between it and the Pest Neolog Community — by far the country's largest, richest and most powerful *kehilah* — continued unabated. With the retirement of the President of the National Bureau in February 1932, the head of the Pest community since 1929, Samu Stern — Privy Councillor, member of the nation's financial elite (known colloquially as the Butter and Egg King), with exemplary connections to Horthy and the ruling coterie — sought to alleviate disputation between the two bodies by seeking election as principal of the National Bureau. Stern's candidacy was opposed by those seeking to maintain the two offices as separate entities;[62] those harbouring suspicion or resentment against Stern; and those antipathetic to such a substantial concentration of power.[63] Inevitably, Stern's candidacy caused high contention and a turbulent campaign, the first such since the Bureau's foundation over sixty years before.

A widespread misconception regarding the attitude of the Hungarian Jewish elite has been encapsulated by a noted authority who states: "Conspicuously absent from [the] leadership group were the totally assimilated Jewish captains of industry like Leo Goldberger..."[64] This assertion is clearly incorrect. Goldberger's commitment to the leadership of Hungarian Jewry can be attested by a glance at the marble honour roll of the Budapest *kehilah*, where his name is listed alphabetically.[65] This gentleman's activist function and illustrious position in the community was summarised by a contemporary account in the leading Jewish weekly *Egyenloseg* (Equality) thus: *"...Buday-Goldberger Leo pedig ott all a mai zsido elet kozeppontjaban, mint iranyito, vezeto es szervezo ero...az egesz magyar zsidosag halajat tolmacsoljuk..."*[66] ("...Goldberger stands at the centre of today's Jewish life, as guide, leader and organising power...we thus express the gratitude of the whole of Hungarian Jewry...") Not only did Goldberger (1874–1944) contest the presidency of the Pest Neolog community in 1923,[67] but he also challenged Stern for the presidency of the National Bureau at the limited franchise election of May 1932.[68]

The Goldberger candidacy, largely supported by upper *bourgeois* elements, was comfortably defeated by Stern 227 votes to 147, the latter securing the confidence of the Pest Board of Directors (with the notable exception of the Deputy President) and the less affluent segment of the *kehilah*. Accompanied by tumultuous confrontations necessitating police intervention, Stern's victory continued the consolidation process by which the National Bureau became the respected central secretariat and official representative of Hungarian Jewry. In 1939, bowing to reality, the government sanctioned the position and function of the National Bureau, converting its de facto circumstance into an officially ratified *de jure* status. Unification of the twin secular peaks of Hungarian Jewry under Stern proved successful, with the generation of a synergy substantially exceeding that formerly provided by the sum of its component parts. In particular, the Bureau contributed experience in considering and advocating a national Jewish perspective, whilst Pest provided wealth, power and political influence.

It was this highly centralised, hierarchical communal structure, with its nationally respected legitimacy and authority, that was utilised and manipulated by the Germans with such devastating effect during the occupation of 1944. As will be seen, in the absence of mandatory affiliation — in effect, a detailed central register of Hungarian Jews (see Chapter I) — and a tightly structured secretariat commanding well-nigh universal community obedience, there must exist considerable doubt whether Eichmann and his collaborators could have achieved so much of their murderous intent with such unparalleled speed and efficiency.

Communal Organisations

Motivated by the advent of institutional discrimination, and spurred by the urging of the American Jewish Joint Distribution Committee (AJDC, known popularly as "the Joint"), by early 1939 the three denominations of Hungarian Jewry and the *Magyar Cionista Szovetseg* (Hungarian Zionist Federation) had combined to form the *Magyar Izraelitak Partfogo Irodaja* (Hungarian Israelite Welfare Bureau), the MIPI.[69] Resulting from the Stern–Eppler mission to London and Paris in May 1939 (see Chapter II), several major international Jewish aid agencies, such as WIZO (Women's International Zionist Organisation), ORT (Organisation for Rehabilitation and Training) and the Joint, contributed funds to subsidise MIPI's welfare programme.[70] In particular, in June 1939 the AJDC agreed to grant $US25,000 per month to MIPI on the basis of an equal contribution from Hungarian Jewry.[71]

This major restructuring of the community's welfare services led to the government-endorsed formation of a nationwide fundraising enterprise, the *Orszagos Magyar Zsido Segito Akcio* (OMZSA), the National Hungarian Jewish Assistance Campaign. Following Hungary's declaration of war on the United States, the Joint and other Allied sources were obliged to discontinue their grants. Despite this, MIPI's expenditure increased from 3.5 million *pengos* in 1941 to 4.4 million in 1942. In the latter year OMZSA's income was 4.8 million *pengos*, of which 83 percent was contributed by the Neolog, 15 percent by the Orthodox and 2 percent by the Status Quo. Of the total amount, 2.6 million (54 percent) was donated by the Neolog Community of Pest.[72] Despite increasingly virulent institutional Antisemitism, Hungarian authorities — particularly the politically moderate Minister of the Interior, Ferenc Keresztes-Fischer — generally facilitated MIPI and OMZSA's provision of comprehensive welfare services to the needy section of the Jewish community.[73] The *Magyar Zsidok Naptara, 1942* (Hungarian Jewish Diary, 1942) contains an *Omzsa Lexikon*, a directory listing some ninety separate OMZSA subsidiaries.[74] Though Hungary and the USA were at war by 1942, it is interesting to note that included in this listing is OMZSA-DOLLAR, described therein as the American Joint Distribution Committee's assistance to Hungarian Jewry via the donation of dollar currency.[75] Even after the German Occupation, OMZSA and MIPI were permitted to continue functioning, albeit as appendages of the rigidly controlled Jewish Council (*Zsido Tanacs*, Hungarian; *Judenrat*, German).

Figure 3.3 *Testveredet Ne Hagyd El!* (**Do Not Abandon Your Brethren!**)

OMZSA (*Orszagos Magyar Zsido Segito Akcio* **— National Hungarian Jewish Assistance Campaign) poster soliciting donations for Jewish welfare. Note the OMZSA symbol (the Tablets of the Law) and acronym above the grieving woman. The poster is held by Mr Frigyes Porscht, Deputy Curator of the Jewish Museum of Budapest.** (Photo: TDK, 1991)

Antisemitic discrimination generated a flowering of cultural activities within the communal fold. Jewish musicians, artists, authors, actors, singers, dancers and teachers dismissed from government or private institutions found employment within the confines of community-supported organisations such as OMIKE, the *Orszagos Magyar Israelita Kozmuvelodesi Egyesulet* (National Hungarian Israelite Cultural Society).[76] Thus, although communal life was largely restructured to an inward, often introspective perspective, "wartime normality" was barely disturbed. Hungarian Jews as a whole appeared, in effect, oblivious to the fate of their co-religionists within the clutches of the Third Reich,[77] a mood of self-centred insularity dominating the community's collective consciousness.

Zionism

Unlike their co-religionists in the successor states — particularly Poland, Czechoslovakia and Roumania — Hungarian Jewry as a whole maintained a palpable hostility to the Zionist message. As previously discussed, Jewish nationalism, the central tenet of Zionism, was seen to represent a threat to Hungarian Jewry's staunchly held self-conception of being stalwart, patriotic, integral Magyars — albeit of the Israelite faith. Antagonism to Zionism was so intense that not only were teachers and pupils suspected of Zionist sympathies dismissed from Jewish schools,[78] but a foremost spokesman of established Jewry, Bela Fabian MP, publicly declared that "every Zionist is a communist".[79] Moreover, with but small exception, Orthodoxy rejected Zionism via the former's fierce, theologically based opposition to the concept of a secular-induced *Aliya*.[80] As a general rule, Zionism replaced Reform Judaism as Orthodoxy's most feared opponent.[81]

Exacerbating anti-Zionist chauvinism was Hungarian Jewry's insularity and virtual isolation from the international Jewish community, a situation only breached in 1939 by the Stern–Eppler mission to London and Paris. Consequently, despite the pogroms and persecutions of the Trianon epoch, a Jewish ethnic identity — arguably the most important factor in the growth of a viable Zionist movement — was slow in striking roots in Hungary. Unlike their co-religionists elsewhere in the successor states, the political consciousness of Hungarian Jewry remained fixated in its prewar format. Partly as a consequence of established Jewry's steadfast hostility, the Hungarian Zionist Organisation (formed 1903) only received formal government sanction for its statutes in 1927.

Not surprisingly, despite the numerous Jewish journalists, authors, scholars and playwrights in Trianon Hungary, even the capital lacked Hebrew newspapers or publishers of substance.[82] Budapest Jewry's pervasive, intensely acculturated *milieu* simply precluded the development of a secular Hebrew culture in the capital. In 1921, after the pogroms of the White Terror, the Hungarian Zionist Organisation had a total membership of 5,000, 1 percent of the Jewish population. And notwithstanding the most intense persecution for centuries, in that year a mere 103 Zionists emigrated to Palestine. Clearly, Trianon Hungary supports the hypothesis that, in the absence of Jewish national consciousness, even an extended period of Antisemitism is insufficient to generate a mass Zionist movement.

Attempting to circumvent the stigma attached to ideologically based Zionist organisations, in 1927 the *Magyar Zsidok Pro Palesztina Szovetsege* (Hungarian Jewish Pro-Palestine Association) was formed, and achieved the first breakthrough regarding Hungarian Jews' involvement in the rebuilding of their ancient homeland.

Indicating its relative success, the Pro-Palestine Association's apolitical approach, and non-pariah status, attracted members of the Jewish elite into its leadership ranks. Thus, despite internal conflicts and the enduring enmity of established Jewry, the last decade of peace involved significant gains — albeit from a very low base — in the membership, resources and influence of Hungarian Zionism. Aided by this growing respectability, and the continuing momentum of the radical Right, by 1933 the full spectrum of Central and eastern European Zionist endeavour was to be found in Hungary.[83] Of future significance (see Chapter IV), towards the end of the 1930s the various Zionist youth groups had grown to about 2,000 members.[84] In the years 1932–38, some 1,300 Hungarian Jews emigrated to Palestine.[85]

One of the most important developments in Trianon-era Zionism resulted from the transfer, via territorial realignment and illegal immigration, of Transylvanian and Slovak Zionists to Hungary. Generally more dynamic and experienced than their Hungarian counterparts, and thus quickly accepted into the leadership of their respective movements, these pro-active relocated Zionists henceforth committed their energy, and their heightened sense of Jewish ethnicity, to the cause of Hungarian Zionism. One noted early initiative by Zionist leaders transferred from Transylvania, a group that included Dr Rezso (Israel) Kasztner (see Chapter IV), occurred in December 1941, when a meeting of prominent Jews was convened in Budapest to discuss Jewish massacres in Reich-controlled territory, and options for the defence of Hungarian Jewry.[86] The meeting proved unproductive,[87] the War, the increasing number of refugees, institutional discrimination, personality clashes, and ideological conflicts pre-empting the time and energy of participants.

Notwithstanding this meeting, Katzburg summarised overall Zionist attitudes in the period 1939–42 thus: "In retrospect, it seems that even the Zionists were not overcome with a sense of urgency and did not feel that Hungarian Jewry was faced with imminent danger."[88] Recognising, however, the need to co-ordinate operations, and maximise efficacy, via the introduction of a centralised system, in January 1943 a combined Zionist *Va'adat Ezra ve'Hazalah* (Relief and Rescue Committee) was constituted, the organisation becoming the Jewish Agency's official representative in Hungary. Chaired by Otto Komoly, leader of the Hungarian Zionist Organisation, the *Va'ada* assumed responsibility for the formulation and implementation of a co-ordinated Hungarian Zionist welfare programme — including the rescue of Jews trapped in Slovakia.

As discussed above, the Kallay interregnum was notable for reinforcing the rapport between Hungarian Jewry and the government; a rapport exemplified by a Zionist memorandum prepared at the request of the Foreign Ministry, and submitted to the Allies via Zionist contacts in neutral Istanbul. In accordance with the Ministry's wishes, the document requested that Budapest be spared from bombing in view of the Hungarian government's constructive attitude towards its Jewish citizens, and its policy of attempted extrication from the German alliance.[89] Paradoxically, by this request the pragmatically inclined government was, in effect, indicating its belief that international Jewry influenced — if not controlled — both the USSR (via Judeo-Bolshevism) and the western Allies (via international Jewish capitalism). Clearly, the Hungarian regime failed to recognise either the political marginality of international Jewish organisations, or the near-apathy of most Allied leaders towards Jewish suffering at the hands of the Reich (see Chapter VI).[90] With such realisation, the Hungarian government would hardly have risked further alienating Germany by utilising such a memorandum — in effect, a thinly disguised request for assistance from international Jewry.

Despite enormous and continuing evidence to the contrary, the Magyar Establishment's totally unjustified belief in the immense power and influence of international Jewry was, with little doubt, one of the major factors safeguarding Hungarian Jews. Well remembering the trauma of Trianon, the Horthyist's *quid pro quo* for this protection was Allied leniency towards Hungary — both during the conflict and at the conclusion of hostilities. This utilisation of the international Zionist network by the Hungarian government was, in important respects, a hitherto unrecognised precursor to the *SS* plan for the Hungarian Zionist leader Joel Brand in mid-1944 (see below). Informed of Hungary's manoeuvring by German agents in Budapest and Istanbul, it is not unthinkable that Himmler conceived his plan for the Brand Mission — an attempt to generate contact and rapport with the West — via the Hungarian government's example of utilising the Zionist network for the same purpose.[91]

Ironically, it would have appeared to both the Hungarian and German regimes that the Zionist memorandum was effective in achieving the desired *quid pro quo*. The fact that Budapest was free from air attack until Hungarian Jewry was placed in jeopardy was, to both Hungary and the Reich, further evidence that international Jewry directed the Allied war effort.

Jewish Labour Service

As has been discussed, prior to the German Occupation of the country (19 March 1944), Antisemitic laws attacked only the socio-economic circumstance of Hungarian Jews. The sole physical threat to a significant proportion of the community resided in the Labour Service regulations, and the implementation thereof.

The antecedents of the *Munkaszolgalat* (Labour Service — henceforth LS) system were the punitive detachments for "political unreliables" instituted in December 1919 by the White (counter-revolutionary) Commander in Chief, Admiral Horthy.[92] With the increase in European tensions, this concept was resurrected as part of a comprehensive *Honvedelem* (National Defence) mobilisation measure promulgated in March 1939.[93] Providing the legal basis for conscription into labour battalions, this regulation compelled all people aged from fourteen to seventy to contribute to national defence if so ordered, a compulsion tantamount to government fiat. It was this law that provided the legal facade used to justify the draconian measures adopted against Hungarian Jewry during the German Occupation of the country.

In September 1939, the army implemented its own anti-Jewish regimen, including the requirement that commissioned officers and their spouses each prove that both their parents and all four grandparents were non-Jews. For non-commissioned officers, only the parents had to pass such scrutiny. At this time, the 2,300 enlisted Jews constituted 2.3 percent of the 102,000-member armed forces — less than half the Jewish percentage of the population. Although Jews could no longer rise to a rank, those fit for active duty were at this stage still distributed evenly through the combat units,[94] only those found unfit being conscripted to the LS battalions.[95]

Initially the LS legislation thus served as an adjunct to military conscription, the early non-discriminatory intakes involving quarterly periods of service for those twenty-one to twenty-four year old males classified as physically and/or ideologically unfit for military duty. Until the end of 1940, the situation of Jews in the LS units was reasonably tolerable, Jewish conscripts generally receiving the same treatment with respect to pay, clothing and rations as their non-Jewish colleagues. Under the command of Hungarian Army officers, the labour brigades were provided with tools and employed largely in the construction of military projects.

Closer political alignment with the Reich, and increasing pro-German sentiment within the military and Ministry of Defence, saw a marked deterioration in the treatment afforded Jewish conscripts. Although lacking the legal basis for such action, on 2 December 1940 Jewish labour service personnel were segregated into their own separate units.[96] Members of these Jewish Labour Service brigades (henceforth JLS) were now barred from attaining rank, even those conscripts previously holding a commissioned or non-commissioned position in the forces. This decree elicited strong protests from the Jewish community, all of which were to no avail — with the possible exception of Horthy's token exemption of a small group of reserve officers who had been highly decorated in World War I.[97]

Despite such discrimination, and despite the absence of insignia or rank, at Hungary's commencement of hostilities against the USSR in late June 1941, most JLS personnel wore Hungarian military uniform. This situation generated considerable criticism from both the Germans and their Hungarian fellow-travellers, particularly the Hungarian Chief of Staff, General Ferenc Szombathelyi. As a result, in March 1942 the JLS were deprived of their uniforms, ordered into civilian clothing and — for the first time in Hungary since the Middle Ages[98] — Jews (in the JLS) were compelled to wear an indicator of their religion, to wit a coloured armband — yellow for Jews, white for Christian Jews.[99] The sole remaining government provision was an insignia-free military cap. Needless to say civilian clothing, lacking the durability of military uniform, rapidly deteriorated under the combined depredations of extremely harsh winters, arduous physical labour and often sadistic commanders.

From this point, the system became increasingly punitive, especially for those brigades stationed near the eastern frontiers or in German-occupied territory. Along with their uniforms, the JLS were progressively stripped of dignity and rights, the distinguishing armbands enabling army Judeophobes to clearly identify their victims. Although exceptions occurred, as a general rule the further a unit was stationed from Budapest, the more inhuman the attitude of the commanding officer and his subordinates.[100] As shall be seen, however, during the German Occupation the JLS system — with great and unpredictable paradox — provided a relative refuge for its personnel, saving tens of thousands from certain deportation.

In June 1942, the Minister of Defence, Karoly Bartha, increased the pressure on Christian Jews by modifying the JLS legislation to apply to all those classified as Jews under the Nuremburg-inspired Third Jewish Law (see Chapter II). As with most Antisemitic measures, the ultra-Right criticised the proposal as being insufficiently rigorous or discriminatory.[101] For entirely opposite reasons, the nation's small, sadly ineffective moderate elements also opposed some of the regulation's provisions. The following December, the Lower House adopted a Bill imposing an extraordinary war levy on those not engaged in military service. Despite many JLS battalions being subject to enemy action at or near the front-lines, duty in such brigades did not grant exemption from this tax. When considered by the Upper House in November 1943, this situation was reversed and JLS members were duly exempted from the levy.[102]

With little doubt, disenchantment with German performance on the battlefield, the residue of pragmatic opinion in the Upper House, and the need to bolster the regime's diplomatic manoeuvring towards the Western Allies (see Chapter II) were the prime factors motivating this decision. It should be noted that the landmark decision of the *Kozigazgatasi Birosag* (Administrative Court) in September 1943, which ruled that JLS members should be exempt from the levy as labour and military service were equivalent, to a large extent pre-empted parliament's decision. The Court's verdict was, in turn, aligned with the August 1943 ruling of the *Orszagos Tarsadalombiztosito Intezet* (National Insurance Institute), which decided to grant families of deceased JLS conscripts the same benefits awarded fallen members of the military forces.[103] The subsequent review of all previously dismissed claims was greeted with satisfaction by the Jewish community, a satisfaction reinforcing Jewry's faith in the basic integrity of Hungarian institutions.

In December 1941, there were about 14,500 Jews amongst the 23,000 members of the Labour Service. In April 1942, with the dispatch of the 250,000-member Second Hungarian Army to the Eastern Front,[104] the number of JLS conscripts increased tremendously. Particular targets for conscription were "objectionable" elements within the community, even those over forty-two years of age — the legal call-up limit. Frequently, denunciations by corrupt officials and unethical individuals (who sought private or corporate benefit) formed the basis of a conscription notice.[105] As the absence of Jews from the armed forces was considered a privilege, and in response to intense German and ultra-Right pressure, by mid-1942 some 50,000 JLS personnel had been attached to the Second Hungarian Army. Henceforth, all Jewish men of military age were conscripted into the JLS.[106]

Far from government scrutiny, their actions reinforced by military superiors, the attitude of many Hungarian JLS commanders in the Ukraine was particularly deplorable, their orders often grossly violating official guidelines. In a postwar statement, former Chief of Staff General Ferenc Szombathelyi admitted:

> The Jewish question had a catastrophic effect upon the armed forces. It had a terrible corrupting effect. Every value underwent a revaluation. Cruelty became love for the fatherland, atrocities became acts of heroism, corruption was transformed into virtue... There emerged two types of discipline. One was applied to the Jews, against whom any action was permissible...[107]

Szombathelyi's testimony confirmed an official Ministry of Defence Report into the JLS situation in the Eastern Front *circa* mid-1942, the Report concluding: "Brutality, violence and corruption were permanent manifestations in all the front lines."[108] This investigation, allied with Kallay's attempted extrication from the German embrace, resulted in the replacement, in September 1942, of the stridently Germanophile Karoly Bartha by a new Defence Minister, Vilmos Nagybaczoni-Nagy.[109] After an inspection tour of the Eastern Front in October 1942, Nagy publicly demanded legal and humane treatment for JLS brigades.[110] Braham states that during his ministerial tenure (September 1942–June 1943), the benevolent Nagy "did everything in his power to ameliorate their [the JLS] plight".[111] Despite this attitude being consistently undermined, and sometimes even sabotaged, by his subordinates, Vilmos Nagy's endeavours generally had a positive influence on the JLS units stationed within Hungary, although the situation of those brigades beyond the Eastern frontier, and in German occupied Yugoslavia, remained largely unchanged.[112] In particular, the treatment of the 6,000 JLS conscripts in the copper mines at Bor, some 200 km south-east of Belgrade, was especially inhumane.[113]

Under intense German pressure, in June 1943 the government requested Nagy's resignation. His replacement, the Horthy loyalist General Lajos Csatay, although less sympathetic to the Jewish plight, adopted a professional attitude towards the JLS. Through his and his predecessor's endeavours, the JLS thus became a major refuge during the German Occupation, many of its conscripts being saved from certain deportation.

It is pertinent to note that despite the often barbaric treatment by their commanding officers on the Eastern Front, the unarmed JLS — in marked contrast to the Second Hungarian Army — distinguished itself with particular gallantry, especially during the agonising, tortuous retreat from the Don.[114] The reports of, for example, Lieutenant-Colonel Bela Vecsey, commander of the 35th Infantry Regiment, attest that he was

> ...compelled to determine that these Jews are much more disciplined than our *Honveds* [regular military forces]; their readiness to work and their productivity are also better than those of the *Honveds*. The Jews brought out the wounded and the dead *Honveds* in the midst of the greatest fire. A Jewish company [of about 200] had about fifty dead and twice as many wounded.[115]

Reinforcing this opinion, on another occasion Vecsey stated: "The Jewish companies at the front behave very bravely; they leave no Hungarian dead or wounded behind. We shall live to see the day when they will become heroes, while our infantry is constantly on the run."[116]

Despite this heroism, the Germans and their Hungarian fellow-travellers subjected the JLS to senseless, vicious attacks during the retreat. The situation became so deplorable that the commander of the Hungarian forces, General Gusztav Jany, lodged a protest with the head of the German Second Army.[117] Of the 50,000 JLS conscripts attached to the Second Hungarian Army, only 6–7,000 eventually returned to Hungary, a mortality rate of over 85 percent.[118] By contrast, of Hungary's 200,000 combat troops in the East, about 60–70,000 survived, a significantly lower mortality rate of some 65 percent.[119] Never mentioned by Hungarist apologists, however, is the fundamental dichotomy between these two figures: whereas the Hungarian Second Army was decimated by enemy action in the theatre of battle, the JLS casualties resulted largely from the deliberate actions of nominally friendly forces.

As will be realised, the extensive JLS catastrophe was totally beyond the power of Hungarian Jewry to either alleviate or avoid. There was no prospect of Jewish leaders either influencing the Judeophobic military or ameliorating the often inhuman regimen inflicted on the JLS. As in many past — and future — respects, the Hungarian Jewish leadership was in effect trapped, its solitary option being the magnitude of support allocated to the existing Horthyist regime. However, under no circumstances should the inability to influence the course of this tragedy be considered either an acquiescence or acceptance of the treatment afforded the JLS. Even successive Ministers of Defence were largely frustrated in their attempts to rectify the abuses inherent in a system organised and directed by Judeophobes — especially in those areas beyond the country's frontiers, areas dominated by the *SS* and Germany's notorious *Einsatzgruppen*. Consequently, one should reject unreservedly contentions such as those made by Robert Rozett. Whilst discussing the "silence" of the Hungarian Jewish leaders on the JLS question, and without presenting evidence or references, Rozett suggests (amongst other possibilities) that "they might have been merely indifferent to the fate of the Jewish soldiers".[120] As will be seen, the welfare and sustenance of the JLS occupied a prominent position on the agenda of Hungary's Jewish leadership.

Chapter III: Notes

1. Mendelsohn 1983:123.
2. Laszlo 1969:157.
3. As discussed in Chapter II, the term "Jew" was defined by Hungary's Antisemitic legislation to be based on "race" not religion. (As in Nazi Germany, the absurdity that an immutable category — "race" — could only be defined on the basis of changeable affiliation — religion — was conveniently ignored.) Consequently, many people with Christian-born parents were reclassified as Jews, the parents themselves being the offspring of couples who had been baptised into a Christian denomination prior to their children's birth.
4. Laszlo 1969:162. Almost three out of four Jews lived in aggregations of over 1,000 people, but fewer than 10 percent resided in settlements of under 100. Large settlements were defined as those with populations exceeding 500 inhabitants; medium settlements ranged from 100 to 500.
5. Patai 1985:166.
6. Braham 1981:778. For an exposition of the *Jo Pasztor Misszio*, see the testimony of Jozsef Elias, 26 February 1946. (YA 768/3652) Rev. Elias, the *Misszio*'s "leading priest", was himself of Jewish background. As a personal opinion: rather than criticising those who sought security for themselves and their families via conversion, one should instead admire the mass of Jews who, in the face of brutal persecution, remained steadfast to their convictions and heritage.
7. For data regarding Hungarian Jewish demography 1919-46, see "Hungarian Jewry", Publication No. 10, Statistical Department, World Jewish Congress, Hungary. (YA 3/44391)
8. Klein 1966:97.
9. Cited Varga 1990:259.
10. Even if this argument had validity, the relatively small numbers involved would expose the Hungarian government to charges of tokenism. To this response the apologist might counter that the government could only permit exit to those Jews holding appropriate foreign visas, documents that, by that stage of the War, were extremely difficult to obtain.
11. Laszlo 1969:157-58.
12. Karady 1990:110-11.
13. Laszlo 1969:154. That author mistakenly states this figure to be 0.01 percent.
14. Laszlo 1969:155.
15. Katzburg 1981:171.
16. Cited Mendelsohn 1983:102. For comparison purposes: prior to World War II, Jewish intermarriage in Bohemia was 30 percent for men and 26 percent for women. In Subcarpathian Ruthenia, it was under 1 percent for both genders. (Braham 1981:83)
17. The military, a traditional Antisemitic bastion, became almost *Judenrein*. (Don 1986:73) In 1925, the Ludovika Military Academy achieved a state of *Numerus Nullius*. (Laszlo 1969:156)
18. Figures in this paragraph have been selected from Laszlo 1969:146-49. See also Kovacs 1994:49-81.
19. Patai 1985:167. Paradoxically, this meant that less meritorious students, ie: those generally forced to study abroad, often attained academic qualifications from more highly regarded institutions than their more accomplished co-religionists who matriculated to Hungarian universities. For a comprehensive exposition, see Aron Moskovits, *Jewish*

Education in Hungary (1848-1948), New York: Bloch Publishing Company, 1964.

20. Klein 1966:81, n11.

21. Lengyel (1990:239) states that about one-quarter of the Jewish members of the elite were converts.

22. Lengyel 1990:233, table 2. By comparison, non-Jewish Hungarians only managed the second highest position in each category, ie: 37, 34, and 31 percent respectively.

23. Ibid.

24. Figures in this paragraph are from Don 1986:69, tables 1 and 2.

25. The boom was largely confined to the developed, more affluent regions of Hungary. In the impoverished outlying provinces, for example Subcarpathian Ruthenia, the situation for poor Jews remained desperate. To alleviate this hardship, on 26 April 1939 the Orthodox Chief Rabbi of Ungvar (Uzhgorod) wrote to the Jewish Agency requesting assistance for the emigration to Palestine of 100 families, the first step in a scheme involving 1,000 participating families. The Chief Rabbi's letter paints a graphic picture of Jewish suffering in this region, the letter's last line summarising the situation of the prospective emigrants: "Their emigration therefore is an utmost urgency." (CZA S25/5604)

26. Don 1986b:62.

27. Letter from Horthy to Teleki, 14 October 1940. (Szinai and Szucs 1965:150-51)

28. Don 1986:75.

29. Even Horthy's relatives accepted directorships in large Jewish enterprises. (Don 1986b:72, n53)

30. Don 1986:76.

31. Braham 1981:252, n57.

32. Private discussion, 3 November 1989, with Dr Gyorgy Gergely, husband of Leo Goldberger's foster daughter, Edit Popper.

33. Don 1986:75. In 1943, Goldberger's company ordered new plant from Switzerland. (Don 1986:82)

34. Janos 1982:304.

35. In 1938, with prospects of Antisemitic legislation imminent, Samu Stern claimed — with unfortunate hyperbole — that 90 percent of Hungarian Jews lived at the poverty level. (Braham 1981:80)

36. Braham 1977:125, n37. The ranks of these 129 Jewish officers were as follows: 34 Lt-Col., 23 Major, 56 Captain, 15 First Lieutenant, 1 Lieutenant.

37. Cited Janos 1982:302, n134. The same source estimated that, contemporaneously, 51,000 Jewish employees had lost their positions.

38. McCagg Jr 1990:74.

39. Lucas 1988:126-27.

40. Vago (1974:38) states that in Hungary, unlike Poland and Roumania, "no Jewish party came into existence in Hungary and no Jewish lists appeared at any election".

41. Vago 1974:39.

42. Katzburg 1990:42.

43. Vago 1974:39.

44. The only political organisations accepting Jewish members were the Social Democrats and the small Centre parties. (Klein 1966:96) Despite this, and their emphatic support from Jews, the "moderate" groups were not free of Judeophobia. The Social Democratic Party, for instance, concurred with the radical Right's attitude towards *rich* Jews, both groups agreeing that such Jews deserved Antisemitism. (Klein 1966:92-3)

45. Katzburg 1990:42.

46. For example, see Braham 1981:90-103.

47. Because of the considerable differences between Hungary, Roumania and Czechoslovakia, arguments based on analogies between these three countries should be considered with caution.

48. In Czechoslovakia, the Jewish population of 350,000 increased its vote for Jewish parties from 80,000 in 1920 to 100,000 in 1925. In Poland, Jewish and minority parties formed a common list in 1929. Winning four mandates, the alliance divided the spoils, with each partner obtaining two seats. (Vago 1974:42)

49. Katzburg 1990:41.

50. With a community of 800,000 people, Jews comprised about 4.2 percent of the Roumanian population in the interwar period. In the elections of 1931 and 1932, the Jewish party polled about 2.5 percent of the total vote. Vago cites the results of the 1929 elections for the Jewish Council in Cernauti, an important Jewish centre in Roumania, as illustrative of the political affiliation of that country's Jews. The vote was divided as follows: Zionists 25 percent; National Peasant's Party list 22 percent; National Liberal list 9 percent; Socialist Bund 17 percent; five other lists totalled 27 percent. (Vago 1974:37-8)

51. Vago 1974:39:40.

52. This interpretation is confirmed by Macartney 1954:xvii.

53. Vago 1974:25. The alliance of some Jews with the autocratic, Antisemitic and even pro-Nazi Right afforded Transylvanian Jews a modicum of security. Because these parties were competing for Jewish members and donations there was, for a time, a de facto moratorium on organised physical violence against Jews. This arrangement was formalised in the well-known expression: "If you beat up our Jews, then we'll beat up your Jews." (Ibid)

54. McCagg Jr 1990:75.

55. Laszlo 1969:140; Laszlo 1969:157. The famous Rabbis of Munkacs and Szatmar, as well as some 80 percent of Orthodox *Yeshivot*, were transferred to the successor states. (Mendelsohn 1983:100)

56. Laszlo 1969:150.

57. Ibid.

58. Cohen, A 1984:141.

59. By contrast, the Orthodox operated on a relatively modern constitution (enacted 1906) whilst the Status Quo *kehilot* only had their statutes approved in 1928. (Katzburg 1988:264)

60. See Katzburg 1988: 264-68.

61. Katzburg 1988:264.

62. This faction argued that the National Bureau's function included the arbitration of disputes to which the Pest community could be party.

63. Recognising the threat to his campaign, in a political masterstroke Stern defused charges of personal aggrandisement by offering to resign as head of the Pest Community if the president of the National Bureau accepted both positions.

64. Braham 1981:94.

65. Located in the Dohany Street complex of the Neolog community.

66. *Egyenloseg*, 21 March 1931, page 10. (YVA 015/25) Founded in 1881 during the Tiszaeslar fervour (see Chapter I), *Egyenloseg* aimed to combat widespread Antisemitic calumnies. (Ujvari 1929:213)

67. Katzburg 1988:272, n43.

68. Goldberger's opposition to Stern was somewhat surprising, as only a short time earlier he had been on Stern's *Hitkozsegi Part* (Community Party) list for the Pest Neolog Community election of 8 March 1931. Listed as "4171 Dr. budai Buday-Goldberger Leo, *gyarigazgato* [factory director]", the list comprised the Community Party's nominations for 300 Regular Deputies. (JMBA 89.107) For an outline of Leo Goldberger (1874-1945) and his communal and commercial endeavours, see "Dr. Buday-Goldberger Leo" in *Egyenloseg* (Equality), 21 March 1931, written on the thirtieth anniversary of Goldberger's appointment as director of his family's textile concern, founded 1785. (YVA 015/25)

69. Following its formation, the MIPI Executive consisted of five Neolog (including the Chairman, Samu Stern, and Dr Sandor Eppler), four Orthodox (including Samu Kahan-Frankl and Fulop Freudiger), two Zionist (including Nison Kahan), and one Status Quo

representative. Before 1938, the majority of welfare services had been provided on a local basis. (Braham 1981:112, n20)

70. Schwartz 1989:5.

71. Braham 1981:87 and 112, n21. The Joint utilised its Hungarian operations to assist Jews trapped directly in the Nazi empire. As an example, for the *Pesach* (Passover) celebrations of 1941, the Joint's Budapest office shipped 32,000 kilograms of *matzo* (unleavened bread) to Warsaw. (Trunk 1972:138-39)

72. Braham 1981:113, n24. In 1941-42, the *pengo* was officially valued at $US0.20, with the black market rate fluctuating at somewhat under half this figure. (Braham 1981:1,175, n8)

73. Importantly, the government permitted these organisations to assist Jewish refugees and non-citizen Jews residing in Hungary. By November 1943 such refugees numbered an estimated 15,000, many of whom were interned in camps. (Braham 1981:88)

74. *Magyar Zsido Naptara* (Hungarian Jewish Diary), 1942: 375-86.

75. *Magyar Zsido Naptara* 1942:377. As Hungary declared war on the USA in December 1941, it is highly likely that the Diary was published and distributed before the proclamation of hostilities.

76. Eight concerts, five operas and several plays were listed in OMIKE's programme for the 1943-44 artistic season. (Braham 1981:113)

77. Braham 1981:89.

78. Cohen 1986:15.

79. Silagi 1986:194. Silagi, a contemporary Zionist activist, returns in kind by writing on the same page of this reference: "Not only did [the Neolog] leaders make a mockery out of Judaism by denying its ethnic essence, but the majority of the [Neolog] members were near-nonbelievers, ignorant of the religious traditions as well." It is important to recognise that anti-Zionist fervour as displayed by Fabian was not unique to Hungary. For an example of Jewish anti-Zionism in Italy, see Deak November 1992:22-23.

80. *Aliya*: the traditional Jewish word for describing a return to the land of Israel.

81. For a precis of relations between Orthodoxy and Zionism, see Laqueur 1980:407-13.

82. Mendelsohn 1983:112.

83. The four largest Zionist groups competing for the allegiance of Hungarian Jews were *Klal* (General), *Mizrachi* (Religious), *Hashomer Hatzair* (Socialist) and *Mapai* (Labour). (Braham 1981:92)

84. Braham 1971:254-55. Cohen (1986:15) states 1,500-2,000 members. For an exposition of the situation and endeavours of the various Zionist youth groups in Trianon Hungary, see Hava Eichler, "Zionism and Youth in Hungary Between the Two World Wars". (PhD thesis, Bar-Ilan University, 1982).

85. Katzburg 1984b:163, n3.

86. For a summary of Zionist endeavour in the years 1939-42, see Katzburg 1984:161-76. For an emotional exposition of the Spinoza Booklets (theme: Jewry is a nation), the Yellow Booklets campaign, and the failed attempt by the Jewish Work Collective to break the Jewish-Magyar nexus, see Silagi 1986:191-235.

87. Silagi 1986:229; Braham 1971:525.

88. Katzburg (1984b:168) continues his discussion by stating: "Given the circumstances prevailing at the time in Hungary, the Zionists felt that the most important task was to safeguard the Hungarian Jews by strengthening their sense of national self-identification."

89. Braham 1971:525. From its context, apparently the memo was dated *circa* mid-1943.

90. Prominent examples of this disregard were the Evian (July 1938) and Bermuda (April 1943) Conferences; the refusal to accept appropriate numbers of Jewish refugees, especially to Palestine and the USA; the refusal to bomb either the railway line to Auschwitz, or the gas chambers and crematoria in the camp itself (see Chapter VI).

91. At the time of writing, there is no documentary evidence to corroborate this hypothesis. However, circumstantial support is provided by the chronology, symmetry and common purpose in the Hungarian and German endeavours. There is a minority view which

maintains that the Brand Mission was either an adjunct and/or a smokescreen for Brand's companion, the triple agent Bandi Grosz. For a cogently argued exposition of this attitude, see Bauer 1978:94-155, especially p147.

92. Braham 1977:1.

93. Braham 1981:122, n14.

94. Elements of the military high command opposed proposals to exclude Jews from active service, arguing that such a privilege might induce conversions to Judaism from those seeking to evade military duty. This type of suggestion had bizarre echoes during the *Nyilas* era (ie: post-15 October 1944), when ultra-Right propaganda accused Jews of selling yellow stars to non-Jews seeking to avoid military service.

95. Braham 1977:7-8.

96. Katzburg 1981:202-03. Legitimised by executive decree in April 1941, this piece of institutional discrimination applied to all those classified as Jews by the Second Jewish Law.

97. Ibid.

98. The Buda Synod of 1279 required Jews to wear an identification mark, a red circle of cloth fixed onto the upper garment. (Katzburg 1984:7)

99. Prior to this protocol, company commanders employed their discretion regarding the wearing of armbands. Some JLS conscripts thus wore armbands displaying the national colours — red, white and green.

100. Braham 1977:viii; Rothkirchen 1968:xxi.

101. Certain minor categories classified as Jews were exempt, viz: "racially" Jewish Christian clergy, and war veterans who were either highly decorated or of 50 percent invalid status. (Katzburg 1981:204.)

102. Katzburg 1981:205-06.

103. Katzburg 1981:207.

104. Berend and Ranki 1973:522.

105. Kovacs 1994:126; Braham 1981:308-09. Even the physically and mentally unfit were conscripted.

106. Braham 1981:325.

107. Quoted Braham 1981:317.

108. Rothkirchen 1968:xix.

109. Braham 1981:321.

110. Rothkirchen 1968:xix-xx; Kovacs 1994:126-27. For extracts from Nagy's speeches advocating reform of the JLS system, see Braham 1977:40-41.

111. Braham 1981:321.

112. Rothkirchen 1968:xx; Braham 1977:41; Braham 1981:323. For a comprehensive eyewitness account of the brutalities inflicted on JLS company 110/34 stationed in the Ukraine, see Singer 1995:15-53.

113. For a detailed exposition of the tragic Bor episode, see Nagy, Gyorgy 1995:55-127.

114. An anonymous source who departed from Budapest in July 1943, and is described as "an industrialist with good connections to Hungarian political circles", confirms that these facts were not unknown in contemporary civilian circles. The source correctly reported in mid-1943 that the last order to the Second Hungarian Army from its commanding General stated that "Hungarian troops did not fight with the traditional Hungarian gallantry, thereby disgracing the name of the Hungarian people." In strong terms, the General castigated Hungarian soldiers and concluded with the words: "On the other hand it cannot be denied that the conduct of the Jewish forced labour companies was very disciplined." (CZA S/25/9285)

115. Quoted Braham 1981:319.

116. Ibid.

117. Braham 1981:320.

118. Katzburg 1981:201, n1.

119. Braham 1981:318.

120. Rozett 1987:46.

CHAPTER IV

THE RACE AGAINST TIME[1]

With the succession of German battlefield disasters, by March 1944 Hungarian Jews were facing the future with increasing confidence. To all but partisan ideologues, German defeat appeared but a matter of time: furthermore, the community's rapport with the most powerful force in the country, Horthy and his government, had improved noticeably; institutional expropriation had not generated mass impoverishment; Hungarian Jewry's most implacable enemy, the pro-Nazi Arrow Cross, was in significant decline, its leadership enervated and membership well below 100,000;[2] Jews still sat in the Upper House; and the formalities of what may be termed Hungary's semi-authoritarian "guided democracy" continued functioning, sometimes with surprising vigour. In particular, up until the Occupation, Hungary maintained a multiparty political system that had, via the parliament and the press, the power to seriously embarrass the government and effect changes in policy, as happened (for example) in the case of the Delvidek massacres (see Chapter II). Similarly, the Hungarian press was able to express a wide diversity of political and ideological opinion. Although Communist views were prohibited, there remained a choice amongst Socialist, liberal, conservative, Monarchist, Catholic, Fascist and several National Socialist publications, some of these organs being openly critical of the chronically sensitive Reich.[3]

Thus although successive Hungarian governments had — to a formerly greater and recently lesser extent — instigated institutional Antisemitism, Hungarian Jewry acknowledged the absence of the intense discrimination inflicted upon their co-religionists elsewhere in the German domain. And above all, with the notable exception of the Jewish Labour Service conscripts, the physical safety of Hungarian Jews remained largely unimpaired. *Ergo*, with a degree of justification that can only be negated with the benefit of hindsight, the Jewish community's prevailing attitude to its situation was encapsulated in the oft-used term *Megusszuk* — literally, we'll swim through.[4]

The Occupation

Operation Margarethe I, the Germans' "restricted Occupation" of Hungary which commenced on the 19 March 1944, is too well chronicled to warrant repetition in this book.[5] However, the reasons for the Occupation and, in particular, the importance of the "Jewish Question" in motivating the German invasion, remain matters of considerable controversy.

One end of this divergent spectrum of opinion, exemplified by Macartney and Deak, ignores the "Jewish Question" as a factor motivating the Occupation.[6] This view considers that the Kallay government's dalliance with the Allies, and the inexorable approach of the Red Army towards the Carpathians, presented the Reich with the prospect of a Hungarian *volte-face*, which for political, military and economic reasons Hitler had to pre-empt. According to this view, although the *Endlösung* was applied in Hungary with particular speed and ferocity, despite German rhetoric and pressure (see Chapter II) the Final Solution was a consequence of, and not the motivation for, the invasion. A corollary of this position is the contention that had Kallay been perceived as a loyal ally, the German Occupation and the massive deportation of Hungarian Jewry could have been substantially averted — if not totally avoided. Accordingly, this school of thought generates a tragic paradox: Kallay's valiant attempt to extricate Hungary from the Axis alliance — and, *inter alia*, safeguard Hungarian Jewry — not only proved counterproductive for the country, but was the catalyst facilitating the catastrophe that befell Hungarian Jews.

In analysing this point of view, one should realise that there was never any real prospect of avoiding an immense German incursion into Hungarian territory. The Red Army's inexorable advance from the East pushed the Germans over the Carpathian Mountains. To counteract this advance, reinforcements streamed into Hungary from *Wehrmacht* reserves to the West. Consequently, one can safely assume that even in the absence of a formal Occupation, Germany would inevitably, for a period, have become the paramount military power in Hungary. Assuming a situation of *ceteris paribus* in variables other than the date of German military ascendancy in Hungary, the probable several months' delay in the attainment of this military dominance may have been sufficient to save very substantial numbers of Jews from deportation to Auschwitz. The prospect of Jewish deportation to elsewhere in the Reich's domain remained extant.[7]

The opinions of Professors Braham and Vago exemplify the centrist view that the *Endlösung*, whilst of some significance, was not the prime motivation for the Occupation. Braham summarises his position thus: "The Germans' decision to occupy Hungary resulted from a series of complex political-military factors; the 'unsolved' Jewish question, though important, was not the determining one."[8] The fact that the *Sonderkommando*[9] commanded by *Obersturmbannführer-SS* (Lieutenant-Colonel) Adolf Eichmann — head of RSHA (Reich Security Head Office) Jewish Department IV B4 — consisted of a mere 200 persons, does not necessarily lend credence to this point of view. The Reich doubtless recognised the prospects of very substantial collaboration from wide sections of Hungary's military, bureaucracy and society. As such, the Germans may well have believed the *Sonderkommando* to be sufficient in number — especially when Eichmann's renowned expertise and efficiency were taken into consideration.

At the other end of the spectrum are those who regard the "Jewish Question" in Hungary to have been a primary determinant instigating the German action of 19 March 1944. Generally, historians adopting this position are quite forthright in their opinion. For example, Gyorgy Ranki states: "...the Occupation was aimed at a final solution of the Jewish Question...it was one of the essential specifics of the Nazi Occupation."[10] Possibly enhancing the credibility of this view is the fact that there is, of course, consensus regarding both the importance and the effectiveness of the *Endlösung* subsequent to the Occupation. As a point of emphasis, the German Plenipotentiary in Hungary during the Occupation, *SS* General Edmund

Veesenmayer, devoted 30 to 40 percent of his reports to the implementation of the Final Solution in Hungary.[11]

This divergent spectrum of opinion has ossified over the decades, the paucity of additional information hardening the respective positions. However, recently a new, highly controversial perspective — unpublished at the time of writing — has been provided by Shlomo Aronson.[12] According to Professor Aronson, an elaborate Allied disinformation campaign increased pre-existing German apprehension about the prospects of a Western landing in the Balkans. Aronson argues that the Nazi hierarchy considered that the Western powers, for their own vital interests, would obstruct a Soviet Occupation — and hence likely monopoly — of South-East, East and Central Europe. The German invasion of Hungary was thus a function of this apprehension and consideration. That is, the Reich's primary military motivation for the Occupation was the attempt to pre-empt the West's anticipated Second Front invasion of the Balkans, an incursion that (according to the Germans) generated for the Western powers the distinct additional advantage of forming a bulwark against Soviet expansion.

Aronson links this military analysis with the radical crux of his hypothesis, the claim that the major political factor behind the German Occupation was Hitler's gross misinterpretation of the reasons motivating the establishment of the US War Refugee Board (WRB) in January 1944.[13] Instead of recognising it as a token political gesture, according to Aronson the *Führer* considered the WRB to be a clear indication of US willingness to negotiate the fate of Jews under German control. But by early 1944 the Reich's domain was virtually *Judenfrei*, the closest substantial number of Jews within German grasp being the 800,000 residing across a lightly guarded border in Horthy's bailiwick. *Ergo*, the crux of Aronson's radical reappraisal: "The creation of the War Refugee Board *invited* the German invasion of Hungary."[14]

By the Aronson Hypothesis, Hitler pre-empted an anticipated Western invasion of the Balkans; captured 800,000 Jews residing in relative safety beyond his control; and, simultaneously, acquired what in his Judeocentric consideration was a very substantial negotiating lever vis-à-vis the Allies. To the question of why Hitler would, with unprecedented speed and magnitude, liquidate his newly attained negotiating power, Aronson has a not unreasonable response. The deportations were a means of exerting pressure on the Allies: the greater the virulence of Judeophobia, the greater the prospect of the Allies being drawn into negotiations.[15] And if the Allies refused to negotiate, then at least another country would become *Judenrein*. Hitler thus achieved a win-win situation, a position he was constantly striving to attain.

Aronson is on firm ground with regard to the military component of his hypothesis. The noted Hungarian authorities Gyorgy Ranki and Gyula Juhasz[16] both confirm Hitler's fears of an Allied invasion of the Balkans, as does the memorandum of 12 February 1943 from the Hungarian Chief-of-Staff, General Ferenc Szombathelyi, to Horthy. The General reported on his recent trip to Germany thus: "...in the spring the Anglo-Saxon powers will attempt *a landing in the Balkan peninsula*... I think a landing is likely already from the end of March. Führer and Chancellor Hitler is also of the opinion that such a landing is very likely..."[17] (emphasis in the original) Juhasz also dismissed the prospect of a Hungarian armistice with the Soviets.[18]

Yehuda Bauer, one of the few authorities aware of Aronson's theory at the time of writing, dismisses the Aronson Hypothesis on the basis that it lacks supporting documentation.[19] Yet despite this rejection, Bauer concurs with one his colleague's critical contentions — the prospect of German interest in negotiating the release of Jews trapped within their domain.[20] It should be understood that Aronson does not claim that the formation of the WRB was the sole reason for the invasion, but that it was a prime catalyst in a multifactorial matrix. Aronson's cogent, incisive and insightful analysis places the "Jewish Question" at the centre of German foreign policy vis-à-vis the Western Allies — again, a not unreasonable proposition. In contrast, opposing theories deny this centrality — a not entirely uncontroversial contention.

To conclude: whilst the lack of documentary evidence is a substantial deterrent to the acceptance of the Aronson Hypothesis, when one considers that Hitler's *modus operandi* frequently eschewed formal documentation,[21] refutation of Professor Aronson's analysis is far from a mere formality. At the very least, his innovative evaluations have injected valuable new thinking into a formerly ossified subject. Although not stated as such by its author, the Aronson Hypothesis also generates a tragic paradox, viz: the *Endlösung* in Hungary was a bi-polar function generated by Allied ambivalence to Jewish suffering — an ambivalence often indistinguishable from indifference[22] — and Nazi willingness to negotiate with the West (see Chapter VI). More specifically, the Occupation of Hungary — and hence the destruction of Hungarian Jewry — was a consequence of the increasingly enervated Reich's involuntary propensity (guardedly promoted by *SS* Chief Heinrich Himmler) to reintroduce its pre-*Endlösung* policy of materially exploiting Jews trapped within its domain.

The Consequences of Occupation

Although an examination of the relationship between Hungary and Germany during the Occupation is beyond the scope of this book, it is pertinent to outline the effects of this relationship on Hungarian Jewry. The Occupation can be delineated into three distinct phases: 19 March to 7 July, when Horthy banned further deportation of Jews; 8 July to 15 October, when Horthy's attempted armistice with the USSR led to his downfall; and the Szalasi era, 16 October to (effectively) the liberation of Buda in mid-February 1945 by the Red Army of Marshal Rodion Malinovsky.

The first phase, from 19 March to 7 July, is notable for encompassing the peak of German power in Hungary, a period in which Germany was, in effect, largely unchallenged as the paramount determinant of the nation's affairs. Negotiations with the Allies ceased; Hungarian independence — especially in foreign policy and Jewish affairs — was virtually abandoned; Horthy withdrew almost entirely from politics and public life; and, immediately after the Occupation, the Kallay government was replaced by a Quisling regime led by the pro-Nazi Dome Sztojay (originally Sztojakovics: born 1883; executed as a war criminal in Budapest, 1946), Hungary's military attache in Germany (1927–33) and thence envoy to Berlin (1935–44).[23] Although omitting Szalasi and the Arrow Cross at Horthy's insistence, Sztojay's cabinet, composed of non-*Nyilas* radical Rightists, governed in the interests of the Reich, particularly with respect to the implementation of the *Endlösung*. Accepting the ideology of *Magyar-Nemet sorskozosseg* (the Hungarian-German common destiny — see Chapter II), in a very real sense the Sztojay regime's exuberant collaboration and reign of terror pre-empted the need for substantial German interference in Hungarian affairs. In his memoirs, former Prime Minister Miklos Kallay characterised his successor's career thus: "Sztojay was heart and soul with the Germans; it used to be said that he, not the German minister, represented Germany's case in Hungary."[24] In particular, with regard to the "Jewish Question", the appointment of the fervently Antisemitic Andor Jaross as Minister of the Interior — that is, the minister most responsible for the Jewish community[25] — and the equally Antisemetic Laszlo Baky and Laszlo Endre as his two Secretaries of State,[26] provided the Germans with a degree of institutional collaboration probably unequalled by a nominally independent power during the Holocaust.[27] With only token exceptions, the Hungarian bureaucracy and *Csendorseg*[28] (gendarmerie) collaborated with the SS to instigate a Nazi-modelled *Endlösung* with a fervour the Germans described as "Asiatic brutality".[29] According to Eichmann, his close friend Laszlo Endre "wanted to eat the Jews with paprika".[30]

On 29 March Jews were physically marked, being compelled by law to attach permanently a ten-centimetre yellow Star of David onto their outer garments.[31] Following their economic expropriation and loss of civil liberties, in mid-April provincial Jews began to be physically segregated by being herded into regional ghettos, such establishments typically being located in brick factories, distilleries or sugar refineries; that is, close to railway sidings and in facilities destructive of health and hygiene. Generally existing from three to seven weeks, these regional ghettos were physically isolated from both Budapest and their neighbouring ghettos, existed in a political vacuum bereft of independent intelligence, and were thus totally dominated by Germany's much practised, highly refined and tragically effective disinformation campaign and manipulation process. These regional ghettos were also used as torture chambers, the gendarmerie subjecting inmates to horrendous beatings as a means of thieving the Jews' remaining valuables.[32]

Mass deportation of Hungarian Jews was organised on the basis of the nation's ten gendarmerie districts, commenced on 15 May 1944 with the Jews of District VIII in the north-east, and continued with each individual district being evacuated in turn.[33] After their extreme physical and psychological brutalisation, it is little wonder that ghetto inhabitants were not unwilling to board the cattle wagons transporting them to what they thought and hoped was "resettlement in the East". The circumstance of German Occupation; fulsome Hungarian collaboration; the Jews' total physical, social and political isolation; the ghettos' impoverishment, and the inhabitants' physical and psychological degradation; the Jewish men of military age being in the Jewish Labour Service; the short time available to organise a survival network; and, possibly most importantly, the lack of an indigenous resistance movement; all these factors combined to preclude the possibility of physical resistance in the regional ghettos.

Through his intimate relationship with Hitler, Sztojay knew from the autumn of 1942 that the Final Solution involved extermination in the East.[34] It is thus especially relevant to note that, when planning the deportations, although the Germans originally suggested two trains per day to Auschwitz, the Hungarians requested six. The negotiations compromised on a figure of four, each train eventually transporting up to 3,000 deportees for several days under appalling conditions. Thus, at its height, the *Endlösung* was consigning some 10–12,000 Jews per day to

Auschwitz.[35] In a period of seven weeks — 15 May to 7 July — some 450,000 Jews residing in Hungarian territory were deported to the infamous death camp.[36]

To maintain the apparent legitimacy of its puppet regime, the Germans' "restricted Occupation" policy retained the facade of Hungarian independence. This was designed to not only soothe the nation's notoriously chauvinistic sensibilities but also, more importantly, to minimise the prospect of disrupting Hungary's increasingly important contribution to the Reich's war effort. As such, the Germans consigned the notion of anointing Szalasi and a *Nyilas* regime to an option of last resort and preserved Horthy as Head of State. By retaining his position and maintaining the established forms of government, Horthy — the embodiment of historic Hungary — in effect assured the success of the Nazi plan. Quite simply, Horthy's official presence legitimised the invasion by conferring upon the Sztojay regime the aura of constitutional continuity.

By the time of the Occupation, there was some doubt as to the state of the Regent's mental faculties. According to one of Veesenmayer's first reports as Plenipotentiary, Horthy, who was seventy-six years of age, "repeats himself constantly, often contradicts himself within a few sentences, and sometimes does not know how to continue".[37] Notwithstanding this assessment, and despite German intimidation and his relative isolation, except for his October 15 debacle Horthy was to display considerable cunning in safeguarding his position and outmanoeuvring German and domestic opponents in his ultimate phase as Head of State, 7 July–15 October.

As a conscious act, during the first phase of the Occupation (19 March–6 July) the Regent adopted a low profile, largely withdrawing from active involvement in public affairs.[38] Thus it was that on 29 March — a date of critical importance regarding the smooth implementation of the *Endlösung* — Sztojay announced to the Council of Ministers (the Cabinet) that "His Excellency the Regent has given full discretion to the Government under his guidance with regard to all anti-Jewish decrees, nor does he wish to exert any influence in this respect."[39] By presenting Sztojay's Quisling regime with this *carte blanche*, Horthy, in effect, consigned Hungarian Jewry to the whims of the *SS* and their fanatical Hungarian collaborators. Although continuing to countersign the government's edicts, Horthy was able to maintain his Pontius Pilate posture regarding the "Jewish Question", measures against the Jews being implemented by ministerial decree and thus, constitutionally, not requiring the Regent's signature.[40]

It is beyond the scope of this work to investigate why Horthy withdrew from the activist national role he had forged for himself over the decades since the White Terror of 1919–20. Whether caused by German intimidation, psychological trauma, creeping senility, Kallay's advice to refrain from participating in matters of state,[41] or a combination of these and other factors, Horthy's abandonment of Hungarian Jewry after the Occupation — their time of greatest need — was the prime catalyst facilitating the destruction of the nation's provincial Jews. This is, of course, not quite the equivalent of indicting Horthy for being an agent of that destruction. However, having noted this aspect of his career, it is equally appropriate to note that, as shall be seen, the Regent's return to the national stage, and his dismantling of the *Endlösung* machinery, was the lifeline by which Budapest Jews managed to survive Nazi and *Nyilas* machinations until his tragic debacle of 15 October.

As with his withdrawal, Horthy's re-emergence into political activity was similarly the product of sundry influences. With regard to the *Endlösung*, the Regent's banning of further deportations seems to have crystallised as a result of appeals by local and foreign dignitaries, particularly the former PM Istvan Bethlen, Pope Pius XII (25 June), President Roosevelt (26 June),[42] and King Gustav V of Sweden (30 June); his disdain for the Nazis and their "uncivilised" Antisemitism; the Allies' massive 700-plane bombing raid on Budapest (2 July);[43] the successful Allied landing in Normandy (6 June); the severely faltering prospects of a German victory; the additional revelations — via the Auschwitz Protocols[44] — regarding the real nature of the *Endlösung*; the fact that Hungary had become free of the mainly "ethnic" Orthodox *Ostjuden* concentrated in the provinces, a group for whom the Regent felt nothing short of contempt; and, possibly decisively, the attempted *coup d'etat* of 6 July by the National Socialist Party stalwart and Head of the Gendarmerie, Laszlo Baky.[45] It should be noted that Horthy displayed considerable proficiency in pre-empting the action of the gendarmes that Baky had massed in Budapest, utilising loyal army officers such as Generals Karoly Lazar and Geza Lakatos to reinforce his orders and neutralise Baky's influence.[46]

The Regent originally indicated his intention to ban further deportations at the Crown Council meeting of 26 June. On 4 July, at a two-hour session with Veesenmayer, Horthy not only argued for restoration of national sovereignty via the Gestapo's removal from Hungary, but also expressed strong dissatisfaction with Sztojay, Baky and Endre.[47] The Regent's decision to prohibit further deportations was publicly proclaimed on 7 July. Despite Eichmann's fury at this interference in his domain, with the exception of several thousand additional Jews in effect smuggled out of the country (see below), this crisis in German-Hungarian relations was resolved by a humiliating German acceptance of Horthy's authority. Not content with this renewed show of strength, the Regent now abandoned the role of passive figurehead and continued to reinforce his position by once more participating actively in the affairs of state.

Enraged by this defiance, on 17 July Hitler instructed Veesenmayer (via von Ribbentrop) to insist on the deportation of Budapest Jews and to warn that dismissal of the Sztojay government would be a treasonable act leading to the Reich's forceful involvement in Hungary's affairs, an involvement that could not guarantee Horthy's personal situation.[48] Despite this attempt at personal and political intimidation, Horthy refused to submit regarding the "Jewish Question". After dismissing Baky and Endre — whom he called "filthy sadists"[49] — in early July, in early August he dismissed their equally extreme Minister, Andor Jaross. And notwithstanding another personal *Note* from Hitler (21 August) which explicitly warned against reconstructing the Hungarian government, the very next day Horthy responded by advising the Germans that any attempt to deport Budapest's Jews would be resisted, by arms if necessary.[50] To add injury to insult, emboldened by Roumania's smooth *volte-face* on 23 August, the Regent dismissed Sztojay and six days later commissioned his loyal officer General Geza Lakatos (former commander of the First Hungarian Army) to form a new administration. Lakatos' brief was simple, straightforward, and impossible to implement without enraging the Germans, viz: to restore Hungarian sovereignty; to cease persecution of the Jews; and to extricate Hungary from the War.[51] That night Himmler acquiesced in the cessation of further Jewish deportations;[52] the next day Eichmann and his *Sonderkommando* left Hungary.

Needless to say, during the life of the Lakatos government the situation of the surviving Jewish remnant — now, with the exception of the JLS, overwhelmingly located in Budapest — improved dramatically. Of particular significance, neutral legations, especially the Swiss and the Swedish, were permitted to issue protective documents (*Schutzpässe*) which granted a legally dubious — though initially effective — protection to the recipients (see below). Once again Hungary commenced secret negotiations with the Allies, an armistice mission leaving for Moscow at the end of September. German intelligence, aware of these discussions, planned political and military precautions (Operation *Panzerfaust*). Upon Horthy proclaiming his well-intentioned but ill-prepared and ill-timed armistice in a state broadcast on 15 October,[53] *SS* Colonel Otto Skorzeny — famous through liberating Mussolini after the Italian dictator's capture by partisans — kidnapped Horthy's sole surviving son (Miklos Jr), rolled him in a carpet, and dispatched him on a freight train to Berlin. Deserted by the bulk of his officers — an act of treason to the *Legfelsobb Hadur* (Supreme War Lord) unparalleled in Hungarian history[54] — and unable to rouse popular support, Horthy's immediate, inevitable resignation enabled the Germans to implement their option of last resort, the elevation to power of the *Nyilas* leader, Ferenc Szalasi.[55]

During Szalasi's fiercely pro-Nazi regime, the Jews of Budapest were subject to a hitherto unprecedented burst of systematic discrimination and indiscriminate terror. Eichmann returned (18 October); two ghettos were instituted (the "International Ghetto" for *Schutzpass* holders and the "Common Ghetto" for the rest); the infamous Death Marches to Austria commenced; and in the final, terrifying, chaotic two months of German Occupation, roaming bands of bloodthirsty *Nyilas* brigands slaughtered 10–15,000 Budapest Jews[56] — at random and in cold blood. The balance of this volume will focus on the period of German Occupation, its main concern being an examination of the dilemmas and options confronting Hungarian Jewry, and an analysis of the manner in which the leadership and certain pivotal individuals responded to these unprecedented challenges.

The Jewish Council

Of all the controversies embroiling Hungarian Jewry, none is argued with greater passion than the issue of Jewish leaders during the Holocaust — particularly the leadership (or lack thereof) of the Nazi-appointed Jewish Council (*Zsido Tanacs*; *Judenrat*). Opinions encompass an extreme spectrum, the nadir exemplified by Nicholas Nagy-Talavera's vituperative judgement, viz:

> The Jewish leadership failed utterly... The Jewish leaders of Budapest especially feared the consequences of jeopardizing their own privileged position. It was a repulsive sight to see those collaborating creatures running about their headquarters, wearing their yellow badges, and threatening their fellow Jews with the Gestapo in case of disobedience. S Stern...was the worst of the collaborators, but not the only one by far. Their work contributed greatly to the efficiency of the Final Solution just a few weeks before liberation... The Jewish Council went to the extreme in collaboration...the groveling, cringing, self-seeking Jewish leaders of Budapest...[57]

The majority of commentators adopt a centrist, less judgemental position, their generally bi-polar assessment condemning the Jewish Council (henceforth JC) for excessive reliance on passive legalities as their defence mechanism, but simultaneously acknowledging — unlike the above school of thought — the supremacy of pro-Nazi forces seeking the community's destruction.[58] That minority of commentators who appraise the JC in a non-negative manner emphasise Hungarian Jewry's predetermined, inexorable situation consequent upon the realities of the Occupation, and the impossible nature of the tasks confronting Jewish leaders. Bela Vago exemplifies this school of thought when he writes:

> ...the majority of the Jews in Hungary perished not because of the weakness or the faults of the Jewish leadership... There is no evidence that the absence of a more adequate leadership, or that collaboration and treason in Hungary contributed to the dimensions of the catastrophe... It was not the leadership that shaped Jewish reality, but the other way round.[59]

Instituted by the Germans on 21 March, the *Magyar Zsidok Kozponti Tanacsa* (Central Council of Hungarian Jews, the JC) consisted of eight prominent community leaders who, collectively, comprised a rough cross-section of Hungarian Jewry, viz: Samu Stern (President), Drs Erno Peto, Erno Boda and Karoly Wilhelm — Pest Neolog representatives; Samu Kahan-Frankl and Fulop Freudiger — Pest Orthodox; Dr Nison Kahan — Zionist; and Dr Samu Csobadi — Buda Neolog.[60] Although the two Orthodox leaders represented the denomination whose greatest numbers resided in the provinces, no specific provincial Jewish leader was appointed; the regions were to have their own *Judenräte* even though the Budapest JC's jurisdiction covered the whole of Hungary's Jews.

The most important initial factor impinging on the JC, and one that is frequently — if not invariably — overlooked by its trenchant critics, is that the realities of the invasion, at the proverbial "one fell swoop", left Hungarian Jewry politically isolated and physically bereft. The Kallay government resigned and some of its members, along with other anti-Nazi elements, were arrested; strict censorship was introduced; the *SS* arrested over 3,000 Jewish hostages and banned Jews from travelling;[61] and, upon enquiring at the relevant ministries, the Jewish Council was informed that the community would have to submit to German orders.[62] At their first formal meeting with Jewish leaders — an assembly of 200 delegates on 21 March at 12 Sip Street, Neolog national headquarters[63] — the Germans pointedly confirmed their de facto hegemony, Eichmann's deputy Hermann Krumey stating that henceforth the Germans "would decide on Jewish matters" and emphasising that Jews "were forbidden to accept directions from others; contact with Hungarian authorities had to go through them..."[64] Although acting so as to dispel panic — in particular, by promising that religious and communal life would continue unhindered and that there would be no deportations — the Germans reinforced their authority by threatening to execute those disobeying orders and "promoting sabotage".[65]

Ergo, with the removal of the Horthyist factor from the political equation, and on the basis of explicit instructions from both the Hungarian authorities and the Germans' universally acknowledged apparatus of ruthless terror, it is patently clear that Hungarian Jewry's carefully nurtured defence mechanisms and survival networks — networks and mechanisms that had proven their worth over several generations — were smashed and rendered useless. In particular, the appointment of known, dedicated Antisemites (Jaross, Endre and Baky — see above) to command of the Interior Ministry eliminated the JC's access to the highest level of the government apparatus most critical to the survival of Hungarian Jews.[66]

Quite simply, in keeping with the well-established, oft-practised and highly successful Nazi formula, during the initial phase of the Occupation Hungarian Jewry was politically isolated, physically marked, impoverished and brutalised; and, as a corollary, the JC was encumbered with a thoroughly entrapped, demoralised mass constituency. Like Hungary's subdued Left, prior to 19 March 1944 the Jewish leadership (with overwhelming communal support) had shunned illegal, underground or anti-government activity as counterproductive, and potentially disastrous for the community; every Jew consciously avoided giving credence to "The Jews are traitors" catchcry. Devoid of allies, understandably lacking experience in resistance, and with the impossibility of organising mass flight, the JC was faced with terrible problems, insurmountable in the short term. In his postwar testimony Samu Stern characterised the JC's position as "utterly helpless",[67] a description entirely appropriate in the first months of the German Occupation.

Yet even during the period of German hegemony, the JC made distinct — albeit of necessity selective and often only marginally productive — attempts to frustrate Nazi policy. Following the Germans' approval of a few travel documents, the JC, despite explicit prohibition, took advantage of the chaos following the Occupation and issued many hundreds if not thousands of unauthorised — and hence illegal — travel permits, such papers permitting a not inconsequential number of provincial Jews to reach the relative safety of Budapest.[68] Furthermore, Christian sympathisers and young Zionist volunteers were utilised as illegal couriers to convey funds and information to the provinces and, in turn, to obtain intelligence regarding provincial conditions.[69]

The progressive emergence of Hungarian officialdom from its political hibernation — a hibernation interrupted by the need to prevent Germany continuing to monopolise the expropriation of Jewish assets — saw the development of two increasingly distinct and divergent Antisemitic power bases, the Hungarians and the Germans gradually becoming embroiled in a progressively intensifying rivalry over the confiscation of Jewish assets. Taking advantage of this situation, from 20 May two executives of the JC, Captain Miksa Domonkos and Dr Janos Gabor,[70] proceeded to submit weekly reports to the Ministry of Commerce regarding German demands on the Council — despite explicit orders from the *SS* prohibiting, on pain of death, the disclosure of such intelligence. In detailed submissions, Domonkos listed requisitions fulfilled and those subverted. Even though German demands expropriated immense Jewish wealth, Domonkos' reports clearly indicate that his courage — which, evidently, is a feat of passive resistance and fiscal subversion, if not sabotage — saved Jewish assets of enormous value.[71] In a very real sense, this stratagem helped intensify contention between the Antisemitic rivals; and, as will be seen, this antagonism generated a commensurate increase in the JC's degree of manoeuvrability, thereby contributing to the Council's increasing freedom of action.

The Quisling regime's initial major formal attempt to redress Germany's dominance over the "Jewish Question" in Hungary was incorporated in their 19 April reconstruction of the JC. Although infuriating Eichmann at this trespass into his formerly exclusive domain, the restructuring was justified on the basis of restoring Hungarian sovereignty, and providing constitutional legality to the solution of the "Jewish Question" in Hungary. This action also abolished all Jewish organisations with a non-religious function and transferred their responsibilities to the JC, that body henceforth taking orders from both the *SS* and Hungarian authorities. Forming what is sometimes called the Second *Zsido Tanacs*, the terms of reference of this body are considered by Jeno Levai to have been drafted by Zoltan Bosnyak, prominent pro-Nazi publicist, and Rabbi Bela Berend, formerly an obscure, provincial Neolog Rabbi whom Bosnyak successfully nominated to membership of this second Council.[72]

Formally appointed by Laszlo Endre, joint Secretary of State at the Interior Ministry, and first meeting on 15 May — the day mass deportations to Auschwitz commenced — the new JC consisted of Samu Stern (president), Dr Erno Peto, Dr Karoly Wilhelm, Fulop Freudiger, Samu Kahan-Frankl, and new members Rabbi Bela Berend, Dr Sandor Torok (representing Christian Jews[73]), Dr Jozsef Nagy and Dr Janos Gabor. Berend's appointment by Endre was a result of the Rabbi's idiosyncratic and not infrequent contact with Hungarian Antisemitic circles. Beyond doubt, Berend was the pro-*Nyilas* authorities' monitor on the Council, a hoped-for source of intelligence regarding German instructions and the JC's response thereto. Rabbi Berend's endeavours merit consideration below; however, suffice it to say (for the moment) that his appointment was a highly disruptive influence on the restructured Council. Reviled and ostracised by his fellow Councillors as a *Nyilas* agent, Berend's appointment caused the JC to, in effect, cease functioning as an integrated executive body, most decisions henceforth being taken at informal gatherings which deliberately excluded Berend."[74] In particular, as the JC disintegrated, an unofficial "Presidential Council" of Stern, Peto and Wilhelm assumed primacy within the official Jewish leadership. Despite this substantial restructuring — a situation reinforced by the necessity of formulating swift responses to frequent emergencies — it should be noted that each of these leaders held frequent (albeit informal) *ad hoc* discussions amongst themselves and with other of their JC colleagues.[75]

The JC has been severely lambasted for sundry aspects of its behaviour, a criticism often based on impressions, rumours, and *post facto* judgements rather than detailed, dispassionate analysis. General allegations, for example by John S. Conway, that the JC was the Gestapo's critical instrument in targeting Jews for deportation, cannot withstand scrutiny.[76] Through what can be reasonably interpreted as a lack of information and/or understanding, critics such as Hannah Arendt fail to realise that Hungary's abiding system of mandatory religious affiliation, when reinforced by the three Jewish Laws, ensured that from birth to death virtually every contact Jews had with government and statutory authorities involved a declaration of religion.[77] Consequently all municipal and military authorities, hospitals, schools and educational institutions, professional associations, police stations etc, and particularly the Interior Ministry, had detailed information on Jews falling within their jurisdiction. Furthermore, the Germans had more than sufficient spies and collaborators, especially in the bureaucracy, to remain independent of the JC in matters pertaining to Jewish demography and registration. *Ergo*, there was a multiplicity of means and sources by which the *SS* could have obtained (and in fact did obtain) authentic, comprehensive registers of Jews without having to rely on the JC.

One specific bitter criticism related to the registration question concerns the Council's involvement in summoning several categories of Jews (mainly journalists and lawyers) to report to the *SS*, such involvement being deemed by many critics as acts of collaboration. The facts, however, contradict such allegations. It is clear from discussions with credible, authoritative eyewitnesses (Drs Elizabeth Eppler and Gyorgy Gergely) that Jews thus summonsed were selected by the Germans and not the JC. The evidence is clear that over a period the *SS* provided the Council's Liaison Office with six lists, a total of some 700 Jews required to report for internment at 26 Rokk-Szilard Street, formerly the Neolog Theological Seminary.[78] Gyorgy Gergely, whom Berend accused of providing Eichmann with lists of people to be deported, stated that the inclusion of deceased people, and the frequency of misspelled names, proves that such registers were provided by *Nyilas* informants and not Jewish — or official Hungarian — sources.[79]

Considering the circumstances, Samu Stern's postwar testimony gives a not unreasonable defence of the *Zsido Tanacs*' involvement in this list controversy.[80] After accepting that many Jews would accuse the JC of collaboration, Stern concluded that a refusal to "act as a postman" for the *SS* would have changed nothing.[81] In this assertion Stern is demonstrably correct. In view of German dominance, the unquestioned obedience of the police and gendarmerie, and the effusive nature of Hungarian collaboration — particularly within the Interior Ministry — Eichmann would have had little difficulty rounding up the relatively small number (700) targeted in this *Aktion*. Refusal by the JC "to act as a postman" would have resulted in, at best, a temporary impediment to Eichmann's strategy. Conversely, with little doubt, it would have exposed the JC — if not the Germans' 3,000-plus Jewish hostages and/or the community as a whole — to the *SS*' well-known penchant for brutal retribution.

In contrast to critics, the testimony of an eyewitness, Dr Elizabeth Eppler, indicates that the handling of the "list issue" may, if anything, bestow merit rather than huge detriment upon the JC's reputation. According to Eppler, her colleague Dr Janos Gabor, a fellow member of the JC's Liaison Office with the *SS*,[82] returned from Eichmann's office "white as a sheet", announced that he had been given a list containing the names of some sixty Budapest lawyers, and stated that the JC was ordered to inform such individuals that they had been summonsed by the Germans to appear at Rokk-Szilard Street.[83] Utilising the JC's courier system — young boys (14–18), some with bicycles, who ran errands and conveyed messages — there was an immediate, deliberate attempt by the Liaison Office to alert people on the list, the messengers warning each person contacted to disappear prior to their receipt of an official summons. Eppler herself went to warn three listed friends: one declared that his Order of Maria Theresa award provided him with immunity and "kicked her out"; another took a small case, reported to the lunatic asylum and gained admittance;[84] the third also heeded her advice and survived. Eppler states that, according to her knowledge, many lawyers accepted the Warning, made alternative arrangements and so increased their chances of survival.

This attempt to sabotage the German action resulted from a consensus amongst the four pro-active (as opposed to reactive) members of the JC's Liaison Office — Drs Eppler, Gabor, Gergely and Laszlo Peto — all of whom were young university graduates.[85] Eppler characterises their relationship thus: "There was complete co-operation and communication between us. We acted in unison." The warning scheme collapsed due to the intervention of Dr Zoltan Kohn, acting Executive

Secretary of the JC, who warned that such behaviour exposed the entire Council to SS reprisals.[86]

Samu Stern, in his postwar testimony, confirms the import of Eppler's narrative, using this episode to defend the Council against charges of collaboration. After noting that the JC was presented with a list of those to be summonsed,[87] Stern continued:

> We had to cope with a difficult dilemma... If we refused to carry out the order, the unexpected rapes [ie: arrests] would continue as before, Jews being carried off without the least preparation. If we forwarded the call-ups, one would have a fixed day for reporting to Rokk-Szilard camp and time to run away or go into hiding. But even those not so minded at least would have an opportunity to procure some equipment, likely to render their bad situation more tolerable. A previous notice [ie: prior warning] may even enable some to get into some clinic or obtain a certificate from some medical officer. Thus we had no doubts whatever that we had to accept the criticism of our brethren about our part as postmen, had to hand over the summons to report, and had to do this for the benefit of our brethren. The wording was to the effect that the summons was based on higher order and included the objects to be taken along. Thus everybody knew what it was all about, could make up his mind about what to do: disappear or report.[88]

Stern concluded his narrative of this episode by noting that, whilst many listed Jews did not present themselves as ordered, the overwhelming majority unfortunately obeyed the summons.

Allied to the list controversy, but generating far greater intensity and passion, is the generally harsh, unrelenting criticism directed at the JC for its alleged role in what Braham terms the "Lulling of the Jewish Masses".[89] Critics accuse the Jewish leadership of awareness of the *Endlösung* elsewhere in the Nazi domain, yet of failing to inform the community as to the fate of their co-religionists in neighbouring countries;[90] of totally neglecting to devise safeguards or contingency plans in the event of a German Occupation; of maintaining the delusion that Hungarian Jewry, whilst enduring expropriation and suffering, would survive because of its "special category" status; of defending the community by continuing to issue obviously ineffective pleas appealing to legal precepts and human decency — that is, of defending Jews with a wall of paper; and, by following German orders, of acquiescing in the *Endlösung* process and hence being an agent in the destruction of Hungarian Jewry. An analysis of this criticism is necessary for the development of a comprehensive perspective, such perspective in turn generating an objective assessment of the JC, its personnel and policies.

Firstly, there is no question that Hungarian Jewish leaders had a more than passing knowledge of German policies and tactics well before 19 March 1944. Samu Stern's testimony states that prior to the invasion:

> ...I knew the [SS] activities to be a long, long sequel [ie: sequence] of murders and robberies... I had heard enough about the methods of the Gestapo's ill-famed Jewish department to know that they always shunned sensation, disliked creating panic and fear, worked noiselessly, coolly and in deepest secrecy, so that the listless, ignorant victims be without an inkling of what is ahead of them even whilst the wagon is travelling with them towards death. I knew their habits, deeds and terrific renommee [ie: reputation]...[91]

It appears that Neolog leaders had concrete evidence about the *Endlösung* some two years before the German Occupation. Elizabeth Eppler recalls that in early April 1942 two young escapees from Polish ghettos visited her father Sandor, then Secretary-General of the Pest Neolog Community, and described in detail Nazi policies vis-à-vis the brutalisation and subsequent mass extermination of Polish Jews. In response, Sandor Eppler invited the top echelon of the Budapest Neolog leadership to hear these eyewitness reports. Held at the Eppler home on the third day of *Pesach* (mid-April 1942), attendance at this secret meeting included, amongst others, Stern, Wilhelm, Peto and Ribary (Director of OMZSA). Elizabeth Eppler relates that all of the attendees, except possibly Stern, were "dumbstruck" at the refugees' news and that "no one believed it with the exception of my father and possibly Stern".[92]

The Orthodox leadership also received one of its earliest — if not its first — piece of information from Polish sources. Arthur Stern relates that his father Leo (born in Poland, no relation to Samu), a leader of the Orthodox community,[93] invited Orthodox (generally including Fulop Freudiger) and Zionist (sometimes including Rezso Kasztner) leaders to Sunday luncheon at his home.[94] Occasionally refugees from various countries, especially Poland, would be invited to provide direct eyewitness testimony as to the Jewish situation in their nation of origin. In particular Arthur, who regularly attended these gatherings, states that at least eighteen months before the Occupation he — and consequently the Orthodox and Zionist leadership — knew about the deportations from Warsaw and the gas chamber exterminations at Treblinka.[95] Additionally, information accrued through international Jewish contacts — particularly Bratislava, Poland, Geneva, Istanbul and Palestine (frequently via Istanbul) — and via the Zionists' remarkable nexus with the Hungarian branch of German military counterintelligence, the *Abwehr*. Consequently, Freudiger's claim in November 1972 that "by the time we learned the truth about Auschwitz, the first phase of the deportations, involving some 310,000 Jews, was already over",[96] can be dismissed as either the deceit of memory or, more probably, a self-serving obfuscation regarding his pre-Occupation knowledge of the *Endlösung*.

Although not a defence of the Budapest *Judenrat*, it should be noted that Jewish leaders in other countries also had prior warning regarding German intentions vis-à-vis the "Jewish Question". In France, for example, leaders of the UGIF (*Union Generale des Israelites de France*), although unaware of Auschwitz, knew about mass deportations and exterminations in eastern Europe and did not inform their Jewish constituents. Jacques Adler, a member of the Jewish Communist underground in France, comments: "The UGIF chose a policy designed to placate public fears and to ensure that the Jewish population did not resort to extreme responses; the UGIF leaders deliberately chose a policy of silence."[97]

Although no direct comparison should be made between Hungary and France — for one, Kallay was no Petain — doubtless the necessity of avoiding the creation of mass panic also guided Stern and his colleagues.[98] More importantly, the hierarchical nature of the Hungarian Jewish community — a reasonable though far from exact reflection of the wider social structure — and the long, honourable tradition of *noblesse oblige* which guided that community's leadership, ensured that a nurturing but decidedly paternalist administrative culture developed (see Chapter I) and then prevailed (see Chapters II and III) within the ranks of Hungarian Jewry's official leaderships. Arguably, this unconditional acceptance of full responsibility for the welfare of their constituency (see below) was one of the factors motivating Stern and his colleagues to maintain silence about Germany's nefarious activities elsewhere in Europe. A corollary of this argument has also found support, in particular by the Hungarian survivor-historian Dr Ilona Benoschofsky. This school of thought attempts to explain the JC's reticence by speculating that in a situation of doom, one precluding mass escape or resistance, it was humane to spare the victims the agony and desperation generated by knowledge of their ultimate destination and destiny.[99] Unfortunately, such sensitivity for the victims' emotional state in effect complied with German policy, which also attempted to keep knowledge of the *Endlösung* a deathly secret. *Ergo*, accusations against the JC of acquiescence and collaboration.

Another, and substantially more powerful, reason for the Jewish leadership's silence — and one seemingly unappreciated by critics of the JC[100] — was the sheer impossibility of Jews mounting an awareness campaign about the Reich's *Endlösung* without generating a firestorm of *Nyilas* and German vituperation and calumny against Hungarian Jewry, such Judeophobia doubtless stereotyping Jews for their traitorous propaganda, defeatist conspiracies and "stab in the back" philosophy. Clearly, an *Endlösung* awareness campaign — in effect aimed against Hungary's partner in the life-and-death crusade against what was universally perceived as rampant, aggressive, Judaic-influenced international Communism — may have generated unforeseen and, at worst, possibly catastrophic consequences. One inevitable result, however, would have been a massive boost to the already strong German pressure on Hungary. Quite conceivably this new, heightened antagonism would have destabilised Kallay's ministry, forced Horthy to seek a new, invariably more pro-Reich PM, and — possibly — precipitated a *Nyilas* and/ or German takeover of the country. Considering the circumstances and without the benefit of hindsight, few reasonable people could have justified the destabilisation of the most powerful non-Nazi force in the country (see Chapters II and III) in exchange for the uncertain but possibly disastrous consequences of a campaign outlining the *Endlösung*. Moreover, by proclaiming the death penalty for those "who spoke of deportation",[101] after 19 March 1944 the Germans effectively precluded the possibility of an official campaign exposing the realities behind "resettlement in the East".

It should be recognised, however, that classified information regarding German atrocities in eastern Europe, particularly with respect to the treatment of Jews, was filtering through to the community with some consistency. Sources of such information included eyewitness reports from survivors of the Kamenets–Podolsk (August 1941) and Delvidek (January 1942) massacres (see Chapter II), refugees (particularly from Poland), members of the JLS and the *Honvedseg* on leave from the Eastern Front, and broadcasts from the BBC, the Voice of America and Moscow's Radio Kossuth.[102] Notwithstanding this consistency, and although tens of thousands of Jews must have been exposed to some of these narratives, atrocity testimonies were almost invariably discounted or dismissed as either Allied propaganda, the products of vivid imaginations,[103] or else, whilst pertinent to Poland's *Ostjuden*, not relevant to a Hungary where Jews had been residing for over a millennium. Even those few accepting the truth of such narratives generally concluded that Hungary, an independent partner in the Axis alliance, could not be compared with defeated and occupied Poland, an enemy Slav nation traditionally treated by the Germans with derision and contempt.

In association with these factors, it is important to recognise that people — individually or collectively, in leadership positions or private life — will generally avoid facing facts which expose them to massive destabilisation. This, which might be termed the Moratorium on Reality Syndrome, incorporates the individual and collective phenomena of psychological dissimulation, repression and denial of evidence. Barbara Tuchman gives several catastrophic examples of the collective aspect of this principle in practice.[104] The French General Staff before 1914 maintained inappropriate military strategies despite obtaining authentic documents indicating German invasion plans. The Russians ignored their masterful double-agent in Tokyo, Richard Sorge, when he forwarded the exact date of the forthcoming German invasion. Tuchman comments: "...his warning was ignored because the Russians' very fear of this event caused them not to believe it. It was filed under 'doubtful and misleading information.'" The same syndrome caused Washington to ignore reports regarding the true situation in postwar China, America's consequent alliance with Chiang Kai-shek exacerbating the Cold War and freezing US-China relations for over a generation.

Regarding individual Moratoria on Reality, the French Holocaust survivor, Michel Mazor, relates a conversation he held with a Professor of History during the great deportation wave from Warsaw in August 1942. Both individuals knew with "absolute certainty" about deportation and Treblinka "but the professor refused to accept undeniable facts and talked instead about the numerous examples in world history of collective anxiety psychoses afflicting groups of people facing non-existent dangers."[105] As Jonathan Steinberg has stated: "Holocaust records show that Jews themselves often refused to believe what was happening in spite of the evidence of their own eyes."[106]

Tuchman's analysis supports the view of Yehuda Bauer, who distinguishes between the different levels of consciousness, and hence the disparate type of response, generated by "information" and "knowledge". In discussing this dichotomy during the Holocaust, Bauer states that knowledge of the *Endlösung* was attained by a multifaceted process, the initial phase of which involved the dissemination of information. Only after a transitional conditioning period, during which evidence was integrated into the individual and collective consciousness of potential victims (ie: information was comprehended and thus transformed into knowledge), could an objective course of action be considered and implemented.[107] Although not stated as such by its author, Bauer's theory implies a mechanism inhibiting the speed and intensity of such transformation.[108] This inhibiting function — which I term the Moratorium on Reality Syndrome (MoRS) — is doubtless generated by a complex socio-psychological amalgam of dissimulation, repression and denial, the syndrome in turn preventing the acceptance, assimilation, objective interpretation, and utilisation of evidence.[109] Clearly, two of the major factors generating MoRS in potential victims are terror and high uncertainty, the resulting all-pervasive bewilderment and dread often producing a paralysis of thought, will and action.[110]

When the above factors were combined with the necessity of conceiving the inconceivable (the Final Solution) and believing the unbelievable (Auschwitz),[111] it is little wonder that the substantial number — albeit minority — of Hungarian Jews exposed to evidence of the Final Solution rejected the information's implication of a collective death sentence on themselves, their family, friends and community.[112] Especially when that sentence was passed by a power whose defeat was conceded to be inevitable and reasonably imminent. Tragically, Moratorium on Reality is evident even *in extremis*. Asher (Istvan) Aranyi, a leader of the *Habonim* branch of the *Halutz* (young Zionist Pioneer) movement, relates that one night in mid-1944 he and some colleagues came upon a stationary deportation train near the Hungarian border. As the Hungarian guards and their German cohorts were carousing nearby, many in a drunken state, leaving the train unguarded, the *Halutzim* seized the opportunity and opened several wagons. Notwithstanding their suffering in the ghettos, the wagons and at the hands of the gendarmes, and despite the *Halutzim* offering them money, false papers and assistance, not one deportee took the opportunity to escape.[113]

To summarise the multifactorial, multifunctional, potentially devastating phenomenon discussed above: the Moratorium on Reality Syndrome appears to be a widespread, if not universal, social vector; is generated by factors such as terror and high uncertainty; operates on an individual and collective level; encompasses a complex socio-psychological amalgam of dissimulation, repression and denial; obstructs the acceptance, integration, objective interpretation and utilisation of evidence (ie: inhibits the transformation of information into knowledge — Bauer's Theory); and, ultimately, subverts rational thought and action with an all-pervasive disorientation, bewilderment and dread. Notwithstanding the tenuous nature of existing circumstance, in its ultimate phase the Moratorium on Reality Syndrome generally produces either a widespread paralysis of spirit and/or a rigid reinforcement of the status quo.

Many critics accuse the JC of "lulling the masses" by conveying German instructions to the community, the admittedly unwilling conveyancing of such orders in the official JC journal still, according to such critics, constituting acts of collaboration. This argument is patently specious. As previously outlined, during the first phase of Occupation — the period of German hegemony — the JC was trapped, defenceless, totally devoid of allies, and utterly helpless. Unable to resist Eichmann's demands without exposing itself, thousands of Jewish hostages and possibly the community as a whole to the certainty of a probably ferocious German retribution, it is clear that the JC succumbed to the same devastating power that had overwhelmed most of Europe. Transparently, publication of German instructions to the community constitute neither co-operation nor collaboration but an act of surrender.

Surrender to invincible force is not a dishonourable estate but a universally accepted and legitimate means of attempting to prevent further, possibly greater, tragedy. Additionally, and critically, a survey of the JC's widely distributed publication, the Nazi-authorised and censored *A Magyar Zsidok Lapja* (The Hungarian Jewish Journal — henceforth HJJ) reveals the hitherto unrecognised subversion of German intentions. From its very first issue of 23 March 1944, the HJJ stated that its function was to "promptly and accurately inform Hungarian Jews about official instructions and orders issued by the authorities". In other words it immediately, clearly and unequivocally warned readers that it was a mouthpiece of the Nazis and their Hungarian collaborators and not a gazette of independent opinion, impartial interpretation or objective advice.

In unmistakable confirmation of its tragic function, in early April the JC circulated to the heads of all major Jewish communities a communique that included the following declaration: "We draw your attention to the fact that the Central Council of Hungarian Jews of Budapest [the JC] implements the instructions received from the higher authorities and that the members of the Council are personally responsible for their immediate and thorough implementation under pain of drastic consequences."[114] Furthermore, on 6 April the HJJ published on page one a manifesto which, whilst calling for obedience, proclaimed starkly: "Each and every member of the Central Council [the JC] is responsible with his life for the exact implementation of [the authorities'] instructions... Consequently, the Central Council is not an authority but only the implementing organ of the authorities."[115]

Given the circumstances, the above extracts constitute nothing if not an astonishingly frank admission that the JC and its members were, in effect, hostages of the Nazis, lacked any semblance of independence, and had no alternative but to act as helpless pawns, and a conduit for the authorities' machinations: a declaration that precludes any possible interpretation but that the JC's instructions to the community would emanate from the Nazi invaders and their Hungarian collaborators, would be in the Judeophobic interest, and should be treated with all caution and scepticism.

Randolph Braham assesses the HJJ's 6 April manifesto as an appeal "designed at once to reassure the Jews and cajole them into submission".[116] Whilst a cursory reading might justify this assessment, Professor Braham fails to explain how a reasonable reading of a manifesto containing the above extract could sustain his interpretation. On the contrary, despite the HJJ's pro-forma pleas for calm and obedience,[117] one cannot construe the above excerpts as providing other than a distinct, unequivocal warning regarding the source of the pronouncements and instructions emanating from a totally subservient JC. Equally, one can discount the point of view expressed by Asher Cohen who, whilst discussing the situation of provincial Jews, states that "they could not imagine that the Jewish press was being censored, and at times its contents even dictated by the Gestapo."[118]

One cannot but conclude that the JC deliberately and audaciously exceeded its extremely circumscribed authority in attempting to forewarn the community and place individual Jews on guard. Furthermore, it should be noted that this forewarning appears never to have been rescinded. Hence, if the JC is to be condemned for attempting to lull the masses via the *SS*-imposed HJJ, at the very least it should be commended for several conscious, courageous and resourceful attempts — albeit unsuccessful — to enlighten its constituents as to the *real-politik* of their situation.[119] Although appearing in hindsight as distinct and unequivocal, tragically, the JC's warnings were neutralised by the turmoil of the times, and overwhelmed by the criminal alliance between effusive Hungarian collaboration and Eichmann's devastatingly proficient stratagem.

Regarding criticism that Hungarian Jewish leaders were totally deficient in neglecting to devise safeguards or contingency plans in the event of a German Occupation, the same critique can, with equal if not greater validity, be made of Hungary as a whole. After the *Anschluss* of March 1938 (see Chapter II), the nation avoided *in toto* any rational debate or analysis regarding the repercussions of a common frontier with the Reich, much less the potential geopolitical and military consequences of Nazi expansionism. As previously discussed, Hungary became engulfed by the German-orchestrated "Spirit of the Times", this maelstrom magnifying the nation's pre-existing fervour towards a rampant, chauvinistic Magyarorszag. The Moratorium on Reality Syndrome was alive and well and thriving throughout rump-Hungary. Hungarian Jews, whose destiny was intimately entwined with their country of birth, were trapped. Unable to emigrate, abandoned by the West, enveloped by a society in which large, growing and influential sections considered the Reich with conspicuous favour, the Jewish leadership's sole viable lifeline to the future was its nexus with the Horthy–Kallay group, the strongest non-Nazi force in the country.

Critics are particularly insistent in condemning Jewish leaders, pre and post-19 March 1944, for failing to undertake precautionary measures against possible catastrophe at the hands of the Nazis.[120] Unfortunately, such critics fail to specify just what viable, meaningful, non-counterproductive options were available to Jewish leaders. In April–May 1939 the Neolog leadership, via their emissaries Stern and Eppler, attempted to abandon the Hungarian community's historic isolation and develop contacts with international Jewry (see Chapter II). As previously discussed, through no fault of Hungary's Jewish leaders, such contacts were only productive in the field of social welfare. Subsequent to this lack of wider success, do critics seriously suggest that Stern and his colleagues should have abandoned their nexus with Horthy in favour of an alliance with the marginal, powerless, splintered forces of the Hungarian Left? Or independently purchased arms, trained self-defence militias, established bunkers, and fomented insurrection; or printed millions of fake Aryan papers;[121] or committed suicide, as per Adam Czerniakow, head of the Warsaw *Judenrat*? Significantly, no critic has yet attempted to analyse the prospect of organising security for those Jews in greatest danger of deportation — the hundreds of thousands of unassimilated, "ethnic", Orthodox *Ostjuden* in the provinces, a group characterised by their distinct visibility, insularity, political apathy, rigid way of life, and "otherworldliness".

In actual fact, Jewish leaders accepted the challenge of safeguarding their constituents via the only viable, non-counterproductive options available for *mass* survival, viz: the reinforcement of their de facto alliance with Horthy and his followers, and the instigation and development of an intense, comprehensive, and unified welfare programme. Overcoming abiding and seemingly intractable intra-communal rivalries and hostilities, the resultant OMZSA organisation (see Chapter III), provided — via an impressively organised, all-embracing, nation-wide infra-structure — genuine, meaningful and consistent support mechanisms for many tens of thousands of needy Jewish families, in both peace and war. Importantly, such services were freely provided to the some 15,000 Jewish refugees residing in Hungary.[122] What other viable, meaningful, non-threatening options were available to Jewish leaders? Critics are conspicuously silent on this pivotal question.

Immediately after the 28 March meeting at 12 Sip Street between Hungarian Jewish leaders and the *SS*, Fulop Freudiger, head of Budapest's Orthodox Community, confided to his Nagyvarad counterpart, Alexander Leitner:

> I do not believe that we shall suffer the same fate that befell the Polish Jews. We shall have to give up our wealth, we must be prepared for many sorrows and deprivations, but I am not worried for our lives. Finally, even this war will end and we will start there, as in the year 1919.[123]

With little doubt, Freudiger's belief in the community's physical survival was generated by his largely understandable but — with the benefit of hindsight — tragically misplaced confidence in the constant flow of albeit generally accurate intelligence provided by the non-Zionist, ultra-Orthodox Rabbi Dov (Michael) Weissmandl, joint leader of the Bratislava *Pracovna Skupina*.[124] Known popularly as the Working Group (henceforth WG), this underground rescue organisation developed from the *Ustredna Zidov* (the official *Judenrat* established by the Slovak parliament in September 1940) and encompassed wide elements of Slovakian Jewry.[125] Negotiations between the WG and *SS* representative Dieter Wisliceny were apparently initiated by the former,[126] commenced in mid-1942 — that is, shortly after the advent of mass deportation of Slovakian Jews — and resulted in the eventual formulation of the Europa Plan, a scheme whereby the deportation of European Jews would be halted upon the *SS* receiving payment of two million US dollars.[127]

Bargaining between the WG and Wisliceny for the saving of Jewish lives continued from mid-1942 until September 1943. After 19 March 1944 these negotiations were, in effect, transferred to Hungary and continued under the auspices of Wisliceny's superior, Adolf Eichmann. Though hardly recognised as such, it was this continuation that produced the well-known and thoroughly documented sagas involving the Hungarian Zionist leaders Joel Brand and Rezso Kasztner.[128] On this basis it is difficult to refute that the Brand Mission and its political satellite, the Kasztner Transport, were descended from a Slovakian Jewish initiative instigated some two years prior to Eichmann's infamous "Blood for Trucks" ransom offer to Joel Brand.

For a matrix of somewhat uncertain reasons, the mass deportation of Slovakian Jews ceased for almost two years — from late October 1942 until 30 September 1944.[129] With little doubt, amongst the amalgam of important factors generating this cessation were appeals from local clergy and the Vatican;[130] the bribing of local authorities (especially Dr Anton Vasek, head of Department XIV in the Interior Ministry[131]); the establishment of Jewish work camps in Slovakia;[132] support from the Ministers of Education, Justice and Finance;[133] and, possibly crucially, the request by Slovakian officials to visit deportees who had been "resettled in the East".[134] Rozett states that it is not possible to determine the importance of negotiations and payments to Wisliceny in the halting of deportations from Slovakia to Auschwitz. With the benefit of hindsight, and by extrapolating from our knowledge of the Holocaust elsewhere in the Nazi domain, it is difficult to place much credence on the lowly *Haupsturmführer* (Captain) Wisliceny playing a pivotal role in the cessation. In all probability, he acted as a long-range intermediary or minor catalyst for his ultimate superior, *Reichsführer-SS* Heinrich Himmler[135] who, in a signed memorandum dated December 1942 stated: "I have asked the *Führer* about the absolving [*Loslösung*] of Jews against hard currency. He has authorised me to approve such cases, provided they bring in genuinely substantial sums from abroad."[136] On this basis, there may have been genuine prospects of mutual utility in the WG–Wisliceny negotiations. At all events, it is clear that key figures in the WG, including Weissmandl and his distant relative, Gisi Fleischmann, "believed in the possibilities of buying Jewish lives and that Wisliceny could be trusted. In letters that followed, into 1944, they continued to evince this belief."[137]

It is apparent from Freudiger's post-19 March behaviour that he also subscribed to these attitudes. His opinion was reinforced on 21 March when he successfully intervened with Wisliceny to secure the release of his older brother, Samuel, a hostage in the Gestapo prison at 26 Rokk-Szilard Street.[138] Moreover, at a private meeting towards the end of March, Wisliceny presented Freudiger and Nison Kahan (Zionist member of the JC) with a letter in Hebrew from Weissmandl which strongly recommended continuing negotiations for the saving of Jewish lives, via the Europa Plan, with Wisliceny, "who could be trusted".[139] The 1 October 1944 testimony of Freudiger and two other Hungarian Orthodox leaders, written after their successful escape to Roumania on 10 August, summarised Weissmandl's recommendations thus:

> The person with whom the negotiations were to be conducted was named and precise instructions were given as to the lines which these discussions were to take. Furthermore, indications were given regarding the financial arrangements and the form they were to take. The information received stated that everything had been settled with the person in question, Baron von [sic] Wisliceny, and that the basis for the realization of these plans had been laid... Information received from Weissmandel confirmed that by making a payment of two million dollars the Hungarian Jews could in all probability be saved.[140]

It is pertinent to note that Freudiger studied at the Bratislava *Yeshiva* and, being the son-in-law of that city's Orthodox Chief Rabbi, over the years he naturally acquired numerous relatives, friends and contacts in that country. Freudiger summarised his attitude to Slovakian Jewry thus: "Many of the [Slovakian] leaders were my personal acquaintances, and, accordingly, they made special claims to my helping them, which I did, whenever and as much as I could."[141]

The extent of Weissmandl and the WG's influence on Hungarian Jewish leaders — largely via Freudiger — is attested by the fact that, despite growing financial difficulties, by mid-April the JC "unofficially collected" and paid the Germans $224,000 — $200,000 to the *SS* and $24,000 as "commission" to the *Abwehr*.[142] Thus was the WG's misconception regarding Captain Wisliceny's power and *bona fides*, and the influence of relatively paltry bribes in preventing deportations, transferred to Hungary and hence tragically compounded.[143] Freudiger's continuing faith in Wisliceny is confirmed by the fact that on several occasions he presented the *SS* Captain with boxes of sweets containing his family jewellery as well as the more usual sort of bonbons. Finally bereft of jewels, on two subsequent occasions Freudiger gave Wisliceny 50,000 *pengos* in cash.[144]

Ergo, it must be recognised that the JC's belief in the "special category" status of its constituency was a bi-polar phenomenon generated by the community's traditional particularities — its ancient history, manifold contributions to Hungary, special relationship with the Magyar establishment etc (see previous chapters) — and a hitherto unacknowledged factor: the fervent advice and apparently extended contemporary success of Slovakian Jewish leaders in halting the expulsion of their community. An apparent success that, it must be emphasised, commenced in October 1942 and continued for six months after the German Occupation of Hungary. Furthermore, with the end of hostilities clearly in sight, enveloping such considerations was Eichmann's cunning, highly practised, universally proficient and apparently reasonable disinformation campaign.[145] With Eichmann, as with Lucifer in Milton's *Paradise Lost*:

But all was false and hollow, though his tongue
Dropp'd manna, and could make the worse appear
The better reason, to perplex and dash
Maturest counsels...[146]

Until the commencement of mass deportations on 15 May, the JC was hopeful that a combination of Hungarian Jewry's "special category status", negotiations with the Germans,[147] and the severe shortage of railway capacity[148] would avert mass expulsion. Even after 15 May Eichmann and his henchmen kept repeating that if Jewish leaders behaved sensibly, arrangements would be concluded in Germany to ensure that deportees remained unharmed.[149] Considering these factors, it is little wonder that, for several months after the invasion, Freudiger and his co-leaders retained their faith in the physical survival of the community. Only with the benefit of hindsight can this attitude be rejected unequivocally by the postwar armchair theorist.

Accusations against the JC of defending its constituents with a wall of paper — that is, of deliberately basing its defence strategy on futile appeals to legal precepts and human decency — have little merit or validity. As previously discussed, during the first phase of the German Occupation the JC's freedom of manoeuvre was extremely limited. One of the very few non-counterproductive options available to Jewish leaders was the issuing of appeals to Hungarian society and government. The war was in its final stages, Germany faced certain defeat, and Allied retribution, now with a distinct War Crimes component, was assured.[150] In the absence of realistic meaningful alternatives, the issuing of appeals to the authorities, and to pragmatic elements of society mindful of the near future, was a natural and logical initiative;[151] albeit one that enthusiastic Hungarian collaboration and the Moratorium on Reality Syndrome ensured remained tragically ineffective during the first phase of the Occupation. However, it should be noted that the JC's barrage of pleas, complaints, and attempts to enlighten non-Nazi opinion as to horrendous Jewish suffering in Hungary were forwarded to the neutrals and, hence, passed on to the Allies.[152] Although the reasons are multifaceted and subject to conjecture, it is an objective fact that both Allied and Neutral powers subsequently applied significant and ever-mounting pressure on Horthy to intervene in the *Endlösung*. On this basis the JC's wall of paper may well have been a not inconsequential factor in Horthy's emergence from his largely self-imposed political hibernation,[153] in his reacceptance of the authority inherent in his position and, consequently, in the eventual neutralisation of Adolf Eichmann and his machinations. Certainly the JC's repeated entreaties, intelligence and pressure were of consequence in the institution by the neutrals of the famous *Schutzpass* (protective document — see below) system.[154]

Considering the above factors, it is clear that, prior to Horthy's re-emergence from the political shadows, the JC had the will but not the power or meaningful opportunity to oppose the *Endlösung*. From 7 July — that is, during the second phase of the Occupation — despite continual difficulties, the JC seized the opportunity created by Horthy's re-emergence to reconstitute and then reinforce its de facto alliance with the Regent. A particularly noteworthy example of this alliance in action involved the Kistarcsa internment camp. Containing hostage, arrested and non-citizen Jews, the Kistarcsa detention centre, located some twenty-five kilometres north-east of Budapest was — with considerable paradox — commanded by a humane police officer, Istvan Vasdenyei.[155] On 12 July Vasdenyei notified a representative of the Jewish welfare organisation MIPI that, despite Horthy's cessation order, an *SS*-planned deportation of 1,500 Budapest Jews was imminent — 1,000 from Kistarcsa and 500 from 26 Rokk-Szilard Street.[156] On being informed, the JC immediately alerted not only the Regent but also Jusztinian Cardinal Seredi (Catholic Primate of Hungary), Vilmos Apor (Bishop of Gyor), Monsignor Angelo Rotta (the Papal Nuncio) and those neutral powers still retaining representatives in Budapest.[157] Defending his previous order banning deportations and/or influenced by the "massive intervention"[158] generated by the JC's pre-emptive publicity, on 14 July Horthy ordered his Interior Minister, the pro-Nazi Andor Jaross, to abort the deportation. As a result, gendarmerie Captain Leo Lullay intercepted the deportation train at Hatvan (some fifty kilometres north-east of Budapest) and ordered its driver back to Kistarcsa — an occurrence unique in the history of the Holocaust.[159] Upon receiving news of their successful intervention, "great exultation prevailed at the council" at the rescue of 1,500 Jews from deportation.[160]

Furious at this crucial blow to his authority engineered by the JC, Eichmann decided to refine his original plan. Ordering the entire Council to report to his headquarters (the Majestic Hotel in the Svabhegy district of Buda) at 8 am on 19 July, the JC was, in effect, held prisoner by *Hauptsturmführer-SS* Otto Hunsche, and only released at 8 pm that evening when a newly organised deportation from Kistarcsa was beyond the Hungarian border.[161] The JC, neutralised by being kept incommunicado, was unable to repeat its previously successful, legally based strategy, which had halted Eichmann's *aktion*. Unlike the initial attempt, the second *aktion* succeeded, being implemented without opposition by *Hauptsturmführer-SS* Franz Novak, Eichmann's transportation specialist.[162] The Hungarian regime, shaken by international reaction, protested strongly to Germany about this infringement upon its sovereignty, declared that the deportation occurred without its approval, and stated that in future the "Jewish Question" in Hungary would become the sole prerogative of the Hungarian government.[163] Notwithstanding these edicts, on 24 July a contingent of 1,500 prisoners was — with similar illegality — deported from the Sarvar internment camp.[164]

Despite these successful (in effect) kidnappings of Jewish prisoners, the reaction generated by the JC's persistent and skilful interventions managed to preclude further German-organised mass expulsions.[165] Denied support from the Hungarian apparatus of state — particularly the some 20,000 gendarmes[166] — Eichmann was rendered largely helpless, henceforth being limited to organising small-scale deportations commensurate with his limited independent capacity (a mere 200 *SS* personnel) to physically arrest, detain and transport Jews.[167]

Thwarting the original Kistarcsa *aktion* was far from an isolated example of the JC's successful disruption of the *Endlösung* process during the Occupation's second phase (8 July–15 October). In mid-August, upon the Germans concentrating troops and armour in Budapest's environs, *Alezredes* (Lieutenant-Colonel) Laszlo Ferenczy — gendarmerie officer in charge of provincial deportations, and a political chameleon *par excellence*[168] — discussed with the JC high command Eichmann's strongly rumoured plan to recommence deportations on 26 August.[169] Pressured by Stern, Ferenczy — possibly seeking protection from postwar retribution and/or attempting to ingratiate himself with the increasingly ascendant JC–Horthy alliance — agreed to prevent this endeavour provided the Council secured him an audience with Horthy,[170] the purpose of which was to determine the military resources available for any attempted counteraction. At the audience Horthy endorsed a highly secret, sophisticated disinformation strategy, devised by Ferenczy and the JC's Presidential Council (Stern, Peto and Wilhelm), in which the Hungarians would feign co-operation with the *SS*, recommission the Bekasmegyer detention centre, and transfer gendarmes, (loyal) Hungarian troops and railway rolling stock to Budapest. Then, as the *coup de grâce*, the Regent would intervene to reconfirm his prohibition on further deportations.[171]

To augment the anti-Nazi alliance, additionally and of its own volition the JC introduced Ferenczy to leaders of prominent leftist groups, who also pledged to oppose Eichmann's plan.[172] On this basis, the *Alezredes* informed the *Obersturmbannführer-SS* that any attempt to reinstitute deportations would be countered by force. To reinforce the pressure on the Germans, and to pre-empt any last-minute wavering by Horthy and Ferenczy, the Council successfully influenced the neutral legations (led by the Vatican diplomat, Papal Nuncio Angelo Rotta) to hold a convocation and pass a joint resolution protesting strongly to the Regent against the Germans' intended *aktion*.[173] With Horthy — as previously agreed — then banning the planned deportation, Eichmann, once again outmanoeuvred and humiliated by a JC-organised coalition, sought advice from Berlin. On 24 August Himmler, taking cognisance of, *inter alia*, the profoundly altered Hungarian political vista, issued instructions to abandon further deportations.[174]

In marked contrast to communal perception, by this stage the JC's authority had grown to such an extent that there was substantial Jewish input into the official Hungarian *Note* submitted in late August to the German plenipotentiary, *SS* General Edmund Veesenmayer. Outlining Hungary's radically revised attitude to the "Jewish Question", the *Note* consisted of five major points — including prohibition of further deportations, *SS* withdrawal from Hungary, and surrender of all Jewish assets confiscated by the Germans.[175] Indicating the then intensity of the JC–Horthy alliance, on 31 August the Zionist chief Otto Komoly noted in his diary that, during discussions at JC headquarters regarding Stern's consultation with the Regent, "...Stern reported that at yesterday's audience the Governor assured him of his greatest goodwill. He [Horthy] would do everything on behalf of the Jews."[176]

It should be emphasised that the Presidential Council's (henceforth PC) strategy to rescue Budapest's Jews involved not inconsiderable risks to the JC and its reputation. As Stern writes in his testimony:

> Around the Capital the rolling stock required [for the deportation] assembles, Wisliczeny's [sic] detachment arrives also, and the much-feared "cock hats", the gendarmes, too, turn up in Budapest's streets... Jewry is horribly upset, fear and despair have overwhelmed it. We [the JC] are being attacked, accused of impotence, and we must keep our mouths shut even towards our own brethren, for we are aware of being surrounded by informers...[177]

In an attempt to pre-empt another successful Council intervention, on 17 August Eichmann paid the PC triumvirate (including the then bedridden Stern) the unmistakable tribute of arresting them and their families. This pre-emptive arrest clearly indicated the *SS* leader's apprehension at the JC's willingness and ability to successfully block his *aktions*. Unfortunately, Freudiger's sudden escape to Roumania on 9 August and these arrests — events Budapest's Jews understandably interpreted as the certain precursor to a general deportation — further lowered the JC's reputation within the Jewish community.

Released next day on Horthy's order,[178] the final obstacle to success of the JC-engineered anti-expulsion strategy was the prospect of the Jewish community becoming enveloped in a possible military confrontation between German and Hungarian forces. Stern assessed this risk thus: "It may come to a clash, when unavoidable [sic]; but it was believed utterly unlikely that for the Jewish question the Germans would risk a breach [with their Hungarian allies]."[179] In this assessment the JC was spectacularly vindicated, even to the then hardly foreseeable extent of *Reichsführer-SS* Himmler ignominiously withdrawing Eichmann from Hungary. For the remaining Jews of Hungary (now overwhelmingly concentrated in Budapest), the prospect of physical survival — "The Race Against Time" — once again appeared favourable.

Notwithstanding this successful co-operation between the JC and the gendarme commander, the Council — unlike the highly respected Zionist chief, Otto Komoly — retained a healthy scepticism regarding Ferenczy and his motives,[180] a suspicion amply justified by events during the Szalasi era. As a consequence of this, the JC's attitude remained as per mid-July, when Ferenczy informed the Council that the authorities had granted permission for some 2,600 Jews to emigrate to Palestine and, as a preliminary procedure, such people would be relocated into special houses. Because of their suspicions the JC decided to obstruct the relocations until, finally unable to resist further pressure, the Council allocated some dwellings for this purpose. These buildings came to form the basis of the International Ghetto,[181] the residential prerogative of those eventual 30,000 Jews holding a *Schutzpass*, a protective document of dubious legality either issued by a neutral power or forged by the *Halutzim* (see below).

In their defensive measures, the Council also successfully utilised the commonly accepted element of Nazi ideology which claimed that the Allies were fighting the War on behalf of the Jews. By convincing the authorities that creation of a ghetto in Budapest would permit the Allies to bomb the rest of the metropolis with impunity,[182] the creation of a dangerous concentration of Jews in the city was delayed for some five months, until the Szalasi junta's inescapable order of late November.

Notwithstanding Horthy dismissing Sztojay and commissioning his trusted former commander of the First Hungarian Army, the non-Nazi General Geza Lakatos, as PM (29 August); and notwithstanding the Jewish Council regaining access to the Home Secretary and Interior Minister, the JC maintained a judicious suspicion of *SS* intentions and played a pivotal role in obstructing the Germans' agreement with the Lakatos government for the concentration of Budapest Jews in provincial camps. In a secret private meeting with the Regent in mid-September, Samu Stern convinced Horthy of the proposed camps' vulnerability to German bombing, and the prospect of more Kistarcsa-type kidnappings from such isolated locations. Swayed by Stern's cogent argument, Horthy reaffirmed — and maintained until his capitulation (15 October) — his commitment that further deportations were prohibited. Additionally, the Regent promised that, contrary to the Lakatos–German agreement, Budapest's Jews would remain in the capital.[183] Once again, Stern and the JC had utilised their nexus with Horthy, and on this occasion also with the Red Cross,[184] to successfully pre-empt German machinations.

The final major venture at resistance by Stern's *Zsido Tanacs* involved its association with the Independence Front, the Horthy regime's feeble, incompetent and poorly organised attempt to extricate Hungary from the Axis alliance.[185] Not only did the JC contribute 100,000 *pengos* to this enterprise, but Samu Stern authorised secret negotiations between Dr Gyorgy Gergely (a senior executive of the JC) and General Karoly Lazar (trusted commander of Horthy's palace guard) regarding the arming of 25,000 JLS members stationed in the vicinity of Budapest. Through no fault of the JC, this plan — a remarkable attempt at Jewish armed resistance unique in the history of the Holocaust — collapsed with Horthy's debacle of 15 October (see Chapter V).

After the German-inspired, organised and conducted coup, the Jewish Council — now headed by Lajos Stockler[186] — not only lost Horthy's patronage but, simultaneously, was confronted by Szalasi's fervently pro-Nazi *Nyilas* junta. Again menaced by Eichmann, its painfully reconstructed defence network again smashed, the JC was once more involuntarily relegated to its role in the first phase of the Occupation: the issuing of largely ineffectual pleas for justice and humanity and the amelioration of its constituents' increasingly desperate circumstances.[187] This third phase of Occupation witnessed a marked fragmentation and diminution of the JC's authority, its leadership and power largely devolving to the official Zionists (particularly Otto Komoly), the underground *Halutzim*, and an assortment of mainly neutral, non-belligerent, non-threatened, international organisations henceforth increasingly involved with protecting the Jews of Budapest. Such organisations — many of whose personnel, unlike the Jewish leaders, were protected by diplomatic immunity — included the neutral legations (especially the Swiss, via Charles Lutz, and the Swedish, via Raoul Wallenberg), the International Committee of the Red Cross (ICRC) and the Papal Nunciature (via the Nuncio, Angelo Rotta).

Szalasi's reign of terror as Hungary's *Führer* — during which possibly 100,000 Jews lost their lives[188] — provided a distinct contrast to the carefully structured, highly systematic persecution prevalent in the first phase of German Occupation. During the *Nyilas* junta's brief, tumultuous tenure, initiative for Judeophobia — apart from the notorious Foot Marches to Austria — devolved throughout the pro-Nazi hierarchy. Often individuals and small groups of armed, bloodthirsty Antisemites took brutal summary action, such brigands neither seeking approval nor fearing government retribution for their atrocities.[189] Yet even in this chaotic phase the JC, now markedly diminished in authority, continued its attempts at social amelioration and resistance. In particular, it established public kitchens that fed many thousands[190] and, through the falsification of Ferenczy's signature, "warded off many dangers".[191] Furthermore, it was the Council's incessant demands and warnings to Pal Szalay, Police Chief of Budapest, that obtained a police guard for the Common Ghetto. With great paradox, the *Nyilas* regime's police were largely responsible for inhibiting further *Nyilas* raids on, and the pillage and massacres of, the ghetto's defenceless inhabitants.[192]

Assessment of the Jewish Council

As previously discussed, assessments regarding the JC encompass a widely divergent spectrum of opinion. The nadir of such judgements, which may be termed the Diatribe School of thought, characterise the Council as a group of servile, cringing collaborationists whose obsessive grovelling and fixation on self-preservation ensured the success of the Final Solution when Germany was on the verge of defeat. Possibly the most succinct formal rebuttal of such appraisal was provided in 1945 by the Budapest Bar Association's little-noted investigation of the three lawyer members of the JC, Messrs Boda, Peto and Wilhelm. Lasting several days and conducted in a period when memories were fresh and witnesses plentiful, the Bar Association (*Ugyvedi Kamara*) not only unanimously acquitted all three of collaboration indictments but also concluded that they had done all they could to help the Jews under the given circumstances.[193] Moreover, in 1945–46 Budapest Police Headquarters seriously considered indicting the JC for collaboration, and collected evidence and testimony for this purpose.[194] It should be noted that, despite numerous war crime trials in this era, with the notable exception of Rabbi Bela Berend — who was indicted, sentenced to ten years' imprisonment, and then acquitted on appeal (see below) — no official charges were ever laid against the JC or any of its members.[195] Considering the available evidence, the Bar Association's verdict and the police decision to forgo indictments, one can readily dismiss the Diatribe School's opinion of the JC.

The majority point of view, which may be termed the "More in Sorrow than in Anger" school of thought, argues that the JC was a body dominated by elderly, frightened, conservative, upper-*bourgeois* men of limited vision who, despite basically good intent, proved tragically ineffective when confronted with their admittedly Herculean tasks. Again, on the evidence, one is compelled to reject such an overall simplistic evaluation. When the period of German Occupation is divided into its three distinct phases — an important division either overlooked or ignored by critics — at best this opinion can only apply to the first and third phases.

Regarding the initial phase, as is evident from the available evidence, the politically isolated JC possessed the will but neither the influence, allies, manoeuvrability nor opportunity to oppose the *Endlösung* in any meaningful manner. In marked contrast, during the second phase Eichmann was neutralised due to the enterprise, initiative and authority of the JC–Horthy alliance, the latter quality supplied by the Regent but the two former attributes provided largely by the Council. In particular, the alliance's enterprise from July to the advent of Szalasi was an integral factor in Himmler banning further deportations from Hungary. In this period the Council's record, whilst indicating some failure (see below), also reveals more than a modicum of courage, dedication, vision, political skill and success — on occasion to a very high order. Furthermore, despite *Nyilas* brigands murdering many thousands of Budapest Jews after the *putsch* of 15 October (in largely uncoordinated acts of brutality), and despite some notorious footmarches to the Austrian frontier,[196] for a variety of reasons — including the cumulative efforts of the JC throughout the whole of 1944 — the third phase of Occupation (the Szalasi era) did not include the systematic mass extermination of Jews. Quite simply, upon liberation, Budapest's 120,000 remaining Jews was the greatest concentration of Jewish survivors from any city formerly under direct Nazi control.[197]

At the non-negative, largely non-judgemental end of the spectrum is that minority of commentators who form what may be termed the Determinist School, a group emphasising Hungarian Jewry's predetermined destiny consequent upon the remorseless realities of the Occupation, and the impossible nature of the tasks confronting Jewish leaders. The Determinist school of thought rightly recognises that the greatest ability, clearest vision and most inspiring leadership count for naught when confronted with determinants such as overwhelming power; the resources of critical state apparatuses; an overwhelmingly apathetic or hostile non-Jewish populace;[198] political isolation and the paucity of allies; the indifference or, at best, token concern of the Christian clergy;[199] the physical and psychological brutalisation, financial impoverishment and physical isolation of the community; the men of military age — the element critical for physical counteraction — having been conscripted into the JLS; the lack of local armed resistance; and the extremely limited time available to marshal resources and formulate viable alternatives to the Germans' well-honed and highly successful *Endlösung* strategy.[200] Supporting this school of thought is the undeniable fact that despite half a century, and the benefit of considerable hindsight, no critic has yet enunciated a coherent set of viable, meaningful, non-counterproductive policy alternatives available to the JC subsequent to the German invasion. Conversely, one frequent deficiency in the Determinist analysis is the lack of recognition accorded the JC's initiative, courage and enterprise.[201]

Is it then impossible to resolve the controversy regarding the *Zsido Tanacs*? Although differing interpretations of the same facts and actions will remain, a largely compelling yet surprisingly neglected study by Helen Fein facilitates an objective evaluation of the JC. In her investigation — an attempt to determine the reasons for differing survival rates amongst Jews of different nationalities — Fein analysed twenty-two states and regions occupied by and/or allied to the Reich, and concluded: "The principal intervening factor accounting for the extensiveness of Jewish victimisation during the Holocaust was the isolation of the Jews, which was not attributable to German control alone but is best accounted for by state co-operation to segregate Jews that was not checked by native resistance."[202] With specific reference to her detailed statistical analysis of Hungary, Fein concluded that "almost two-thirds of the processing of Jews towards their destruction — definition and stripping — occurred in Hungary prior to the German Occupation of 1944."[203] But again, it is simplistic and highly misleading to base sectional evaluations on Fein's overall national figure. For realistic specific assessments, Hungarian Jewry must be divided into its two great segments, the populace in the provinces and that in the capital. For the former — many of whose Jews were highly visible Orthodox residing in easily isolated small towns or villages — the predetermined prospects of survival were substantially lower than for Jews in Budapest. In the capital the largely assimilated, more affluent, far less visible Budapest Jewish Community resided in a complex metropolis in direct contact with, and under the surveillance of, potential allies such as neutral legations and the Papal Nuncio. Consequently, if the overall level of *Endlösung* processing in Hungary prior to 19 March 1944 was almost two-thirds, one can reasonably assume that, because of the far greater opportunities for survival in the capital (via assuming false identity, living underground, utilising support networks etc), the respective processing figures for Budapest and the provinces would be of the order of 30 percent and 90 percent respectively. When integrated, these percentages produce Fein's resultant average of "almost two-thirds" for Hungary as a whole. This sort of differential is supported by the fact that at the conclusion of hostilities, although 120,000 Jews had survived in Budapest, the provinces were classified as *Judenrein*.[204]

Fein's quantitative study thus confirms the qualitative analysis of the Determinist minority. With Palestine closed to mass immigration, with the Allies in effect apathetic to Jewish torment, and with widespread, exuberant Hungarian collaboration, the vast bulk of Hungary's provincial Jews were doomed from the moment of German Occupation. In conjunction with these determinants totally beyond Jewish control, mandatory affiliation, the three Jewish Laws and a generation of largely unmitigated Antisemitic propaganda had reinforced social differentiation and isolation, prepared the non-Jewish populace for a radical solution of the "Jewish Question", and dangerously pinpointed Hungary's provincial Jews. At the complete mercy of a determined, ruthless and highly experienced predator, the vast majority of these over half-million highly visible, often reviled, politically apathetic, unsophisticated, largely poor or impoverished people could not have been saved except by an Allied destruction of the Auschwitz gas chambers or the systematic bombing of the railways leading thereto. In the circumstances, without resolute and consistent Allied intervention — before or after 19 March 1944 — no Jewish skill, vision, leadership or power on earth could have saved the provincial Jews of Hungary. Considered in context, only a calumny of the highest magnitude could conclude otherwise.

[Due to Germany's continuing military debacles, and due to ever more intense bombardment by partisan action and Allied air forces, there is little doubt that the *Endlösung* in 1944 tied up some amount of the Axis' increasingly scarce railway capacity.[205] Consequently, it is difficult to refute the concept that before and immediately after the Allies' D-Day (6 June) invasion of France, the transportation of hundreds of thousands of Jews across vast tracts of occupied Europe reduced the manoeuvrability and hence the military efficacy of German forces. In particular, mass Jewish deportation from Hungary (15 May to 7 July 1944) encompassed a period when retaining maximum railway capacity for military purposes was essential for Nazi forces — especially as *Wehrmacht* reserves were scattered over a huge area (the Allies' point of invasion was uncertain), and as increasingly significant amounts of war material were being abandoned by the Germans due to insufficient transport capacity. There is also little doubt concerning the Allies' realisation that, without the *Endlösung*, the "Jewish-occupied" railway capacity would revert to the Reich's war effort. Pondering the Allies' considered and adamant refusal to bomb Auschwitz or the railway lines leading thereto — and it should be noted that the Allies not only bombed vast tracts of the Nazi domain,[206] but also bombed Auschwitz, *by accident*[207] — one cannot easily dismiss the argument that the Allied command was placed in a severe dilemma, viz: disruption of the *Endlösung* may indirectly have generated increased Allied casualties via some small improvement in the *Wehrmach's* manoeuvrability, and hence its fighting capability.[208] Although beyond the scope of this book to discuss either this dilemma or the Allies' resolution thereof, a brief analysis in included Chapter VI.]

Because the head of the *Zsido Tanacs*, Samu Stern — eminent businessman, long-term leader of the largest, most prosperous and influential Jewish community in Hungary, Counsellor of the Hungarian Royal Court, and confidant of Admiral Miklos Horthy — had such a critical role in the JC's deliberations, it is appropriate to briefly examine the character, calibre and leadership of this pivotal individual. Braham presents a cogent precis of Stern's personal qualities, viz:

> Stern's generosity, combined with his ability to collect large amounts of money for Jewish causes, earned him universal esteem... He remained conscious of his deep Jewish roots and did everything *legally* possible [Braham's emphasis] to advance the cause and interests of the Jews of Hungary...in many ways Stern showed great

personal courage in dealing with the *Moloch*, and did everything possible to win that which was, to his mind, decisive — the race with time.[209]

In his postwar testimony, Stern presented a compelling justification for accepting — and retaining — leadership of the *Zsido Tanacs*, viz:

> ...a prisoner at the mercy of the jailer is not in a position to object to the cell into which he is thrown... In my eyes, it would have been cowardly, unmanly and unjustifiable, selfish and running away [ie: spineless] on my part to let down my brethren in the Faith in the very instant when they are in the dire necessity to be conducted [ie: provided with leadership], when men having both experience and connection, and ready to [make] sacrifices too, may prove useful to a certain extent.[210]

Stern was to demonstrate the courage of his convictions. Unlike several colleagues on the JC — Samu Kahan-Frankl, who "soon disappeared" and stayed underground until liberation; Dr Nison Kahan, who emigrated to Palestine; and Fulop Freudiger who, with the assistance of his *SS* contact, Captain Dieter Wisliceny, escaped to Roumania[211] — Stern maintained his position for as long as was feasible. Presentation of this comparison does not imply criticism of these three individuals for attempting to save their lives. Rather it should be interpreted as a tribute to Stern's staunch commitment to the responsibilities of command — with little doubt, the zenith of *noblesse oblige* in the long and honourable history of Hungarian Jewish leadership — as well as an acknowledgement of Stern's redoubtable disregard for his private welfare and personal safety, despite being a prime target for *SS* intimidation and arrest.[212] Very importantly, it should be noted that Stern accepted exhausting, crushing responsibilities despite his seventy years of age, continual ill health — a contemporary observer noted: "Stern was permanently coughing, thin as a rake and looked like death warmed up."[213] — and an attempt to retire from his official positions, because of deteriorating health, in late 1940.[214]

Allegations regarding Stern's fixation on self-preservation are easily dismissed. With his wealth and connections, Stern could have left Hungary with his family at any time prior to 19 March 1944. Furthermore, as proven by the Weiss, Chorin[215] and Freudiger families, safe departure for the prominent was also possible after the Occupation. Yet even the most bitter critics of the Jewish leadership in Hungary have never accused Stern of attempting to scuttle and run. Moreover, despite torrential criticism levelled at the JC, there exist very few accusations regarding Stern's involvement in corrupt practices. Possibly the only credible suggestion of Stern utilising his public position to advance his private interest is contained in Otto Komoly's diary. As requested by Stern the previous day, on 6 September Komoly asked Miklos Mester, State Secretary in the Ministry of Education and Religious Affairs, about Stern, Peto and Wilhelm's application for the restoration of their property rights.[216] Whilst a morally dubious request, it should be noted that this episode occurred in phase two of the German Occupation, that is after deportations had been banned by Horthy and pressure on the Jewish community had been substantially reduced. Far from a machination aimed at criminal gain, this was clearly an attempt to restore gainfully obtained assets; moreover, an attempt involving no physical danger or financial detriment to the Jewish community. Considering the Hungarian Jewish leadership's firmly established tradition of *noblesse oblige*, it is quite conceivable that a portion of the income derived from these properties would have been donated to the hard-pressed community, either then or after the cessation of hostilities.

Granting insight into Stern's request is the testimony of his grand-daughter, Mrs Marika Bosnyak, who recently enunciated her grandfather's hitherto unrecognised financial (and social) plight thus:

> The war left Samu impoverished. He had nothing. He lived in one room in distressing circumstances, Mrs Rosi Alpar looking after him in her small flat at 8 Nador Street. All his wealthy friends and acquaintances abandoned him after the War. None came to his assistance. He died in virtual poverty. We emigrated [from Hungary] practically without a penny. On arrival in Australia my mother obtained manual work in a textile factory. So much for Samu Stern's great wealth.[217]

In a lengthy discussion Mrs Bosnyak confirmed the corollary of this narrative: Stern never used his position to smuggle funds out of the country. In an era endemic with corruption, Stern's request to Mester, whilst doubtlessly condemned by some, would, equally doubtlessly, be classified by others — including Mester — as a harmless bagatelle, a trifling manifestation of human weakness understandable in the circumstances.[218]

Of little consequence is the invective mounted against Stern and his Neolog colleagues by, for example, Denis Silagi, a Betar (right-wing Zionist youth) activist. After pronouncing judgement that "not only did [the Neolog] leaders make a mockery out of Judaism by denying its ethnic essence, but the majority of the members were near-nonbelievers, ignorant of the religious traditions as well", Silagi continues by characterising Stern as "indeed the boss, a despot as intractably self-willed as he was conceited, and thirsty for power too...an autocrat [whose] behaviour would have fitted Haman rather than Mordecai...he dictatorially pursued policies aimed at holding back the Jews in the country and thwarting attempts at Jewish emigration."[219]

Neglecting his blanket delegitimisation of the Neolog community, and the canard that Stern was akin to Haman (an infamous ancient enemy of the Jewish people), Silagi is demonstrably incorrect in his wild, unsupported assertions. Far from thwarting Jewish emigration, Stern was paramount in attempting to facilitate its growth. Previous discussion has shown that one of the integral motivations for Stern's historic mission to London and Paris in May 1939 (see Chapter II) — a quest by which Hungarian Jewry's abiding isolation was relinquished — was his concern to assist those overwhelmingly impoverished Hungarian co-religionists who were considering emigration. Furthermore, it was Stern who requested that Hungarian Jewry's potential emigrants be included on the Evian Conference agenda, a plea denied by the chairman of that conference's Inter-governmental Committee on Refugee Resettlement (see Chapter II).

Regarding his alleged despotic lust for power, it is clearly untenable to classify Stern with someone like Chaim Moredechai Rumkowski, the consummately ego-centric, generally reviled and ultimately tragic head of the Lodz (Poland) *Judenrat*, a leader who consciously, despotically and sometimes brutally implemented a policy of "*Arbeit Macht Frei*" ("Work Liberates") in attempting to save his ghetto's inhabitants.[220] Although assertive and resolute, Stern, unlike Rumkowski, never attempted to generate a personality cult about himself. Neither did he utilise his position with the Germans to eliminate ideological, political or bureaucratic rivals.

On the contrary, within the dictates of prudence, continual emergency and the necessity of frustrating informers, Stern delegated authority to, and shared responsibility with, his long-term bitter opponents, the Zionists and the Orthodox.[221] As Asher Cohen states: "a large number of senior Zionist activists worked within the framework of the Judenrat..."[222] Of the JC's members, only Rabbi Bela Berend was ostracised from the centrum — by consensus and for particularly cogent reasons (see below). Far from suffering a despotic yoke via the autocratic imposition of Stern's *Weltanschauung*, during early April the JC engaged in heated debate regarding the appropriate response to German demands and orders.[223] Importantly, upon allegations in August of the JC favouring the affluent and neglecting its poorer constituents, an inquiry panel consisting of Erno Boda and Lajos Stockler, the latter an enemy of Stern, was instituted to examine these accusations.[224]

Notwithstanding Stern's stringent legal orientation in his official duties, and although the JC dismissed extra-legal activity as potentially disastrous for the community,[225] it is false to assume that Stern completely eschewed unofficial or illegal measures. For instance, in March 1944 Rezso Kasztner stated in correspondence with Istanbul that funds to bribe Hungarian border guards, and thus facilitate the entry of Polish Jewish refugees into Hungary, were provided by the "Head of the Neolog Community"[226] — clearly Stern. Subsequently, in keeping with his "Race Against Time" strategy, Stern instituted a policy of judiciously delaying or obstructing fulfilment of the Germans' insatiable demands for *matériel*.[227] It is equally clear that as head of the community, Stern, for highly cogent reasons, refrained from personal involvement with certain unofficial actions — in particular, the attempted arming of the JLS units (see below) — yet his approval, or condoning of such actions, was an essential lubricant facilitating their implementation.

Despite his age, infirmity and adamant predilection for "correct procedure", Stern displayed considerable vision and flexibility in the fulfilment of his official duties. The foresight and social conscience manifest in his prewar mission to London was reinforced by his integral involvement with, and dedicated support for, the great OMZSA welfare programme. Other instances could be cited, for example his courageous welfare-motivated attack on the government — and consequently the pro-German Prime Minister Laszlo Bardossy — at the general assembly of the Budapest Neolog Community in August 1941.[228]

Perhaps the most authoritative non-Jewish Hungarian testament to Stern's foresight, eloquence, courage and *modus operandi* is provided in Prime Minister Miklos Kallay's postwar memoirs. Writing of the tense, confused period immediately prior to the German invasion, Kallay stated that at a private discussion:

> Stern of the Jews declared openly that he had one duty: to draw my attention to the fact that the country, our constitutional existence, our economic and social structure might bear the strain of and survive a German domination, but the Jews would be annihilated to the last man. If I could not prevent that, the great historic responsibility would be mine. If up to then it had been possible to save their lives, to which end the Hungarian Jews had brought unparalleled sacrifices and had borne suffering, to let them down at the last minute would mean the mockery and failure of my entire policy. Any concession could be made to the Germans and they would not reckon that against Hungary or me because I would be acting under duress. But to abandon the Jews would be an irreparable crime that history would never pardon. After saying that, Stern left the room sobbing.[229]

The question thus inevitably arises: what should — or could — the JC have done differently? Despite the nation collectively dismissing the possibility of a German invasion, and even without the benefit of hindsight, it is obvious that Horthy, Kallay and their prominent non-Nazi colleagues should have been kept far more fully informed about the *Endlösung*. Whilst Horthy's coterie doubtless dismissed much of its information about the Jewish situation in Reich-controlled territory as war hysteria or anti-German propaganda, the Jewish leadership's prompt, detailed, and long-term enunciation to the "pragmatic" establishment of Germany's universally applied *Endlösung* policies *may* have resulted in Horthy expediting his ban on deportations. This argument is enhanced by the postwar testimonies of both Veesenmayer and Horthy. At his trial in Nuremberg, Hitler's plenipotentiary claimed that Germany continued to treat Hungary as an ally even after 19 March 1944. Horthy's testimony at the same trial reinforced Veesenmayer's account, the Regent stating that "the Germans only made requests to the Hungarians and did not give them any orders".[230] Accepting these statements *in toto*, one authority argues compellingly that:

> In retrospect, it is truly astounding to realise how much (invariably underutilized) discretionary power and authority over political and military matters was available to Admiral Horthy even in the darkest hours of March, the summer and October of 1944 — yet whatever he did was too little and came too late.[231]

The German acquiescence to Horthy's 7 July ban on further deportations to Auschwitz confirms the crux of this analysis. Still, it is dubious whether the Regent would have acted before the Allies proved D-Day a success by breaking out of the Normandy beach-heads. Certainly there was no great prospect of Horthy acting prior to the Allied invasion of France, especially as "only" provincial Jews were then being deported. Ferenczy confirms the thrust of this argument by testifying that at a private audience in mid-August 1944, the Regent, with his usual "pragmatic Antisemitism" — and despite his by-then acquaintance with the Auschwitz Protocols[232] — declared: "I do not care what happens to the little [ie: provincial] Jews, but I certainly don't want the valuable and wealthy [Budapest] ones to be taken out of the country."[233]

The benefit of hindsight suggests the possibility that judicious, selective implementation of illegal, unofficial and hazardous methods on a micro rather than a macro scale — for instance, the development of bunkers and escaping across borders — *may* have made *some* difference to the survival rate of *certain* sections of provincial Hungarian Jewry.[234] Whilst benefiting a minority in the provinces, the inevitable detection of such endeavours — invariably classified by pro-Nazis as a treasonable Jewish conspiracy — may well have provoked or forced the authorities to institute policies severely counterproductive to the community as a whole. These arguments are, of course, matters of speculation. Beyond doubt, however, is the fact that Stern and his fellow Councillors were political and social conservatives leading a conservative, insular, isolated, deeply divided community suddenly thrust into a maelstrom beyond known historical experience. As Asher Cohen has rightly enunciated with regard to Hungarian Jewry: "No individual, much less an entire community, can be expected to change their life-rooted credos in the space of two or three months."[235] Is it thus appropriate, valid or meaningful to criticise isolated, defenceless people trapped in such remorseless circumstances for displaying what postwar armchair critics — utilising hindsight — might term "conceptual inertia" ?

As has been shown, no *additional* amount of conceptual or ideological flexibility, political acumen, personal integrity or sense of responsibility by the JC could have saved the provincial Jews of Hungary. Considering the Allies' attitude and the other factors discussed above, the *Endlösung* in Hungary could have been prevented only if the non-Jewish population had behaved in a manner akin to the people of Bulgaria, another Axis partner. With the signing of an agreement in February 1943 to deport 40,000 Bulgarian Jews, anti-Nazi forces in that country publicly proclaimed: "Take your stand in front of your Jewish neighbours' homes and don't let them be led away by force. Hide their children and do not hand them over to the executioners! Crowd the Jewish quarters and demonstrate your solidarity with the oppressed Jews."[236] When Bulgarian police attempted to enforce the agreement, the Police Chief reported that throughout the country "...the native Bulgarian population expresses its complete solidarity with Jews and is taking part in their [non-compliance] actions. Every attempt to deport the Jews has met not only with the people's indignation but also with their resistance. We are forced to give up our plan to resettle the Jews in Poland."[237]

Tragically, not only was there no such indigenous support forthcoming for the JC but the Hungarian populace overwhelmingly adopted a diametrically opposite attitude, either approving or, at best, passively witnessing the *Endlösung* process. Although denunciations in the tens of thousands exposed Jews in hiding, as well as those Hungarians suspected of aiding the persecuted, not one single non-Jewish protest was registered with the authorities.[238] As confirmation of the vast difference in national attitudes, the Bulgarian resistance — in marked contrast to Hungary's minuscule anti-Nazi effort — contained an underground of 200,000 which, in turn, supported 20,000 partisans. It is pertinent to note that Bulgarian Jews played such a prominent anti-Nazi role that "in Bulgaria today there is hardly a city without a street named after a Jewish partisan hero who fell fighting the Nazis".[239]

Possibly the most well-informed, non-partisan, credible and highly respected eyewitness regarding the calibre and endeavours of Stern and the Presidential Council of the JC was the Swiss diplomat Carl Lutz. [Arriving in Budapest on 2 January 1942 to represent the UK, the USA and some dozen other countries which had severed relations with Hungary, Lutz (1895–1975), together with Miklos Krausz — representative of the Jewish Agency in Budapest, and a leader of the Mizrachi (religious Zionist) movement — initiated the *Schutzbrief* (collective passport) scheme which later evolved into the famous multinational *Schutzpass* enterprise (see below). Refusing to abandon his responsibilities, Lutz stayed in Budapest for the duration of hostilities and, in 1965, was recognised by Yad Vashem as a "Righteous of the Nations". It is estimated that Carl Lutz's endeavours facilitated the rescue of some 20,000 Jews, possibly the greatest number by a "Righteous Gentile" in the annals of the Holocaust.[240]] In an apparently totally overlooked interview (conducted in Istanbul in mid-April 1945), Lutz was reported thus:

> Three outstanding Jewish leaders, according to Mr Lutz are: Dr Wilhelm President of the Judenrat [sic], Moise [Miklos] Krausz who represents the Zionist and orthodox elements and Samuel Stern, who had for many years been president of the Judenrat. These men represented the Jewish community staunchly and bravely risking their personal safety in the months preceding the Russian siege.[241]

Considering the totality of the above evidence and analysis, one can only concur with Bernard Klein's conviction that the JC "indulged in noble and sometimes heroic deeds in their attempts to save Jewish lives".[242] Furthermore, states Klein, "the *Judenrat* played an important part in whatever resistance Germans encountered in Hungary".[243] Quite simply, Samu Stern and the *Zsido Tanacs* were principal agents in saving the majority of those Hungarian Jews whom it was possible to save.

[The question thus arises: why have an overwhelming percentage of commentators been so negative, if not condemnatory, with regard to the JC? An important part of the answer lies, I believe, in such commentators' understandable fixation on the tidal wave of Jewish blood that engulfed the community's leadership, a tidal wave the JC was unable to stem. Additionally, many of those Hungarian Jewish historians who survived this maelstrom — especially if they lost family members — may have a subconscious psychological need to distance themselves from individuals or institutions appointed by, or associated with, the Nazis.[244] Dispassionate, objective analysis often requires the passing of one or more generation to emerge.

Associated with these considerations is a bandwagon factor impinging upon postwar Jewish analysis. The post-Holocaust era saw the rapid and understandable emergence of a well-nigh Zionist hegemony through great parts of the Jewish world.[245] Consequently assimilationist, Bundist or non-Zionist advocates, leaders and philosophies were exiled "beyond the Pale". Possibly the most noted example of this phenomenon is the tragic case of Dr Marek Edelman, last surviving deputy commander of the Warsaw Ghetto uprising, who is either unknown or a non-person throughout the Jewish world. With little doubt, except for his determined, non-contrite Bundist views, Dr Edelman would occupy a position in the Jewish world akin to what the Japanese term "A Living National Treasure". Largely tarred with the same brush as Edelman, the non-Zionist Hungarian Jewish leaders — albeit leaders of different calibre operating in a different ethos under markedly different parameters to Edelman — have likewise been relegated to historical purgatory and denied the recognition their efforts deserve.[246]]

The Orthodox

Not unexpectedly, enormous amounts of Hungarian records were destroyed in the concluding stages of the War, particularly during the Soviet siege of Budapest (December 1944–February 1945). Included in the destruction were most of the archives of, amongst others, the Demographic Registry Office, the Supreme Council of National Defence, the Ministry of Defence, and the Ministry of Foreign Affairs. Levai comments that "piles of documents were still burning for days during the liberation in front of the palace of the Ministry of the Interior, in the Fort section of Budapest. In the same manner, the other ministries also burned large parts of their archives."[247] The archives of the *Zsido Tanacs* and the Budapest Orthodox Community also failed to survive the conflict. The writer's enquiries with the presidents of both the Neolog and Orthodox communities in Budapest revealed that subsequent to the fall of Hungarian Communism, no significant additional documentation had emerged relating to either group's leadership or activities during the Holocaust epoch.[248]

The historiography of Orthodox endeavours in Hungary during the War has been largely eclipsed by the substantially greater information provided via the far more numerous Neolog and Zionist testimonies, the latter being reinforced by much detailed correspondence between Zionist executives in London, Jerusalem, New York, Geneva and Istanbul. (In turn, the latter two neutral cities acted as a two-way conduit for intelligence between Zionist leaders in Budapest and in British-occupied Palestine.) Since the conclusion of hostilities, knowledge of Hungarian Orthodox activities during the Holocaust epoch has been based largely on affidavits by Fulop Freudiger (1900–1976) who, in 1939, succeeded his father Abraham as president of the Budapest Orthodox Community and, in 1944, became a foundation member of the JC. Recently, however, the hitherto unpublished testimony of Arthur Stern, elder son of the prominent Orthodox leader Leo Stern, has revealed significant new insights into and details of the endeavours and attitudes of Hungarian Orthodox leaders during the cataclysmic period 1942–45.[249]

Prior to the Occupation Leo Stern (no relation to the president of the JC, and henceforth referred to as Leo in order to distinguish him from Samu Stern), was one of seven elected directors of the Budapest Orthodox Community, being appointed honorary director responsible for economic and financial matters. Concurrently, he was also president of the *Bikur Cholim*, the Orthodox National Health-Protection Society founded in 1871.[250] Subsequent to the illegal entry of Slovakian Jewish refugees into Hungary, Leo and his brother Herman[251] became foundation members of the Orthodox *Va'ada Ezra ve'Hazalah* (Relief and Rescue Committee).[252] Resulting from a suggestion in late 1941 by Rabbi Rabinowicz of Munkacs, the Orthodox Rescue Committee was formally inaugurated in early 1942 with Fulop Freudiger as its foundation chairman. Reflecting Orthodox attitudes, the Committee included two Rabbis; and, in keeping with the Orthodox leaders' agenda and non-insular perspective, the Committee also included Slovakian representatives.[253]

Primary focus of this covert group, in which Leo Stern played a prominent role,[254] was resolving the many problems encountered by Jewish refugees sheltering illegally in Hungary. Consequently, such people were provided with appropriate forms of assistance, including identity papers, documents, accommodation, sustenance, contact with a pertinent social circle, and — where possible in a minority of cases — employment. Following the December 1942 visit to Hungary by Gisi Fleischmann, a leader of the Slovakian Working Group (WG), the Orthodox somewhat reluctantly donated 100,000 *pengos* to the WG.[255] In mid-November 1943 the Orthodox Rescue Committee combined with its Zionist counterpart to form a joint clandestine Zionist-Orthodox rescue and welfare operation (henceforth the *Va'ada*), the combined body being formed to co-ordinate the often illegal efforts to rescue Jewish refugees — predominantly from Slovakia and Poland — and to provide more effective welfare services to the approximately 15,000 such people then sheltering in Hungary.[256]

Although the endeavours of the *Va'ada* and the official Zionist leadership are well documented, it should be realised that the low-profile, and relatively small scale, of the Zionist-Orthodox rescue effort permitted a freedom of action that would have been inappropriate and/or counterproductive for either a mass-rescue operation or the socially conspicuous, and high-profile, Neolog and JC leadership. It will be recalled that in the first phase of Occupation, the politically isolated JC — the body held responsible by the Germans for the safety of thousands of hostage Jews, as well as the Jewish community in general — was forced to officially eschew illegal or legally dubious forms of activity available to the *Va'ada*, a small body not accountable to the community as a whole.

Arguably, the two most important factors generating the Zionist-Orthodox coalition[257] — a union of two traditionally bitter ideological enemies — were each group's international perspective and its positive attitude towards activist, innovative, non-authorised endeavour. By contrast, as discussed above, force of circumstance compelled the Neolog leadership and then the JC — largely isolationist bodies lacking either international perspective or contacts — to pursue authorised, legally oriented defensive methods via formal, traditional channels.

This dichotomy between what critics lacking perspective may term "Neolog legality" versus "Orthodox activism" was exemplified by a plan in June 1944 to print and distribute a circular to the non-Jewish populace, the leaflet detailing the Jewish plight and pleading for assistance. Although initially approving the scheme, Samu Stern subsequently reversed his position, citing the impossibility of the circular obtaining clearance from the government censor. Disregarding Stern's instructions, Rabbi Fabian Herskovits and three assistants used the typewriters and mimeograph in the Orthodox headquarters to reproduce 2,000 circulars and, with help from Zionist youths, managed to distribute the eloquent, heartrending leaflet to numbers of prominent Hungarians. Obtaining a copy, the police arrested the scheme's main participants, who remained in Hungary due to Horthy's order of 7 July banning further deportations.[258] With the benefit of hindsight, it is clear that the circular was of no practical benefit to the Jewish community.

As previously mentioned, before the Occupation Leo Stern's office and residence became an unofficial, informal meeting place for the Orthodox, Zionist and refugee hierarchies, leaders from these groups attending Leo's Sunday luncheons and weekday evening gatherings on a reasonably regular basis.[259] Freudiger states in his postwar memoirs that he initially met the de facto head of the *Va'ada*, Dr Rezso Kasztner, at the Leo Stern abode.[260] It is pertinent to note that, due to ideological incompatibility, Neolog leaders hardly ever attended these gatherings. The *Va'ada* connection, and the fact that a few Orthodox were also Zionists, enabled the Orthodox-Zionist ideological chasm to be bridged.

Arthur Stern states that Leo, like the great majority of Hungarians, was tremendously surprised by the German invasion of Hungary. Arthur recalls that on the afternoon of Occupation day (Sunday, 19 March 1944), his father was visited at home by a Polish general, a legal refugee in Hungary who had obtained sanctuary subsequent to his country's defeat by the Germans. The general, a non-Jew whose name is unfortunately no longer recalled, utilised underground contacts in his native country to provide Leo with regular, reliable and up-to-date information regarding the Jewish situation in Poland. Knowing standard German practice, the general predicted that many Jewish notables would be arrested by the Gestapo at 5 am next morning. Leo was warned to hide immediately, remain underground until after the initial flurry of arrests, and then obtain documents — generally available to select individuals subsequent to a German takeover (see Figs. 4.6 to 4.10) — which would provide reasonable security until the inevitable commencement of deportations.[261] Accepting this advice, Leo and his family spent several days at the writer's parents' residence in Csaky Street[262] before moving to the home of Leo's brother Jozsef for about a week until finally returning to their own apartment at the end of the month.

Subsequent to the invasion, although not formally resigning from the *Va'ada*, Leo Stern withdrew from active participation in that body. Warned by sundry people that involvement with the *Judenrat* would expose him to physical dangers and accusations of collaboration, Leo maintained his financial directorship of the Budapest Orthodox Community in Dob Street but withdrew entirely from political activity. Arthur states that the Polish general was particularly influential in his father's decision, Leo accepting the general's advice that a high political profile would expose him to the German spotlight, would not exempt him or his family from deportation and, if surviving the War, might subject him to accusations of traitorous conduct. Consequently, although Leo maintained regular contact with Freudiger,

Testvér!

Munkatáboros testvéreinkre újból ráköszöntött a tél. Keményen dolgoznak és nincs módjuk, hogy lerongyoló-dott ruhájuk helyébe újat szerezzenek maguknak.

Tőled, a testvértől várják a meleg ruhát,

amely megvédi testüket és lelküket a maguk és mind-annyiunk számára a megfagyástól.
A Honvédelmi Minisztérium nagyobb mennyiségű ruhát és lábbelit utalt ki most részükre, de nincs pénzünk, hogy megvehessük.

Rajtad, a Te pénzbeli adományodon múlik,

hogy a Minisztérium jóindulatával éljünk és a szükségeset beszerezzük.
Juttasd el tehát — **erődön felül juttasd el** — a csatolt befizetési lapon pénzbeli adományodat, hogy

megmenthessük férfiaink színét-virágát, akik most egyedül ránk vannak utalva.

Légy rajta, hogy az élet és egészség győzzön a betegség és pusztulás fölött és

ne engedd, hogy munkaszolgálatos testvéred csalódjon benned, mert ő érted is, mind-annyiunkért dolgozik!

ORSZÁGOS IZRAELITA IRODÁK HADVISELTEK BIZOTTSÁGA:

Müller Rezső
az országos pénzgyüjtés
vezetője.

Fábián Béla
elnök.

A BUDAPESTI AUT. ORTH. IZR. HITKÖZSÉG ELÖLJÁRÓSÁGA:

Stern Leó
elöljáró.

óbudai Freudiger Fülöp
hitk. elnök.

Figure 4.1 *Testver!* (Brother!)
Advertisement requesting donations for the JLS winter clothing appeal. The Orthodox were represented in this community-wide campaign by Fulop Freudiger and Leo Stern. (Source: Ferenc Glatz [ed.], *Az 1944. Ev Historiaja* [History of 1944]. Budapest: Historia evkonyv, 1984; p 115)

after the Occupation Arthur never again saw Kasztner at his father's residence. Thus, whilst still engaged in Orthodox communal activities, Leo henceforth concentrated on safeguarding his family and personal reputation. In keeping with this policy, on 30 June Leo Stern and his family, in company with some 1,700 other Jews, left Hungary on the Kasztner transport (see below).

Arthur states that the relationship between his father and the president of the Pest Orthodox Community, Fulop Freudiger, was based on social contact, shared religious conviction and a personal friendship which also extended to the men's wives. Moreover, Leo's brother Odon was general manager of the Freudiger textile factory.[263] After the War the relationship cooled between the two former friends, doubtless partly due to Leo becoming very reserved about his experiences in 1944. This cooling is clearly indicated in a recently discovered exchange of postwar letters between the two men, this correspondence succinctly elucidating Orthodox involvement in illegal and quasi-legal rescue and relief activities in Hungary during the War.[264] Writing on 4 August 1954 from his home in Jerusalem, after the usual pleasantries Freudiger explained to his former colleague that as a potential witness in the Kasztner trial he required details regarding Orthodox endeavour in wartime Hungary. Consequently, Leo Stern's former superior asked to be informed of:

1. The approximate amount donated to Polish refugees and the number of such people thus supported.
2. The amount of funds received from Kasztner's group.
3. The situation of the Slovakian refugees with respect to the above matters.
4. The amount donated *biklal*[265] and the date(s) of such donation(s).
5. Whether or not there were any complaints about the Kasztner group with respect to financial matters.

Freudiger continued his letter thus:

> With regard to the first two questions you are in a position to remember, because these functions were conducted by yourself on behalf of the committee, and possibly you can add something pertinent to the other questions. I remember that the second or third negotiation with Kasztner occurred at your home and that is where it was agreed that he would contribute money to our work. Can you remember the approximate date when this occurred?

Replying on 12 August 1954 from his home in Geneva, Leo commenced by reproaching Freudiger for not maintaining their formerly close contact, and continued by stating:

> I can contribute nothing concrete towards the matters raised in your kind letter. I also remember that once or twice Kasztner had dinner with me, when you were also present, but what was discussed unfortunately escapes my recollection... I personally never discussed monetary matters with Kasztner and I have no idea what he contributed to the Orthodox.

Leo continued his letter by noting that on occasion he was forced to borrow directly from the Orthodox community's funds in order to aid refugees in urgent need. By this statement Leo Stern, in effect, confirmed his crucial involvement, authority and prerogative vis-à-vis the financial aspects of Orthodox activity on behalf of Jewish refugees in Hungary during the Holocaust period. Stern concluded the substantive portion of his letter by asserting — perhaps accurately, in light of the Neolog leaders' preference, and need, to eschew even quasi-illegal activity during most of this period — that "Hungarian Orthodoxy provided refugee assistance above its proportionate resources, unlike the Neolog who did not even come close to fulfilling their proportionate obligations."[266]

In his postwar memoirs, Freudiger corroborates a portion of Stern's declarations by stating:

> I met Dr Kasztner at Leo Stern's because I wanted a member of our committee to be present. Before concluding the [*Va'ada*] agreement, Dr Kasztner asked: "How much money would the Orthodox give for the joint work?"... I didn't promise any definite sum or percentage but that we would continue our efforts of raising whatever we could.[267]

It appears that Freudiger was unable to obtain the information sought from Leo Stern via alternative sources, as no specific financial details relating to his queries are revealed in this or any other of his testimonies. These omissions provide strong circumstantial evidence that such financial responsibility was largely, if not exclusively, the province of Leo Stern.

Regarding questions of finance vis-à-vis his father, Arthur could not provide direct evidence but only information obtained through personal discussion with a range of relevant people, and on observation of Leo's activities, such pursuits being divided between his home and office. However, Arthur does state that to his knowledge:

> A great deal of Orthodox money was involved in the *Va'ada*. But this group was not a rigidly structured organisation. It was a shadowy group — of necessity and because of its agenda. Consequently I don't know whether the money went through a central administration or whether it was distributed on an informal or an *ad hoc* basis. Nothing was formal, there were no minutes taken.[268]

The tone of the above correspondence indicates a marked reserve, if not hostility, in the postwar relationship between the two wartime Orthodox leaders. Arthur suspects that the deterioration was instigated by the arrest of his paternal uncles, Leo's brothers Jozsef and Salamon, by the Germans in mid-June 1944 whilst the brothers were fleeing with their families to Roumania. Leo, aware of Freudiger's access to Wisliceny, considered that his friend and *confrère* was insufficiently vigorous in attempting to prevent his brothers' subsequent deportation by the Germans.[269]

Leo's response to Freudiger was consistent with a distinct postwar reticence he maintained about his endeavours in the period 1942 to mid-1944; in particular, he refused to testify at either the Kasztner or (Hermann) Krumey trials. Despite being an indefatigable correspondent,[270] and despite being at the centre of Hungarian Orthodoxy's top administrative hierarchies, Leo Stern never documented either his role or the community's endeavours during the War. Arthur assumes that the main factors generating this reticence were his father's understandable wish to avoid the intense public criticism levelled at other Hungarian Jewish leaders, his ardent desire to protect his reputation, and the obligation to prevent his family becoming embroiled in emotional turmoil and public furore. Whilst not discounting the validity of such argument, it should be noted that as a highly successful businessman and company director in the prime of life, a person with a wide reputation for financial acumen and attention to detail, it is hardly likely that Leo Stern could not have answered Freudiger's questions in some detail, should he have so desired.[271]

One of the frequent criticisms levelled at Freudiger in particular, and the Hungarian Orthodox leadership in general, has been enunciated by Yehuda Bauer thus: "...Freudiger seems to have been more interested in saving the members of his own Orthodox group than in a general rescue effort."[272] Whilst Professor Bauer is doubtless correct in his assessment, it must be emphasised that there were cogent reasons for Orthodox particularity towards rescue operations, such reasons not necessarily resulting from resentment, bitterness, jealousy, or attitudes of superiority towards the non-Orthodox sections of Hungarian Jewry.[273] Firstly, a "general rescue effort" was not only beyond Orthodox resources, but — as has been shown — in the prevailing circumstances would have been quite impractical, if not counterproductive. Furthermore, in a highly stratified and largely insular society like Hungary, group affiliation/particularity was an important basis for social life. Consequently, as expected in such situations, members of each segment of Hungarian Jewry generally had stronger rapport and trust with their ideological *confrères* than with Jews outside their particular group.

[This differentiation sometimes generated significant divisions of responsibility regarding rescue and relief operations — even within the one group. For example, in the chronically split Hungarian Zionist movement, for cogent reasons the official leadership concentrated on negotiating with the Germans (the Kasztner or "Big Line", ie: mass rescue) whilst the Halutz endeavours included the *Tiyul* (literally "trip", or escape across borders; of necessity a selective, small-scale operation; see below.)]

A practical consequence of such socio-ideological delineation occurred in mid-1944 during the allocation of seats on the Kasztner transport, a train originally meant for 600 but eventually conveying some 1,700 Hungarian Jews to ultimate freedom in Switzerland. Kasztner initially divided the available places into ten categories, the resultant division essentially embracing three major groups: the Zionists (including 250 Halutzim, each constituent movement distributing its awarded quota amongst its own members); prominent personalities, communal activists, and the widows and orphans of JLS conscripts (this group included the highly controversial allocation of 388 places to Jews from Kolozsvar, Kasztner's home town); and those still sufficiently affluent to purchase seats, this category funding a substantial portion of the overall venture.[274] These major groups were in turn subdivided into sundry subgroups, each resultant subset being allocated to a different segment of Hungarian Jewry. Consequently, apart from those mentioned above, Neolog, Orthodox, academic, artistic, and even Jewish refugees in Hungary, were allocated a quota on the train, each such quota being distributed by the subsets' leaders amongst their respective constituents.

It must be recalled that the Orthodox community, being considerably smaller, less powerful, significantly more inward-oriented and ideologically inflexible than its Neolog counterpart, was in reasonable consensus regarding its agenda and objectives. And unlike Samu Stern and his colleagues, the Orthodox leadership lacked traditional access to the topmost hierarchy of Hungarian politics. Not unexpectedly in such circumstances, Fulop Freudiger utilised his connection with Wisliceny to include some eighty Orthodox Jews in the Kasztner transport.[275] For Freudiger not to have interceded in such a manner would have, in all likelihood, exposed him to criticism for the dereliction of duty vis-à-vis his constituents.

Arthur Stern presents a cogent analysis of the Hungarian Jewish community's socio-ideological orientation thus:

> [Particularity] was typical of all groups. Zionists, Neolog and Orthodox tried to save their members. It was inherent in the system. There was a lot of lip service to saving all Jews, but in reality people tried to save the social circle to which they belonged.[276] In the *Va'ada* there were primarily two efforts, with the Orthodox looking after the Orthodox refugees and the Zionists after the Zionist refugees.[277]... It's human nature to favour family and friends. It was a generally accepted thing. Anything different would have been surprising.[278]

Although this delineation — or fragmentation, or lack of integration, or division of responsibility; the term depending on one's proclivities — generated suspicion and lack of confidence amongst some, if not most, segments of Hungarian Jewry, Arthur concluded his analysis by stating that even without such divisions the fate of Hungarian Jewry would, in all probability, have remained unchanged.

In largely dissolute Horthyist Hungary, *protekcio* (patronage, nepotism, corruption) was a well-nigh institutionalised commodity, with falsification of business activity being an endemic fact of economic life — especially after the advent of war-generated shortages and the growth of the black market. The Orthodox, like wider sections of Hungarian society, took advantage of such circumstance to protect themselves and their affiliates. In particular, after 1942 the Freudiger textile works — which employed some hundreds of people and was thus considered a large facility by Hungarian standards — provided employment for several dozen Polish Jewish refugees sheltering in Hungary under "Christian" papers.[279]

Apart from providing employment, activist Jews in business utilised the country's endemic corruption to achieve illegal, or quasi-legal, welfare objectives. For example, Arthur Stern states that his uncle Odon (brother of Leo, and General Manager of the Freudiger textile works) sold single rolls of fabric, at rock bottom prices, to needy Orthodox who, in turn, disposed of the material on the open (black) market. In general, an average family could survive on the proceeds of such an individual-roll transaction for some three to four months. Odon accomplished this, at considerable risk to himself, by understating the Freudiger factory's production input and output reports to the government by a factor of about two-thirds. As such, over half the factory's actual fabric production was effectively hidden from the authorities. Arthur continued:

> That's how Odon achieved a deserved reputation as a *Tzadik* [a righteous person]. Thousands of people were dependent on him. He would rarely have done that for someone who wasn't Orthodox. This selective activity, because it was unknown to the wider Jewish society, didn't cause bitterness in non-Orthodox circles. Its relatively small scale and secret nature kept knowledge within the strict confines of the Orthodox community, only single rolls being passed to individuals every three to four months.
>
> This activity was known and condoned, if not wholeheartedly approved, by Freudiger. Odon was the chief executive, knew the business and could not be dismissed.[280] I heard reports of differences between the two men over this [support] policy.[281]

In a very real sense, particularity was a defence mechanism helping to maintain the secrecy — and hence continuity — of such illegal activity. Obviously, participants sharing a common affiliation with the organisers of such endeavour, and hence known and trusted, would be far less likely to emerge as government agents. In particular, clearly the authorities would have had considerable difficulty infiltrating an illegal relief enterprise consisting entirely of Orthodox participants. Hence secrecy, closely followed by common affiliation, were the *sine qua non* of success, with care and discretion being the order of the day; it was not unknown for such operations to be unravelled by the authorities. For example, Arthur relates that Miksa Mayer, joint proprietor of a textile factory substantially larger than the Freudiger establishment, was arrested for involvement in a similarly illegal operation, sent to prison and died in gaol. To preclude such a possibility, the Freudiger operation used bribery to pre-empt investigation, those people accepting bribes becoming "stinking rich".

It should be noted that aiding illegal refugees was a serious crime in Hungary, subject to internment without trial in a detention centre.[282] Even minor assistance to illegal refugees resulted in entire families being incarcerated in such establishments.[283] [As mentioned above (see Chapter II), the authority charged with suppressing such crime against the state was the oppressive, feared and efficient KEOKH (*Kulfoldieket Ellenorzo Orszagos Kozponti Hatosag*, National Authority for Alien Control), a special department within the Hungarian police.[284] Under KEOKH's auspices, in July 1941 some 18,000 "non-citizen" Jews were registered, interned and (often brutally) deported in freight trains to the recently "liberated" area of Eastern Galicia where, in late August, the large majority were massacred.] Importantly, and without doubt, operations such as those centred on the Freudiger works — that is, long-term programmes consciously opposing the impoverishment of the community and the detection of illegal Jewish refugees sheltering therein[285] — should not be trivialised as mere fiscal deceptions, but acknowledged as systematic strategies for frustrating the Holocaust process. Consequently, it must be acknowledged that entrepreneurial Jews utilised Hungary's endemic socio-economic corruption to initiate, organise and sustain deliberate, systematic and meaningful acts of Jewish resistance to the Nazi *Endlösung*.

Arthur Stern

Immediately following the Allies' first great air raids on Budapest,[286] on 4 April 1944, the joint Secretary of State at the Interior Ministry, Laszlo Endre, demanded that the JC evacuate 500 Jewish apartments in districts VIII and IX in favour of Christians made homeless by the bombing. Ordered as an act of vengeance on Budapest Jews, and to garner popularity by providing shelter, furniture and households goods to non-Jews dispossessed by Allied raids, the JC was allowed twenty-four hours to fulfil this demand. After an all-night meeting which concluded that such instruction could not be ignored, the JC appointed a banker, the forthright Rezso Muller, to head a housing requisition department.[287] On 5 April, the day the wearing of the Yellow Star became compulsory, the Hungarians arrested two members of the JC (Wilhelm and Kahan-Frankl) and increased their original demand to 1,500 apartments.[288] Henceforth, a succession of orders and requisitions ensured that the Housing Department grew to become one of the JC's largest sections.

In early May, Endre decided to order the registration of all Jewish dwellings in Budapest, a plan that was secretly communicated to the JC by Counsellor Jozsef Szentmiklossy, humane head of the Budapest Municipality's Social Policies Bureau.

Grateful for this intelligence, and impressed by his previous goodwill, at a secret meeting the JC convinced Szentmiklossy to forego his opposition to Endre's policies and accept appointment as government director of housing registration and sequestration.[289]

To the Antisemites' rage, registration figures published in June indicated that Jewish households — constituting some 20 percent of the capital's population — occupied 48,000 rooms (40 percent of Budapest's total) in 21,000 apartments (40 percent of the total), whilst the balance of the capital's populace (80 percent) had some 70,000 rooms (60 percent) in 32,000 apartments (60 percent).[290] Due to fears concerning the targeting of exclusively Christian areas by Allied air forces, the government rejected the concept of a self-contained ghetto. As an alternative, on 15 June the authorities ordered the concentration of Budapest Jews into 2,700 so-called Yellow Star (*Sarga Csillag*) Houses — some 8 percent of the capital's residential buildings — initially allocating a week for the relocation. Individual Christian protests against their buildings being classified as Yellow Star saw the allocation reduced from 2,700 to about 2,000, some 5 percent of Budapest's residential building stock.[291]

Charged with effecting the resettlement, the JC directed the dynamic chief of the Housing Department, Rezso Muller, to oversee a Herculean co-ordination, transportation and relocation operation, affecting some 200,000 people, which had to be completed by 24 June. Shortly thereafter, the government proclaimed drastic new restrictions on the community's freedom of movement, Jews being confined under virtual house arrest for most of the day.[292]

As indicated above, and as expanded below, individual staff and even departments of the JC sometimes used the resources and facade of the Council to hinder implementation of the *Endlösung* process in Hungary. Thus it is clear that, far from being employed by an authoritarian entity controlled through a rigidly centralised secretariat, individual and group initiatives of some JC staff gave rise to a largely unstructured, informal, often autonomous *ad hoc* resistance within the precincts of JC headquarters at 12 Sip Street. As expected, due to the constrictions of time and circumstance, such operations were sometimes, if not frequently, unknown — officially or otherwise — to Samu Stern and his fellow directors. Although originally of only marginal utility, the aggregate of these frequently self-contained covert activities centred on the JC was instrumental in "illegally" saving several thousand people from oppression and deportation.

Considering the number of Jews in Hungary, even a charitable interpretation would not assess the sum of these operations as anything other than a concordant note in a cacophony of persecution. However, the important principle is that, as with the upper-echelon Liaison Office, lower-echelon attempts at tactical and strategic resistance — albeit only marginally successful in the totality of dreadful circumstance — were implemented and accomplished. In addition to rescue operations, activist middle management and employees of the JC used the prevailing chaos of the Occupation to alleviate, and sometimes even neutralise, German demands and impositions. Thus, far from being a submissive entity with a rigid lineal command structure, the JC was a complex, multifaceted phenomenon, disparate layers working independently to evolve covert, often analogous — albeit sometimes only temporary — solutions to some of the critical problems confronting Hungarian Jewry.

The hitherto undocumented testimony of Arthur Stern is a particularly valuable contribution elucidating the covert activities emanating from the lower echelons of JC headquarters. Not only was Arthur one of the few Orthodox activists who worked in the official JC *milieu*, but he was also in the rare position of being personally involved in field-work resistance whilst, through family connections, having access to the deliberations of the top Orthodox and Zionist hierarchy. Very few activists or eyewitnesses would have had such a comprehensive perspective on Jewish attitudes and endeavours during the Occupation's first phase, Arthur having a foot — as it were — in all three segments of Hungarian Jewry.

Although Leo Stern refused active association with the JC, he did not attempt to dissuade his elder son from volunteering to work at 12 Sip Street, the Council's Budapest headquarters.[293] Motivated by the prospect of obtaining protective documents available to many of its employees, Arthur, then eighteen and of adventurous spirit, welcomed the additional freedom of movement, and the consequent increase in his options that such papers would provide. Commencing at the JC in the chaotic period towards the end of March, Arthur cannot recall the exact circumstances of his acceptance but suggests that, as a university student, his employment resulted from membership of the Hungarian Jewish Students' Association — the MIEFHOE (*Magyar Izraelita Egyetemi es Foiskolai Hallgatok Orszagos Egyesulete*), encompassing Hungary's then forty-eight Jewish university students as full members[294] — rather than through the intervention of his father. As a member of this elite group, Arthur was allocated a variety of responsible assignments by JC officers, worked extended hours and frequently spent the night with his co-workers in a big office at 12 Sip Street. The JC paid its employees reasonably well but, as with other members of wealthy families, Arthur worked in an honorary capacity. Two particular endeavours, apartment requisition and false document activity — respectively official, overt and unofficial, covert — highlight Arthur's work at the JC.

As has been seen, shortly after the Occupation both German and Hungarian authorities commenced requisitioning, amongst other things, Jewish residential accommodation. The job of selecting apartments, and informing the occupants thereof, was delegated to some fifty young people, including Arthur Stern, employed by the JC.[295] Members of this group would frequently sleep at JC headquarters, and attend a daily meeting at 6–7 am during which teams of two would be allocated a city area to canvass. Each team would be given a map, a list specifying the number and type of dwellings requisitioned, and an inventory (drawn from JC files, and invariably larger than the actual requirement) listing the name, address and type of residence of Jewish households in the team's respective area. University students were considered an elite group and afforded considerable latitude in the accomplishment of their duties. Consequently, Arthur and his student colleagues were granted the substantial authority of fulfilling their quota according to the results of their investigations. After independently finalising their selections, generally by the very early afternoon, teams would report to a central bureau in 12 Sip Street. Sometimes quotas were unable to be met, but Arthur cannot recall being criticised or penalised for such failure. It should be noted that, where possible, the JC attempted to minimise disruption by listing for investigation larger residences containing relatively few people, and that neither German nor Hungarian authorities ever interfered with, or became involved in the requisition process, at the team level.

Arthur comments that there existed a covert, unofficial tendency for the teams to favour "overt" Jews by selecting the homes of Christian or "nominal" Jews, that is converts or those classified as Jews not by voluntary allegiance but by Hungary's racial laws. Arthur stresses that this initiative was strictly contrary to policy, the JC's officials actively discouraging such behaviour. Despite manifestations of discrimination, the teams were permitted to retain their prerogatives so as to enable appropriate consideration to be extended in special circumstances.

With the introduction of the Yellow Star House (non-contiguous ghetto) concept, Arthur was transferred to the department charged with selecting Star buildings. Allocated to the heavily Jewish Lipotvaros neighbourhood, an affluent area on the Pest side of the Danube, Arthur was appointed a senior representative in this region and given a small staff of assistants. Commenting that this was a "tremendously powerful position" for an eighteen-year-old, Arthur recalled "indescribable, heartrending scenes" when people attempted to influence his decisions. Braham notes that the Housing Department was "constantly inundated with demands and complaints",[296] and Samu Stern, in his postwar testimony, confirms the anguish generated by the requisition procedure, writing that:

> The "Lodgings office" swiftly became incredibly unpopular with the suffering Jews... It is but natural that those banned from their dwellings found fault with the Council's new office, though it only did what it could not help doing: carrying out the authorities' orders... Concentrating people in pre-fixed places meant an appalling confusion. An unimaginable onslaught set in against us, everybody expecting us to make the building he lives in a starred house...those turned out of their lodgings vented their anger by scolding the Council, and the Council alone.[297]

Despite amelioration policies, including encouraging people to locate new living quarters through relatives, friends or their own initiative, and subsidising or paying relocation expenses; despite saving many provincial Jews, living illegally in Budapest, by listing them as homeless air raid victims and allocating them a "legal" residence; and despite threats by Endre that non-compliance with his orders would result in the demands being implemented by the *SS* and the Gendarmerie, the bitterness directed at the JC because of its requisition activity is indicated by the following grievous joke, which swept the Jewish community:

> At 3 am a furious hammering erupts on the door of a Jewish household in Budapest.
> "*Achtung*! Open immediately. It's the Gestapo."
> "Oh, thank goodness" sighs the householder, fumbling with his key. "For a moment I was terrified it was the Jewish Council."

In his assessment of the situation, Arthur Stern presents a cogent rationale of the JC's housing relocation policy:

> At the time it didn't really occur to us that our requisition activities would one day be labelled as improper or a collaboration. We did it because we felt it was a means of mitigating the hurt, and we did it with a degree of pride that we were minimising suffering. It was an attempt to avoid the radical steps which the authorities would have undertaken. We felt we had no choice. We were convinced that some at the Jewish Council would have been shot and the Germans and Hungarians would have got the apartments anyway... We obtained apartments in a reasonably professional

and compassionate manner, attempting to concentrate on large apartments inhabited by few people, giving priority to big families with small children. We felt the job we were doing was in the best interests of the community.[298]

There is little doubt that the Germans and their Hungarian collaborators, having control of the Gendarmerie and the critical instruments of state during this period, could have inflicted harsh vengeance on the Jewish community in the event of the JC refusing to comply with their sequestration demands. Typical of the Germans' attitude and *modus operandi* was the statement made to the JC shortly after the Occupation. Upon their orders for certain difficult-to-obtain commodities remaining unfulfilled, *SS* officers drew their revolvers and stated:

> If our demand is not met by five pm to-day, we will have the responsible leaders shot. You must realise that, if it is possible to execute 10,000 Jews within ten minutes, a demand of this nature can be met within an hour and a half. Quite apart from that, we don't know the meaning of the word "impossible".[299]

Even with the benefit of hindsight, Arthur Stern's analysis is thus difficult to refute. Rather than endangering Jewish lives, the JC's policies were aimed at maintaining their "Race Against Time" strategy, preventing the formation of a separate, integral ghetto in Budapest, and minimising the prospect of reprisals by ensuring Nazi ferocity was satiated with material commodities rather than Jewish lives. Simply stated, the JC's pro-active requisition programme attempted to distribute the inescapable burden over the community as a whole. The only alternative option — a consequence of JC non-compliance — was to, in effect, inflict upon the community an indiscriminate, unpredictable but doubtless vengeful Nazi implementation of their sequestration orders.

Concurrent with his official, overt duties at the JC, Arthur Stern was immersed in unofficial, covert activities involving false document processing and distribution. Even before the War, individuals in Hungary — whether Jewish or otherwise — were compelled to possess sundry identity papers. Police could, and did, stop people at will and demand to inspect their documents. Subsequent to the invasion of March 1944, if a Jew wanted to retain privileges permitted non-Jewish citizens — particularly entitlements pertaining to travel, employment and residence — a comprehensive set of credible documents became a mandatory requirement. As a corollary, it was essential for Jews to have such papers if attempting to live underground, a primary purpose of false documents after the German Occupation. In particular, a good set of false papers would pre-empt the physical examination of males introduced by Occupation authorities, circumcision being confined overwhelmingly to Jewish males and hence considered *prima facie* evidence of "non-Aryan" identity.

The three most important components of a comprehensive set of identity papers were an individual's *Polgari Szemelyi Lap* (Civil Identity Card — the primary form for personal identity; see Fig. 4.11), housing registration form (see Fig. 4.2) and birth certificate.[300] Regarding the second mentioned, it should be noted that the superintendent of an apartment building not only maintained the property, but also performed sundry official and unofficial duties. Amongst his official functions was the quarterly distribution of food ration cards and the certification of an individual's change of address form, the *Bejelentolap*. By law, this residential certificate had to be registered with the police within twenty-four hours of relocation to a new, even

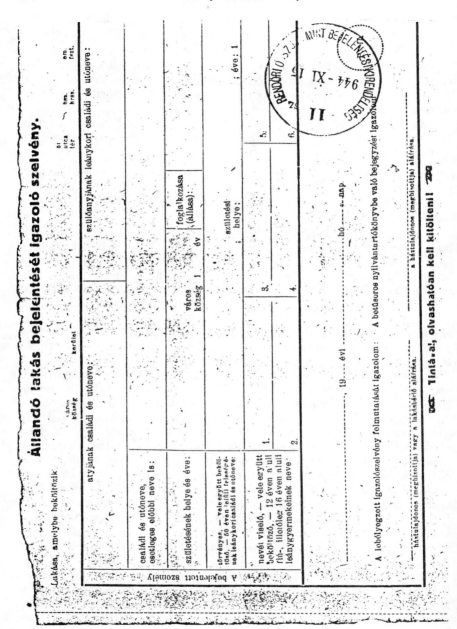

Figure 4.2 *Allando lakas bejelenteset igazolo szelveny.*
Blank housing registration form (*Bejelentolap*), unsigned but pre-stamped with a Hungarian police imprint dated 15 November 1944. (Source: JMB 65.859)

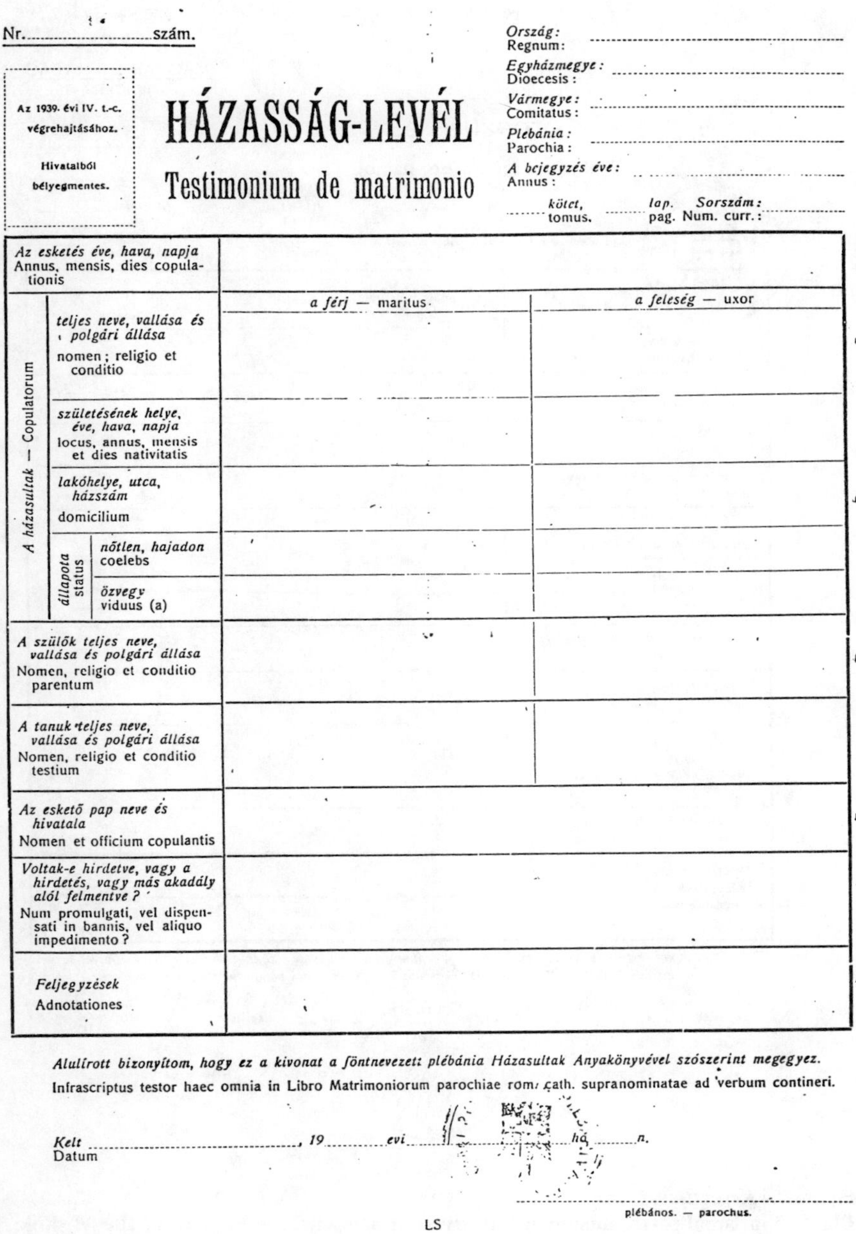

Nr. .... szám.

Ország:	
Regnum:	
Egyházmegye :	
Dioecesis :	
Vármegye :	
Comitatus :	
Plébánia :	
Parochia :	
A bejegyzés éve :	
Annus :	

Az 1939. évi IV. t.-c.
végrehajtásához.

Hivatalból
bélyegmentes.

HÁZASSÁG-LEVÉL

Testimonium de matrimonio

	kötet,	lap.	Sorszám :
	tomus.	pag.	Num. curr. :

		a férj — maritus·	a feleség — uxor
Az esketés éve, hava, napja Annus, mensis, dies copulationis			
A házasultak — Copulatorum	teljes neve, vallása és polgári állása nomen ; religio et conditio		
	születésének helye, éve, hava, napja locus, annus, mensis et dies nativitatis		
	lakóhelye, utca, házszám domicilium		
	állapota status — nőtlen, hajadon coelebs		
	özvegy viduus (a)		
A szülők teljes neve, vallása és polgári állása Nomen, religio et conditio parentum			
A tanuk teljes neve, vallása és polgári állása Nomen, religio et conditio testium			
Az esketö pap neve és hivatala Nomen et officium copulantis			
Voltak-e hirdetve, vagy a hirdetés, vagy más akadály alól felmentve ? Num promulgati, vel dispensati in bannis, vel aliquo impedimento ?			
Feljegyzések Adnotationes			

Alulírott bizonyítom, hogy ez a kivonat a föntnevezett plébánia Házasultak Anyakönyvével szószerint megegyez.

Infrascriptus testor haec omnia in Libro Matrimoniorum parochiae rom. cath. supranominatae ad verbum contineri.

Kelt .... , 19 .... évi .... hó .... n.
Datum

LS

plébános. — parochus.

Figure 4.3 *Hazassag-level.*
Blank marriage certificate, unsigned but pre-stamped with illegible Hungarian imprint. Note that the religion (*vallasa*) of the bride, groom, respective parents and witnesses had to be declared. (Source: JMB 65.861)

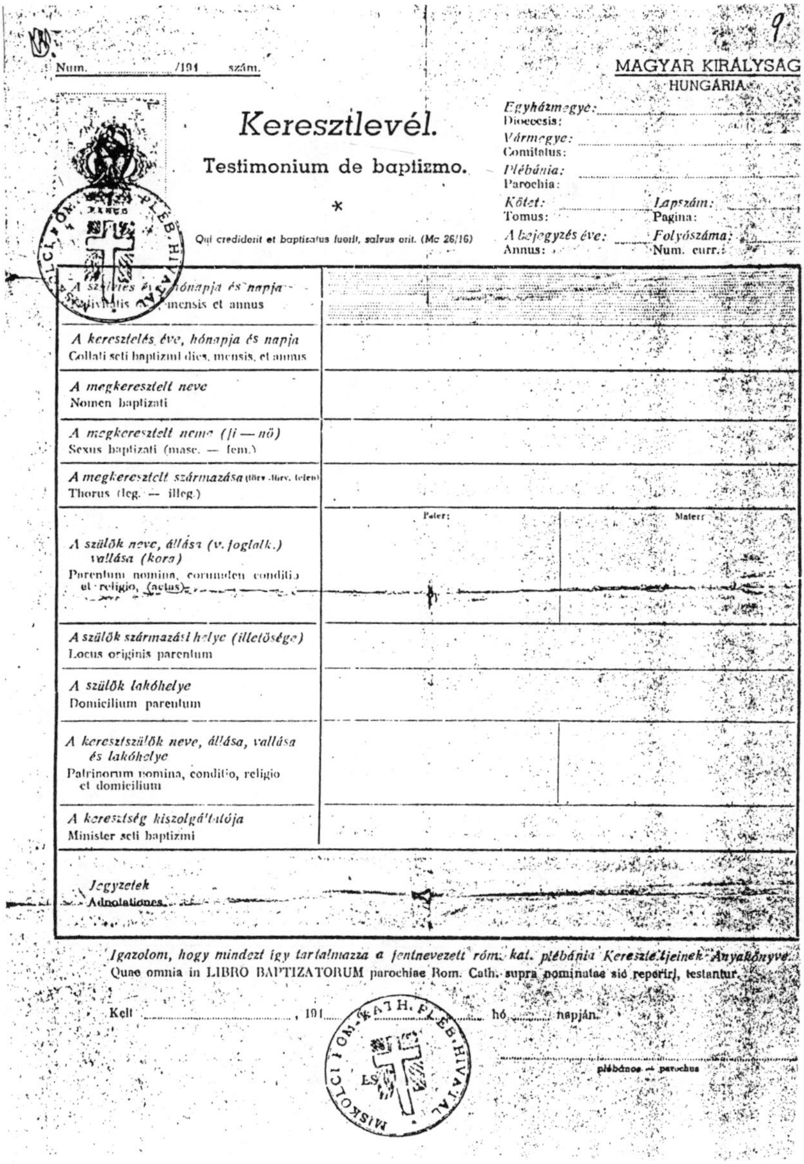

Num. _____ /191 szám.

MAGYAR KIRÁLYSÁG
HUNGARIA

Keresztlevél.

Testimonium de baptizmo.

✳

Qui crediderit et baptizatus fuerit, salvus erit. (Mc 26/16)

Egyházmegye: _____
Dioecesis: _____
Vármegye: _____
Comitatus: _____
Plébánia: _____
Parochia: _____
Kötet: _____ *Lapszám:* _____
Tomus: _____ Pagina: _____
A bejegyzés éve: _____ *Folyószáma:* _____
Annus: _____ Num. curr.: _____

A születés éve, hónapja és napja Nativitatis mensis et annus	
A keresztelés éve, hónapja és napja Collati seti baptizmi dies, mensis, et annus	
A megkeresztelt neve Nomen baptizati	
A megkeresztelt neme (fi — nö) Sexus baptizati (masc. — fem.)	
A megkeresztelt származása (törv.-törv. telen) Thorus (leg. — illeg.)	

A szülők neve, állása (v. foglalk.) vallása (kora) Parentum nomina, eorundem conditio et religio, (actas)	Pater:	Mater:
A szülők származási helye (illetősége) Locus originis parentum		
A szülők lakóhelye Domicilium parentum		
A keresztszülők neve, állása, vallása és lakóhelye Patrinorum nomina, conditio, religio et domicilium		
A keresztség kiszolgáltatója Minister seti baptizmi		
Jegyzetek Adnotationes.		

Igazolom, hogy mindezt így tartalmazza a fentnevezett róm. kat. plébánia Keresztelteinek Anyakönyve.
Quae omnia in LIBRO BAPTIZATORUM parochiae Rom. Cath. supra nominatae sic reperiri, testantur.

Kelt _____ , 191 ____ hó ____ napján.

plébános — parochus

Figure 4.4 *Keresztlevel.*
Blank baptismal form, unsigned but pre-stamped with the imprint of the Miskolc Catholic Parish (some 150 km north-east of Budapest). The slight discontinuity on the central-left portion of the stamp's circumference — a break more visible in the full-size original — is a clear indication that the stamp is non-genuine. Consequently, when completed, this form would have provided low credibility to the bearer. (Source: YVA 015/5)

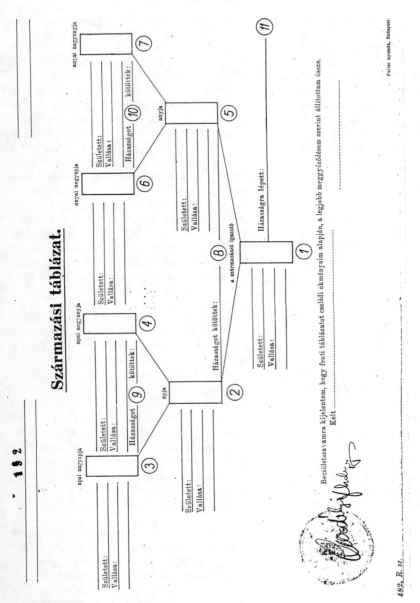

Figure 4.5 *Szarmazasi tablazat.*
Blank "Family Tree" certificate, signed and pre-stamped with an illegible Hungarian imprint. Note that the religion (*vallasa*) of each antecedent on the document had to be declared. As such, these forms were useful adjuncts in verifying that the bearer was excluded from the provisions of the Third Jewish Law (see text). The number stamped in the top left corner may have been deliberately smudged so as to hinder the verification of authenticity. (Source: JMB 65.851)

temporary, abode. Additionally, most superintendents also acted as unofficial police informers, constantly surveying their tenants and reporting suspicious activity to the authorities.

Blank *Bejelentolap* forms were readily available from retail tobacconists; the problem for illegal (underground) residents and their supporters was obtaining the appropriate police registration stamp. Initially, pre-stamped forms were purchased from the underworld, a practice soon discontinued because of high costs and the danger of blackmail. Next priority for "illegals" was a birth certificate. Early underground residents borrowed genuine certificates from family and friends, a daunting habit endangering both parties. Because of its hazards, this practice was soon replaced by safer *modus operandi*, a popular method being for an individual to enter the registry office during peak hours and request a replacement birth certificate for a fictitious person. When the clerk, harassed by the War-induced labour shortage, was unable to locate the fictitious name, the requester would volunteer to locate the request in the office register. Under this pretext many genuine names, addresses and pertinent details were copied and passed on to appropriate individuals. Such people subsequently presented themselves at the registry and obtained a government-issued birth certificate in the name of a real person who approximated their relevant particulars. Importantly, a credible birth certificate enabled people to obtain a genuine work permit, thus providing their claimed identity with additional validity.[301]

For on-the-spot credibility, false papers had to withstand a telephone check to various government registries. Different documents provided differing degrees of security, and hence were classified as of either primary or secondary importance. Regarding proof of Christian status, the former included, as appropriate, the birth and marriage certificates (see Fig. 4.3) of self and parents as well as the latters' death certificates. Secondary documents — including baptismal (see Fig. 4.4), school (primary and secondary), military release or exemption, "Family Tree" (see Fig. 4.5) and employment certificates — although of lesser importance, were still significant adjuncts to the verification of a claimed identity. In general, the greater the number of credible papers, the greater a person's degree of security — assuming that the accosted individual used the documents in a confident and appropriate manner.[302] [For a selection of such papers see the following pages. Unfortunately, apart from the genuine passes provided by Arthur Stern, in no instance was the real — as opposed to the apparent — origin of these documents indicated by the archives from which they were obtained.]

Shortly after commencing work at the JC, Arthur Stern became involved with unofficial, covert activities centred on false document processing and distribution. Of necessity, he acquired two sets of papers, the combination providing him with a freedom of movement considerably above and beyond that permitted non-activist Jews. Arthur's usual *modus operandi* involved concurrently carrying both sets of documents, the (false) non-Jewish papers in his right pocket, the JC-issued *Schutzpass* (protective pass) in his left. Outside the JC building he wore an overcoat or raincoat onto which was sewn the regulation Yellow Star, but his jacket underneath was bare. Consequently, Arthur retained the ability to change identity virtually at will, simply by removing or donning his outer coat. An easy, convenient and safe method for effecting such change was to enter a building that extended between two streets, either don or remove the outer coat whilst in the building, and emerge from the building's other exit onto another street. This method was in general use by people switching between overt and covert activity, Arthur and his colleagues memorising a list of appropriate buildings in Budapest having entrances from two separate street frontages.

Early in the Occupation there were five grades of false papers circulating within the Jewish community. Fifth grade documents — the majority then in circulation — were of such poor quality that a policeman could detect them as false through cursory observation (see Fig. 4.4). Of necessity, Arthur possessed first class false papers, thus permitting movement as a non-Jew with considerable security and psychological confidence. In general, first class papers enabled a Jew to adopt "Aryan" identity to the extent that an investigating policeman had appreciable difficulty in challenging the document's authenticity. Often such papers were of genuine government issue — that is, not obtained by bribery — having previously belonged to a non-Jew from a remote province who shared common physical characteristics with the Jewish bearer. For example, Arthur Stern's non-Jewish papers originally referred to a young Swabian (ethnic German) from a village near Sopron (far Western Hungary) who had been listed by the military as missing at the Eastern front. Consequently, any check with the relevant civilian authorities would confirm that the papers were valid, as they had in fact been issued to the original recipient in the appropriate manner.

However, enquiries with the military would, in all likelihood, have created problems, the "listed as missing" classification arousing suspicions regarding Arthur's *bona fides*. Thus, whilst first class false papers provided a relatively high degree of security, they were not without risk to the bearer. The closest approximation to unquestioned acceptance was generated by documents genu- inely issued in a remote province to a now dead Christian citizen of similar characteristics to the Jewish bearer, the deceased person not being known as such to the police or other authority.[303] It should be noted that there were techniques by which photos on government-issued documents could be successfully replaced by a photo of the subsequent bearer.

Arthur Stern's false document activities were concurrent with his official duties at the JC, were conducted largely in his spare time, and commenced shortly after his engagement at Sip Street. On the basis that Arthur was employed very shortly after the institution of the JC, it appears likely that he was amongst the foundation members of this particular covert, unofficial, hitherto unrecognised resistance centred on JC headquarters. Arthur states that after about a month of experience vis-à-vis false document procurement and distribution, techniques improved to such an extent that early batches of false papers were thereafter classified as of fifth grade quality.

It should be noted that, as discussed below, the Halutz false document endeavour was instituted in response to the needs of illegal Slovak and Polish refugees sheltering in Hungary. Consequently, refinement of the Halutzim *modus operandi* in this field commenced largely before the German invasion. As a result of the JC-centred group and the Halutz being at different stages of what might be termed "the false document production learning curve", one can conclude with reasonable confidence that these groups engaged in largely separate but parallel operations in this field of resistance.[304] Consequently, it should be recognised that both Zionist and non-Zionist youth made distinct contributions in the rescuing of

Hungarian Jews via false documents. Eventually the Halutzim came to dominate this activity (see below), providing many tens of thousands of false papers to Jews, as well as thousands for individuals and organisations outside the Jewish community.

As with the original Halutz efforts, initially the JC groups distributed their documents to family, relatives, friends, ideological *confrères*, colleagues and neighbours; that is, those who were trusted to accept and use the papers and — even more importantly — not inform the authorities. Consequently and inevitably, there was a significant element of *protekcio* (patronage) during the initial period of operations, a phase when false papers were in limited supply. Arthur Stern comments on this period, largely coinciding with the first phase of Occupation, thus:

> You couldn't deal in matters of this type except with people whom you trusted. There were risks to all parties involved which had to be minimised. However there was also an attempt to target those Jews at greatest risk. For example, when it was learnt that the Jews of Ujpest [a suburb of Budapest containing about 14,000 Jews[305]] would be eliminated, some of us went there, attempted to warn them, and gave false papers to those who listened. Tragically, many of them failed to heed our warnings.[306]

In stark contradistinction to the Halutz' later attempt at mass rescue via an avalanche of false papers — the young Zionists eventually producing over 100,000 *Schutzpässe* — the JC group's efforts were distinctly selective and discreet. Contemporaneous with the first phase of the German Occupation, this selective, what might be termed micro rescue strategy — as opposed to the Halutz' later macro (mass) operation — was centred on several dozen young employees operating on a covert, unofficial basis at JC headquarters. Expenses were covered by selling papers whenever possible, the cost depending upon the recipient's ability to pay. Initially, Jewish printers were used to produce blank certificates. Unfortunately, they were not able to supply the stamps required to complete and authenticate such forms. Consequently, contacts in the bureaucracy were quickly developed, bribery of lower-echelon government officials henceforth becoming the favoured method of obtaining completed documents. Although this produced higher-class papers — that is, of government issue though generally in fictitious names — of necessity, such papers were available in only micro (limited) quantities. As will be seen, the Halutzim produced their avalanche of false papers after mid-1944, the neutral legations' *Schutzpässe* scheme providing the necessary facade for validating the Halutz macro strategy.

As with the Zionist youth, the JC group distributed their false documents to both individuals and organisations, the latter redistributing such papers to their own members. However, unlike the tightly organised, ideologically based Halutz structures, the JC groups were informal, non-ideological, largely leaderless networks of young activists. Lacking a secretariat or formal organisation, these loose circles utilised interested friends, colleagues, families and trusted acquaintances to facilitate their operations. Recognising the mortal dangers inherent in the ghettoisation process, both the Halutz and JC groups attempted to warn Hungary's provincial Jews. Despite both parties dispatching emissaries from Budapest with warnings and false papers, and despite some intrepid Jews accepting the advice and the proffered documents, as previously discussed, the great mass of provincial Jews remained welded to the status quo.

Interestingly, Arthur notes the anomaly that in some cases, especially in the provinces, people requested false papers testifying to a Jewish rather than a Christian status. This apparently counterproductive request highlights the dilemma of those Jews wanting the security of false documents yet unwilling to abandon their Jewish identity. Consequently, such people were prepared to continue living as Jews, albeit under the generally reduced risk of a false name and address.[307]

Regarding the JC groups' non-Budapest endeavours, Arthur Stern states that, although personally never venturing outside the capital and its suburbs, he knows that:

> These missions to the provinces were informal, often individual actions, usually by people with local knowledge. They weren't co-ordinated by a central bureau and, being highly illegal, nobody kept statistics. There were numerous informal circles, based on friendship, ideology or personality, often operating independently of each other. No one considered the needs of future historians asking questions and requesting details of our actions.[308]

Although unable to quantify results with any precision, Arthur states that the JC groups' false documentation operations helped save many hundreds of families. According to his testimony, a total of possibly several thousand people were thus spared the horrors of deportation. As a matter of principle, priority was allocated to those at greatest risk, in particular those who "looked Jewish" — that is, conformed to the commonly accepted Jewish physical stereotype — and were prepared to risk living underground.

During extensive discussions, Arthur recalled personally supplying about two dozen families with false papers, one large family requiring seven separate sets of documents.[309] Despite their relatively extensive activity, it appears that none of the JC-based youth activists ever encountered difficulties with either the Hungarian or German authorities. It should be noted that Arthur was never involved with bribing Germans, his bribes being directed exclusively at Hungarian officials, in particular a bureaucrat at the Interior Ministry who "appeared to have access to everything".[310]

In unexceptional circumstances, an apparent lack of supporting documentation presents a very substantial impediment to the acceptance of oral testimony. Regarding the lower-echelon resistance centred on the JC, the problems generated by the lack of documentary evidence can be overcome by considering the special factors pertinent to illegal operations in occupied Hungary. The keeping of records or files by the few dozen activists would have jeopardised not only their operations but also their lives, and probably the lives of their contacts and those assisted. Additionally, it should be noted that, on a percentage basis, only an insignificant number of the some 200,000 Jewish survivors of the Holocaust in Hungary wrote memoirs or deposited testimony regarding the circumstances of their survival. These factors, when combined with the relatively small scale and highly secret nature of the JC-based operations, the authorities' apparent inability to detect such activities, and the fact that some activists — probably including the dedicated long-term operatives — would not have survived the German Occupation,[311] Budapest ghetto, *Nyilas* terror and Soviet siege, indicates that the absence of documentation confirming Arthur Stern's oral testimony is quite in accord with reasonable expectations.

Consequently, in such situations, rather than dismissing the oral testimony *per se*, one should consider the eyewitness and the given testimony on their intrinsic

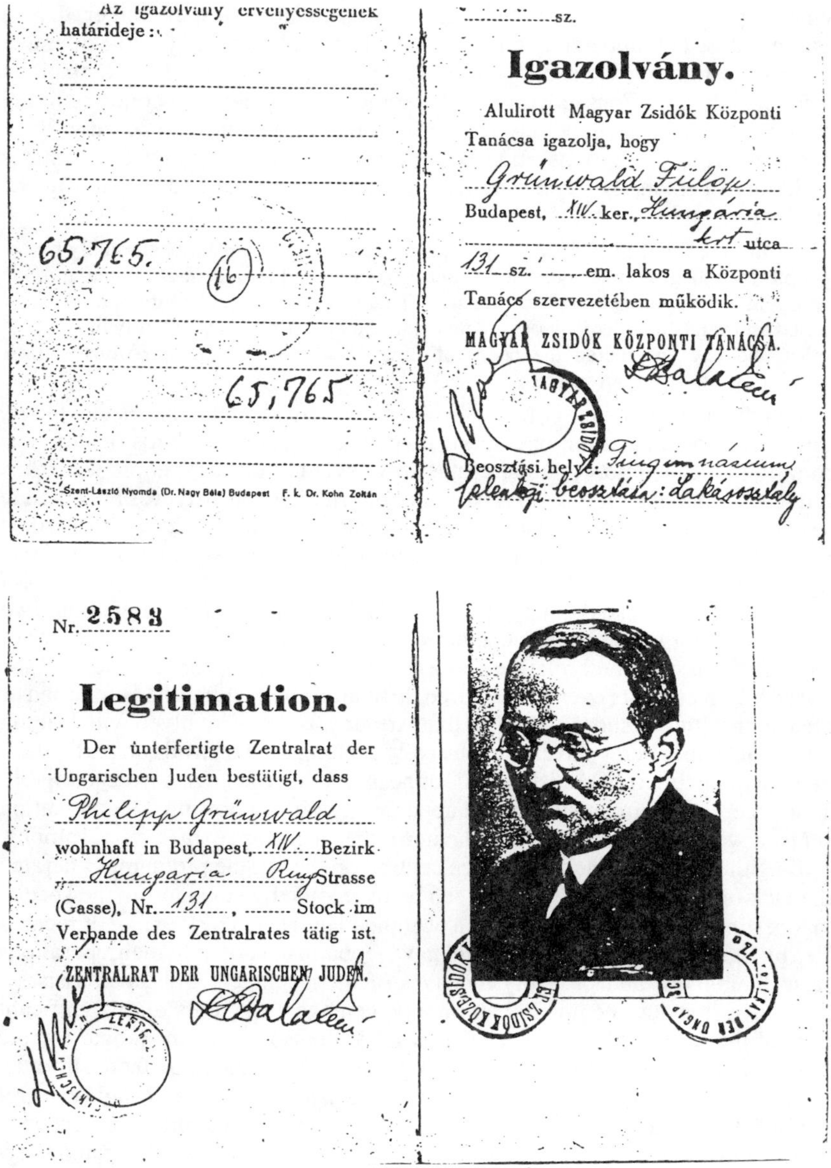

Az igazolvány érvényességének
határideje :

.... sz.

Igazolvány.

Alulírott Magyar Zsidók Központi
Tanácsa igazolja, hogy

Grünwald Fülöp

Budapest, XIV. ker. *Hungária*
.... *kört* utca

131 sz. .... em. lakos a Központi
Tanács szervezetében működik.

MAGYAR ZSIDÓK KÖZPONTI TANÁCSA.

Beosztási helye: *Tungimnásium*
jelenlegi beosztása: lakásosztály

Szent-László Nyomda (Dr. Nagy Béla) Budapest   F. k. Dr. Kohn Zoltán

Nr. 2583

Legitimation.

Der unterfertigte Zentralrat der
Ungarischen Juden bestätigt, dass

Philipp Grünwald

wohnhaft in Budapest, XIV. Bezirk
Hungária Ring Strasse
(Gasse), Nr. 131 , ... Stock im
Verbande des Zentralrates tätig ist.

ZENTRALRAT DER UNGARISCHEN JUDEN.

Figure 4.6 *Igazolvany.*
**Protective pass with photograph in the form of a Registration certificate
(*Igazolvany* — no. 2583) provided by the *Magyar Zsidok Kozponti Tanacsa* (Jewish
Council) to one of its officers. The recipient, Fulop Grunwald, worked as an
executive in the Housing Department (Lakasosztaly). Illegible date, but probably
issued in the first months of the Occupation.** (Source: JMB, 65.765)

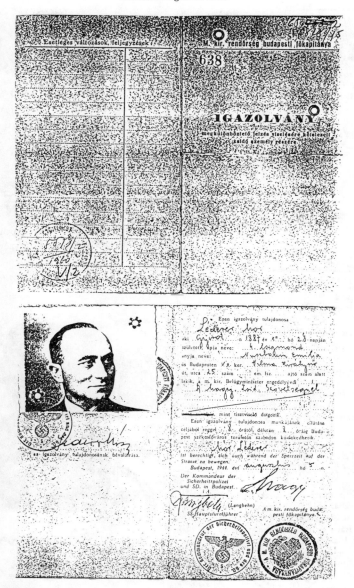

Figure 4.7 *Igazolvany.*
**Protective pass with photograph in the form of a Registration certificate
(*Igazolvany* — no. 638) dated 5 August 1944. Issued by the Royal Hungarian Police
Headquarters of Budapest (*m. kir. rendorseg budapesti fokapitanya*) and counter-
signed by an *SS-Hauptsturmführer* (Captain), the pass states that the bearer,
Mor Lederer, is an official of the "*Magy. Zsid. Szovetseg*" [Hungarian Jewish
Association] and is thus permitted unrestricted movement throughout Budapest
between 8am and 8pm — whilst on official duties.** (Source: JMB, 65.828)

Jene Angehörige, die mit dem Ausweis-
inhaber im gemeinsamen Haushalt wohnen
und ❚❚ schützen sind :

Az igazolvány tulajdonosával közös háztartásban élő és vele együtt védett hozzá-
tartozók :

Frau Leo Stern geb.
Berta Frankfurter Buda-
pest 1901.

Söhne: 1) Artur Stern geb.
1925. Budapest.

2) Robert Stern geb.
1928. Budapest.

F. k. Stern Samu

Nr. *95.*

IMMUNITÄTS-AUSWEIS

für Angehörige des Zentralrates
der Juden in Budapest.

MENTESSÉGI-IGAZOLVÁNY

a Zsidók Budapesti Központi
Tanácsához tartozók részére.

Der Inhaber dieses Ausweises

Leo Stern

geboren am *20. IV. 1897.*
in *Sokolowka*   ist Angehöriger
des Zentralrates der Juden in Budapest.
Es ist von allen Massnahmen gegen diese
Person und gegen seinen (ihren) in gemeinsamen Haushalt wohnenden Angehörigen
Abstand zu nehmen, bzw. ist mit der unterzeichneten Dienststelle Verbindung aufzunehmen.

Ennek az igazolványnak a tulajdonosa
Stern Leó
aki *1897. IV. 22.*-én *Sokolowka*-n
született, a Zsidók Budapesti Központi Tanácsához tartozik. Tartózkodni kell minden
rendszabálytól, amely ezen személy vagy a
vele közös háztartásban élő hozzátartozója
ellen irányul, olyan esetben a jelen igazol-
ványt kiállító hatósággal kell nek érintkezésbe.
Budapest, 1944.

S. Kállai
aloszt. vez.?

SS Obersturmbannführer.

Figure 4.8 *Mentessegi Igazolvany.*
**Joint Hungarian-German Exemption Certificate (No. 95?) with photograph of Leo
Stern, dated March 1944 (day not specified) and stamped 4 April. The Certificate
testifies that the recipient is associated with the Jewish Council, bears the
signature of** *Obersturmbannführer-SS* **(Lieutenant-Colonel) Krumey, and provides
immunity for Leo and Berta Stern, and their two sons, Robert and Arthur.**
(Source: private files of Arthur Stern)

Namenliste der geschützten Familien-
angehörigen:

A védett családtagok névjegyzéke:

Ehefrau: Berta Stern, geb.
Frankfurter 1901

Kinder: Arthur Stern – 1925.
Robert Stern – 1928.

Bruder: Jonas Stern – 1904
Schwägerin: Fr. Anna Stern, geb.
Adler – 1914.

ihre Kinder: Killy Stern – 1935
Andreas Stern – 1937.

Felesége: sz. Frankfurter Berta 1901
Fiai: Stern Arthur – 1925
" Robert – 1928
Fivére: " Jonás – 1904
Sógornője: Stern Jónásné sz. Adler
anna – 1914.
gyermekeik: Stern Killy 1935
" Andor – 1937

Der Kommandeur der Sicherheitspolizei und des SD in Budapest.

Magyar Királyi Állambiztonsági Rendészet.

Der Inhaber dieses Ausweises

Leon Stern

geboren *1897* in *Szokolofka*

wohnha

arbeitet unterzeichnete Dienststelle.

Es ist von allen Massnahmen gegen den
Inhaber dieses Ausweises, sowie gegen die
umseitig angeführten Familienangehö-
rigen Abstand zu nehmen, bzw. ist mit
der unterzeichneten Dienststelle **vor**
allfällig zu ergreifenden Massnahmen Verbindung aufzunehmen.

Az igazolvány tulajdonosa

Stern Leó

született *1897*-ben *Szokolofka*n

lakik

alulírott hatóság részére dolgozik.

Ezen igazolvány tulajdonosa, valamint
annak a hátlapon feltüntetett családtagjai
és hozzátartozói ellen minden eljárástól el
kell tekinteni, illetve ilyen eljárás okvetlen
szüksége esetén **előbb** a kiállító hatósággal érintkezésbe kell lépni.

Figure 4.9 *Mentessegi Igazolvany.*

Joint Hungarian-German Exemption Certificate No. 207 with photograph of Leo Stern. This certificate provides protection for Leo, one of his younger brothers, Jonas, as well as their wives and children. Note that the document bears neither date nor Leo's address (*lakik*). Furthermore, the German signatory's title is not included. On this basis, the certificate's authenticity is dubious.

(Source: private files of Arthur Stern)

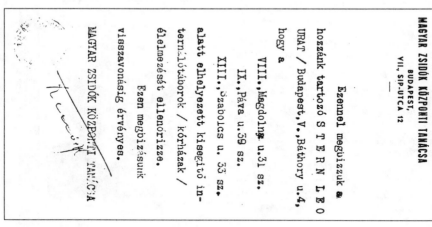

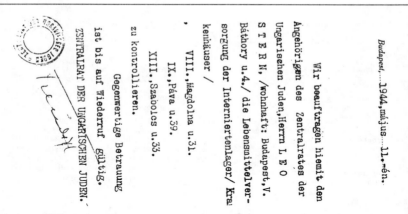

Figure 4.10 **Certificate of Office.**
**Certificate issued by the Jewish Council on 11 May 1944, testifying that Leo Stern
is in charge of food supply and distribution at 31 Magdolna Street, 39 Pava Street
and 33 Szabolcs Street, addresses located in the VIII, IX and XIII districts of
Budapest respectively.** (Source: private files of Arthur Stern)

187

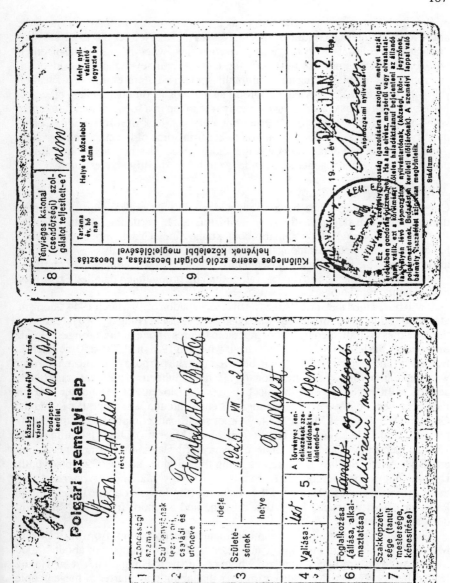

Figure 4.11 *Polgari Szemelyi Lap*.
Civilian Identity Card No. 6606944 issued to Arthur Stern by the Hungarian
government on 21 January 1942. Note that over the years his occupation
(*Foglalkozasa*, section six) was altered from school pupil to university student,
with the final classification being war work. The dates of these changes are not
recorded. Section four refers to the card-holder's religion, the abbreviation *izr.*
indicating Israelite (ie: Jewish). (Source: private files of Arthur Stern)

merits. In this regard, detailed discussions over many hours with Arthur Stern did not reveal any internal contradictions in his statements. Neither did these sessions produce any conflicts with previously verified fact, whether published or otherwise. Furthermore, unlike some other informants, Arthur never denigrated ideological opponents, displayed personal antipathies, claimed a pre-eminence or leadership role, refused to acknowledge appropriate merit or accomplishment in others, or became heated in his claims. His testimony was given in a sober, coherent manner, with forthright admissions of uncertain memory and lack of information. Consequently, despite lacking documentation to confirm some of his statements, Arthur Stern's intimate and detailed knowledge, thorough consistency, and unquestioned personal involvements generate confidence in his credibility and testimony.[312]

The Halutzim

Considerable research has been conducted on Zionist endeavours in Hungary during World War II, especially by Israeli historians. In particular, Halutz (Hebrew for "pioneer"; plural Halutzim; in this context, the Zionist Youth movement) efforts have been chronicled by (amongst others) Dr Asher Cohen, many of whose works are now available in English. Consequently, this section will concentrate on filling gaps and elucidating controversies, rather than on producing a detailed exposition of the Halutzim in Hungary.

It will be recalled that, prior to the German Occupation of 19 March 1944, Zionism, at both the adult and youth levels, was a marginal entity in Hungary.[313] The extent of this weakness is indicated by the membership figures of one of the strongest Halutz movements, the left-wing Hashomer Hatzair which, in 1941, had 200–250 members in Budapest. The majority of this group believed that the purpose of Halutz endeavour was preparation for *Aliya* (emigration to Palestine), rather than political or anti-Nazi activities. In accordance with this belief, some dozens of Hashomer Hatzair members went on *Aliya* between Hungary's entry into the War (June 1941) and the German Occupation of March 1944.[314] Other significant components of the Halutz movement included Maccabi Hatzair (henceforth Maccabi), Dror-Habonim (some 150 members in 1942, mainly in Budapest; henceforth Habonim),[315] Hanoar Hatzioni, and Bnai Akiva, the last group representing the religious sector of Zionist youth. Despite not inconsiderable differences in ideology and *modus operandi*, all these groups were affiliated with the Histadrut (the Jewish Labour Federation in Palestine) and, as such, had contact with, and support from, the Histadrut delegation in Istanbul.

As previously mentioned, commencement of deportations from Slovakia in March 1942 resulted in the significant illegal influx into Hungary of about 10,000 Slovakian Jewish refugees, many of whom could speak Hungarian.[316] One Halutz leader, Perecz Revesz (Maccabi), estimates that about one quarter of these people — including some Polish Jews who had previously escaped the German Occupation of Poland — arrived via the various Halutz smuggling networks.[317] Included in this influx were Slovakian Halutzim, many with leadership experience. Importantly, these Slovak Zionist youths were accepted unconditionally by their *confrères* in the respective Hungarian movements. As conscription into the JLS created a substantial void in the leadership of Hungary's Zionist youth groups, it was these foreign Halutzim — both legal residents from Transylvania and illegal refugees from Slovakia and Poland — who, despite their precarious (often illegal) existence, largely energised, organised and commanded the Halutz response to the Nazi pressures on Hungarian Jews.[318]

As indicated above, the primary imperative of those supporting illegal refugees was to provide shelter, documents, wherewithal and secure social contacts for their charges. After the German Occupation, there developed an additional option for safeguarding people in danger — the *Tiyul* (Hebrew for "trip"; plural, *Tiyulim*) networks, the often Halutz-inspired and organised expeditions that smuggled Jews to the relative safety of Roumania, some of whom then attempted to reach Palestine.[319] Initially, systematic smuggling focused on Polish Halutzim sheltering in Hungary,[320] that is those activists with the greatest experience of German methods and the least security due to their unfamiliarity with Hungarian customs and language. Contemporaneously, Slovak Halutzim organised a so-called re-*Tiyul*, a return of Slovakian refugees to the then relative security of Slovakia.[321] As with many Halutz endeavours, *Tiyulim* were financed by the *Va'ada*, the principal origin of such funds being Zionist delegations in Istanbul and Geneva.[322] It should be noted that partisan activity in Yugoslavia in effect precluded *Tiyulim* to that country, the Germans and their guerilla opponents turning the Hungarian-Yugoslav border region into heavily patrolled areas of persistent conflict.

Tiyul activity by Habonim was largely representative of Halutz endeavour in this field of resistance.[323] Habonim's initial attempts involved those members born in Transylvania and thus familiar with Roumanian customs and language. Once securely in Roumania, these members and their Roumanian *confrères* developed smuggling, reception and support networks to help subsequent escapees reach the relative security of the capital, Bucharest. One Habonim leader, Asher Aranyi, was based in the Hungarian city of Nagyvarad (currently Oradea Mare, in Roumania), 200 km to the east of Budapest. Forming connections with local Roumanians — mainly smugglers who travelled back and forth across the border — in a period of under two months Aranyi accompanied some 350–400 individuals from Budapest to Nagyvarad, generally in groups of ten to twelve people. Placing each group under the guidance of a smuggler on the Hungarian side of the border, Aranyi continued this activity until arrested by the Gestapo on 23 May 1944. Confessing to smuggling Jews for money, Aranyi was released from prison on 23 June — apparently the Gestapo could not conceive of a Jew smuggling fellow Jews — and returned to Budapest with a genuine Gestapo document, albeit one that prohibited him being less than fifteen kilometres from the Roumanian border. Subsequent to this arrest, Moishe Alpan re-established Asher Aranyi's operation, which proved to be the most important route of the Roumanian *Tiyul*.[324]

Tiyulim, in effect, ended abruptly on 23 August when Roumania announced an immediate switch to the Allied side of the War, the *volte-face* creating a war zone along the frontier with Hungary. Note that unlike the isolated attempts at reaching Yugoslavia, or the more systematic re-*Tiyul* to Slovakia, escapes to Roumania were purely rescue missions, with no thought of the participants engaging in armed resistance. Importantly, *Tiyulim* were initially attempted as a centrally co-ordinated Halutz endeavour. Proving unsuccessful, this centralised format quickly devolved into a cellular matrix, one whereby each movement tended to organise the escape of its own members, supporters or selected participants. However, elements of co-operation remained, notably between Habonim and Maccabi, and Bnai Akiva and Hanoar Hatzioni.[325]

Considerable controversy exists regarding the actual numbers rescued by the Halutz-organised smuggling operations. David Gur (originally Grosz), a Hashomer Hatzair leader in wartime Hungary and, at the time of writing, Secretary of The Society for the Research of the History of the Zionist Youth Movement in Hungary, states that in the period 19 March to 23 August 1944, the Halutzim smuggled about 16,000 Jews into Roumania. Gur adds that, contemporaneously, about 500 returned to Slovakia, where the large majority participated in the Slovak national uprising.[326] It is a matter of appreciable distress to Gur that historians do not accept these figures. Asher Cohen estimates that the Roumanian *Tiyul* saved some 7,000 Jews.[327] After noting the impossibility of quantifying numbers saved, Robert Rozett concludes — somewhat ambiguously — that "apparently at least 4,000 refugees from Hungary reached Rumania and at least 2,000 through the Tiul", without clarifying whether the second figure is included within, or additional to, the first.[328] Whilst stating that "the Halutzim are generally very credible in their claims...on the whole they did very important work", Professor Yehuda Bauer accepts Roumanian figures which indicate that approximately 5,000 Jews escaped from Hungary into Roumania, about half of these being saved by the Halutzim.[329] Professor Randolph Braham praises the Halutz movement for being "responsible for what were by far the shiniest hours in the tragic wartime history of Hungarian Jewry", but gives no figures regarding the *Tiyul* endeavour.[330]

Prior to 1944, there existed relatively little co-ordination amongst the various Halutz movements, although there was a general awareness of respective activities. The main factors inhibiting co-operation were ideological differences, competition for members, funds and *Aliya* certificates,[331] and Hungary's somewhat inconsistent wartime attitude towards Zionism, the adult movement being tolerated in Budapest but provincial and youth organisations being repressed by the government. Consequent upon Kallay's attempted extrication of Hungary from the German embrace (see above), in December 1943 these bans on Zionist endeavour were lifted, a decision that resulted in a burst of Halutz activity.[332]

In February 1944, the Istanbul *Va'ada* dispatched $US10,000 to the Halutz movements in Hungary and, concerned about the prospects of a German invasion of that country, issued instructions to prepare for such an eventuality by establishing a centralised leadership, the Haganah, and undertaking pre-emptive defence measures. All elements of Zionist youth accepted this order, the resulting central hierarchy consisting of a leader, Moishe Rosenberg (Hashomer Hatzair), supported by a ministry of Slovak refugees Mano Klein (Maccabi) and Moishe Alpan (Hashomer Hatzair), and Polish refugees Dov Abramczik (Bnai Akiva) and Leon Blatt (Hatzioni).[333]

Such a structure quickly proved unwieldy, especially in situations of urgency and risk. Consequently, under pressure from the German Occupation, this cabinet was superseded by a mixed format, with individual movements once again tending to organise their own acts of resistance. Importantly, despite this devolution of command, Halutz activities were still centrally financed, with elements of co-ordination and decision making — particularly the systematic production of false documents — remaining as a tangible legacy of the Jewish Agency's February instruction.[334]

As previously discussed, Christian identity was an essential prerequisite for all forms of underground endeavour. As such, "Aryanisation" of the entire Halutz membership, via the provision of false documents, became an urgent priority. It will be recalled that Zionist youth involvement in false document production and distribution commenced with the influx of illegal refugees (that is, well before the German Occupation), was far more extensive, and demonstrated an intense, committed professionalism compared with the similarly altruistic but relatively small-scale, largely decentralised operation conducted by non-Zionist youth from the Jewish Council's headquarters at 12 Sip Street.

Led by David Gur of Hashomer Hatzair,[335] a small Halutz cell built a remarkably proficient enterprise which, despite severe difficulties and hazardous conditions — including arrests, and the need to physically relocate the operation's headquarters fifteen times during the ten months of Budapest's Occupation — eventually produced and distributed a wide assortment of over 200,000 false documents. According to identical lists provided in Budapest by Gur (1946) and Hashomer Hatzair (1948),[336] these included:

Birth Certificates	10,000
Marriage Licences	8,000
Civil Identity Cards (*Polgari Szemelyi lap*)	10,000
Catholic Baptismal Certificates (see Fig. 4.4)	3,000
Catholic Marriage Certificates	1,500
Protestant Baptismal Certificates	1,200
Protestant Marriage Certificates	750
Polish Birth Certificates	300
Slovak Birth Certificates	80
Slovak Baptismal Certificates	80
Croat Baptismal Certificates	5
Swiss Birth Certificates	5
Death Certificates	80
University Index (Registration) Certificates	25
Work Cards (with photographs, assorted factories)	7,400
Foreign Office Certificates	25
El Salvador Consulate Certificates	50
Paraguay Consulate Certificates	50
Swiss Consulate Certificates	120
Swiss Protective Passports (*Schutzpässe*)	120,000
Swedish Protective Passports (*Schutzpässe*)	30
Vatican Protective Passports (*Schutzpässe*)	450
USA Citizenship Documents	15
Slovak Citizenship Documents	30
Slovak Passports	12
Gestapo Certificates	20
Nyilas (Arrow Cross) Documents (two types)	420
Housing Registration Forms (see Fig. 4.2)	60–80,000
Demobilisation Cards	180

Additionally, 3,500 Military Exemption Certificates and 170 Execution Decrees were printed, the latter enabling Halutzim — dressed in stolen *SS* and Hungarian uniforms — to spirit comrades from prison without bureaucratic entanglement or delay.[337]

It is important to note that this Halutz endeavour involved both macro and micro aspects of resistance. The imperative to protect the great mass of Budapest Jews led to the overwhelming majority of false documents falling into two categories, Swiss *Schutzpässe* (120,000) and Housing Registration Forms (60–80,000). Despite this necessity, the needs of small Jewish minorities sheltering illegally in Budapest were not neglected, as indicated by, for example, the tiny volume of Croat Baptismal (five), Swiss Birth (five) and Slovak Passports (twelve) that were produced. The number and variety of documents manufactured clearly indicates a comprehensive, systematic endeavour to negate the *Endlösung* process. Very few, if any, elements of the Jewish community were neglected by this Halutz resistance cell.

A critical precursor to the success of this endeavour was the neutral legations' well-known *Schutzpass* scheme (discussed below). Miklos (Moishe) Krausz, controversial head of the Palestine Office in Budapest, initiated this scheme with the unstinting co-operation of the Swiss consul, Charles Lutz,[338] who was repeatedly criticised by his superiors at the Swiss Foreign Ministry for exceeding his authority in safeguarding Budapest's Jews.[339] It should be noted that, during the War, Switzerland represented various Allied powers in Hungary, including the United Kingdom, Lutz being the Swiss legation officer in Hungary who handled Palestine visas issued by the British government. On 26 June 1944 the Hungarian government, hoping to alleviate Allied and neutral pressure regarding the appalling Jewish situation in Hungary, approved the emigration of 7,800 Jews. This figure was deliberately misinterpreted by Krausz and his Jewish colleagues as referring to 7,800 families, thereby hoping to increase numbers involved in the scheme to about 30,000 people. A month after the government's approval, the Swiss Legation opened an annex at 29 Vadasz Street — premises formerly utilised as a glass warehouse, and henceforth popularly called the Glass House — in which 7,800 families were to be registered as participants in the migration scheme. As an annex of the Swiss Embassy, the Glass House was formally protected by its extra-territorial status, being classified as the "Swiss Legation, Foreign Interests Section — Department of Emigration".

Knowledge of legal migration possibilities spread rapidly, with thousands of Budapest Jews besieging the building in an attempt to register themselves and their families as participants.[340] The Halutz false documentation cell, recognising this demand and ignoring strict legalities and diplomatic niceties, seized the opportunity created by the emigration scheme and manufactured many tens of thousands of Swiss *Schutzpässe* which were then distributed to the Jews of Budapest via the Halutz network. Whilst not valid under international law, possession of such a document conferred an aura of protection and "extra-territoriality" upon the recipient, the genuine Swiss *Schutzpass* stating that the holders were "included in a collective Palestine passport and until their departure under the protection of the Swiss Legation".[341] Importantly, without Krausz' initiative, and the facade of legality provided by Lutz at the Swiss legation, it is unlikely that this aspect of the Halutz resistance could have achieved much significance.

In early November 1944 Szalasi's *Nyilas* junta, suspicious of the number of protective passes then circulating within the Jewish community, decided to segregate *Schutzpass*-holders into a so-called International Ghetto, specially designated Yellow Star apartment blocks centred around Budapest's Pozsonyi Road. By that stage the junta, desperate for political legitimacy, had attempted to obtain the neutrals' diplomatic recognition by permitting neutral powers to issue a total of 15,000 *Schutzpässe* — 7,800 Swiss; 4,500 Swedish; 2,500 Vatican; 700

Portuguese; and 100 Spanish.[342] The *Nyilas* junta had gambled that, as a *quid pro quo*, the neutral nations would grant them diplomatic recognition, which, in turn, would provide their regime with the desperately desired facade of political legitimacy.

Paradoxically, because of its magnitude — the Halutz false document endeavour was one of the largest, if not the largest, such enterprise in German-occupied Europe[343] — questions arise as to its ultimate benefits. With hindsight it may be argued that, by providing the majority of Budapest Jews with false papers — a defence mechanism meant for a small minority of their co-religionists — the protection afforded this minority was significantly devalued via the severe erosion of the genuine documents' credibility.[344] Numerous reports indicate that *Nyilas* brigands, emboldened by suspicions surrounding the number of dubious *Schutzpässe* in circulation, refused to recognise foreign protective documents and systematically raided the buildings constituting the International Ghetto.[345] Asher Cohen broaches this subject thus: "When the protected houses were set up, the privileged residents were subject to the harassment of the Fascists no less than the others. Still it is difficult to ascertain with any certainty if the houses under Swiss patronage suffered any more than the others."[346]

No such doubt was entertained by Miksa Domonkos, heroic head during the Szalasi era of the Jewish Council's Technical Services Department, the department that included the Jewish ghetto police.[347] At Szalasi's postwar trial, whilst answering questions concerning the notorious footmarch deportations of Buda-pest Jews following the *Nyilas* coup of 15 October 1944, Domonkos stated that "*A gettobol keveset vittek, hanem a getton kivuli reszekbol, az ugynevezett vedett hazakbol.*"[348] ("Few were taken from the [Common] ghetto, but from districts outside the ghetto, from the so-called protected houses.") Circumstantial evidence supports this assessment of *Nyilas* selectivity. In early January 1945, about 10,000 Jews protected by Sweden, Portugal, Switzerland and the Vatican were transferred by these powers from the International Ghetto to the Common Ghetto, presumably (according to Braham) in the interests of increased safety.[349]

Thus, according to Domonkos' overlooked testimony — and he, via the reports of his ghetto police, was in a position to know — the Halutz false documentation endeavour inadvertently proved counterproductive to some of the 15,000 Budapest Jews holding genuine *Schutzpässe*. However, even accepting Domonkos' state-ment that most deportees during the Szalasi era were seized from protected Yellow Star buildings, one cannot assume that in the absence of the Halutz false document enterprise, the *Nyilas* brigands would not have vented their fury on the Jewish majority herded into the Common ("non-protected") Ghetto.

With regard to this aspect of the Halutz resistance in Hungary, it is reasonable to conclude that, during the Occupation period prior to the Szalasi era, Halutz-produced false documents increased the manoeuvrability and security, and lifted the morale, of many thousands of Jews. Moreover, during the Szalasi era thousands of pragmatic (or opportunist) Hungarians — including members of the police, military and public service — sought security and/or alibis via papers produced by the Halutzim,[350] such people thus moderating their behaviour towards Budapest's remaining Jews. In particular, apart from the police guarding the Glass House environs in Vadasz Street,[351] some Hungarian army units not wanting to be sent West to defend Germany provided weapons to the Halutzim in exchange for either money or false documents. Such weapons were either kept for Halutz purposes or else given to various elements of the small, ineffective non-Jewish resistance. According to David Gur, included in the weapons obtained in this manner was a tank! — which was subsequently used by Halutzim in military uniform to release Jews held captive by *Nyilas* brigands.[352]

Despite a possibly counterproductive — though undoubtedly inadvertent — aspect to their false document production, no such caveat can be levelled at other Zionist youth endeavours during the Occupation period. In particular, Halutz co-operation with Otto Komoly, head of the Hungarian Zionist movement and director of Section A of the International Red Cross (IRC) in Hungary, resulted in the successful maintenance of some thirty Childrens' Homes in Budapest. Originally intended for orphaned and abandoned Jewish youngsters, these IRC-protected Homes saved about 4,000 Jewish children plus over 1,000 adults who sheltered under its auspices.[353] It was primarily Halutz leadership, initiative and enterprise that provided the guards, equipment and psychological stamina needed to maintain the viability of this rescue enterprise.[354] Above all, this endeavour was accomplished in Szalasi's Budapest, a period noted for its administrative chaos, virtual social anarchy, critical food shortage, and rampant *Nyilas* brigandry. A period in which the havoc, hysteria and homelessness produced by the Allies' ferocious aerial bombardment was exacerbated by the 300–400,000 desperate, impoverished refugees from eastern Hungary who poured into Budapest after fleeing the advancing Soviet forces.[355]

One of the critical factors determining Jewish survival in Budapest during this epoch was the provision of food. The Red Army's progressive capture of Hungary's agricultural provinces continually reduced available food supplies until, on 24 December 1944, Soviet encirclement commenced a bitter siege that prevented further deliveries to the city. Utilising Jewish funds transmitted to Budapest via the IRC and the Swiss Legation,[356] and operating under the protective aegis of Komoly's Section A (the Red Cross), the Halutzim prepared for the inevitable Soviet blockade by initiating and conducting a massive procurement, transportation and distribution effort that resulted in remarkable quantities of food being supplied to Budapest's Jewish populace — before, during and after the siege.[357] Using the knowledge, experience and stock of prominent Jewish food wholesalers,[358] as well as bribes, threats of retribution and promises of postwar payment and protection, the Halutzim procured foodstuffs and regularly thwarted the marauding *Nyilas* brigands (who were themselves in genuine need) by guarding shipments in purloined German or Hungarian uniforms.[359] One particularly successful Halutz tactic for obtaining provisions was to promise postwar payment in full, a promise that was fulfilled via funds provided by international Jewish agencies. Non-Jewish wholesalers and businesses generally provided supplies on the basis of self-interest, realising that their warehouses would probably be looted by combatants or destroyed in the theatre of battle.

Despite the concurrence of oral testimony,[360] there exists a school of thought sceptical about the significance of the Halutz food procurement enterprise, a school exemplified by Hungarian historian Laszlo Karsai. Whilst claiming that the Halutz were marginal providers, supplying less than 10 percent of food consumed by Budapest's Jews in the Szalasi period, Karsai commented: "I feel sorry for [David] Gur because he is currently attempting to construct his own statue and I'm afraid I can't contribute to the endeavour. He attempts to take advantage of the lack of [supporting] documents... Documents prove that [Raoul] Wallenberg provided tonnes of food."[361] When assessing this point of view, it should be noted that Karsai's contention regarding the critical importance of Wallenberg's provisions is contradicted by a Swedish Consulate Report (7 December 1944, to the Ministry of Foreign Affairs in Stockholm), and by some of Wallenberg's close associates in Occupied Hungary, including the Swedish diplomat Per Anger.[362]

Comprehensive details of Halutz food procurement during the Szalasi era no longer survive.[363] However, Karsai's opinion can be examined in the light of the remaining records of Rudolph Weisz, Halutz transport manager from the beginning of November 1944.[364] Weisz' surviving registers indicate that for the period 28 November to 23 December over 300,000 kg of foodstuffs and provisions were delivered to various Jewish locations in Budapest, primarily the 12 Sip and 7 Wesselenyi Street buildings in the Common Ghetto (see Fig. 4.13).[365] Quantified deliveries included:

```
30 November ........................................................... 14,550 kg flour
3 December .............................................................. 6,000 kg beans
7 December ........................................................... 10,000 kg pasta
11 December ...................................................... 9,000 kg oat-flakes
13 December .............................................................. 500 kg cheese
15 December ................. 5,000 kg tinned tomatoes; 15,000 kg flour
.............................................. 200 straw mattresses; 2,000 kg coke
16 December ......................... 10,000 kg flour; 14,415 kg dried peas
............................................................................. 20,000 kg beans
19 December .......................... 20,400 kg flour; 10,200 kg corn flour
20 December ...................................... 1,100 kg eggs; 465 kg cheese
.......................................................................... 10,000 kg white beans
21 December .................................. 4,500 kg coke; 4,500 kg wood
22 December ................. 100,000 kg marrow; 20,000 kg hulled peas
23 December .......................... 10,000 kg salt; 200 straw mattresses
```

Additional to the above were unquantified items, such as: 3 December — "*egy fuvar kulonbozo elelmiszer*" (one delivery of assorted foodstuffs); 8 December — "*1 vagon sutotok*" (1 wagon pumpkins); and 23 December — "*egy fuvar tisztitoszerek*" (one delivery of cleaning agents). Importantly, the significance of Halutz deliveries should be considered in light of Macartney's statement that by September 1944 the fuel situation was "extremely serious", and Budapest's food supply had suffered "substantial deterioration...in practice many foodstuffs vanished from the market altogether".[366]

David Gur ardently maintained that the supply by Halutzim of foodstuffs and provisions to the besieged Budapest Jews during the Szalasi era was an undertaking unique in the history of Jewish resistance during the Holocaust epoch.[367] Whilst an evaluation of Gur's claim is beyond the scope of this book, knowledge of certain parameters regarding the Budapest Jewish population permits a broad evaluation of Karsai's belief regarding the Halutz food enterprise. One may assume that for the period of the above list (28 November–23 December) the capital had adequate water supplies[368] and contained 100,000 officially registered Jews[369] leading a largely sedentary existence, many of whom were tending towards starvation.[370] Note that Budapest's two ghettos had a disproportionate number of youngsters, women, the ill and the aged, most people of military age (sixteen to sixty) having been conscripted into the JLS, gone underground, or been deported via footmarches.[371] From its institution (15 October) to the commencement of the siege of Budapest (24 December), the Szalasi regime deported some 80,000 Jews for labour to Germany.

The writer's discussion with medical authorities revealed that, under then prevailing circumstances, the "average" Jewish inhabitant of Budapest would have required a monthly supply of six to eight kilograms of basic foodstuffs to survive.[372] The upper figure possibly errs on the generous, a conclusion implied by Macartney's statement that for non-Jews — invariably allocated a higher official ration than Jews[373] — in early December "the bread ration was down to 150 grams per day [ie: 4.5 kg per month]; milk, meat and fats [were] practically non-existent and prices on the black market fantastic".[374] However assuming that the "average" registered Jew consumed eight kilograms of food in December, the Jewish population of Budapest consumed some 800,000 kg of food that month. Consequently, taking cognisance of Rudolph Weisz' register, one may reasonably conclude that the over 300,000 kg supplied by the Halutzim constituted at least one-third of the food consumed by Budapest Jews in December 1944. On the basis that some food was supplied after 23 December[375] — albeit from urban stockpiles, and probably in reduced quantities due to the Soviet siege which commenced the next day — and that nine deliveries listed on Weisz' register were unquantified, there is a distinct possibility that this proportion may have been significantly higher. Certainly, if average consumption is taken at six kilograms per month — an assumption in keeping with Braham's statement that "*in theory*, ghetto dwellers were to receive 100 to 150 grams of bread a day" (emphasis added)[376] — then the Halutz contribution to total consumption in December 1944 (600,000 kg) would have exceeded 50 percent.[377] At the very least, the above evaluation has a sufficient order of accuracy to refute Karsai's marginalisation of the Halutz food endeavour, and to conclude that without the initiative, courage and enterprise of the Halutzim, many thousands of Jews would have perished of starvation during the bitter winter months of Szalasi's brutal reign.[378]

With regard to Karsai's contention that Wallenberg provided tonnes of food, Gur, whilst minimising neither Wallenberg's heroism nor his contribution, asked rhetorically: "From where did Wallenberg obtain his food supplies? Who went to the countryside, in German and Hungarian uniforms, to procure, transport and distribute foodstuffs to Budapest's Jews?"[379] Apart from this implied Halutz co-operation with Wallenberg's organisation (which, in turn, consisted largely of Jews), Gur mentioned a little-noted benefit of the Halutz food distribution process. Trucks and carts delivering provisions to Jews — those herded into appalling internment camps before being footmarched to the Reich, or those actually on a footmarch — often returned with Jews rescued from such situations.[380]

In addition to the rescue and resistance activities discussed above, the Halutzim instituted contingency measures, possibly the most important of which involved the creation of bunkers, and liaison with the small, split Hungarian Communist Party. The latter was not only an attempt to co-ordinate anti-Nazi activity, but also an effort to develop relations with a political grouping which, the Halutz leadership realised, would become an inevitable, legitimate and highly significant factor in Hungarian politics upon the Soviet Occupation of the country. Such relations, it was hoped, would legitimise, and benefit, Zionism in postwar Hungary.

One of the significant conduits from the Halutz to the Communist movement was a Hashomer Hatzair leader Jozsef Meir, a left-wing political activist at the grass-roots level. After mid-1944, Meir became Hashomer Hatzair's liaison with Gyorgy Non, a principal of the then illegal Communist Party's military wing, a marginal body with several hundred members.[381] Through Christian contacts at the Csepel heavy industry centre, Meir, in exchange for false documents, obtained weapons which were either retained for Halutz defence purposes or transmitted to the Communist underground.[382]

Meir was also involved with a proposed national uprising planned after the Szalasi coup of 15 October 1944. Organised by an assortment of anti-Nazi Hungarians, this movement included military officers, social democrats and trade unionists. Significantly, this planned uprising — which never eventuated — was opposed by the Moscow-controlled Communists, ostensibly on the grounds that it would cause a blood-bath.[383] Meir states that whilst other Halutz had contacts with the small (non-Jewish) resistance, the only Zionist youth movement involved in this particular network was Hashomer Hatzair.

Despite elements of central direction, each Halutz movement retained some of its own particular policies and tactics. Habonim, for example, developed bunkers which were maintained as a matter of principle, and as refuges for those unable to be "Aryanised". In contrast, Hashomer Hatzair opposed bunkers because of their inherent dangers, and the difficulties in supplying provisions — particularly electricity — to the occupants.[384] As an alternative, Hashomer Hatzair utilised its Socialist and Communist contacts to locate underground sanctuaries for "un-Aryanisable" Jews.[385]

Notwithstanding the terror generated by the Germans and their Hungarian collaborators during the Occupation, some conflict remained amongst the disparate elements of Hungarian Zionism. In particular, enmity between the Halutzim and the adult movement was predicated upon differences in ideology and *modus operandi*, such disparities being exacerbated by personality clashes and the generation gap. One of the most extended disputes involved Miklos Krausz, Secretary of the Palestine Agency in Hungary, and concerned Krausz' controversial allocation of *Aliya* certificates (see Fig. 4.12) to the various Halutz movements.[386] Well before the Occupation, complaints and conflicts generated by Krausz' allegedly improper activities had reached such intensity that Chaim Barlas, Jewish Agency and Youth Aliya representative in Istanbul, was repeatedly forced to intervene. Indicative was the intervention of 26 January 1943, in which Barlas telegrammed Budapest: "Re Krausz imperative appointing Committee arranging participation General Zionists Misrachi and left stop Receiving complaints against Krausz please investigate."[387] Despite attempting to resolve the discord by allocating the limited number of *Aliya* certificates on the basis of a special Halutz membership census (August 1943), frictions between many Halutz sections and Krausz remained unresolved.[388] In the Szalasi epoch this antagonism extended to the Halutz false *Schutzpass* endeavour, the intensity of confrontation being elucidated by Yehuda Weiss (Hashomer Hatzair) thus:

> Hahomer Hatzair and the other pioneering youth movements thought that this document should be distributed as widely as possible. The bureaucrats who were in charge of "our Legation" [the Palestine Office] thought otherwise and sabotaged all our efforts. Again there were arguments and clashes in "The Glass House". We had to sever all contact with the vicious bureaucracy of the assimilated Jews.[389]

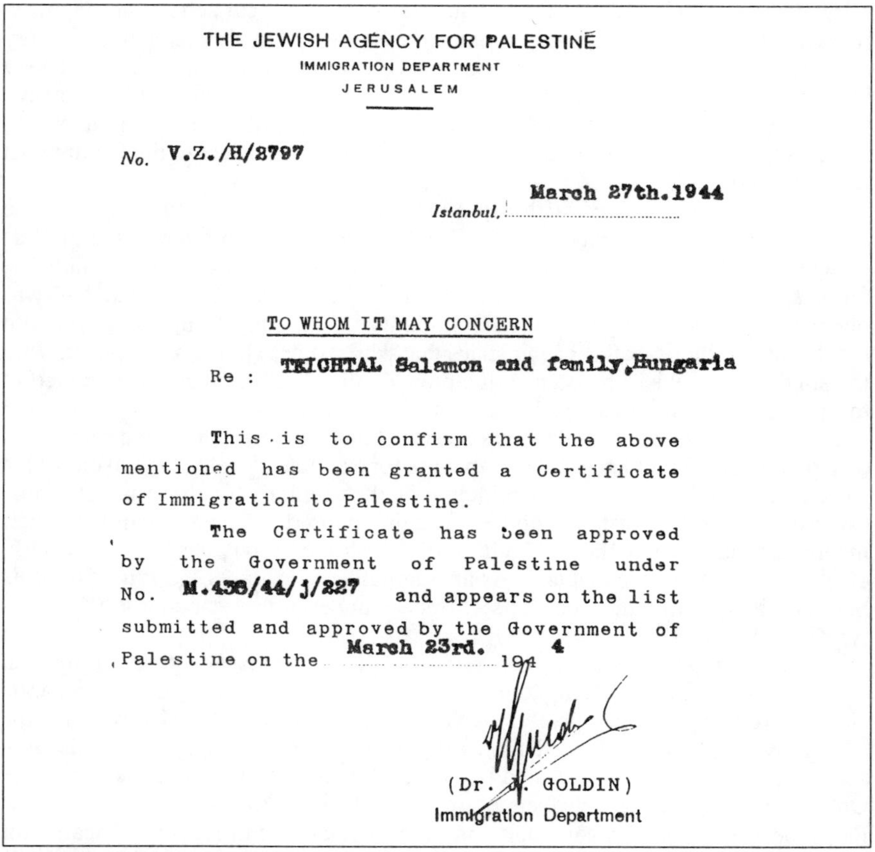

THE JEWISH AGENCY FOR PALESTINE

IMMIGRATION DEPARTMENT

JERUSALEM

No. V.Z./H/2797

March 27th.1944

Istanbul, ...

TO WHOM IT MAY CONCERN

Re : **TEICHTAL Salamon and family,Hungaria**

This is to confirm that the above mentioned has been granted a Certificate of Immigration to Palestine.

The Certificate has been approved by the Government of Palestine under No. **M.436/44/J/227** and appears on the list submitted and approved by the Government of Palestine on the **March 23rd.** 19**4**4

(Dr. J. GOLDIN)

Immigration Department

Figure 4.12 *Aliya* **certificate.**
**Certificate of Immigration to Palestine, No. VZ/H/2797, issued 27 March 1944,
by Dr J Golden, Immigration Department, The Jewish Agency for Palestine,
Jerusalem. Note that this certificate, which refers to Salamon Teichtal and family
of Hungary, was approved and issued subsequent to the German occupation of
Hungary (19 March 1944).** (Source: CZA L15/224)

In general, the Halutzim were frustrated by what they considered were Krausz' ineffectual and indulgent legalisms, and disdainful of the *modus operandi* of the Palestine Office in Budapest. Adding to mutual antagonism, there appeared little acknowledgement by Zionist youth of the reality that Krausz, who negotiated with the Interior Ministry, the Police and foreign legations for visas and other relevant emigration papers, had to eschew illegality and operate in a government-sanctioned manner in order to preserve his organisation's official status.[390]

Similar generic contentions existed between the *Va'ada's* Rezso Kasztner and the Halutz leadership. This conflict was highlighted during the first phase of the Occupation when a senior member of Hashomer Hatzair was captured by the Germans whilst attempting to reach Yugoslavia. Totally committed to the mass rescue of Hungarian Jews (the *nagy vonal* or macro line), Kasztner demanded that the Halutzim refrain from activities which could jeopardise his negotiations with the SS. In turn the Halutz movements, contemptuous of German promises, rejected Kasztner's attempted interference in their micro rescue (*kiss vonal*) endeavours, particularly the *Tiyul*.[391]

Even during the Szalasi era — with the benefit of hindsight, the period of greatest physical danger to Budapest Jews — contention between the youth and adult Zionist leaderships remained extant. Possibly the most notorious example was the *contretemps* between the Halutzim and the directors of the Glass House at 29 Vadasz Street. After its establishment in late July 1944 as an annex of the Swiss legation, the Halutzim gradually abandoned meeting in public arenas to centralise many illegal operations at these premises.[392] Not only was the building's Swiss extra-territoriality a convenient facade for rescue activities but, as Swiss employees, Halutz staff members of the annex enjoyed significant privileges and near-exemption from anti-Jewish legislation.[393]

Arthur Weisz, director of official operations at — and proprietor of — the Glass House, like his colleague Miklos Krausz of the Palestine Office, considered illegal activity a threat to the government-sanctioned emigration scheme for which the annex was originally instituted. Consequently, not infrequent altercations occurred between the largely pro-active youth and the often reactive adult leaders, both sides deprecating each other's *modus operandi*.[394] These disputes were of such intensity that they came to the attention of Otto Komoly, head of the Hungarian Zionist movement. In his diary entry of 6 September 1944 Komoly notes that on 4 September Krausz and Weisz "allegedly threatened with the police to remove Pil and Efra [Agmon; two Hashomer Hatzair leaders] from the [Glass House] building".[395] Accordingly, on 6 September Komoly discussed the Halutz-Glass House situation with Arthur Weisz.[396] Although sufficiently concerned about the situation to label this dispute a conflict, Komoly's diary does not elaborate on his discussion with Weisz. Notwithstanding this mediation by the respected Hungarian Zionist leader, the frictions continued. On 14 September Komoly, again without elaboration, noted in his diary: "Cat and mouse games between Krausz' clique and the left wing. Complaints of Erzsi Eppler and Dundi [Deutsch] over incorrect work assignments, the appointment of new and unknown workers, and the possible firing of those who signed the letter addressed to the leadership."[397]

Although receiving no mention in her testimony, Dr Elizabeth (Erzsi) Eppler, who was seconded to the Glass House on 24 July 1944,[398] elaborated upon these incidents in private discussions with the writer. Commenting that the Halutzim had "real fights" with Krausz and Weisz, Eppler states that the fundamental problem resulted from the latter attempting to coerce Halutzim into working within officially approved channels. In turn, the Halutz leaders not only rejected Krausz and Weisz' "passivist" ideology but also resented their coercive attitude. This mutual antagonism led to what Komoly called the "cat and mouse games between Krausz's clique and the left wing". Furthermore, according to Eppler, Weisz took advantage of his position — and power of patronage — to stack the Glass House hierarchy with his relatives and friends, invariably non-Zionists from the upper stratum of Budapest's Jewish society. These people were unknown to the Halutzim; of unknown ideology, calibre and capacity, and not necessarily to be trusted with intimate details of their secret, illegal and highly dangerous rescue operations.

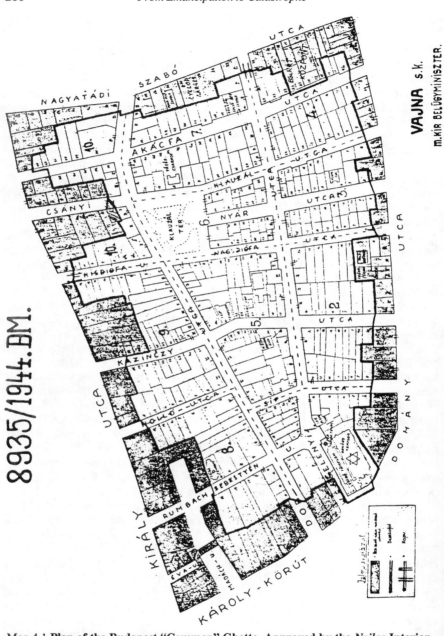

Map 4.1 **Plan of the Budapest "Common" Ghetto. Approved by the *Nyilas* Interior Minister, Gabor Vajna, and established on 29 November 1944, the ghetto contained 4,000 apartments spread over 3 of Budapest's 200 sq km.**[399] **On 17 January 1945, Soviet forces liberated its 70,000 remaining inhabitants. The legend *"Kapu"* indicates a gate.**

GAZDASAGI HIVATAL
V., vadász-u. 29.

Budapest, 1944. december 25.

E L S Z A M O L A S.

XII. 15.-22.-ig szállitott kenyér 3107 kg. á 4.-- P. 12,428.--
    raktári kenyér kg.4000 "   " "   " 16,000.--
    nyomdaszámla   " 1,707.90
    hurkaszámla   " 361.20

                         Összesen: P. 30,497.10

a hiányzó cca. P. 10,000.-- részben Zieglernél van, amiért nekünk még
kenyér jár, részben nagy fuvarelszámolás a holnapi nap folyamán lesz
benyujtva.

Kaptunk: P. 57,400.-- t.
Z₁egler I. előleg: P. 20,000.--
Ziegler II. "   " 20,000.--
165 kg. margarin: " 9,075.--
hurkaszámla: " 361.20   ♦ 49,436.20

                         különbözet: P. 7,963.80

Figure 4.13 *Elszamolas* (Accounts). Accounts for the period 15-22 December, drawn
up by the *Gazdasagi Hivatal* (Finance Department) of the Glass House, 29 Vadasz
Street, on 25 December 1944. Amongst the total expenditure of P(*engo*) 30,497.10,
the ledger shows the following disbursements: P12,428.00 for 3,107 kg of bread
@ P4.00 per kg; P16,000 for 4,000 kg *raktari kenyer* (long-life black bread generally
used by the military); and P1,707.90 for printing costs. The document also indicates
that additional bread deliveries were owing via Ziegler, and that large transport
bills were expected in the near future. (Source: Moreshet Archive DI4668/2)

Eppler characterised the Weisz-appointed group, whom Komoly called the "new
and unknown workers", as "irresponsible people, lacking ideology or commitment,
who only came to the Glass House to save their own skins". Komoly's phrase
"incorrect work assignments" refers to the employment of such individuals in
positions of authority within the Glass House. In particular, the Weisz-appointed
Chief Security Officer was subsequently suspected by Eppler of selling *Schutzpässe*
for his (the appointee's) personal gain.[400]

Consequent to these contentions, a letter protesting against Arhtur Weisz'
actions was sent to the *Va'ada*. This protest finally resulted in such disputes being
largely resolved; Weisz' independence of action was curtailed and his unilateral
power of appointment withdrawn. This, in effect, victory over Weisz resulted in a
considerable increase in the Halutz freedom of action vis-à-vis their Glass House
operations. Notwithstanding appalling conditions, and Weisz' original objections,
from early November until liberation by the Red Army (17 January 1945), numbers
sheltering permanently within the building surged from several hundred to some 2–
3,000 people.[401] Furthermore, despite the intrigues of police informers, the Halutzim
not only fed the inhabitants (see Fig. 4.13), but built a bunker in the basement and
resolved to use their weapons in armed resistance if attacked.[402]

In Central and eastern Europe, Jewish underground movements operating within
the Nazi domain generally had to plead with the local non-Jewish resistance for
assistance, arms and refuge. In the words of David Gur: "Jewish resistance was the
step-child in the anti-Nazi family."[403] It is equally clear that in Hungary these roles

were largely reversed. Not only did the Halutzim rescue many thousands of their co-religionists,[404] but the Jewish underground's infrastructure and experience — unique in Hungary prior to the German Occupation of 19 March 1944 — preceded, and facilitated the development of, the fledgling Hungarian (non-Jewish) resistance.

Despite the deliberate — and highly understandable — avoidance of documentation by underground operatives,[405] Halutz leaders interviewed by the writer were in agreement that it was they who provided anti-Nazi Hungarians with thousands of false documents. Additionally, Zionist youth also supplied the political Left — particularly the Communist groups — with arms and ammunition. Importantly, whilst often harbouring mutual suspicions and ideological hostilities, all non-Jewish anti-Nazi factions during the Szalasi epoch trusted the Halutz movement not to betray their members or secrets to the authorities.

One may conclude that, at the very least, the Halutz were an important, integral part of the anti-Nazi matrix in Hungary. There is no doubt that postwar Hungarian historians who refuse to recognise the centrality of Jewish participation in the fight against Nazism in Hungary — for instance, as late as 1986 Istvan Pinter did not include a single recognised Jewish name in the index of his book on Hungarian resistance during the German Occupation — are attempting to generate collective amnesia whilst engaging in a blatantly untenable historical revisionism.[406]

Chapter IV: Notes

1.This title was suggested by Samu Stern's postwar testimony (Budapest, 1945). Stern characterised his term as president of the Nazi-appointed Jewish Council (*Judenrat*) thus: "I was aware that a race with time was on." (p 3) For an English translation of his testimony, see Yivo 768/3627.

2. Nagy-Talavera 1970:194-96.

3. Janos 1982:306.

4. The word implies that, although caught in a raging torrent, through some means the speaker will survive. This attitude pervaded both Orthodox and Neolog sections of the community, "*Megusszuk*" being the contemporary equivalent of the traditional Jewish refrain "This too shall pass".

5. The Germans formulated two invasion strategies. Margarethe I, a "restricted" Occupation, was the option eventually approved by Hitler. Margarethe II was classified as a "total" Occupation.

6. Macartney 1957:II, 222-23; Deak 1989:37. Deak calls "the deportation of the Jews *perhaps* the greatest human tragedy in Hungarian history..." (Ibid, emphasis added) It would be interesting to discover Professor Deak's considered alternatives to that inglorious title.

7. This is, in fact, what occurred when deportations to Auschwitz were no longer an available option. After the "Szalasi coup" of 15 October 1944, Budapest Jews were herded on death marches to the Reich. Although many thousands died thus, the prospect of an Auschwitz-type genocide occurring on German territory is a matter of speculation.

8. Braham 1981:362. Vago (1969:202) states: "Next to the military and political considerations for the Occupation of Hungary, the Jewish Question was decidedly secondary." According to this body of opinion, the main military motivation was to thwart the collapse of Germany's south-eastern front, a possible consequence of a Hungarian armistice. Politically, Hitler was concerned about the further loss of German prestige. The prime economic motivation for the Occupation was the retention of Hungary's agricultural, mineral and industrial contributions to the Reich's war effort.

9. A special *SS* detachment, in this case charged with implementing the Final Solution in Hungary.

10. Ranki 1985:316.

11. Private discussion with Yehuda Bauer, Jerusalem, December 1990.

12. Shlomo Aronson's arguments will be contained in his forthcoming book *The Quadruple Trap*. I wish to express my particular gratitude to Professor Aronson for generously providing me with a pre-publication manuscript of his forthcoming work.

13. It is pertinent to note that had Roosevelt been seriously interested in rescuing European Jews from the Nazis, not only would the WRB have been established years earlier, but US policy throughout this era would have been fundamentally different. The WRB was established as a result of the US Secretary of the Treasury, Henry Morgenthau — himself a Jew — presenting the US president with a secret memorandum entitled "Acquiescence of this Government in the Murder of the Jews". As history has shown, establishment of the WRB was largely a grand gesture by Roosevelt; a gesture having the advantage of increasing his popularity with US Jews in 1944, an election year. More importantly, it masked the machinations of Antisemitic elements in the US State Department, particularly of Breckenridge Long, an Assistant Secretary of State. Arthur D. Morse summarised US policy in this era thus: "In the years between 1933 and 1944 the American tradition of sanctuary for the oppressed was uprooted and despoiled. It was replaced by a combination of political expediency, diplomatic evasion, isolationism, indifference and raw bigotry which played directly into the hands of Adolph Hitler even as he set in motion the final plans for the greatest mass murder in history." (Morse 1968:86) At the Evian Conference of July 1938 — an attempt to facilitate Jewish emigration from Germany — Australia, less hypocritical than most participants, announced: "As we have no real racial problem, we are not desirous of importing one." (Morse 1968:174) See also n 22 in this chapter.

14. Private discussions with Prof. Aronson, December 1990–February 1991, Jerusalem and Tel Aviv. Recently, Aronson (1997:97) appears to have retreated somewhat from this position.

15. This aspect of Aronson's analysis is in general accord with Eichmann's attitude. The leader of Budapest's Orthodox Community, Fulop Freudiger, relates that "Dr Kasztner pleaded with Eichmann to halt the deportations, arguing that there should be Jews to barter when [Joel] Brand returned from his mission. Eichmann didn't accept this; he said that instead the thumb screw had to be applied, otherwise International Jewry would not be willing to deliver the wanted goods." (Freudiger 1972:268)

16. Ranki 1984:278; Juhasz 1984:216.

17. For the full text of Szombathelyi's memorandum to Horthy, see Szinai and Szucs 1965:211-20. The quoted extract is on page 214. Even three months after the Western Allies' successful landing at Normandy (6 June 1944), the Hungarian government (now led by the pro-Horthyist General Geza Lakatos) believed in a Western landing in the Balkans. Otto Komoly's diary of 9 September 1944 notes: "...[according to official sources] the Hungarian Government believes that the most suitable time for the extrication from the War would be the sixth day after the Adriatic landing of the Anglo-Saxons..." (Komoly 1944:222)

18. Juhasz (1984:216) comments: "We have not paid enough attention to the fact that neither Hungary's internal condition nor the situation on the eastern front at the time were sufficient reasons for an urgent Occupation of the country in March 1944... Did the German High Command possibly fear an imminent breakthrough in the Carpathians? There is no written evidence to support such a hypothesis."

19. Private discussion with Prof. Y. Bauer, Jerusalem, January 1991.

20. Bauer 1978:154.

21. Marrus summarises Hitler's *modus operandi* thus: "...Hitler had a positive aversion to orderly procedures...the Nazi dictator was reluctant to commit himself to paper with concrete ideas and preferred always to give orders orally..." (Marrus 1988:33)

22. Regarding the rescue of European Jews, the unmistakable import of US (and Allied) refugee policy was enunciated on 17 August 1944, by J.W. Pehle, head of the US WRB. Writing to Under Secretary of State Edward Stettinius, Pehle declared: "As I previously indicated to you, I feel strongly that we cannot enter into any ransom transactions with the German authorities in order to obtain the release of the Jews." (Document 11, in Mendelsohn and Detwiler 1982b:101) See also n 13 in this chapter.

23. Pamlenyi 1973:629. The Germans' original nomination of Bela Imredy as PM was rejected by Horthy. Sztojay was accepted by both sides as a mutually agreeable alternative. (Klein 1956:42)

24. Kallay 1954:362.

25. Under Sztojay, responsibility for the Jewish community was transferred from the Ministry of Education and Religious Affairs to the Ministry of the Interior.

26. Within the Interior Ministry, Baky was appointed Secretary of the Political Department, and Endre the Secretary of the Administrative Department. (Braham 1981:402) Baky, a secret agent of the SS and Gestapo, thus gained control over both police and gendarmerie. (Braham 1981:408)

27. Certainly from nowhere else were some 450,000 Jews deported to a death camp (in this case Auschwitz) in a mere seven weeks (15 May-7 July 1944). Without German-Hungarian uniformity of purpose, and totality of co-operation, such a result would not have been possible.

28. The Gendarmerie (*Csendorseg*) maintained law and order everywhere except in Budapest, the municipalities and county seats. In these places such responsibilities were the function of the police.

29. Cited in Handler 1982:22.

30. Quoted Braham 1981:403.

31. Levai 1948:66.

32. For an indication of the brutalities inflicted on provincial ghetto inhabitants, see Levai 1948:144-45.

33. Braham 1981:410.

34. Sakmyster 1984:301. Despite this knowledge, adds Sakmyster, Sztojay "nonetheless believed that Hungary must contribute actively to the realisation of this policy".

35. Levai 1948:146.

36. For this privilege the Hungarian government paid the Reich some 2.5 billion marks. (Klein 1956:55)

37. Quoted Braham 1981:375.

38. Handler 1982:22.

39. Minutes of the Cabinet, 29 March 1944; quoted Levai 1961:67.

40. Braham 1981:374.

41. Kallay (1954:433-34) relates that having failed to convince Horthy of the need to resign ("I begged him earnestly to abdicate..."), he then suggested the Regent adopt the position of King Christian X of Denmark and withdraw into isolation.

42. This *Note* reinforced US warnings of 24 March and 12 June 1944. On 14 July, the US admonished that Hungary stood "condemned before history" and "cannot escape inexorable punishment". (Documents on American Foreign Relations, Vol. 7, 1944-45, New York, 1976, p 251; cited Vago 1983:41, n6)

43. Vago 1983:41, n4. It should be recalled that, as discussed in Chapter III, there existed a widespread belief that international Jewry directed the Allied war effort. The massive bombing raid was thus misinterpreted as a *quid pro quo* for Jewish suffering. Yehuda Bauer believes this raid was Horthy's prime motivation in banning further deportations. (Private discussion with Prof. Bauer, 24 July 1991, Sydney)

44. On 7 April 1944 two Slovakian Jewish prisoners, Walter Rosenberg (subsequently Rudolph Vrba) and Alfred Wetzler (subsequently Josef Lanik), escaped from Auschwitz.

Managing to reach Slovakia, their eyewitness testimony regarding the operations of that death camp came to be called the Auschwitz Protocols. Although this report was taken to Horthy's palace by Sandor Torok and Erno Peto, there is controversy regarding the date at which Horthy first received a copy. Tzvi Erez states that Horthy's daughter-in-law recorded in her diary that she received the document on 2 July, immediately gave it to Mrs Horthy who read it and suffered a nervous collapse. On being informed, the Regent took the Protocols, disappeared for two and a half hours and, when he reappeared, the daughter-in-law notes that he was ashen-faced and trembling. (Private discussion with Tzvi Erez, 8 January 1991) An assessment of the evidence, however, leads one to concur with Braham's assertion that Horthy first saw the Protocols in the second half of June, having received them via his son. (Braham 1981:718)

45. Both Jews and Arrow Cross warned Horthy of the attempted plot; the former to ensure the Regent's survival, the latter to thwart the plans of their hated National Socialist rivals. (Macartney 1957:II, 304-05)

46. One of the main thrusts of the *coup* was to ensure the deportation of Budapest's Jews.

47. For Veesenmayer's version of this meeting see "Telegram from Veesenmayer to Ribbentrop concerning a conference with Horthy on 4 July 1944", NG 5684; Document 186 in Braham 1963:419-24 (in German). (Translation from German by Ursula Healy, Sydney. Unless otherwise indicated, future German to English translations in this book will be courtesy of Mrs Healy.)

48. For Hitler's instructions, see "Telegramme from Ribbentrop to Veesenmayer regarding Hitler's orders to safeguard the interest of the Reich in the event of Horthy's moves against the Hungarian government", NG 2739; Document 199 in Braham 1963:450-54 (in German). Macartney (1957:II, 307) called this *Note* "one of the most formidable messages ever addressed to a Head of State from a nominal ally".

49. Horthy used this expression at the Crown Council meeting of 26 June. (Macartney 1957:II, 303)

50. Macartney 1957:II, 318.

51. Evidence given by Lakatos in Szalasi's postwar trial; cited Macartney 1957:II, 320. Horthy (1956:221) states that the Roumanian *volte-face* gave him "the long sought opportunity to act".

52. According to documentary evidence produced at Veesenmayer's postwar trial, Himmler accepted the following five Hungarian proposals: Hungarian authorities to regain control over Jewish affairs; where possible, Budapest Jews to be employed in the country; unemployable Jews to be relocated in Red Cross camps outside Budapest; release of Jews in internment camps; and restoration of Jewish property under German control. (Macartney 1957:II, 321)

53. Typical of the high farce to which this drama degenerated, the land mines positioned around the Regent's palace were installed largely by *Nyilas* sympathisers who removed most of the detonators. Macartney (1957:II, 427) states: "In all, only three or four mines ever went off, and they by accident."

54. Private discussion with Tzvi Erez, 8 January 1991, Tel Aviv. It should be noted that the Hungarian military did not swear allegiance to the Crown, country or constitution but to Horthy, the *Legfelsobb Hadur.*

55. For possibly the most comprehensive exposition and analysis in the English language of the last six weeks of Horthy's reign (the Lakatos era), see "Horthy Agonistes" in Macartney 1957:II, 319-443.

56. Affidavit by Rudolph (Reszo) Kasztner, sworn 13 September 1945, International Military Tribunal, Nurnberg, Exhibit 242, 2605 PS: page 10. (Document 439 in Braham 1963:906-921)

57. Nagy-Talavera 1970:240-41.

58. For an example of this centrist point of view see Braham 1981:418-79.

59. Bela Vago "Jewish Leadership Groups in Hungary and Romania During the Holocaust — Their Reactions to Nazi Policies". (Yivo Archive 9/74358, p 33-34, nd)

60: Stern 1945:3. The members of the JC were well acquainted, having been MIPI directors for the previous five years. (Freudiger 1972:244)

61. Braham 1981:481.

62. Testimony of Erno Peto (1956:50); Stern (1945:2) confirms this Hungarian attitude. Ministries approached included Religious Affairs, Interior, Prime Minister, and the Police Department.

63. Paradoxically, tragically and with great irony, this assembly was the first and last formal gathering of Hungarian Jewry since the Jewish Congress of 1869 (see Chapter I).

64. Peto 1956:50.

65. Stern 1945:2.

66. Peto (1956:52) states: "The Hungarian authorities and ministries did not receive us. We stormed them with telegraphic appeals."

67. Stern 1945:6.

68. Stern (1945:20-21) states that "many thousands" of false papers were issued by the JC. Levai (1948:129) accepts that "many hundreds" of provincial Jews managed to reach Budapest with the aid of these illegal travel permits. Rozett (1987:67) cites testimonies which indicate that, for a period, over 100 provincial Jews arrived in Budapest per day. The possession of these false documents became counterproductive once the *SS* became aware of their existence.

69. Stern 1945:8.

70. At this stage Domonkos was Manager of the JC's Technical Department, whilst Janos Gabor, previously a member of the Liaison Office, the body charged with maintaining contact with the *SS*, had recently been appointed an executive member of the JC.

71. Levai 1948: 184-86. Apparently individual Germans indulged in private acts of expropriation to such an extent that, on Domonkos' recommendation, Eichmann issued an order on 24 May forbidding the JC "to hand over any sums of money whatsoever to any German official organisation or person without previously obtaining particular permission, both verbal and in writing, of the above office". (Ibid)

72. Levai 1948:103; Braham 1981:448.

73. Torok was appointed due to the Christian Churches lobbying for their Jewish members to have either a separate *Judenrat* or, alternatively, their own representative on the JC.

74. Private discussion with Gyorgy Gergely, 30 October 1990. Henceforth, private discussions involving the writer will be noted as "PD:TDK-XY, date".

75. Braham 1981:422.

76. In a tendentious and judgemental article, Conway (1986:29-30) alleges that the JC's actions "were indispensable for future deportation plans".

77. Arendt appears unaware of the critical importance of mandatory religious affiliation and the three Jewish Laws to the *Endlösung* process in Hungary. Furthermore, Arendt's book is strewn with inaccuracies and misinterpretations regarding Hungary, eg: "The Zionist movement had always been *particularly strong* in Hungary..." (Arendt 1963:180; emphasis added) and "...Eichmann and his men *invited* the Jewish leaders to a conference, to *persuade* them to form a Jewish Council". (Arendt 1963:178; emphases added) As has been shown, the Zionist movement in Hungary, far from being particularly strong, was particularly puny. Moreover, it is an absurdity to claim Eichmann "invited" or attempted to "persuade" Jewish leaders, people for whom he had nothing but contempt. His very presence, inherent authority and brutal demeanour intimidated and commanded in the most naked manner.

78. See Braham 1981:555-58.

79. PD:TDK-Gyorgy Gergely, 14 May 1992.

80. Fulop Freudiger (1972:259-60) gives a similar interpretation to Stern.

81. Stern 1945:7.

82. The JC's Liaison Office with the *SS* consisted of Drs Eppler, Gabor, Gergely and (Laszlo) Peto. Eppler's father, Sandor, was Secretary-General of the Pest Neolog community for over a decade until his untimely death in 1942. Elizabeth Eppler attributes her father's early demise to the treatment he received in the JLS, to which he was conscripted in 1940. Gabor's father, Gyula, was Sandor Eppler's predecessor as Secretary-General of the Pest Neolog community. (PD:TDK-Elizabeth Eppler, 17 December 1990)

83. The (poor) English translation of Eppler's postwar testimony leaves the source of this list unresolved. No such irresolution marked the writer's interviews with Dr Eppler, viz: "One day Janos [Gabor] came back from Eichmann's office with a sheet and said he had been given a list containing the names of lawyers in Budapest..." Unless otherwise specified, this and subsequent information regarding the "list" episode is taken from the writer's discussions with Dr Eppler, December 1990–January 1991.

84. Similarly, Fulop Freudiger (1972:260-61) relates how he warned his personal lawyer, Dr Dach, who also took refuge in a mental asylum. After being warned, another of Freudiger's lawyer acquaintances, Dr Frank, avoided reporting by arranging for a huge plaster cast to be placed on each leg.

85. Eppler at twenty-three was the youngest; Gergely, at thirty, possibly the oldest. The nominal head of the Liaison Office, the elderly lawyer Dr Jozsef Vagi — a specialist in ecclesiastical law as applied in the Hungarian legal system — was in charge of the JC's legal department and generally not consulted. Eppler states: "Vagi didn't even know what we were doing. He never went to the Gestapo." Braham's contention (1981:441) that Gabor assumed the Chair of the Liaison Office primarily because of his excellent command of German is vigorously contested by both Eppler and Gergely. The latter states that as he had a German governess from the age of four, and as he subsequently studied in Berlin, his German was the equal of, if not better than, that of Gabor. (PD:TDK-Gyorgy Gergely, 1 August 1991) Certainly Gergely's archive contains numerous official reports and correspondence which he wrote in German.

86. The officially appointed Executive Secretary, Dr Erno Munkacsi, was ill at that stage. Prior to the Occupation, Dr Kohn was superintendent of the Pest Neolog Community's school system.

87. Stern (1945:7) states that the list of lawyers was prepared by MUNE, the National Union of Lawyers.

88. Stern 1945:7. I have taken the liberty of correcting the grammar and rectifying some obscurities in this and future extracts from Jacques Sarlos' rather poor English translation of Stern's testimony.

89. Braham 1981:434-36.

90. For example, John S. Conway 1986:3. See also n 100 in this Chapter.

91. Stern 1945:3.

92. PD:TDK-Elizabeth Eppler, 23 December 1990.

93. Leo Stern was Financial Director of the Budapest Orthodox Community and president of their *Orszagos Bikur Cholin*, the National Health-Protection Society. (PD:TDK-Arthur Stern, 10 February 1991)

94. Freudiger (1972:243) states that he first met Kasztner at Leo Stern's residence.

95. Arthur Stern relates the case of a typical eyewitness at a Stern Sunday luncheon, a Polish refugee who had escaped from his work detail at a death camp by jumping off a truck. The refugee chronicled horrific experiences, including the functioning of gas chambers, in considerable detail. Arthur adds that he was instructed to treat such news in the strictest confidence. (PD:TDK-Arthur Stern, 10 February 1991)

96. Freudiger 1972:285.

97. Jacques Adler, *The Jews of Paris and the Final Solution* (New York: Oxford UP, 1987), 46-47 (henceforth Adler).

98. A statement by Erno Munkacsi supports this view. (Cited Braham 1981:719)

99. PD:TDK-Ilona Benoschofsky, 17 January 1991. (Dr Benoschofsky, a pioneer historian of the Hungarian Holocaust, is also Director of the Jewish Museum of Budapest.) For the same reason Rabbi Dr Leo Baeck, of the Terezin *Judenrat*, also adopted a non-disclosure policy. (Kulka 1984:299)

100. See, for example, a tendentious, judgemental article by John S. Conway (1986:1-48). By posing questions such as "Why were the Jews of Budapest able to survive while their less fortunate compatriots in the provinces were daily deported to Auschwitz by the thousands?" (p 3), Conway broadcasts his knowledge of the Holocaust process in Hungary. Even a brief historical overview reveals that during implementation of the *Endlösung* Hungary was divided into ten gendarmerie districts, each individual district being evacuated of Jews in sequence. For cogent strategic reasons, the Germans planned the final deportation to be a short, swift *aktion* against the Budapest community — but only after the provinces had become *Judenfrei*. Despite Conway's efforts, this strategic decision had nothing to do with either Stern or the *Zsido Tanacs*. See Conway 1986: 22, 29, and 36-37 for further examples of his scholarship.

101. Braham 1981:425.

102. The BBC's initial series of *Endlösung* revelations were broadcast by the famous novelist Thomas Mann in December 1941-January 1942. (Feingold 1970:168)

103. As an example, in my father's family was the case of a female cousin who had married a Polish Jew and gone to live with her husband in Poland. She returned to Hungary in 1942 and related how her husband and his family had been slaughtered in cold blood. Her testimony was dismissed, the story being considered an excuse for absconding from a bad marriage. (PD:TDK-Imre Kramer, 19 March 1991)

104. See Tuchman 1982:291.

105. Laqueur 1980:149, footnote*. Current examples in Western society of individual denial and/or repression of evidence would include the widespread ignoring of suspicious signs of ill health (eg: lumps, bleeding etc), and the persistence of cigarette smoking.

106. Steinberg 1990:50. A psychologist, Leon Festinger, formulated the term "cognitive dissonance" to describe this type of phenomenon. Relating cognitive dissonance to the threat to mankind posed by environmental degradation — a threat now readily apparent to all who choose to see — the ecologists Anita Gordon and David Suzuki state that "the mind intervenes to ease the conflict by denying the importance of the condition, reconciling the discrepancies or refusing to be convinced and demanding more and more evidence". With poignancy excruciating for Holocaust scholars, Gordon and Suzuki conclude: "When the issue is extinction, such denial can be deadly." (Anita Gordon and David Suzuki, *It's a Matter of Survival* [Sydney: Allen and Unwin, 1990], 4.)

107. Lecture, Prof. Y. Bauer, Yad Vashem, 11 January 1988. See also Bauer 1978:18 and 106.

108. The existence of this moratorium syndrome in bystanders is self-evident. Lord Dacre (Hugh Trevor-Roper), a member of British Intelligence during World War II, described his bystander moratorium thus: "I well remember the moment when I first saw the evidence — a fragment of the evidence — about the extermination of the Jews. It was explicit, factual, documented. But could it be believed? Between the reception of evidence and belief in its conclusion there is a great psychological gulf; and in wartime, when so much is uncertain — when hatred breeds passion and passion is exploited by propaganda — it is prudent to suspend judgement. I recall that I suspended my own judgement and only gradually, many months later, drew from that dreadful evidence the conclusion which it entailed." (*The Listener*, 1 January 1981; quoted Gilbert 1984:110, n3)

109. Many of the conundra and paradoxes inherent in the syndrome have been synthesised in a statement by Amos Manor, sometime head of Israeli security services. Deported from Hungary at the age of seventeen, Manor stated: "If I had known what Auschwitz was, no power on earth could have gotten me on that train, but there was no

power on earth that could have convinced me that Auschwitz was possible and indeed existed." (Cited by Gideon Hausner, in Yisrael Gutman and Gideon Greif [eds], *The Historiography of the Holocaust Period*. Jerusalem: Yad Vashem, 1988; p 443)

110. The Moratorium syndrome even occurred in Auschwitz. Regarding a collective instance, Kulka (1984:296) states: "Artisans among the inmates who could enter the 'family camp' [in Auschwitz-Birkenau] from time to time informed the deportees from Terezin about what was really happening in Birkenau. Although the 'family camp' was less than a kilometre from the crematoria, and flames flared from the chimneys night and day, the inmates of the 'family camp' did not want to believe that the bodies of Jewish deportees were being cremated there. Even when they later found out that this was indeed the case, they kept trying to silence their fears by convincing themselves that they would be treated as 'privileged characters'." Clearly, this response involved the collective restructuring of normality, a transformation that integrated the abnormal into the commonplace.

111. In an article entitled "On Disbelieving Atrocities", the famous Hungarian-born author Arthur Koestler wrote in the January 1944 *New York Times Magazine* that "atrocity stories which went beyond the limits of previous historical experience could not be linked with the realities of daily life and were consequently discounted as fictional fabrications". (Cited John S. Conway 1986:6)

112. An analogous situation appears to pertain to many, if not most, European countries under German domination. For example, in France — where information regarding the *Endlösung* seems to have been far more widespread than in Hungary — Georges Welles, survivor of Auschwitz and Director, *Centre de Documentation Juive Contemporaine*, comments that prior to the mass deportation of French Jews, which commenced after July 1942, "everyone knew of Radio London's broadcasts about the gas chambers, and other means of extermination were known, but no one could believe them." (Quoted Adler 1987:47) Regarding the *Yishuv* (Jewish community in British-controlled Palestine) during the War, Avishai Margalit writes: "What was known about the Holocaust in the *Yishuv*? The information about the killings was available and was published... Belief and denial, however, could paradoxically exist at the same time... The evidence tempts one to say that many in the *Yishuv* knew about the extermination yet did not believe it." (Avishai Margalit, "The Uses of the Holocaust." *The New York Review of Books*, 17 February 1994, 8)

113. PD:TDK-Asher Arayi, 3 January 1991. Note that a not insignificant number of deportees — the elderly, ill, young, severely tortured, infirm, insane, pregnant etc — would have been in no state to attempt flight.

114. Braham 1981:445. A slightly different translation of this passage can be found in Levai 1948:97.

115. Ibid.

116. Braham 1981:446.

117. The 6 April edition of the HJJ, that is the edition containing the manifesto, carried an editorial entitled "Calm and Discipline, Self-Sacrificing Fulfilment of Duties". (Braham 1981:446)

118. Cohen 1986:78. Even without the information provided above, Dr Cohen's point is unconvincing. Subsequent to the Occupation, newspapers and publications were either banned or subject to severe restrictions. Relatively few Jews, irrespective of where they resided, would have been unaware of these facts. In particular, on 6 April the *Orthodox Zsido Ujsag* (Orthodox Jewish Newspaper) informed its readers that, due to reasons beyond its control, the paper would cease publication. (Braham 1981:472, n52)

119. It is not clear why the Germans permitted publication of details that destroyed the facade of Jewish self-government. Several possibilities arise, including a combination of overconfidence, inefficiency and incompetence in the Germans' censorship system. Elizabeth Eppler, who as a member of the JC's liaison office with Eichmann would be in a position to know, states that the HJJ was vetted by Eichmann's batman! (PD:TDK-

Elizabeth Eppler, 17 December 1990) As such, the above reasons appear a reasonable hypothesis for this breakdown in the Germans' much-vaunted system.

120. For example, see Braham 1981:91, 97, 424, 440, 775, etc.

121. Residents needed several papers to prove their identity. Consequently, millions of fake documents would have been required to "Aryanise" Hungary's 800,000 Jews.

122. This figure is Asher Cohen's estimate of refugee numbers. (Cohen 1988:254)

123. Quoted Braham 1981:436. In extreme contrast was the JC's Zionist representative, Nison Kahan, who contemporaneously expressed the small minority's point of view, viz: "Our fate is not only material ruin, and not even only a chain of physical and mental tortures and the beating down of the last fibres of our human dignity, but rather *certain physical annihilation*." (Ibid. Emphasis in the original)

124. See Freudiger 1972:253. It should be noted that Kasztner also had good contacts in Bratislava, including Weissmandl and Fleischmann, amongst others.

125. Obtaining information from the clandestine messages of Slovakian deportees, in early 1943 the WG exposed the death camps at Sobibor, Majdanek and Treblinka, and, in May 1944, distributed the Auschwitz Protocols, eyewitness testimony disclosing the intimate workings of that infamous death camp. (Rothkirchen 1983:7) Indicative of the WG's diversity were its two most prominent leaders, Rabbi Weissmandl and his distant relative, the secular, female Slovakian Zionist leader Gisi Fleischmann.

126. Rozett states that most sources indicate that Rabbi Weissmandl initiated these discussions by approaching Wisliceny. The latter broached the subject with Himmler who granted permission to conduct negotiations. Eventually $US40-50,000.00 was paid to Wisliceny, some of these funds being raised in Hungary. (Rozett 1987:160-61)

127. Braham 1981:471, n20.

128. For a convincing and vigorously argued exposition of the Brand Mission, see Bauer 1978:94-155. For Kasztner's affidavit (London, 13 September 1945), see doc. 2605-PS, in Braham 1963:906-921.

129. Dagan 1984:xxxvi-xxxviii.

130. One of the Vatican's earliest sources of information on the *Endlösung* were the alarming reports from the Slovakian Apostolic Delegate, *Monsignor* Giuseppe Burzio, which detailed the Nazi extermination programme. As a result, the Holy See addressed several *Notes* to the Slovakian government, a regime headed by a Catholic priest, Father Josef Tiso. (Rothkirchen 1983:7)

131. Rothkirchen 1983:5.

132. Instituted at Jewish request, at their height the three Slovakian work camps contained 4-5,000 Jews. As Jews had a significant degree of authority in their administration, these camps should not be considered analogous to the JLS system in Hungary. (PD:TDK-Robert Rozett, 19 December 1990)

133. Lipscher 1984:209. The Education Minister, Dr Jozef Sivak, was particularly supportive.

134. In his postwar interrogation, Wisliceny states that the Slovakian PM's questions regarding the situation of Jewish deportees in Poland resulted, in late July, in his (Wisliceny's) return to Berlin for consultations. As a consequence, Wisliceny was ordered by his superior, Adolf Eichmann, to hinder the Slovakian request via delaying tactics. According to Wisliceny's testimony, it was on this trip that he first learnt the real meaning of deportation. As proof, Eichmann revealed Himmler's Top Secret order to Heydrich instigating the "biological extermination of the Jews". (Wisliceny 1945:6-9)

135. In his postwar interrogation Wisliceny declared that abridged reports of his Europa Plan negotiations were submitted by Eichmann to Himmler. Furthermore, Wisliceny stated that in early November 1942 "I was shown an order from Himmler that was signed by his adjutant, Suchanek. It stated that the twenty thousand dollars would be delivered immediately and that I should attempt to elicit another large sum from [Slovakian] Jew[s]."

(Wisliceny 1945:12-13) It is hardly conceivable that an official of Himmler's power and rank would personally intervene regarding such a paltry sum without a higher, ulterior purpose.

136. Quoted Manvell and Fraenkel 1965:134-35.

137. Rozett 1987:162.

138. Freudiger 1972:241-42.

139. Freudiger 1972:245. It should be noted that after meeting Wisliceny and reading Weissmandl's letter, Freudiger went to 12 Sip Street to inform the JC. (Freudiger 1972:246)

140. Freudiger, Diamont and Link 1944:93-94. With Wisliceny's help, Freudiger, Sandor Diamont and Gyula Link escaped to Roumania on 10 August 1944.

141. Freudiger 1972:239.

142. Freudiger, Diamont and Link 1944:94. For Freudiger's version of how the JC decided upon this payment to the *SS*, see Freudiger 1972:246-48.

143. With little doubt, the prime reason preventing Weissmandl and the WG's influence on the Hungarian Jewish leadership receiving due recognition is the absence of the WG from mention in almost all postwar testimonies of Hungarian Jewish leaders. Such absence is, however, entirely predictable. Very few leaders, whatever the circumstance, want to admit being influenced by failed policies, especially those leading to disaster. A similar situation occurred with regard to the postwar Polish Jewish diaspora. In that scattered community of survivors, Bundist philosophies were swept away to such an extent that the Bund's prime competitor, Zionism, achieved — and retains to this day — a position of almost total ideological hegemony.

144. Freudiger (1972:266) comments on this strategy thus: "My Poles [ie: Jewish refugee informants from Poland] were right, it was worthwhile."

145. For example on 31 March, at his Majestic Hotel headquarters in the Svabhegy district of Buda, Eichmann told a JC delegation (Stern, Peto, Boda and Gabor) that "his major concern was that industrial and war-industrial production be expanded, for which purpose he would set up workers' units. If Jews showed a proper attitude, no harm would befall them... After the War, the Jews would be free to do whatever they wanted." (From shorthand notes taken at the meeting by Erno Boda; quoted Braham 1981:437-39)

146. *Paradise Lost* II, 112.

147. Macartney 1957:II, 301.

148. Stern 1945:7 After receiving concrete information from Weissmandl regarding the contract between Slovakian and Hungarian railway authorities for the transportation of 310,000 Jews to Nazi-occupied Poland, the JC engaged in a "heated debate...about the reliability of this information". Even after the former Chief Inspector of the Hungarian Railway Directorate (a Jew, forcibly retired by anti-Jewish edicts) confirmed the conclusion of such an agreement, the JC wanted further information. The conclusive confirmation regarding the import of this railway contract was obtained from Hungarian officials on 14 May, one day before the commencement of mass deportations. (Freudiger 1972:255-56)

149. See Freudiger's testimony at the Eichmann trial, 25 May 1961; quoted Hilberg 1972:193.

150. For example, the USA issued several warnings to the Sztojay regime regarding the Jewish situation in Hungary, the first by Roosevelt on 24 March 1944. Subsequent warnings were issued, for example, on 12 June and 14 July, the latter stating that the Hungarian government stood "condemned before history" and "cannot escape inexorable punishment". (*Department of State, Bulletin*, vol. XI, p 59; cited Vago 1983:41, n6) In his *Note* of 26 June, Roosevelt wrote to Horthy: "Hungary's fate will not be like that of other civilised nations...unless the deportations are stopped." (Quoted Braham 1981:754)

151. For an eyewitness account of such endeavours see Peto 1956:52-53. The JC devoted considerable time and energy to opposing the *Endlösung* process, and in attempting to ameliorate the Jewish condition in occupied Hungary. Typical were the 27 April, 3 May and 12 May submissions to the Interior Minister (Andor Jaross) and other government officials

detailing, amongst other things, the horrors inflicted upon the inhabitants of the provincial ghettos, and pleading for permission to alleviate such suffering. These initiatives were either ignored or their arguments and evidence denied. (Klein 1960:38)

152. Stern 1945:10. For an example, see the JC's 23 June appeal to Horthy, in Levai 1948:192-96.

153. See Stern 1945:15. Klein (1960:39) agrees with this view.

154. Klein (1960:38) concurs that the JC's reports to the neutral powers eventually saved many lives.

155. Built for 200 prisoners, Kistarcsa generally contained some 1,500-2,000 Jews. (Levai 1948:252-53)

156. Before 19 March 1944, 26 Rokk-Szilard Street housed the Neolog's National Rabbinical Institute.

157. Stern 1945:17. Horthy was notified through his son, Miklos Jr, who in turn had been informed of developments (via his secret telephone) by Dr Erno Peto. (Peto 1956:57)

158. Braham 1981:773.

159. Testimony, Dr Sandor Brody, OMZSA Director, ET 1993:957.

160. Freudiger 1972:271.

161. For eyewitness testimony, see Stern 1945:17-18, Peto 1956:57, and Freudiger 1972:271-73. All three narratives agree on the essential details of this episode.

162. For details of this second Kistarcsa *aktion*, see Levai 1948:256-57.

163. Macartney 1957:II, 309.

164. Braham 1981:774.

165. Using lorries under the cover of night, Eichmann's final deportation attempt occurred at Foutca prison. Alerted in time, Horthy successfully surrounded the prison with police and blocked the road to Vienna with gendarmes and tank traps. (Macartney 1957:II, 309)

166. Braham 1981:751.

167. It should be noted that small-scale deportations were conducted on independent German initiative before, during (15 May–7 July), and after the cessation of mass expulsions. Organised without Hungarian assistance, the strictly limited dimension of these deportations indicates the critical importance of Hungarian collaboration in the *Endlösung* effort. The Krumey-Hunsche trial (Frankfurt, 1969) revealed that such small-scale deportations from Hungary to Auschwitz occurred up to November 1944 and involved an aggregate of several thousand Jews. (PD:TDK-Sari Reuveni, 19 December 1990) For additional information see Sari Reuveni "Exceptional Deportations and Late Trains from Hungary to Auschwitz, 1944", (in Hebrew) in Yalkut *Moreshet* 1985:123-34.

168. Stern (1945:19) characterised Ferenczy as "an opportunist rotten to the marrow".

169. Except for the JLS, by this stage Hungary was, in effect, *Judenrein* outside of the capital. Consequently, this plan was limited to the deportation of Budapest Jews.

170. The audience was granted within twenty-four hours, via Dr Erno Peto's connection to Miklos Horthy Jr.

171. According to Stern (1945:20) only seven people were aware of this counteraction: the JC triumvirate (Stern, Wilhelm, Peto), Horthy and his son Miklos Jr, and Ferenczy and his deputy, Captain Leo Lullay. For eyewitness accounts of this episode from the JC point of view, see Peto 1956:60-67 and Stern 1945:18-22. For evidence that Lullay kept the Zionist leader Otto Komoly informed of the broad situation, see Komoly's Diary for 21 and 23 August 1944, in Komoly 1944:147-48 and 156-57 respectively.

172. Peto 1956:62.

173. For the neutral legations' protest *Note* of 21 August, see Levai 1948:319.

174. Braham 1981:797. Doubtless, Himmler's attempt to establish negotiations with the Western Allies was also a factor in his decision (see Chapter VI).

175. For a precis of this *Note* see Braham 1981:790-91.

176. Komoly 1944:195.

177. Stern 1945:20.

178. After their release, Stern, Peto and Wilhelm decided not to sleep at their homes, with Peto seeking a different abode every night. (Peto 1956:73)

179. Stern 1945:19. History has proven Stern's assessment to be correct. As one authority noted: "The retention of Hungary in the Alliance and the full exploitation of its military and natural resources were vital considerations in the strategy of the Germans." (Braham 1981:764)

180. For material on Komoly's trust in Ferenczy and Lullay, see Komoly's Diary entries of 6 September (1944:210) and 9 September (1944:223). In particular, on the latter date the Zionist chief told Rev. Albert Bereczky (an important conduit between Komoly and government authorities) that "...one can now trust in them". (Ibid)

181. Braham 1981:788-89.

182. Even the commander of Budapest's anti-aircraft defences protested to Laszlo Endre about the creation of a ghetto. (Stern 1945:13)

183. Stern 1945:23.

184. Over an inspection period of six weeks, the Red Cross Chief Physician, Lajos Langmar, was used to certify that every proposed campsite was below European standards and hence unfit for the concentration of people. (Peto 1956:70-71; Stern 1945:22)

185. The Extrication Bureau (*Kiugrasi Iroda*) was headed by Horthy's sole surviving son, Miklos Jr.

186. Informed by a succession of people — including Stockler, Domonkos and gendarmerie Captain Leo Lullay — that Ferenczy wanted them eliminated, Stern and Peto disappeared underground whilst Wilhelm successfully sought refuge in the Swiss Embassy. (Peto 1956:73-74) Note that after 15 October, Szalasi placed Ferenczy in charge of Jewish affairs.

187. For example, the JC maintained 6,000 children who had been herded into the Budapest (Common) Ghetto. (Klein 1956:95-96)

188. Bauer 1994:240.

189. *Nyilas* atrocities were "unparalleled in any other satellite country except Croatia". (Vago 1989:230)

190. See Levai 1948:385-86.

191. Klein 1960:41.

192. Klein 1956:96.

193. Braham 1981:470, n11; Freudiger 1972:285. Braham's account acquits the three lawyers whilst Freudiger clears the lawyers *and* the JC. As the Bar's jurisdiction and indictments refer only to the three individuals, Braham's version appears much the more probable. See also R.L. Braham (ed.), *The Hungarian Jewish Catastrophy* (New York: Social Science Monographs, 1984), p 105, no. 550.

194. Testimony: Mrs Oszkar Rado, Interior Department of the National Police, Budapest, 20 May 1946. (YVA 015/19)

195. Braham 1981:968.

196. Involving tens of thousands of debilitated Budapest Jews, footmarches were horrendous attempts to conscript labour for the construction of Vienna's defence installations.

197. Varga 1990:262.

198. Vago 1989:229.

199. Although most clerics were concerned exclusively (if at all) with those Jews converted to their own denomination, there were a handful of honourable exceptions who attempted to prevent all Jewish suffering, notably the Calvinists Bishop Laszlo Ravasz and pastor Albert Bereczky.

200. Hungarian deportation was "speedier than in the entire history of the Holocaust". (Cohen 1986:56)

201. Gyorgy Gergely, a member of the JC's Liaison Office with the *SS*, supports this assessment when he states that "the survival of [Budapest] Jews was altogether due to the machinations and shrewdness of the Jewish senate [the JC]...the avoidance of the deportation of Budapest Jews has been attributed to all sorts of other people who had nothing to do with the matter." (Gyorgy Gergely 1987:73a)

202. Fein 1979:141.

203. This quote, and the following encapsulation, is contained in Helen Fein, "Genocide in Hungary: An Exchange", *New York Review of Books*, 27 May 1982, 54-55. Fein's general conclusion states that "two variables alone explained most of the difference [amongst the survival rates of Jews of different nationalities]: the success of the pre-War anti-Semitic movement before 1936 in each state and the *SS* grip over that state in 1941 which was inversely related to its political status." Though contentious in some respects, Fein's analysis clearly refutes suggestions that the *Endlösung* was accelerated by *Judenrat* "co-operation" with the Germans. (See Fein 1979:121-42, "The *Judenräte* and Other Jewish Control Agents".) Vago (1981:329) concurs with these conclusions.

204. The provincial figure excludes those 40,000 JLS survivors originally from the provinces and the 6,000 provincial deportees who survived deportation. See Table 32.1 in Braham 1981:1,144.

205. Levai (1961:43) states that "deportations from Greece took place simultaneously with those from Hungary, and the requisitioning of trains for that purpose caused grave disturbances with the southern army of Weichs. For want of transport facilities and due to the jamming of the railway lines by the trains of deportees, their war material and supplies were captured by Greek partisans."

206. See Gilbert 1984:302, map 14. The map depicts the Allies' "Operation Frantic" air raids of 6, 7 and 17 August 1944, as well as Allied airborne aid to Warsaw on 8 August. Note that Auschwitz is either directly under, or in the vicinity of, several of these flight paths.

207. Gilbert 1984:315. As discussed above, the Auschwitz complex was overflown by Allied aircraft on several occasions. In particular, US aerial photographs — first taken in April 1944, prior to the commencement of mass deportations from Hungary on 15 May — clearly indicated the crematoria and gas chambers at the camp. Between clenched teeth Conway (1986:13) concedes that "at the time this information was ignored".

208. Allied commanders probably had insufficient information to formulate a conclusive assessment. Consequently, could they have dismissed the argument that the Germans' deportation regimen reduced the *Wehrmacht's* efficacy via the utilisation of scarce tracktime, locomotive time, and manpower? Unlike Germany, the USA prohibited the use of military resources to achieve non-military aims (see Chapter VI).

209. Braham 1977b:276-77. Despite this equitable assessment, Braham (1981:422) appraises Stern's postwar affidavit under the emotive, tendentious heading "The Rationalisations of Samu Stern".

210. From "Why had membership of the council to be accepted?", Stern 1945:3. Braham (1977b:284-85) presents a cogent, succinct analysis of Stern, Peto and Wilhelm's dilemma, viz: "Conversely, it is safe to assume that had Stern and his associates refused to undertake the tasks assigned to them by the Germans, and by some miracle still survived the ordeal while hundreds of thousands of Jews were massacred, they would certainly have been condemned by other survivors for having held positions of power only while there was prestige and honour associated with them, and for having abandoned the community in its darkest hour..."

211. Peto 1956:50.

212. Stern finally went underground after the coup of 15 October, when impeccable sources warned Peto that the JC's PC was on Ferenczy's death list. (Peto 1956:73-74)

Kasztner's testimony at Nuremburg provides additional confirmation of the threat to Stern's life. Immediately prior to the siege of Budapest "Eichmannn, accompanied by [*Hauptsturmführer-SS*] Hunsche, came to the Ghetto to look for Hofrat Stern, the President of the Jewish Council, whom he personally wanted to exterminate. When he could not find Stern, he finally left Budapest." (Testimony of R. Kasztner, *Interrogation Summary no. 2817*, Office of US Chief Counsel for War Crimes, APO 696-A, Evidence Division, 18 July 1947, p3)

213. PD:TDK-Elizabeth Eppler, 17 December 1990. Stern's grand-daughter, Mrs Marika Bosnyak, confirms this observation, stating that her frail grandfather had chronically weak lungs, was very prone to bronchitis and respiratory infections, and suffered from numerous fevers. (PD:TDK-Marika Bosnyak, 6 August 1991)

214. PD:TDK-Marika Bosnyak, 6 August 1991. Stern's colleagues, realising his experience, contacts, calibre and valuable contributions to Hungarian Jewry, compelled him to stay. (Ibid)

215. For an account of the transfer to *SS* control of Hungary's foremost industrial complex — the Manfred Weiss works of over 40,000 employees — see Braham 1981:514-24. It was this transfer that enabled the interrelated Weiss and Chorin families, controllers of the Manfred Weiss business, to leave Hungary.

216. Komoly 1944:212.

217. PD:TDK-Marika Bosnyak, 6 August 1991.

218. In his diary Komoly noted Mester's response to Stern's request as "(Smiling) Small human weakness". (Komoly 1944:212)

219. Silagi 1986:194-96.

220. For a deeply moving account of Rumkowski and his tragic fiefdom, see Alan Adelson and Robert Lapides (eds), *Lodz Ghetto. Inside a Community Under Seige* (New York: Viking, 1989).

221. For example, the JC's Provincial Department and Information Office was assigned to the Zionists. (Braham 1981:445)

222. Cohen 1986:132. Cohen (1986:147) reinforces this point by stating that "between July and the middle of October [1944], the co-operation became even stronger, and [Zionist leader Otto] Komoly was in almost daily touch with the leaders of the Jewish Council".

223. Levai 1948:96.

224. Levai 1948:316.

225. Klein 1956:86.

226. Cohen 1986:17 and 253, n3.

227. One eyewitness reported: "Stern adopted tactics of delay whenever the Gestapo made demands on the Council for the supply of goods and services, eg: typewriters, furniture etc within twenty-four or forty-eight hours. He sometimes drew out [the provision of] such supplies for days. Stern's attitude was that time was working against the Nazis and every hour gained helped people to survive." (Private correspondence: Dr Elizabeth Eppler to TDK, 23 January 1993)

228. Stern attacked the government for the deplorable effects of the First and Second Jewish Laws on Hungarian Jewry. For excerpts of this address, see Katzburg 1981:165-66.

229. Kallay 1954:412.

230. *Trial of War Criminals*, American Tribunal, Nuremberg, p 2,706, 13322, NG 2,973; quoted Klein 1956:42.

231. Tokes 1984:291.

232. In his memoirs, Horthy (1956:219) claims that only in August did he learn "the truth about these extermination camps". For compelling argument that Horthy and his officials received such information well before August 1944, see Braham 1981:716-718.

233. Quoted Levai 1948:315. In their postwar testimony, both Veesenmayer and Baky confirm Ferenczy's statement regarding Horthy's attitude. At his own trial the former stated:

"Horthy himself told me that he was interested only in protecting those prosperous, the economically valuable Jews in Budapest. However, as to the remaining Jewry — and he used a very ugly term there — he had no interest in them..." (Quoted Braham 1981:379) In written testimony, Baky stated that Horthy had told him: "The Germans have cheated me. Now they want to deport the Jews. I don't mind. I hate the Galician Jews and the Communists. Out with them, out of the country!" (Ibid)

234. Only with the benefit of hindsight can one state unequivocally that these dangerous options were less hazardous for the provincial Jews than maintaining the *status quo*. As hindsight has shown, the JC's policy during the second phase of the Occupation was of great benefit to the Jews of Budapest.

235. Cohen 1984:136. Cohen's argument applies equally to Hungarian society and its Antisemitic ethos.

236. Quoted Ainsztein 1974:xxi.

237. Ibid.

238. Vago 1989:229. Cohen (1984:143, n7) accepts that the authorities received no fewer than 35,000 denunciations. Vago (1989:229) states: "The ghettoizaton and deportation of some 600,000 Jews, carried out with the utmost brutality, was the crime of the Hungarian authorities, aided and abetted by the population at large."

239. Ainsztein 1974:xxi.

240. Commenting on Carl Lutz's endeavours during the Occupation, an executive of the JC's Liaison Office, Gyorgy Gergely, states that Lutz "was one of the most important men in Hungary for Jewish purposes, and whose help can never be exaggerated. Unfortunately, when Wallenberg is mentioned, Lutz is completely forgotten." (Gergely 1987:38a)

241. "Interview with Mr Charles Lutz", CZA S25/5604, p 6. Lutz was technically incorrect in calling Wilhelm president of the *Judenrat*. As previously mentioned, during the *Nyilas* era that office was officially occupied by Lajos Stockler.

242. Klein 1956:81.

243. Klein 1960:41.

244. In this context, note that both my parents were survivors of the Holocaust in Hungary, with my father losing his mother, sister and six brothers, plus virtually all his very large extended family.

245. Exceptions to this phenomenon include some small ultra-Orthodox groups.

246. Whilst commenting upon Tom Segov's book *The Seventh Million, Israel, and the Holocaust* (Hill and Wang, 1993), an Israeli writer Amos Elon states that "despite the pervasiveness of the subject in Israeli life most serious works by Jewish writers on Nazism were written by non-Israelis and — perhaps because they did not fully conform with current formulas — only a handful of those were translated into Hebrew, nearly always belatedly." Referring to the tendency of preferring "simplistic versions to more nuanced ones", Elon notes that "it took more than a generation to produce Israeli historians able to detach the history of the Holocaust from their own biographies." [Amos Elon, "The Politics of Memory", *The New York Review of Books* (7 October 1993), 3]

247. Levai 1966:263.

248. These enquiries were conducted in 1991.

249. I would like to thank Arthur Stern for his kind hospitality and the forthright provision of information regarding his father Leo, Fulop Freudiger, and the Orthodox leadership. Unless otherwise specified, all such information was provided by Mr Stern during private discussions with the writer, 7-14 February 1991.

250. For details regarding the *Bikur Cholim*, see *Hetven Ev A Betegek Szolgalataban 1871-1941* (Seventy Years in the Service of the Ill 1871-1941), published in 1941, in Budapest, by the *Bikur Cholim* Society. This book was kindly provided by Leo Stern's younger son, Dr Robert Stern.

251. As Secretary-General of the Budapest Orthodox Community, Herman Stern

(second oldest to Leo of the six Stern brothers) was the community's chief administrative officer and highest-paid executive. (Private correspondence: Arthur Stern to TDK, 16 August 1993, p 5-6)

252. Freudiger 1972:242

253. Rozett 1987:65-66.

254. Leo Stern's elder son, Arthur, states that Fulop Freudiger "may have been the nominal head of the Relief and Rescue Committee at its inception, but in fact my Father became the acting and working chairman of the Committee and was, in my memory, always referred to as such. Freudiger's claim to have been chairman probably had its foundation in the early days of the Committee but it was under my Father's direction that things actually happened... Because he wore a small beard which instantly identified him as a Jew, Freudiger preferred not to undertake certain tasks publicly and sometimes requested my Father to act instead of him, particularly when visiting government authorities... It should be noted that, starting maybe in 1942, my Father spent an increasing portion of his time on relief activities. By late 1943 these activities occupied most of his time. He had to neglect his business..." (Private correspondence: Arthur Stern to TDK, 16 August 1993, p 6) In independent correspondence to the writer (22 October 1993, p 22-23), Leo Stern's younger son, Dr Robert Stern, concurs with this statement.

255. Rozett 1987:170. Fleischmann returned to Slovakia bitterly disappointed by the Hungarian Jewish leaders' attitudes. Arguably, however, foreign Jewry's alleged frugality towards the WG may have been, according to some Jewish sages of the highest repute, at least partly consistent with general Jewish ethics. In commenting on the verse "Thou shalt surely open thy hand unto thy poor and needy brother, in thy land" (Deuteronomy XV 11), the great medieval Spanish sage Abraham Ibn Ezra (born 1092) states that "one's first duty lies towards a brother, then relatives, then the needy of one's country, and finally come those of other countries". The great medieval French sage Rashi (Rabbi Shelomoh Yitzsachaki, born 1040) appears to concur with this principle. Discussing priorities regarding charity (Deuteronomy XV 7), Rashi states that "a fellow townsman must be considered before an applicant from another city". (Rabbi Dr S. Frisch, "The Book of Deuteronomy", in Rev. Dr A. Cohen [ed], *The Soncino Chumash* (London: The Soncino Press), 1966, pp 1,071 and 1,070 respectively.)

256. Braham 1981:108-09.

257. Arthur Stern states that the Zionist-Orthodox coalition should be described as a quasi-merger "because the merger was never complete: the Orthodox committee participated in joint committee meetings with Zionists but never abandoned its own identity and its members met frequently without the Zionists present. Hence [Leo Stern] was referred to as Chairman of the Orthodox committee and as Vice Chairman of the combined committee..." (Private correspondence: Arthur Stern to TDK, 16 August 1993, p 6-7)

258. Klein 1956:87. See also Braham 1981:630-32. For Rabbi Herskovits' testimony, see Yivo 768/3581.

259. Private correspondence: Arthur Stern to TDK, 16 August 1993, p 8.

260. Freudiger 1972:243.

261. Private correspondence: Arthur Stern to TDK, 16 August 1993, p 8-9.

262. Leo Stern's wife Bertha was the eldest sister of the writer's mother.

263. Freudiger 1972:260.

264. The letters were discovered by Arthur Stern in the 1980s, in the Geneva files of his late father Leo.

265. "*Biklal*": Hebrew for "in general". (Private correspondence: Arthur Stern to TDK, 16 August 1993)

266. Eventually the relationship between Leo and Freudiger regained its warmth, the latter visiting the Stern residence in Switzerland on several occasions. (PD:TDK-Arthur Stern, 10 February 1991)

267. Freudiger 1972:243-44.
268. PD:TDK-Arthur Stern, 7 February 1991.
269. Arthur Stern states that he, his father and some other relatives approached Freudiger to plead for intervention on behalf of the arrested Stern brothers. (Ibid) Freudiger referred to the deportation of Jozsef and Salamon Stern in some detail during his testimony at the Eichmann trial. For a precis of, and extracts from, this testimony, see "Postcards from Waldsee" in Hilberg 1972:191-99.
270. This assessment is based on the writer's personal knowledge.
271. This observation is clearly supported by Arthur Stern's statement: "Being responsible for the Finance and Economic Affairs portfolio, [Leo] was certainly aware and in control of every substantial financial action. Since all implementation (issuing payment orders, making detailed fund allocations, collecting funds, etc.) was through his brother Herman, nothing of significance escaped his attention." (Private correspondence: Arthur Stern to TDK, 16 August 1993, p 9)
272. Bauer 1981:390. For details of Orthodox rescue activities, see Rozett 1987:115 and 140.
273. Certainly the Orthodox resented, and rightly so, their characterisation by some of their assimilated co-religionists as "primitive *Ostjuden*" (backward provincial Jews from eastern Europe).
274. Cohen 186:101; Braham 1981:952-57 and 1,015, n90. Such a "Kasztner seat" cost 100,000 *pengos*. (Freudiger 1972:266)
275. For Freudiger's version of these events, see Freudiger 1972:255.
276. Freudiger, obviously aware of, and sensitive to, such criticism, contradicts this claim by stating that "a large number of the refugees were Orthodox but we distributed them [Hungarian and/or Christian papers] to everyone who asked for them". (Freudiger 1972:242) More specifically, he further asserts: "Conducting *Hatzala* on a party basis was alien to us, and we ourselves had abandoned the separation principle of the Orthodoxy in view of the sacredness of this work." (Freudiger 1972:244)
277. The minor overlap was the *Mizrachi*, an Orthodox Zionist organisation.
278. PD:TDK-Arthur Stern, 10 February 1991.
279. Freudiger 1972:252.
280. In subsequent correspondence with the writer, Arthur Stern elaborated upon the relationship between Freudiger and his uncle Odon thus: "...the Freudigers couldn't do without Odon, he was indispensable to them and therefore he could do as he saw fit, provided only that he delivered enough money to the numerous branches of the Freudiger family to keep them living in the style to which they were accustomed." (Private correspondence: Arthur Stern to TDK, 16 August 1993, p 12)
281. PD:TDK-Arthur Stern 10 February 1991.
282. Freudiger 1972:242.
283. Cohen 1986:24.
284. As expected, police activity and supervision increased as the War progressed, with the police force's most efficient agencies being the KEOKH and the political department. (Cohen 1986:25)
285. Cohen (1986:27) states that illegal Jewish refugees often worked for Jewish employers "who chose to turn a blind eye to the origins of their new employees".
286. It will be recalled that prior to the German Occupation, the Allies had an implicit understanding with the Kallay government, viz: Hungary remained unbombed, whilst Allied aircraft penetrating Hungarian airspace remained unmolested.
287. After criticising his behaviour and management style, Elizabeth Eppler (1946:5) states that "Muller's administration absorbed immense amounts of money". The JC's Chief Secretary, Erno Munkacsi, is more specific, on 21 August 1944 writing to Samu Stern thus: "I admit that extreme necessity and compulsion justify many things which otherwise would

not be possible but in serving the Germans many expenses were incurred, for which neither the excuse of extreme necessity nor the excuse of compulsion can be advanced." (Levai 1948:184) Whist not discounting the possibility of greed and/or corruption permeating its operations, it should be noted that the Housing Department's "immense apparatus" was created at a few hours' notice by conscripting personnel from "all [Jewish] community institutions". (Stern 1945:12) Such overworked, abused (if not terrified) staff, largely inexperienced in requisition and allocation, could not be expected to operate at optimum efficacy, especially in the chaos then prevailing amongst Budapest's Jews.

288. Eppler 1946:4.
289. See Braham 1981:487-90.
290. Levai 1948:182.
291. Ibid.
292. For an itemisation of these restrictions, see Levai 1948:186-87.
293. Unless otherwise specified, information in this section was provided by Arthur Stern during a series of private discussions with the writer, 7-14 February 1991.
294. The MIEFHOE also contained several hundred associate members, this category consisting of Jewish graduates from *gymnasia* (high schools) excluded from university by the various anti-Jewish Laws. Only full members had the right to vote at MIEFHOE meetings. (PD:TDK-Arthur Stern, 7 February 1991)
295. Samu Stern 1945:12; PD:TDK-Arthur Stern, 7 February 1991.
296. Braham 1981:443.
297. Stern 1945:12-13.
298. PD:TDK-Arthur Stern, 10 February 1991.
299. Levai 1948:81. The demands included 300 mattresses, 600 blankets and 30 printing compositors.
300. As the primary means of identification, the *Polgari Szemelyi Lap* was generally the first document demanded from an individual. Subsequent demands involved papers containing verification and/or information not contained on this card. When requisitioning apartments, "the people living in an abode frequently denied that they were Jewish, sometimes alleging to be 'born Christians'. In such cases we asked for their *Polgari Szemelyi Laps*." (Private correspondence: Arthur Stern to TDK, 16 August 1993, p 4)
301. See "Acquisition of Hungarian documents by Slovakian Refugee", 28 June 1943. (CZA S25/7844)
302. Apart from illegal refugees, many Hungarian Jews also needed instruction on how to use their false papers in a credible and confident manner. (PD:TDK-Arthur Stern, 7 February 1991)
303. Such papers could be obtained, for example, from corpses killed in air raids. Ideally, the corpse had to be disposed of in a secret, permanently secure and non-traceable manner.
304. As some MIEFHOE members were Zionists, there may have been a degree of cross-fertilisation between the Halutz and JC-based false document operations. (PD:TDK-Arthur Stern, 7 February 1991)
305. Braham 1981:672.
306. PD:TDK-Arthur Stern, 10 February 1991.
307. One of the most common examples of this phenomenon was provincial Jews using false papers to live illegally in Budapest. Such papers "seldom if ever caused suspicion, whereas aryan papers on a person who looked Jewish [sic] could cause all kinds of investigations." (Private correspondence: Arthur Stern to TDK, 16 August 1993, p16)
308. PD:TDK-Arthur Stern, 7 February 1991.
309. Arthur Stern recalled that the best set of papers he ever supplied was for a Jewish family named Tarnoky residing in Fasor Road, Budapest. Considered a "non-Jewish" name, these papers originally referred to a Christian Tarnoky family, of similar characteristics to their Jewish namesakes. Paradoxically, the Jewish Tarnoky family were thus provided with

a Christian identity in their own name, that is they obtained a genuine set of authentic false papers. (PD:TDK-Arthur Stern, 7 February 1991) [The papers in question did not refer to the Jewish Tarnoky family, so they were obviously false. However they were of proper government issue, so they were also genuine. And since they referred to the Tarnoky family, they were authentic. Consequently, the documents in question were a genuine set of authentic false papers.]

310. PD:TDK-Arthur Stern, 10 February 1991.

311. Having left Hungary on the Kasztner Transport, Arthur Stern's eyewitness testimony is limited to the first three and a half months of the Occupation.

312. This assessment is reinforced via the writer's personal experience and private knowledge. Having known Arthur Stern over many years, I can vouch for his reputation as a person of honesty and integrity.

313. In March 1944, Zionist youth movements had a mere 500 members in Budapest. (Braham 1981:998)

314. PD: TDK-Jozsef Meir, 3 January 1991. At the age of 13-14 Meir joined Hashomer Hatzair in northern Transylvania, before that region was annexed to Hungary. As the movement was prohibited in the annexed territories, in 1941 Meir (then aged nineteen) and several of his Transylvanian Hashomer Hatzair colleagues moved to Budapest, where they maintained a somewhat precarious activist existence.

315. Formerly separate groups, Dror and Habonim amalgamated in 1943. Prior to the Hungarian Occupation of Transylvania, Habonim did not exist in Hungary. In Transylvania, Habonim was considered a strong movement, with about 8-900 members, some of whom moved to Budapest upon the Hungarian annexation to organise the movement in the capital. (PD:TDK-Asher Aranyi, 3 January 1991)

316. Braham (1981:105) states that approximately 10,000 Slovak Jews entered Hungary during 1942. He believes that, at the end of 1943, 6-8,000 still remained in the country. (Braham 1981:109) The Maccabi leader Perecz Revesz estimates that in the period March 1942 to March 1944, 10-15,000 Slovakian Jews crossed into Hungary. (PD:TDK-Perecz Revesz, 4 January 1991)

317. PD:TDK-Perecz Revesz, 4 January 1991.

318. The notable exception to this phenomenon was the Habonim movement, whose leadership remained largely Hungarian and Transylvanian. (PD:TDK-Asher Aranyi, 3 January 1991)

319. By this time the Roumanian government was distancing itself from Germany. Consequently, there was a moderation in Roumania's attitude towards Jewish refugees and the "Jewish Question" in general.

320. Cohen 1981:253.

321. Some 200 Halutzim reached Bratislava via the re-*Tiyul*, with an unknown number reaching other parts of Slovakia. The re-*Tiyul* ceased with the defeat of the Slovak uprising in October 1944. (Rozett 1987:136)

322. Cohen 1986:87.

323. One noted exception was Habonim's non-involvement in re-*Tiyul* to Slovakia, the lack of Slovakian-speaking members precluding this option. (PD:TDK-Asher Aranyi, 3 January 1991)

324. PD:TDK-Asher Aranyi, 3 January 1991.

325. PD:TDK-Rafi ben Shalom (originally Friedl) of Hashomer Hatzair, 5 January 1991.

326. PD:TDK-David Gur, 8 January 1991.

327. Cohen 1986:244. Cohen (p 265) aptly notes that it is "impossible to estimate how many Jews crossed the border on their own initiative, after realising that the *He-Halutz* had been successful in their attempt."

328. Rozett 1987:141-42.

329. PD:TDK-Yehuda Bauer, 24 July 1991 (Sydney).

330. Braham 1981:998. Despite this sterling commendation, in this 1,269 page book Braham devotes a mere five pages to the section entitled "The Rescue Activities of the Hehalutz Youth" (see pp 998ff). Cohen (1986:249, n2) comments on this work thus: "Although [Braham's] two volumes are rich in detailed information based on abundant sources, they lack adequate information on the Halutz Resistance."

331. See Rozett 1987:122-34.

332. Cohen 1981:249; Cohen 1986:47.

333. PD:TDK-Rafi ben Shalom, 5 January 1991.

334. Ibid.

335. The son and grandson of produce merchants, David Gur (originally Endre Grosz) was born in 1926 and arrived in Budapest in 1943. He became head of the Halutz documentation department in April 1944. (PD:TDK-David Gur, 8 January 1991)

336. These lists are contained in Gur 1946:10-11 and Hashomer Hatzair 1948:18-20.

337. Weiss 1963:332.

338. For an example of Lutz's highly supportive attitude, see Cohen 1986:204.

339. Klibanski 1983:358.

340. For an indication of the crowds besieging the Glass House, see the photographs in Levai 1948:41.

341. Cited Braham 1981:1,080.

342. Braham 1981:847.

343. According to David Gur, the Halutz false document endeavour was the largest such enterprise in the whole of the Nazi domain. (PD:TDK-David Gur, 8 January 1991)

344. This argument was put to the writer by Laszlo Karsai, who claimed that by November 1944 "the false papers were worthless". (PD:TDK-Laszlo Karsai, 16 January 1991)

345. Braham 1981:848-49.

346. Cohen 1986:193.

347. Braham 1981:858. See also Braham 1981:830-31.

348. Karsai and Karsai 1988:605. For extracts from Domonkos' testimony, see pp 604-08. Domonkos' diary of his period at the JC was held in the private archives of the respected Hungarian historian, the late Elek Karsai. At the time of writing, the diary was held by Elek's son, Laszlo Karsai, who was only prepared to grant the writer access to it for "diamonds", ie: a large sum. (PD:TDK-Laszlo Karsai, 16 January 1991). The offer was refused. It is interesting to note that Elek Karsai permitted Robert Rozett access to his archives during the latter's PhD research on the Holocaust in Slovakia. (PD:TDK-Robert Rozett, 19 December 1990)

349. Braham 1981:849.

350. Pill 1946:3. Note that some authorities spell this Halutz leader's name as "Pil". However, "Pill" is the spelling on his signed Budapest testimony.

351. Pill 1946:2.

352. PD:TDK-David Gur, 8 January 1991.

353. Cohen 1986:270-71.

354. For a summary of the Children's Homes endeavour, see Cohen 1986:170-81.

355. Macartney 1957:II 346-47; Cohen 1986:203.

356. Amongst the largest donors were Jewish philanthropic organisations based in the USA, particularly the American Jewish Joint Distribution Committee, known popularly as the Joint.

357. For a summary of the Halutz food supply endeavour, see Cohen 1986:182-94.

358. Cohen 1986:183.

359. Uniforms were also obtained from deserters, generally for payment or in exchange for false papers.

360. During the writer's discussion with former Halutz leaders and members, there was

not a single individual who disputed the critical importance of Halutz food procurement to Budapest's Jews.

361. PD:TDK-Laszlo Karsai, 16 January 1991.

362. Per Anger negates the thrust of Karsai's argument thus: "...towards the end he [Wallenberg] also worked to protect the inhabitants of Budapest's general or so-called sealed ghetto, where around 70,000 had been forced together. He could *sometimes arrange* for food deliveries to the starving..." (Emphasis added) (Anger 1981:92) A report by three of Wallenberg's senior executives supports Anger regarding the spasmodic nature of Wallenberg's food supplies. This report states: "It was a grave blow to the Swedish and other protected people when the Arrow Cross in mid-December, occupied and totally looted [Wallenberg's] largest food store at Szentkiraly-utca... Subsequently it was barely possible to secure some meagre food supplies for the proteges..." (Report by Drs Andor Balog, Endre Szanto and Aladar Feigl, nd but probably *circa* late December 1944–January 1945; cited Levai 1948a:254) It should be noted that this misfortune was not confined to Wallenberg's organisation, the International Red Cross' food stores similarly being the frequent target of *Nyilas* raids. (Braham 1981:861) The Swedish Consulate's Report of December 1944 clearly indicates the relative importance of Wallenberg's food supplies to Budapest's 100,000-plus Jews, viz: "It was arranged earlier that [Jewish] House residents would be supplied with food from a common kitchen. Breakfast, lunch and dinner have been supplied daily to about 1,500 people." [Swedish Ministry for Foreign Affairs, *Raoul Wallenberg* (Swedish Institute, 1988), 35]

363. Cohen 1986:272, n3.

364. Cohen 1986:183. Rudolph Weisz operated under the aegis of Section A of the International Red Cross, the section headed by the Zionist leader Otto Komoly.

365. Hashomer Hatzair 1948:10-11. This listing includes the address of each delivery.

366. Macartney 1957:II 346.

367. PD:TDK-David Gur, 8 January 1991.

368. Although it appears water was a not a major problem, one inhabitant of Szalasi's Budapest reported utilising snow for drinking purposes. (PD:TDK-Gyorgy Gergely, 10 September 1993)

369. This figure refers to people formally registered as Jews (70,000 in the Common Ghetto, 33,000 in the International Ghetto [Macartney 1957 II:451]), and thus the recipients of Halutz relief activities. It does not include JLS members or those Jews living an underground existence outside the two ghettos.

370. PD:TDK-Gyorgy Gergely, 9 September 1993. As discussed in the following chapter, Dr Gergely was in Budapest during the whole of 1944. Despite being a high official of Section A of the International Red Cross, and consequently having freedom of movement and residence outside the ghettos, during the later stages of the Szalasi era Gergely and his immediate family were forced to eat pancakes made from perfumed rice powder — a substance originally intended for use as talc!

371. Andre Biss (1973:197-98) states that upon the creation of the Ghetto "Jews, men or women, fit for labour and fighting, were immediately evacuated; the others were led into the ghetto."

372. PD:TDK-Dr George Foster, 4 September 1993. Dr Foster, who was born in Budapest and is vice-President of the Australian Association of Jewish Holocaust Survivors, emphasised that people can survive for an extended period on small quantities of food provided they have adequate water supplies.

373. For example, Jews were prohibited from purchasing fats, butter and oil. (Biss 1973:201) At the same time, Hungarian authorities (theoretically) allocated Jews less than half the food provided to convicts in Hungarian prisons — 690 calories versus 1,500 calories, respectively. (Levai 1961:177)

374. Macartney 1957:II 461. Levai (1961:177) supports a lower estimate, viz:

"Municipal provisioning [of the ghetto] was to begin on December 8. The ghetto then made an inventory of its stocks. As shown by records, there were no noteworthy food reserves... From that day an arduous, relentless struggle was carried on continually to ensure provisions for the ghetto... However, the food continued to grow poorer, both in quality and quantity, particularly in January, when all municipal supplies came to an end."

375. The writer was unable to discover any evidence, oral or documentary, to contradict this assumption.

376. Braham 1981:860. This assumption is reinforced by a report by Miklos Gellert. Dated 30 December 1944, Gellert noted that "Mr Secretary Wallenberg asked the Council Delegate whether provision of food to the ghetto was as inadequate today as in previous days. I told him that the inhabitants of the ghetto got daily one bowl of food, usually soup and one thin slice of bread, as the bread portion was not able to be delivered over the past few days." (Levai 1948a:279)

377. Even the figure of six kilograms per month may be an overestimate. For example, in early 1942 the monthly basic bread ration in the Warsaw Ghetto varied between 2 kg (January) and 2.25 kg (March), although a minority received supplements via welfare allocations, smuggling and the black market.

378. This analysis assumes a reasonably equitable nutritional distribution of the foods listed. In other words, people would have been provided with a variety of listed foods and not just one or two types.

379. PD:TDK-David Gur, 8 January 1991.

380. Confirmed by Cohen 1986:207-09.

381. Cohen 1986:216.

382. PD:TDK-Jozsef Meir, 3 January 1991.

383. Many postwar Hungarian historians obfuscate Communist opposition to an independent Hungarian uprising during the Szalasi era. See, for example, Pinter 1986:199.

384. Asher Aranyi of Habonim states that the main difficulty with maintaining bunkers was providing electricity. Generally this was accomplished via a system of batteries, which had to be regularly removed and recharged. (PD:TDK-Asher Aranyi, 3 January 1991)

385. PD:TDK-Jozsef Meir, 3 January 1991. Such Jews were, of course, also provided with false papers.

386. See Rozett 1987b:83-98. See also CZA L15/224.

387. CZA S6/1640/3.

388. Rozett 1987b:91.

389. Weiss 1963:328.

390. Note that Krausz had his defenders. For example, in February 1944 Otto Komoly stated that, despite his deficiencies, Krausz was a conscientious worker. (Rozett 1987:129)

391. Cohen 1986:88.

392. Pill 1946:2.

393. Braham 1981:1,000-01.

394. Pill 1946:2.

395. Komoly 1944:210. Rafi ben Shalom states that his relations with Arthur Weisz deteriorated to such an extent that the latter instructed police guarding the Glass House to prevent him (ben Shalom) entering the building. (PD:TDK-Rafi ben Shalom, 5 January 1991)

396. Komoly 1944:219.

397. Komoly 1944:232. Dundi (Bertha) Deutsch was the secretary of Dr G. Polgar, director of MIPI. When Polgar left Hungary on the Kasztner Transport, Deutsch transferred to the Glass House. (PD:TDK-Elizabeth Eppler, 23 December 1990)

398. Eppler 1946:7.

399. Cohen 1986:223.

400. PD:TDK-Elizabeth Eppler, 23 December 1990.

401. Pill (1946:3) and Braham (1981:1,001) state that the residents eventually numbered

about 2,000, whilst Cohen (1986:193) claims over 3,000 from early December. The Glass House's extra-territoriality was eventually extended to the neighbouring building, 31 Vadasz Street. (Cohen 1986:193)

402. Pill 1946:3.

403. PD:TDK-David Gur, 8 January 1991.

404. Cohen 1986:247. Note that this figure relates solely to the Halutz false document endeavour.

405. The avoidance of incriminating documentation was a cardinal principal of Halutz policy. (PD:TDK-David Gur, 8 January 1991.)

406. For examples of collective amnesia regarding the Holocaust in Hungary, see Katzburg 1988c:369-86.

CHAPTER V

THE ENDEAVOURS OF DR GYORGY GERGELY, 1939 TO 1945

One of the most significant difficulties confronting Hungarian Holocaust scholarship is what might be termed the compartmentalisation of testimony. The large majority of survivors can provide direct eyewitness evidence on only a relatively narrow selection from the multitude of factors and events impacting on Hungarian Jewry during the Occupation era. In particular, there has been a paucity of comprehensive contemporary written testimony from those few activist leaders in the upper echelon of the Jewish hierarchy whose experience encompassed a wide range of responsibilities and endeavours. Until now, the exemplar of this category has been the Zionist leader Otto Komoly, whose diary outlines events, issues and individuals in a generally forthright though unfortunately often all too brief manner. Possibly another inclusion in the same category is the senior JC executive Miksa Domonkos, whose diary of the Occupation period was, at the time of writing, unavailable to historians due to being under private control.[1] However, as shall be seen, this paucity and narrow focus has been rectified to a substantial extent via the documentation and testimony of Dr Gyorgy Gergely. After over four decades in his private files, the majority of Gergely's material is now available for scholarship at the Archive of Australian Judaica within The University of Sydney.

Born into an upper *bourgeois* Hungarian Jewish family on 6 July 1914, Gyorgy Emile Gergely had an upbringing considered appropriate for the son of an affluent, thoroughly assimilated, patriotic Hungarian Jewish family of that class and era.[2] After completing high school in Budapest, Gergely spent a year in Berlin studying commerce. Transferring to Vienna shortly after the appointment of Hitler as German Chancellor, Gergely continued his studies for six months before returning to Hungary and enrolling at the Peter Pazmany University in Budapest. Some years before he received a doctorate in political science in 1938, Gergely's father Gyula secured his son employment at the *Magyar Altalanos Hitelbank* (General Credit Bank of Hungary), at which institution Gyula Gergely occupied a senior position.[3] At the Bank Gyorgy Gergely met Count Gyorgy Pallavicini Jr, a fellow employee of similar age whose father (and namesake) was a leading Legitimist (pro Hapsburg restorationist) politician and a former member of Count Istvan Bethlen's Vienna-based group of White Counter-revolutionaries (see Chapter II).[4] Because of their common interests, in particular a shared antipathy to the ultra-Right, Gergely and

Pallavicini Jr soon developed a close camaraderie. It was through the political standing of the Pallavicini family, and their trust and confidence in him, that Gergely became involved in the venture to arm the JLS brigades, an attempt at Jewish armed resistance unique in the annals of the Holocaust (see below).

As a result of Hungary's anti-Jewish legislation, Gergely was dismissed from the Bank in August 1939. Notwithstanding such blatant discrimination, as a staunch Hungarian patriot Gergely used this opportunity to travel to *Tatarhago* (the Tartar Pass) in the newly regained portion of Slovakia, the place where the conquering Magyar brigands originally entered Hungary in the latter part of the ninth century. Apart from various attempts at earning a living, Gergely utilised his time to compose polemics expounding his views on the Jewish situation in Hungary. After writing a seven-page tract advocating a Jewish counter-propaganda bureau to combat the influence of ultra-Right media, in July 1940 he distributed copies to the presidents and Rabbis of Hungary's Jewish communities.[5] Receiving a large number of positive responses, Gergely personally conveyed the written replies to the prominent Jewish leader Dr Geza Ribary, foundation head of OMZSA (see Chapter III), upon which the latter invited Gergely to join a committee of communal elders concerned with Jewish affairs.

This invitation was Gyorgy Gergely's entry into the official Jewish community. The youngest of some fifty elderly male participants — which included Ribary and Dr Erno Munkacsi, Chief Secretary of the Pest Jewish Community — Gergely regularly attended the committee's deliberations at Neolog headquarters, 12 Sip Street. Impressed with his input, Ribary and Munkacsi requested Gergely to prepare a pamphlet outlining the Jewish contribution to Hungary over the ages. Shortly before being conscripted into the JLS Gergely produced a lengthy tract, an effort that resulted in his formal introduction to Hungarian Jewry's foremost leader, Samu Stern.[6]

After being dismissed from the Bank, Gergely maintained friendly relations with his former colleague Pallavicini. Their personal relationship was reinforced by a reciprocal business arrangement for, contemporaneously with Gergely's dismissal, Pallavicini had become secretary to the General Manager of *Hazai Fesufono*, one of Hungary's largest spinning and weaving enterprises. From this position Pallavicini supplied *Hazai Fesufono* fabrics to Gergely who, in turn, supplied Pallavicini with difficult-to-obtain drive belts used in the textile mill's manufacturing facility. Apart from business encounters, Gergely visited his friend on private occasions, amongst others on 4 April 1941, the day following the suicide of young Pallavicini's uncle, the former Prime Minister Count Pal Teleki (see Chapter II).[7]

As with other eligible male Jews, after 1940 Gyorgy Gergely was conscripted into the JLS, his brigade spending much of its duty periods near the Roumanian border in the newly regained region of northern Transylvania. Notwithstanding his lack of formal qualifications, Gergely became medical orderly to his company of some 220 men, as well as the sole provider of medical aid to the border village of Sosmezo.[8] Resulting from this responsibility, Gergely's JLS duties included periodic travel to Budapest to replenish the brigade's medical supplies, such material being provided by the *Orszagos Izraelita Irodak Hadviseltek Bizottsaga* (National Bureau of Jewish War Veterans, henceforth NBJWV) headed by the former MP, Dr Bela Fabian, and operating from the community's headquarters at 12 Sip Street.

The genesis of the NBJWV occurred in November 1939, shortly after the commencement of the labour service system, when the Pest Jewish Community established a Jewish War Veterans' Committee. Liaising with OMZSA and MIPI, Hungarian Jewry's great national social-action consortium (see above), the committee evolved into the multifaceted NBJWV organisation. As the government no longer supplied uniforms for Jewish labour conscripts, in September 1942 the Interior Ministry, responding to the pleas of Jewish leaders, authorised the Jewish community to collect winter clothing for needy members of the JLS. The resulting intensive nationwide campaign soliciting donations was conducted by the NBJVW (see Fig. 4.1). Tragically, it appears that little if any of the clothing collected reached the JLS brigades in most need — those stationed in the Ukraine and Yugoslavia.

Towards the end of 1943, whilst in Budapest replenishing his JLS brigade's medical stores, Gergely was advised by Fabian to see the Chief Secretary of the Pest Jewish Community, Dr Erno Munkacsi, and request inclusion in a Budapest-based "Special Labour Company" then being formed within the NBJWV to provide support for the JLS.[9] Accepted by Munkacsi, from then until the German Occupation (19 March 1944) Gergely was stationed in Budapest and worked at the Jewish War Veterans' offices writing articles and publicity material on behalf of the Bureau. In addition, he helped administer the collection and distribution of used civilian clothing to needy members of the JLS.[10]

The National Bureau of Jewish War Veterans

Gyorgy Gergely's appointment as a publicist and advocate for the NBJWV appears eminently understandable. Apart from his doctorate in political science, discussion with Gergely revealed his deep and abiding interest in politics and the political process — particularly those facets affecting Jewry. Confirming this assessment, his archives contain articles, speeches and correspondence vis-à-vis the "Jewish Question" that span over half a century. As early as 1935, for instance, at the age of twenty-one, Gergely commenced correspondence with Henry S. Haskell, assistant to the Director of the Carnegie Endowment for International Peace.[11]

Subsequent to his July 1940 tract advocating a Jewish counter-propaganda bureau, Gergely's writings included a forty-three page treatise *Faj vagy Vallas?*[12] (Race or Religion?; June 1941) followed, in September 1941, by a vigorous nineteen-page attack on the first Yellow Booklet, a publication released in July 1941 by the Jewish Work Collective (*Zsido Munkakozosseg*), a small (fifty members) Budapest-based Revisionist-Zionist group.[13] Notwithstanding the consternation generated within the Jewish community by the contemporaneous, racially based Third Jewish Law (see Chapter II), Gergely echoed the large majority of his compatriot co-religionists by vehemently rejecting the Zionist view that Jews formed an ethnic — as opposed to a religious — minority in Hungary. Denouncing the Revisionists' repudiation of the community's cherished Magyar-Jewish symbiosis, Gergely rejected the concept of *Aliya* by proclaiming: "We shall beat our chests that we are Hungarians until everybody acknowledges us. Whatever happens, wherever we find ourselves, we shall always say: 'God bless Hungary.' "[14]

Despite the strength of such patriotic statements, a discernible diminution in Gergely's intense nationalism — and consequent anti-Zionist stance — is apparent from an undated but probably contemporary speech contained in his archive. In this seven-page tract, Gergely concluded that despite the latest anti-Jewish legislation — a probable reference to the Third Jewish Law of August 1941 — Jews remained firm Hungarian patriots and, whilst nothing could alter this attitude, there was a creeping realisation within the community that "the mother-country is only a step-mother".[15] Irrespective of his then ideology, however, Gergely's attitude never constrained his close future co-operation with Otto Komoly, as the Hungarian Zionist Chief's authoritative diary clearly reveals (see below).

A clear verification of Gergely's contemporary status within institutional Jewry occurred on 17 March 1942, when two OMZSA executives formally invited him to the inaugural meeting of the OMZSA Youth Committee, a group formed to involve Hungarian Jewish youth in OMZSA and MIPI activities.[16] His track record, taken in conjunction with his writings — for example, his twenty-four page treatise "*A zsidosag es a szocialis kerdes. Tervezet.*"[17] (Jews and the Social Question. Plans.) — indicate that his appointment to the social action-oriented NBJWV was both understandable and entirely appropriate.[18] Presented in speech format, in this treatise Gergely clearly revealed his social conscience by proclaiming every individual's right to be free from hunger, to be clothed and decently housed, to have children, to provide self and family with medical care, to have sufficient wherewithal and free time to facilitate personal development and leisure activities, and for these rights to be independent of an individual's possible unemployment, injury, illness, age or other such circumstance.

Shortly after commencing at the NBJWV, in December 1943 Gergely wrote a thirty-six page *Jelentes* (Report) for that organisation which outlined its work and, in effect, attempted to stimulate the social conscience of Hungarian Jews and thus encourage greater support for the JLS conscripts and their families.[19] As far as can be determined, Gergely's Report is the most comprehensive document available on the endeavours of the NBJWV, an organisation then at the centre of institutional Jewry's concerns and obligations.

Section I of the Report, headed "*Elso a Munkaszolgalatos!*" (First the JLS Conscripts!), outlined the bitter winter conditions faced by JLS members, and stated that the NBJWV's responsibilities towards these Jewish conscripts and their families included: collection and equitable distribution of clothing; protection against war-induced socio-economic difficulties; hospital visits and social net-working; support for civil and military prisoners; advice and legal aid; and national fundraising campaigns.[20] Noting that the Hungarian government's withdrawal of army uniforms from the JLS meant that Jewish conscripts were forced to clothe themselves whilst on active duty — an obligation many were unable to fulfil — the Report quotes Samu Stern's official statement of 15 December 1943 to the effect that the community could not permit the JLS to suffer and die through lack of adequate clothing and that "All our troubles and sufferings are subordinate to this emergency".[21]

According to the Report, in the period 17 November 1942 to December 1943, apart from contributions distributed within Hungary, the NBJWV dispatched twenty-eight wagons of donated merchandise to JLS brigades stationed in the Ukraine.[22] Aggregate figures reveal that, of these 262,000 collected items, 196,000 — about 75 percent — were allocated to benefit JLS members on the Eastern Front. It is thus clear that the majority of clothing collected by the NBJWV was dispatched to foreign-based JLS brigades rather than reserved for the benefit of their families or Hungarian-based colleagues. As previously mentioned, despite precautions

— in particular, to ensure that requests for clothing went to the "needy and not greedy"[23] — wholesale theft by the Hungarian and German military meant that little if any of these foreign shipments reached their intended recipients on the Eastern Front.[24] This may not have been the case with merchandise dispatched to JLS units based in Hungary,[25] due to the proximity of central authorities and the absence of Germans from the scene.

After emotional descriptions of JLS deprivation and suffering — which, the Report notes, were in stark contrast to opulent displays by affluent civilians in elegant urban precincts — the Report's first section admonished the community by presenting a stark choice: it could support either private greed or the public saving of life. In effect, Gergely invited Hungarian Jewry to choose between, on the one hand, an inhumane, antisocial apathy or, on the other, the acknowledgement of heroic sacrifice by providing unstinting material support to those suffering in the JLS on the community's behalf.[26]

Section 2 of the Report deals with the NBJWV's endeavours on behalf of JLS conscripts' families (especially widows and orphans) who, since June 1943, were no longer supported by welfare authorities and had become the NBJWV's responsibility.[27] Despite providing assorted forms of financial assistance (both emergency and systematic) to individuals and organisations, the prime aim of the Bureau was to supply a comprehensive matrix of social services, including health care, support for mothers, foster parenting, employment and retraining. Funds for these programmes were obtained largely from communal contributions, cultural performances and markets, with support being effected by both volunteers and paid administrators. As with many other NBJWV endeavours, health care, ante and post-natal protection,[28] pharmaceutical subsidies and ambulance services were introduced because JLS conscripts' dependants were ineligible to receive government welfare benefits.[29]

The Report's final portion (Section 8), headed *Orszagos Penzgyujtes* (National Fundraising), explained that although individual departments of the NBJWV were involved in some fundraising, overall responsibility for obtaining donations was vested in a national campaign sanctioned by the Interior Ministry, the initial campaign being approved for the period 15 March to 15 April 1943. Taking ten days to organise and implement, the campaign was thus, in effect, restricted to twenty days of public activity. Involving all three denominations of Hungarian Jewry, by utilising word of mouth, pamphlets and public meetings, the initial campaign raised 800,000 *pengo* — the lion's share donated by Budapest Jews — for an expenditure of 19,317 *pengo*, a commendable ratio of costs to income of some 2.5 percent. As previously indicated, the major portion of nett proceeds was allocated to providing clothing for the JLS.[30]

As the sum raised proved inadequate to satisfy continuing needs, the Interior Ministry granted permission for another fundraising effort. To conclude on 31 January 1944, and again lasting one month, a separate department was created by the NBJWV to oversee this second national campaign. Because of existing shortfalls, the second campaign was budgeted to raise nett proceeds of 3,000,000 *pengo*, which was required urgently for (amongst other items) 25,000 boots, 10,000 metres of textiles and 10,000 suits.[31]

The Report concluded by criticising those with negative attitudes towards the NBJWV's fundraising efforts, particularly those maintaining "I don't want anything, I won't give anything, leave me alone"; "A close friend in need didn't receive anything"; and "Parcels were not received in the Ukraine." As per his occasional wont, Gergely was unapologetic in responding to what he perceived were unwarranted excuses:

> We are not perfect, we can only allocate priorities, of whom the first is the JLS. Our warehouses are empty. We have to rebuff those to whom we are the last resort. Remember the orphans, widows and the *Munkaszolgalatos* [JLS]. We seek merely your clothing and money, not your happiness or lives. Additionally, however, the time and skills of volunteers are required to advance social welfare. Hopefully, this will need to be our last appeal.[32]

The Jewish Council

Immediately upon the German Occupation, Gergely again approached Dr Munkacsi, Chief Secretary of the Pest Jewish Community, this time requesting a transfer from the NBJWV to a more responsible position, one commensurate with the change in the Jewish Community's circumstances. Aware of his fluency in German, the Chief Secretary transferred Gergely to what, in effect, became the Liaison Bureau, an office consisting of four young university graduates — Drs Elizabeth Eppler, Janos Gabor, Gyorgy Gergely and Laszlo Peto. Strategically located within the President's Department at Community headquarters in 12 Sip Street, the Liaison Office quickly evolved into the prime formal conduit between the JC, Eichmann and the *SS Dienststelle*.[33] Based at the JC for some four months, towards the end of July — after Horthy's order banning further deportations had diminished the need for constant contact with the *SS* — Gergely's reputation was such that he was transferred to the Swedish legation to become secretary to their recently arrived emissary, Raoul Wallenberg (see below).[34]

Through his archive, and in private discussion with the writer, Gergely was at pains to emphasise that despite his formal position as a Liaison Officer, exigencies quickly restructured his actual duties and responsibilities at the JC. In particular, after noting his frequent contacts with "everybody who counted" within the Jewish hierarchy, and regular reports to the JC,[35] Gergely described his position thus: "I was not a member of the Senate [JC], I was purely a...let's call myself an executive, because it would not express my position properly were I to say I was a liaison officer. I was the negotiator as well...[and liaison with the *SS Dienststelle*] was only a smaller part of my activities..."[36] There is powerful support for this contention, particularly via the immediate postwar testimony of Lajos Stockler, member of the JC and Samu Stern's opponent and successor who, in an official affidavit, stated: "Dr Gyorgy Gergely was also a member of the liaison group with the authorities. He prepared the secret instructions. He was the Council's man who knew everything."[37]

In keeping with Stockler's statement, permeating Gergely's testimonies and private discussions with the writer were cogent, detailed and wide-ranging analyses of the Hungarian Jewish situation during the German Occupation, especially the JC's formation, membership, infrastructure, reconstruction and endeavours. For example, in the 1958 testimony he prepared for two important War Crime trials in West Germany (see below), Gergely provided details on a broad spectrum of subjects — including the layout and functioning of *SS* headquarters, the Kistarcsa operations (see Chapter IV), Eichmann's contempt for the puppet Sztojay government (eg: *"Was interessiert mich euer Zigeunerregierung!"*), the "complicated operation" that prevented the deportation of Budapest Jews, and Krumey's briefing of the Jewish leadership on 20 March 1944.[38] It should be noted that this information was provided well before the Eichmann Trial of 1961 publicised many of these events.

Having attended the early, critical meetings between the *SS* and Jewish leaders, in his testimony Gergely provided primary evidence regarding the German disinformation campaign vis-à-vis the safety and security of Hungarian Jews.[39] At the formal gathering held on 21 March in the Assembly Hall of Community headquarters at 12 Sip Street, Gergely witnessed *SS* representatives Hermann Krumey and Dieter Wisliceny inform the top echelon of Hungarian Jewry that the "Jewish Question" was of secondary importance to the Reich, a problem to be resolved but only after the cessation of hostilities. According to the Germans, as the War effort was the current prime focus, the Jewish Community would be subject to discipline but all co-operating Jews would remain safe and secure — including those Jews arrested so as to assure appropriate behaviour by their co-religionists.[40] In his oral testimony, Gergely's narration of this topic concludes with the poignant comment: "It was much easier to believe."[41]

Assessing the impact of this meeting, Gergely stated that the approximately 200 Jewish leaders present[42] accepted that the Reich's prime concern was to win the War, the consensus being that the Germans would behave rationally and conscript all available resources — including Jewish labour — towards that end.[43] Certainly Fulop Freudiger's discussion on 28 March with his Nagyvarad counterpart (see Chapter IV) was in full keeping with this assessment. Equally, Freudiger's flight to Roumania in August 1944 (see Chapter IV) clearly represented the Jewish leadership's changed attitude towards German assurances. This revised evaluation, states Gergely, was based on the leaders' eventual acceptance that their security was but a transitory phenomenon, a temporary exemption from deportation which would terminate upon the destruction of their community. In a later testimony, Gergely emphasised that, by mid-1944, "this was absolutely accepted knowledge".[44]

During the Occupation's initial stages, Gergely and the Liaison Office maintained regular contact with Eichmann, the latter personally directing major matters affecting the Jewish community. With the *Endlösung* strategy in place, considerable authority was delegated to Eichmann's deputy, *Obersturmbannführer* Krumey, ensuring that the latter became the first point of contact between the JC and the *SS*. Subsequently, with the erosion of German hegemony over Hungarian Jews (see Chapter IV), the corrupt Laszlo Koltay of the State Security Police was delegated to represent Hungary's interests at Eichmann's headquarters, the Majestic Hotel in Buda. In principle, with this appointment all future communications between the JC and the *SS* were to be conducted via Koltay,[45] although in practice only relatively minor questions were referred through him.[46]

As one of their first acts, the Germans in effect unified the Community by subordinating it to the supreme authority of a *Judenrat* (JC). Imposing the *Führerprinzip* upon Hungarian Jewry, in turn the JC's leader became responsible to Eichmann for the successful implementation of German orders and the maintenance of discipline within the Community. Relating one of their early meetings, Gergely states that Eichmann ordered the JC to produce a Constitution to this effect within forty-eight hours[47] — thus fulfilling the German strategy of dealing with the solitary leader of a peak body, instead of a convoluted matrix of leaders and organisations.

Touching upon the German-Hungarian rivalry over the sequestration of Jewish wealth, Gergely referred to the decree of early April that compelled Jews to permanently attach a six-pointed Yellow Star on the left side of their outer garment.[48] In accordance with his orders from Krumey, Gergely submitted a model of the Yellow Star to the *SS* for approval. As some three million such badges would be required for the 800,000 people officially classified as Jews, upon acceptance of the prototype the Hungarians assigned a monopoly on Yellow Star production to a co-operative society. This decision was promptly vetoed by the *SS* so as to prevent several million Jewish *pengos* flowing into Hungarian coffers. Consequently, states Gergely, every Jewish household was permitted to produce its own Yellow Stars.[49]

Although Gergely's writings and 1987 narrative discuss the major German figures in the saga of Hungarian Jewry, most details regarding *Obersturmbannführer-SS* Hermann Krumey and *Hauptsturmführer-SS* Otto Hunsche, two prominent members of Eichmann's *Kommando*, are contained in his 1958 testimony. Resulting from a request by Dr Frigyes Gorog, foundation head of the World Federation of Jews of Hungarian Descent and Head of the Budapest AJDC (the Joint) at the end of hostilities,[50] Gergely's 1958 testimony was prepared for the then forthcoming trials of Krumey and Hunsche in West Germany. Shortly thereafter Gergely received the same request from Dr Siegfrid Roth (Chief Secretary, European Division — World Jewish Congress). Of special note, the Krumey and Hunsche cases have been assessed as by far the most important trials regarding the Hungarian Jewish tragedy conducted in West German courts.[51]

On 24 January 1958, Dr Gorog wrote to Gergely from New York requesting the latter's testimony on Krumey and Hunsche's activities in Hungary, explaining that such testimony was to be used as evidence at their forthcoming trials.[52] Replying on 12 April 1958, Gergely enclosed his typewritten nine foolscap page testimony with a closely argued, soul-searching and sometimes emotional two foolscap page covering letter which expressed his moral misgivings concerning the proposed trials.[53] Primary amongst these was his concern at the apparent policy of "hanging the executioners" whilst setting the judges free, aptly summarised in his poignant refrain "Whatever happens to them [Krumey and Hunsche], justice will not be done".[54]

Shortly after commencing work at the Liaison Office, one of Gergely's fundamental tasks was to request "audiences" with Krumey so as to submit diplomatically worded memoranda on various issues affecting Jews — especially the situation of those arrested and/or deported. Krumey's general response to these submissions was to react politely, occasionally express indignation at the documented brutalities, and reiterate that as the resolution of such charges was the responsibility of various German authorities, the JC could not be involved in redressing the complaints. Discussing the *modus operandi* of the *SS* hierarchy, Gergely commented that, in contrast to Eichmann's consistent psychic brutality, Krumey generally adopted a civilised demeanour. Despite this apparently reasonable attitude, Gergely emphasised that Krumey's numerous commitments to rectify documented outrages remained unfulfilled.[55] Notwithstanding continual rebuffs, in the absence of any viable alternative — Eichmann and Koltay making no secret of their ferocious, pathological hatred of Jews — the Jewish leadership persevered with their supplications to Krumey who, despite his polite manner, proved a conscientious servant of the *Endlösung*.

Prior to leaving the JC, Gergely was also in contact with lower-ranking members of the Eichmann *Kommando*. Included in this category was *Hauptsturmführer-SS* Otto Hunsche, whom he saw with respect to minor complaints or when Krumey was unavailable to deal with urgent matters. Two other *SS* officers mentioned by Gergely in some detail in his 1958 statement were *Hauptsturmführers* Krieger and Bethge. The former, an argumentative type, shared Eichmann's brutal demeanour, Nazi philosophy and rabid Antisemitism. In particular, as a stalwart Nazi, Krieger unabashedly proclaimed that not only was Roosevelt a Jew, but that Jews ruled the world, caused the War, and should be eliminated.[56] Bethge, a graduate of the elite *Reichsführerschule* in Berlin (a school for especially talented *SS* members), was a historian whose brief was to record the saga of Hungarian Jews whilst the community still existed.[57] Accordingly, Gergely gathered comprehensive data on Hungarian Jewry — demography, socio-economic development, denominational differences etc — which Bethge received in a courteous, appreciative manner.[58]

Gergely concluded his 1958 testimony by listing those additional events upon which he could present detailed evidence if required — including the arrests of Jewish hostages, deportations from the Rokk-Szilard Street detainment centre, confiscation of Jewish residences, the death marches from Budapest to the Reich in late 1944, and *Nyilas* atrocities during the Szalasi era. Such detail is absent from his 1958 testimony, argued Gergely — surely correctly — because it was impossible to produce at short notice a history of Hungary during the German Occupation. This telling point is followed by a somewhat controversial assertion: despite being in a highly advantageous position to do so, Gergely claimed that his prominent government appointments in postwar Hungary (including First Secretary, Ministry of Trade; see fig. 5.4), and subsequent demands upon his time and energy as a migrant in Australia, prevented his memoirs being written in the immediate postwar years.[59]

Frigyes Gorog responded to this testimony on 8 May 1958, replying that he had received evidence from Fulop Freudiger, Erno and Laszlo Peto, Imre Reiner (the Orthodox community's legal counsel[60]), and Samu Kahan-Frankl. Additionally, other important informants — including Joel Brand, Jeno Levai and Andre Biss — had undertaken to provide testimony at the German consulate closest to their residence.[61] Amongst other information, Gorog related Freudiger and Reiner's assertion that Eichmann's order exempting the families of JC members from deportation was subverted by Krumey and Hunsche. Consequently, amongst others, Kahan-Frankl's mother and sister and Karoly Wilhelm's sisters and family were deported and gassed.[62] The thrust of Gorog's letter was the suggestion that Gergely revise his testimony in eighteen specific respects, generally to reduce and/or eliminate those points which were either irrelevant or weakened the case against Krumey and Hunsche.[63] Furthermore, he requested Gergely to provide information on various additional aspects of the Occupation era, including Hunsche's role in the Kistarcsa deportation of 19 July 1944, and Krumey's acceptance of a $200,000 bribe (see Chapter IV).[64]

Quite independently, on 16 May 1958 Dr Siegfrid Roth (Chief Secretary, European Division — World Jewish Congress) wrote to Gergely from London informing him of the Krumey–Hunsche defence claim that both defendants thought deportations were for labour purposes only, and that neither knew about Auschwitz or its gas chambers. Roth continued by stating that apart from the deceased Janos Gabor, Gergely, an executive of the Liaison Office, would have been the person in most frequent contact with the two defendants. Thus, because his evidence could be of crucial importance, Gergely was requested to officially deposit a relevant, comprehensive affidavit at the nearest German consulate, such testimony paying particular attention to Krumey's role in the deportations. Furthermore, because the Frankfurt judiciary examining this case had formally requested the WJC to provide evidence, Roth considered that the prosecution might call Gergely as a witness.[65] The letter concluded with an appeal to help locate other witnesses, both Jewish and otherwise, so as to provide independent corroboration at the trial.

Roth's subsequent letter to Gergely came surprisingly quickly, being dated 3 June 1958. From this correspondence, it is obvious that Gergely had responded to Roth's 16 May requests at some time between these two dates. Roth's letter clearly indicates that Gergely's response had included a draft affidavit which, upon receiving Roth's approval, Gergely would formally lodge at a German consulate. From the short time between Roth's two letters, it is reasonable to assume that this draft affidavit was substantially — if not completely — the same as Gergely's submission to Gorog. One may surmise that this probable redundancy was a prime reason for the second affidavit being absent from Gergely's various archives. After requesting additional information on Bethge ("he could be a useful witness"), Roth again concluded with an appeal for assistance in locating additional witnesses.[66]

The above cordial exchanges appear to comprise Gergely's extant correspondence with Messers Gorog and Roth.[67] It is pertinent to note, however, a possible antagonism — if not animosity — harboured by Gergely against Gorog. Although its time of commencement is uncertain, friction is clearly evident in Gergely's testimony narrated some thirty years subsequent to their correspondence. In this narrative Gergely, after commenting that "he [Gorog] was not dirtied by dangerous jobs which others had to do during their work",[68] attacked Gorog's alleged passivity during the Occupation, and deprecated postwar claims of Gorog's wartime resistance activities.[69]

Rabbi Bela Berend and the "Zionisation of Antisemitism"

One of the most emotive — though almost totally neglected — aspects of the Holocaust in Hungary concerns the activities of Rabbi Dr Bela Berend. Although a detailed study of Berend is beyond the bounds of this discussion, because of Gergely's integral role in the Berend case, a precis of the latter's attitudes and endeavours is in order.[70]

Bela Berend (originally Presser, 12 January 1911–June 1987[71]) graduated from the Rabbinical Seminary of Budapest in 1936 and the following year was appointed Rabbi of the Neolog community of Szigetvar (a small town in south-west Hungary), where he remained until shortly after the German Occupation. To the great consternation of established Jewish leaders, on 8 May 1944 this provincial Rabbi, a person about whom highly detrimental suspicions had already circulated, gained access to the supreme hierarchy of Hungarian Jewry via his appointment to the Hungarian-reconstructed Jewish Council (see Chapter IV). As it was accepted that Berend had been appointed to the JC due to his association with, and at the behest of, the Hungarian ultra-Right — in particular, the rabid Antisemites Zoltan Bosnyak and Laszlo Endre — even before his arrival at 12 Sip Street, the JC triumvirate (Stern, Peto and Wilhelm) may have pre-empted Berend's access to confidential documents by having such material destroyed.[72] But certainly, in line with his deep concern, Stern instructed Gyorgy Gergely to intercept Berend's mail and report on its contents. This tactic quickly revealed Berend's close association with a senior gendarmerie officer in Szigetvar,[73] Gergely intercepting a particularly ominous letter from Berend to the officer which stated: "Sir, I arrived into this dirt hole [JC Headquarters] and the instructions you gave me during our talks are very clearly in my mind. They will be carried out to the letter, and this place needs a big clean-up. That clean-up will happen, and I will keep you informed."[74]

Based on his now proven fraternisation with Antisemitic officials and *Nyilas* leaders, the JC considered Berend an informer in its midst and, in effect, quarantined itself, conducting its discussions in secret or during Berend's absence. The threat posed by what was considered Berend's high treason became so great that, towards the middle of the year, Gergely attempted to eliminate Berend's influence and — on his own initiative, so as to prevent the JC being implicated — formed an "Action Committee" towards that end.[75] Consisting mainly of university graduates who were Gergely's contemporaries, the Committee, condemning Berend for high treason, resolved to utilise German-Hungarian rivalry to neutralise Berend and the power of his *Nyilas* patrons.[76] Three members of the Committee, including Gergely, contacted Franz Weinzinger, a timber merchant known for his powerful German connections, and informed him that Berend's spying for the Hungarian authorities prevented the JC complying with Eichmann's orders, via the Hungarians pre-emption of German demands — especially upon Hungarian Jewry's rapidly dwindling assets. Upon receipt of Weinzinger's report, the *SS* arrested Berend; yet despite *SS* involvement, Endre's subsequent intervention secured Berend's release.[77]

Upon gaining his freedom, Berend resumed his position at the JC and continued associating with his *Nyilas* contacts until he became "practically a *persona grata*" at the Interior Ministry.[78] At the end of July 1944 he gave an interview to the virulently Antisemitic *Nyilas* publication *Harc* (Battle; see fig. 5.1), edited by his *Nyilas* contact Zoltan Bosnyak, in which he supported the *Nyilas* view that conversion was a religious and not an ethnic metamorphosis. In his postwar defence, Berend stated that this interview was aimed at preventing mass conversions and, hence, retaining the unity of the Jewish community.[79] It is pertinent to note that Bosnyak was the founding director of the highly Antisemitic, state-supported Institute for Researching the Jewish Question, having been appointed to that post by Laszlo Endre, a violently Antisemitic joint Secretary of State at the Interior Ministry.

For the balance of the Occupation Berend, whilst often performing yeoman social service — especially during the Szalasi era[80] — maintained his singular political and ideological activities, remaining in Budapest until the city's liberation by the Red Army. Arrested by the Budapest police in mid-May 1945, Berend was charged with eight counts of collaboration and brought to trial in August 1946. Although in November of that year he was found guilty on two counts (participating in *Nyilas* raids and giving the *Harc* interview[81]) and sentenced to ten years' gaol, Berend's subsequent appeal to a higher court (the National Council of People's Tribunals — the NOT) quashed these convictions. Following his release

Mikor 24 zsidó pribék diktált
Magyarországon

Hogyan került a bolondokházába egy
magyar — a rizs és a zsidók miatt?

Biharban már 1941-ben is
gettót követeltek

Figure 5.1 *Harc* (Battle). Masthead and main headline of the extreme Antisemitic newspaper *Harc*, 1 July 1944. Published by the state-supported Institute for Researching the Jewish Question, *Harc* was edited by the director of the Institute, Zoltan Bosnyak. Note the newspaper's logo, a lightning bolt splitting the traditional Jewish symbol, the six-pointed Star of David. The front page contains a cartoon which — with clear homage to that abiding anti-Jewish canard, the ritual murder blood libel — depicts a well-fed Jewish plutocrat fertilising his fortune by squeezing the blood from defenceless, emaciated Hungarians. The top headline on the right reads: "When 24 Jewish Henchmen Dictated in Hungary". (Source: YVA 015/25)

in April 1947, Berend emigrated to the USA, changed his name to Albert Belton, and spent a not inconsiderable amount of time and energy during the next forty years adamantly defending his activities during the German Occupation. Clearly indicative of Berend's attitude is his letter of 3 November 1972 to Professor Braham in which he stated:

> As a friendly warning, I repeat: <u>I SHALL SUE anyone</u> making or just repeating, quoting or re-printing any defamatory statement or characterization, even if such statements are just being "recorded for history" and published only in scholarly volumes of Holocaust Literature. Anyone who tells, repeats, spreads, prints, publishes damaging statements or allegations, is just as guilty as the one who originally invented, told and spread those unsubstantiated stories in 1944 and at any time thereafter [on] any spot of the globe.
>
>   N.O.T. pronounced the FINAL VERDICT in the case, upon the conclusion and termination of two year long pre-trial imprisonment by EXONERATING Dr Berend of any wrong doing, and at the same time and in the same document, also establishing his merits, good deeds, noble motivations and heroic rescue efforts.[82]

In line with this "friendly warning", Berend initiated several court cases in attempts to defend his reputation or, according to his opponents' not unreasonable interpretation, in attempts to silence his critics. Of particular note, Berend brought two unsuccessful cases against Professor Randolph Braham.[83]

The issues involved in Berend's legal tribulations are many, varied, complex, liable to subjective interpretations, and often well beyond the boundaries of this discussion. Inherent in these controversies, however, is the issue of the integrity of the immediate postwar Hungarian judicial system, both lower and upper courts. In precis, Berend maintained that the NOT (appeal court) acquittal constituted the final verdict on his activities during 1944, whilst Berend's opponents maintained that his acquittal resulted from political pressure applied by postwar Jewish leaders who, despite their personal antipathy to the defendant, abhorred the very thought of a Rabbi being declared a Nazi collaborator. In this context it is pertinent to note Braham's statement, with which Gergely concurred, that most of the Wartime leaders and officials of the JC had "for some unknown reason, not been invited to testify at [Berend's] trial".[84]

Believing that the established Jewish leadership in 1944 represented the affluent, urban communities, Berend claimed his interventions with *Nyilas* leaders were on behalf of the disenfranchised poor, the Jewish lower classes without power, influence or representation. As an ardent Zionist, Berend considered that he and the *Nyilas* had a common agenda to the extent that both parties, as ethnic nationalists, considered Jews an alien element in Hungarian life and, hence, wanted the Jewish community eliminated from Hungary — Berend via migration to their ancient homeland, the *Nyilas* via deportation to the East. According to Berend's conception, there were prospects of resolving Hungary's perennial "Jewish Question" by the mass migration of Hungarian Jews to Palestine after the War, a solution satisfying both Zionists and the ultra-Right.[85] Thus his association with *Nyilas* leaders, a strategy he classified under the oxymoronic designation "Zionising Antisemitism".

The term "Zionising Antisemitism" suggests that Berend's attitude may, in his own mind, have been derived from the writings of Theodor Herzl, co-founder (with Max Nordau) of modern political Zionism. Late in the nineteenth century, Herzl argued that Antisemites should be encouraged to support the establishment of a Jewish state in Palestine and, in turn, their views and support should be utilised to hasten the state's establishment.[86] The problem for the JC, in the perilous circumstances of the Occupation, was Berend's idiosyncratic interpretation, and unilateral implementation, of his self-appointed role. Despite his doubtless good (albeit supremely naive) intentions, by acting as a *Nyilas* informer, Berend destabilised the JC, severely compromised the secrecy of its deliberations, and added to the already relentless pressures bearing upon Jewish leaders. Clearly, whatever the merits of Herzl's policy during a time of peace, hindsight confers a harsh judgement on Berend and his strategy, for Hungarian collaboration either matched or exceeded *SS* Judeophobia.[87] In precis, critics are surely correct in denouncing Berend's scheme for developing rapport, and a common agenda, with the murderous *Nyilas* as an absurd, counter-productive delusion.[88]

Understandably, Berend received prominent mention in Gergely's postwar testimonies, invariably in a hostile or highly damaging manner. In turn, during his court case against Braham, Berend engaged in the following exchange with the defence attorney, Gerald Zuckerman:

Question [Zuckerman]: This was by Mr Gerbly [Gergely]. Who was Gerbly?
Answer [Berend]: He was a young lawyer and a war criminal because —
Mr Zuckerman: Objection.
The Court: Sustained.
Question: He was the liaison man for the Jewish Council and the gestapo?
Answer: Yes and he wrote down the list of those people to be arrested.[89]

In this exchange Berend identified Gergely, an official of the JC, as a collaborator and war criminal for providing the *SS* with lists of Jews to be deported. Yet elsewhere, in a written response on the same subject, Berend significantly contradicted this statement thus:

...the *Judenrat* in Budapest, appointed by Eichmann, [sent] out summons to fellow Jews to be arrested, interned, and in the end deported. The Stern *Judenrat* accepted such a list almost daily from both the German as well as the Hungarian Gestapo (Laszlo Koltay) and ordered those fellow Jews to report at Rokk-Szilard Street 26 for internment.[90]

Clearly, by acknowledging that the JC's role was the *submissive acceptance* of orders rather than the *active provision* of raw material for German machinations, Berend's written response negates the allegation of collaboration inherent in his courtroom testimony. Consequently, even if one neglects Berend's hostility towards the JC's executives and policies,[91] on the basis of these mutually incompatible testimonies, one must conclude that Berend is an unreliable witness whose claims should be treated with considerable caution. This evaluation is reinforced by Berend's failure to provide independent corroboration for his claim, and by the knowledge that Berend's informants were *Nyilas* and not *SS* officials. As such, his information regarding *SS* actions would probably have been derived from secondary (*Nyilas*) rather than primary (German) informants, these ostensible allies often being in fierce economic competition, each with a vested interest in destabilising their opponent by the spread of misinformation.

Wallenberg

Influenced by the request of US authorities,[92] thirty-two year old Raoul Wallenberg arrived in Budapest on 9 July 1944, two days after Horthy had banned deportations to Auschwitz. Prior to his departure from Stockholm, Wallenberg had been appointed special Third Secretary at the Swedish legation with a specific brief to provide diplomatic support and physical relief to Hungary's remaining Jews. Importantly, Wallenberg's mission was facilitated by: his diplomatic status; his family's highly influential position in Sweden, a powerful, industrialised and strategically important neutral state; Germany's desperate need for Swedish war *matériel*; his exemption from diplomatic niceties, including the ban on bribery;[93] the donation to his mission of $100,000 by the AJDC (the Joint);[94] an abundance of sterling personal qualities including courage, energy, determination, intelligence, wit, initiative, and *chutzpah*; his fluent German; and the fact that Swedish diplomats represented Hungary in all the Allied countries.[95]

Commencing as Wallenberg's secretary *circa* late July 1944, Gergely was the second person to hold this post, replacing the initial appointee Laszlo Peto[96] when the latter's position became untenable around the time of the Kistarcsa deportation (see Chapter VI). Due to Eichmann's growing suspicions that Laszlo Peto —

Gergely's former colleague at the Liaison Office and son of the prominent JC member Erno Peto — was the conduit for confidential information conveyed from the JC to Wallenberg, the two former colleagues in effect exchanged jobs, Gergely transferring to the Swedish Legation and Laszlo Peto returning to work at the JC.[97]

Despite sleeping at the Legation and being Wallenberg's close associate for some two months, Gergely's documents contain relatively little about the indefatigable Swedish diplomat, quite possibly due to the archive's understandable focus on those events in which Gergely was directly involved. It should be noted that Wallenberg's main accomplishments occurred during the Szalasi era, by which time Gergely had transferred to the International Red Cross (see below). At all events, it is clear that whilst paying due homage to Wallenberg's well-documented courage, organisational skills and heroic personal interventions, Gergely deprecates the fact that populist — often exaggerated — assessments of the Swedish diplomat's attainments has obscured the greater achievements of the Swiss Consul, Charles Lutz,[98] and the valuable work of the Vatican's representatives, Nuncio Angelo Rotta and his secretary *Monsignor* Gennaro Verolino.

Possibly adding to Gergely's reticence is what he terms the "*Intelligenzliste* Affair", a hitherto apparently undisclosed instance of possible corruption within the upper echelons of Wallenberg's hierarchy. Towards the end of Gergely's tenure at the Swedish Legation, Wallenberg decided to draw up a register of the scientific and cultural elite of Budapest Jewry, the *Intelligenzliste* (people to be protected), and placed his personnel manager Mr (?) Forgacs in charge of the enterprise. In turn Forgacs delegated the detailed responsibilities to his brother, an employee of the Jewish hospital. Upon being shown the selected names by a reluctant Forgacs at the embassy, Gergely was appalled that the list consisted largely of nonentities, that is unknown people lacking either accomplishment or public recognition. In his 1987 narrative, Gergely clearly implies that inclusion on the *Intelligenzliste* was not determined by either achievement or objective criteria but by willingness to pay a consideration, possibly to one or both Forgacs brothers.[99] Confronting Wallenberg with his suspicions, Gergely declared the list a scandal and suggested that "Forgacs should be called to task". Gergely concludes his exposition of this episode thus:

> Nothing of the sort happened, Wallenberg has become angry and our relationship has become less good than before. In fact I was told not to stay in the main building but go to another building of the Swedish legation — to the outskirts of the Swedish legation... Well that broke our relationship with Wallenberg.[100]

Dismissing the prospect that Wallenberg was personally corrupt ("This is not possible, he did not need it, he did not get it"[101]), with the benefit of hindsight Gergely recognised the potential for such controversy to destabilise — if not devastate — Wallenberg's overall strategy. Acknowledging the potential of the *Intelligenzliste* issue to generate public scandal, Gergely correctly assessed that such a furore would not only have damaged Wallenberg's — and the Swedish Legation's — credibility, but also jeopardised the safety of thousands of Jews holding Swedish *Schutzpässe*. Consequently, whilst genuflecting towards *realpolitik*, Gergely concluded (surely correctly) that Wallenberg's non-action was the appropriate response in the circumstances — especially when one accepts the impossibility of withdrawing *Schutzpässe* issued to individuals on the *Intelligenzliste*, people who also had a right to life.

Figure 5.2 *Igazolvany* (**Exemption Certificate) No. 7545/1944.**
Interior pages of an *Igazolvany* **issued to Dr Gyorgy Gergely by Budapest Police**
Headquarters and countersigned by a *Hauptsturmführer-SS*, **31 August 1944. On the**
rear page (not shown) Gergely, as an executive of the Royal Swedish Legation, was
endorsed as having unrestricted movement throughout Hungary. (Source: GGA)

Although it appears that mention of this episode is unique to Gergely's testimony — and, as such, cannot be compared to other eyewitness narratives and interpretations — the context of this testimony is confirmed by the fact that Vilmos and Dr Bela Forgacs were associates of Wallenberg.[102] In particular, Vilmos is described as the first recipient of a Swedish provisional passport (in mid-June 1944[103]) and one of Wallenberg's three closest co-workers.[104] Reinforcing this information, Braham states that Bela and Vilmos Forgacs had been appointed Swedish subjects and "played an important role in rescue work, especially as intermediaries with the Hungarian authorities".[105]

On this basis, Gergely is correct in placing the Forgacs brothers at the centre of Wallenberg's operations. Furthermore, Wallenberg dealt with Gergely's suspicions in much the same manner that he handled another allegation of corruption within his orbit. Levai relates this episode thus:

> The oldest protected official of the Embassy, Mrs Istvan Engelmann, discovered ...during the negotiations [to open a hospital] that certain Hungarian officials of the Swedish Red Cross were pursuing their own interests. She reported this to Wallenberg who...decided to call off the joint hospital action. Soon after his Humanitarian Department set up its own hospital.[106]

Once again, probably because of the potential impact on his organisation and the wider Swedish interest, Wallenberg apparently decided not to bring a matter involving breach of trust and/or profiteering into the open, a response in keeping with his reaction to Gergely's suspicions.[107]

The most congruent circumstantial evidence for Gergely's misgivings, however, is provided by Wallenberg himself. In his Report of 29 September 1944 (a document, it should be noted, contemporaneous with Gergely's suspicions and subsequent transfer to the International Red Cross), Wallenberg stated that "according to information some persons have made economic sacrifices in order to obtain safety or provisional passports" — a clear reference to financial considerations ("economic sacrifices") influencing the allocation of Swedish *Schutzpässe*. The Report states that several individuals, not employed by the Legation but claiming connection with "certain members of the staff", have charged "very high fees to deal with applications for safety passports... Two persons on the staff of the Department who have been mentioned in this connection have thus been dismissed."[108]

With little doubt, Gergely's testimony is well in keeping with Wallenberg's Report, the two narratives being in general harmony, lacking fundamental contradictions and, arguably, describing different aspects of a common scenario. Notwithstanding the possible validity of such suspicions, one may conclude that, in a Hungary endemic with graft and *protectio*, even with the isolated allegations mentioned above, Wallenberg and his largely Jewish staff of some 400[109] remained remarkably free from the taint of corruption.

Attempted Arming of the JLS Brigades, September–October 1944

The genesis of this episode — an attempt at mass Jewish armed resistance unique in the Holocaust, in which a vassal regime decided to arm Jewish conscripts to defend itself against the Germans and their collaborators — occurred after Gergely left Wallenberg's staff to become a senior executive at the International Red Cross (see below). It should be noted that despite Gergely's changes of position and locale, in line with his general responsibilities and personal inclinations, he kept in close touch with his contacts at the JC, including the president, Samu Stern.

On 18 September — during the Lakatos interregnum, when Horthy and his loyalists were seriously manoeuvring to extricate Hungary from the disastrous Axis alliance — Gergely met his friend and anti-Nazi *confrère*, Count Gyorgy Pallavicini Jr (see above). Not having seen each other for some time, Pallavicini mentioned that he had become an executive member of the Hungarian Front, a broad underground coalition encompassing Horthyists and other anti-Nazi, non-Communist groups.[110] Admitting that the lack of reliable manpower was a considerable handicap to the Front's plans, Pallavicini responded positively to Gergely's proposal to arm the JLS, stating that he would submit this "interesting though complicated question" for consideration. Taking leave of his friend, Gergely immediately saw Samu Stern to inform the president of this discussion. Obtaining Stern's approval in principle, Gergely was authorised to proceed with negotiations should he again be contacted. Importantly, Stern specified that the negotiations were to be conducted solely by Gergely, in absolute secrecy, and none other than he (Stern) was to be informed of developments. Whilst lending his name, position and full support to arming the JLS, Stern clearly indicated the necessarily unofficial nature of his patronage, Gergely's account stating: "He [Stern] also warned me quite bluntly that whilst he can authorise clandestine negotiations unofficially, he cannot risk the official involvement of the Jewish authorities for in case of trouble the consequences would be catastrophic. If the matter comes into the open, he will have to disclaim all knowledge."[111]

Within forty-eight hours Pallavicini had arranged for discussions amongst himself, Gergely and Count Jozsef Palffy at the highly elitist National Casino, an old-established gentlemen's club catering exclusively for members of Hungary's "historic classes".[112] At this meeting Palffy, also a member of the Front's executive, revealed that the proposal to arm the JLS had been appraised by various Front leaders. As a result the military director of the Hungarian Front, General Karoly Lazar, Commander of the Regent's bodyguard, wanted to see Gergely for further discussions. Consequently, at 12.30 pm on 30 September, Gergely presented Palffy's letter of recommendation to General Lazar at the Regent's Palace. In their discussion, a courteous Lazar proved wary of Gergely's proposal to transfer the bulk of JLS units to the capital or its environs, the General considering the potential repercussions so great that only the Prime Minister could authorise such a move. Despite this justified caution, Lazar retained the option of future action — albeit of limited scope — by requesting the addresses of JLS units already stationed in or near Budapest.[113] In his 1971 memoir Gergely comments that, apart from the JC, Lazar could only have obtained such a listing from the Defence Ministry, an organisation thoroughly infiltrated by pro-German agents and sympathisers.

After obtaining the requested list, a task accomplished via Samu Stern's forceful intervention with a recalcitrant Dr Bela Fabian of the NBJWV,[114] on 4 October Gergely presented Lazar with the required information, a register encompassing some 26,000 men. In his 1945 Report, Gergely emphasised his pressing upon Lazar the urgent necessity of arming the JLS so as to help pre-empt a widely anticipated *Nyilas* putsch. In response, once again the General counselled caution, being apprehensive of German forces in the vicinity of Budapest. Not mentioned in Gergely's 1945 report, although raised in both his 1971 and 1987 memoirs, is the concern inherent in Lazar's question "What do you think the [JLS] companies would do if they suddenly found themselves in possession of arms?"[115] Prefacing his reply with the point that his assessment was based on the personal experience of two years in the JLS, Gergely responded that JLS members blamed the Germans for their misery, and would fight for the Hungarian Front if provided with weapons. As an indication of goodwill, and to facilitate logistics, Gergely undertook to ensure that appropriate orders would be conveyed to those JLS units selected to receive arms.[116]

Irrespective of Lazar's doubts, or perhaps because Gergely was able to resolve them, the Front decided to arm JLS units stationed near the capital. By this decision, and the decision's mode of implementation (see below), the Hungarian Front resolved to confide in, and co-operate with, the JC — a decision, in effect, underwritten by the JC–Horthy compact (see Chapter IV). Note that whilst the Hungarian resistance was represented in negotiations by executive committee members Counts Pallavicini and Palffy, and the military commander General Karoly Lazar, the JC was represented solely by Samu Stern's personal confidant, Gyorgy Gergely, who had been granted executive powers and sworn to secrecy.

Pallavicini's next contact was on 13 October, when he told Gergely to attend the Hungarian Front meeting at the National Casino the following evening,[117] where he would receive concrete instructions. In line with his commitment to General Lazar concerning the distribution of marching orders to JLS units, Gergely contacted his lifelong friend, Dr Gyorgy Heltai, informed him of the negotiations, and delegated the responsibility of distributing the JLS order to Heltai and Dr Janos Beer, Heltai's personal friend and political associate on the far Left of politics.[118] In his 1971 testimony, Gergely points out that he kept these plans from Stern "just in case something would go wrong..."[119]

On the evening of 14 October Gergely joined a group of about 100 in the cellar of the National Casino. After a solemn opening speech, the gathering was informed that the Regent would proclaim an armistice the next day and that relevant people would receive pertinent orders forthwith. Gergely received three instructions from Pallavicini: write a Proclamation to the JLS, arrange its printing, and organise that it be distributed the next morning. Unfortunately, at that stage Pallavicini had still not received either the list of labour units selected for arming or the addresses of their weapons caches, both sets of intelligence being provided by Lazar that evening. At 8 am the next morning, 15 October, Gergely would receive both lists at the "Kings Office", 2 Apponyi Square, Budapest. Having completed all these commitments as required, despite the limited time at his disposal,[120] to Gergely's astonishment and chagrin the scheme collapsed. Failure resulted from Pallavicini's arrest by the Germans after the meeting, the list remaining with Lazar and thus unable to be delivered to Gergely for further distribution.[121] As a consequence of the debacle, Gergely decided to live underground at various changing locations. The wisdom of this move was confirmed in 1946 when Pallavicini revealed that the Germans tortured him until he disclosed the names of the plotters, including that of Gergely.[122]

In his assessment of the above venture's potential, Gergely, after noting correctly that the bulk of Horthy's loyal brigades were stationed at the front lines,[123] argued that the JLS could have guarded or destroyed Budapest's bridges and important facilities, particularly the National Radio station.[124] After Horthy concluded his armistice proclamation on national radio at about 1 pm on 15 October, Gergely surmises that with the wireless station secured or destroyed, there was a chance the German-supported *Nyilas putsch* may have proceeded differently. This view is based on Gergely's suggestion that if the Regent's proclamation of an armistice had not been publicly countermanded on National Radio, even after a Horthy resignation there were prospects that some Horthyist units, loyal to the Supreme Commander, may have yielded at the front, thus allowing the Red Army to break German lines and pour through to Budapest — hence either pre-empting or truncating the Szalasi epoch.[125] In this context it is pertinent to note Braham's assessment that "by the summer of 1944, German troop strength in Hungary was greatly diminished, and no longer represented a real threat".[126]

Of additional moment, Gergely states that 20,000 armed JLS members would have afforded significant protection against *Nyilas* brigands who, under Szalasi, terrorised Budapest Jews, killing over 10,000 and looting their property. This opinion parallels that of Otto Komoly's confidant Albert Bereczky, as well as that of postwar authority Bela Vago.[127] Komoly's diary notes that on 28 August 1944, whilst discussing Horthy's anticipated armistice, Bereczky stated that upon its declaration "one would immediately have to arm the Jewish labour service men. I am convinced that we would find them to be excellent soldiers."[128] Doubtless Bereczky, unlike many postwar critics, realised that, despite the lack of military training given the JLS units, prior to Hungary's anti-Jewish Laws of the late 1930s Jewish men were conscripted into the military in the same manner as non-Jewish males. Moreover, Jews with World War I experience, that is men in their mid-forties, were conscripted into the JLS, some of these being former officers. Consequently, the JLS had a significant reservoir of members with military training, some of whom had had combat experience. Regarding the negative aspects of the plan, Gergely concedes the inevitability of losses but notes that confrontation with German forces was to be avoided, and that — with the benefit of hindsight — after Horthy's debacle many (unarmed) JLS units still disappeared.[129]

Gergely concluded his 1945 testimony on this topic by noting that he received formal written corroboration of the facts in his account from Count Jozsef Palffy.[130] In his far more expansive 1971 memoir, he mentions that such explicit documentation was required to qualify for the *Szabadsagrend* (Order of Liberty), a decoration awarded to members of the anti-Nazi resistance. Although clearly entitled to do so, Gergely states that he did not submit an application for the Order because irregularities conferred the decoration on those clearly lacking entitlement.[131]

When assessing the credibility of Gergely's narrative regarding the proposed arming of the JLS, the first factor to note is the consensus of postwar testimony and historiography regarding the centrality of his role in the venture. Probably the first major chronicle of this episode was by Erno Munkacsi, a prominent Jewish leader closely associated with — and a postwar critic of — the JC. In his authoritative book *Hogyan Tortent?* (How Did it Happen?) published in 1947, Munkacsi — the man, it should be noted, who introduced Gergely to Samu Stern[132] — acknowledged that his account of this episode was based on Gergely's involvement,[133] an acknowledgement readily confirmed by even a cursory comparison with the latter's 1945 Report. This acknowledgement, in association with the fact that

Munkacsi's entire exposition of this venture is published in italics, raises the distinct prospect that his narrative may have been taken well-nigh verbatim from Gergely. This prospect is strengthened by Gergely's statement — made several times during discussions remote from this agenda — that shortly after the War Munkacsi requested from him a report on the workings of the JC during the Occupation, a document that Gergely provided before the publication of *Hogyan Tortent*.[134]

With only minor variations, Munkacsi's acceptance of Gergely's central role is supported by Erno Peto (prominent member of the JC),[135] Jeno Levai (noted postwar chronicler of the Hungarian Holocaust)[136] and Professor Randolph Braham.[137] Even the Halutzim who, though playing no appreciable role in the saga, were generally well informed via Otto Komoly, acknowledge Gergely's critical role in the planned uprising.[138] Importantly, there appears to be a total lack of evidence or testimony contradicting this consensus.[139]

In addition, five pieces of circumstantial evidence support Gergely's account: Gergely was a well-established, trusted friend and political confidant of Count Gyorgy Pallavicini Jr, whose father was a pivotal member of the Hungarian Front's executive; Lazar's cautious approach to arming the JLS, as described by Gergely, is reflected in independent testimonies which reveal the General's procrastination about arming the workers;[140] Counts Palffy and Pallavicini were entrusted by Lazar with the distribution of arms; Macartney, presumably from non-Jewish sources, confirms that "arms were to be issued to the Jewish Labour Battalions";[141] and finally, as far as can be ascertained, there has been no objection to Munkacsi's account, a narrative placing Gergely at the centre of a unique strategy involving many thousands of Jewish conscripts combining with a satellite government in armed resistance against the Germans — a plan unique in the annals of the Holocaust and of World War II. Although an analysis of Horthy's 15 October debacle is beyond the scope of this narrative,[142] it is clear that Hungarian Jewry, substantially via Gergely's efforts, collaborated with and fulfilled its commitments to the Hungarian Front resistance. As has been seen, the collapse of the movement to arm the JLS brigades was entirely beyond the control of the Jewish Community or its representative.

The International Red Cross in Hungary

Throughout most of World War II, the International Red Cross (henceforth IRC[143]) headquarters maintained the attitude that its legal and moral obligations were defined by the Geneva Convention of 1929, a protocol focusing the organisation's endeavours onto matters concerning prisoners of war.[144] The protection of persecuted minorities was considered so far beyond the IRC charter that no protest was lodged when, at the beginning of the War, the Germans separated captive Polish officers of the Jewish faith from their non-Jewish colleagues. This silence was despite the fact that any act of segregation or discrimination — not to mention mass murder — was a patent breach of the Geneva Convention, a document specifying that POWs be treated according to rank, physical condition and professional qualifications, not "race" or religion.[145] Thus, despite overwhelming evidence documenting the grotesque persecution of Jews, the IRC maintained its traditional commitment to "objectivity, prudence and discretion" vis-à-vis the combatants.[146] Importantly, as a consequence of its refusal to classify Jews herded into ghettos or concentration camps as civilian internees, the IRC abrogated the possibility of providing food and medical aid to the interned. Such IRC action, states Braham, possibly conservatively, might have saved hundreds of thousands of Jewish lives. As shall be seen, it was not until mid-1944, by which time the Reich was obviously facing defeat, that the IRC considered implementing discrete attempts to safeguard Jews persecuted as such.[147]

Following stringent Geneva guidelines, the IRC Delegate in Budapest, Jean de Bavier, adhered strictly to the imperatives of "impartiality", "discretion", and a narrow focus on POWs. By this stringent interpretation, de Bavier considered the Jewish plight in Hungary during the German Occupation a purely internal, civilian, political matter, an interpretation precluding IRC intervention. The non-German speaking de Bavier was replaced by Friedrich Born in May 1944, a succession stimulated by Germany's looming defeat and by Miklos Krausz (see Chapter IV) informing the Swiss press of Nazi atrocities in Hungary.[148] Under Born the IRC's policy gradually became less rigid, two divisions — departments A and B, both concerned with the protection of Jewish children — eventually being created within the IRC structure. Section A, directed by the Zionist leader Otto Komoly, eventually employed some 550 people and utilised dozens of buildings to safeguard 5–6,000 children of the Jewish religion;[149] Section B, directed by Rev. Gabor Sztehlo of the (Protestant) Good Shepherd Committee, safeguarded children of Jewish converts to Christianity.[150] Established in early September 1944, and supported by the JC via funds provided by the AJDC, the original catalyst for creating these departments occurred in mid-July, when the JC received a Spanish offer to accept 500 Hungarian Jewish children as emigrants to Spanish Morocco.[151] Seizing the opportunity, the JC convinced Born that this offer provided the IRC with a legally valid opportunity to take foreign-protected children, and others, under its protection.[152]

In accordance with its policy of attempting to garner international recognition and goodwill (see Chapter IV), on 30 October the Szalasi regime conferred extra-territorial status on IRC-supported buildings and institutions (orphanages, hospitals, public kitchens, homes etc), under the aegis of Sections A and B. Henceforth, such places were marked with a sign in Hungarian, German, French and Russian stating "Protected by the International Committee of the Red Cross". Contemporaneous with the establishment of the Budapest ghetto, in December 1944 Hans Weyermann was appointed to Hungary by the IRC headquarters in Geneva. Shortly after his arrival, the Hungarian capital was divided into two zones of authority, Born controlling Buda and Weyermann becoming responsible for Pest, the region containing both the Common and International ghettos.[153]

Gyorgy Gergely states that he met Friedrich Born through the president of the Jewish Council, Samu Stern.[154] Circumstantial evidence for this assertion is provided by Otto Komoly's Diary which, on 6 September 1944, notes that Stern requested that he (Komoly) attend negotiations the next morning with Born and the JC's representative Gyorgy Gergely.[155] Komoly's Diary for 7 September is quite explicit regarding Gergely's role and status in the consequent lengthy, wide-ranging meeting.[156] Discussion commenced by reviewing plans for the transport of 500 children to Morocco,[157] a proposal that Gergely had commenced planning with Born on 29 July.[158] In his diary Komoly, after referring to a telegram tabled by Gergely which was received from Tangiers by Dr Imre Reiner (legal counsel for the

Hungarian Orthodox Community), noted that "Dr G[ergely] does not believe Dr I[mre] R[einer] competent in this matter and did not bring him along".[159] Significantly, Gergely's authority for making such decisions was unchallenged by either of the two other participants. Furthermore, this passage clearly indicates Gergely's central role in negotiations conducted amongst the JC, IRC and the Orthodox, Reiner having assumed a leadership position after the Orthodox representative on the JC, Fulop Freudiger, fled to Roumania in early August 1944 (see Chapter IV). Gergely's capacity and authority is further confirmed when, towards the end of the meeting, Komoly notes thus: "Dr G raises the question of concentration [of Jews] and asks B[orn] to demand an audience with the Nuncius [Papal representative, Angelo Rotta] this very morning. B[orn] agrees..."[160] Once again Gergely's prerogative (and judgement) in presenting, in effect, an order to the director of the IRC in Hungary, remained unchallenged — an assessment confirmed by Born's acceptance of Gergely's proposal. With such rapport, and the obvious trust of the IRC's supreme leaders in Hungary, it is no surprise that, less than two months after leaving Wallenberg, Gergely was appointed to the IRC's top echelon. Designated *Oberreferent* of Section A on 11 November 1944 (see Fig. 5.3), in this position Gergely was subordinate to only two people — Born and Komoly.[161]

Although containing gaps, Gergely's period at the IRC is the most thoroughly documented aspect of his endeavours during the German Occupation. Apart from his inclusion in Komoly's Diary — a document that appears to have gained universal favour regarding its veracity — Gergely's archives contain numerous reports and documents attesting to his position and activities on behalf of the IRC. Particularly significant is Komoly's official directive of 11 November 1944, in which Gergely is charged with organising all IRC-Section A institutions in Hungary (see Fig. 5.3), including children's homes, hospitals, infirmaries, public kitchens, food stores, workshops, emigration camps, branches and central offices. Two further written directives from Komoly, dated 19 November and 8 December, confirm and enhance Gergely's seniority and responsibilities.[162] Significantly, the signature on these documents was authenticated by Komoly's only child, Mrs Leah Furst, in Israel.[163] Although conscious of the plethora of false papers circulating in Szalasi's Budapest, Mrs Furst was not aware of any instance in which her father's signature had been forged.

Additional confirmation of Gergely's position is provided by his name being listed as a senior staff officer on three IRC documents held in the *Magyar Orszagos Leveltar* (Hungarian National Archives).[164] Despite Gergely granting the Archive documented permission to release his particulars to the writer, specific details were withheld "because particulars are under the protection of the Human Rights Agreement".[165] Further proof is generated by Gergely's Reports of this period, such Reports in turn confirming numerous aspects of his 1987 oral testimony (see below).

In accordance with his policy of maintaining close contact with Stern, on 7 September Gergely sent a communique to the president of the JC outlining his meeting that day with Born and Komoly.[166] In this dispatch, Gergely expands considerably the information on these discussions provided by Komoly's Diary entry of that date. According to Gergely's Report to Stern, information Stern could have readily verified with both Born and Komoly, after discussion of the Spanish offer to accept 500 children, Gergely informed Born of his considerable apprehension regarding the proposed concentration of Budapest's Jews (see Chapter IV). To

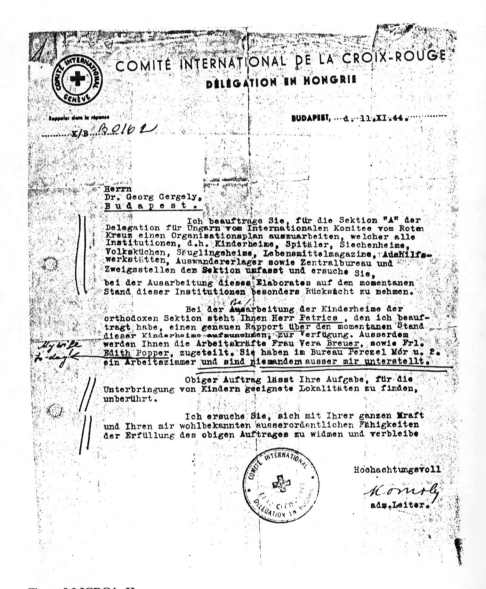

Figure 5.3 **ICRC in Hungary.**
**Otto Komoly's directive of 11 November 1944 appointing Gyorgy Gergely in charge
of organising all IRC-Section A institutions in Hungary. Handwritten English
annotation by Gergely.** (Source: GGA)

this effect, after handing Born a memorandum advocating collective action by neutral legations to prevent the resumption of deportations, Gergely suggested an urgent meeting with the Apostolic Delegate, Angelo Rotta.

In clear contrast to the impression generated by Komoly's diary entry, Born responded in a highly negative manner, stating that the plan to concentrate Jews, and thence make Budapest *Judenrein*, was irrevocable. Moreover, Born opposed IRC intervention as — technically — the organisation had not been requested to participate in either implementing or supervising the plan. Notwithstanding these objections, Born and Gergely saw Angelo Rotta at 12.45 pm that day, at which meeting Gergely read a statement and then presented his memorandum to the Nuncio.[167] Ensuing discussion revealed that Rotta echoed Born's opinion regarding the inevitability of Jewish concentration. Furthermore, the Apostolic Delegate stated that his frequent representations to various Ministers regarding the "Jewish Question" had gained him a reputation as a Jewish hireling, thus reducing his influence and effectiveness as a lobbyist. Nevertheless, Rotta made a commitment that at a personal meeting with the Prime Minister the following Monday, he would make a further appeal in the name of the Diplomatic Corps (of which he was the Dean), informing the PM (Geza Lakatos) that anti-Jewish measures not only transgressed Christian principles and humanitarian values but were contrary to the political interests of Hungary. From this meeting Born and Gergely visited various embassies, including the Swiss and Spanish, to hold discussions and present Gergely's memorandum.[168] It should be noted that in a postwar addendum, Gergely stated that he was Komoly's subordinate only regarding Section A, and not with respect to his various liaison endeavours. Accordingly, it was appropriate for Gergely to communicate directly with the IRC Delegate as, for example, on 9 October 1944, when he wrote to Born requesting welfare assistance for the JLS.[169]

Gergely's evident dissatisfaction with the IRC — primarily due to Born's resolutely legalistic approach to safeguarding Jews (see below) — was alleviated with Hans Weyermann's appointment to Budapest. Apparently contemporaneous with Gergely's Report of 16 December to Weyermann — in which the later is addressed as *Herr Sonderbeauftragter* (special representative)[170] — is a directory listing the locations of over 130 institutions under the protection of the IRC.[171] One can reasonably assume that the logistics governing these premises resulted largely from Komoly's 11 November directive to Gergely, in which the former charged the latter with responsibility for organising all institutions pertaining to the work of the IRC's Section A.

A much more comprehensive report to Weyermann is dated 28 December and signed by Gergely as *Oberreferent*.[172] Reviewing the work of Section A in considerable detail, Gergely's Report lists (amongst others) thirty-three children's homes, five factories manufacturing children's clothing, a cheese factory, twenty-five hospitals, ten public kitchens, three old-age nursing homes, a home for the deaf and dumb, ten public kitchens and fifteen food depots, all of which were operating under the aegis of the IRC. Despite some figures being approximate due to the chaotic situation in Budapest causing continually fluctuating numbers, it is clear that Komoly's Section A operation constituted an integrated, comprehensive programme of massive scale. Excluded from this listing are five IRC houses outside the Common Ghetto, in the Lipotvaros district of Pest, sheltering some 3,500

Schutzpass holders. After noting that all IRC institutions were currently operating under threat, the Report continued by describing the infrastructure and operations of Section A. Apart from Otto Komoly's office at 19 Munkacsi Mihaly Street, three other important bureaux included 6 Merleg Street, at which location was based Rudolf Weisz (see Chapter IV), Komoly's transportation manager. Gergely thus confirms previously mentioned testimony that the Weisz-managed food distribution enterprise operated under the facade of IRC protection.

In this Report to Weyermann, Gergely discussed in detail Section A's decentralised administrative structure — four central bureaux, one of which, 35 Benczur Street, was Gergely's then principal location.[173] This particular office was responsible for (amongst other matters) liaison with assorted authorities and embassies, reports and communications, and for admissions to the IRC-protected houses in the Lipotvaros district of Pest. Despite this multiplicity of responsibilities, Gergely's main burden as *Oberreferent* was admissions into the protected houses.

It should be noted that this comprehensive Report ranks only one executive above Gergely in the Section A hierarchy — namely, Otto Komoly, the Director. Furthermore, of the top echelon, only one individual (Gergely) has the title of *Oberreferent*. On the basis that the writer of such a report could hardly have misrepresented himself to Weyermann, this is convincing evidence supporting Gergely's statement that, with regard to Section A, he was subordinate to none other than Komoly. By corollary, Gergely was thus the IRC's third-highest ranking officer in Hungary from 11 November 1944, being subordinate to only the Delegate (Born) and Komoly. With the appointment of Weyermann in December 1944, this ranking slipped to fourth.

In the Report's general summary, Gergely stated that Section A had several integrated priorities: to provide food and medical attention to its institutions and the (Common) ghetto, and to retain all such institutions and existing offices, especially those outside the ghetto. After noting that it was the JC's legal responsibility to supply food and health care to the ghetto, Gergely stated that Jewish organisations helped finance IRC operations in Hungary via funds donated by, for example, the US-based AJDC. Despite this co-operation, despite many former employees of the JC being employed by the IRC, and despite most current JC employees having obtained Red Cross passes, in practice the IRC and the JC were strictly separate in their operations, unfortunate political factors preventing closer co-operation.

Regarding the then progressive concentration of Budapest's Jews, Gergely stated that support from the neutral legations in negotiations with Hungarian authorities had, so far, prevented a total relocation of Jews into the ghetto. However, such a resettlement had to be completed by 31 December, an unavoidable deadline considering the recent *Nyilas* attack on the Children's Home at 5/7 Munkacsi Street. Thus, Gergely notes, was terminated the struggle to maintain official Jewish institutions outside of the ghetto. As contact with authorities, embassies, food and transport companies etc could only occur outside the ghetto, Gergely's final comment emphasised the absolute necessity for two new outside offices to be obtained as compensation for those outside locations closed by the authorities.

An integral, critical part of Gergely's endeavours involved liaison with the neutral legations.[174] One particularly important instance of this was his *Note* of 20 December 1944, which he handed to the Portuguese *Charge d'affaires*.[175] After minor amendments, this was then submitted in the form of a *Note Verbale* to the Hungarian Interior Minister, a submission endorsed by the Apostolic Delegate, the Spanish, Swedish and Portuguese Legations, the Swedish Red Cross and the IRC. The *Note* undertook that Section A's Children's Homes outside the ghetto would be evacuated of adults sheltering therein, it being an open secret that on occasion these homes contained more adults than children.[176] As this matter fell within his department's responsibility, Gergely directed the relocation of the evicted adults, an operation having to be completed within thirty-six hours. In order to prevent these people being forced into the Common Ghetto, Gergely asked Born to issue a *Schutzpass* that granted the holder IRC protection. Born refused on the technicality that the IRC, not possessing any territory to which passholders could emigrate, would be infringing provisions of Hungary's *Schutzpass* scheme. Gergely overcame Born's legal pedantry by the simple expedient of obtaining three additional houses in the International Ghetto (from Rezso Muller on 19 November[177]) and then issuing some 3,500 of his own *Schutzpässe* — a document authorised and signed on behalf of the IRC by the *Oberreferent* of the IRC, Dr Gyorgy Gergely. The deputy Police Chief Janos Solymossy, either ignoring or possibly unaware of official regulations, permitted the transfer of Gergely's 3,500 *Schutzpass* holders into five buildings in the International Ghetto. After several days, Gergely's documents became known as Red Cross *Schutzpässe*, and his buildings as International Red Cross Houses.[178]

In his 1987 narrative, Gergely describes his pass in some detail. Stating that the holder is an authorised resident of an IRC-protected building, Gergely's *Schutzpass* was formatted with text in two vertical columns, one Hungarian the other German. At the bottom of the certificate was a butt with a printed serial number, which also appeared at the top of the certificate, the butt being given to the house supervisor and the main certificate being retained by the pass recipient. Gergely states that the large majority of his *Schutzpass* holders survived the Szalasi era.[179]

The final epoch of Szalasi's rule, contemporaneous with Weyermann's appointment to Hungary, saw death and destruction inflicted upon Budapest's Jews. Gergely, in his 1987 narrative, relates his tragic eyewitness experiences of this era in a distinctly straightforward manner. The *Nyilas* attack on the Munkacsi Mihaly Street orphanage, he states, resulted in scores of murdered children, including some handicapped youngsters. Deaths in greater numbers occurred at his Perczel Mor Street office. Such *Nyilas* attacks, plus air raids, death marches, malnutrition and the conscription of females for labour companies, left large numbers of orphans and abandoned babies. Towards the end of the Soviet siege, the police delivered 200 babies to Gergely's then office at 2 Perczel Mor Street. Despite frantic attempts to provide sustenance, the only food procurable was cabbage juice. After three days, all the babies had died.[180]

In the immediate aftermath of liberation, Gergely composed a comprehensive account of his period as *Oberreferent* of the IRC in Hungary. Dated 13 May 1945, this eighteen-page *Jelentes* (henceforth Report) gives unrivalled detail concerning the problems, dilemmas and *modus operandi* pertaining to his particular responsibilities within Section A. Although addressed to recipient(s) unknown, Gergely's text indicates that the Report was most probably written in response to the IRC's request for information regarding financial reconciliations and/or compensation claims, the latter possibly from landlords seeking payment for the IRC's wartime use of their premises. This interpretation stems from the Report's considerable discussion of specific addresses, their fiscal particularities,[181] the often futile attempts to negotiate leases in the chaos of Szalasi's Budapest, and the resulting confusion in the IRC's secretariat regarding the actual location of the organisation's premises. Gergely commented thus: *"...a Titkarsag sem tudta hogy hol van otthon es hol nics"*.[182] ("The secretariat itself did not know the location of the [Children's] homes.")

Importantly, the *Jelentes* is basically a commentary upon forty-three separate letters and communiques, these documents having been dispatched simultaneously with the Report. That all such documents were issued by Gergely on behalf of the IRC during the period 11 November 1944 (the day he became *Oberreferent*) to 13 January 1945 (several days before Liberation, by which time communications had become impossible),[183] is clear indication that the Report was written in response to official IRC request. Unfortunately, in the absence of these forty-three addenda (which appear to be no longer extant), the detail provided by Gergely's commentary is sometimes insufficient to either justify or fully elucidate his context and conclusions. On occasion, without giving details, Gergely merely notes that a particular communique warrants attention on several counts.

In the first portion of this Report, which largely concerns the weeks immediately following his appointment as *Oberreferent*, Gergely complained of poor or nonexistent communication among the various divisions of Section A. According to his assessment, the paucity of information regarding agreements with landlords (vis-à-vis their properties being incorporated into Section A's network of buildings) was deserving of particular condemnation. Despite Gergely's sharply worded (*eleshangu*) protest letter of 18 November to Komoly — a protest resulting in the reconfirmation of Gergely's authority — the Report notes that, in practice, nothing changed as a result of this complaint. Consequently, on 27 November Gergely produced a circular requesting information as to the terms and conditions under which individual IRC buildings operated, and sent it to each listed location of Section A. Although 120 circulars were dispatched, very few responses were received. Another circular of similar intent was disseminated on 21 December, but by this time, concedes Gergely, Section A's executives were struggling with far more serious issues than formal administration. Thus, comments Gergely, was lost the last chance to inform the IRC secretariat as to which facilities actually functioned and which existed only on paper.

Another concern expressed in the Report was the unjust distribution of food and Red Cross passes — issues raised with Komoly on more than one occasion — with Zionists, comments Gergely, often being favoured over their non-Zionist co-religionists.[184] It should be noted that Gergely distinguishes in this Report, as he does elsewhere in his archives,[185] between what he calls the aggressive, self-centred Zionist youth who forcibly occupied his building in Merleg Street, and the dynamic, altruistic Halutz leadership. On several occasions the Report mentions Gergely meeting an "Efra", "Rafi", and "Perecz", most probably the prominent Halutz leaders Efra Agmon, Rafi ben Shalom, and Peretz Revesz (see Chapter IV).[186]

Of considerable significance, and clearly indicating his responsibility for liaison with the neutral legations, was Gergely's *Note* of 17 November to the Papal Nuncio.[187] In a telephone discussion between the two men the next evening, Gergely urged the Vatican to intensify its involvement in protecting and increasing the number of Children's Homes. Gergely's 1987 narrative provides some additional detail on his liaison with the Nuncio. In this memoir he mentions a *Note* (of unspecified date) in which, amongst other matters, Gergely argued against permitting the concentration of Budapest Jews in a ghetto. Emphasising that Hungary was a signatory of the Geneva Convention on the Red Cross whereas the USSR was not, Gergely asserted that if Hungary broke the Convention by violating IRC-protected institutions then the Russians would have no inhibitions about analogous actions. Gergely's contention was on the cogent basis that a non-signatory (the USSR) could not be expected to respect a convention more than a signatory (Hungary).[188]

From information provided in the May 1945 Report, one can now estimate that Gergely's IRC *Schutzpässe* were most probably issued in the period late November to mid-December. Consequently, this *Jelentes* not only confirms important details contained in Gergely's *Note* of 20 December to the Portuguese *Charge d'affaires* (see above), but also enables his *Schutzpass* activity to be dated with a degree of precision not otherwise possible. Analysing the *Note* and the *Jelentes* in association, one can determine with certainty that such activity occurred after 19 November (the date Gergely obtained additional buildings in the International Ghetto[189] — see above) and before 20 December (the date of his *Note* to the Portuguese *Charge d'affaires*, in which his *Schutzpass* is first mentioned[190] — see above), with probability favouring the fortnight between the end of November and mid December.[191] In keeping with Gergely's attitude to Friedrich Born, the Report states that even without support from the centre (presumably Born), over 3,000 people were saved by passes issued in defiance of Born's orders.[192] The *Jelentes* concluded with the courteous statement that the undersigned was at the recipient's service should any further questions arise in the future.

Assessment
Gyorgy Gergely During the German Occupation

It is clear that Gergely's archives constitute a conspicuous portfolio, some 250,000 words written by a dynamic, self-disciplined, productive and extremely well-informed activist operating at the highest level; an eyewitness chronicle to the Holocaust in Hungary, an event described by Sir Winston Churchill as "[without doubt] probably the greatest and most horrible crime ever committed in the whole history of the world".[193] Importantly, as has been seen, much of the archive was composed contemporaneously with the events described therein.

Without repeating detail, it is clear that Gergely's career during the War followed a logical progression that formally commenced with a humble position at the National Bureau of Jewish War Veterans and ended at the uppermost levels of Hungarian Jewry's activist hierarchy. Numerous independent, authoritative sources (including Gergely's wartime colleagues) have produced evidence corroborating many critical aspects — and hence the overall veracity — of Gergely's testimonies and documents. Reinforcing this assessment are Gergely's career, achievements and writings, these elements combining to provide the most extensive, most multifaceted individual eyewitness archive to emerge from the Hungarian Holocaust. As expected from an abundance of material written over almost half a century, inevitable discrepancies and inconsistencies can be discovered (see below). Overall these are of minor moment, being confined largely to dates and chronology. If anything, such features tend to confirm Gergely's *bona fides* and veracity for, as

Deborah Lipstadt has written: "It is axiomatic among attorneys, prosecutors and judges that human memory is notoriously bad on issues of dimensions and precise numbers but very reliable on the central event."[194] Because of these discrepancies, a brief assessment of the more controversial aspects of Gyorgy Emile Gergely's career and credibility is in order.

As previously mentioned, uncontradicted expert testimony as to Gergely's position, involvements and reputation is provided by the affidavit of Lajos Stockler (prominent member of the Jewish Council and Samu Stern's successor as president) who stated: "Dr Gyorgy Gergely was also a member of the liaison group with the authorities. He prepared the secret instructions. He was the Council's man who knew everything."[195] In line with this deposition, the World Jewish Congress (see above), Yad Vashem[196] and the Frankfurt-am-Main War Crimes Tribunal[197] requested the benefit of Gergely's eyewitness testimony. Such requests can be interpreted as nothing other than the formal recognition of Gergely's expertise, knowledge, reputation and personal involvement in major events of the Hungarian Holocaust. Even if these accolades were neglected, Rabbi Bela Berend's allegation of Gergely collaborating with Eichmann over the deportation of professional groups cannot withstand scrutiny.[198] Braham effectively disposes of Berend's accusation thus:

> It was Koltay's office [the Hungarian Gestapo] that on its own initiative and in response to [35,000[199]] denunciations prepared the many lists of Jewish newspapermen, lawyers and other professionals who were called to report to the "transient camp" of the National Theological Institute at 26 Rokk-Szilard Street. (This proved to be the first stop to Auschwitz for many.) The lists were handed over to the Jewish Council, which was compelled to send out the military-type notices to the unfortunates on the list.[200]

The undisputed fact that Gergely retained the intimate confidence of the top echelons of Hungarian Jewry's activist hierarchy; his senior position with Wallenberg and the IRC; the lack of evidence, testimony or independent corroboration supporting Berend's accusations; and the fact that the anti-Nazi postwar Hungarian government utilised his services as a top public servant negotiating Foreign Trade treaties with the West (see Figure 5.4) — all these factors combine to vindicate Gergely and refute Berend's unsubstantiated allegations.

In similar measure, Gergely's centrality in the attempt to arm the JLS is without question, as is his involvement with the IRC. Scattered throughout his extensive documentation on the latter organisation, however, is possibly the most controversial aspect of Gergely's relationship with, and attitude towards, the IRC Delegate in Hungary, Friedrich Born. In his usual forthright manner, Gergely is not averse to questioning the reputation of popular figures, Born having been granted a Righteous of the Nations award by Yad Vashem in 1987. Gergely's criticism of Born's ineffectiveness and legal pedantry when confronted with *Nyilas* Judeophobia[201] is not without independent support. Levai, although on occasion a questionable source (see below), states:

> Born showed no inclination to accept the defence of the protected Jews, currently under Swedish protection, even in spite of the fact that the Swedish Embassy at Gyopar-utca was attacked. He said: "This is not the way to do it. I must be asked to act on behalf of the Swedish Government or asked by the King of Sweden, otherwise I cannot intervene in this matter."[202]

Hans Weyermann's appointment to Hungary by IRC headquarters in Geneva reinforces questions about Born. In particular, confirming Gergely's attitude is Weyermann's retrospective Report of August 1945 in which "the implicit criticisms of Born become increasingly frequent and severe as the account proceeds".[203] Arieh Ben-Tov, main advocate of Born's Righteous of the Nations award, defends his nominee thus: "In general, I think that Weyermann's assessment of Born's work suffered from the fact that he had only recently arrived in Budapest and was much less familiar with the overall situation than was Born."[204] In this appraisal, Ben-Tov is demonstrably incorrect. By August 1945 Weyermann had been stationed in Budapest for some nine months, consequently his Report was not written in the heat of the moment or without the benefit of reflection. Furthermore, as has been seen, Weyermann had access to Gergely's comprehensive and detailed Reports, such *communiqués* providing thorough context and perspective on Born's attitude and activities regarding the "Jewish Question" in Hungary. At all events it is clear that, with the division of responsibility between the two men (see above), Weyermann obtained responsibility for protecting Budapest's Jews whilst Born was, in effect, removed from involvement with the "Jewish Question" by being confined to the Buda area. Nowhere has the writer discovered any document, testimony or comment protesting against Born's transfer to Buda — a protest surely inevitable following the removal of an effective, sympathetic and trustworthy defender of Pest's persecuted Jews. On the contrary, according to Gergely, Jewish leaders were so dissatisfied with Born that they requested IRC headquarters to appoint another representative to Hungary.[205] Nor are these criticisms of Born isolated instances. Miklos Krausz, head of the Palestine Office in Hungary (see Chapter IV), took the unusual — if not desperate — step of criticising Born to Robert Schirmer, the IRC Delegate in Berlin.[206] Ben-Tov himself concedes that Saly Mayer, prominent Jewish leader in Switzerland, had a "negative attitude" regarding Born.[207] On this basis, it can be seen that Gergely's disposition towards Born is clearly not unique, being supported by activists of no small authority. And although an examination of Born's career is beyond the scope of this chronicle, it is pertinent to note that the political department of the Swiss Foreign Office suspected Born of corruption.[208] Perhaps this suspicion explains Weyermann's sudden appearance in Budapest, an appointment that Ben-Tov concedes was thrust upon Born as a *fait accompli* — surely unusual treatment of a trusted leader, but entirely understandable for one about whom there are serious doubts. The above may indicate the reasons Saly Mayer, on 4 December 1944, entrusted Weyermann and not Born with five specific tasks to be accomplished in Hungary.[209] At all events, Born left Budapest in April 1945 having become *persona non grata*, the Russians deprecating his "too cordial" relations with both Szalasi's regime and the German authorities.[210]

Despite its substantial content, it is clear that Gergely's archives contain numerous gaps. Of the many missing papers now presumably lost forever, possibly the most important absence is the *Schutzpass* he issued as *Oberreferent* of the IRC. As Budapest was awash with numerous types of false papers towards the end of 1944, someone with Gergely's connections would have had little difficulty in obtaining 3,800 *Schutzpässe* printed to his required specifications. Writing to the United Restitution Organisation in Sydney on 13 March 1958, Gergely stated of his *Schutzpässe*: "I still have one in my possession having a current number of 4807. They were all signed by me."[211] This statement is a clear indication of Gergely's credibility, it being well known at the time that the United Restitution Organisation demanded evidence from its applicants. With little doubt, Gergely made the above assertion in the clear understanding that, where possible, documentation would be required on all aspects of his submission.

Gergely's *modus operandi* supports the assertion that the issuing of *Schutzpässe* was a natural extension of Section A's activities. Although not stated as such, Gergely corroborates this assessment by explaining that his involvement with the IRC can be divided into two periods. During the first, he acted on behalf of the Delegate and the Jewish Community in a formal, administrative manner. In the chaotic second period, "everyone was for himself, there were no orders coming from anywhere, each person did what he could. That was the more profitable, more important part of my work for the IRC." In particular, his greatest independence came after the *Nyilas* had murdered Otto Komoly at the end of December 1944. Gergely comments that, as no one took Komoly's place, "the agile honorary members of the IRC did what they wanted, and were their own bosses. So was I."[212]

In the tumult of Szalasi's Budapest, it is hardly likely that there would have been problems with his IRC superiors had Gergely issued his *Schutzpässe* in the second period. This favoured timeframe correlates closely with the estimate (see above) that Gergely's passes were most probably issued between late November and mid-December. Significantly, Gergely classifies these *Schutzpässe* as his "greatest concrete achievement".[213]

[To its great shame the IRC archive in Geneva is, to say the least, decidedly unco-operative — if not obstructionist — in the provision of information about the Holo-caust in Hungary. Specific, detailed questions regarding Gergely, presented to the IRC on 3 July 1990, elicited the response on 30 August 1990 from Geneva that "we immediately undertook a thorough search of our archives, unfortunately without success...we found no file (or trace) of Dr Gergely..."[214] In subsequent correspond-ence, on 4 September 1990 Geneva refused the writer access to material mentioned in Arieh Ben-Tov's book.[215] In another rebuff, on 16 October the IRC stated:

> Any researcher allowed access to the ICRC's archives has to give a written undertaking not to divulge any part thereof, not to issue any analysis of the documents consulted without the ICRC's prior consent. He/she must therefore submit the text in its entirety to the ICRC before making it public or publishing any part of it, and must remove any passages which the ICRC might direct him/her to delete.[216]

This was a clear indication of the censorship, and/or self-censorship, necessarily inherent in any research project based on IRC archives. Adding insult to injury, with Orwellian flourish the letter concludes: "We are always willing to carry out research in our archives for information on clearly specified subjects and forward the results to you without the need for any of the above-mentioned formalities."

Notwithstanding the conspicuous absence of information or co-operation, the dispatch to Geneva of photocopies pertaining to Gergely's IRC activities produced the response on 3 January 1991 that another search — one obviously more thorough than the thorough search mentioned in the IRC's letter of 30 August 1990 — did, in fact, discover Gergely's name on a list.[217] Despite the written commitment to provide information, neither a photocopy nor a description of this list was ever received. The January 1991 letter did, however, provide the remarkable intelligence that individual files or correspondence on Otto Komoly and Gyorgy Gergely were unavailable "because the main office of the delegation in Budapest caught fire when Pest was taken in January 1945 and all the records perished in the flames".[218] The writer's response of 18 April 1991 — "Surely the destruction of Budapest records would only have affected the copies of correspondence, the originals of such material being safely maintained in Geneva. Please clarify this important point."[219] — effectively ended a futile ten-month correspondence with the ICRC.]

It will be recalled that *Oberreferent* Gergely's Bureau had two major responsibilities within the IRC: protection of Jewish children and liaison with the Papal Nuncio and the neutral legations. Braham summarises the IRC's endeavours during the Occupation thus: "By far the most important contributions of the IRC to the Jewish community in Budapest were the sheltering of children and the safeguarding and supplying of Jewish institutions..."[220] Being directly responsible for the first task, it is clear that Gergely deserves a substantial portion of the credit for organising and directing one of the IRC's most important successes in Szalasi's Budapest, the protection of Jewish children. Continuing to discuss the IRC's *modus operandi* during the *Nyilas* era, Braham comments: "The effectiveness of the IRC during this time was greatly enhanced by its co-operation with the Papal Nuncio and the representatives of the neutral states."[221] With little doubt, a significant portion of the credit for this increased effectiveness should also be allocated to Gergely, his liaison work contributing substantially to the success of another IRC endeavour.

Possibly the major question concerning Gergely's credibility is raised by his almost total absence from the books of Jeno Levai — highly influential chronicler of the Hungarian Holocaust in the early postwar period — of whom Asher Cohen wrote in 1986: "Levai was a Jewish journalist and his books published at the end of the 1940s were until recently the widest source of the history of Hungarian Jews during the Holocaust."[222] Gergely has a not unreasonable explanation for this absence, stating that his omission resulted from refusing Levai's request to provide details of his activities during the Occupation period. At the time of Levai's approach, Gergely was planning his own commercial writing venture, also a history of Hungary during the Occupation. Not unnaturally, on this basis Gergely considered Levai a competitor and withheld material and documents about himself, a decision largely precluding his inclusion in Levai's postwar historiography.[223] This absence was not compensated by his substantial mentions in Erno Munkacsi's 1947 book *Hogyan Tortent?* (How Did it Happen?) which, unlike many of Levai's numerous publications, remains available only in Hungarian. His close connection with Wallenberg, as mentioned in the July 1947 issue of the *Reader's Digest*,[224] similarly appears to have generated little long-term attention.

This lack of public awareness throughout the postwar decades cannot, of course, be equated with a lack of expert interest in his testimony. In addition to requests for information from authorities mentioned above, on 7 June 1980 Randolph Braham wrote to Gergely thus:

> I just got your letter of May 6, and the valuable materials on your activities within the framework of the International Red Cross, which you mailed in a separate envelope. Unfortunately, they arrived too late for incorporation (or corrections) in the first edition of the Politics of Genocide. Hopefully, another edition will make possible their use. In the meantime, I shall place them in my appropriate files. Needless to say, they might be used for a separate study on the IRC's role during that tragic period in Hungarian-Jewish history.[225]

One cannot assess Braham's letter as anything other than a wholly positive evaluation of Gergely's indeed valuable IRC materials. Significantly, the phrase "incorporation (or corrections)" — note the plural — clearly indicates Braham's acknowledgement that his comprehensive work *The Politics of Genocide* requires modifying and/or correcting in light of Gergely's documentation. Probably the most significant such correction required concerns Braham's attribution of some of Gergely's most important endeavours to Sandor Gyorgy Ujvary, a writer–journalist

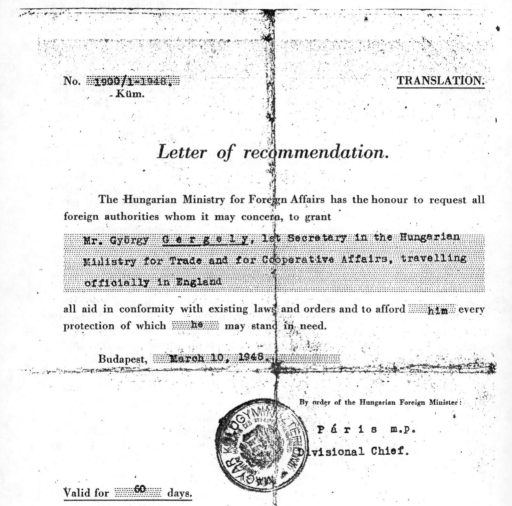

No. 1900/1-1948.
- Küm.

TRANSLATION.

Letter of recommendation.

The Hungarian Ministry for Foreign Affairs has the honour to request all foreign authorities whom it may concern, to grant

Mr. György G e r g e l y, 1st Secretary in the Hungarian Ministry for Trade and for Cooperative Affairs, travelling officially in England

all aid in conformity with existing laws and orders and to afford him every protection of which he may stand in need.

Budapest, March 10, 1948.

By order of the Hungarian Foreign Minister:

P á r i s m.p.
Divisional Chief.

Valid for 60 days.

Figure 5.4 **Letter of Recommendation, No. 1900/1-1948.**
Letter of Recommendation issued to Gyorgy Gergely on 10 March 1948 by the Hungarian Ministry of Foreign Affairs. As First Secretary in the Ministry of Trade, Gergely was issued this document for travel on official business to the United Kingdom. (Source: GGA)

and publisher. Although allegedly associated with the IRC from October 1944,[226] Ujvary is totally absent from Section A's senior executive list contained in Gergely's Report of 28 December 1944 to Hans Weyermann. As information on Ujvary in *The Politics of Genocide* appears to be based solely on Levai's writings,[227] even without Gergely's documentation Braham's acceptance of Ujvary's alleged achievements should be treated with caution. Asher Cohen succinctly summarises many authorities' attitude to Levai thus:

> [Levai's] books contain no footnotes, and in most cases Levai does not cite his sources. In numerous cases these works contain errors of fact which in part cannot now be verified. There is no doubt that the abundant material in Levai's books, written soon after the events, are important sources of information. Nevertheless, for the reasons mentioned above, I have used this source with caution.[228]

Reinforcing Gergely's credibility, and the value of his archive, is the quite remarkable coherence of his matrix of documents, correspondence and testimony. Despite its over four-decade timeframe, the archives lack a major internal contradiction or incompatibility. The relatively minor discrepancies contained therein (as previously mentioned, largely confined to dates rather than people or places) are quite expected in documents spread over such an extended period, some of which were — of necessity — composed under extraordinarily urgent and traumatic circumstances.

Axiomatic to historiograhic practice is the assumption that contemporaneous documentation generally generates significantly greater credibility than narratives composed several decades after the event. As such, in this analysis Gergely's wartime and early postwar writings take precedence over his oral testimony of mid-1987. Reinforcing this decision is the unfortunate circumstance that Dr Gergely's oral testimony was dictated some eighteen months after he had lost his visual acuity, the power to read and, consequently, the ability to access his files. Considering this severe handicap, and the four-decade interval, there is a remarkable congruence between Gergely's contemporaneous documentation and his 1987 narrative — especially as the latter was dictated without preparation and entirely from memory. The basic disparity between these two sets of documents is the marked difference in tenor sometimes displayed by Gergely during the two eras. Whereas his former compositions are generally cogent, tightly controlled in content and demeanour, dispassionate, and closely argued (as official reports warrant), the 1987 narration is free-flowing, prone to emotive judgements,[229] and sometimes confused and confusing — the inevitable product of fading memory and the unfortunate inability to prepare material. Despite these difficulties, his oral testimony forms a useful and expansive adjunct to his previous documentation. Gergely's non-involvement with the Sydney Jewish community; his detachment from history conferences, Holocaust associations and Survivor gatherings; and the absence of Holocaust books and journals from his library, indicate that his oral testimony is not coloured unduly by the possibly distorting influence of consensus or non-eyewitness judgements. His attitude towards Samu Stern and Friedrich Born clearly denotes ability to withstand the pressures of current perceived wisdom.

It must be realised that the bulk of Gergely's archives remained largely hidden for some forty years, remaining under his private and — of late — unfortunately far from meticulous control. This fact, in itself, enhances credibility; for as Gergely rightly emphasises, such disposition clearly indicates that "I was in no hurry to obtain praise or advantage of any kind..."[230] With such inherent negativity towards self-aggrandisement, one can understand the emotion in his 1987 narrative when he discusses those (for example Janos Beer) who have attempted to misappropriate his achievements unto themselves. These decades-long and hitherto often generally successful attempts to exclude Gergely from his rightful place in the history of the Hungarian Holocaust appear to have generated an alienation, disillusion and cynicism in the gentleman's old age. In contradistinction to his youthful disposition, Gyorgy Gergely's recent attitude is encapsulated thus: "In history, only that which did in fact happen matters, and not even this is always certain."[231]

Chapter V: Notes

1. At the time of writing, Domonkos' Diary is "owned" by Laszlo Karsai of Budapest. Unlike his respected late father, the authoritative historian Elek Karsai, Laszlo was only prepared to grant access to Domonkos' Diary, and for material on Gyorgy Gergely in Elek Karsai's archives, for substantial amounts (PD:TDK-Laszlo Karsai, 16 January 1991, Tape XXIV). Consequently, no information on either Gergely or Domonkos was obtained from the Karsai archive.

2. Shortly after emigrating to Australia in mid-1949, Gyorgy Gergely (henceforth GG) Anglicised his name to George Gregory, the English equivalent of his Hungarian name. He passed away in Sydney, 1995. Transcript and editing of Dr Gregory's 1987 oral testimony (henceforth GGT 1987) by his son-in-law, Dr Andrew Parle; pagination by TDK. I would like to thank Sr Marianne Dacy, Curator of the Archive of Australian Judaica, for providing the writer with a copy of this testimony. Unless otherwise stated, all references to Dr Gergely are from documents contained in this archive.

3. GGT 1987:9.

4. Braham 1981:16.

5. GG July 1940.

6. GGT 1987:13-14.

7. GG 1971:1.

8. GGT 1987:34-35.

9. By this action Dr Fabian probably saved Gergely's life. Subsequently, Gergely's JLS brigade was dispatched to the Ukraine, where the large majority perished. (GGT 1987:36)

10. GGT 1987:37.

11. Although Gergely's letters to The Carnegie Endowment For International Peace appear to be no longer extant, his private archive contains five letters he received from this organisation, the letters encompassing the period 8 May 1935 to 8 November 1938. The earliest of these letters was received from New York; the subsequent four were written in French and received from Paris, three of which emanated from Malcolm W. Davis, the organisation's *Directeur-Adjoint*. At the time of writing, Dr Gergely's private archive contained material not deposited with The University of Sydney. I would like to express my appreciation to Dr Gergely for generous and unrestricted access to his private files (henceforth referred to as GGPA).

12. GGPA.

13. Katzburg 1984b:169. For a sometimes intemperate and self-serving exposition of the Jewish Work Collective and its activities (including the two Silagi-authored Yellow Booklet publications), see Silagi 1986:191-235.

14. GG September 1941 (annotation by Yehuda Feher).

15. GG, nd (annotation by Yehuda Feher). The tract's first line — *"Melyen tisztelt Holgyeim es Uraim!"* (Deeply esteemed Ladies and Gentleman!) — clearly indicates a spoken format. Unfortunately date(s) and place(s) of presentation are not specified.

16. Letter from Drs Tibor Neumann and Dezso Weisz to GG, 2 March 1942, one page, typewritten, in Hungarian.

17. GG nd.

18. GG nd:22-23.

19. Although the NBJWV's Report is anonymous, Gergely confirmed his authorship of that document on several occasions, in particular during a discussion with the writer on 10 November 1993.

20. GG's NBJWV *Jelentes* (henceforth Report) 1943:4.

21. Report 1943:5-6. Stern was supported by the leadership of all three Jewish denominations. (Ibid)

22. Report 1943:6-8. Included in shipments to the Ukraine were 8,200 blankets; 10,900 winter coats; 10,500 jackets; 21,300 trousers; 4,400 shoes and boots; 30,500 winter gloves; 52,000 shirts; 25,100 winter underpants; 25,300 scarfs; and 18,800 ear muffs. Of these items, the following totals were collected: 15,200 blankets; 12,500 overcoats (not necessarily all of winter weight); 20,200 jackets; 34,500 trousers; 14,000 shoes and boots; 33,400 gloves; 66,600 shirts; 33,100 winter underpants; 25,600 scarfs; and 19,000 ear muffs. Also dispatched were assorted medicines and 23,400 cakes of soap.

23. See Report 1943:9-12.

24. For the situation of JLS company 108/84 stationed at Bor, Yugoslavia, see Nagy, Gyorgy 1995:79-80.

25. See Report 1943:9-12.

26. Report 1943:14.

27. Report 1943:14a. (Pagination by TDK)

28. In the latter stages of pregnancy, wives of JLS conscripts were admitted to either maternity homes or hospitals. Upon birth, each baby was presented with a "glory box", the mother retaining the box for eight months, after which its contents were taken for refurbishment before being presented to another newborn infant. Subsequently, to enable needy mothers of young children to participate in the workforce, the NBJWV's Family Protection Division placed children in an institution appropriate to their age and circumstances: either a crèche, kindergarten, day care centre, or children's home. (Report 1943:17)

29. Report 1943:15-17.

30. Report 1943:31.

31. Report 1943:32-33.

32. Report 1943:35-36.

33. GG 1971:3. After a brief period in Pest (mainly at the Hotel Astoria), Eichmann moved his headquarters to the Majestic Hotel, located in a beautiful, secluded villa area of Buda.

34. Wallenberg arrived in Budapest on 9 July 1944, two days after Horthy suspended deportations.

35. GGT 1987:52.

36. GGT 1987:72a. In his writings, Gergely consistently refers to the JC as the "Senate".

37. Deposition of Lajos Stockler, Political Criminal Division, Budapest Police, No. 5356/1946, 14 May 1946; in Braham 1986:325.

38. GG 1958a:1-3. With regard to Krumey's instructions of 21 March 1944, Gergely states that the meeting decided to accept German demands "in order to avoid provocation and retaliation..." (GG 1958a:4)

39. See GG 1958a:1-2.

40. Ibid.

41. GGT 1987:39.

42. Levai 1948:81.

43. PD:TDK-GG, 20 June 1993.

44. GGT 1987:68a. Possibly utilising hindsight, Gergely supports the view that by March 1944 the Germans recognised that the War was lost. As such, he states, their primary war aim became the Final Solution, a "war" that could still be won and one which would present a glittering victory — the destruction of European Jews. (GGT 1987:39)

45. GGT 1987:71a-72a. See also Braham 1981:406-07.

46. GG 1958:5.

47. PD:TDK-GG, 20 June 1993. Eichmann accepted the submitted Constitution with the order that it be implemented until further notice. Established by German fiat, it was this "until further notice" caveat that caused the official title of the JC to include the word "Provisional". (GGT 1987:69a) The reconstructed JC formed by Hungarian edict in mid-May also contained the word "Provisional", viz: *A Magyarorszagi Zsidok Szovetsege Ideiglenes Intezobizottsaga* (The Provisional Executive Council of the Association of the Jews of Hungary). (Braham 1981:451)

48. GG 1958:6.

49. GGT 1987:54-55.

50. See Braham 1981:1,148-49 and 475, n130.

51. Braham 1981:1,171.

52. Letter from Frigyes Gorog to GG, 24 January 1958, typewritten, one page. On the letter is a handwritten addendum from Gorog requesting personal information on Gergely and commenting that the latter's wife, Edith, has owed Gorog's daughter, Vera, a letter for some years.

53. Amongst other moral dilemmas, Gergely notes that Hunsche probably saved his life by issuing an order countermanding his dispatch to the Ukraine. (GGT 1987:44)

54. GG 1958b:1. In his covering letter Gergely wrote that, whilst initially hesitant about providing testimony, he decided to co-operate due to the firmly expressed opinion of many friends that the presentation of testimony is the act of a witness and not of a judge.

55. GG 1958a:6-7. The solitary, token exception to this policy was Krumey's release of Bela Fabian's mother, an intercession that Gergely organised.

56. GGT 1987:43.

57. GGT 1987:47. As a graduate of the *Reichsführerschule*, Bethge wore a black stripe with the inscription *"Reichsführer"* on the arm of his uniform.

58. After noting that Bethge was the only *SS* member who ever called him *Sie* (as opposed to *Du*), Gergely comments that Bethge was convinced Germany would lose the War. (GG 1958:8)

59. GG 1958:9.

60. Braham 1981:86.

61. Letter from Frigyes Gorog to Gyorgy Gergely, 8 May 1958, four typewritten pages, in Hungarian; page 1. Translation by Nora David. Henceforth Gorog 1958.

62. Gorog 1958:3.

63. For example, Gorog rightly corrects Gergely's mistake regarding the date of an early meeting with the *SS*. (Gorog 1958:2) In his testimony, Gergely states the meeting occurred on 19 March whilst the evidence is clear that it took place the next day. (See Braham 1981:420-21)

64. Gorog 1958:3. The last request is headed "Kasztner-Brand *fele penzek*" (The Kasztner-Brand money). In an interview, Gorog related how he obtained 3 million forints from Stern when Kasztner required the money for bribing the Germans. (Interview with Dr Gorog by Yehuda Bauer, 2 April 1968. Page 2, File 47/15, Oral Documentation Centre, Institute of Contemporary Jewry, Hebrew University of Jerusalem.)

65. Letter from Siegfrid Roth to GG, 16 May 1958, two pages, typewritten, in Hungarian.

66. Letter from Siegfrid Roth to GG, 3 June 1958, two pages, typewritten, in Hungarian.

67. Apart from The University of Sydney, other relevant archives examined for further correspondence included Yad Vashem, The Hebrew University of Jerusalem, University of

Haifa, Lochamet Ha'Gettot, Moreshet, the Zionist Central Archives (Jerusalem), Yivo, Pest Neolog Community, the Jewish Museum of Budapest, and the Hungarian National Archives. Despite Roth's written commitment to answer the writer's questions, no answers were ever received. (Letter, SJ Roth to TDK, 2 April 1991.)

68. GGT 1987:70a. Gergely also criticises Dr Erno Munkacsi, Chief Secretary of the Pest Neolog Community, for the same reason. Additionally, he accuses Munkacsi of refusing a position on the JC because of cowardice and the fear of postwar retribution.

69. GGT 1987:71a.

70. At the time of writing, it appears that the sole English-language publication regarding Berend's activities is Braham 1981:452-62.

71. The date of Berend's death was communicated to the writer by Professor R.L. Braham. (Private correspondence to TDK, 1 July 1990.)

72. Eppler 1946:7. It should be noted that Eppler's assertion of confidential material being destroyed appears to lack corroboration.

73. GGT 1987:59. Whilst the officer's name is not recalled, Gergely suggests he was a Colonel.

74. GGT 1987:57.

75. Elizabeth Eppler (1946:7) comments upon Berend's activities re the JC thus: "From the later behaviour of Berend it became manifest that he was a traitor indeed."

76. GGT 1987:59. Committee members included a young Rabbi (name not recalled), Vera Gorog (daughter of Frigyes Gorog) and her close friend Edit Popper who, in 1947 in Paris, became Mrs Gyorgy Gergely.

77. GGT 1987:61.

78. Braham 1981:500-01.

79. Braham 1981:456. The interview was published in the 29 July 1944 issue of *Harc*.

80. Braham (1981: 457-58) states that whilst Berend undoubtedly saved many Jews from almost certain death, he was embroiled in unsavoury allegations regarding his contemporaneous activities, eg: removing valuables from corpses, being present in *Nyilas* raids on Jews, and taking advantage of women.

81. Braham 1981: 475, n126.

82. Private correspondence from Bela Berend (then named Albert Belton) to Prof. Randolph Braham, 3 November 1972, typewritten, single page. Emphasis in the original. Letter by courtesy of Prof. Braham.

83. Berend launched his first suit against Braham in December 1973, claiming that the latter's publishing of Samu Stern and Erno Peto's testimonies constituted a libel. Berend lost both the case and the subsequent appeal. In a private discussion with the writer, Professor Braham stated that the last fifteen years of Berend's life were spent conducting a vendetta against him (Braham). (PD:TDK-R. L. Braham, 24 January 1991)

84. Braham 1981:460.

85. In his 1 April 1944 letter to Endre, Berend concluded by asking: "The goal is the same; why should we not do it together?!" (Braham 1981:474, n101)

86. Raphael Patai, *The Jews of Hungary* (Detroit: Wayne State University Press, 1996), 349.

87. Braham (1981:461-62) comments on this aspect of the Occupation thus: "The SS were amazed by the speed and efficiency with which the Hungarian Nazis had acted, stating that in no parts of occupied Europe had they gotten such co-operation." Testifying in February 1946, *Standardtenführer-SS* Kurt Becher, Himmler's economic representative in Hungary, supported this assessment thus: "Eichmann once said to me that Endre was an even more fanatical person than he himself was." (Becher 1946:3).

88. PD:TDK-GG, 18 November 1992. Of the several dozen activist survivors of the Hungarian Holocaust interviewed by the writer, not one was prepared to defend Berend's actions during this period.

89. Transcript, Berend (Plaintiff) versus Braham *et al* (Defendants), page 135-36, Belton

[Berend] — cross examination, *circa* February 1979; transcript by courtesy of Professor Braham. Note that the court reporter consistently misspelt Gergely's name as "Gerbly".

90. Letter, Dr Albert Belton (formerly Bela Berend), *The New York Review of Books*, 27 May 1982; 54.

91. For example, one of Berend's written commentaries on the JC is headed "Horrible Crimes of Samu Stern". (YVA 0-56/5434, R7)

92. Particularly Iver Olsen, representative in Sweden of the United States War Refugee Board and the Office of Strategic Services (OSS) — the latter being the predecessor of the US Central Intelligence Agency.

93. Lester 1985:151. See Levai 1948a:41-42 for the agreement between Wallenberg and the Swedish Foreign Ministry regarding the former's terms of appointment to Hungary.

94. Lester 1985:147.

95. Braham 1981:1,084.

96. Wallenberg and Laszlo Peto had met as students during a summer holiday at Thenon-les-Baines in France. (Peto 1956:58)

97. GGT 1987:77.

98. Gergely correctly states that Lutz issued four to five times more *Schutzpässe* than Wallenberg, approximately 20,000 to 4,000 respectively. (GGT 1987:78) Consequently, the following assessment of Wallenberg is the type to which Gergely objects: "Only in Budapest in the hellish winter of 1944 did the Jews have an official advocate [Wallenberg] from the civilized world..." (Lester 1958:147) In this context Gergely is clearly correct. Such misinformation manifestly denigrates Charles Lutz and a handful of other stalwart, humanitarian diplomats from neutral countries.

99. GGT 1987:80.

100. Ibid.

101. Ibid.

102. Levai 1948a:78.

103. Levai 1948a:46-47.

104. Levai 1948a:246.

105. Braham 1981:1,087.

106. Levai 1948a:77.

107. After the War, Gergely met one of the Forgacs brothers (name unspecified) in the presence of Laszlo Peto. During their discussion, Forgacs pressed Gergely for information on Wallenberg, such questions angering Peto, who repeatedly told Gergely to remain silent. (GGT 1987:80)

108. CZA CU/314, 29 September 1944. Wallenberg concluded this section of his Report by stating "There are no proofs [sic] that they [the two dismissed individuals] had any influence on decisions regarding passports." One should treat this claim with caution. In the absence of proof, surely the individuals would not have been dismissed.

109. At its height, Wallenberg's organisation included 355 employees, 40 physicians, two hospitals and a public kitchen. (Braham 1981:1,087)

110. Note that the Halutz were never affiliated with the Front.

111. GG 1971:4-5. Gergely comments on Stern's provisos: "He was absolutely right and I never expected it otherwise." (Ibid)

112. Probably on the basis of some apprehension regarding the then domestic Hungarian political situation, in his 1945 *Beszamolo* (henceforth Report II) Gergely emphasised that he, as the representative of the JC, negotiated with Count Palffy solely on the basis of the latter's membership of the Hungarian Front, and not because of Palffy's alignment with pro-Hapsburg forces. (Report II 1945:36) Report II was provided by courtesy of Professor Randolph Braham.

113. Report II 1945:36.

114. For details of the altercation between Fabian and Gergely over the list, and Stern's resolution of the issue in favour of the latter, see GG 1971:7-8.

115. GG 1971:12. See also GGT 1987:110.

116. GG 1971:12.

117. Ibid. Gergely (Report II 1945:36) is obviously mistaken when stating that this contact was on 15 October around noon. By the evening of 15 October the Szalasi *putsch* had succeeded.

118. Gergely states that, by this stage, both Heltai and Beer were living underground. Some months before this meeting, Gergely received a joint invitation from both men to join their political cell, an offer he refused. After the War, Heltai became deputy Foreign Minister during Imre Nagy's Prime Ministership, whilst Beer was deputy Lord Mayor of Budapest for two years and thence Secretary of State at the Ministry of Justice. (GG 1971:13)

119. Ibid.

120. By the morning of 15 October, 250 Proclamations had been printed and some 14 students assembled for their distribution. (GG 1971:15)

121. Gergely received this news at 10 am on 15 October, at the Kings Office, from Pallavicini's private secretary, Otto Draksich, to whom Gergely gave the Proclamations. (Report II 1945:37)

122. GG 1971:19.

123. See Macartney 1957:382-85.

124. The *Nyilas* occupied the radio station shortly after Horthy's broadcast. (Peto 1956:73) Stern (1945:24) confirms that the city bridges and radio station "were next to unguarded".

125. PD:TDK-GG, 18 November 1992.

126. Braham 1981:816, n126.

127. Vago 1970:97.

128. Komoly 1944:184.

129. GG 1971:18.

130. Report II 1945:37.

131. GG 1971:19. For example, Gergely states that a Mr (?) Udvarhelyi was awarded the Order of Liberty even though he "spent most of the time in a Children's Home of the Red Cross under my direction, with a broken leg". (Ibid)

132. GGT 1987:14.

133. Munkacsi 1947:238.

134. PD:TDK-GG, 20 August 1990. Unfortunately, this report to Munkacsi appears to be no longer extant.

135. See Peto 1956:73.

136. See Levai 1948:331.

137. See Braham 1977:68 and Braham 1981:284, 990 and 997.

138. See Rozett 1988:284.

139. A few accounts attempt to associate another person with Gergely during these negotiations. Peto's candidate for such a Jewish negotiation team is Istvan Lengyel (Peto 1956:73), an individual conspicuous by his apparent total absence from testimonies or documents of this period. Levai (1948:331) and Braham (1981:284 and 290) nominate Janos Beer, at that stage a little-known individual without any apparent position or power. It seems far-fetched to believe that Lazar, a cautious person in a highly sensitive position, was prepared to negotiate with unknown people apparently representing nobody but themselves.

140. See Pinter 1986:185.

141. Macartney 1957 II:384.

142. Apart from his assumption that Hungary's officer corps would remain loyal to himself as Supreme Commander, it appears that Horthy's major error was his sudden, unexpected decision of 14 October to bring forward the *volte-face* from 18 October to 15 October. Plans were disrupted: in particular, loyal troops could not be transferred to Budapest in time and the JLS and the workers remained unmobilised.

143. The International Red Cross (IRC) is also known as the International Committee of the Red Cross (ICRC).

144. Braham 1981:1,057-58.

145. Carr-Gregg 1989:11.

146. Carr-Gregg 1989:15.

147. Braham 1981:1,057-58.

148. Braham 1981:1,059.

149. Braham 1981:984.

150. Braham 1981:1,062.

151. Komoly 1944:216.

152. Braham 1981:1,062.

153. Braham 1981:1,063.

154. GGT 1987:82.

155. Komoly 1944:213.

156. The meeting commenced at 10 am with Komoly's next appointment being at 1 pm at the Ministry of Cults. One can thus reasonably assume that Born, Gergely and Komoly's discussion probably lasted some two hours.

157. For Gergely's original notes on this and subsequent discussions with Born on the Spanish proposal, see Munkacsi 1947:208-12. These notes appear to be no longer extant elsewhere.

158. Braham 1981:1,092.

159. Komoly 1944:214.

160. Komoly 1944:215.

161. GGT 1987:88.

162. Letters from Otto Komoly to *Herrn* Dr Georg Gergely, both single page, typed on *Comite International De La Croix-Rouge, Delegation En Hongrie* letterhead, signed by Komoly as "adm. Leiter"; Budapest 19 November and 8 December 1944.

163. PD:TDK-Leah Furst, 8 January 1991. Comparing photocopies of Gergely's documents with Otto Komoly's signatures in her possession, Mrs Furst declared: "There is no doubt in my mind that the signatures on Gergely's papers are authentic."

164. Private correspondence to TDK from department heads, Hungarian National Archives, Budapest; 5 November 1991, and no date but received 13 June 1991.

165. Ibid. Gergely granted permission for the release of his details to TDK via a Statutory Declaration, 13 September 1991.

166. Gergely to Samu Stern, two pages, typewritten, in German; Budapest, 7 September 1944.

167. Several times in this Report to Stern, Gergely refers to the document he presented to Rotta as "my memorandum". The statement Gergely read to Rotta was based on this memorandum.

168. About twenty minutes were spent with the Spanish *Chargé d'affaires*, with Gergely seeing Charles Lutz at the Swiss Legation the following day.

169. Gergely to Born, one page, typewritten, in Hungarian; Budapest, 9 October 1944.

170. *Communiqué* from Gergely to Weyermann, in German, four pages, Ref. Dr G/D4 No 254; Budapest, 16 December 1944.

171. As the three pages of this directory were loose in Gergely's archive, and not attached to a covering letter, a precise date of composition cannot be determined.

172. *Bericht* (Report) from Gergely to Weyermann, in German, seven pages; Budapest, 28 December 1944.

173. Section A's four central offices were Komoly's at 19 Munkacsi Mihaly Street; Gergely's at 35 Benczur Street; the financial, supply and medical office, and headquarters of Rudolph Weisz, at 6 Merleg Street; and the personnel department, under Dr Sandor Grozinger, at 52 Baross Street.

174. The Gergely Archive contains an English and a German translation of reference

Wy/NP No 708 from Hans Weyermann. Dated 16 June 1945 (by which time Born had left Hungary), the English translation states: "The Delegate for Hungary of the International Red Cross Committee certifies herewith that Dr George Gergely is acting in our Delegation since September 1944. The Delegation has entrusted Dr Gergely with various responsible duties — among others, to represent the Committee to the Foreign Diplomatic Corps — which he has fulfilled to our greatest satisfaction. The Delegate testifies that Dr Gergely has discharged all his duties even under the most difficult circumstances most conscientiously and that he enjoys the Delegate's absolute confidence. Signed H Weyermann." The original of this reference is no longer extant. As noted in the text, the IRC archive in Geneva (which possibly contains a copy) refused to co-operate in this study.

175. *Note* presented by Gergely to the Portuguese Legation for submission, in turn, to the Hungarian Interior Minister; three pages, in German; Budapest, 20 December 1944.

176. Ben-Tov 1988:325.

177. Report May 1945:9.

178. GG May 1945:9-10.

179. GGT 1987:91 Amongst these survivors was his father, Gyula Gergely, who was placed in charge of one of his son's IRC-protected houses.

180. GGT 1987:86.

181. For example, in his discussion of the IRC office at 6 Merleg Street, Gergely emphasised that equipment missing from these premises was clearly stolen during a major *Nyilas* raid. With the Report, Gergely enclosed three documents (nos 34, 35 and 36) relating to this address. (Report May 1945:13) Whilst discussing the premises at Benczur Street, Gergely stated that the telephone, gas and electricity accounts were not yet available, and thus had yet to be paid, but the house was only occupied on 12 December and the light failed on 31 December. Rent at this location was 6,700 *pengos* per month. (Report May 1945:16)

182. Report May 1945:2.

183. Appendix A, Report May 1945.

184. Report May 1945:4.

185. See, for example, GGT 1987:84-85.

186. Efra is mentioned on pages 6 and 14, Rafi on page 16, and Perecz on pages 7, 10 and 11. (Report May 1945) It is a matter of conjecture as to why the Halutz are so conspicuously absent from elsewhere in Gergely's archives.

187. See Report May 1945:8-9. Gergely's *Note* was accepted by the Nuncio's Deputy, *Monsignor* Gennaro Verolino, as at the time the Nuncio was in conference with Szalasi. Braham (1981:1,074) confirms that on 17 November the Nuncio did, in fact, have a meeting with Szalasi.

188. GGT 1987:91.

189. Report May 1945:9.

190. See Addendum, Gergely's *Note* of 20 December 1944, p3.

191. This estimate is based on Gergely's statement that he obtained three additional buildings to house his *Schutzpass* holders on 19 November. (Report May 1945:9) On the basis that his pass was of original design, it would have taken about a week or so to produce. Plus several days to issue to individual holders, *ergo* the estimated timeframe.

192. Report May 1945:9.

193. See Chapter I, n1.

194. Deborah Lipstadt, *Denying the Holocaust. The Growing Assault on Truth and Memory* (New York: Free Press, 1993), 134.

195. Deposition of Lajos Stockler, Political Criminal Division, Budapest Police, No. 5356/1946, 14 May 1946; see also Braham 1986:325. Stockler arrived in Australia at the end of 1957 and died in 1961. His son George, who was twelve when Budapest was liberated in early 1945, refused to discuss his father's activities with the writer, stating: "I have some books which were sent to me and which contain references to my father. I didn't even bother to read them. I live in today's world and I can't change history. These things are totally

unproductive." (Telephone conversation, TDK-George Stockler, 27 August 1991)

196. Letter from Zoltan Moor, Yad Vashem's Hungarian Archivist, to Gyorgy Gergely, 12 March 1961; single page, typewritten, in Hungarian.

197. Although the original request is no longer extant, Gergely's response is contained within his archive, in a Statutory Declaration entitled: "Following a Request received from *Das Landgericht* [the Higher Court] Frankfurt am Main as outlined in the Letters of *Landgerichtarat* Grabert, dated 8 th and 28 th June, 1960 regarding the prosecution of former *Obersturmbannführer-SS* Herman Krumey and former *Hauptsturmführer-SS* Otto Hunsche, reference 4a Js 586/56 of *Das Landgericht*."

198. Gergely states that his modest financial circumstances — a condition to which the writer can attest — prevented him taking legal redress against Berend's accusation. (PD:TDK-GG, 14 October 1993)

199. Levai 1948:99.

200. Braham 1981:407. Additionally, and importantly, it should be noted that numerous lists of many Jews were readily available, having been maintained by professional and business associations, and government departments, in order to implement the quota system introduced by Hungary's Antisemitic legislation.

201. For examples see GGT 1987:81a.

202. Levai 1948a:168.

203. Ben-Tov 1988:342

204. Ibid.

205. GGT 1987:81a. Gergely's critique of Born is clearly echoed by Iver Olsen, War Refugee Board representative in Stockholm. In a letter of 14 August 1944, Olsen writes of his recent conversation in Stockholm with the First Secretary of the Swedish Legation in Budapest, then home on a brief leave. Olsen states that the First Secretary "indicated, and please keep this as personal, that we should not take without a grain of salt the hopeful enthusiasm of the IRC man there [Friedrich Born], who apparently drinks a lot and has delusions of grandeur, but very little in the way of practical judgement in approaching the problems [facing Hungary's Jews]". (Wyman 1990:11)

206. Braham 1981:1,126, n20. In this reference Braham cites other criticisms of Born contained in Levai's *Feher konyv* (White Book).

207. Ben-Tov 1988:293.

208. PD:TDK-Yehuda Bauer, 24 July 1991 (Sydney).

209. Ben-Tov 1988:339.

210. Ben-Tov 1988:377.

211. GG 1958:2.

212. GGT 1987:82. "Agile honorary members" refers to the Halutzim.

213. GGT 1987:96.

214. Letter to TDK from Florianne Trunninger, Research Officer, ICRC, Geneva (Henceforth ICRCA); 30 August 1990. Ref. DDM/RECH 90/233 FT/av.

215. Letter to TDK from ICRCA, 4 September 1990. Ref. DDM/RECH 90/240 FT/av.

216. Letter to TDK from ICRCA, 16 October 1990. Ref. DDM/RECH 90/280 FT/av.

217. Letter to TDK from ICRCA, 3 January 1991. Ref. DDM/RECH 90/327 FT/av.

218. Ibid.

219. Letter from TDK to ICRC, 18 April 1991.

220. Braham 1981:1,062.

221. Braham 1981:1,063.

222. Cohen 1986:249, n1.

223. GGT 1987:1.

224. The *Reader's Digest* writes: "On January 16, he [Raoul Wallenberg] told Gyorgy Gergely of the International Red Cross he was going to the Russian Commander, Marshal Malinovsky, at Debrecen..." ("Raoul Wallenberg, Hero of Budapest", in *Reader's Digest*, July 1947, 100. Ralph Wallace, condensed from *True*.)

225. Letter from Randolph Braham to Gyorgy Gergely, 7 June 1980, single page, typewritten. Unfortunately, Braham's 1994 edition of his 1981 work *The Politics of Genocide* (see Bibliography) leaves these matters uncorrected.

226. Braham 1981: 1,075-77.

227. See Braham 1981:1,128, n 70-73.

228. Cohen 1986:249, n1. Agreeing with Dr Cohen's assessment, this writer utilised Levai for either confirmation purposes or where no alternative source exists. As expected, Gergely deprecates Levai's publications, calling them "journalistic quick-books, money making operations". (PD:TDK-GG, 19 March 1990) Unfortunately, even Levai's work published long after the conclusion of hostilities (and therefore written with the benefit of hindsight and reflection), may contain substantial errors. For example: "This is how Eichmann succeeded in obtaining 150 trains for the deportation of Hungarian Jews in 1944. As a result, following the extrication of the Rumanians from the War, the Balkan Army of Gen. Maxmilian von Weichs could not be resupplied and did not receive sufficient trains for the forced retreat that became necessary. The deportation of the Jews continued at a record pace while Gen. Weichs was compelled to destroy his artillery and ammunitions and to retreat in the midst of great infantry battles, suffering great losses." (Levai 1973:284) Levai is demonstrably incorrect in several important aspects of his analysis. The Roumanians did not "extricate" themselves from the War; they changed allegiance from the Axis to the Allies on 23 August 1944 and continued combat activities, now supporting Soviet forces against the Germans and Hungarians. It will be recalled that as Horthy banned further deportations to Auschwitz on 7 July 1944, only small numbers of Jews were deported from Hungary thereafter. Levai's claim that the "deportation of [Hungarian] Jews continued at a record pace [after 23 August]" is thus simply not true. Clearly, General Field Marshal Maxmilian Freiherr von Weichs' (1881-1954) problems with railway transportation after the Roumanian *volte-face* were unrelated to the Jewish situation in Hungary.

229. For example, in 1987 he sometimes gives unbridled rein to his emotions, on occasion calling a few selected individuals in his disfavour "absolutely stupid and repulsive" or "an uneducated idiot". (GGT 1987:106 and 104 respectively)

230. GG 1971:1.

231. GG 1971:19.

INTERNATIONAL NEGOTIATIONS AND THE 'RESCUE MATRIX'

DUPLICITY, HIDDEN AGENDAS, CALCULATED TOKENISM OR GENUINE RESPONSE?

It is ill-recognised in many histories of the Holocaust — if recognised at all — that peace overtures were a virtually constant feature of World War II, such attempts beginning at the very commencement of military activities.[1] During the first phase of conflict, the so-called *Sitzkrieg* (Phony War), the West retained a significant residue of sympathy towards negotiating a settlement with Germany.[2] Hitler did little to discourage such thinking, transmitting vague proposals to the UK indicating the Reich's willingness to negotiate a compromise peace and to recognise a new Polish state, albeit of substantially reduced area.[3] Chamberlain, in turn, for a short time hoped to utilise these feelers as a means of dividing the Nazi leadership. All such strategies, as well as interventions by individual intermediaries (notably the Swedish industrialist Birger Dahlerus), and several neutral countries (particularly the increasingly apprehensive Holland and Belgium), proved equally unproductive.

The USSR, Italy and Spain, each wanting a halt to German expansionism, attempted to convince the West that a policy of accommodation generated benefits to both warring factions. Such cajoling elicited sympathy in right-wing French circles (especially those surrounding Pétain), elements in the British Conservative Party, some US State Department officials (in particular, Joseph Kennedy, US Ambassador to Great Britain) and wealthy US industrialists belonging to the Liberty League. Roosevelt, conscious that 1940 was a presidential election year and aware of the political power of his domestic isolationist lobby, in February 1940 dispatched two prominent US businessmen to negotiate in Berlin and London. A month later, after Germany had intimated that it may consider favourably a US proposal to end the conflict, it was clear to Roosevelt that Chamberlain, Mussolini and the French Premier, Edouard Daladier, would accept a peace agreement guaranteed by the US. Despite this, Roosevelt continued to maintain a non-intervention ("hands-off") policy regarding the European conflict.

Germany's attack on France in May 1940, Mussolini's subsequent withdrawal of his offer to mediate, and the appointment of the principal British foe of appeasement, Winston Churchill, as Prime Minister, reduced the prospect of a negotiated settlement. Notwithstanding these factors, and although reticent in public, during private discussions Hitler continued to express admiration for England's "mission for the white race" and the desire for an accord with the British.[4]

With the succession of German victories in the West, at the end of May the French suggested to Churchill that Italian mediation be accepted.[5] Subsequently, the British government weathered a series of crises over the wisdom of accommodating Germany, especially after France requested an armistice on 17 June. Although Hitler ceased his peace offers with the French defeat, contacts between Great Britain and the Reich continued, especially via Switzerland and the Vatican.[6] A blustering speech by Hitler in the *Reichstag* on 19 July, however, generated a hostile reaction in Britain and led to the discontinuation of talks in Washington between the British ambassador and the German *charge d'affaires*.

From August 1940, attempts at reconciliation were largely brokered by European neutrals, including Sweden (persisting until December 1940), the Swiss, Turkey and Spain. Even the Japanese, in February 1941, attempted to intervene and broker negotiations. The Vatican was especially active in attempting to reconcile the warring parties. Churchill, however, refused on principle to accept the Vatican's auspices, stating that the Curia, being dominated by Italians, was pro-Mussolini and supported Italy's policy of conquest.

The British PM had cogent reasons for questioning the *bona fides* of the Vatican's leadership. Of special concern were the views of Eugenio Pacelli — Papal Nuncio to Weimar Germany, 1920–29; Vatican Secretary of State, 1930–39; and Pope (Pius XII, 1939–58) — who, as the Vatican's Foreign Minister, was instrumental in negotiating a concordat with Nazi Germany in July 1933, shortly after Hitler's advent to power. An acknowledged Germanophile, Pius XII notedly failed to pursue — much less emphasise or elaborate upon — his predecessor's encyclical *Mit Brennender Sorge* (With Deep Anxiety), a pointed attack on Hitlerism and the Nazi State which Pope Pius XI issued in March 1937. Doubtless Churchill realised that Pius XII's Germanophilia was reinforced by the Vatican's abiding, fervent anti-Communism and the Pontiff's conception of the Holy See's paramount financial and political interests.[7] Apart from Pacelli's general statements criticising the Treaty of Versailles and his calls for a re-enlarged Germany, in 1940 Pius XII gave a formal address in which he once again stated his attitude that the frontiers established at Versailles were not a mandatory prerequisite for peace. After Operation Barbarossa in June 1941, the Pope considered the Nazi regime to be a necessary bulwark against international Communism and, following the German debacle at Stalingrad in early 1943, the Holy See consistently supported a negotiated settlement.[8]

The War's most spectacular peace overture occurred on 11 May 1941, when Hitler's deputy, Rudolph Hess, in a startling and apparently individual (non-authorised) initiative, parachuted into Scotland in an attempt to commence negotiations with the British. Hitler dismissed this action as an instance of lunacy, an explanation utilised by Churchill to keep Hess' revelations secret, thus inhibiting further controversy in Britain regarding a negotiated settlement. Hess' initiative did, however, generate a permanent residue. The Soviet dictator, Josef Stalin — invariably suspicious of "international capitalist conspiracies" — suspected Hess and the British of concluding a secret, mutually beneficial agreement at Soviet expense. Reinforced in this view by Hitler's surprise attack on the USSR in June 1941, Stalin demanded of Churchill a binding pact that neither country would negotiate a separate peace with Germany. In an attempt to reassure the Soviets of their good intentions, the British revealed to Stalin Hess' statement that his journey was concerned solely with peace on the Western Front — the obvious corollary being that Germany, by making peace with Great Britain, wanted to avoid a war on two fronts. As may have been expected of the often paranoid Soviet dictator, this revelation proved counterproductive, the news intensifying Stalin's apprehensions and suspicions regarding British policy. The significance of Hess' bizarre endeavour has been succinctly summarised thus:

> The presence of the Nazi emissary on English soil was constantly to poison relations between the British and the Russians — aside, that is, from the animus Stalin already bore Churchill for the latter's dispatch of British troops to Russia to fight the infant Red Army in 1918. The Soviet leader obviously feared that Hess was being groomed to replace Hitler and promote an Allied-German combination against the USSR.[9]

During the *Blitzkrieg* invasion of the USSR, Hitler was preoccupied by the Eastern Front, being obsessed with his quest for *Lebensraum* (living space for Germans in the East). As such, peace feelers to the West were foregone, all efforts being devoted to the destruction of Communism (frequently referred to by the Nazis as Judeo-Bolshevism). The Nazi crusade against the USSR, however, generated considerable support for peace between the UK and Germany, with numerous European diplomats, industrialists and politicians of Rightist persuasion considering the defeat of Stalin more important than the replacement of Hitler. Again in the forefront of attempts to reconcile Great Britain and Germany were Turkey and Spain, whose efforts were supplemented by the Vatican, Switzerland, Sweden, Vichy France and, repeatedly, British business interests.

Following Japan's surprise attack on Pearl Harbor in December 1941, and the subsequent American entry into the War, US military experts further deprecated the possibility of Soviet resistance against the German *Blitzkrieg*. This attitude increased the reluctance of the US public to aid the USSR, the world's prime purveyor of atheistic Communism. The fall of Stalin was considered so probable that plans were formulated for a democratic Russian government-in-exile.[10]

The Reich's military position — and, consequently, its political leverage — was considered to be so powerful in this period that the Atlantic Charter, an eight-point declaration of human rights and policy aims announced by Great Britain and the USA on 14 August 1941 was, *inter alia*, designed to ambush a German peace offensive. To reinforce this policy, to neutralise the calls for peace by pro-German sympathisers, and to answer his British critics — including the press baron, Lord Beaverbrook, and a faction of the Labour Party — in a special address in October, Churchill restated his policy of continuing the War until Hitler was defeated. Acting in tandem, Roosevelt maintained his attacks on US isolationists. Despite these developments, official contacts were maintained between the German legation and the British consul in Zurich until Ribbentrop, possibly motivated by petty Anglophobia, banned further discussions. On 1 July 1942, Churchill's policy of refusing to negotiate with the enemy was supported by a large majority of the House of Commons, a motion of no confidence in his government being heavily defeated.

The eventual decline of Germany's military ascendancy stimulated concern in numbers of Hitler's domestic opponents. These small, disaffected bands — which included *Wehrmacht* generals, *Abwehr* (military intelligence) agents, a few diplomats (importantly, the ambivalent former Chancellor Franz von Papen, Ambassador to Turkey, April 1939–August 1944) and even some individuals in the *SS* hierarchy — commenced to manoeuvre for position. To reinforce Allied resolve and to pre-empt further peace overtures, at the Casablanca Conference, 12–23 January 1943, Roosevelt and Churchill promulgated a demand for the Reich's unconditional surrender.

Perhaps paradoxically, this declaration energised German anti-Nazi circles into taking tentative steps to implement their opposition to Hitler, all of which foundered on the West's absolute demand for unconditional surrender even in the event of the Nazi dictator's fall from power. Recognising this impediment, in March 1943, shortly after Germany's catastrophic debacle at Stalingrad, Franz von Papen made a speech that highlighted the common dangers resulting from a Soviet expansion into Europe, emphasised the mutual benefits of an American-European symbiosis and, *inter alia*, recognised the principles enunciated in the Atlantic Charter. Papen's message generated waves, being featured in the foreign press and receiving support from elements within the *SS* intelligence service. Yet despite Churchill having second thoughts about the wisdom of demanding unconditional surrender, Papen's overture came to naught — primarily, it appears, because of the need to maintain Allied solidarity, all three major Allies being concerned at the prospect of a secret German peace offer to one of their number.[11] The Western Allies, in particular, remembered vividly the Nazi-Soviet Pact of August 1939, a treaty that, in effect, led to the outbreak of World War II.

Yet despite (or perhaps because of) this attitude, the manoeuvring continued. Elements within the OSS — Office of Strategic Services, the US secret intelligence bureau[12] — were increasingly apprehensive at what they considered was Roosevelt's too pro-Soviet attitude. With the decline in Germany's military supremacy in the East, these OSS elements — like some members of German intelligence — became convinced of the need to counterbalance the growing Soviet threat to postwar Europe. Consequently, in the (northern) spring of 1943, Allen Dulles, OSS chief in Europe, held three conferences in Switzerland with semi-official German agents, one of whom was a representative of Walter Schellenberg, head of the *SD*, the intelligence branch of the *SS*. During these negotiations, and at a meeting with Papen in early October 1943, Dulles made verbal concessions to his German counterparts, concessions primarily motivated by the American's perception of the need to pre-empt another Nazi-Soviet Pact and so abort the formation of a huge Eurasian faction.

Western concern at the possibility of a German-Soviet understanding was so great at this time that at the Foreign Ministers' Conference in Moscow in late October 1943, the British insisted upon an immediate and comprehensive exchange regarding German peace offers. According to Martin and Havens, "of all the nations involved, it was the USSR most of all that toyed with the idea of a separate peace... the most frequent motif [being the USSR's] fear of encirclement by the capitalist nations."[13] Accordingly, Stalin was never reticent about his demand for territorial expansion, which he couched in terms of the necessity for buffer zones to protect the USSR against future aggression. As early as December 1941, the Soviet dictator, in his conference with the British Foreign Minister Anthony Eden, insisted that in any postwar settlement the USSR should regain Tsarist Russia's western frontier of 1914. During these discussions, Stalin drew a distinction between Hitler and Germany, thus lending further credence to the West's suspicions regarding the prospects of a separate peace on the Eastern Front. The implication of Stalin's delineation was clear: unless the West agreed to his territorial demands, the USSR would conclude an agreement with the German regime.

Western suspicions proved well founded for, in March 1942, the Soviet approached the Reich for an immediate armistice. Although German intransigence prevented progress, contact was maintained between the parties. In December 1942, Peter Kleist (attaché to Ribbentrop) received another Soviet armistice offer and, in early 1943 — towards the end of the fateful Stalingrad campaign — the Soviet directed an overture to the German legation in Stockholm. The Japanese, who were not at war with the USSR, remained anxious to mediate and/or broker an armistice on the Eastern Front but were rebuffed by Stalin, who preferred to deal directly with Berlin. In December 1942 and April 1943, Italy, now fearful about the fate of her troops in both Russia and north Africa, was equally unsuccessful in persuading Hitler to accept an accord in the East. The *Führer's* fanatical refusal to negotiate with the Soviet was doubtless connected to what he perceived as his life's quintessential *raison d'être* — a crusade to the death against the heinous gorgon of Judeo-Bolshevism as represented by the USSR. Although disheartened by its previously unsuccessful efforts, Japan continued attempting to broker a German-USSR accord until July 1944.

Despite these manifestations of Hitler's intransigence, the German-Soviet talks in Stockholm continued until June 1943 when, notwithstanding Ribbentrop's desire to continue the exploration process, they were aborted by the Germans. Unfortunately for the Reich their great hope, the *Zitadelle* offensive on the Eastern Front in July 1943, was smashed when the Red Army inflicted another substantial defeat over the increasingly faltering *Wehrmacht*. As a consequence, even the pessimists within the Soviet leadership acknowledged that the Germans had lost the initiative in the East. Yet notwithstanding their increasing military momentum, in September 1943 the USSR opened another channel of communication, this time via V. G. Dekanozov, former Soviet ambassador in Berlin. In a joint appraisal, two authorities have summarised Stalin's attitude in this period thus: "It can hardly be doubted that the Soviets in 1943 truly wanted an accord with the Germans under conditions the Western Allies would never grant."[14] It should be noted that by this stage Himmler had achieved the capacity to communicate with the Allies, including via contacts originally established by anti-Hitler circles in Germany.

Not unnaturally, from early 1944 the growing prospects of a Second Front in western Europe — which occurred at Normandy (France) in June 1944 — combined with the Red Army's rapid advances in the East, substantially diminished Stalin's desire for another Nazi-Soviet accord. Perhaps equally naturally, the *Führer's* undiminished obsession with his once-in-a-lifetime opportunity of destroying

Communism, the Red Army's acknowledged and growing ascendancy over the *Wehrmacht*, and Churchill's steadily increasing apprehension about Soviet territorial intentions in Eastern and Central Europe, combined to revive the notion of an agreement between the Western Allies and Germany. As late as 1944, such an accord was considered favourably by elements within the West's armed forces and intelligence services. Reinforcing this attitude, some anti-Roosevelt circles in the USA viewed a strong Germany as a necessary impediment to Communist expansion into Europe — a philosophy harboured by significant elements within the Reich, including some in the Nazi hierarchy.

When Anglo-American forces breached Germany's 1938 frontiers in September 1944,[15] Ribbentrop, conscious of (apparent) overlapping interests and with Hitler's possible approval, proposed that Germany unite with the West in a crusade against rampant Communism. Envoys were dispatched to Sweden, Switzerland and Spain, but Ribbentrop's offer came to naught — as did proposals by Himmler, Göring and Göbbels.[16] By that stage of the conflict, the Soviet in particular had realised that Germany's unconditional surrender was merely a matter of time.

As has been seen, whilst Anglo-American leaders after the resignation of Chamberlain — especially Churchill — maintained a consistent and resolute refusal to bargain with Hitler, until late 1943 Stalin played the role of a consummate pragmatist. Only with the undisputed ascendancy of the Red Army over the *Wehrmacht*, the consequent immense gains in formerly German-occupied territory, and the definite agreement regarding a Second Front in Europe, did the Soviet dictator become averse to negotiating with his Nazi counterpart. Following the successful Anglo-American invasion of France in June 1944, the failure of Colonel Claus Graf von Stauffenberg's attempt on 20 July 1944 to assassinate Hitler was a relief to both Stalin and the *Führer*. With the Western Allies established on the Continent, one of the last things Stalin desired was a new non-Nazi, anti-Communist and pro-Western regime in Germany whose probable priority would be to conclude an accord with the West to contain Soviet expansion. Hitler, although initially willing to reach agreement with the British, became progressively more intransigent until, in effect, prospects for his acceptance of a negotiated peace settlement were extinguished with Operation Barbarossa (Red Beard), his June 1941 invasion of the USSR. The failure of Stauffenberg's assassination attempt resolved the struggle for power between the Nazi Party and the *Wehrmacht*. Henceforth, until Germany's unconditional surrender in May 1945, Hitler and the Party maintained an unchallenged ascendancy over the Reich's politically acquiescent armed forces.

The "Blood for Trucks" Proposal

As previously discussed (see Chapter IV), with the Occupation of Hungary the Europa Plan negotiations in Bratislava between the *SS* (represented by *Hauptsturmführer* Dieter Wisliceny) and the Slovakian Working Group (led by the ultra-Orthodox Rabbi Dov Weissmandl and the Zionist leader Gisi Fleischmann) were, in effect, transferred to Budapest. Due to Germany's deteriorating military position, which necessitated a negotiator of higher profile and greater authority, Wisliceny — who was frequently in the countryside organising the deportation of Hungary's provincial Jews — was replaced in the Budapest discussions by his notorious commanding officer, Adolph Eichmann.

Continuing Himmler's policy of utilising international Jewish organisations as a conduit to contact Western intelligence services (see below), on 25 April 1944 Eichmann summonsed Joel Brand, a leading member of the Budapest *Va'ada* (underground Jewish Relief and Rescue Committee), to discuss the ransoming of Hungarian Jewry. Consequent upon this and several other meetings between these two protagonists, on 17 May — two days after the commencement of mass deportations from Hungary to Auschwitz — Brand left Budapest under German auspices and arrived in Istanbul two days later. Carrying three letters of introduction from Hungarian Jewish leaders, Brand was accompanied on his mission by a shadowy multiple intelligence agent, Andor "Bandi" Grosz (sometimes known by the alias Andre Gyorgy).

Despite lacking a Turkish visa, Brand met the representatives of various international Zionist organisations in Istanbul and revealed what has become infamous as Eichmann's "Blood for Trucks" offer. According to Eichmann, Germany was prepared to spare the lives of Hungarian (and possibly Roumanian) Jews in exchange for various suggested commodities, viz: 10,000 army trucks (that Eichmann promised would be used exclusively on the Eastern Front), 800 tons of coffee, 200 tons of tea, two million bars of soap, and unspecified minerals and materials. Upon receipt of the Allies' readiness to negotiate such an arrangement, the Auschwitz gas chambers would be destroyed and an initial instalment of 100,000 Jews would be released and permitted to travel to any Allied territory except Palestine, which was explicitly excluded due to the Nazi alliance with the Mufti of Jerusalem, Amin el-Husseini.[17]

After a convoluted sequence of incidents, the Turkish authorities, suspicious of Brand's motives and guarding Turkey's neutrality from encroachment, held Brand in protective custody from 25 to 31 May, thus preventing his access to the US ambassador, Laurence Steinhardt, in Ankara. On 1 June, Grosz left Istanbul, arrived in Syria and was promptly arrested by the British. Four days later, after receiving assurances that the British would not impede his return to Hungary, the Istanbul *Va'ada* apparently persuaded Brand to travel to Palestine for discussions with the Jewish Agency executive. Despite receiving a British visa, on 7 June Brand was arrested upon reaching Aleppo in British-controlled Syria and, shortly thereafter, sent to Cairo for intensive interrogation by Western intelligence. Only in early October, months after the Allies had, in effect, unconditionally rejected the German overture, was Brand finally permitted to reach Palestine. An understanding of this multifaceted and still highly controversial episode requires an analysis, in historical context, of the convoluted motivations, strategies and responses of the disparate protagonists involved.

Anglo-American Reaction

Notwithstanding the Grand Alliance hierarchy being fully aware of the *Endlösung* (Final Solution) by March 1944, and despite Churchill being the Allied leader most in sympathy with the Jewish plight under the Nazis, British policy remained decidedly cool towards the first potential opportunity to rescue/ransom substantial numbers of Jews trapped within the Reich's domain. The tenor of British policy towards the "Blood for Trucks" offer was set very early in the piece by the Foreign Office official R.M. Hankey. Writing on 27 May, just eight days after Brand and Grosz arrived in Istanbul, Hankey assessed the German proposal in a totally derogatory manner, classifying it as a "stunt" utterly devoid of redeeming virtue, viz:

It seems likely that this fantastic offer is just a political warfare stunt by the Germans. They must know that it would be almost impossible to move a million Jews from eastern Europe across France to Spain and Portugal without preventing our bombing of French railways, interfering with the Second Front, embarrassing our relations with Spain and Portugal, using shipping in the Mediterranean and Atlantic, upsetting the supply position in Spain and Portugal and (if the refugees went to the Middle East) very probably precipitating troubles in Palestine and the Middle East which would immobilise British divisions otherwise available for offensive operations. Even if we did accept, there would be no means of sending the lorries to Germany without interfering again with shipping and military operations. Finally, if once we were to agree to be blackmailed in this way we should not have an appeal for a mere [sic] million Jews, there would be Poles, Frenchmen, Dutchmen, etc, etc.[18]

Hankey's unconscionable and inhumane response — note his callous reference to the surviving Jewish remnant as a *mere* million — neglects alternative options to mass migration. Jews could, for example, have been maintained safely in specially designated locations within Hungary or elsewhere in the Reich's domain, the inhabitants therein being supervised by neutral countries, the International Red Cross and/or the Vatican. Such a solution would have obviated problems with the Arabs and caused little if any interruption to Allied military operations. On the contrary, any disruption would have been largely at the expense of the Axis' war effort and so would have benefited the Allies, possibly to a significant extent.

As must have been realised by Hankey, it is not unusual in diplomatic, political and commercial negotiations for opening gambits to be either substantially modified or even negotiated away. The demand for trucks was, clearly, an opening gambit by the Germans. However, even in the highly unlikely event of the Allies deciding to supply a quantity of trucks, any such cargo could have been shipped in neutral vessels sailing under neutral flags and thus not interfering with Allied maritime capacity. Furthermore, as must have been known to Hankey, no other ethnic category under German control — whether Poles, French, Dutch etc — was under the collective death sentence imposed upon Jews. And possibly, once the precedent had been set, those non-Jews at risk could have been included in the same, or a similar, rescue scheme.

A somewhat more reasoned response came from Hankey's colleague A. W. G. Randall, Head of the Foreign Office's Refugee Department. Doubtless conscious of 1944 being a US presidential election year, and aware of the importance of the Jewish vote to Roosevelt, Randall noted the wisdom of consulting with the Americans as opposed to merely issuing a unilateral British rejection of the German approach. The British Foreign Minister, Anthony Eden, whilst agreeing with his Department's broad thrust, decided to take the matter to Cabinet.[19]

Shortly thereafter, on 31 May, at the meeting of the War Cabinet's Committee on Refugees — held in the absence of Churchill and Eden, but with A.W.G. Randall in attendance — both the Colonial and the Foreign Office rejected the German overture. According to the official minutes, the Committee not only accepted the opinions of both Hankey and Randall but, in addition, refused exploratory discussions with the Germans in order to pre-empt the possibility of "a [further] offer to unload an even greater number of Jews on to our hands".[20] Meeting the next day, less than a week before the Anglo-American invasion of France created the Second Front in Europe, the War Cabinet concurred with the Committee and classified the proposal as one meant to inhibit the Allies' prosecution of the War. Notwithstanding this decision, no public statement was to be issued until the matter had been discussed with the Americans. With Churchill present, however, the Cabinet agreed to investigate the provision of shelter in Spain and Portugal for a small number of Jews from Nazi territory whose acceptance would not prejudice the Allied war effort. Yet despite these attitudes, the Cabinet also decided to refrain from issuing an outright rejection until Brand's revelations, and the implications thereof, had been assessed.

Having agreed upon their stance, on 3 June the British transmitted the German proposal to the US State Department and commented that, in their opinion, the offer was attempted extortion and/or devious, multifaceted political warfare, namely either a venture to trade civilian lives for war material, a diabolical public relations exercise, a bid to sabotage Allied military operations, an attempt to split the Grand Alliance, or a convoluted combination thereof. Contemporaneously Chaim Weizmann, head of the Jewish Agency (for Palestine) — and, subsequently, the first President of the State of Israel — was informed of the Brand–Grosz mission, his initial response being that it seemed like another German attempt to embarrass the Western Allies.[21] On 7 June, Weizmann conferred with Eden and told the British Foreign Minister that although he had no knowledge of Brand, the emissary could well be trustworthy. Resulting from this meeting, the British agreed to permit Brand to be interviewed by Moshe Shertok, Head of the Political Department of the Jewish Agency (see below).[22]

During his discussions with Eden, Weizmann requested that Britain direct an official warning to the Sztojay regime regarding the perilous situation of Hungary's Jews. Shortly before, this suggestion had also been made by Laurence Steinhardt — US Ambassador to Turkey (1942–45), the USSR (1939–41), and himself a Jew — who had been informed of the German proposal by the Jewish Agency. Suspicious of possible collusion by Jewish circles, A. W. G. Randall resumed his political theme mentioned above and noted on 7 June: "It has to be remembered that the US Ambassador in Angora [Ankara] has declared his intention of winning the Jewish vote in New York for the Democrats..."[23]

Despite agreeing with the thrust of the British attitude, the United States — doubtless largely influenced by domestic political considerations — decided not to reject the proposal outright but to explore the possibility of utilising the German offer for the relief and/or rescue of the trapped Jews. Consequently, Ira Hirschmann, a prominent Jewish businessman, notable Roosevelt supporter, a US delegate at the 1938 Evian (Refugee) Conference, and Special Assistant, National War Labor Board (1942–44), was dispatched to Turkey on 11 June as Special Representative of the US War Refugee Board (see below) with instructions to interview Brand and convey to him America's concern and empathy. Although this unilateral response appeared to imply a degree of US flexibility, Ambassador Steinhardt was informed that the German offer could only be considered, much less accepted, in consultation with both the UK and USSR governments. Furthermore, to preclude any possible misunderstanding of their position, simultaneously with Hirschmann's departure to Turkey the State Department informed Lord Halifax, Britain's Ambassador to the USA — and a member of the British War Cabinet whenever home on leave[24] — that the German proposal was unacceptable and that Hirschmann's trip to Turkey was "merely an expedient for gaining time".[25]

Shertok's promised meeting with Brand took place in Aleppo (Syria) on 11 June, the former questioning the latter for six hours. Apart from revealing Eichmann's proposals and the potential implications thereof, and discussing in detail the situation of Hungarian Jewry, Brand emphasised the following amalgam of fact, fiction and conjecture to Shertok: Jews deported from Hungary were being kept alive, thus far, for ransom purposes; the German prohibition on Jews entering Palestine was due to the Reich not wishing to alienate the Arabs; German belief that the intensity of Antisemitism in a country was determined by the percentage of Jews in that country's population meant that, according to the Reich's prevailing ideology, the emigration of a million European Jews would increase Jew-hatred elsewhere in the world, and hence fulfil another Nazi goal; as the inevitable Allied victory was becoming increasingly obvious, Germany was attempting to use the Jews to rehabilitate its image throughout the world and, simultaneously, undermine the Allies by increasing their Jewish populations; and refusal by the Allies to negotiate would be the death sentence for Hungarian Jews, as would his (Brand's) failure to return to Hungary.

On 12 June, the day after Shertok had interviewed Brand in Aleppo (in the presence of a British Army officer), Britain's Ambassador to Turkey, Sir Hugh Knatchbull-Hugessen, reported to the Foreign Office on his discussions with Laurence Steinhardt. The US Ambassador, stated Sir Hugh, had no intention of taking the proposal seriously, being of the opinion that Eichmann's scheme was impractical, absurd, and nothing other than a half-baked attempt at blackmail. However, in an addendum of the very next day, Sir Hugh reported that the US Ambassador, influenced by the US War Refugee Board, now believed that the door should be kept open on the German proposal in order to see what eventuated.[26] The British Cabinet, guided by: Churchill's sympathy for the Jewish plight; Eden's concern at the propaganda windfall to Germany of an unilateral British refusal to save Jews; the certain Arab hostility — and probable rebellion — at the possible massive influx of Jews into Palestine; and by Roosevelt's domestic political objective vis-à-vis the Jewish vote, decided to close ranks with the Americans and maintain a low profile for the moment, to see what may ensue.

To safeguard their position and credibility with Stalin, in mid-June the Western Allies informed the USSR of the German proposal, but without revealing all the details. In a swift, predictable response, on 18 June the USSR, in effect, vetoed any significant exploration process by stating that it was "neither expedient nor permissible" to negotiate with the German government on any aspect of Brand's revelations.[27] The Soviet reaction had its desired impact, particularly on the War Refugee Board (henceforth WRB), the organ of US government most intimately concerned with the plight of Hungarian Jews. On 21 June, John Pehle, the WRB's Executive Director, cabled Ambassadors Steinhardt (Turkey) and Harriman (USSR): "Please take no, repeat no, further action of any nature with respect to this [Brand] matter pending further instructions."[28] Thus ended Phase I of the "Blood for Trucks" saga. Although lasting a mere four weeks, as shall be seen, Phase I set the main parameters, and the primary perimeter, of Allied response to possible Jewish rescue via international negotiations.

To summarise: by mid-June, it is clear the Western Allies had the dilemma of attempting to reconcile what appeared to be two fundamentally incompatible objectives. Both the British and the Americans were faced with accommodating their apparently insurmountable reservations regarding the German proposal with their need to be seen taking meaningful action to save the remaining Hungarian Jews. Acting largely in unison, the West was thus hoping — and certainly gambling with a vast number of Jewish lives — that the strategy of appearing to consider the "Blood for Trucks" offer would be sufficient response to postpone deportations from Magyarorszag. The West's "game plan" to safeguard Hungarian Jews from Eichmann's clutches — a plan that was, in effect, to remain unchanged until the Red Army forced the *Wehrmacht* from Hungary — was up and running.

Thus, whilst the West was struggling to decipher the *SS'* real intentions, and to formulate an appropriate response acceptable to a diverse range of apparently irreconcilable interests — including the UK, USA, USSR, the Germans, the Arabs, and (in the very minor league) the Jewish Agency — the proposal's instigators were displaying signs of increasing irritation and frustration at the conspicuous absence of progress. This change in *SS* attitude was conveyed to the American Embassy in Turkey by Chaim Barlas of the Jewish Agency. Accordingly, on 22 June, US Ambassador Steinhardt notified Cordell Hull, US Secretary of State, of Barlas' information that the Gestapo was "very angry" at the lack of headway, as the Brand–Grosz mission was merely a precursor to future negotiations in Lisbon by Freiherr Kurt von Schroeder, a German banker with powerful *SS* associations. Barlas also stated, reported Steinhardt, that the deportation of Hungarian Jews was continuing unabated and that unless both emissaries returned immediately to Budapest "all efforts are useless".[29] Further pressure in this direction was applied to Cordell Hull the next day by Somerville Pinkney Tuck, US Envoy Extraordinary and Plenipotentiary to Egypt. Tuck cabled the US Secretary of State that both Shertok and Hirschmann, each now having interviewed Brand, believed the emissary "to be entirely trustworthy and reliable". Furthermore, concluded Tuck, "I believe it important that Brand should be allowed to return to Budapest. In accordance, I ask that it be recommended."[30]

After over a month of examination and consideration, in a memorandum of 26 June the British Foreign Minister, Anthony Eden, accepted that the "Blood for Trucks" proposal had originated from within the top Nazi echelon. Once again, Eden assessed the proposition as either a contemptuous attempt to split the Allies (particularly the USSR from the West) or, in the event of Allied rejection, a plot to engineer Allied complicity in the destruction of Hungarian Jews. Despite the offer being delivered by two inconsequential individuals, Eden concluded that a non-counterproductive response would be appropriate to ensure that the Allies could not be accused of indifference (at best), or collusion (at worst), with Germany's Final Solution programme. Consequently, on 1 July, the USA was advised by Eden that Britain would now permit Brand's return to Hungary so as to inform his contacts that the Allies would examine realistic propositions to aid Jews. Additionally, in this little-noted exchange Eden suggested that the following counterproposal be conveyed officially to Germany via the Swiss government, the power representing both UK and US interests in Hungary:

a) 1,500 Jewish children under German control to be given temporary refuge in Switzerland.
b) The German government to grant 5,000 Jewish children from South eastern Europe, plus an appropriate number of adult chaperons, exit visas to Palestine.
c) Germany to guarantee safe passage to the above transports.

    d) The release of Jews in German territory who had previously received valid visas to Palestine, transport arrangements for this group to be organised by the UK and USA.[31]

Transparently, Eden's counteroffer reduced the potential number of entrapped Jews to be saved from over one million to a tiny fraction of that number. Equally clearly:

    1. Both the UK and the USA realised that Germany's alliance with the Palestinian Arab leader, the ardent pro-Nazi Amin el-Husseini, almost certainly precluded Germany accepting point (b) above. Note that, as previously mentioned, Brand had specifically emphasised that Jewish migration to Palestine was prohibited.

    2. Eden's suggestion did not contain a *quid pro quo* reward for German acceptance.

    3. The large majority of Jews in category (d) above were no longer alive.

Whilst accepting the main thrust of the British Foreign Minister's proposition, particularly regarding Brand's return to Hungary, the Americans requested modification so as to avoid the impression that only an "unduly limited" number of Jews would be accepted under the scheme. As an alternative, the US proposed that "the UK and US governments would be willing, with due regard to military necessities, to consider measures for the reception of all Jews permitted to leave areas under the control of Germany..."[32]

Notwithstanding the appearance of considerably greater generosity to the Jewish plight, the US proposal was rendered well-nigh hypothetical by an insistence that "the matter must be cleared in advance with the Russians". It is inconceivable that the Americans had forgotten the USSR's insistence of 18 June that it was "neither expedient nor permissible" to negotiate with the German government on any aspect of Brand's revelations (see above). In marked contradistinction, Eden's telegram neither specified Soviet acquiescence as a mandatory requirement of his plan, nor did it refer even indirectly to consulting Stalin. On this basis it is reasonable to assume that, at this stage, Eden may well have considered that a response through the Swiss would overcome — technically at least — the USSR's prohibition, and his own aversion, to negotiations with Germany. Alternatively, with the recent fulfilment of Stalin's constant demand for a Second Front in Europe, the British Foreign Minister may have been prepared to risk the Russian dictator's wrath regarding his humanitarian initiative — a (relatively minor?) plan to, in effect, save 6,500 children under sentence of death.

As indicated by the above exchange, the difference between the two Western Allies at this stage appeared profound. Assuming for the moment some German flexibility of intent, the British proposals, whilst restricted to less than 10,000 souls, presented an initial tender that may have been the catalyst for progress towards some sort of negotiation; the US proposition, whilst potentially far greater in humanitarian scope, clearly depended on Stalin's approval, an endorsement that both sides of the Atlantic knew would not be forthcoming.

[To relate this international manoeuvring back to the Hungarian context, it will be recalled that Admiral Miklos Horthy was subjected to concerted international pressure during the last week of June 1944 to alleviate the desperate situation confronting Hungary's remaining Jews. As discussed in Chapter IV, leaders lodging appeals with the Regent included Pope Pius XII (25 June), President Roosevelt (26 June), and King Gustav V of Sweden (30 June). This international campaign was reinforced in early July via the exposure in Switzerland — by the Transylvanian Jewish businessman Georges Mantello, First Secretary of the El Salvador Consulate in Geneva — of what has come to be called the Auschwitz Protocols, a comprehensive, detailed report on the Death Camp's operations by two former inmates, Walter Rosenberg (later Rudolf Vrba) and Alfred Wetzler (later Josef Lanik), who successfully escaped from Auschwitz on 7 April 1944.[33]

[Reaching Slovakia on 21 April, the escapees' testimony was checked and typed by the Jewish Council and, after an unfortunate delay of some weeks, eventually distributed to the Jewish Agency in Istanbul, the Papal Nuncio in Bratislava (*Monsignor* Giuseppe Burzio), the Halutz representative in Geneva (Nathan Schwalb), and Kasztner in Budapest. Meanwhile, the Rosenberg–Wetzler Protocol had been confirmed (and updated regarding the Hungarian deportations) by another two Jewish prisoners, who had escaped from Auschwitz on 27 May.[34] Importantly, however, the Western leaders received irrefutable, extensive testimony regarding the *Endlösung* well before mid-1944. One of the most notable earlier eyewitness informants was Jan Karski, a Lieutenant in the Polish Army, who lived underground in Warsaw during 1941–42 and served as a courier between Warsaw and the London-based Polish Government-in-Exile. At the request of Jewish leaders in Poland, Karski travelled to America and, on 28 July 1943, personally gave Roosevelt a comprehensive exposition of German policy towards European Jewry. Tragically, as has been seen, the US president — in effect — remained unmoved. Karski's courage and efforts on behalf of entrapped European Jews came to naught.

[After Brand and Grosz arrived in Istanbul, increasing information emerged regarding the fate of Hungarian Jewry and the role of Auschwitz, sometimes relayed via the West's diplomatic missions in neutral countries. These included a report to London in which the British Minister in Berne (Switzerland), on 26 June, described the Auschwitz *modus operandi* and stated accurately that of Hungary's 800,000 Jews some 400,000 had already been deported to the Death Camp.[35] Subsequent independent confirmation was provided by, amongst others, the Czechoslovak and Polish Governments-in-Exile, the latter forwarding to the Foreign Office on 3 July accurate information based on reports received from the non-Communist Polish underground.[36] In the UK's public domain, important details of the Death Camp's operations were broadcast by the BBC on 18 June, and, on 27 June, the *Manchester Guardian* published a report, "Fate of Jews in Hungary. Massacre Begins", which stated that 100,000 Jews had been murdered at Oswiecim (Auschwitz) during May 1944.[37]]

Notwithstanding the relatively modest nature of Eden's rescue proposals to the Americans, on 1 July — the very day the proposals were referred to the USA — Herbert Morrison, the British Home Secretary (a Labour member), noted unequivocally: it is "essential that we should do nothing at all which involves the risk that the further reception of refugees here might be the ultimate outcome".[38] Chauvinism in general, and anti-Jewish sentiment in particular, were strong undercurrents in both the UK and the USA — and overtly rampant in the USSR — during this era, and continued thus well beyond the conclusion of hostilities.

A further blow to the prospect for negotiations occurred on 7 July, when the Americans informed the USSR of Eichmann's commitment not to utilise the trucks against the West. The US relayed this previously undisclosed information despite

British opposition, the UK realising that such news — which clearly indicated that the trucks would be used exclusively against the USSR — could only heighten Stalin's abiding suspicion regarding a possible anti-Soviet conspiracy between Germany and the West. Once again the difference between the UK and the USA had come to the fore: whilst having substantial reservations, at this stage the British were prepared to keep the door open and see what may eventuate, whilst the USA — probably motivated by the desire to share the future costly invasion of Japan (against whom the USSR had not yet declared war) — clearly desired not to risk Stalin's trust, confidence and co-operation.[39]

The USA's fear of upsetting Stalin was clearly confirmed the next day by Britain's Ambassador to Portugal. Subsequent to the arrival of 32 wealthy Hungarian Jews in Lisbon (see below), the Ambassador, Sir Ronald Campbell, notified London on 8 July that the US State Department was alarmed that this group's arrival constituted a German plot to plant suspicion of separate negotiations in Soviet minds. In marked contrast, on the same day, 8 July, Churchill minuted Eden regarding the situation confronting Hungarian Jews: "I am entirely in accord with making the biggest outcry possible."[40]

Because of its importance and urgency, the report on Grosz' debriefing was presented to the British War Cabinet's Refugee Committee on 13 July, immediately upon its receipt in London.[41] During interrogation, Grosz maintained that he was the main emissary, and that his was the main mission, with Brand's story merely a convenient facade to disguise the delegation's primary intention. The mission's real purpose, stated Grosz, was to arrange a meeting between senior *SS* and Western — preferably US — intelligence operatives in a neutral country in order to negotiate an armistice. Any top German security officer, except Himmler, would be made available for such discussions.[42] Notwithstanding Churchill's sympathy, on the basis of Grosz' revelations and the need to maintain Allied solidarity, the British resolved their attitude: the "Blood for Trucks" proposal was a thinly disguised attempt to split the Western Allies from the USSR via the institution of separate peace talks between high-ranking members of Germany's and the West's intelligence services. The results of this resolution were profound. Eden abandoned his vaguely inquisitive stance and condemned the proposal outright as an intrigue aimed at splitting the Grand Alliance, a devilish ruse hiding behind an apparently humanitarian facade. On a matter of such perceived importance, Churchill supported his Foreign Minister and banned negotiations via the Swiss or any other government.[43]

Consequent upon these decisions, for security reasons the British retained Brand in custody (until 5 October), thus preventing his early return to Budapest. However, in an attempt to extend some succour to Hungary's Jews, immediately upon the Refugee Committee's meeting of 13 July the British Foreign Office contacted Moscow. Noting that "the Germans are in no way desisting from their barbarous treatment of the Jews", the Soviet government was requested to issue an unambiguous and frank declaration that retribution for these horrendous crimes would enter Hungary with the Soviet army.[44] Stalin ignored the request.

Having thus abandoned its previous policy of what may be termed "cold comfort consideration" in favour of total rejection, the British faced the problem of preventing a German propaganda victory at the Allies' refusal to investigate even the possibility of rescuing Jews. As is common in the world of politics and diplomacy, consequent upon an important government decision the bureaucracy quickly prepared material justifying the new policy. And, as often practised in the frequently duplicitous arena of international relations, in all probability such material was reserved until an opportunity arose which would magnify the material's impact and reduce its negative connotations. For the British rejection of 13 July, that opportunity came very quickly.

It will be recalled that, after the consolidation of the Kallay government (see Chapter IV), the Hungarian Prime Minister began to manoeuvre cautiously towards extricating Hungary from the Axis alliance. Because of the Horthy coterie's Anglophile attitude, because the UK's politico-economic influence in Hungary before the War had far surpassed that of the US, and because Great Britain was considered the paramount diplomatic and strategic Western power in Central Europe, Kallay's policy favoured a rapprochement with the UK, the USA remaining the reserve option. Thus, having taken cognisance of Germany's "release" of 1,700 Hungarian Jews on the Kasztner Transport of 30 June, and having a vastly inflated notion of the power of "International Jewry", on 18 July Admiral Horthy offered to allow, according to Anglo-American interpretation, some 40–50,000 Jews to leave Budapest conditional upon the Western Allies making the necessary technical arrangements, that is providing transportation, provisions, finance, visas etc.[45]

Immediately on receipt of the Horthy Offer, some senior officials in the British Foreign Office, Home Office and Colonial Office became "panic-stricken" at the thought of a flood of Hungarian Jews clamouring for entry into Palestine, or possibly even England.[46] Jews liberated from Hungary could, surmised these bureaucrats, eventually arrive in Britain and Palestine either legally or illegally, thus generating intractable political problems, and unexpected but substantial financial expenditures, both at home and abroad. In short, as with the "Blood for Trucks" proposition, UK reservations to the Horthy Offer were based on Britain's abiding policy of strictly limiting Jewish entry into Palestine and the UK, on the fear that those rescued would not be accepted into neutral countries, on the obvious cost and logistic difficulties involved, and on the possibility of spies and saboteurs infiltrating the refugee transports.

Notwithstanding such serious misgivings, for Britain the Horthy Offer had substantial advantages over Eichmann's proposal. Most importantly, as the maximum number of Jews potentially involved was slashed from 1,000,000 to 50,000, the cost, organisational difficulties and possible military disruption to the West was slashed proportionately. Additionally, as Horthy's scheme did not appear to necessitate direct negotiations with Germany, it reduced both British and American reservations, and the chance of incurring Stalin's wrath. Furthermore: the source of the offer (Horthy) was clear and unmistakable; no *quid pro quo* was demanded, so there were no complications vis-à-vis either aiding or negotiating with the enemy; and a peace proposal, either overt or covert, was not involved. Finally, as Britain had already concluded a secret provisional armistice with Hungary in September 1943 (see Chapter IV), the Horthy Offer presented a potential opportunity to advance on that agreement, thus possibly reducing German capacity to continue waging war and possibly inhibiting Soviet influence in postwar Hungary. On this basis the British, having secretly jettisoned the Brand revelations, now undertook to examine the Horthy Offer.

Britain's perceived dilemma regarding the Regent's proposal was succinctly encapsulated by the Minister for the Colonies (1942–45), Oliver Stanley, the official most intimately involved with the question of refugee admission to Palestine. At the Cabinet's Refugee Committee meeting of 4 August, Stanley argued: "It is impossible to reject the proposal because this would gravely harm Britain in domestic and American opinion. To accept is also impossible, because its implementation would lead to civil war in Palestine..."[47] Yet notwithstanding this equivocation in Committee, Stanley proved himself an intractable opponent of liberalising Palestinian visa quotas, writing privately to Eden on 5 August — one day after the Committee meeting — of his uncertainty whether or not "this move of Horthy is not inspired or approved by Hitler as a plan to get rid of Jews and plant them on us or others...whatever happens we should not be manoeuvred into a position in Palestine which breaks faith with the Arabs..."[48] By his "breaking faith" remark, Stanley was referring to the White Paper quota of 1939, which restricted the admission to Palestine of 75,000 Jewish immigrants during the next five years, at a maximum rate of 15,000 arrivals per annum. As a counterproposal, the Colonial Office suggested that visas be issued to some 10,000 Jews, 85 percent being allocated to children and the rest to adults. Although Horthy's Offer was, for many weeks, at the forefront of topics discussed by the Cabinet Committee on Refugees, forces opposed to the scheme eventually prevailed.

After considerable contention, if not recrimination, within and between the Western Allies — in particular, Britain objecting to America "signing a blank cheque [regarding the absorption of refugees] which we could not honour" — on 17 August, a month after its formal announcement, the US and UK issued a joint response which, whilst presenting a humanitarian facade, in effect left the situation of Hungary's remaining Jews unchanged.[49] Shortly thereafter, the Roumanian *volte-face* of 23 August (see Chapter IV) made emigration via the Balkans well-nigh impossible.[50] After five weeks of fitful existence, military developments — and Allied apathy, intransigence and self-interest — had scuttled the Horthy Offer.

Consequent upon their decision of 13 July to align themselves with the US and USSR in rejecting the "Blood for Trucks" proposal, the British sought an opportunity to pre-empt a propaganda coup by Germany based on the Allied refusal to negotiate the fate of Jews remaining under Axis control. That opportunity came on 18 July with the news of Horthy's Offer. The opportunity was dramatically reinforced that same day when the Foreign Office learned of Horthy's 7 July decision to ban further deportations to Auschwitz, thus apparently lifting the death sentence on Hungary's remaining Jews. Without pause for reflection, on the same day, 18 July, the Foreign Office informed the State Department of Cabinet's decision of 13 July, thus confirming that both Western Allies were now in agreement that the Brand–Grosz mission was a "political warfare trap" to split the Grand Alliance. To further indicate their unequivocal total rejection, the British cable to Washington stated that, for security reasons, the "Gestapo agent" Brand now would be retained in custody.[51]

As the hoped-for final *coup de grâce* to Brand's revelations, the West's unanimous interpretation and policy was leaked to the news media. The following day, 19 July, the story was broken in the UK by the BBC, and in the US by the *New York Herald Tribune*.[52] As in these initial revelations, subsequent media reports in both countries castigated the Germans for their "monstrous attempt" to use Jews to blackmail the Allies. Significantly, these reports were noted with considerable interest in Berlin (see below). Thus ended Phase II of the "Blood for Trucks" proposal. Just as Phase I had lasted one month and was ended by the Soviet veto, with considerable symmetry Phase II also lasted one month and was ended by the Western veto. In contrast, as shall be seen, Phase III was to linger fitfully for some nine months, until Germany's unconditional surrender in May 1945.

The USSR

Until the unprovoked German invasion of the Soviet Union in June 1941 (Operation Barbarossa), the USSR had been a non-belligerent nation. Reeling in confusion from the ferocious attack, the unprepared Red Army initially suffered devastating defeats, with enormous losses of men, equipment and territory.[53] Yet despite the Soviet leaders being conversant with the treatment of Jews under Nazi control, and despite claims to the contrary by postwar apologists, no priority was allocated to evacuating the endangered Jewish population from the western regions of the USSR. On the contrary, some noted historians claim that there was intervention to prevent the evacuation of Jews from those areas under German threat. To exacerbate matters, due to political considerations arising from the infamous Nazi-Soviet Pact of August 1939, Soviet Jews had been kept in ignorance regarding the fate of their co-religionists in German territory until after the commencement of hostilities.[54] This, of course, prevented endangered Russian Jews placing appropriate priority on the need to flee the German advance. Even after June 1941, most Soviet media reports obfuscated the specific Jewish dimension of German atrocities by vague references to the Nazis' slaughter of peaceful, innocent people.

On the other hand, it should be noted that after the German-Soviet conquest of Poland in September 1939, some 350,000 Jews fled from western Poland into the Polish eastern region occupied, and then annexed, by the Soviet Union. This unrestricted mass migration continued until late October, when the German-USSR border was finally established and closed to free movement. From then on, Jewish and other refugees were refused entry into Soviet territory as a matter of policy. During the great deportations of 1940–41, some 400,000 "unreliable" Jews — including those refugees classified by the authorities as "politically suspect" — were arrested and exiled to labour camps in Siberia and Soviet Asia.[55] With great paradox, despite the death of many tens of thousands in the harsh camp system, it was transportations to Siberia and elsewhere that (inadvertently) saved the majority of deportees from being captured and murdered by the Germans.

According to Dov Levin, the percentage of Jews escaping capture was, in general, related to the length of time between the German attack and the retreat of Soviet forces. Lithuania, for example, was occupied by the *Wehrmacht* in three days and only about 15,000 (6 percent) of Lithuania's 250,000 Jews escaped into Russia. Yet in Estonia, which was occupied four weeks later, some 3,000 (65 percent) of Estonia's 4,500 Jews managed to flee the Germans.[56] Needless to say, time proved a vital factor in enabling Soviet authorities to overcome chaos and to integrate mass evacuation strategies into their scorched earth policy. Jews were included in such evacuations, but only as members of the local population. Importantly for any assessment of Soviet rescue policies, Jews were not allocated any priority in transportation to the east, even though Soviet leaders were aware that the notorious German *Einsatzgruppren* brigades had targeted Jews for liquidation, irrespective of age, gender or state of health.[57] Still, notwithstanding this lack of priority, Levin states that 70–90 percent of Jews in Central and Eastern Ukraine managed to escape German capture.[58]

Although there were token exceptions, Soviet partisans in German-held areas were either indifferent to the Jewish plight or, more often, systematically discriminated against Jews. As has been well documented, such prejudice frequently resulted in the guerrillas murdering Jewish refugees fleeing Nazi persecution. In analogous manner, several thousand Hungarian Jewish Labour Service conscripts captured by Soviet forces were treated harshly as enemy prisoners. This is despite JLS members wearing civilian clothing and the yellow armband, not being equipped with weapons, not having received military training, not being military personnel, and having been treated viciously by their German and Hungarian officers.

As a ruthless and brutal dictator, Stalin never permitted humanitarian issues to impede policy implementation. His attitude towards the great Ukrainian famine of 1932–33; his massive, unprecedented terroristic purges of the late 1930s; his policies of relentless industrialisation and totalitarian collectivisation; and the deportation to, and death of millions in, his notorious Gulags (slave labour camps), all indicate Stalin's total lack of concern for the human dimension. On a personal level, his treachery and hypocrisy knew few, if any, bounds. As one example: following the infamous Nazi-Soviet Pact of August 1939, on 31 December of that year at Brest Litovsk the USSR delivered to the Gestapo several hundred German and Austrian Communist activists who had found refuge previously in Soviet territory.

Neither was Stalin averse to exploiting the Antisemitism of Russians, Ukrainians, and other ethnic groups in the USSR, who, like Antisemites elsewhere, traditionally regarded Jews as aliens, traitors, defeatists, and the "economic exploiters of the toiling masses". After the consolidation of his dictatorship, Jewish religious, cultural and Zionist activities were repressed under Stalin's orders. Dissatisfied with the results, during his great purges of the late 1930s, Stalin initiated the liquidation of Jewish institutions, and prominent leaders, until only a vestige of former numbers remained. And despite the devastation of the Holocaust, from 1948 until his death in 1953, Stalin systematically destroyed all Jewish cultural institutions — and many Jewish intellectuals — which had either survived the 1930s or were established during the War.[59] Following this increasingly rabid phase of Soviet Antisemitism, it is generally considered that Stalin's death in March 1953 prevented an even greater disaster for Soviet Jews.

Yet notwithstanding his attitude, neither was Stalin backward in exploiting Jewish nationalism to further Soviet interests. After the German attack, he established the Jewish Anti-Fascist Committee to help the War effort and, in 1948, he supported the founding of Israel in an attempt to erode Britain's position in the Middle East. Consequently, despite his Antisemitism, Stalin had no difficulty in issuing several joint statements with Churchill and Roosevelt warning of severe retribution for Germany's barbaric policy towards the Jews.[60]

None of the above should be utilised to deny, or even minimise, the Red Army's crucial, heroic effort in emancipating — and thus ensuring the survival of — Hungarian Jewry's remaining remnants, the Jews of Budapest and the Jewish Labour Service conscripts. It must be recognised, however, that this emancipation did not result from specific Soviet policy but was a by-product of the Red Army's general advance into eastern and then central Europe. In short, Soviet policy during World War II, although based on numerous factors, was overwhelmingly determined by Stalin's perception of national self-interest. With great tragedy, the desire to rescue Jews as Jews was an insignificant element in the Soviet dictator's matrix of considerations.

The Germans: "Pragmatists" versus Ideologues?

Despite manifold difficulties in obtaining foreign entry visas, over 400,000 Jews (300,000 German and 120,000 Austrian) obtained permission from the Nazi state to emigrate from German territory before World War II. The earliest official stimulus to this exodus was the PALTREU agreement of August 1933, by which all Jews leaving the Reich for British-controlled Palestine deposited a percentage of their assets with Germany's PALTREU, the Palestine Trust and Transfer Company. Upon reaching Palestine, these immigrants received German goods and services to the value of their deposit. With the increasing virulence of German Antisemitism, and the consequent increase in Jewish desperation to emigrate, the percentage of Jewish capital permitted to leave Germany was reduced until, with the declaration of war by Britain, the PALTREU agreement was finally revoked.

In late 1938, Germany intensified attempts to extrude Jews from its territory. Dispatched to Vienna in August, Adolph Eichmann instituted the *Zentralstelle für Jüdische Auswanderung* (Central Bureau for Jewish Emigration) and was so successful in thrusting Jews from Austria that, in January 1939, the Bureau was moved to Berlin with Eichmann as director. Subsequently, *Zentralstelle* methods were also applied in Czechoslovakia. In precis, it is clear that for the period 1933–38 German policy was to stimulate Jewish emigration via heightened Antisemitism and the ever-increasing economic repression of its Jewish residents. For the period 1939–40, however, German Jewish policy changed to one of forced emigration, including deportation to Polish ghettos subsequent to the partition of Poland.[61] As previously discussed, the policy of exterminating Jews *en masse* began with Operation Barbarossa in June 1941.

Prior to adopting the *Endlösung*, it is clear that Hitler approved of the simultaneous persecution, exploitation and physical departure — that is, the brutalisation and financial expropriation before expatriation — as a means of removing Jews and their influence from Germany whilst benefiting the Reich's coffers. Quite simply, until early 1941 Jews were treated officially as a commodity to be exploited for the Reich's benefit.[62] Accordingly, not inconsiderable numbers of German, Austrian, Czech and (only a few) Polish Jews continued to leave German-controlled territory until well after the commencement of hostilities in 1939. Departures ebbed towards the end of 1940 until, consequent upon war with the Soviet Union, Jewish emigration was finally terminated in July 1941. As previously noted, the chief obstacle to this flow, even after the outbreak of war in September 1939, was the indifference and/or hostility of the world towards the very concept of accepting "alien Jewish refugees".

It will be recalled that, as discussed in Chapter IV, negotiations between Jewish leaders in Bratislava and *Haupsturmführer-SS* (Captain) Dieter Wisliceny began in mid-1942, shortly after the commencement of mass deportations from Slovakia. This attempt to rescue Jews from "resettlement in the east" resulted in the formulation of the Europa Plan, a scheme whereby the deportation of surviving European Jews would be halted upon the *SS* receiving payment of two million US dollars. These Europa negotiations, which lasted until August 1943, may have been a significant factor in deportations from Slovakia being halted in September 1942 for a period of almost two years. Yehuda Bauer surmises that Wisliceny's ultimate *SS* superior, *Reichsführer-SS* Himmler, approved the cessation due to the prospect of negotiations eventuating with the American Jewish Joint Distribution Committee (AJDC, the Joint).[63] Stating that there was an undeniable connection between payment of $50,000 to the *SS* by Jewish leaders in Bratislava and the stoppage of deportations from Slovakia, Bauer concludes that Himmler's primary aim "may in fact have been political... It seems obvious to me that the *SS* did not regard the $2 million dollars as anything but an opening gambit for something they really wanted."[64] Whilst controversial, this assessment appears to be supported by the final German demand in June 1943 — $2 million and direct talks with AJDC representatives. As will be evident from previous discussion, neither the Jewish Agency in Palestine — who believed the German offer to be serious — nor the AJDC were in a position to fulfil these conditions. Not only was $2 million not available to Jewish organisations but, even if such a sum could have been raised, the Allies' comprehensive — and strictly enforced — economic blockade would have prevented its transfer to Germany.

In February 1944, shortly before the German occupation of Hungary, Hitler dismissed Admiral Wilhelm Canaris as head of *Abwehr,* the foreign and counterintelligence department of the *Wehrmacht* High Command.[65] Transferring the *Abwehr* to Himmler's control — thus significantly enhancing the *Reichsführer-SS*' status in the Nazi pecking order — Himmler, in turn, merged his newly acquired asset with the *SD*, the intelligence branch of his *SS*, and appointed the "pragmatic" *SS* General Walter Schellenberg as director of the combined group. This was of particular significance to the Budapest *Va'ada* (Relief and Rescue Committee), as one of its leaders, Joel Brand, had developed close contacts with *Abwehr* operatives in Hungary.

On 14 March 1944 the Budapest branch of *Abwehr,* which thus far had managed to remain quasi-independent from the *SS*, informed Brand about the imminent German occupation of Hungary. Confirming his importance to its continuing viability, on 19 March Budapest *Abwehr* agents abducted Brand, together with documents in his possession, and spirited him to a safe house for several days. The abduction prevented Brand's immediate arrest[66] — by either Eichmann or his rival, the *SD* head in Budapest, *Obersturmbannführer* (Lieutenant-Colonel) Otto von Klages (sometimes Clages) — and thus pre-empted many awkward questions to both Brand and the *Abwehr.* It also maintained the latter's monopoly on contacts with international Jewry's representatives in both Budapest and Istanbul. Unfortunately for its cause, however, the *Abwehr* was unable to prevent Bandi Grosz from being arrested by the *SD*.[67]

With the invasion successfully accomplished, Himmler instituted a tri-polar strategy for Hungarian Jewry, each pole being supervised by a specialist *SS Obersturmbannführer* — Eichmann, responsible for deportations; Klages, responsible for initiating contacts with Western intelligence via Hungarian Jews; and Kurt Becher, responsible for the expropriation of Hungarian Jewish assets. In early May, the *SD* decided to eliminate competition from its *Abwehr* rival in Budapest, and charged the latter with corruption, smuggling and collaboration with international Jewry. It seems reasonable to accept Bandi Grosz' admission to the British in Cairo that it was he (probably under considerable duress whilst detained by the *SD*) who disclosed details of the *Abwehr*'s secret relationship with various Jewish individuals and groups.[68]

Note that in addition to his contacts with UK, US, Japanese, and Polish intelligence operatives in the Balkans (especially Istanbul), Grosz became associated with the *Abwehr* in January 1942, and with Hungarian military intelligence in September 1942.[69] As further indication of his worth and versatility, in October 1942 he became responsible for the *Va'ada*'s communications and clandestine operations with Istanbul, a position mainly concerned with the smuggling of cash and correspondence.[70] As a successful, experienced multiple agent and smuggler, one who made a total of eight trips to Istanbul, Grosz had undoubted survival skills, arguably most important of which was the instinct for reading the direction and force of the prevailing political wind. The *SD*, after receiving information about the Budapest *Va'ada* (in all likelihood from Grosz), then interrogated Brand on three separate occasions, *circa* 1, 4, and 10 May.[71]

According to Grosz' revelations in Cairo, it was Klages, in the presence of two *SD* subordinates, who ordered him in mid-May to contact US or Jewish agents in Istanbul and arrange a meeting — in effect, a peace preamble — in any neutral country, between two or three senior US (preferably) or British intelligence operatives and their German counterparts. When Grosz enquired why an unknown like himself, and not Franz von Papen (German Ambassador to Turkey) was entrusted with such a momentous task, Klages replied that the contacts sought were with intelligence officers and not diplomats. Klages, said Grosz, explained that Brand was a facade to disguise his (Grosz') own mission — the true purpose of the Istanbul initiative — from Himmler's bitter rival Ribbentrop and the German Foreign Office. If Brand was successful in obtaining goods, services or money for Germany, Ribbentrop's objections to Himmler's attempted Western strategy would be neutralised. Additionally, Klages also ordered Grosz to instruct the AJDC, and other international Jewish organisations, to commence a campaign in the Western press praising Germany's altered policy towards the Jews.[72]

Throughout his interrogation, Grosz maintained that, according to Klages, his (Grosz') orders had come directly from Himmler. This apparently brazen claim enhances Grosz' credibility, for impeccable German sources confirm Himmler's personal involvement from the beginning of the initiative. Immediately after news of the Istanbul mission was broadcast by the BBC, on 20 July the German Foreign Ministry informed their Plenipotentiary in Hungary, *SS* General Edmund Veesenmayer, that Ribbentrop desired to be informed about the facts of the Istanbul matter. On 22 July, Veesenmayer responded:

> I have been confidentially informed [by Himmler's representative, *SS* General Winkelmann, Higher *SS* and Police Leader in Hungary] of indications that the broadcast from London is accurate, and that there are two SS emissaries currently in Turkey. The matter has resulted from secret orders received from the Reichsführer-SS.
>
> Legation Counsellor Grell [Theodor Grell, expert on Jewish matters in Germany's Budapest legation] informed me today that he had heard that negotiations in Turkey were proceeding well, and that the Reuter [newspaper] report was apparently only being published in order to camouflage the matter from the Russians, but that, in fact, the Western powers were ready to agree to such a transaction.[73]

It should be noted that Grell's optimistic assessment regarding the progress of the Istanbul talks resulted from the calculated disinformation spread by leaders of the *Va'ada* in their desperate attempts to keep the mission from being aborted through the lack of a positive Western response.[74] Apart from Grell's optimism, Veesenmayer's cable is also problematic from several other points of view. Most importantly, the reference to Winkelmann's information clearly, though indirectly, implies that Veesenmayer disclaimed prior knowledge of the Istanbul initiative, and hence, in effect, distanced himself from Himmler's strategy. If true, this disclaimer reflects adversely upon Joel Brand's credibility, as Brand claimed, in Cairo in mid-June 1944, to have met Veesenmayer (accompanied by Winkelmann and Eichmann) before departing for Istanbul.[75] However, if Brand's claim about having met Veesenmayer is true, then the latter certainly knew the details of the former's mission. Thus, if Brand is correct, the logical conclusion is that Veesenmayer's response to Ribbentrop was a premeditated act of dissimulation.

Because of the reflection upon Brand's credibility, the question has to be asked: did Veesenmayer meet Brand? Although no definite conclusion can be reached with the information currently available, two pieces of circumstantial evidence give pause for consideration. Firstly, is it feasible that Veesenmayer remained in ignorance whilst his underling — the relatively humble Legation Counsellor Grell — and his *SS* subordinates Eichmann, Wisliceny and Klages, were informed of Himmler's strategy in considerable detail? The corollary of an ignorant Veesenmayer is that the petty criminal, smuggler and multiple agent Bandi Grosz' sources of information were superior to those of the German Plenipotentiary regarding strategic policy, and the formation thereof, at the top of the *SS* hierarchy. Whilst theoretically possible, neither of these hypotheses generates confidence.

Despite some troubling contradictions in Brand's testimonies,[76] on the balance of probability we may conclude that the two did in fact meet at least once, even though Veesenmayer later denied that any meeting took place.[77] One straightforward and compelling interpretation of the Plenipotentiary's probable feigned ignorance (of Himmler's Westward manoeuvring), was so as to distance himself from — and appear uninvolved with — a strategy known to be opposed by his nominal director, the German Foreign Minister, who (at that stage) still favoured an accord with the Soviet (see above). As is readily apparent, Veesenmayer had dual allegiances — as Plenipotentiary in Hungary, to Ribbentrop; and as an *SS* General, to Himmler. It seems reasonable to conclude that feigning ignorance may have been the most convenient — and least risky — solution to Veesenmayer's potentially stormy bureaucratic predicament.[78] At all events, up to this point the whole Istanbul episode was in accord with Himmler's usual *modus operandi*, which was to keep rivals in the Nazi hierarchy uninformed of his intentions. He succeeded to such an extent that Ribbentrop had to seek information on the initiative from one of Himmler's own *SS* generals, Edmund Veesenmayer.[79]

Notwithstanding the uncertainties outlined thus far, it is appropriate to draw some important conclusions at this stage. Firstly, Bandi Grosz told the truth in Cairo regarding Himmler's involvement in the Istanbul strategy. Postwar research confirms this conclusion as both logical and unavoidable. Equally, the fact that such a Top Secret was revealed to Grosz indicates his importance to Himmler's initiative. It is hardly conceivable that a nobody like Grosz — uncertain what the British did or did not know, completely at their mercy, but certain that they knew of his association with enemy intelligence — would have risked his credibility and freedom, if not his life (the British could have sent him back to Hungary), by inventing such an audacious claim to fame. Receiving orders, in effect, from one of Hitler's most powerful disciples does not require embellishment or magnification, and Grosz did neither.

This is not the solitary instance of hindsight proving that the much-maligned petty criminal Bandi Grosz did not necessarily lack credibility or integrity in a matter of great moment.[80] Joel Brand himself stated at the Eichmann Trial that it was Grosz who advised him that the *Va'ada* should switch from the *Abwehr* to Klages' *SD*. Being aware of the machinations within the German intelligence community, Grosz told Brand the truth: the *Abwehr* group had become powerless to assist the *Va'ada* in its attempts to save Hungarian Jewry.[81] As befitting a successful multiple agent, Grosz also, on occasion, knew when to remain discreet. As a notable example: although he delivered to the British the secret message of Lieutenant-Colonel Antal Merkly, of Hungarian intelligence, that elements in Hungary would defect to the Allies if the USSR did not enter Hungarian territory, Grosz refrained from revealing this confidence to the Germans. Neither did he disclose to the Germans that Merkly had instructed him to arrange a meeting in Istanbul between Hungarian intelligence officers and their British counterparts.[82]

Clearly, Ribbentrop was not Himmler's only rival in the Nazi hierarchy. It will be recalled that one of the primary motivations behind Germany's Occupation of Hungary was the economic exploitation and appropriation of Jewish assets for the Reich's benefit. The jewel in the crown of Hungary's manufacturing and commercial sector was the vast Weiss Manfred industrial complex, owned by the Baron Weiss, Baron Kornfeld, Chorin and Mauthner families. All of Jewish origin, by 1944 the four families — via conversions and marriages to non-Jews — included individuals who were classified as "Aryan" by Hungary's Antisemitic legislation.

With over 40,000 employees, Weiss Manfred was a huge, diversified, vertically integrated mining, heavy and light engineering, armaments (including aircraft) and banking conglomerate that bestrode the Hungarian economy.[83] To protect their interests against anti-Jewish legislation, the four families established the Weiss Manfred Trust, a holding company with 51 percent of its shares registered in the names of the families' "Aryan" members. By the commencement of hostilities, the Weiss Manfred conglomerate was thus classified as an "Aryan" entity and, as such, legally exempt from the numerous requirements of Hungary's anti-Jewish laws.

Even before the Occupation, Weiss Manfred's heavy involvement in the production of war *matériel* — including Messerschmidt fighter planes — attracted the acquisitive attention of various German interests. Included in this coterie was the most rapacious Nazi of all, the corpulent *Reichsmarschall* Hermann Göring, *bon vivant* and Commander-in-Chief of the *Luftwaffe* (Air Force), who wanted to incorporate Weiss Manfred into his own immense industrial fiefdom, the Hermann Göring Works. Neither Göring nor the Hungarian regime realised, however, that shortly after the Occupation, secret negotiations commenced between the four Weiss Manfred families and the *SS* for Himmler to gain control of Hungary's paramount military-industrial conglomerate.

Unfortunately for the Germans, maintenance of Hungary's internal sovereignty during the Occupation was not infrequently demanded by the Sztojay regime, particularly with regard to the ownership and distribution of seized Jewish assets. Notwithstanding this potential impediment, after several weeks of negotiations between Ferenc Chorin (representing shareholders) and Kurt Becher (representing Himmler), on 17 May 1944 the 51 percent "Aryan" holding in Weiss Manfred Trust was transferred to the *SS* for twenty-five years. As *quid quo pro*, in late June some forty individuals from the four families were flown to neutral territory by the Germans, with a portion of their personal valuables and an *SS* promise for $600,000 and 250,000 Reichmarks to be paid in several instalments.[84] Naturally, the grotesque troika of Göring, Ribbentrop and the Hungarian regime was incensed at Himmler's audacious aggrandisement — but all to no avail: Hitler had approved the deal.[85]

Regrettably for Himmler's Istanbul strategy, the arrival of the "Weiss Manfred Jews" in Lisbon on 25 June was viewed by the West as yet another instance of cynical Nazi self-interest, rather than an indication of the *Reichsführer-SS*' new *bona fides*. Concerned at the implications of this development, and its effect on Brand's stalled mission, Jewish leaders in Palestine formulated an "Interim Agreement" based on the Europa Plan, and dispatched it to Rezso Kasztner in Budapest. Kasztner, who had assumed leadership in negotiating with the Germans after Brand departed for Istanbul, received the Agreement on 7 July and promptly showed it to Kurt Becher. Because of Brand's detention by the British, the Istanbul and Budapest *Va'adas* had devised a strategy for negotiations to be held in Portugal between Becher, Kasztner, a US national (Dr Joseph Schwartz, European representative of the AJDC), and a British subject (Eliyahu Dobkin, member of the Jewish Agency's Executive in Palestine).[86]

The Jewish initiative was almost aborted in late July, when both US and UK governments prohibited their nationals from participating in talks with the enemy. In the USA, this recommendation originated from, and was promoted by, John W. Pehle, Executive Director of the United States War Refugee Board (henceforth WRB). On 27 July, Pehle, the bureaucrat primarily responsible for American efforts to rescue European Jews from destruction, wrote to Edward R. Stettinius, Deputy Secretary of State, thus: "I strongly urge that definitive instructions be sent which will effectively prevent any meeting between Schwartz and the German representative. I would also urge...that the British be informed of our decision."[87] On the same day, Stettinius confirmed in writing his acceptance of Pehle's recommendations. To overcome this obstacle, Roswell McClelland, WRB head in Switzerland, successfully proposed that a Swiss citizen, the conservative, taciturn and somewhat haughty Saly Mayer (retired lace manufacturer, and AJDC representative in Switzerland since 1940), be authorised to negotiate on behalf of the West's Jewish leadership. Mayer's task was made decidedly onerous, if not unattainable, by the WRB, the AJDC, and the US and Swiss governments (amongst others) imposing severe restrictions on his negotiating manoeuvrability. As examples: the US Secretary of State prohibited Mayer from negotiating in the name of any US organisation, including the AJDC; the Red Cross told Mayer that it would boycott any individual or group using illegal means to rescue Jews; and Heinrich Rothmund (Chief, Swiss Alien Police) vetoed any ransom proposal and claimed that entry visas would be restricted to Jews having relatives in Switzerland.[88] In effect, Mayer lacked the authority to either commit anything, or to accept anything, of substance. Essentially, his main prerogative was the double-edged freedom to extend and/or obfuscate the negotiations, in the hope of postponing deportations. Quite simply, along with Samu Stern in Budapest, Mayer was involved in a race against time.

In an attempt to advance the talks, provide Himmler with an opportunity to prove his *bona fides*, and to save some lives, Kasztner suggested to Becher that the 1,700 "Kasztner Transport Jews" — those who left Budapest by train on 30 June (see Chapter IV) and were now detained, under moderate conditions, in a special section of the Bergen Belsen concentration camp — be permitted to reach neutral territory. After flying to Berlin for consultations with Himmler, Becher returned to Budapest on 2 August and informed Kasztner that an initial group of about 500 "Kasztner Transport Jews" would soon leave Belsen for Switzerland, and, despite the Allies' negativity towards his Istanbul strategy, Himmler would still permit Jews to leave Europe upon delivery of appropriate merchandise.

To maximise the public relations impact, the first German-Jewish "Blood for Trucks" meeting was scheduled to coincide with the arrival in Switzerland of the initial Kasztner Transport group. Unfortunately for the Nazis' cherished theory of Jewish power and influence throughout the world, Saly Mayer could not obtain Swiss visas for Becher and his associates. Consequently, on 21 August near St Gallen, the Germans were subject to the indignity of being forced to negotiate with Mayer and Kasztner on the middle of a bridge linking Switzerland and Austria. After an exchange of previously enunciated views, Becher, who emphasised that he was negotiating as a personal representative of Himmler, suggested that Jews could leave Europe in the empty ships that had delivered the trucks to Germany. In accordance with his brief, Mayer's responses were, of necessity, non-committal. As expected considering the gap between the parties, the first round of talks ended inconclusively, although both sides agreed to resume discussions after receiving further instructions.

Notwithstanding the lack of progress, and despite Mayer clearly stating that he was negotiating exclusively on behalf of a Swiss charity (the largely nominal Swiss Support Fund for Refugees),[89] Becher's report of 23 August to Himmler contained reasons for German optimism. Although noting Mayer's pronouncement that the US government would never agree to providing 10,000 trucks, Becher stated that the arrival in Switzerland of a portion of the Kasztner Transport group had generated credibility for the Reich, and defused Jewish scepticism regarding the genuineness of the offer. As a substitute for the unobtainable trucks, Becher supported Mayer's (unauthorised) suggestion that the Germans request other urgently required *matériel* — chrome, nickel, ball bearings, machine tools, tungsten, aluminium etc — which could be obtained from neutral countries, as had occurred before the Allies' prevention of such trade. Importantly, Becher emphasised that recommencement of deportations would place his negotiations in considerable jeopardy.[90] In swift response, on 25 August Himmler banned all further deportations from Hungary[91], and, on 26 August, permitted negotiations to continue in the same vein.

Becher's optimism appeared to be justified when, on 1 September, Roswell McClelland (WRB head in Switzerland) informed Mayer that the WRB had assigned $2 million to assist the talks. This fund, however, could only be used with the WRB's prior approval and, as such, was unavailable for ransom purposes. Making the most of this equivocal development, at the second St Gallen meeting (3–5 September, which Becher did not attend), Mayer announced his willingness to place 5 million Swiss francs at the disposal of his Swiss charity, and to use his good offices to facilitate *SS* purchases of Swiss *matériel* in Switzerland. Although no issues were resolved at the second meeting, the German negotiators departed with the distinct feeling that progress had been made, and that international Jewry (and, by implication, their Western associates) genuinely intended to continue exploring Himmler's initiative. Needless to say, this was exactly the impression Mayer, and the Jewish leadership throughout the world, was attempting to create. Similarly, the third meeting (29 September) also appeared to give the Germans cause for optimism. Mayer stated his readiness to place funds in a Swiss bank for Germany's use in Switzerland, on three conditions: a halt to deportations from Slovakia (which had recommenced following the Slovak national uprising of 28 August); abandonment of plans to deport Budapest Jews; and the balance of the Kasztner Transport group to be freed.

Because of adverse developments for Jews in Slovakia (renewed deportations) and Hungary (Szalasi usurping Horthy, Eichmann's return to Budapest), another meeting — 4 November, held on Swiss territory at St Gallen with entry visas arranged by McClelland — commenced in a mood of considerable apprehension. Possibly sensing heightened scepticism regarding his *bona fides*, and/or possibly continuing his "carrot and stick" policy, Himmler authorised Becher to announce that the balance of the Kasztner Transport group would be released to Switzerland. The most enticing event for the Germans, however, occurred the next day in Zurich, when Himmler's delegate, Kurt Becher, finally met an official representative of the US government, Roswell McClelland, who was accompanied by Saly Mayer. At this discussion, Mayer showed Becher a recent cable from the US Secretary of State, Cordell Hull, which revealed that twenty million Swiss francs would be released for Mayer's purposes. Needless to say, the highly restrictive terms and conditions imposed on Mayer's use of these funds (most importantly, prohibition on ransom payments and the supply of goods) were kept secret from Becher. Despite this precaution, unfortunately for the Jewish strategy the Germans quickly discovered that Hull's promised funds were inaccessible. Another blow to the Jewish negotiators followed on 16 November, when the US State Department and the WRB jointly ordered that "no (repeat no) funds from any source" could be utilised to implement any negotiated proposal.[92] At one blow, Mayer had lost his prime — and possibly his sole — bargaining chip.

Being a skilled negotiator, Becher was doubtless suspicious of Mayer's by now apparent obfuscation and stalling tactics, yet — equally doubtless for his own postwar purposes — the devious, duplicitous, opportunistic Becher kept such suspicions from the *Reichsführer-SS*.[93] In a case of symmetry (or parallel evolution), Saly Mayer, like Kurt Becher but for vastly different reasons, also kept his overseers distanced from reality by keeping significant details of the negotiations from Roswell McClelland, WRB chief in Switzerland. Quite simply, Mayer substantially exceeded his authority by censoring his reports to ensure that only aspects largely within his official guidelines were revealed to McClelland. And so the subterfuge continued.

Following discussions with Himmler, on 26 November Becher announced that the *Reichsführer-SS* had halted the Final Solution and had ordered the decommissioning of the Auschwitz gas chambers. Due to the obvious lack of effective progress in the talks, doubtless the primary influence on Himmler's decision was the Red Army's proximity to the Death Camp, and the Germans' frantic efforts to destroy all evidence of the *Endlösung*. After further desultory discussions in Switzerland at the end of November, the arrival on Swiss territory of the remaining 1,400 Kasztner Transport Jews (7 December) — an arrival that Hitler did not attempt to prevent — was viewed as confirmation of Himmler's interest in continuing negotiations. On 13 December, the Director of European Operations for the AJDC, Dr Joseph Schwartz, in association with other Jewish leaders, convinced McClelland to recommend that the Joint be permitted to transfer $5 million, via the International Red Cross, to help support those Jews still trapped in the Nazi domain. When the State Department finally approved the recommendation on 7 January 1945, it emphasised that the previous conditions imposed on the use of funds continued to apply. Mayer was informed of these continuing restrictions after the Red Army had liberated Budapest. Thus concluded his transactions with Becher.

For the rest of the War, Kasztner chose to remain in Nazi-held territory in his continued attempts to rescue Jews, largely focusing on those still imprisoned in concentration camps.[94] Although liberation by the Red Army ended the importance of international negotiations to the surviving Jews in Budapest, it is revealing to briefly summarise the balance of Himmler's increasingly urgent quest to find negotiating partners in the West. One of his most important alternative routes was via Jean-Marie Musy, former Swiss President and Nazi sympathiser, whom Himmler had met in 1940. Meeting again on 3 November 1944, Musy claims Himmler stated that the 600,000 Jews still at his disposal could be released without Hitler's specific approval provided trucks and/or other suitable goods were received in exchange. Musy's claim is not unreasonable as, by these terms, Himmler basically restated the conditions put to Joel Brand back in May. The significant difference is that, on this occasion, Himmler raised the always sensitive question of Hitler's attitude towards a core issue (see below). The "Grosz Agenda" was inherent in the Himmler–Musy discussion by the *Reichsführer-SS'* undoubted realisation that a substantial release of Jews would, virtually by definition, lead to important political connections in the West. It will be recalled that the Grosz part of the Brand–Grosz equation was the search for Western contacts with whom to negotiate a separate peace.

Working at the instigation of, and in conjunction with, Orthodox Jewish aid organisations in Switzerland and America — primarily, the New York-based Union of Orthodox Rabbis' Emergency Rescue Committee — on 18 November Musy wrote to Himmler stating that 20 million Swiss francs was available for the release of Jews, and that these funds could be used to purchase Germany's desired *matériel*. Musy's chief contact in Switzerland, and his conduit to US Orthodoxy and their funds, was the Swiss Orthodox leader Issac Sternbuch, a pointed opponent of Mayer and the AJDC. In an exploratory request, on 6 January, Musy and Sternbuch asked McClelland to sanction the use of $1 million to obtain the release of all Jews remaining in Germany. Although opposing the request because of its vagueness, and because of Musy's pro-Nazi reputation,[95] McClelland still interpreted this development as an indication of Himmler's intense desire to connect with the West.[96] Shortly thereafter, in mid-January 1945, Sternbuch claimed that Musy could obtain the release of 300,000 Jews for $5 million, on the basis of 15,000 people being liberated monthly in exchange for payments of $250,000 per month.[97] Several days prior to this claim, Musy had again met Himmler, who informed the Swiss politician that, due to current negotiations, Jews under Nazi control had been re-allocated from heavy to ordinary labour, thus significantly reducing their mortality rate. In early February, two of Mrs Issac Sternbuch's brothers (Jakob and Joseph Rotenberg) were released through Himmler's intervention. Significantly, after Musy had once again travelled to Germany (21 January), on 7 February some 1,200 Jews from the Czech ghetto Theresienstadt arrived in Switzerland. There is little doubt that this release resulted directly from the Musy–Himmler negotiations.[98]

As stated by Musy, Himmler's requested *quid pro quo* for the Theresienstadt release was revealing indeed: acknowledgement in the Swiss and Western press of Germany's positive humanitarian gesture towards the Jews. Himmler's terms and conditions for the release of Jews had eroded substantially since Brand left Budapest in mid-May 1944. Explaining a significant component of Himmler's problem/quandary is his *Note* of 18 January: "Who is really the one with whom the American government actually maintains contact? Is it a rabbinical Jew or is it the Joint [AJDC]?"[99] Apart from his obvious ignorance of the US power structure, clearly the *Reichsführer-SS*, despite all evidence to the contrary, was still vastly overestimating Jewish authority and influence in the West. The Theresienstadt release, which received wide publicity in Switzerland, resulted in Hitler banning further such "gestures". Yet despite this major setback, Himmler maintained his efforts — particularly via Becher — to secure goods, money and negotiating partners via the utilisation/exploitation of Jews remaining within the Nazis' rapidly contracting domain.

Himmler's other major attempt to forge a link with the West was via the Swedes, this time involving seriously ill Scandinavians under German control being repatriated to either Sweden or their homeland. Circumventing the German Foreign Office and its now substantially diminished Minister, the Swedish government approached Himmler via the latter's personal masseur, the ubiquitous Felix Kersten.[100] As a consequence, in December, fifty Norwegians, fifty Danes and three Swedes were released to Sweden. In response, on 16 February 1945 Count Folke Bernadotte (1895–1948), Deputy Director of the Swedish Red Cross and a relative of Sweden's King Gustav V, arrived in Germany for discussions with both Himmler and Ribbentrop.[101] This arrival occurred a week after Sweden announced that it would receive all Jews remaining in concentration camps, especially those imprisoned in Theresienstadt and Bergen Belsen.[102]

In response to the Swedish initiative, and to Bernadotte's subsequent trip to Berlin, Himmler relocated Scandinavian detainees in Germany at the Neuengamme concentration camp near Hamburg, in preparation for their repatriation to Sweden. On 2 and 21 April, Bernadotte again met Himmler for talks. It seems, however, that Hitler had intervened regarding the Neuengamme release, as the Scandinavians in question had been transported to Denmark, their release to Sweden becoming contingent upon Denmark becoming a war zone. A few hours before his 21 April meeting with Bernadotte, Himmler met Norbert Masur — a Swedish citizen representing the World Jewish Congress — and promised to release 1,000 Jewish women.

In the tumult and confusion of the final weeks before Germany's capitulation — especially after Hitler had decided to remain in his Berlin bunker (22 April) — Himmler obviously felt less constrained regarding his freedom of action. As a result, Sweden was able to rescue about 20,000 people from Germany, of whom some 6,500 were Jews.[103] Notwithstanding Himmler's lengthy and varied attempts to find Western negotiating partners, in the end the *Reichsführer-SS*' solitary accord was with Felix Kersten, his private masseur! Signed secretly in early March 1945, and known derisively as the Himmler–Kersten Agreement, by this the *Reichsführer-SS* promised — "in the name of humanity" — not to destroy the concentration camps, to surrender them peacefully to the Allies, to cease killing Jews, and to permit Sweden to provide food parcels to individual Jews.

The final hectic, chaotic phase of the "Thousand Year Reich" saw a continuation of efforts by, amongst others, Kasztner, Becher, Schellenberg, and the International Red Cross, to alleviate conditions for both Jews and concentration camp inmates within German-held territory. In his last will and testament of 29 April 1945, Hitler expelled both Heinrich Himmler and Hermann Göring from the Nazi Party for traitorous conduct, namely for having done "immeasurable harm to the country and the whole nation by secret negotiations with the enemy, which they have conducted without my knowledge and against my wishes..."[104] On 8 May 1945, Germany capitulated; and on 23 May 1945, the ogre Himmler committed suicide.

International Jewish Leadership

Irrespective of their affiliation or location of operations, the leaders of international Jewish organisations engaged in mass rescue attempts were, as has been discussed, invariably trapped between the relentless German hammer and the monolithic Allied anvil. Yet despite this fearful realisation, and notwithstanding a clear appreciation of their powerlessness (apart from a modicum of moral authority with the West), international Jewish leaders continued their efforts to save Jews in occupied Europe. As has been seen above, and as will be elaborated below, most leaders of established multinational Jewish groups with close ties to UK or US government officials — the noted exception being the Swiss Saly Mayer of the AJDC — based their *modus operandi* on recognised procedures conducted via authorised channels. In contrast, the smaller, less institutionalised organisations with less of a governmental nexus — and hence with less to lose regarding recognition by, and access to, senior politicians and government bureaucrats — adopted positions that sometimes eschewed the Allies' legal rigidities. One of the foremost examples of the latter was the Swiss HIJEF (Society for the Aid of Refugees Abroad), agent for the US Orthodox Rabbinate's Emergency Rescue Committee, run by a Swiss Orthodox troika consisting of brothers Issac (Yitzhak) and Elias Sternbuch, and Issac's wife Rachel Sternbuch. The situation of international Jewish leaders thus closely paralleled the dichotomy in wartime Hungary, where leadership was split between the predominantly formal, legalistic attitude of the establishment Neolog directors on the one hand and, on the other hand, the flexible (semi-underground) policy of the Orthodox minority's *Va'ada*, and the end-justifies-the-means (underground) approach of the radical, anti-establishment Halutzim (Zionist youth).

The magnitude of the task confronting Jewish leaders campaigning for a pro-active Allied response to the extermination of Jews was clearly indicated by the Allies' attitude to the mass atrocities committed by Germany's *Einsatzgruppen* death squads in Russia. Despite full knowledge that Jews were being slaughtered *en masse* from July 1941, it was only on 17 December 1942 that the Allies made their first public declaration regarding (*postwar*) retribution for German atrocities. This war-time indifference was further confirmed by the outcome of the Bermuda Conference held in April 1943. Convened to discuss ways to aid the victims of Nazism — a euphemistic term for Jews — the Conference finally issued its nebulous report in mid-November 1943. The leader of the British delegation, Richard Law, then Parliamentary Undersecretary for Foreign Affairs, commented after the War that the Bermuda Conference "was a conflict of self-justification, a facade for inaction".[105] As at its predecessor, the Evian Conference of July 1938, the Allies had, once again, distanced themselves from the Jewish plight, being especially concerned about too close an identification with Jews and, at Bermuda, about the accusation of waging war on behalf of Jewish interests.

In an attempt to overcome such impediments, in late 1942 the Jewish Agency's Jerusalem Rescue Committee established the *Eretz*-Israel Delegation in Istanbul (henceforth IRD — Israel Rescue Delegation) as its official representative in Turkey.[106] Istanbul was selected by the Jewish Agency (henceforth JA) as the centre of its relief and rescue activities for several cogent reasons, including: its proximity to both Palestine and the Nazi domain; the benefits of Turkish neutrality; and the presence of delegations from the Allies, the Axis, the Neutrals, European Governments-in-Exile, the Vatican, and the International Red Cross. But due to the Turkish government's refusal to authorise the Delegation's activities, it was forced to operate illegally — and hence below maximum efficiency. However, because the Delegation's Director, Chaim Barlas, received recognition from the Turks (and the British) as the JA's official representative in Turkey, Barlas was able to provide the IRD with the semblance of legality.

The lack of general recognition forced all Barlas' colleagues, including Venya Pomerantz (Communications Director) and Menachem Bader (Treasurer), to adopt the guise of private businessmen. As such, not only were IRD members restricted in their activities — much of which were, of necessity, illegal — but they were continually apprehensive about the possibility of being arrested and/or expelled from Turkey. Notwithstanding these structural obstacles to efficient operations, Istanbul became one of the most important centres of the JA's relief and rescue activities, particularly with regard to Jewish immigration to Palestine. The flow of migrants — both legal (via the Palestine Office, *Aliya* Department) and illegal (via what became known as *Aliya Bet*) — was organised, for the balance of the War, by IRD representatives in Istanbul. Not unnaturally, the conflict served as an impetus for illegal immigration but hindered the organised flow of legal refugees.

The Delegation's attempts to assist occupied Diaspora communities were continually constrained by Allied indifference, Turkish hostility, lack of funds, and the belief that "the *Yishuv* and its leadership did not fully comprehend the gravity of the situation".[107] Needless to say, the heterogeneous ideologies represented on the IRD, plus the need to maintain absolute secrecy with respect to illegal activities — especially regarding contacts with secret agents, smugglers and couriers — sometimes generated considerable internal tension. This was exacerbated by disagreements amongst the IRD's constituent — and often competing — Zionist factions over the equitable distribution of both funds and Palestine visas. To eliminate the turbulence caused by these disputes, and hence increase the efficiency and effectiveness of operations, IRD members worked towards adopting a unified, non-factional approach to issues and activities.

Unfortunately, sometimes this attempted consensus in turn led to further conflict. With reference to Hungary, for example, Menachem Bader, IRD representative of the left-wing Zionist group *Hashomer Hatzair* — a movement characterised by intense party solidarity — became embroiled with the Hungarian leaders of that movement due to the latter's refusal to join a unified Hungarian Rescue Committee. *Hashomer Hatzair* in Hungary rejected co-operation because of their special agreement with Miklos (Moishe) Krausz, head of the Palestine Office in Budapest, who controlled the precious Palestine visas (*Aliya* certificates, see Chapter IV).[108] Exacerbating this problem were the almost inevitable conflicts between the JA and those Jewish organisations, particularly Orthodox groups, who claimed that Zionists were receiving preferential treatment in the allocation of Palestine visas and places on refugee boats. Another not infrequent cause of disunity was the split between the advocates and opponents of shipping to Palestine Jewish refugees lacking permits or Red Cross protection.

Yet despite substantial internal problems and external impediments, the IRD's achievements in Istanbul were not inconsequential. These included: maintenance of dependable two-way communications with Jewish communities in Nazi-controlled territory, especially (but not exclusively) Hungary, Roumania and Slovakia; the dissemination of reliable intelligence to the Allies, Neutrals, Governments-in-Exile, the Vatican, the International Red Cross, and the *Yishuv*, concerning developments affecting Jewish communities under Nazi control; and the dispatch of funds to these communities. Although a matter of controversy, Menachem Bader claimed that, during the War, the IRD transferred £1,500,000 (pounds sterling) to the occupied Diaspora, of which, he estimated, two-thirds came from the *Yishuv* and the balance from the AJDC. This figure is disputed by some authorities as being an exaggeration.[109] Also subject to controversy is the number of refugees rescued/transported through Istanbul. Although estimates range up to 20,000, the most realistic figure for the years 1943–44 appears to be 11,000, this number originating as follows: Bulgaria 1,618; Greece 969; Hungary 319; Poland 282; Roumania 4,488; Turkey 3,234.[110]

Notwithstanding its leading role in the actual relief and rescue of refugees, and in the gathering of authoritative secret intelligence, the IRD was excluded from top-level negotiations with the Allies, these being conducted primarily by the JA's top hierarchy and supplemented by the leaders of US-based international Jewish organisations. But being on the spot in Istanbul, a principal focus of intelligence operations by all parties, sometimes enabled the IRD to exercise significant authority, especially in cases of urgency or emergency. One particularly fateful instance of this prerogative occurred on 29 May 1944, when three of the IRD's leading figures (Barlas, Bader and Ehud Avriel) signed a Protocol with the recently arrived Joel Brand. By this compact, Brand was authorised to inform Eichmann of an in-principle agreement, by representatives of the Jewish Agency, to hold negotiations providing deportations ceased immediately and that permission was received to dispatch food, clothing and medical supplies to ghettos and camps. In return, the Germans were offered payment of $400 per person evacuated to Palestine, and $1 million per 10,000 persons evacuated to neutral territory.[111]

Shortly thereafter, on 11 June, after a long debriefing in Aleppo (Syria), Moshe Shertok, Director of the JA's Political Department, accepted Joel Brand's analysis that although the Germans were decidedly interested in receiving goods, their prime intentions were political. This claim was reinforced by Bandi Grosz' revelations concerning the political nature of his own mission. Consequently, Shertok informed the JA that Brand was a facade for Grosz, the latter's assignment constituting the real purpose of the Germans' Istanbul initiative. On this basis, Shertok stated, "we have to maintain that it is possible to save Jews and to postpone deportations without making a commitment".[112] Accordingly, in his subsequent meeting with

Sir Harold MacMichael, British High Commissioner in Palestine, Shertok stressed that it was of the utmost importance to arrange a meeting between German representatives and, on behalf of the Allies, either the Intergovernmental Committee for Refugees, the International Red Cross, or the US War Refugee Board (see below).[113]

In line with this attitude, at the end of June the JA formulated an "Interim Agreement" based on the Bratislava-developed Europa Plan (see Chapter IV), and dispatched it to Rezso Kasztner in Budapest, who then showed it to Kurt Becher (Himmler's confidant) in early July. Because of Britain's continuing detention of Brand, the Istanbul IRD and the Budapest *Va'ada* had, by this Agreement, devised a strategy for negotiations between Becher, Kasztner, a British subject (Eliyahu Dobkin, Co-Director of the JA's Immigration Department), and a US national (Dr Joseph Schwartz, European representative of the AJDC) to be held in Portugal. Dobkin, in Spain at the time, was informed by Kasztner via cable that the Germans were pressing for negotiations, and that the *SS* was prepared to send high-ranking agents to a place of Dobkin's choice so as to meet Jewish representatives, namely Kasztner, Dobkin and Schwartz. Kasztner's — and the Germans' — credibility was reinforced when *SS* operatives in Spain located Dobkin and informed him that not only were their superiors prepared to meet him but, to expedite negotiations, were also willing to provide a plane and fly him at short notice to Switzerland.[114]

In a co-ordinated pre-emptive strike aimed at this, and any future, unwelcome German initiatives, in late July the Western Allies, determined to maintain unfettered control over negotiations, prohibited their nationals from meeting German representatives. To mask their real intentions, and hence to lessen the negative public relations impact of this Western veto, it will be recalled that in August the US Secretary of State appointed Saly Mayer, AJDC representative in Switzerland, to negotiate with German representatives on behalf of international Jewish leaders. Thus, with considerable paradox, it was the West's veto of a German initiative to inaugurate German-Jewish negotiations that was the catalyst for the commencement of those very negotiations — albeit under the highly restrictive commission imposed on Saly Mayer (see above).

Brand's mission, his proposals, and the implications thereof, were discussed intensively by the JA from late May to 19 July when, as previously discussed, press leaks in the UK and US effectively terminated prospects for the mission's success. The anguish generated in Jewish leaders conversant with the facts was succinctly summarised on 20 July by Yitzhak Gruenbaum, Director of the JA's Labour Department, who declared: "What they [the West] did in publicizing these things is an unmatched villainy. They ignored the blood of our brethren altogether."[115] Yet despite this crucial blow to the possibility of mass rescue, the JA, a Jewish organisation under strict British control, considered it had no alternative but to maintain its British-imposed policy of avoiding direct contact with the Germans.

In marked contrast to the JA's generally compliant public attitude and restricted *modus operandi*, the New York-based Union of Orthodox Rabbis' Emergency Rescue Committee of USA and Canada (henceforth ORRC — Orthodox Rabbis' Rescue Committee) adopted an assertive approach towards the rescue of European Jews. On 17 May 1944 — two days after the commencement of mass deportations from Hungary, and the day Brand departed Budapest for Istanbul — the ORRC forwarded a wide-ranging set of pro-active rescue and relief proposals to John

Pehle, Executive Director of the War Refugee Board (WRB), and to Adolf A. Berle, US Assistant Secretary of State. Concerning the peril faced by Hungary's Jews, the ORRC stated bluntly to Berle: "The relief necessary, cannot be accomplished through individuals, organisations or agencies... Our government must, if success is to be achieved and rescue effected, react to this problem [of saving Hungarian Jews] and utilize measures which it would use in matters pertinent to our own national interest."[116] By this declaration, ORRC was clearly challenging Allied policy of not utilising military means to achieve civilian goals, the Allies maintaining that the most effective method of aiding the persecuted was to reserve the military exclusively for the War effort, thus ensuring the quickest possible collapse of the Reich. Typical of the obstacle confronting international Jewish rescue organisations was the response of John Pehle who, in a July 1944 Report, "What We Have Done With Respect to Hungary", informed Henry Morgenthau Jr, US Secretary of the Treasury:

> At this stage of the War, it did not seem proper [sic] to suggest to the War Department the diversion of military equipment or military personnel to non-military purposes. Furthermore, aerial and paratroop raids of this kind [on the death camps] must entail casualties on the part of the raiders and we did not feel justified in asking the War Department to undertake a measure which involved the sacrifice of American troops.[117]

In similar manner, the International Red Cross (IRC) also refused to assist Hungarian Jews *per se*, classifying them "civilian detainees", that is, a group embroiled in domestic politics and, as such, not war victims qualifying for its protection. This attitude was succinctly summarised by Leland Harrison (US Minister, Bern) who on 13 April 1944, three weeks after the German occupation of Hungary, informed the US Secretary of State that the IRC "has not considered sending to Hungary a special delegation with instructions to [protect Hungary's Jews] since under the present circumstances such a mission might be considered as unrelated to the [IRC] committee's traditional and conventional competence. The committee [will not intrude] into the domestic policy of any state..."[118]

Confronted with widespread indifference towards the plight of Jews under German control, the ORRC — established in 1939 to raise funds for *Yeshivot* (Jewish seminaries) and Polish Orthodox refugees in Lithuania — substantially expanded its operations after Germany's invasion of the USSR in June 1941. During 1943, it supplied aid worth $114,000, plus cash remittances totalling $49,000, to some 4,000 mainly Orthodox refugees, most of whom had obtained sanctuary in Siberia, Turkestan and other provinces of Asiatic Russia. Due to economic factors, this relief effort was directed mainly through the ORRC's representatives in Teheran and Palestine.[119] Additional ORRC donations during 1943 included: $91,000 to maintain 465 Rabbis and *Yeshiva* students in Shanghai; $13,000 to aid refugees in Palestine and elsewhere; and $55,000, of which $47,000 was directed through Switzerland, for rescuing people from Axis territory and protecting those still under Axis control. According to the ORRC's Budget Bulletin of June 1944, its rescue efforts within the Nazi domain during 1943 may have saved the lives of up to 1,000 people. From a total revenue of $373,000 in 1943, $325,000 was spent on rescue and relief efforts, and $42,000 on fundraising, promotion and administration.[120]

After considerable discussion at its Annual Conference in January 1944, the ORRC approved a 1944 budget forecast of $1,250,000 (up from $750,000 in 1943, a

67 percent increase), and decided to re-orientate its main activity from relief to rescue operations. Accordingly, the budget for general rescue work in Europe was expanded from the $55,000 spent in 1943 to a forecast minimum of $500,000 in 1944, a massive nine-fold increase. Of special significance regarding its planned future *modus operandi*, with this re-orientation the ORRC emphasised that "the objects of rescue were to be Jews of any kind [sic] and not merely [sic] Rabbis, scholars or leaders".[121] In keeping with this restructured emphasis, the numbers aided in the USSR during 1944 was to remain fixed at the 1943 total of 4,000 people. Somewhat surprisingly in view of its new policy, however, the amount extended to this group was to be increased from an actual $114,000 in 1943 to a forecast $414,000 in 1944, a budgeted rise of 363 percent, meaning a growth in per capita aid to Russia from $0.55 per week in 1943 to a budgeted $1.99 per week in 1944. In even more startling fashion, the 465 refugees ("mere" Rabbis and *Yeshiva* students) in Shanghai had their allocation increased from $91,000 in 1943 to a budgeted $180,000 in 1944, a per capita increase of 98 percent, from $3.76 per week to $7.44 per week respectively.

In a tentative financial statement contained in its June 1944 Budget Bulletin, the ORRC stated that, of $237,000 total expenditure for the period January–March 1944 inclusive, $121,000 (51 percent) had been remitted to Switzerland for rescue work in Europe.[122] Whilst discussing its rescue activities, the ORRC commented pointedly that "it pioneered new and untried, often dangerous, methods of rescue, expects to continue doing so to the the limit of its financial ability, and *is prepared to disregard any consideration other than the rescue of the maximum possible number of Jews"*.[123] (emphasis added) The portion of this claim in italics, whilst possibly containing elements of bravado and self-promotion, is certainly valid to the extent that by mid-1944 the ORRC, like its Hungarian counterpart (the *Va'ada Ezra ve'Hazalah*), had refused to be constrained by "legal niceties" and, as such, had adopted the use of unauthorised channels and methods in its rescue endeavours. Accordingly, in deliberate contravention of US regulations, on occasion the American-based and funded ORRC, amongst other things, illegally avoided dealing through Roswell McClelland (WRB representative in Switzerland), raised funds in the USA for (illegal) ransom purposes, and illegally used the diplomatic facilities of the Polish Government-in-Exile to facilitate its rescue efforts.[124] To emphasise this distinctiveness, and to distinguish its pro-active strategy from what it considered to be the timid, ineffective and legalistic attitudes of other Jewish rescue organisations, the ORRC — in a revealing public glimpse of the internecine conflict fracturing US Jewry — stated tersely in its Budget Bulletin of June 1944: "No co-operation in <u>rescue work</u> exists between the Vaad [ORRC] and the [A]JDC or the Jewish Labour Committee."[125] (emphasis in original)

Consequent upon the Sternbuch–Musy nexus with Himmler in late 1944, by mid-January 1945 the ORRC had, in accordance with its philosophy, transferred over $250,000 to the Sternbuchs in anticipation of pro-rata ransom payments to Germany. Indicating his general disapproval, Roswell McClelland, strongly suspecting both the ORRC and its Swiss representatives of unauthorised/illegal procedures, wrote to a correspondent in late December 1944: "Whereas I fully appreciate your desire to be of assistance to persons persecuted by the Nazis, I must confidentially advise you to handle any propositions coming from Frau Sternbuch with *extreme circumspection*."[126] (emphasis added)

In mid-January 1945 the ORRC, cognisant of the dangers involved in violating America's "Trading With the Enemy" legislation, officially revealed its rescue strategy to the US Assistant Secretary of State. According to a Memorandum by Florence Hodel, the WRB's Assistant Executive Director, by this revelation the ORRC considered itself "absolved" from illegalities, including those that deliberately kept its unilateral actions hidden from US authorities.[127] It is pertinent to note, however, that the Orthodox Rabbis' rescue organisation was not unique in favouring the (assumed) benefits of confidentiality. Thus, although the ORRC notified the WRB of the Sternbuch–Musy–Himmler negotiations on 25 November 1944, the US only informed the UK and USSR ten weeks later, on 10 February 1945 — that is, three days after 1,200 Jews released from the Czech ghetto of Theresienstadt arrived, with a fanfare of publicity, in Switzerland.[128] In similar vein, although the first meeting between Saly Mayer and *SS* representatives occurred on 21 August 1944, the US only revealed these negotiations to the UK and USSR on 21 October 1944.[129] One can reasonably assume that such intelligence was withheld from the UK and USSR because the USA believed that it obtained some advantage, or prevented some disadvantage to itself, by keeping the information secret.

In any assessment of Jewish rescue organisations, it must be realised that relatively small, relatively low-profile groups lacking developed connections with senior government officials — such as the ORRC — had (as in Hungary) relatively little to lose by the secret use of unauthorised/illegal channels and methods. In marked contrast, the JA, AJDC, the World Jewish Congress (WJC) and other relatively large, well-established, high-profile organisations, because of their potential for substantially greater losses of official access, intelligence, government support, public sympathy etc, refrained from either alienating government officials or transgressing national policies. This apparent need for circumspection by "establishment" Jewish organisations was heightened in January 1944 when Roosevelt — motivated by his Treasury Secretary (Henry Morgenthau Jr), and largely for domestic political reasons — established the War Refugee Board, an organisation that, despite its name, focused on the issue of Jews in occupied Europe.

Of special note, the WRB was empowered — at least in theory — to engage in any endeavour promoting the relief and rescue of Jews trapped within Nazi territory.[130] This considerable freedom of action was enhanced, again in theory, via the assistance of US consulates and delegations overseas, and by the Board including very senior representatives of the State, War and Treasury Departments. Thus, despite the USA's stringent wartime blockade and boycott of the Axis, the WRB had a theoretically powerful special mandate — personally authorised by President Roosevelt — both to assist and rescue Jews under Nazi control. This mandate, which was in significant contravention of US anti-Axis legislation, included powers to negotiate with the enemy, to transfer funds into German-held territory, and to obtain priority for the shipping of refugees.[131]

Yet despite its powers and specific commission, throughout the War the WRB's attitudes and operations were largely subordinated to the US government's underlying indifference to the fate of European Jews. Typical of the WRB's disposition is an undated Memo regarding the saving of Hungarian Jews — composed after the German occupation of Hungary, and probably *circa* April–May 1944 — which declared: "Hungarian Jews may, however, be saved with the active co-operation of Hungarian civil servants, soldiers, police staff and peasants. They must be spurred on to active co-operation with the Jews and passive resistance against the Gestapo."[132] In the WRB's estimation, this co-operation was to be achieved by a publicity campaign conducted via Voice of America radio broadcasts to Hungary. Also included in the Board's Memo was the recommendation that "American propaganda" [sic] give full credit to the achievements of Hungary's anti-German "resistance" prior to the Occupation of 19 March 1944.[133] With the mass of information on the *Endlösung* available to US authorities by mid-1944, the WRB's attitude can, at best, be characterised as tragically naive. Nowhere in Nazi Europe, even in those occupied countries with an active, well-organised anti-Nazi resistance — a factor certainly absent in Hungary — did the WRB's recommended strategy prevent either collaboration or deportations.[134] Clearly, the WRB's Memorandum reflected abiding US policy of refusing to save Jews by either providing temporary shelter in America or utilising military means to disrupt deportations.

This policy was endorsed by Henry Stimson, US Secretary of War, in all probability shortly before the above (undated) Memorandum was composed. On 9 March 1944, ten days before the German occupation of Hungary, the Director of the WRB (John Pehle) discussed with Stimson the possibility of rescuing Jews by the establishment of transient (temporary) refugee camps in the USA. According to official documentation by Pehle, the powerful Secretary of War declared that:

> America should not accept further [Jewish] immigration after the War and stated that if we set up refuge camps in the United States to which large numbers of people were admitted there would be strong pressure brought on Congress, particularly by Jewish organisations, to change the immigration laws to allow such persons to enter the United States.[135]

After mentioning the possible difficulties in shipping refugees to the US, Stimson, not surprisingly, did not oppose the establishment of transient camps in Palestine.[136] On 31 March, a mere twelve days after the German occupation of Hungary, Stimson in a *Note* to Pehle reinforced his opposition to transient refugee camps for Jews in the USA, this time by pronouncing that US immigration laws prohibited altering the relative proportions of "racial stocks" then existing in the country.[137] By this unabashed declaration, the Secretary of War was aligning himself with attitudes then widespread amongst the chauvinist-isolationist segment of American society, a politically influential element harbouring Antisemitic views and strongly opposing the liberalisation of strict US immigration quotas.

Clearly, Stimsonite attitudes heavily influenced the WRB's Memorandum on the saving of Hungary's Jews, the Board's recommendations failing to even mention the concept of transient refugee camps or the use of military measures to disrupt Nazi deportations. Equally clearly, the words of President Roosevelt whilst inaugurating the WRB on 22 January 1944 — "it is policy of this government to take all measures within its power to rescue the victims of enemy oppression who are in imminent danger of death...to effectuate with all possible speed the rescue and relief of...victims of enemy oppression..." — were rapidly proving themselves a sham.[138]

Long conversant with Allied indifference and dissimulation, the sudden, unexpected Brand–Grosz mission left many, if not most, international Jewish leaders well-nigh dumbstruck. Instead of recognising it as probably the last opportunity for the USA, the WRB and the UK to regain some credibility by saving Hungarian Jewry from its inevitable fate under the Germans, the initial response of international Jewish leaders was generally hesitant, equivocal and far from decisive. Not untypical was the reaction of David Ben Gurion and Moshe Shertok of the Jewish Agency — in effect, respectively the *de facto* Prime Minister and Foreign Minister of the *Yishuv* — who, at the end of May in Jerusalem, met Sir Harold MacMichael, British High Commissioner in Palestine, to discuss the Brand Mission and its implications. When asked by MacMichael whether the Jewish Agency required any action from Britain other than communicating the facts of the matter to two international Jewish leaders, Chaim Weizmann and Nahum Goldmann, Ben Gurion and Shertok replied in the negative.[139] In similar vein, when Anthony Eden disclosed Brand's revelations to Dr Weizmann in London on 5 June, Weizmann's initial reaction was to label the episode a Nazi plot to embarrass the Allies. However, at a subsequent meeting with Eden the very next day — a clear indication of Weizmann's ready access to the topmost strata of the UK's political hierarchy — Weizmann obtained a promise from Eden that Britain would keep the door open on the German offer to see what may eventuate.[140]

Receiving Brand's revelations at the end of May, it took the JA over a month — during which period more than 350,000 Hungarian Jews were deported to Auschwitz — to present the Allies with an integrated set of recommendations for action on Himmler's proposal. This occurred on 30 June, at a meeting in London with George Hall of the Foreign Office, when Weizmann and Shertok proposed that the Germans be informed, via the Swiss, that the Allies were prepared to discuss the principle of rescuing Jews. As such, recommended the Jewish leaders, the WRB — whom, the JA realised, possessed authority to negotiate with the enemy — should meet German representatives, but only on condition that deportations from Hungary ceased forthwith. Additionally, the JA leaders also proposed that the Final Solution be disrupted by air force bombardment of the extermination facilities at Auschwitz, and that Hungarian railway workers be warned by radio broadcasts not to transport Jews to death camps.[141]

It should be noted that the concept of bombing Auschwitz, and the railways leading thereto, was largely — though not exclusively — related to the saving of Hungarian Jewry. The idea appears to have originated in mid-May 1944, being proposed by a Slovakian Jewish leader virtually unknown in the West, the ultra-Orthodox Rabbi Michael Weissmandl of Bratislava (see Chapter IV). In early June, Weissmandl's proposal was transmitted to the USA by two apparently unconnected sources, Yitzhak Gruenbaum of the JA and Issac Sternbuch, Swiss representative of the ORRC.[142] The scheme quickly gathered support from some international Jewish leaders, and was subsequently powerfully supplemented by Churchill in a Memo to his Foreign Minister. Having read a report on the extermination operations at Auschwitz, on 29 June the PM wrote to Eden in distress: "What can be done? What can be said?" Shortly thereafter, Eden, influenced by Churchill's interest and involvement in the issue, suggested that as they both supported the bombing proposal, the scheme should be investigated. Churchill replied on 7 July: "You and I are in entire agreement. Get anything out of the Air Force you can and invoke me if necessary. Certainly appeal to Stalin."[143] Unfortunately for those imprisoned in Auschwitz, the British Air Ministry responded to Eden's prompt Memo by claiming that bombing the death camp was technically untenable. The Foreign Minister, in some dudgeon, summarised the RAF's response as "characteristically unhelpful".[144]

The British air force response was entirely in accord with prevailing American attitudes. Shortly before the Churchill–Eden exchange of early July, on 24 June the Director of the WRB, John Pehle, raised the bombing issue with John J. McCloy, Assistant Secretary of War. After expressing doubts as to the worth and efficacy of such a scheme, Pehle emphasised to McCloy that the WRB was only investigating the proposal and not requesting action. A mere two days later, the Operations Division of the War Department General Staff replied that the proposal was "impractical [because] it could be executed only by diversion of considerable air support essential to the success of our forces now engaged in decisive operations". Clearly, for the Department, the saving of Jews condemned to death was neither essential nor worth consideration. For good measure, and to reinforce existing US policy, the War Department added that "the most effective relief to victims of enemy persecution is the early defeat of the Axis, an undertaking to which we must devote every resource at our disposal".[145] Note, however, that the Department never claimed that the USAF could not accomplish such a mission *if so directed.*

Without presenting a detailed analysis of the military and operational technicalities involved in bombing the death camps, it is pertinent to note that by April 1944 the Allies had defeated the *Luftwaffe* and, in effect, gained mastery over the skies of Europe.[146] As stated by US Air Force historians, after this date US bombers attacked enemy targets without being deterred by probable losses.[147] Furthermore, from early May 1944 — that is, before the commencement of mass deportations from Hungary to Auschwitz — the US Fifteenth Air Force based in Italy had the range and capacity to bomb the Auschwitz area. For example, on 7 July 452 Italian-based US bombers flew along railway lines leading to Auschwitz and attacked the huge synthetic oil refineries and rubber installations associated with the death camp. This operation was in keeping with the advice of General Ira Eaker, commander of Allied air forces in Italy, who, on 8 May, informed US Air Force headquarters in England that such bombing attacks were feasible.[148] In precis, during the period July–November 1944, over 2,800 Allied bombers attacked the synthetic oil and rubber installations, and other selected targets, within the vicinity of Auschwitz.[149]

The effectiveness of German opposition to air attacks in this region is indicated by the morning raid of 20 August, when 127 US Flying Fortresses, accompanied by 100 Mustang fighters, successfully dropped 1,336 500-pound high explosive bombs on the factory areas of Auschwitz, less than eight kilometres (five miles) from the gas chambers. Only one plane, a bomber, was lost in the operation. Yet despite the WRB's commission/obligation to investigate all life-saving options for Jews trapped in Axis territory, and although the air raids on Auschwitz were reported in the US press, it appears the Board did not monitor such operations.[150]

After examining the issue of whether or not aerial bombardment could have been sufficiently precise to eliminate the extermination facilities at Auschwitz–Birkenau, two authorities, David S. Wyman and Stuart G. Erdheim, both conclude in the emphatic affirmative.[151] In cogent analyses, both scholars establish that the long-range, highly accurate USAF Lightning P38 dive bomber, the aircraft responsible for destroying the heavily defended oil refineries at Ploesti in Roumania, could have wrecked the sparsely shielded gas chambers and crematoria in Auschwitz with only limited collateral damage (prisoner casualties). The RAF's fast fighter-bomber, the Mosquito, could also have accomplished the operation. With usual contra-distinction, however, there are a few who support the Allies' no-bombing policy, two of the most prominent being James H. Kitchens III and Richard Levy, the latter claiming that "it was beyond the power of any force the Allies could possibly bring to bear to interrupt the Hungarian railways by bombing".[152] Yet when asked at the US Holocaust Memorial Museum in Washington about the possibility of destroy-ing Auschwitz' extermination facilities from the air, Levy unhesitatingly replied: "They [the Allies] could have plastered it [Auschwitz]."[153] There was, in fact, no need to "plaster" (carpet bomb) Auschwitz-Birkenau, as aerial photographs required by the Allies to avoid prisoner barracks were available from 31 May 1944.[154] Conclusive support for the technical feasibility of bombing was provided by Sir Arthur Harris, Chief of the RAF's Bomber Command, who, in a postwar statement, confirmed that similar objectives to Auschwitz had been bombed "with pinpoint accuracy and great success", notably the Amiens prison in France.[155]

The conclusion that bombing Auschwitz was a feasible option to save Jews imprisoned therein should be considered in association with the fact that, as previously mentioned, mass murder in Auschwitz continued until Himmler's order closed the gas chambers in late November 1944. It is important to note that the machinery of death, the gas chambers and crematoria, originally took eight months to install in Auschwitz–Birkenau. Furthermore, this installation occurred at a time of considerably greater availability of materials, transportation and skilled labour. Demolition of these lightly defended "facilities" in mid-1944 would have rendered the machinery of death useless for either many months or, more probably, for the rest of the War.[156] Circumstantial German confirmation is provided by Rudolph Höss, commandant of Auschwitz, who, in postwar testimony, stated that several priority projects were not built at the camp in 1944 due to a shortage of materials.[157]

Needless to say, the technical feasibility of bombing Auschwitz only became clear to civilians with the relatively recent release of previously secret World War II military archives. Being deprived of concrete information, Jewish leaders and their organisations during the War were, not surprisingly, disunited on the wisdom of military action. One of the most important instances of an internal split was the convoluted polarisation within the Jewish Agency. At a meeting of the JA executive in Jerusalem on 11 June 1944, during the height of the Hungarian deportations, the only member to support bombing was Yitzhak Gruenbaum, Director of the JA's Labour Department (1935–48), and Head of its Rescue Committee (1939–45). According to Ben Gurion's non-emotive precis of the meeting: "The view of the Board is that we should not ask the Allies to bomb places where there are Jews." However, by Gruenbaum's passionate, bitter account

> I was forced to consult with the [JA] colleagues and they all expressed their opinion that we should not request a thing like that because Jews might get killed in the death camps! I explained to them that in such places all the Jews are about to be killed. They didn't listen to me. They do not want to take such a responsibility upon themselves. They prefer not to prevent mass murder for fear that Jews will be killed by bombs.[158]

Yet, in a dramatic *volte-face* some three weeks later, the JA's most senior executives in London, Weizmann and Shertok, proposed to the Foreign Office

(30 June) and the Foreign Minister (6 July) that the extermination facilities at Auschwitz be destroyed by Allied bombing.[159]

Another high-profile international Jewish organisation with a similar dichotomy was the World Jewish Congress (WJC). Leon Kubowitzki, Head of the WJC's Rescue Bureau, had two objections to aerial bombardment, namely, the risk to Jewish prisoners and the propaganda coup to Germany if it should eventuate that Jews were killed by the Allies. As an alternative to bombing, on 28 June Kubowitzki proposed to the WRB that either Soviet paratroops and/or Polish guerillas launch a concerted ground attack to destroy the death facilities. Kubowitzki's appeal was not even referred to the US War Department. As explained by John Pehle to Treasury Secretary Morgenthau two months later, the WRB did not feel justified in requesting an operation that would result in the "sacrifice" of Allied troops. Regarding Kubowitzki's proposed Polish action, Pehle stated:

> In view of the apparently [sic] deep-rooted anti-Semitism on the part of a large segment of the Polish Government and underground movement, it seemed most unlikely that the Poles would, in good faith, undertake to attack the death centers effectively unless strong political pressure involving political support were asserted.[160]

One can reasonably conclude that the WRB Director felt secure in the knowledge that appropriate political support for Jews imprisoned in Auschwitz would not be forthcoming from the Allies.

Notwithstanding Kubowitzski's disavowal of bombing on 28 June, six weeks later, on 9 August, the WJC appealed to the WRB to bomb the death facilities in Auschwitz and the railways servicing the camp.[161] Replying on 14 August, the US Assistant Secretary of War, John McCloy, rejected the appeal. Apart from the usual objections noted above, McCloy added a new assertion: "...such an effort, even if practicable, might provoke even more vindictive action [sic] by the Germans."[162] With the mass of detailed information about Auschwitz available to the Allies by mid-August 1944, one is left wondering what more vindictive action the US Assistant Secretary of War could possibly have had in mind. Although subsequent attempts to change US policy were equally unsuccessful, in an endeavour to pre-empt further appeals the War Department, on 4 October, responded to another request for bombing with the riposte that such action was the "operational responsibility" of the USSR.[163] Only on the afternoon of 27 January 1945, with the Red Army's occupation of Auschwitz, was the issue finally laid to rest.

Needless to say, significant divisions amongst international Jewish leaders and their organisations on the critical bombing question helped the Allies maintain their hands-off policy towards Auschwitz. In general, Jewish unity was lacking on many issues, not only in North America but also throughout the Western Diaspora. This disunity became so obvious that in 1944 non-Jewish multinational institutions — including the Red Cross — were making jokes about the "disorder and disorganisa-tion" evident in the activities of various Jewish organisations.[164]

One of the most controversial and disruptive intracommunal disputes that em-broiled American Jewry resulted from the activities of a small, radical, high-profile activist group of right-wing Jewish nationalists led by a Palestinian, Peter Bergson (born Hillel Kook, Lithuania 1915). Matters came to a head on 18 May 1944 (three days after the commencement of mass deportations from Hungary to Auschwitz), when Bergson and his seven-member executive — all professed Palestinian or stateless Jews — announced at their Washington "Embassy" the formation of the Hebrew Committee of National Liberation (henceforth HCNL, sometimes called the Bergsonites). Apart from insisting that Palestine be opened immediately to all Jewish refugees, the HCNL sought recognition by the United Nations and demanded that a Hebrew army be permitted to fight against the Axis. As a declaration of the group's general philosophy, Bergson stated at a press conference attended by about twenty reporters that "we speak as Hebrews in exile and not as Americans of the Jewish faith".[165]

Indicating the intensity of opposition, even before the press conference concluded the American Zionist Emergency Council berated the HCNL as the attempt of "a handful of young men to perpetuate a colossal hoax upon the American people...a half dozen adventurers from Palestine with no standing, no credentials, no mandate from anyone unless from the Irgun Zevai Leumi in Palestine, an insignificantly small, pistol-packing group of extremists..."[166] Other established American Jewish organisations were also quick to join the fray, with the Zionist Organisation of America, Dr Nahum Goldmann (representing the Jewish Agency for Palestine, and the American World Zionist Organisation in Washington), Hadassah (the 125,000-member Women's Zionist Organisation of America), and the American Jewish Conference being equally derogatory.[167]

Throughout the Bergsonites' existence, many established US Jewish organisations, especially the American Zionist Emergency Council, spent considerable time and energy attacking the group and attempting to demolish its ideology, influence and credibility. These organisations, although sharing common goals with the HCNL, viewed Bergson's group as a disruptive, undisciplined and dangerous competitor for funds, members and authority, and, as such, one that had to be nullified. Accordingly, American Zionists, the American Jewish Committee, and — not surprisingly — the British Embassy urged the US State and Justice Departments to neutralise Bergson by conscripting him into the armed forces. Intervention by his supporters in Congress, however, ensured that Bergson was neither conscripted nor deported.[168]

Acrimony between the HCNL and their opponents intensified when Bergson submitted resolutions to the US Congress urging the development in Palestine of temporary emergency camps to shelter Hungarian Jewish refugees. Although securing important supporters in both Houses when the resolutions were introduced on 24 August, the HCNL's campaign disintegrated due to the unremitting hostility of both established American Jewry (especially the Zionists) and the State Department.[169] The anti-Bergsonites, despite acknowledging the desperate need to secure a transient haven for Jews fleeing Nazi persecution, attacked the resolutions as compromising Jewish rights to settle permanently in their ancient homeland. Indicative of this opposition was the American Zionist Emergency Council's identical letters of 8 September to Senator Robert A. Taft and Congressman Hugh Scott Jr, sponsors of the Bergson-initiated congressional resolution. Written by Abba Hillel Silver and Stephen Wise, the letters expressed the view that:

> What is necessary is not the creation of temporary refugee camps in Palestine for Jews in Hungary, but the opening of Palestine to Jewish refugees wherever they may be... [The resolutions] are premised on the condition that Jews shall be brought to Palestine for temporary internment in refugee camps, but subject to ultimate removal elsewhere.[170]

The letter concluded with a vitriolic personal attack on Bergson, calling him a self-appointed spokesman of the "Hebrew" [sic] nation, a fake and a fraud who indulged in one publicity stunt after another.

The conflict between pro and anti-Bergsonites was, in significant ways, representative of the intracommunal conflicts confounding and enervating American Jewry during the Holocaust era. In particular, Orthodox feuded with non-Orthodox, and Zionists battled amongst themselves and with non-Zionists. The WRB quickly realised that one of the biggest difficulties involved in co-operating with Jewish organisations was getting Jews "to work together and stop fighting among themselves".[171]

It should not be thought that the divisions within American Jewry were generated exclusively, or even largely, by secular-religious antagonism. The lack of co-ordination — and hence co-operation — between, for example, the WJC and the AJDC was due mainly to the latter organisation's conservatism, this division, according to Yehuda Bauer, probably preventing greater success in overall relief and rescue operations.[172]

Yet despite some debilitating intracommunal convulsions, there were also substantial areas of Jewish confluence. One notable example of complementary collaboration transcending ideological barriers related to the monthly aid parcels dispatched to Jewish refugees in the Soviet Union, such parcels being sent by both the Orthodox Rabbis' Rescue Committee and the AJDC. Regarding these refugees, whilst the former utilised its special expertise, reputation and connections to fulfil the unique needs of Orthodox Jews, by mid-1944 the latter was sending over 6,000 parcels per month to all categories of Jewish refugees sheltering in the USSR. Notwithstanding their diametrically opposed rescue philosophies, by this time the Orthodox organisation was sufficiently impressed by the AJDC's relief activities for the ORRC's Budget Bulletin of June 1944 to advocate that the ORRC "discuss and integrate" its relief programme with that of the AJDC.[173]

Although funded by American Jewry, it should not be thought that the AJDC restricted its donations to specifically Jewish causes. Of particular significance, the US War Refugee Board received $15 million directly from the AJDC, and another $5 million from other organisations, most of whom were subsidised by the AJDC. Contrary to popular belief at the time, the Board received little funding from either government or non-Jewish sources. Upon its inauguration, the US administration allocated $1,150,000 to the WRB, of which $603,000 was returned at the cessation of hostilities.[174] Neither should it be thought that the WRB restricted its operations to refugee matters, Jewish or otherwise. Included in the Board's non-refugee activities was the funding of anti-Nazi activities in northern Italy and the provision of medical supplies to the French underground.[175]

In short, the WRB's operations were financed overwhelmingly by Jewish philanthropic organisations, such groups donating almost $20 million during the Board's existence. Apart from the AJDC's $15 million, the next largest contributors were the Union of Orthodox Rabbis (over $1 million) and the World Jewish Congress ($300,000).[176] Consequently, it should be recognised that, despite being an official US government body, the WRB was funded almost entirely by American Jews. In particular, Roswell McClelland's discretionary fund of $260,000, which he used to foster underground operations in Occupied areas, was donated by the AJDC, as was the $100,000 received by Raoul Wallenberg in mid-September 1944, via US Treasury licence, for his use in the relief and rescue of Hungarian Jews.[177]

Created in response to Hitler and Nazism, the WJC was convened by Rabbi Stephen Wise, president of the American Jewish Congress, in August 1932 and formally founded in August 1936.[178] Aid activities in Axis territory commenced shortly after the outbreak of war, when the WJC established a committee in Geneva to assist both Polish Jews and Jewish refugees from Poland. This effort was augmented shortly thereafter by a relief bureau based in New York. In marked contrast to the conservative, legalistic-oriented AJDC, the WJC, despite the Allies' economic and financial blockade of occupied Europe, raised and clandestinely transmitted substantial sums to Axis territory to aid Jews trapped therein.[179]

Yet notwithstanding the WJC–ORRC concord regarding clandestine funding for Jewish victims of Nazism, the secular WJC was hardly sympathetic to its fraternal organisation run by Orthodox Rabbis. The zenith of this discord commenced on 8 January 1945 when Rabbi Irving Miller of the American Jewish Congress (AJC) telephoned Benjamin Akzin of the WRB to enquire if the ORRC was justified in seeking financial contributions for its campaign to rescue Jews trapped in occupied Europe. Akzin sidestepped the question, responding that he "could not comment on the merits of any campaign by any relief organisation, and that if a comment of the Board is desired, the American Jewish Congress could send us any material regarding which they wish to have our opinion."[180] When pressed by Miller for his personal views, Akzin replied that, personally, he believed that the ORRC "had done very useful work in connection with the rescue of individuals..." After this response, Akzin noted that Rabbi Miller "rang off with every evidence of being disappointed".[181] The next day, 9 January, Akzin was telephoned by the WJC's Kurt Grossman, who enquired about rumours circulating in New York that the ORRC was raising funds to ransom 300,000 Jews and, in particular, whether this fundraising was conducted with the consent of the government. Once again Akzin avoided the issue, this time by stating that he did not comment on unsubstantiated rumours.[182]

Obviously dissatisfied with these developments, two days later, on 11 January, Dr Nahum Goldmann, co-founder of the World Jewish Congress (and its president, 1949–77), met Florence Hodel, Deputy Director of the WRB, and enquired whether the Board was familiar with the ORRC's plan to ransom Jews in occupied Europe and, in particular, if the plan had been approved by the government. Hodel, more forthcoming than her subordinate Akzin, advised Goldmann that "no such specific project had been presented to us or approved by the Board." On the other hand, she also informed Goldmann in explicit terms that the ORRC was "licensed to conduct certain rescue operations from Switzerland and is regularly making remittances to Switzerland to finance such operations". Furthermore, she continued, the WRB would continue to liaise with the ORRC "in the hope that further concrete programs could be worked out".[183] Clearly, these official responses indicated that the WJC strategy to involve the US government in its rivalry with the ORRC had failed.

Benjamin Akzin assessed the WJC's attempt to erode the ORRC's credibility and reputation, and the discord amongst American Jewry's aid organisations, as follows:

> On its face, the purpose of Rabbi Miller's and Mr. Grossman's calls was to obtain some statement from a member of the Board's staff which could be quoted to discourage contributors to a rival organization from contributing to it and to

encourage them to devote their contributions to the organizations in which these gentlemen are interested — a practice which, unfortunately, is very frequent among Jewish relief organizations. This is why I was particularly careful not to give either of the gentlemen any answer of which they could make use for their own ends.[184]

The not infrequent enmity amongst American Jewish foreign aid organisations was, not surprisingly, also reflected in their operations outside the USA. Switzerland, one of the most important centres for Jewish relief and rescue activity on behalf of entrapped Jews, is a particular case in point. Overseas Jewish aid groups operating in neutral Switzerland included the Palestine Office of Switzerland (Director 1940–45, Chaim Posner), Hehalutz World Centre (Director 1939–45, Nathan Schwalb), World Jewish Congress (Director 1936–45, Gerhard Riegner), American Jewish Joint Distribution Committee (Honorary Director appointed 1940, Saly Mayer), and ORRC (Directors, the Sternbuch brothers).

Severely constrained by the Allies' stringent currency transfer restrictions, precluded from local finance by the need for the Swiss community of 17,000 Jews to support the growing number of their co-religionists grudgingly admitted as refugees into Switzerland, and beholden to a Swiss government swayed by local Antisemitism and German power, overseas Jewish aid organisations in Switzerland were represented by small-scale operations with low budgets and minimal staff.[185] As an additional restraint, non-citizen Jewish leaders working in Switzerland were continually apprehensive about jeopardising their residency via the undermining of Swiss relations with the Reich by, for example, publicising the *Endlösung*, news of which reached them in 1942. Their position was further weakened by the conflicts and lack of co-operation amongst the organisations they represented, which, in turn, were amplified by the absence of a central or even co-ordinating secretariat. Basically, individual groups communicated solely with their own headquarters and usually kept their activities secret from perceived Jewish rivals. In general, Jewish aid organisations thus operated independently and in isolation from each other, which, in turn, exacerbated their rivalries and consequently further eroded the effectiveness of both individual organisations and the overall Jewish effort.

Realising the limitations inherent in independent operations controlled by competing, secretive bureaucracies, from 1942 the Jewish Agency attempted to co-ordinate the endeavours of international Jewish aid organisations, but with only marginal success.[186] Thus, until the concluding stages of the War, when Germany's defeat was perceived as inevitable, international (and local) Jewish leaders in Switzerland had only token influence on events they were working to shape.

It was, however, not only foreign Jewish leaders in Switzerland who were concerned about their status with, and the reactions of, national officials. Corresponding burdens afflicted Jews in leadership positions throughout the Western world, especially those engaged in government service. An appreciation of the pressures — or divided loyalties, as it was described frequently — impinging upon Jewish leaders in Western countries can be discerned from the attitude and actions of the most powerful government official of Jewish background in the Allied world, the US Secretary of the Treasury, Henry Morgenthau Jr (1891–1967).[187] Apart from his well-known intervention with Roosevelt which led to the creation of the War Refugee Board in January 1944, a lesser-known case of Morgenthau's honourable role in changing shameful US attitudes towards Jews occurred in November 1942, and related to the recently liberated French colonies in north

Africa. After the US refused to intervene in the colonies' "internal affairs", Morgenthau's intercession was largely responsible for removing the discriminatory Vichy (pro-Nazi) policies that continued to afflict north African Jews even after liberation from German control.[188] Notwithstanding his overall international perspective, it should be noted that much of the time and energy expended during 1944 on the "Jewish Question in Europe" by Morgenthau, and many of his co-religionists in the US and UK, related to their attempted saving of Hungarian Jews, Hungary being one of the few areas in the Nazi domain whose Jewish population remained basically intact until mid-May 1944.

The pressures upon Morgenthau, and his responses thereto, are clearly indicated in the twenty-four page verbatim transcript of a meeting concerning WRB matters, held on 27 February 1945 between the Secretary and his senior staff. Primary discussion focused on the dilemmas generated for both Morgenthau and the WRB by Musy's negotiations, and the ORRC's actions, in attempting to save Jews under German control. Morgenthau's initial emphasis indicated his concern with the politico-financial aspects of rescue, viz: "Now wait a minute. What I want to know, particularly on the money transactions, is what part the Treasury and Foreign Funds [Bureau] had in any of this."[189] This deficiency regarding details is not necessarily a criticism of Morgenthau's commitment to rescue. A Secretary's prime attention generally concerns the "Big Picture", with responsibility for detailed implementation consigned to senior subordinates. However, one must question why, at the end of February 1945, Morgenthau, as revealed in the transcript, remained ignorant of the critical and highly sensitive Mayer negotiations (viz: "What were their [the Germans'] talks with Saly Mayer about?"[190]) — especially as the talks had commenced six months ago, on 21 August 1944 (see above).

After Florence Hodel of the WRB summarised the recent history of rescue negotiations, she reassured Morgenthau by emphasising her strict order that licences to transfer funds to Switzerland for rescue purposes would only be issued upon collective written approval from the State Department, the Treasury and the WRB.[191] Satisfied with this response, the Secretary next turned his attention to domestic political considerations regarding the rescue of Jews. This concern he enunciated thus:

> The Chicago Tribune [newspaper] has about got this, and the story they are talking of running is that Henry Morgenthau, the Jew, is dealing with Himmler to bring out Jews, and Jews only, see, that I am dealing with Himmler... And the War Department will just shrug their shoulders. O'Dwyer [successor to John Pehle as WRB Director] isn't very crazy about this, and neither is the State Department.[192]

Once again, Morgenthau's anxieties were both valid and reasonable. There is little doubt that significant elements of US society would have deprecated an American Jew apparently exploiting his high government position for the exclusive liberation of his co-religionists, especially if the endeavour involved reaching agreement with the satanic Nazi Himmler. Thus, whilst supporting the transfer of funds to Switzerland, in subsequent discussion Morgenthau showed a natural concern to remain distanced from the direct, sole responsibility for authorising monetary transfer abroad to rescue Jews, and to ensure that the State Department and the WRB also approved such authorisation. The Secretary's caution was reinforced when Pehle stated:

These [ORRC] negotiations were not handled by the United States government, but by intermediaries, and we were never advised of the full facts. All we know is that some human lives were saved. Now, there are side currents, and people doing things for the worst motives, I have no doubt. I have no doubt Musy is a scoundrel... And they [the ORRC] have their own means of communicating [with Switzerland] not subject to [US government] censorship.[193]

From subsequent discussion, it is clear that one of the major factors contributing to Morgenthau's political anxieties was the uncertain lines of authority regarding the overseas transfer of rescue funds. A complex, convoluted and uncertain bureaucratic structure devolved responsibility to such an extent that, ultimately, a political explosion would catch the Secretary exposed whilst his senior subordinates remained unscathed, collectively protected by their indeterminate, overlapping obligations. The meeting revealed that nobody in the hierarchy either understood the process or knew clearly the persons whose approval was required to transfer funds abroad. Morgenthau expressed his concerns thus:

I agree it is risky... The trouble is the personnel of the Treasury and War Refugee Board are so mixed up I don't know which is which, and I want to tighten up my own lines so I'll know what is happening within my own Department... [Furthermore] Who is going to be blamed? Are they [the Chicago Tribune] going to say 'These Orthodox people [the ORRC] are going through non-censored avenues [the Polish Embassy] directly to Himmler...'?[194]

Further discussion enabled Morgenthau to clarify, and thence rectify, these politically hazardous deficiencies. His ultimate domestic and international concerns, however, were succinctly summarised towards the end of the meeting: "The thing [exposition] that you gave can be given an interpretation that will make it impossible to do anything more for any Jews...",[195] and "But if the thing [rescue attempt] goes wrong — not only the future treatment of Jews in Europe is at stake, but the whole question of anti-Semitism in this country..."[196] Morgenthau's solution to this complex, troubling matrix was cogent and direct, but not necessarily easy to implement. In the meeting's final address he stated: "Well, anyway, the only way the [WR]Board can do the job is to be sure that it moves, as far as the Administration is concerned, on a united front, [with] both [Secretary of War] Stimson and the Secretary of State. Now, we will see."[197]

The Secretary's final statement of concern, and the urgent need to politically safeguard the Administration, were considered of sufficient importance for a rare meeting of the WRB's ranking hierarchy to be called the very next day, 28 February 1945. Only the sixth meeting of the WRB held since its inception in January 1944, the government departments, and their attending personnel, were: Treasury — Secretary Morgenthau (Acting Chair) and Assistant Secretary Gaston; War — Secretary Stimson and Assistant Secretary McCloy; State — Acting Secretary Grew; WRB — Executive Director William O'Dwyer and Assistant Executive Director Florence Hodel; plus John Pehle (Assistant to the Secretary of the Treasury, and O'Dwyer's predecessor) and George Warren (Special Adviser on Refugees to the Secretary of State).[198]

The meeting was arranged on Morgenthau's request, ostensibly to discuss the ORRC's application to transfer $937,000 to its Swiss representative, Issac Sternbuch. After some discussion, the WRB's Executive Director recommended the application be approved with the caveat that the funds be directed to a joint account in the names of Sternbuch and Roswell McClelland (WRB representative in Switzerland), and with the usual proviso (see above) "that no expenditure or commitment for expenditure be made without the prior authorisation of the War Refugee Board".[199]

Not unexpectedly, despite these onerous conditions Stimson maintained his previously discussed recalcitrance, querying if the application would ultimately benefit the enemy and questioning whether or not the Treasury would issue a licence for the payment of ransom. Morgenthau defused the challenge by stating that Treasury would not approve any such licence. After "thorough considera-tion", Acting Secretary of State Grew moved that the Board approve the application providing that, under no circumstances could any portion of the money be used for ransom payment. Stimson, either satisfied or sensing his minority position, agreed, upon which Morgenthau, as Chairman, concurred with the decision. The resolu-tion, in effect, solved Morgenthau's dilemma: all necessary instruments of government approved his objectives, his unique exposure to criticism was eliminated, and his position was safeguarded by means of a collective administra-tive consensus.[200] Yet despite this apparent breakthrough, even with Stimson and his cohorts outmanoeuvred, Morgenthau still failed to achieve the ultimate purpose of the exercise. His strategy, whilst successful on its own terms, failed to change America's abiding passivity towards the *Endlösung*. For the remnant of European Jews still trapped by the Nazis, it was another case of American assistance being too little and too late.

The steadfast tokenism inherent in US policy was exemplified by the case of Oswego, the USA's sole refugee camp. Selected personally by Roosevelt in June 1944 to house refugees, Oswego was an abandoned army base — Fort Ontario, in northern New York State — that had been established before the American civil war. A total of just under 1,000 refugees (of whom some 900 were Jews) were brought to the USA in August 1944 — and interned in Oswego "under appropriate security restrictions" — on the basis that all were to be repatriated to their "homelands" upon the cessation of hostilities. To place this gesture in perspective, in mid-1944 the USA had a quota of 55,000 unfilled immigration places from Occupied Europe; and in October 1943 Sweden, a country with a population and land area only 5 percent of the USA, had accepted 8,000 Jewish refugees from Denmark.[201] It should also be noted that emergency internment camps in the US, which ultimately held 425,000 prisoners of war, operated outside the official immigration system and thus avoided the question of quotas and visas.[202] That Jewish refugees were not permitted access to this classification is merely another indication of American attitudes towards Jewish escapees from the Nazis' charnel houses. Clearly, US policy regarded European Jews to be less worthy of consideration than the soldiers of Axis powers.

Assessment

As has been seen, by the time Joel Brand revealed Himmler's infamous "Blood for Trucks" proposal, the Western Allies had developed a justified suspicion of the Reich's diplomatic manoeuvrers. The sudden, unexpected German overture raising the prospect of mass Jewish rescue, however, caught both Britain and the US unprepared. Thus, as admitted to Shertok by Lord Moyne, British Minister Resident in the Middle East, the UK's response to Brand's disclosures was both confused and confusing. Such an admission implied indecision, a lack of co-ordination, and the inadvertent or deliberate withholding of full information from British policymakers.[203] Nothing summarised Britain's attitude in this period more clearly than Lord Moyne's comment to Brand in Cairo: "What shall I do with those million [Hungarian] Jews? Where shall I put them?"[204] US policy was similarly indistinct until, a month after Brand's arrival in Istanbul, the Western Allies closed ranks with Stalin, denounced Himmler's overture as a monstrous trick, and, in effect, scuttled any prospect of rescuing substantial numbers of Jews remaining under Nazi control.

The West adopted this policy despite the distinctly favourable impression that Brand generated amongst his British, American and Jewish interrogators.[205] Typical was the assessment of Ira Hirschmann, Roosevelt's special WRB attaché in Turkey who, in his comprehensive twenty-four page report of 22 June 1944, stated that Brand impressed him as "honest, clear, incisive, blunt and completely frank... In short, Brand's disclosures are to be accepted in my view as truthful, without reservations."[206] The crux of Hirschmann's report was as follows:

> Brand's statement that the proposal connected with ten thousand lorries and other commodities was mentioned in an off-hand way and in effect "pulled out of the hat" by one of the German officers is a clear indication that this is not concrete or to be taken seriously. Immunity or some reference to immunity may be considered seriously as a bargaining point... Plans should be considered for a possible meeting between the Nazi representatives and British and Americans at some neutral point as soon as desirable. Brand should attend this meeting.[207]

Clearly, these assessments were reinforced by the following exchange between the two men:

Hirschmann: "Did you see any evidence on the part of the German leaders that they were becoming fearful or desperate?"

Brand: "Yes, decidedly, I see it in their talk and protestations; in the fact that a high German officer tells the Jew, Brand, 'We need things — go and get them.' "

In Brand's considered opinion, reported Hirschmann, this attitude appeared "to be a great confession of [German] weakness".[208] Accordingly, in his letter of 3 July to Pehle, Hirschmann emphasised that "it [is] of utmost importance that Brand be returned to Hungary without delay".[209] Subsequent discussion with Brand in Jerusalem — on 7 October 1944, shortly after the British released Brand from prison — confirmed to Hirschmann his earlier assessment, viz:

> I was again convinced of his [Brand's] frankness and integrity; that he was an impassioned young man, ready to risk his life for the sake of his people. His testimony taken in Cairo by me has now been confirmed as having been truthful... I am confident...that he has connections in Hungary which could render any possible illicit movement of refugees out of Hungary a feasible operation.[210]

Inadvertently or otherwise, Hirschmann's analysis alluded to one of the West's primary fears regarding the "Blood for Trucks" offer: that constructive engagement with the Istanbul overture risked producing a substantial exodus of Jews from Hungary — an exodus, the West feared, that could result in tens of thousands of impoverished Jewish refugees eventually reaching the US, UK and/or Palestine. Thus, paradoxically, recommendations by Hirschmann, Shertok and others for a positive humanitarian response to the German proposal, whilst given in good faith, may have been counterproductive through alerting Western policy makers to the highly unwelcomed possibility that negotiations could lead to a flood of distressed and destitute Jews from Nazi territory to Western control and/or responsibility. By corollary, the possibility remains that less optimistic or positive analyses may have led the Anglo-Americans to treat the overture more seriously and/or with less hostility, thus leading to the survival of substantially greater numbers than was eventually achieved.

In summary: one of the primary factors in the West's refusal to consider seriously the rescue of Hungarian Jewry was the suspicion that Germany was prepared to release Jews *en masse*.[211] We are thus confronted with the (paradoxical?) hypothesis that the West's fear of the consequences of successful negotiations may have been sufficient to doom Himmler's overture to rejection. Note that the existence, or otherwise, of a German readiness to release Jews is irrelevant to the hypothesis: the mere suspicion amongst Western policy makers that Germany might permit substantial Jewish emigration appears to have been sufficient catalyst for the West's refusal to countenance negotiations.

In the last two decades, there has been heavy emphasis in research on whether or not Himmler was prepared to release substantial numbers of Jews. Whilst important for scholarship, this emphasis is misconstrued regarding the potential rescue process. As stated by Brand, and as accepted by Hirschmann and others, the issue of providing trucks was a mere opening bid in the negotiation process — the salient factor through which a formula to rescue Jews *en masse* might have been devised. Rejecting this analysis, the Allies, in brutally simple terms, refused the opportunity to explore the possibility of liberating Europe's entrapped Jews. As noted by John Pehle, Executive Director of the WRB, in his *Memorandum* of 17 August 1944 to Deputy Secretary of State Stettinius: "As I have previously indicated to you, I feel strongly that we cannot enter into any ransom transactions with the German authorities in order to obtain the release of the Jews."[212] By this statement Pehle was expressing the consensus of the Grand Alliance — no negotiations, no ransom payments, Jews to be left to their fate.

This is not to say that Western leaders neglected to create a concerned, humanitarian facade regarding the Jewish plight. On 17 December 1942 the House of Commons stood in silent tribute to Jews murdered by the Nazis and their collaborators.[213] This sixty-second testimonial set the tone for future Allied responses — in effect, an up and down motion whilst maintaining the same position. Subsequently, apart from proposing postwar judicial retribution for the perpetrators of what the West acknowledged to be unprecedented mass murder, Western policy makers refrained from meaningful unilateral initiatives regarding Jewish rescue. Thus despite Roosevelt's rhetoric, and Churchill's sympathy for "this martyred race", Jews remaining in the Reich's domain — who, after March 1944 were concentrated primarily in Hungary — were abandoned to the mercy of the Nazis and their collaborators.[214]

This abandonment is clearly indicated by the controversy surrounding the use of Allied air power to aid victims of German persecution. It is now apparent that by the commencement of deportations from Hungary to Auschwitz in mid-May 1944, Allied air forces were — at relatively little cost — in a position to not only seriously disrupt the railway servicing the camp but also destroy the camp's lightly defended death facilities. Yet in early August 1944, just two weeks after the British Air

320

Staff negated bombing Auschwitz, the RAF engaged in substantial special operations to aid the (non-Communist) Polish uprising in Warsaw — operations of substantially greater magnitude and risk than required for bombing the gas chambers and crematoria at Auschwitz.[215]

For cogent political reasons, Britain and the US were determined — notwithstanding Stalin's resolute opposition — to provide the insurgents with all possible support before the Red Army reached the Polish capital. Thus, in August and September 1944, RAF squadrons based in Italy flew aid to Warsaw via a total of 181 bombers, of which thirty-one were lost. Unfortunately for the insurgents, much of this attempted air-supply fell into German hands. On 18 September, 107 USAF Flying Fortress bombers parachuted 1,284 containers of war *matériel* to the Warsaw insurgents, about 1,000 of which were captured by the *Wehrmacht*. Before the commencement of Anglo-American operations — in which the USSR refused to participate — the RAF commander in Italy, Air Marshal Sir John Slessor, predicted that such missions would result in a "prohibitive rate of loss" without causing any possible effect on the War. After their conclusion, Slessor's assessment was that the effort had "achieved practically nothing". Moreover, because of adverse weather conditions and other factors, the USAF mission of 18 September withdrew over 100 heavy bombers, and their personnel, from regular military activity for some nine days — a rate of withdrawal described as extremely high.[216]

Of particular note, whilst agreeing with Air Marshal Slessor's military assessment, the US Strategic Air Force's Director of Intelligence justified the USA's Warsaw airlift on the basis of fulfilling a moral imperative:

> Despite the tangible cost which far outweighed the tangible results achieved, it is concluded that this mission was amply justified... America kept faith with its ally. One thing stands out, from the President down to the airmen who flew the planes, America wanted to, tried, and did help within her means and possibilities.[217]

In tragic contrast, one of the principal reasons for the West's refusal to bomb Auschwitz, or the railway leading thereto, was the alleged impracticality of diverting necessary air capacity from decisive military operations. Notwithstanding the establishment of the WRB, the Allies decided that meaningful aid to European Jews (unlike meaningful aid to Polish insurgents) lacked moral imperative, was a misallocation of scarce resources, and an unwelcome diversion from the task at hand — the pulverisation of Germany into unconditional surrender in the shortest possible time. With the benefit of hindsight, it is evident that the Grand Alliance's refusal to utilise air power to disrupt the *Endlösung* was based on political considerations and not technical difficulties. American hypocrisy, in particular, was magnified by Roosevelt's warning that "full and swift retaliation in kind...[would follow]...any use of gas by any Axis power".[218] When approached regarding the gassing of Jews, the WRB declared that the issue of gas was a military matter and thus beyond its jurisdiction; and, in tandem, the US Joint Chiefs of Staff stated that the question was one beyond its "cognizance".[219]

This was not the only occasion on which the WRB and the US military, by acting in tandem, negated a meaningful response to the *Endlösung*. Reporting to Secretary Morgenthau in early September 1944, Pehle accepted the War Department's rejection of several Jewish requests to bomb the railway servicing Auschwitz because "Railway lines are quickly and easily repaired unless subjected to constant bombing. Furthermore, if the Germans are bent on exterminating Jews, it is not necessary first to concentrate them in existing extermination centres."[220] Military expertise is not required to realise that the War Department-WRB argument was bogus and probably deliberately deceitful. Clearly, "constant bombing" was required in western Europe, where there existed dense rail (and road) networks that provided numerous optional, alternative transportation routes. This bombing protocol, however, was not required for the far less-developed railways of central and eastern Europe. Not only was special repair equipment, and skilled personnel, substantially less available in the east, but disruptions to deportation schedules could not be readily overcome by simply switching to alternative routes or modes of transportation. Moreover, as Allied intelligence doubtless realised by September 1944, efficient industrial processing was required for both mass extermination and, because of the Red Army's relentless advance, the necessary destruction of incriminating "by-product". After mid-1944, alternatives to the Auschwitz "production line" were no longer readily available to the Germans — especially for the efficient elimination of incriminating evidence, the untold mass of Jewish corpses. It is thus not unreasonable to contend that destruction of the gas chambers and crematoria at Auschwitz in mid-1944 would have led to a substantial slowing — if not a moratorium — on mass murder, and almost certainly on gassing, until Himmler himself terminated gassing operations in mid-October 1944.[221]

How, then, are we to assess Himmler's "Blood for Trucks" strategy? For an assessment in overall context, it must be realised that, stimulated by the Stalingrad debacle (January 1943) and subsequent military disasters on the Eastern Front, there gradually emerged two divergent attitudes within the Nazi hierarchy. One faction, which for the sake of convenience can be labelled the "Pragmatists", recognised that the War was lost unless there was a decisive restructuring of the Reich's priorities. The "Pragmatists'" emphasis was to terminate conflict with the West, and join the Anglo-Americans in a joint crusade against rampantly expanding international Communism, as represented by Stalin's USSR. Centred mainly in the upper *SS* echelons, the guiding lights of this faction included Schellenberg, Klages and Becher, who orbited around the often cautiously supportive Himmler. Although "pragmatic" relative to the Party's true believers, the "Pragmatists" remained dedicated Nazis. In particular, despite all evidence to the contrary, they still accepted Party ideology that Jews were immensely powerful via "International Jewry's" control of both the West (via international capitalism) and the USSR (via Judeo-Communism).

In their increasingly desperate attempts to disengage from a disastrous two-front war, the "Pragmatists" believed, despite all evidence to the contrary, that the Reich's remaining Jews were a trump card to be exploited in achieving their restructured priorities. Increasingly motivated by the Axis' continuing military catastrophes, and their consequently growing apprehension about their own postwar fate, by May 1944 the "Pragmatists" favoured reverting to Germany's prewar policy of exploiting Jews for the material and political benefit of the Reich. After all, the Holy Grail of Nazi ideology, the "Final Solution of the Jewish Question in Europe" — by extermination or expulsion, either would suffice — could only be attained if Nazism survived the ever-growing military crisis. Even the "Pragmatists'" hardline opponents — the unwavering ideologues orbiting around Hitler, who included Ernst Kaltenbrunner (1903–46, successor to Reinhard Heydrich as chief of the *SD*) — whilst continuing to believe that Jews should be exterminated, were, because of Germany's critical material and labour shortages, on occasion prepared to temporarily alter tactics regarding the *Endlösung*.

Himmler was thus encouraged in his quest to the West by various developments regarding official attitudes towards Jews, including: Hitler's permission in December 1942 to ransom Jews in return for substantial financial gain; Hitler's promise, in April 1944, to provide 100,000 Hungarian Jews to construct, and work in, six huge underground aircraft factories (the *Jägerstab* plan); Kaltenbrunner's order to Eichmann, in June 1944, for Hungarian Jews to be diverted from Auschwitz for war work in Austria (known as the Strasshof group and eventually numbering some 20,000 workers, about 75 percent of these Jews survived the War); Hitler's acceptance of Ribbentrop's proposal to permit the release of Hungarian Jews to Sweden, Switzerland and the US (but not Palestine); Himmler's successful acquisition of Hungary's paramount industrial complex, the Weiss Manfred Corporation, via the ransoming of Jews; the Foreign Office instructing Edmund Veesenmayer, German Plenipotentiary in Hungary, to demand the release of Germans interned in Allied territory as a *quid pro quo* for permitting the emigration of some Hungarian Jews; and the suggestion to Hitler by Himmler's rival, Ribbentrop — generally a slavish devotee of the *Führer's* thinking — that, as a propaganda coup, all surviving Jews be donated as a gift (legacy, offering) to Roosevelt and Churchill.[222]

Consequently, there was some justification for Himmler concluding that a reversion of Germany's tactics towards Jews, from *Endlösung* back to exploitation and/or selective release, was feasible on a temporary — albeit probably only partial — basis. His initially cautious, but progressively more open attempts at rapprochement with the Anglo-Americans were reinforced by several overlapping considerations, including a determination to rehabilitate his satanic image in the West. Increasingly concerned at his postwar future, Himmler blamed concerted Jewish propaganda for his appalling international reputation, a perception that could be rectified, he thought, by the West recognising him, and his *SS*, as a bulwark against rampant Communism, and by his amelioration of the Jewish situation in Axis territory. Without doubt, this notion was reinforced by Himmler's consideration that, through the imperatives of *real-politik*, the West was allied to the monster Stalin via a grotesque, sharply oscillating and obviously transient marriage of convenience. Postwar developments, including the Cold War — and the Allies' employment of German rocket scientists, *SS* intelligence officers, and Nazi war criminals — indicate that Himmler was premature in some of his thinking.

Apart from the above, three other factors were also significant in encouraging the *Reichsführer-SS* to persevere with his strategy: the prospect of Hitler approving an ideologically acceptable "blood for blood" transaction — for example, the exchange of Jews for ethnic Germans residing in Roumania who, by mid-1944, were threatened with deportation to Siberia by the advancing Red Army; Hitler's approval, on 12 September 1944, of Himmler's proposal for separate peace negotiations; and, although not involved in either plotting against Hitler or in preventing such plots, Himmler's awareness of conspiracies against the *Führer* doubtless influenced him to prepare for a possible post-Hitler epoch and/or keep his options open regarding a change in priority towards Jews.[223] All these were additional, cogent reasons for Hungary's remaining Jews being kept alive for possible contingencies — in particular, as ransom for future negotiation purposes.

As with many issues discussed above, Holocaust historians are divided — in some cases, sharply so — regarding the motivation behind Himmler's "Blood for Trucks" enterprise. Raoul Hilberg's attitude is in keeping with his general posture that Jewish representatives and institutions were, inadvertently or otherwise, mere extensions of Germany's bureaucratic machinery of destruction. Accordingly, Hilberg accepts Eichmann's claim that Himmler's initiative was an attempt to blackmail "International Jewry" to, in effect, motorise two *Waffen-SS* cavalry divisions — the *Florian Geyer* and the *Maria Theresia*, both of which were stationed in Hungary.[224] As a corollary, this attitude views both Brand and Grosz as mere couriers in a nefarious blackmail ploy by Himmler.

Those few supporting this simplistic analysis either ignore, or lack cognisance of, two important factors, viz: the acquisition of Hungary's pre-eminent military-industrial manufacturing complex (the Weiss Manfred Works, with 40,000 employees) by the *SS* in mid-May 1944, negated any need for Himmler to debase himself (according to Nazi ideology) by haggling with Jews over trucks; and the paltry significance of 10,000 lorries in the overall drama unfolding inexorably before the *Reichsführer-SS*. To place this number into material perspective: the Roumanian *volte-face* in August 1944, which was only one in a long sequence of German military routs, resulted in the estimated loss of 338 planes, 830 tanks and self-propelled guns, 5,500 artillery pieces *and* 33,000 trucks.[225] Compared with Germany's overall *matériel* losses and needs, Himmler's opening gambit for 10,000 trucks was conspicuously modest. Quite clearly, even the initial number suggested (not demanded) in the "Blood for Trucks" overture would have meant little in the overall military (that is, non-political) scheme of things, and was hardly intended, from the German perspective, to be either onerous, intimidating or materially debilitating to the West. It is hardly reasonable to conclude, as does Hilberg, that Himmler's real motivation, at such a critical juncture of the War, was a marginal improvement in the Reich's *matériel* stockpile. Moreover, it is equally unreasonable to dismiss out of hand, as does Hilberg, the profound political implications of Himmler's overture to the West, the Reich and, above all, to the Jews.

Writing in 1988, forty-four years after the event, Michael Marrus expressed the opinion that "little is known for certain about what motivated Germans [behind the overture]", and quotes his private correspondence with Martin Gilbert, in which the latter made the amazing claim that the offer was "a clear ruse...to neutralise the potential resistance of a million people".[226] In marked contrast to the views of Hilberg, Marrus and Gilbert are the analyses of Randolph Braham and Yehuda Bauer, scholars with considerable specialist expertise on the *Shoah* in Hungary. Like Shlomo Aronson (see Chapter IV), Braham deserves recognition as one of very few historians relating Himmler's unfolding strategy to the establishment, in January 1944, of the US War Refugee Board. Both maintain that this development probably influenced the *Reichsführer-SS* to believe that the US had resolved to become more pro-active in the rescue of European Jewry, the "Blood for Trucks" initiative flowing from this belief. This position makes sense, as does Schellenberg's enunciation, in 1951, of the imperative behind Grosz being appointed the peace emissary. According to Schellenberg, a positive Western response would, most probably, have progressed negotiations at a higher level (without Grosz), whilst a rejection would have enabled Himmler to escape hazardous political turbulence by dismissing Grosz, the multiple agent, as a petty criminal and inveterate liar.[227] Whilst acknowledging the significance of the Grosz mission, Braham's attitude towards Brand's role is left up in the air; he merely notes that the *SS* allegedly attempted to camouflage Grosz' "important mission" with the "Blood for Trucks" offer.[228]

In sharp contrast to the large majority of historians, Yehuda Bauer has integrated the apparently disparate Brand and Grosz missions into a single, coherent strategy. Bauer achieved this by establishing that Grosz was one of the very few low-profile, readily disownable operatives, with connections to both Western intelligence and representatives of international Jewry, still available to Himmler in mid-1944.[229] Grafted onto this base is Bauer's acceptance of Bandi Grosz' claim — an assertion, incidentally, accepted by the West — that Brand was a smokescreen to the main task at hand. The real purpose of Himmler's overture, as revealed to Grosz by Klages (*SD* chief in Budapest, see above), was for Grosz to initiate negotiations between the *SS* and his Anglo-American contacts, preferably those in Western intelligence, but, if that was not possible, with representatives of "International Jewry". Accordingly, Bauer dismissed Brand's counterclaim that Eichmann's order to obtain goods was the Istanbul overture's prime purpose.[230]

The use of Brand's attempt to obtain needed goods as camouflage for Grosz' peace mission meshed with Himmler's requirement for protection against Hitler and the orbiting hardcore ideologues, particularly Kaltenbrunner and Ribbentrop. Thus, although pressured to preserve all his options by the incessantly deteriorating military balance, Himmler continued to oscillate between, on the one hand, obsequious loyalty to his mentor Hitler and, on the other hand, acting upon the fallacious belief that his postwar survival depended upon changes in German emphasis. The *Reichsführer-SS* thus continued to appease the *Führer* yet, driven by Nazi mythology regarding the power of international Jewry, Himmler devoted considerable time, energy, and not some little risk, in chasing the chimera of Allied sympathy for the plight of European Jews.[231] His wild goose chase was aided and abetted by Nazi "Pragmatists" such as Schellenberg, whose particular fantasy was to reinvent Himmler into an acceptable negotiating partner with the West.[232] Like other Nazis, Schellenberg and his ilk believed that Jewry controlled the Allies; but unlike Hitler and the hardcore ideologues, the "Pragmatists" accepted that, as a consequence of this belief, the *sine qua non* of successful negotiations with the Anglo-Americans was the exploitation — as opposed to the extermination — of their perceived trump card, Europe's surviving Jews.[233]

Note that although seemingly separate initiatives of apparently disparate intent, the Brand and Grosz missions were, in effect, analogous to the two sides of the one strategic coin. Clearly, Himmler accepted that without the prospect of an *en masse* release of Jews, his peace overture would come to nought. Consequently, both sides of the strategic coin were crucial to Himmler's plan — one side (Brand) to placate both Hitler and, with breathtaking paradox, "International Jewry", the converse side (Grosz) to appease the anti-Communist West. Hence both sides were necessary, and neither side was sufficient by itself, to achieve the *Reichsführer-SS*' primary objectives of extracting Germany from a disastrous war on two fronts whilst simultaneously ensuring his own postwar future. In the end, however, Himmler's attempted grand slam in Istanbul — an attempt to generate a win-win-win-win situation for Germany, himself, the Allies and the Jews, with only Stalin a loser —

stumbled over the author's *unreal-politik*. Yet notwithstanding the Grand Alliance's public rejection, to the end Himmler persevered with his increasingly audacious, increasingly desperate attempts to achieve some sort of accommodation with the West. Unlike his rival Ribbentrop, who retained delusions about resuscitating his greatest triumph (the Ribbentrop–Molotov Pact of August 1939), both poles of Himmler's integrated (bi-polar) strategy — the Brand ransom offer and the Grosz peace overture — were directed solely against Stalin and the "rampaging Judeo-Communist menace".

Unfortunately for trapped European Jews, substantial tactical pitfalls lurked within Himmler's seemingly well-crafted strategic conception. One inherent weakness was the choice of Grosz as the peace emissary. Despite the paucity of alternative choices, even superficial consideration of the West's sensitivities would have revealed the political difficulty for the Allies' to act upon momentous information supplied by a petty criminal, a highly dubious multiple agent secretly employed by both the Nazis and themselves. From the Allies' blinkered perspective, the scenario was ideal for either a German propaganda coup, a blackmail attempt, or both. The critical factors for the Anglo-Americans in the "Rescue Matrix", however, were generated by the following two interrelated elements:

A: The supply of trucks or *matériel* (the Brand objective) would have resulted in the mass rescue of Jews, as would have an armistice with the West (the Grosz objective). Accordingly, Jews were not only the common factor but also the common impediment to both poles of Himmler's bi-polar strategy — the common impediment because no single country, or group of nations, was prepared to accept a mass influx of impoverished Jewish refugees. Rejecting Himmler's overture as a satanic attempt at blackmail was a simple solution for Allied politicians determined to avoid the distasteful question of "what shall we do with a million Jews?". But even if secure havens could be located, a mass exodus of Jews from the Reich would, according to the West, have obstructed — possibly severely — Allied military operations.

B: A separate peace with the West, and the consequent suspension of hostilities, also implied an unacceptable mass release of Jews by the Reich — plus the even more unthinkable: Stalin's wrath and the highly probable collapse of the Grand Alliance.

Consequently, for the the sake of the West's primary strategic concern (the undisrupted continuation of the Grand Alliance's campaign to pulverise Germany into unconditional surrender), both the Brand and Grosz objectives had to be quickly and effectively quashed. And, apart from token gestures, that is exactly what happened — brutally, ruthlessly and efficiently.

Historians rejecting the concept of Himmler utilising Jews in a genuine armistice strategy often base their opinion on the *Reichsführer-SS*' admitted duplicity and paucity of *bona fides*. In turn, such rejectionists propose several alternative motivations behind the Istanbul endeavour, motivations in keeping with the *Reichsführer-SS*' Machiavellian nature. Stripped of its convoluted matrix, they assert, Himmler simply attempted to split the Grand Alliance. This is not a valid objection; in fact, it is quite the reverse. As enunciated above, due to Stalin's renowned antipathy towards Jews, Himmler (in effect) required an East–West schism for his peace strategy to succeed. Furthermore, because he wanted to split the Allies' united front does not mean that Himmler was not seriously interested in negotiating an accord (temporary or otherwise) with the West. After all, what better way to achieve a desperately needed armistice than by driving a wedge between Stalin and the West? And, from Nazi ideology, what better, faster means of forcing negotiations than by dangling occupied Europe's remaining Jews before international Jewry and the West?

Another objection relates to the furious speed at which Hungarian Jews were deported to Auschwitz. If Himmler was genuine about forcing the West into negotiations, why was his so-called trump card — Hungary's Jews, the only substantial Jewish community remaining under Axis control — exterminated at such a frantic tempo? Consequently, as a corollary, was not the Istanbul endeavour simply a smokescreen, a distraction to the Holocaust continuing at an even more rapid rate? Whilst apparently cogent points, these are not valid objections either. Rapid deportation worked in Himmler's favour. As Eichmann stated to Freudiger (see Chapter IV), the faster the rate of extermination, the greater the pressure on International Jewry, and their Anglo-American associates, to commence negotiating.[234] With catastrophic defeat and terrible retribution advancing with the triumphant Red Army, Himmler could not afford the luxury of a leisurely timetable. Besides which, the Reich remained the master of European Jewry's destiny. Clearly, Himmler did not need a smokescreen for the Holocaust to continue.

The final major objection is based on Himmler's admittedly duplicitous nature, particularly as revealed by his faithful acolyte, the "pragmatic" Kurt Becher. During postwar interrogation, Becher testified that Himmler instructed him to "take everything you can get from the Jews; promise them whatever you want. As for what we shall carry out, that's an entirely different matter."[235] Although, once again, an apparently cogent point, the instruction must be placed into appropriate context. Given early during the Istanbul endeavour, this is exactly the sort of order expected from someone who, like Himmler, was attempting to keep his real intentions secret, safeguard his position with Hitler, keep his predatory rivals at bay, and simultaneously effect a risky policy manoeuvre. Moreover, there is no real reason to believe that the statement "what we shall carry out, that's an entirely different matter" should be treated as anything other than dissimulatory, a precaution against information, and Himmler's real intentions, being leaked to his voracious adversaries. The *Reichsführer-SS*' real *bona fides* in this matter should be assessed from late June 1944 onwards — once the West had secured the long-awaited Second Front in France.

In early July, Himmler — for a variety of reasons — instructed Eichmann to accept Horthy's order banning further deportations to Auschwitz. In this context, it must be recalled that Himmler's subsequent formal suspension of deportations from Hungary occurred four days after the apparently promising commencement of negotiations, in Switzerland, between his personal representative, Kurt Becher, and Saly Mayer of the AJDC. Not surprisingly, the suspension order was issued immediately after Becher informed the *Reichsführer-SS* on 25 August that further deportations of Hungarian Jews would cause the Swiss talks to fail. To reinforce his *bona fides*, and to reassure his representative, on 26 August Himmler ordered Becher to continue his negotiations "in the spirit of your message".[236] Neither was it accidental that the start of Becher's discussions coincided with the arrival in Switzerland of the first Jews released from the Kasztner Transport. Clearly, Himmler's plan to reinvent himself for Western consumption, display his new-found flexibility, prove his capacity to deliver on his promises, and generate *bona fides* in the West, was up and running.

Himmler's order forbidding further deportations of Hungarian Jews was reported to Veesenmayer, who immediately informed Ribbentrop.[237] Even though news of the banning must have reached Hitler fairly quickly, it is significant that the *Führer* did not rescind the *Reichsführer-SS*' order. The latter's changed attitude towards Hungarian Jews was exemplified by the exceptional treatment provided Kasztner Transport passengers during their incarceration in the notorious Bergen Belsen concentration camp.[238] Significantly, this attitude persisted during the brutal Szalasi era. Moreover, upon being notified by Becher in November that Eichmann's marching of Jews from Budapest to Austria were, in effect, death marches, Himmler immediately forbade their continuation.[239] To reinforce his authority over a recalcitrant subordinate, at a meeting between Himmler, Becher and Eichmann, the *Reichsführer-SS* deliberately humiliated Eichmann, shouting at him "If up to now you have murdered Jews, and if I now give you the order to care for the Jews, you tell me whether you are going to carry out this order or not." Eichmann acquiesced: "Certainly, *Reichsführer.*"[240] Clearly, Himmler was not going to permit the intractable Eichmann to frustrate his higher strategy because of a "pathetic remnant" of Jews.

When it became clear that the *Wehrmacht* could not hold Hungary, Himmler extended his "attentiveness" to all Jews under German control. This policy was confirmed by the postwar interrogation of surviving *SS* leaders, who testified that Himmler tried to prevent the mass murder of surviving Jews. Whilst evidence from such sources is generally problematical, it must be recognised that, at the cessation of hostilities, some 150–200,000 Jews were liberated from the concentration and labour camp system controlled by Himmler. There was no necessity for the camps to surrender meekly to the Allies; in fact, quite the opposite. By annihilating the camps' (by now) physically debilitated inmates, the *SS* could have eliminated the surviving eyewitnesses to Germany's crimes against humanity. Yet, motivated by the advancing Red Army, the *Reichsführer-SS*' attempts to reach an accommodation with the West grew "more and more frantic".[241] Moreover, apart from his previously discussed endeavours in Turkey and Switzerland, Himmler also attempted separate initiatives in Italy, Sweden (for the ransom of 2,000 Latvian Jews), and with Allen Dulles, head of US intelligence in Switzerland.

One crux of the complex "Rescue Matrix" is thus posed: was Himmler, the consummate bureaucrat and satanic demon — the cautious strategist who obtained Hitler's permission to ransom Jews in December 1942, that is, shortly before the German catastrophes on the Eastern Front — prepared to release substantial numbers of Jews after mid-1944 in return for an Allied *quid pro quo*? For a determination, one must consider the evidence of his recurring initiatives, the concerted actions of his "pragmatic" subordinates, the continual erosion of his "demands", and the desperation required for the *Reichsführer-SS* to, in effect, haggle with the menial representatives of the despised Jews. For Himmler, the very act of negotiating on the basis of equality with what the entire Nazi hierarchy perceived to be Jewish racial vermin, was akin to an act of humiliation — a transparent indication of his desperation and haste to open discussions with the West in the short time available before Germany's clearly inevitable collapse. The leader of the omnipresent *SS* — Hitler's terrifying praetorian guard, and a state within the state — debased himself in full view of the Nazi elite. Notwithstanding the Allies' contemptuous rejection of his Istanbul overture in mid-July 1944, such was the intensity of Himmler's motivation that he permitted the consequent talks to drag on indefinitely.

Arguably, the most important factor to consider is the number of Jews he released from mid-1944 until the Reich's final collapse. Increasingly desperate to generate *bona fides*, in this period Himmler, of his own volition, liberated some 10,000 Jews from Axis territory, the large majority without any *quid pro quo*.[242] But without an incentive from the West, Himmler remained ensnared in a trap woven from his loyalty to, and psychological dependence upon, his beloved mentor and *Führer*. Virtually until Germany's death knell, Himmler's instinct for postwar preservation was largely mesmerised by Hitler's ruinous embrace. The highly suspicious *Führer* made a shrewd assessment of his *Reichsführer-SS*: despite the SS accumulating vast power, Hitler never felt threatened by his cautious satrap Himmler, the failed chicken farmer.[243] Conversely, there is little doubt that the West's indifference to the fate of European Jews substantially reinforced Himmler's loyalty and deference to Hitler. The potent amalgam of loyalty, psychological subordination, lack of incentive, and the Allies letting Auschwitz continue unabated, inhibited — but did not extinguish — the *Reichsführer-SS'* propensity for initiatives beyond the limited perimeters authorised by Hitler. Notwithstanding substantial impediments, Himmler, amongst other things, independently commenced, and continued, negotiations with Jewish representatives; decommissioned, and did not replace, the Auschwitz gas chambers; released some 10,000 Jews from German control; and ordered that Jews within the concentration camp system be treated with previously non-existent consideration.[244] Undeniably, in aggregate, a significant measure of change to the status quo.

Clearly, no one can say with confidence how Himmler, the "Pragmatists" and the *Wehrmacht's* non-Nazi officers, would have reacted to an early, genuine and meaningful Allied response to the Istanbul initiative. Certainly, all these elements were in a state of flux prior to the attempted assassination of Hitler in mid-July 1944. Following a successful attempt, Himmler, doubtless encouraged by the "Pragmatists", may have been emboldened to propound separate policies towards Jews and foreign affairs for his SS, an organisation that, by the final stages of the War, threatened to take precedence over the state, Party, and armed forces alike.[245] Not withstanding such imponderables, from the known context one can only agree with Yehuda Bauer's longstanding assessment that negotiations "might have secured the survival of very many Jews" and that the SS was "most probably" prepared to release Jews as ransom for materials.[246]

With some justification in principle, historians rejecting this analysis ask "where is the documentation?" In this particular instance, however, the question is hardly valid. Surrounded as he was by ideological opponents and predators, Himmler would have been an absolute simpleton to document his manoeuvrings.[247] And, as has been seen, the *Reichsführer-SS* was indeed, and in deed, a cautious satrap. Just as documentation from Hitler ordering the *Endlösung* will, most probably, never be discovered, it is hardly conceivable that the *Reichsführer-SS* would have issued written Memoranda regarding his real intention towards the possible liberation of European Jews. Bauer is surely correct in his view that analysis of rescue prospects must consider Himmler's extended initiatives, and his intimate involvement in the eventual release of some 10,000 Jews. A release, it should be noted, for which he received precious little incentive, acknowledgement or gratitude from the Allies. In short, based on objective fact, the question of substantial additional release was most probably available for genuine exploration, should the Allies have so deigned.

Thus is posed the second crucial question of the "Rescue Matrix": was the fanatical ideologue Hitler prepared to sanction the survival of a substantial number of Jews? From previous discussion it will be recalled that, as early as December 1942, Hitler had authorised the ransom of Jews for the benefit of the Reich. Moreover: in April 1944 he excluded 100,000 Hungarian Jews from deportation to Auschwitz for work on the *Jägerstab* project; he did not veto the release of the 1,700-member Kasztner Transport, nor did he castigate Himmler for so doing; and, in keeping with his statement "The West entered the War to prevent us going East, not to have the East come to the Atlantic", in mid-January 1945 he authorised Ribbentrop to negotiate peace with the Anglo-Americans.[248] In this context, Richard Breitman's statement should be noted: "Hitler had to have Jews remain [alive] as hostages in the hope of controlling the behaviour of Western powers."[249] Additionally, two Nazi perceptions, each based firmly on Nazi ideology, should also be factored into our analysis: Jewish emigrants would increase Antisemitism in their countries of destination (a Nazi policy objective); and it was permissible to trade "blood for blood", typically Jews in exchange for ethnic Germans residing in danger beyond the Reich's borders.

None of this can be interpreted as indicating that the *Führer* may have been prepared to abandon the *Endlösung*. However, it does give us pause regarding the possibility of Hitler, in response to a meaningful Allied *quid pro quo*, permitting Himmler a larger perimeter in which to manoeuvre. And this development may well have provided additional opportunities to rescue further (possibly substantial) numbers from the Final Solution.

Any further regression by Hitler (from extermination back to the exploitation of an increased number of Jews) would certainly have been a transient phenomenon, that is, neither a permanent manifestation nor an abandonment of the *Endlösung*. To reiterate: it is clearly beyond reason to assume that, as hardcore Nazis, either Himmler, much less Hitler, were manoeuvring towards philosemitism. But it is certainly reasonable to assume that Himmler — influenced by self-serving "Pragmatists" (like his *SD* Chief Schellenberg), and motivated by the imperative of postwar survival — became increasingly nervous about the outcome of the War. In the incessantly growing crisis facing Germany, a pragmatic tactical manoeuvre regarding Jews may have appeared justified. That is, exploit the Jews, as before 1940, by any means possible so as to benefit the Reich's faltering war effort on two fronts. Nazi racial strategy — the eventual elimination of Jews from Europe — would remain unchanged, but the strategy could be suspended temporarily in order to resolve the immediate and greater (military) crisis confronting the Reich. In considering this scenario, it is critical to distinguish between Nazi *tactics* towards Jews (which could be varied according to need), and the ultimate *strategy* (the Final Solution of the "Jewish Question" in Europe) which remained a core principle of Nazi ideology.

Unfortunately for Europe's entrapped Jews — Himmler's chosen catalyst for redressing Germany's politico-military deficiencies — the *Reichsführer-SS*' initiatives were based on a double fantasy. The fantasy of Jewish power within, and influence upon, the Allies; and the fantasy of the West having sympathy — other than in the form of crocodile tears and sentimental gestures — for the Jewish plight under the Nazis. The (inconsequential) priority accorded rescue was summarised, and the paltry influence of Jewish leaders upon Allied policy was implied, decades after the War by John Pehle, the WRB's founding director: "What we did was little enough. It was late... Late and little, I would say."[250] Exacerbating the problem was the US State Department which, in tandem with the War Department, adopted a persistently obstructionist — if not antagonistic — attitude towards European Jewry. As David Wyman's research confirmed, the State Department's "basic policy was not rescue but the avoidance of rescue".[251]

With few exceptions, this malaise permeated the commanding heights of America's political hierarchy, including President Roosevelt himself. Wyman succinctly summarised Roosevelt's response to the *Endlösung* thus: "He had little to say about the problem and gave no priority at all to rescue."[252] Even Roosevelt's establishment of the WRB — a creation, it should be noted, that came after the death of some five million Jews — was a hasty strike aimed at pre-empting political turmoil generated by his apathy towards the destruction of European Jewry.[253] Motivated by political expediency, Roosevelt paid the WRB scant attention after its establishment, denied it adequate funding, and impeded its effectiveness by not appointing a high-profile public figure as its director. In short, Roosevelt — a master of rhetorical flourish and grand political gestures — consciously distanced himself from the WRB, condoned the continuation of the status quo, avoided the political risk of adopting a pro-Jewish stance, and thus evaded the emotive accusation of waging war on behalf of Jewish interests. The President's attitude towards Jewish rescue was simple and consistent: public concern to mask both private and official indifference, with appropriate concessions at the margins to satisfy political necessity. One can only concur with Wyman's assessment that "in the end, the era's most prominent symbol of humanitarianism turned away from one of history's most compelling moral challenges".[254]

In accord with this pervasive ethos, the WRB, notwithstanding specific authority to rescue Jews by a multiplicity of means, severely compromised its mission and often attempted to act as an "honest broker" between US interests and the Jewish tragedy in Europe. Thus, despite initial hopes generated by the WRB's powerful charter, its potential for the mass rescue of Jews was never realised. It is clear that the WRB accepted American national interest as its primary concern. This is not to deny that some valuable work was accomplished by WRB executives. In particular, Roswell McClelland, WRB representative in Switzerland, used funds donated by the AJDC in an "illegal" manner. McClelland produced false documents, bribed police and border officials, hired smugglers to bring Jews to Switzerland, and smuggled cash, and scarce commodities, to Jews in Axis territory.[255] It appears that, unofficially at least, the WRB condoned bribery and "micro rescue" (the rescue of small numbers via the use of small sums) whilst, in accordance with US policy, mass rescue (via the use of significant sums) was, in effect, vetoed. Doubtless the Board, like its political masters, was distinctly nervous about the political consequences of supplying significant sums to the enemy specifically for the rescue of Jews.

Like the vacuous Bermuda Conference of April 1943, the WRB was part of the public relations smokescreen masking the West's real policies towards European Jewry.[256] Accordingly, the Board failed to institute for Jews the precedents established for non-Jewish refugees. Of particular note, at considerable expense in terms of time, personnel and transport capacity, the West shipped 100,000 non-Jewish Poles, Yugoslavs and Greek civilians to north Africa and the Middle East, and then maintained them in dozens of refugee transit camps.[257] No such scheme was ever approved for Jews during the War. One is forewarned of this omission by examining the internal "culture" of the WRB. At the end of March 1945, Roswell McClelland, writing to a colleague regarding the Musy–Himmler negotiations, referred to Jews under Nazi control as "deportees" and "political detainees".[258] At the end of the War, for McClelland to call Jews under German control "deportees" and "political detainees" is at the very least, after everything that he knew about the *Endlösung*, a trivialisation of the Jewish fate under the Nazis. It is also a very early — if not the first — example of what has come to be called Holocaust universalisation.

The primary problem confronting the West's Jewish leaders was that, despite their lobbying and rallies, they failed to convince their respective governments, or public opinion, that the rescue of European Jews from destruction should be either a war aim and/or a humanitarian priority.[259] In America, Jewish leaders battling against pervasive apathy and antagonism at the top were further handicapped by the indifference of the mass media. Most American newspapers — with the notable exception of the Yiddish press — published very little about the Holocaust, mass circulation magazines virtually ignored the subject, radio coverage was sparse, and Hollywood — despite its numerous Jewish "moguls" (magnates), producers, directors and screenwriters — simply avoided the issue.[260] In particular, the destruction of Hungarian Jews had very little impact on the US public, whose attitude was summarised by an editorial in the *New Republic* of July 1944. Headed "Getting Used to Massacres", the editorial assessed American opinion thus: "Such news is received nowadays with a shrug of the shoulders."[261]

Constrained by this negative socio-political ethos, American Jewish leaders (like those elsewhere in the West) operated with marginal influence and effectiveness — even when their proposals were in full accord with Allied policy. A notable instance occurred shortly after Germany occupied Hungary, when the ORRC suggested to Adolf A. Berle, Assistant Secretary of State, that Jews be exchanged for German civilians interned in Africa and other Allied-controlled territory.[262] Although conforming with Allied policy that a *quid pro quo* offered the Reich should have no military or economic significance, the proposal was never considered seriously. Neither was the question of (Axis) satellite leaders receiving immunity from postwar prosecution in return for freeing Jews, a consideration that may well have appealed to Horthy and Germany's other increasingly nervous allies. In this context, it is poignant to note that at least 500,000 Jews were murdered in Auschwitz in the period May–November 1944, inclusive.[263]

As has been seen, the ORRC, after realising the futility of attempting to involve official US agencies in meaningful rescue endeavours, initiated its self-proclaimed "Stop at Nothing" policy, that is, actions not in conformity with government regulations.[264] Rather than being bound by US fiat, the ORRC was guided by the Jewish religious principle that "He who saves a life saves the world". As a consequence of these "extra-legal" efforts, and the initiative and perseverance of their Swiss representatives (the Sternbuchs), the ORRC, a small, relatively unknown organisation much neglected by postwar historiography, deserves recognition as the main catalyst in facilitating Himmler's release of 1,200 Jews from the Theresienstadt concentration camp. The AJDC, despite its often overly legalistic (compliant) attitude towards rescue, also achieved success. Apart from donating more aid to European Jews than the rest of the world combined, the AJDC also, for example, funded Jewish children hidden in France, and financed International Red Cross operations in Hungary (see Chapter V).[265]

Doubtless, American Jewish leaders could have achieved greater success if granted more funds and support by American Jews. The US community's level of support, and degree of sympathy towards European Jewry, is indicated by the amounts donated to the AJDC: $38,000,000 in 1939-43; $36,000,000 in 1944–45; and $194,000,000 in 1945–48.[266] Clearly, despite the (albeit spasmodic) information available during the War, US Jews (like Jews throughout the Diaspora) only comprehended the enormity of the Holocaust after the conclusion of hostilities. Western Jewish leaders, like their *confrères* in occupied Europe, were confronted with an event unprecedented in recorded history, that is, one beyond both previous conception and experience. In response to such incomprehensible tragedy, doubtless greater urgency, a temporary armistice on the question of Zionism, and the advent of central co-ordination or planning — with its consequent reduction in duplication, suspicions, open squabbling and (possibly) personality clashes — would have increased the effectiveness of Western Jewish organisations involved in the great task of rescue.

Likewise in Palestine, for a substantial part of the War the Jewish community and its leaders generally failed to comprehend the hitherto inconceivable events occurring in Europe.[267] But the real problem was that no nation permitted Jewish leaders to establish either responses or structures appropriate for confronting a tragedy of such vast proportion. In attempting to overcome the Allies' paralysis of policy and compassion, Jewish leaders everywhere agreed that the opportunity to negotiate the rescue of their European co-religionists warranted urgent, comprehensive and meaningful exploration. But faced with the Soviet's absolute opposition, and the West's tokenist response, most Jewish leaders were initially nonplussed. Their eventual attempts to circumvent the impasse foundered on the West's control over contacts with the enemy, and the consequent embargo on Western citizens (including Palestinians) meeting with German representatives — a prohibition, it should be noted, strongly advocated by the WRB.[268]

Paradoxically, this ban resulted in the Mayer–Becher (Jewish-German) negotiations in Switzerland. As has been seen, Saly Mayer, retired lace manufacturer and marginal political entity, was tightly constrained and denied meaningful authority by his US masters, especially regarding the provision of ransom as *quid pro quo* to the Germans. Still, the astute Mayer, through the judicious use of bluff and bluster — and the adroit withholding of non-acceptable details from his WRB controllers — managed to keep Himmler both dangling yet interested. Needless to say, Saly Mayer had his detractors — particularly the executives of rival Jewish organisations. This was to be expected for a somewhat haughty figure operating in an emotionally charged, deeply sensitive, competitive and decidedly controversial arena.[269]

Yet notwithstanding suspicions regarding his sometimes "extra-legal" (non-authorised) *modus operandi*, Mayer retained the WRB's consistent support. Early in the negotiations, on 30 August 1944, the Board cabled Switzerland: "Please express to Saly Mayer the Board's appreciation for the excellent manner in which he is handling a most difficult task."[270] And on 17 January 1945, Florence Hodel (WRB) complimented Mayer for ingeniously continuing the discussions, and using every possible device to stall for time, whilst making no commitments to the Germans.[271] Such forbearance of non-authorised procedures was hardly within the WRB's usual *modus operandi*. Probably, the Board overlooked Mayer's infractions primarily because the large majority of its funding was supplied by Mayer's head office, the AJDC. Thus, as previously mentioned, it must be recognised that the WRB's achievements (such as they were) were financed largely by the American Jewish community and not the US government.

Like its US partner, the UK also dismissed the concept of mass Jewish rescue. In particular, despite Churchill stating in his postwar memoirs that "Ever since the Balfour declaration of 1917, I have been a faithful supporter of the Zionist cause", throughout the War Britain maintained its highly restrictive quota on Jewish emigration to Palestine.[272] Unlike Roosevelt, however, both Churchill and Eden favoured bombing the death facilities at Auschwitz. Tragically, both succumbed to Air Ministry and Foreign Office intransigence, and the proposal was shelved. The issue of bombing Auschwitz was yet another instance of Churchill's sometimes meaningful, compassionate attitude towards persecuted Jews being impeded, if not sabotaged, by the action (or inaction) of ideologically hostile or obdurate subordinates. A not untypical example of Whitehall intransigence towards Jewish rescue was expressed on 1 September 1944 by A. R. Dew of the Foreign Office. In assessing a Board of Deputies of British Jews plea to assist the Hungarian and Roumanian communities, Dew minuted: "In my opinion, a disproportionate amount of time of this office is wasted in dealing with these wailing Jews."[273]

As discussed above, by reasonable standards of assessment Auschwitz remained operational because of political considerations rather than technical difficulties. Destruction of the Auschwitz gas chambers and crematoria in May 1944, besides most probably reducing the speed and volume of deportations from Hungary, would, equally probably, have eroded Himmler's confidence regarding his ability to pressure Jewish leaders and their Western associates. This, in turn, may have resulted in a significant erosion of his negotiating terms well before the camp's actual decommissioning. At all events, it is clear that Auschwitz was a prime factor in Himmler's Istanbul attempt to force the West into negotiations.

Notwithstanding their vast differences in ideology, European Jewish leaders supported the principle of rescue via negotiations. When the Western news media reported the Allies' refusal to barter "Blood for Trucks", the ultra-Orthodox, Slovakian, anti-Zionist Rabbi Weissmandl neutralised the Allied rejection by assuring the *SS* that these reports were a facade to hide the West's real intentions. Himmler not only continued to act on the basis of this assurance, but also continued his attempts to initiate dialogue with the West via the use of Jewish intermediaries.

Transparently, Himmler's attempted metamorphosis from Mephistopheles to the Angel of Mercy via the use of Jewish leaders was the macabre, surrealist illusion of an increasingly beleaguered fantast. Deluded by Nazi ideology regarding the immense power of "International Jewry", Himmler simply failed to recognise that

Jewish leaders were helpless when confronted by Allied intransigence. He also failed to appreciate that the Allies camouflaged their conflicting war aims by deciding (at Casablanca, in January 1943) to insist on Germany's unconditional surrender; that this policy was based on the desire to prevent the Grand Alliance from splintering on the details of a negotiated peace; and that the Allies demanded the physical destruction of Germany, and the total demoralisation of the German people, so as to preclude the possibility of a third rematch on the battlefield.[274]

Rather than viewing the "Blood for Trucks" proposal as an opportunity to rescue Jews under the sentence of death, Western leaders considered that Himmler's initiative — and its mandatory negotiations — not only threatened the Grand Alliance and its military operations, but also raised the highly distasteful prospect of being engulfed by a flood of impoverished alien Jewish refugees. Hence the Allies' subsequent duplicity, disinformation, procrastination, obfuscation, crocodile tears and calculated tokenism. By this process, European Jews were deliberately abandoned to their fate and, in effect, relegated to the status of a historical footnote to World War II.

Jewish leaders in both Palestine and the Diaspora concurred that time could be gained, and additional rescue most probably achieved, by the mere commencement of some form of meaningful negotiations. Even without the benefit of hindsight, one acknowledges the wisdom of this position. With regard to postwar theoreticians who criticise from the certitude of comfortable armchairs, one can only sympathise with Kasztner's heartfelt plea: "Was there anything left for us to do? Did anyone suggest other, better rescue possibilities?"[275]

To summarise: on the one hand, Himmler's lack of political sophistication towards the West, his tenuous grasp of the realities behind the Grand Alliance, and his almost obsessive focus on utilising his fallacious "trump card" (Hungary's Jews), well-nigh programmed his Istanbul overture for contemptuous Allied dismissal as yet another satanic Nazi ploy. On the other hand, the West's political considerations and absolute focus on military priorities — augmented by Soviet Judeophobia, Arab antipathy to rescue, Allied Antisemitism, and the indifference or hostility of Western public opinion — ensured that Jews in Axis territory were caught in a classic lose-lose situation. We are left with the tragic paradox that, for the West, the prospect of successful negotiations negated the very possibility of negotiations. Quite simply, Europe's Jewish remnant remained bound between the relentless German hammer and the impassive Allied anvil.

Chapter VI: Notes

1. Most overtures were motivated by attempts to gain postwar advantage, rather than a desire to halt the carnage.

2. To such an extent that, in Britain, a popular joke referred to Prime Minister Chamberlain as Neville "J'aime Berlin" (I love Berlin).

3. For a precis of such attempted peace settlements, see B. Martin and T.R.H. Havens 1989:372-85. Unless otherwise stated, information regarding these attempts is from this source.

4. In particular, to his Chiefs of Staff, 2 June 1940. (Martin and Havens 1989:375)

5. Italy entered the War on 10 June 1940.

6. For example, Göring proposed that the great powers divide the world into spheres of influence, with Africa to be exploited by an international consortium. In turn, the US State

Department took seriously the German suggestion that, as Germany had achieved hegemony over continental Europe, the USA should advise the UK to negotiate.

7. As has been seen in previous chapters, this attitude even extended to Pius XII's acquiescence regarding the Nazis' persecution and deportation of Italian Jews. One noted authority summarised the Pope's attitude and "endeavours" thus:

> Worst of all, not a single word of public protest issued from the Vatican. Like other Italians, priests, monks and nuns throughout Rome, and indeed, throughout the country, were hiding Jews at great personal risk to themselves. But from the Pope himself, there was only silence.
>
> In fact, the Pope seems to have learned about the pending roundup [of Jews] by at least October 9 [1943], one week before it actually occurred... There is no evidence that Pope Pius XII ever acted on his knowledge. Before the roundup, he never threatened, suggested, or even hinted that he would publicly condemn any SS action to deport the Jews of his own city... Pope Pius XII, however, did not just fail to speak out or exert private pressure before October 16. He also failed to issue a public protest after the roundup had actually occurred... He never publicly condemned the deportation of the Jews who lived beneath his very windows. (Zuccotti 1987:126-32)

The true extent of the Pontiff's ethical stupor was, once again, confirmed in 1944 by his carefully considered refusal to invoke the Papacy's incomparable moral authority — and Christian responsibility? — to condemn the massive destruction of Hungarian Jews.

8. Michael Phayer, "Pope Pius XII, the Holocaust, and the Cold War", *Holocaust and Genocide Studies*, V12 N2, Fall 1998, 236-37.

9. Martin and Havens 1989:378.

10. To be led by Alexander Kerensky, former Prime Minister of the Russian Provisional (post-Tsarist) government.

11. Martin and Havens 1989:379.

12. The OSS was the precursor of the US Central Intelligence Agency (CIA), which was established in July 1947.

13. Martin and Havens 1989:380.

14. Martin and Havens 1989:381.

15. Miller 1945:767.

16. Martin and Havens 1989:382.

17. Braham 1981:945; Bauer 1978:112 and 120.

18. Cited Gilbert 1984:214.

19. Ibid.

20. Cited Gilbert 1984:217.

21. See *Aide Memoire*, British Embassy, Washington DC, 5 June 1944; WRB Records, Box 70, Joel Brand Folder, Franklin D. Roosevelt Library (henceforth WRB-B70:JBF).

22. Shertok, who changed his name to Sharett in 1948, was Israel's first Foreign Minister and a subsequent Prime Minister.

23. Cited Gilbert 1984:223.

24. Winston Churchill, *The Second World War* (London: Cassell & Co, 1959), 372.

25. Cited Gilbert 1984:225.

26. Gilbert 1984:226-28.

27. See Telegram, Ambassador Harriman, US Embassy in Moscow, to US Secretary of State, 19 June 1944, WRB-B70:JBF.

28. See File Memorandum, John Pehle, 21 June 1944, Ibid.

29. Telegram, Steinhardt to Cordell Hull, 22 June, 1944, Ibid.

30. Telegram, Tuck to Cordell Hull, 23 June, 1944, Ibid.

31. Telegram, Anthony Eden, 1 July 1944, Ibid.

32. US analysis of Eden's Telegram, "Points to be made to the British", n.d. but *circa* early July 1944, Ibid.

33. On 19 June, Miklos Krausz in Budapest sent Mantello an abridged version of the Auschwitz Protocols together with his (Krausz') summary of Hungarian Jewry's fate during the Occupation.

34. Gilbert 1984:231, *et al.* Braham (1981:710) mistakenly states that the escape, by Arnost Rosin and Czezlaw Mordowicz, occurred on 27 April.

35. Telegram, Berne to Foreign Office, London; PRO FO WR 75/3/48, 26 June 1944.

36. PRO FO WR 110/3/48, 3 July 1944.

37. Gilbert 1984:252-53.

38. PRO FO 371/42807 WR 170/3/48.

39. In mid-1944, the US programme to develop the atom bomb, the Manhattan Project, was far from completion.

40. Cited Gilbert 1984:276.

41. Established in January 1943, the British Cabinet Committee for Refugees consisted of the Foreign, Home and Colonial Ministers (respectively Anthony Eden, Herbert Morrison, and Oliver Stanley) and their top bureaucrats.

42. Vago 1974a:123-24.

43. Churchill actually banned all such negotiations on 11 July, two days before the Committee meeting. [Winston Churchill, *The Second World War* Vol. 6 (Boston, 1953), 693]

44. Telegram, British Foreign Office to Moscow, 13 July 1944; WRB-B70:JBF.

45. At its meeting of 26 June 1944, the Crown Council approved the emigration of about 8,000 Hungarian Jews. After a flurry of international communications, this was interpreted in the West to mean 8,000 families, hence the idea that refugee numbers would total 40-50,000 individuals. The Red Cross reported from Hungary that the total number of refugees involved would be approximately 41,000. (Ofer 1990:283)

46. Vago 1977:219-20.

47. Cited Ofer 1990:283.

48. Cited Vago 1977:221.

49. Vago 1977:220-21. The joint response stated, *inter alia,* that temporary refuge would be organised for Jewish refugees who arrived in a neutral country or in Allied-controlled territory.

50. Braham 1981:1,117.

51. Telegram, British Embassy, Washington, to State Department, 18 July, WRB-B70:JBF.

52. The *Tribune* reported this under a London by-line of 18 July 1944. Not unreasonably, Yehuda Bauer (1978:149) attributes the leak to Eden.

53. A total of about 20,000,000 Soviet citizens were killed as a result of World War II.

54. Levin 1977:227.

55. Levin 1977:229-30. "Unreliable" and "politically suspect" Jews included those classified as *bourgeois* and those unwilling to become USSR citizens. Despite this policy, the Soviet regime in the newly occupied regions presented Jews with a considerable dilemma. In Lithuania, for example, which the USSR occupied on 15 June 1940, Jews appreciated the Soviet's protection from German and Lithuanian Antisemitism, and the new opportunities for socio-economic advancement that the regime introduced. Yet simultaneously, the Soviet systematically suppressed Jewish religious, cultural and political activities. Matters were exacerbated by the nationalisation law of September 1940, when 83 percent of businesses nationalised had been in Jewish hands. In June 1941, one week before the German invasion, 30,000 people were arrested in Lithuania and sent into exile; 5,000 of these were Jews. (Bauer 1981:117)

56. Levin 1977:234.

57. *Einsatzgruppen* were German mobile killing squads in the USSR that operated in conjunction with the *Wehrmacht*.

58. Levin 1977:235.

59. As a particularly vindictive example: following the secret "trial" of leading Jews — including members of the Anti-Fascist Committee — twenty-six defendants found "guilty" were secretly executed in August 1952.

60. The most notable joint statements by the "Big Three" were issued on 17 December 1942 and 2 November 1943, although the latter did not specifically mention Jews.

61. Included in such forced migration schemes was the Jewish "reservation" near the Lublin area in Poland, and the proposal to deport all Jews to the French island colony of Madagascar. Of particular note was the plan formulated by Hjalmar Horace Greely Schacht, President of the Reichsbank and member of Hitler's cabinet. Subsequent to the Evian (Jewish Refugee) Conference of July 1938, Schacht proposed to promote German exports via the emigration of the Reich's Jewish residents. Despite Ribbentrop's opposition, Schacht's plan received Hitler's approval in January 1939.

62. Most historians consider that the policy of *Endlösung* was decided upon in the period November 1940-April 1941.

63. Rabbi Weissmandl, one of the instigators of the Europa negotiations with Wisliceny, claimed to be in close contact with the AJDC.

64. Bauer 1979:14-15. Although evidence exists to support Bauer, some historians find his reasoning inconclusive. For an example of this contrary attitude, see Braham 1981:914-15. Unless otherwise indicated, all dollar amounts refer to US currency.

65. Admiral Canaris was arrested in July 1944 as a leader of the *Wehrmacht* plot to assassinate Hitler. He was hanged on 9 April 1945 in the Flossenbürg concentration camp.

66. Brand's name was on a prepared list of high-profile and activist Budapest Jews, all of whom were subject to immediate arrest upon the German occupation.

67. Grosz was released due to the intervention of Hungarian intelligence officers. (Vago 1974a:120)

68. It was during his second arrest, several days after his first release, that Grosz apparently testified against the Budapest *Abwehr* and its head, Dr Josef Schmidt. (Ibid)

69. Braham 1981:942.

70. Vago 1974a:115-17.

71. Bauer 1994:165-66.

72. Breitman and Aronson 1993:191.

73. Document No. T/37(151), *Trial of Adolf Eichmann,* 1993 (henceforth ET):1,070.

74. ET 1993:1,071.

75. Interview with Joel Brand, p7, 22 June 1944, Cairo; WRB-70:JBF.

76. Bauer 1994:164-65.

77. Bauer 1994:281.

78. This episode is inextricably enmeshed with the internecine conflict between Ribbentrop and Himmler. Shortly after being appointed Plenipotentiary, Veesenmayer was warned by Ribbentrop that his duties included neutralising Himmler's attempts to interfere with the Foreign Ministry's jurisdiction in Hungary. In an attempt to reinforce his position, Veesenmayer regularly announced that, being personally appointed to Hungary by Hitler, he was directly responsible to the *Führer*. However, as his attempts to operate independently were often thwarted, Veesenmayer generally aligned with the Foreign Ministry and not the *SS*. (Breitman and Aronson 1993:183) Doubtless, this attitude was influenced by the fact that Veesenmayer's bitter rival, *SS* General Otto Winkelmann, was Himmler's representative in Hungary.

79. Breitman and Aronson 1993:191-92.

80. Anthony Eden, for one, was repeating contemporary Anglo-American attitudes when he concluded that Grosz was "a German agent of most dubious reputation". (Vago

1974a:126) Yehuda Bauer (1978:147) is less negative, merely calling Grosz "a worthless lout".

81. ET 1993:1,065.

82. PRO FO WR 324/3/48, 22 June 1944.

83. As a young graduate engineer before the War, my father Jozsef worked for several years in Weiss Manfred's Danube naval division.

84. Nine were flown to Switzerland, the rest to Lisbon. For details of the SS-Weiss Manfred "agreement", see Braham 1981:518. Under Himmler's instruction, nine members of the four families were detained in Vienna as hostages. "Circumstances" prevented most of the monetary promise being paid.

85. Horthy's attempt to block the transfer was unsuccessful.

86. Braham 1981:957. There is some support for the opinion that the Germans attempted a parallel initiative on 8 July, again due to Brand's detention by the British. In this view, an undercover operative in the German legation in Istanbul, Colonel Stiller — whom Braham (1981:1,106) calls the German Consul General in Istanbul — contacted Menachem Bader of the Turkish *Va'ada*, (allegedly) on behalf of the German Foreign Office. Stiller offered to fly Bader, at very short notice, to Berlin (or Vienna or Budapest) to continue the stalled Brand negotiations. Although mentioning this incident, Bauer (1994:191) states that a Colonel Stiller was not listed amongst German personal in Istanbul, and could hardly have represented the German Foreign Office, who opposed the mission. Bauer's conclusion: "no trace has been found of such an attempt in any German archive or testimony. We just do not know." (Ibid) At all events, although it is clear that an approach to Bader was made by someone claiming to represent Germany, the British refused Bader (a Palestinian citizen) permission to negotiate with the enemy.

87. Letter, J. Pehle to E. Stettinius, 27 July 1944; WRB-B70:JBF. For Stettinius' wholehearted acceptance of Pehle's recommendations, 27 July 1944, see Ibid.

88. Bauer 1994:220. In 1938, Rothmund persuaded Germany to distinguish Jews from "Aryan" German travellers by marking German Jewish passports with the red letter "J".

89. The Swiss Support Fund for Refugees (the supposed distributor of AJDC funds to Jewish refugees in Switzerland) was a paper entity consisting largely of Saly Mayer. (Bauer 1994:220)

90. *Note*, Becher to Himmler, 25 August 1944; in Braham 1963:Doc.No. 294.

91. Telegram, Vessenmayer to Ribbentrop, 25 August 1944; in Braham 1963:Doc.No. 214.

92. Braham 1981:962.

93. For a succinct *exposé* of Becher's duplicity and opportunism, see Bauer 1994:206-12 and 239-40.

94. Braham 1981:963-64. After the cessation of hostilities, Kasztner provided substantial assistance to the Allied prosecutors of Nazi war criminals.

95. A WRB report, 28 February 1945, noted McClelland's opinion that Musy "is generally looked upon [in Switzerland] as a potential Swiss Quisling". [Florence Hodel, "Special Negotiations", WRB, 28 February 1945, p3; WRB-B71: Negotiations in Switzerland (henceforth NS).

96. Bauer 1994:230-31.

97. F. Hodel, "Memorandum for the Files", 24 January 1945; WRB-B71:NS. Ms Florence Hodel was the Assistant Executive Director, WRB.

98. This claim, regarding the release of 1,200 Jews from Theresienstadt, was first made on 7 February 1945 by the US Union of Orthodox Rabbis' Emergency Rescue Committee, in a telephone call to the WRB. On 8 February, Sternbuch and Musy stated in a joint press release that the 1,200 Jews had been liberated as a consequence of personal negotiations with Himmler. The same day, McClelland accepted this statement and reported Musy's request that five million Swiss francs be deposited in the Swiss National Bank in his (Musy's) name.

Musy claimed that he was passing on a German request for compensation regarding transportation and evacuation costs, and that the money would not leave Switzerland. On 10 February, the US State Department informed the British and the Soviets of Musy's negotiations. (F. Hodel, "Special Negotiations", WRB, 28 February 1945, p4; WRB-B71:NS)

99. Cited Bauer 1994:231.

100. Kersten gained access to the Nazi hierarchy via his successful treatment of Himmler's frequent and painful stomach cramps. Amongst other Nazi notables whom Kersten treated were Rudolph Hess (gall bladder problems) and Joachim von Ribbentrop (severe headaches, vertigo and digestive disorders). [Louis L. Snyder, *Encyclopedia of the Third Reich* (London: Blandford, 1989), 193-94. Henceforth Snyder.] Before his career as a Nazi, Ribbentrop was a champagne salesman, until he married the boss' daughter.

101. In September 1948, whilst in Palestine attempting to negotiate an armistice between Arabs and Jews, Count Bernadotte was assassinated in Jerusalem by Jewish extremists.

102. Bauer 1994:242-43.

103. Bauer 1994:247-48.

104. Snyder 1989:165-66.

105. Quoted Braham 1981:1,100.

106. *Eretz*: Hebrew term for "the land".

107. Ofer 1977:445.

108. Ofer 1977:446

109. Ofer 1977:448.

110. Ofer 1990:320, Appendix D. As there was no Holocaust in Turkey, it is not appropriate to consider Jewish citizens of Turkey smuggled to Palestine by the IRD to have been rescued from the Holocaust.

111. Porat 1990:193.

112. Porat 1990:198.

113. See *Note*, Mendelsohn 1982:176.

114. Porat 1990:204.

115. Cited Porat 1990:208.

116. WRB-B34: "Persecutions in Hungary" Folder, Hungary No. 1, 17 May 1944, p1.

117. WRB-B34: "What We Have Done With Respect to Hungary" Folder, Hungary No. 1, 6 September 1944, p3-4.

118. Wyman 1990:35.

119. The cash remittances were primarily used to pay custom duties and transport costs on the ORRC's aid parcels. [ORRC Budget Bulletin, June 1944, p1. (Henceforth ORRC:BB, June 1944) The Bulletin, which is contained in the Yeshiva University Archives, can also be found in Wyman 1990:181-84.]

120. The ORRC estimated that of its $42,000 overhead, $34,000 (81 percent) was spent on fundraising. (ORRC:BB, June 1944, p2)

121. ORRC:BB, June 1944, p2-3.

122. ORRC:BB, June 1944, p3.

123. ORRC:BB, June 1944, p4.

124. Wyman 1990:ix.

125. ORRC:BB, June 1944, p4. In contrast to the ORRC's efforts, the (Bundist) Jewish Labor Committee's rescue activities — which were based on its association with underground labour and socialist groups (often non-Jewish) in occupied Europe — were conducted in "close co-operation" with the AJDC. (Ibid)

126. Roswell McClelland to Dr Wilhelm Abegg, Zurich, 20 December 1944; WRB-B62, Union of Orthodox Rabbis, July-December 1944. This advice on handling the Sternbuchs was in keeping with McClelland's cable of 5 August 1944, when he informed the WRB that "we have had to handle them [the Sternbuchs] with considerable circumspection".

127. F. Hodel, Memorandum for the Files, 24 January 1945; WRB-B71:NS.

128. F. Hodel, Report, "Special Negotiations with Gestapo and SS to Save Jews in Europe", 28 February 1945, p3 and p5; WRB-B71:NS.

129. F. Hodel, Memorandum for the Files, 17 January 1945, p4; WRB-B71, Saly Mayer Folder.

130. Ofer 1990:269.

131. Bauer 1978:133.

132. Memorandum, "Persecution in Hungary" Folder, Hungary No. 1, no author, undated but probably *circa* April-May 1944, p6; WRB-B34.

133. Ibid, p7.

134. The unique collective rescue of Denmark's tiny Jewish population of some 8,000 souls, in October 1943, was achieved by methods remote from the WRB's recommended strategy. Note that the Danish rescue preceded the establishment of the WRB in January 1944.

135. The complete document can be found in Wyman 1990:188.

136. Ibid.

137. Braham 1981:1,097.

138. Quoted Eppler 1977:64.

139. Telegram to Foreign Office from High Commissioner, Jerusalem, 26 May 1944, p2; WRB-B70:JBF.

140. Bauer 1978:133.

141. Bauer 1978:137-38.

142. Bauer 1978:139.

143. Quoted Gilbert 1984:270.

144. Erdheim 1997:151. Eden's Memo of 7 July, which was marked "Secret" and "Immediate", stated: "I very much hope that it will be possible to do something. I have the authority of the Prime Minister to say that he agrees." (Quoted Gilbert 1984:272)

145. Quoted Gilbert 1984:238.

146. One of the most conclusive instances of the Allies' overwhelming air superiority was the meagre *Luftwaffe* activity over the beaches of Normandy during the critical Anglo-American invasion of France in June 1944.

147. Wyman 1984:298. The critical factor inhibiting daylight bombing of Axis territory was the absence of fighter protection for bombers raiding enemy installations distant from Allied aerodromes. This problem was solved brilliantly when a supercharged Rolls Royce Merlin engine, and additional fuel tanks of 200-gallon capacity, were fitted to US-built P51 Mustang fighters. The protection provided to Allied bombers by this improvement was so effective that by May 1944 the *Luftwaffe* had been systematically eliminated as a viable defence force. The upgraded P51 provided continual fighter escort for US B17 Flying Fortress bombers flying missions from England to Berlin and return, a total of some 2,300 km.

148. Wyman 1984:298-99.

149. Wyman 1984:307.

150. Gilbert 1984:307, Wyman 1984:299.

151. Erdheim 1997:155; Wyman 1984:302.

152. Levy 1996:290. For Kitchens' views see "The Bombing of Auschwitz Re-examined", in Verne Newton *FDR and the Holocaust* (New York: St. Martins Press, 1996), 183-218. For a comprehensive demolition of both Kitchens' and Levy's arguments, see Erdheim 1997:129-70.

153. Herzstein 1998:335. It was Herzstein who asked Levy this question after a public presentation by the latter at the Holocaust Memorial Museum, Washington. For his part, even the sceptical Kitchens concedes that two RAF squadrons might have successfully bombed the gas chambers and the crematoria at Auschwitz. (Ibid)

154. Gilbert 1984:216.

155. See *Jewish Chronicle*, 16 November 1962 and 11 January 1963. (Cited Hausner 1977:243) Harris' view is supported by Group Captain Leonard Cheshire, VC. (See *Sunday Telegraph*, 4 June 1961; Ibid) Further support is provided by (amongst others) Bertram Schwartz, research and development scientist, and a USAF B25 bomber crew member during World War II. Schwartz states that he recently developed "an attack plan for destroying its [Auschwitz'] four death machines [gas chambers] with minimal inmate casualties". See Bertram Schwartz, "Bomb Birkenau?", in *Holocaust and Genocide Studies*, Volume 13, Number 2, 1999:348-51.

156. Wyman 1984:303-04.

157. Erdheim 1997:170, n135.

158. Ben Gurion's and Gruenbaum's statements are quoted in Levy 1996:271.

159. In their meeting with Eden on 6 July, Weizmann and Shertok — apart from urging that the RAF bomb Auschwitz and its railway network — proposed that the UK provide Jews under Nazi control with "Certificates of Protection", arrange for temporary refugee camps in Allied territories, and warn the Hungarian regime against collaborating with Germany in the Final Solution.

160. Quoted Gilbert 1984:256.

161. Wyman 1984:295. This request was made on behalf of Ernest Frischer, a member of the Czechoslovak Government-in-Exile in London.

162. McCloy's complete response can be found in Wyman 1984:296.

163. Gilbert 1984:321.

164. Braham 1981:1,140, n284.

165. Fred Barkley, "New Group Sets Up a 'Hebrew Nation' ", *The New York Times,* 19 May 1944, p8. Included in the HCNL executive was Samuel Jabotinsky, son of the famous right-wing Zionist pioneer, Vladimir Jabotinsky.

166. Ibid.

167. Ibid.

168. Wyman 1984:346.

169. The State Department opposed the resolutions because of its concern at adverse British and Arab reaction.

170. The complete text is contained in Wyman 1990:191-93. The same letter was also sent to several other members of Congress.

171. Quoted Wyman 1984:347.

172. Bauer 1981:406. Randolph Braham disagrees with Bauer's assessment, see Braham 1981:1,124.

173. ORRC: BB, June 1944, p4. The Budget Bulletin reported that the number of aid parcels dispatched by the AJDC to Jewish refugees in Russia was expected to increase from 6,000 to 20,000 per month. This increase, plus the ORRC's decision to concentrate resources on rescue efforts, was the probable motivation behind the latter's desire to co-ordinate its relief programme with the AJDC.

174. Morse 1968:303.

175. Bauer 1981:405; Morse 1968:308.

176. Morse 1968:308.

177. Bauer 1981:440; Hull to WRB, 8 September 1944, Franklin D. Roosevelt Library, "The Diaries of Henry Morgenthau Jr", 770/246.

178. Eppler 1977:48.

179. Eppler 1977:62.

180. "Inter-Office Communication", B. Akzin to F. Hodel, WRB, 9 January 1945, p1, WRB-B27, *Vaad* Emergency Committee (henceforth ORRC).

181. Ibid.

182. Ibid.

183. F. Hodel, "Memorandum For the Files", WRB, 11 January 1945; WRB-71:NS.

184. "Inter-Office Communication", B. Akzin to F. Hodel, WRB, 9 January 1945, p2; WRB-B27.

185. At the commencement of World War II, there were about 5,000 Jewish refugees in Switzerland. (Bauer 1981:226) Of the 295,000 people allowed to enter Switzerland during the War, some 21,000 were Jewish refugees from Nazism. (Bauer 1981:230)

186. Braham 1981:1,123.

187. It is worthy of note that Morgenthau Jr's father, Hans Morgenthau Sr, was the US Ambassador in Constantinople during the Turkish massacre of 1,500,000 Armenian men, women and children in 1915-16. Writing of this tragedy, Morgenthau Sr stated: "The great massacres and persecutions of the past seem almost insignificant when compared with the suffering of the Armenian race in 1915." [*Ambassador Morgenthau's Story*, quoted in *The Armenian Genocide* (Sydney: Armenian National Committee, 1983), p106.] Henceforth, for the sake of brevity, Morgenthau Jr will be referred to as Morgenthau.

188. "Internal affairs" included German-instituted concentration camps in which Jews were incarcerated. (Bauer 1981:204)

189. Franklin D. Roosevelt Library, "The Diaries of Henry Morgenthau Jr", 823/90-113, 27 February 1945, (henceforth HMD), 3.

190. Morgenthau to Hodel, HMD, 2.

191. HMD, 3-4.

192. HMD, 9-10.

193. HMD, 12-13.

194. HMD, 18-19.

195. HMD, 20.

196. HMD, 22.

197. HMD, 24.

198. Franklin D. Roosevelt Library, "The Diaries of Henry Morgenthau Jr", 824/242-244, 28 February 1945, (henceforth HMD:I), 1.

199. HMD:I, 2.

200. HMD:I, 3.

201. Wyman 1984:265-68.

202. The POW figure is from Wyman 1984:338.

203. Vago 1974a:125-26; Porat 1990:201.

204. ET 1993:1,067. Brand stated that this remark was made to him by Lord Moyne, in the presence of at least fifteen to twenty people, at an Anglo-Egyptian club in Cairo. (ET 1993:1,068.)

205. Bauer 1978:128.

206. Ira Hirschmann, "Memorandum to Ambassador Steinhardt: Interview With Joel Brand, Observations and Recommendations", 22 June 1944, p7-8; WRB-B70:JBF.

207. Ibid, p8 and p11.

208. Ibid, p6.

209. Letter, Hirschmann to Pehle, Ankara, 3 July 1944; WRB-B70:JBF.

210. Hirschmann, "Conversation With Mr Joel Brand", Jerusalem, 7 October 1944, p3; WRB-B70:JBF.

211. As A. W. G. Randall, of the British Foreign Office, noted on 24 December 1943: "Once we open the door to adult male Jews to be taken out of enemy territory, a quite unmanageable flood may result. (Hitler may facilitate it!)" (Cited Gilbert 1984:168.)

212. Pehle to Stettinius, *Memorandum*, 17 August 1944, in Mendelsohn and Detwiler 1982:101.

213. Leni Yahil, *The Holocaust: The Fate of European Jewry, 1932-45* (New York: Oxford University Press, 1990), 404.

214. On 26 July 1944, whilst advocating a special flag for the proposed Jewish Brigade

Group, Churchill, in a Top Secret Minute to the Minister of War, wrote: "I cannot conceive why this martyred race...should be denied the satisfaction of having a flag." (Cited Gilbert 1984:291) The Jewish Brigade was finally established on 19 September 1944.

215. Gilbert 1984:285.

216. Wyman 1984: 306.

217. Ibid.

218. Wyman 1984:295.

219. Ibid.

220. Pehle to Morgenthau, "What We Have Done With Respect to Hungary" Folder, Hungary No. 1, 6 September 1944, p3; WRB-B34.

221. According to Becher's postwar testimony, Himmler ordered gassing to cease in mid-October 1944. (ET 1993:1,119)

222. Braham 1981:516; Bauer 1981:410-11; Bauer 1994:222. For background to the Strasshof group, see Braham 1981:649-52.

223. Bauer 1994:229; Breitman 1997:84; Bauer 1994: 168.

224. Hilberg 1985:1,134 (Vol.3). It is interesting to note Hilberg's admission that "except where indicated otherwise, the entire account of the Brand mission is taken from Alexander Weissberg, *Die Geschichte von Joel Brand*, published in Germany in 1956, some thirty years before Hilberg's edition appeared in 1985. (Ibid, 1,132, n67) As is well recognised, Weissberg's account was released well before many important archives were opened for historical research.

225. Peter Young, *A Short History of World War II, 1939-1945* (New York: Thomas Crowell, 1966), 346.

226. Marrus 1988:186-87. Gilbert's extraordinary claim is neither explained nor clarified. One is simply left perplexed.

227. Bauer 1978:147 and 1994:169. Schellenberg's memoirs (written 1951 [Bullock 1956:15], published 1956) state that, during a private discussion with Himmler in August 1942, he responded thus to the *Reichsführer-SS'* query on how to safely open negotiations with the West: "I explained that such operations could never be conducted through official channels of conventional diplomacy, but should go through the political sector of the Secret Service. Then, in case of misfiring, the persons directly involved could be officially discredited and dropped. On the other hand, it would be essential for the other side to know that the person with whom they would be dealing had real authority behind him." (Schellenberg 1956:353) Schellenberg's memoir, although highly tendentious and blatantly self-serving, does provide insights into the intrigues and machinations within the *SS* hierarchy. Manvell and Fraenkel (1965:159-161) accept Schellenberg's claim regarding the above conversation.

228. Braham 1981:943-44. According to Braham, Grosz' closely concealed personal objective was to escape to free or neutral territory as, by this time, his wife was already in Istanbul. (Ibid)

229. Bauer 1994:168-69.

230. Bauer 1978:147 and 1981:393.

231. Chimera: "monster with lion's head, goat's body, and serpent's tail; a fanciful conception." (*The Concise Oxford Dictionary*, Fourth Edition, Oxford, 1956, 204)

232. ET 1993:1,042 and 1,119. Schellenberg was brought to trial in January 1948 and, in April 1949, sentenced to six years' gaol, the sentence to commence from June 1945. Released in June 1951, he died in March 1952. (Bullock 1956:15)

233. The hardline Kaltenbrunner, with surer grasp of *real-politik,* contemptuously informed the "pragmatic" Kurt Becher that no foreigner would negotiate with a concentration camp commander (Himmler). (For this and other postwar statements by Becher, see "Interrogation of Kurt Becher", No. 929, 7 July 1947, Nuremberg, Office of US Chief Counsel for War Crimes, APO 696A.)

234. The leader of Budapest's Orthodox Community, Fulop Freudiger, related that "Dr Kasztner pleaded with Eichmann to halt the deportations, arguing that there should be Jews to barter when [Joel] Brand returned from his mission. Eichmann didn't accept this; he said that instead the thumb screw had to be applied, otherwise International Jewry would not be willing to deliver the wanted goods." (Freudiger 1972:268)

235. Quoted by Assistant State Attorney Bach, during the Eichmann trial, from Becher's interrogation of 2 March 1948. (ET 1993:1,042)

236. For critical extracts from both Becher's telegram and Himmler's response thereto, see ET 1993:1,090.

237. Ibid.

238. Whilst in Bergen Belsen, the Kasztner Transport's 1,700 members received cigarettes, sausages, a complete exemption from compulsory labour, and daily allocations of bread, margarine and marmalade. Children, and the sick, received milk and adequate medical attention. The group appointed their own camp Council, and were permitted to organise ample cultural activities. (Braham 1981:957)

239. ET 1993:1,117.

240. Cited ET 1993:1,118.

241. Bauer 1979:23.

242. The three major components of this release were 1,700 Jews on the Kasztner Transport; 1,200 from Theresienstadt; and, in April 1945, about 6,500 from Sweden. (The Swedish figure is from Bauer 1994:248.)

243. Bullock 1956:14.

244. For Himmler's order in late 1944 stipulating the "humanitarian" treatment of Jews (an order for which both Schellenberg and Becher claim responsibility), see Höhne 1972:524-25.

245. Bullock 1956:11.

246. Bauer 1979:24, 1978:154, and 1994:255. Recently, Bauer seems to have retreated somewhat from this assessment, writing "...negotiations were a way out, not for the rescue of the majority, to be sure, but for the rescue of some, maybe more than were actually saved... Was rescue, then, possible? On a large scale, no." [Bauer, "Conclusion", in David Cesarani (ed), *Genocide and Rescue* (Oxford:Berg, 1997), 207] As apparent from my main text, I disagree with Professor Bauer's apparent change of emphasis regarding the possibility of further substantial rescue.

247. A noted authority has described the *SS* — a universe containing both supporters and opponents of Heinrich Himmler — thus: "...the world of the secret service and secret police, a world in which nothing was too fantastic to happen, in which normality of behaviour or simplicity of motive were curiosities and nothing was taken at face value, a world in which lies, bribes, blackmail and false papers, treachery and violence were part of the daily routine." (Bullock 1956:9) To a considerable extent, this description applies to the whole Nazi hierarchy.

248. Padfield 1990:560.

249. Breitman 1992:63.

250. Quoted Wyman 1984:287.

251. Wyman 1984:189.

252. Wyman 1984:311.

253. At the suggestion of the Bergson group, towards the end of 1943 identical motions were introduced into the US Senate and House of Representatives which called on Roosevelt to establish a commission to rescue European Jews. To this extent, if no other, the Bergson group played an important part in the creation of the WRB.

254. Wyman 1984:312-13.

255. Wyman 1984:232.

256. At the conclusion of the (private) Bermuda Conference between the UK and USA,

the British delegation reported to London that "after ten days of agreeable discussion...so far as immediate relief to [Jewish] refugees is concerned, the conference was able to achieve very little." (Quoted Wasserstein 1988:348) Despite this, Eden, patently motivated by the imperative of public relations, declared the Conference a "marked success". (Ibid)

257. Wyman 1984:305.

258. "Memorandum", Roswell McClelland to Don Bigelow, 23 March 1945; WRB-B62.

259. One of the largest pro-rescue rallies was organised by the American Jewish Conference, and held at the Madison Square Park, New York, on 31 July 1944. Attended by 40,000 people, the rally called for the immediate implementation of Horthy's offer to release thousands of Jews from Hungary.

260. Jews had such a prominent role in Hollywood's film industry throughout the Nazi era that, during this period, Twentieth Century Fox was known as the Goy (gentile) Studio because its head, Darryl F. Zanuck, was the only non-Jewish mogul in town. Likewise, MGM (Metro Goldwyn Mayer) was known as Mayer's Ganze Mishpoche (Yiddish: Mayer's whole family) for obvious reasons. Why was it that in an era when celebrated films of great social conscience were released, and when Hollywood had so many acclaimed Jewish managerial and creative executives, that the annihilation of European Jewry was either ignored, trivialised and/or universalised away? For an overview of this question, see T.D. Kramer "Hollywood During the Holocaust Era", in *Menorah, Australian Journal of Jewish Studies*, Volume 4 Nos. 1 & 2, December 1990:94-102. For other media, see Wyman 1984:321-27.

261. Quoted Wyman 1984:252.

262. ORRC, "Memorandum to the Honorable Adolf A. Berle", "Persecutions in Hungary" Folder, Hungary No. 1, p3, nd but probably *circa* April 1944; WRB-B34.

263. This conservative estimate is from Hilberg 1985:1,132 (Vol. 3).

264. Wyman 1984:251.

265. Wyman 1984:330.

266. Bauer 1981:458.

267. Ofer 1990:315.

268. On 27 July 1944, John Pehle wrote to the State and War Departments thus: "I strongly urge that definitive instructions be sent which will effectively prevent any meeting between [Joseph] Schwartz [of the AJDC] and the German representative." (Letter, Pehle to Acting Secretary of State Stettinius, and Assistant Secretary of War McCloy, 27 July 1944, p2; WRB-B70:JBF)

269. Regarding objections by historians, Wyman (1990:ix), without elaboration or references, states that Mayer's "claims of achievements must be read with substantial reservations".

270. Cable, WRB to Leland Harrison and Roswell McClelland, 30 August 1944, FDR Library, "The Diaries of Henry Morgenthau Jr", 767/151.

271. F. Hodel, "Memorandum for the Files: Special Negotiations with the Gestapo and SS for Saving the Jews of Europe", 17 January 1945, p4, Saly Mayer Folder; WRB-B71.

272. Winston Churchill, *The Second World War* (London: Cassell, 1959), 971. In the period September 1939–May 1945, only 50,000 Jews entered Palestine, of whom 16,500 were illegal arrivals. (Ofer 1990:318)

273. Quoted Wasserstein 1988:351.

274. For Churchill's defence of the Allies' policy of requiring unconditional German surrender, see Winston Churchill, *The Second World War* (London: Cassell, 1959), 646-49.

275. Porat 1990:190.

CONCLUSIONS

Above all, this study demonstrates that, despite their arrival in Magyarorszag many centuries before the Magyars, Jews remained perennial aliens in the land of Hungary. Even enormous contributions to the nation's development, and conspicuous displays of intense patriotism in periods of national peril, failed to alter Hungarian allegations regarding the Jews' immutable "otherness" and adherence to pernicious foreign doctrines.

As has been seen, subsequent to the government-sponsored Jewish Congress of 1868–69, Hungarian Jewry was, in effect, formally divided into two great "denominations", the Neolog and Orthodox. Whilst the latter focused on the preservation of religious tradition and Rabbinic authority, the former desired an (often cautious) accommodation with changing socio-economic circumstances. These "denominations" formed largely separate and distinct communities, their respective leaders and members divided by the apparently insurmountable religious and ideological divisions formalised by the Congress' deliberations. With tragic irony, the most unified Jewish community in the history of contemporary Hungary was instituted by Nazi fiat shortly after the German Occupation of 19 March 1944. Of critical significance, the principle of mandatory affiliation introduced by the Congress — a principle binding by law upon all of Hungary's Jews — was utilised by the Nazis and their local collaborators with devastating consequences for the Hungarian Jewish Community during the period of German Occupation.

It was the intracommunal turmoil associated with the Jewish Congress of 1868–69 that inaugurated the successful application of innovative political methods by the Orthodox leadership. This success inculcated into subsequent generations of Orthodox leaders the ethos of considering activist and unconventional secular strategies as appropriate and effective political tools. In marked contrast, the modernist, socio-economically progressive Neolog, being the politically dominant grouping and generally having the sympathy of post-Emancipation governments in Hapsburg Hungary, developed a culture of working "passively" through authorised procedures and established channels. To large extent, this dichotomy lasted until Phase II of the German Occupation of Hungary.

The Emancipation era thus provides historical perspective regarding the disparate responses of Orthodox and Neolog leaderships to the pressures inflicted upon Hungarian Jews during World War II. In particular, the final two decades of Hungarian Jewry's "Golden Age" generate insight into why the closest and most significant Jewish co-operation during the Holocaust era in Hungary occurred between Hungarian Jewry's bitterest ideological enemies, the Orthodox and the Zionists. With little doubt, a shared activist ethos, combined with an international

Jewish perspective, were the major factors enabling these two groups to overcome their abiding, hitherto irreconcilable hostilities.

Subsequent to the failed revolution of 1848, Hungary's Jews — especially of the Neolog sector — increasingly perceived themselves as innate Magyar nationals, albeit of the "Israelite" persuasion. According to this self-conception, Hungarian Jews formed an intrinsic element of Magyarorszag, the Hungarian motherland. Mesmerised by this perception, Magyar Jews during the "Golden Age" misinterpreted their constitutional equality as equivalent to an unqualified acceptance. In reality, an informal social contract ensured that Jewish progress was effectively confined to largely delineated sectors of the Hungarian state, Jews remaining emphatically blocked from advancement in many governmental spheres. Thus, despite liberation from a medieval-type pariah status, Hungarian Jewry, in effect, retained significant neo-feudal elements in its social topography. It remained a highly visible, non-integrated social entity, patently distinguishable from other groups within Hungary by its brilliant cultural and economic achievements yet transparently dependent on the continuing goodwill of its Magyar Establishment patron. It was the removal of this patronage following the debacle of 1918 that sanctioned the reactivation of Hungary's endemic — though at that stage covert — Antisemitism.

Until the infamous blood libel of Tiszaeszlar — the last hurrah of medieval Judeophobic superstition in Hungary — Hungarian Antisemitism was based on religious prejudice, and bolstered by those vested interests adversely affected by the development of liberalism, capitalism and the rise of the Jewish entrepreneurial classes. In marked contrast, Antisemitism in the Trianon era was founded on xenophobia, racial Darwinism, and widespread economic avarice. This last factor was exacerbated by the widely known fact that Jews occupied white collar, professional, financial and cultural positions far in excess of their proportion of the country's population.

The debacle of World War I precipitated a dramatic and fundamental transformation in Magyar self-conception. During the *Ausgleich* era it had been largely acceptable in polyglot, monarchist Hungary for minorities — especially the Jews — to adopt Hungarian national identity and still maintain their religious proclivities. Trianon nationalism, however, now rooted in an overwhelmingly homogeneous society motivated by the chauvinistic Antisemitism of the country's guiding ideology, the *Szegedi Gondolat*, rejected the prewar supra-ethnic model of nationhood and, with this rejection, consciously abandoned the previously state-supported concept of religious tolerance. In essence, Hungarian nationalism had metamorphosed from a mobile, "open" form based on voluntary allegiance, to a "closed" format based on a preordained, immutable ethnicity that refused to tolerate intranational diversity. Henceforth, contrary to the abiding and fervent hopes of a traumatised Jewish community, the concept of the Hungarian political state was largely superseded by that of a Hungarian nationhood based on "race".

Despite this metamorphosis, even after the advent of institutional Antisemitism — beginning with the *Numerus Clausus* of 1920, an attempt to restrict Jewish access to higher education — Jewish national consciousness, namely Zionism, remained absent from Hungary. Overwhelmingly, Zionists were reviled by their co-religionists for embracing an alien philosophy — generally referred to as dual or divided loyalties — that was incompatible with Hungarian Israelites' self-perception of being inherent constituents of the Magyar peoplehood. Consequently, with few exceptions, only elements of the less Magyar-centric minorities of Hungarian Jewry — the Zionists and some Orthodox leaders — had the ideological freedom, activist ethos in non-authorised channels, international perspective and contacts to engage in underground activities during the largely pragmatic, non-Nazi Kallay government of 1942–44.

As with Germany, social turmoil erupted in Hungary following the collapse of 1918. The advent of Bela Kun's bolshevik-influenced regime generated a bloodthirsty reaction from the White militia, a counter-revolutionary force organised by the Hungarian Establishment, *déclassé* gentry, xenophobes, professional soldiers and ex-servicemen. As some two-thirds of Kun's Commissars were of Jewish origin, public opinion identified Hungarian Jews with Kun's left-wing dictatorship. The perception of Jews being the spiritual rectors, and temporal facilitators, of Hungarian and international Communism became so firmly embedded in public consciousness that Jewish duplicity became a *sine qua non* of even serious political discussion in Hungary until — at least — the end of World War II.

The White Terror of 1919–20 inaugurated — and Horthy's subsequent career legitimised — institutional Antisemitism in Hungary. For the first time in the modern era, physical brutality became a legitimate means of solving the "Jewish Question" in Hungary. Notwithstanding the fundamental incompatibility of Judaism and atheistic Communism, the fervent patriotism of Hungarian Jews, and the significant Jewish role in anti-bolshevik activity, the White Terror's Judeophobic policy of "national purification and regeneration" dwarfed in magnitude the violence perpetrated on Hungarian Jews by Kun's Red Terror.

Upon its consolidation, Horthy's White regime curbed physical intimidation and embarked upon a policy of institutionally constricting the socio-economic status of Hungary's Jews. The initial instance of this policy, the *Numerus Clausus* of 1920, was the first example of anti-Jewish legislation in post-World War I Europe, and the first breach in Hungarian Jewry's hitherto constitutional equality. Not unexpectedly, the number of conversions to Christianity during the Trianon era correlated closely with two factors: the intensity of Antisemitic agitation and, more importantly, the level of institutional pressure exerted by the government on the community.

Following Prime Minister Bethlen's relatively moderate and pragmatic ministry of 1921–31, during which there was some alleviation of the pressures upon the Jewish Community, the great depression and the advent of Hitler's Germany facilitated the resurgence of Hungary's Antisemitic radical Right. Unable to curb its increasing popularity, from 1938 onwards, successive governments attempted to pre-empt the radical Right agenda by introducing a series of increasingly harsh and restrictive anti-Jewish statutes. The initial such piece of legislation, the First Jewish Law, was motivated largely by socio-economic considerations. Lacking an intrinsically racist basis, it nevertheless attempted to introduce an economic *Numerus Clausus* via the revival of medieval (restricted membership) trade guilds. It appears that, for the first time in the history of the Jewish people, some (Hungarian) Jewish leaders (secretly) advocated the introduction of a (relatively mild) form of discrimination against Jews — in effect, an "affirmative action" on behalf of the Christian majority aimed at pre-empting the far more virulent inequities proposed by the growing ultra-Right. In contrast to the *Numerus Clausus* of 1920, there was to be no recovery or amelioration from the First Jewish Law of 1938.

The Second Jewish Law of 1939 stimulated the first attempt by Hungarian Jewry to emerge from its abiding isolation and seek the assistance of international co-religionists. The priority necessarily allocated by international Jewish organisations to Jewries under greater threat elsewhere in Europe ensured the failure of this historic initiative. Notwithstanding the setback, Hungarian Jewry, acting with notable cohesion, established and then expanded its great social welfare matrix, MIPI and OMZSA.

The Third Jewish Law of 1941 was an overtly racist piece of legislation, one motivated by Nazi race theory as enshrined in Germany's infamous Nuremberg Laws of 1935. Thus there was a clear progression in the aims of the three Jewish Laws. From financial oligopolists of the First Jewish Law, through economic and ethnic opponents of the Second Jewish Law, the Third Law institutionalised Jews as "racial" enemies, ethnic polluters and sexual predators. In less than a generation (1918–41), Hungarian Jewry had been forced from a constitutionally equal partnership generating national progress and development to the status of an alien element corrupting the nation's heritage, birthright and security. For the first time in Hungarian history, Jews were not classified as a religious community but as a "race" or nationality, a category applying equally to many baptised Jews and their descendants. It appears that for the first time in the history of Christianity, Hungary and those governments influenced by Nazi ideology, in effect, abolished the primacy of baptism. That is, secular authority abrogated a Christian Church's right of deciding who was, or was not, considered a member of that particular church. The Christian Churches thus lost the authority of determining who was, or was not, recognised as a Christian in good standing. In Hungary, as in other countries under Nazi influence, the Christian Churches acquiesced in this historic removal of their previously sacrosanct prerogative.

Despite institutional Antisemitism, ultra-Right agitation, and the Kamenets–Podolsk and Delvidek massacres, Kallay's pragmatic policies reinforced the Hungarian Jewish perception of sheltering securely behind a government determinedly resisting German hegemony. Miklos Kallay was so successful in maintaining Hungarian independence and, *inter alia*, safeguarding the country's Jews, that Hungarian Jewry fell into the trap of considering itself to be residing in an island sanctuary, isolated and insulated from the fate of co-religionist communities elsewhere in the Reich's domain.

Along with the wider society, Hungarian Jews never questioned the Horthy regime's ability to withstand *Nyilas* and German pressure. Thus, despite the portents of Kamenets–Podolsk and Delvidek, and in the absence of any viable alternative, official Jewish leaders retained their faith in a *de facto* compact with the supreme authority in Hungary, the Regent and his non-Nazi coterie. The absence of opposition to the Reich's apparently successful neutralisation of Horthy's power in March 1944 smashed this carefully nurtured Jewish survival policy in a single blow. During the Occupation's initial phase, the period of German dominance over the "Jewish Question" in Hungary, Jewish responses to Judeophobic edicts were predetermined by Eichmann's iron grip over the community. Reinforced by *SS* terror, extensive Hungarian collaboration and a comprehensive disinformation campaign calculated to minimise backlash both within and beyond the community, this iron grip proved devastatingly effective in inflicting the *Endlösung* upon provincial Jews. In effect, an isolated, chronically divided, rigidly structured, historically complacent and compliant community, clearly identified via the long-established government policy of mandatory affiliation, was overwhelmed — like its home country — by the Nazis' brutal efficiency and the intensity of Hungarian collaboration.

Official Jewry, led by the German-imposed Jewish Council, was thus encumbered with a terrorised, entrapped, demoralised and defenceless mass constituency mesmerised in accordance with the Moratorium on Reality Syndrome. Like Hungary's enfeebled political Left, before 19 March 1944 the Jewish leadership (with overwhelming communal support) shunned illegal and anti-government activity as counterproductive and potentially disastrous for the community. Consequently, before Sztojay's appointment as Prime Minister, the vast majority of Hungarian Jews lacked even the basic prerequisites for survival — forged documents, reliable contacts and the determination to evade German orders.

Building on foundations laid by various proto-fascist Prime Ministers, Eichmann and his commandos — aided enormously by widespread individual and official collaboration — identified, expropriated and terrorised provincial Jewry with such practised efficiency that, a mere seven weeks after the commencement of deportations, Hungary's provincial regions had, in effect, become *Judenfrei*. Yet even during the period of German hegemony over the "Jewish Question", the JC made distinct — although, of necessity, selective and often only marginally productive — attempts to frustrate Nazi policy. These, and later efforts, were aided by a concerted display of solidarity, as Jewish leaders, under intense pressure from the Germans and their local sycophants, relinquished ideological partialities and accepted former opponents — most significantly, the Zionist leader Otto Komoly — as valid and productive partners in the great enterprise of attempting to ensure communal survival.

Clearly, Horthy's abandonment of Hungary's Jews during Phase I of the Occupation was the prime catalyst facilitating the destruction of the nation's provincial Jewish communities. By corollary of the Regent's still immense personal authority, German ability to implement the *Endlösung* depended on the compliance of the Hungarian political establishment, an acquiescence determined largely by Horthy's assessment of the military balance of power, and the worth to Hungary of the Jews targeted for deportation. Thus foundered Hungarian Jewry's only hope (and consequently its sole viable strategy) for communal survival — the integrity, *in extremis*, of the Regent and the Hungarian state. Conversely, however it must be acknowledged that Horthy's tragically belated — albeit forthright and sometimes courageous — interventions during Phase II of the Occupation were the agencies enabling Budapest Jews to survive Eichmann's depredations until the debacle of 15 October 1944.

Only with Horthy's re-emergence from his political hibernation in June 1944 did Hungarian Jewry regain some freedom of manoeuvre, a freedom that was used by the JC to significant effect in protecting the surviving segment of the Hungarian Jewish community. This study clearly indicates that, in practice, the *Judenrat's* effectiveness varied inversely with *SS* authority. As the tide of war eroded German influence, especially after the successful Allied landing at Normandy in June 1944, during the Occupation's second phase (7 July–15 October) the Jewish leadership's ability and success in frustrating the *Endlösung* rose commensurately.

Contrary to widespread belief, far from being a group of servile, cringing collaborationists whose obsessive grovelling and fixation on self-preservation contributed greatly to the efficacy of the *Endlösung*, when circumstances permitted, the JC displayed courage, dedication, vision and political skill — on occasion of a high order, and (in the circumstances) with remarkable success. Furthermore, despite *Nyilas* brigands murdering many thousands of Jews in largely unco-ordinated acts of demented blood-lust during the Szalasi era, for sundry reasons — including the cumulative efforts of the JC throughout 1944 — the third phase of Occupation did not include the systematic mass extermination of Jews.

Working independently of official Jewry, the underground Halutz movement commenced largely in response to the needs of illegal Jewish refugees sheltering in Hungary before the German Occupation. As the mentors and benefactors of most illegals — particularly with regard to the provision of credible (false) documents — the Halutz' underground experience and infrastructure was well-nigh unique in Hungary before March 1944. Seizing the opportunity presented by the neutrals' *Schutzpass* schemes, from mid-1994 the Halutz false document venture escalated from a micro (small scale) to a macro (mass) rescue enterprise. The number and variety of documents manufactured and successfully distributed clearly indicates a comprehensive, systematic endeavour to negate the *Endlösung* process. Very few, if any, elements of the Jewish community were neglected, particularly after the Roumanian *volte-face* in late August 1944 closed Hungary's southern border, thus preventing further escapes via the largely Halutz-organised *Tiyul* (people-smuggling) networks.

The third great Halutz contribution to Jewish survival in Hungary involved the supply of food to Budapest's Jews during the Szalasi era. The analysis of surviving — and clearly incomplete — records reveal that at least one-third, and possibly over one-half, of the food supplied to Budapest Jews in the critical month of December 1944 was provided by the Halutzim. This finding clearly refutes attempts to marginalise the Halutz contribution to the provisioning of Budapest's besieged ghettos. Beyond their invaluable contributions to the Budapest Jewish community's survival, the numerically tiny Halutz underground preceded, assisted and facilitated the development of the fledgling Hungarian (non-Jewish) resistance after March 1944. At the very least, the Halutzim deserve recognition as a salient, integral factor in the numerically minute anti-Nazi physical resistance matrix in Hungary. Yet despite being substantially more effective, in important respects, than their non-Jewish counterparts, the significant Halutz contribution to fighting Nazism in Hungary remains shamefully unacknowledged — over fifty years after the event — by the great majority of Hungarian historians of the Occupation.

The recently disclosed testimonies of the prominent contemporary leader Gyorgy Gergely, and the student activist Arthur Stern, clearly confirm that non-Zionist elements also participated in resistance endeavours. In particular, Dr Gergely's multifaceted and wide-ranging testimonies, affidavits, correspondence and documents constitute an invaluable primary resource regarding the Hungarian Jewish community during World War II. Despite their somewhat dishevelled state, the hitherto unresearched Gergely archives — a record encompassing some 250,000 words — constitute by far the most comprehensive eyewitness chronicle of the Hungarian *Shoah* by a Jewish leader of the period. Additional to his intimate association with the Swedish diplomat Raoul Wallenberg, Papal Nuncio Angelo Rotta, Zionist leader Otto Komoly, and the uppermost hierarchy of the JC and ICRC,

Gergely was the sole representative of Hungarian Jewry in a venture unique in the history of World War II: an attempt at armed resistance, in which a vassal regime conspired to arm many thousands of Jewish conscripts to help defend the regime's proposed *volte-face* against the Germans and their collaborators. It is clear that Hungarian Jewry, via Samu Stern's authorisation and Gyorgy Gergely's efforts, co-operated with, and fulfilled its commitments to, the dilettantish Hungarian Front resistance. Clearly, the collapse of the plan to arm the JLS brigades was beyond the control of either Stern or Gergely.

The benefit of hindsight, exposing flaws in the official Jewish leadership's procedures, has permitted numerous critics the luxury of *post factum* judgements. But even with fifty years of hindsight, such critics have yet to formulate a viable, non-counterproductive alternative policy to that pursued by community leaders. Given the circumstances of the German Occupation, it is hardly conceivable that any other strategy could have saved a larger percentage of Hungarian Jews from the *Endlösung*. In the critical first phase of the Occupation, Hungarian Jewry's fate was clearly beyond its own control. Psychologically terrorised, clearly identified (especially in the provinces), physically marked, financially crushed, bereft of men of military age, abandoned by the West, defenceless and friendless, Hungarian Jews — despite the looming German defeat — faced the ferocious Nazi and *Nyilas* onslaught in physical and political isolation. In the words of Samu Stern, Hungarian Jews were trapped in a race against time. Evidently, without resolute and consistent Allied intervention after 19 March 1944, no Jewish skill, vision, leadership or power on earth could have saved the provincial Jews of Hungary. Yet despite enormous adversity, exacerbated by testy ideological conflicts and personality clashes, the JC, the Halutzim, and their various associates, were principal agents in saving the majority of those Hungarian Jews whom it was possible to save. Thus, despite the *Endlösung's* ferocious onslaught, thanks in good measure to both official and underground Jewish activists, at liberation Budapest contained a greater concentration of Jews than any other major city occupied by German forces.

Even though direct comparisons between different countries may well be misleading, it is interesting to note that the French Jewish leadership could not formulate a survival strategy over the four years of their nation's Occupation. This is despite France being a country with a long, intense democratic tradition, and a purposeful, egalitarian, viable anti-Nazi resistance — critically, all these factors being absent in Hungary. Realistically then, could the Hungarian Jewish leadership be expected to accomplish such a task in the two months between Occupation and the commencement of mass deportations?

Regarding international efforts to save Hungarian Jews, it must be recognised that peace overtures were an almost constant feature of World War II, such attempts beginning at the very commencement of hostilities. Consequently, by the time Joel Brand and Andor Grosz arrived in Istanbul in mid-May 1944, on Himmler's "Blood for Trucks" mission, the West had developed an understandable cynicism towards German peace overtures. Influenced by this cynicism, by their domestic Antisemitism, and by antipathy towards accepting responsibility for up to a million impoverished Jewish refugees, the Allies quickly rebuffed Himmler's proposals. This rejection was sold to Western public opinion on the basis that the German proposition was attempted extortion and/or devious political warfare, namely either a satanic venture to trade civilian lives for war material, a bid to sabotage Allied military operations, an attempt to split the Grand Alliance, a diabolical public relations exercise, or a combination thereof.

Despite this rejection, for reasons of political expediency the West (unlike the USSR) needed to generate the perception (as opposed to the reality) that steps were being taken to aid Jews trapped within German-controlled territory. Consequently, and to avoid the charge of Allied complicity with the *Endlösung*, both the UK and USA adopted the public relations strategy — in effect, the pretence — of appearing to consider seriously the prospect of saving Hungarian Jewry. To ensure that this simulation remained under firm control, both US and UK governments prohibited their nationals from negotiating with the enemy. To pre-empt any negative public relations impact of this veto — 1944 was an American presidential election year — the USA authorised Saly Mayer (Swiss citizen, retired lace manufacturer, and AJDC representative in Switzerland) to negotiate, under onerous restrictions, with Himmler's economic representative, Kurt Becher. The talks commenced on 21 August 1944. Stalling for time, and with little real bargaining power, Mayer, through a combination of obfuscation, misinformation, and the judicious exceeding of his authority, obtained the release of Kasztner Transport Jews confined in Bergen Belsen and, despite the absence of a *quid pro quo*, still maintained Himmler's interest in continuing discussions with "World Jewry".

Frustrated by his lack of progresss with Mayer, in November 1944 Himmler attempted to promote negotiations via the Nazi sympathiser Jean-Marie Musy, a former Swiss president with strong connections to Orthodox rescue organisations in Switzerland and the USA (the ORRC). Very probably, the ORRC-sponsored Sternbuch–Musy–Himmler negotiations resulted in the release, in early February 1945, of 1,200 Jews imprisoned in the Czech ghetto of Theresienstadt. Himmler's requested compensation for this liberation was revealing indeed: acknowledgement in the Western press of Germany's humanitarian gesture towards the Jews, this demand being a virtual capitulation in Himmler's terms and conditions of release compared with Brand's and Grosz' Istanbul revelations.

In evaluating Jewish rescue organisations, it must be recognised that relatively small, relatively low-profile groups lacking a tradition of co-operation with senior government officials — notably the Halutzim and *Va'ada* (Hungary) and, to a lesser extent, the ORRC (North America) — had relatively little to lose by the judicious use of clandestine (unauthorised) channels and methods, and, as such, sometimes acted accordingly. In marked contrast, the JA, AJDC, and other relatively large, long-established, well-connected high-profile organisations, because of their potential for substantially greater loss of access (formal and otherwise) to government intelligence and support, and public sympathy and funds, refrained as a matter of policy from either alienating government officials or publicly transgressing national policies. This perceived necessity for circumspection by "establishment" Jewish organisations was heightened in January 1944 when Roosevelt, largely motivated by domestic political considerations, established the War Refugee Board, an organisation that, despite its name, focused on the issue of Jews in occupied Europe.

Notwithstanding the Allies' stringent wartime blockade of the Axis, the WRB's charter included the power to negotiate with the enemy, to transfer funds into German-held territory, and to obtain priority for the shipping of refugees. In theory, the WRB's mandate was in fundamental contravention of US anti-Axis legislation; in fact, the theory was never really tested, much less applied. Thus, despite its powers and specific commission, throughout its existence the WRB's attitudes and operations were largely subordinated to the US government's underlying indifference to the fate of European Jews. Notwithstanding the Board's consequent ineffectiveness, and its frequent negativity towards Jewish mass rescue, WRB operations were financed almost entirely by American Jewry. Of the nearly $20 million donated by US Jewish organisations, $15 million was given by the AJDC.

Long conversant with Allied apathy and dissimulation, the sudden, unexpected Brand–Grosz revelations left many international Jewish leaders, and their organisations, dumbstruck, hesitant and disunited. In particular, the JA took over a month — during which time more than 350,000 Hungarian Jews were deported to Auschwitz — to present the Allies with a set of integrated recommendations for action on Himmler's proposals. Included in the JA's submission was a plea to disrupt the Final Solution via the aerial bombardment of the Auschwitz extermination facilities, a proposition quickly rejected, on largely spurious grounds, by both the USAF and the RAF. It is not unreasonable to maintain that destruction of the Auschwitz death facilities prior to mid-1944 may well have led to both a substantial slowing in deportations from Hungary and a reduction in the extermination rate of Jews via industrial (mass) processing. For a deterrent substantially earlier than March 1944, the Allies could have nominated — at no cost either to themselves or their war effort — any number of major air raids on German cities as being in retaliation for the slaughter at Auschwitz.

One of the most honest admissions of the Western attitude towards Jewish rescue was enunciated — albeit inadvertently — by Lord Moyne, who asked Brand in Cairo "What shall I do with those million Jews? Where shall I put them?" By his epigram, Moyne was stating one of the West's primary concerns, namely that a constructive engagement with Himmler's Istanbul initiative risked producing a mass exodus of impoverished Jewish refugees from Hungary, the majority of whom would, legally or otherwise, eventually reach the USA, UK and Palestine. Thus is generated the hypothesis that the Anglo-American fear of the political consequences of successful negotiations may well have been sufficient to doom Himmler's Istanbul overture. Note that the existence, or otherwise, of a German readiness to release a flood of Jews is irrelevant to the hypothesis: the mere suspicion amongst Western policymakers that Germany might permit substantial Jewish emigration appears to have been sufficient catalyst for the West's refusal to countenance negotiations — another instance of an untested Allied perception regarding the "Jewish Question" leading to an inevitable, tragic reality. Accordingly, on 17 August 1944 the WRB's executive director, John Pehle, in a Memo to the US Deputy Secretary of State, formalised Allied policy thus: "As I have previously indicated to you, I feel strongly that we cannot enter into any ransom transactions with the German authorities in order to obtain the release of the Jews." By this formulation, Pehle was expressing the consensus of the Grand Alliance: neither meaningful negotiations nor ransom payments, the Jews (in effect) to be abandoned to their fate.

Firmly committed to forcing Germany's unconditional surrender, the Allies ignored the gradual, cautious emergence of a "pragmatic" element centred largely within the *SS* hierarchy. In their increasingly desperate attempts to disengage from a disastrous two-front war, the "Pragmatists" believed, despite all evidence to the contrary, that Hungary's surviving Jews were a trump card through which their restructured priorities — especially disengagement on the Western Front — could be achieved. Increasingly motivated by the Reich's unrelenting sequence of military disasters, and an ever-growing apprehension as to their own postwar fate, by May 1944 the "Pragmatists" favoured reverting to Germany's prewar policy of exploiting Jews for material and political gain. Generating its own particular surrealism, this transient, Machiavellian about-face clearly attempted to utilise the condemned in order to ensure the executioners' — and hence Nazism's — postwar survival.

Himmler's seemingly separate initiatives — the Brand and Grosz missions, each of apparently unrelated intent — were, in fact, the two poles of an integrated (bi-polar) strategy, being analogous to the two sides of the one strategic coin. Yet notwithstanding his initiatives' contemptuous public rejection by the Grand Alliance, Himmler persevered with his increasingly audacious, increasingly desperate attempts to achieve an accommodation with the West through the use of Jewish intermediaries. The level of this desperation is indicated by the fact that from mid-1944 until Germany's final debacle, Himmler independently initiated, and maintained, negotiations with low-level Jewish representatives; decommissioned, and did not replace, the Auschwitz gas chambers; and ordered that Jews within his concentration camps be treated with a degree of previously nonexistent consideration. Moreover, he eventually released some 10,000 Jews from Axis territory, the large majority without the receipt of any *quid pro quo*. Lacking incentive or encouragement from the West, Himmler remained ensnared in a trap constructed from his loyalty to, and psychological dependence upon, his beloved mentor and *Führer*. With little doubt, this dependency was reinforced by the Allies' calculated indifference to the fate of European Jews.

As discussed, Jews were not only the common factor, but also the common impediment, to both poles of Himmler's bi-polar strategy. Rejecting the *Reichsführer-SS*' initiative *in toto* was the obvious, simple solution for Allied politicians and bureaucrats determined to avoid, amongst other issues, the distasteful question of what to do with up to a million Jewish refugees. And apart from tokenist gestures, the West pursued its policy of rejecting mass rescue — brutally, ruthlessly and efficiently. One can reasonably conclude that the question of substantial additional release was most probably available for genuine exploration, should the Allies have so deigned — especially considering that, in mid-January 1945, Hitler finally authorised Ribbentrop to negotiate peace with the Anglo-Americans. This does not indicate that the Nazis would have been prepared to abandon their core belief, the *Endlösung*. It does suggest the possibility, however, that Hitler, in response to a meaningful Allied *quid pro quo*, and as a temporary tactical manoeuvre, may have permitted Himmler a larger, less restrictive perimeter in which to operate. Whilst possibly too late to benefit Hungarian Jews, this development may have provided additional opportunities to rescue further (possibly substantial) numbers from the Final Solution. In particular, many thousands of Jews remaining under German control may have been saved from perishing on the infamous death marches that commenced in January (mid-winter) 1945.

Although Churchill, and to a lesser extent Eden, attempted to ameliorate the plight of European Jews — especially through bombing the Auschwitz death facilities — a malaise regarding rescue permeated the commanding heights of America's political hierarchy. Of particular note, Roosevelt created the WRB — after the extermination of some five million Jews — for reasons of domestic political expediency. The President's attitude towards Jewish rescue was consistent and unambiguous: public concern to mask both private and official indifference, with (largely tokenist) concessions to satisfy political necessity.

The primary factor inhibiting the West's Jewish leaders was their political marginality, an ethos generated by domestic Antisemitism and the Allies' adamant refusal to elevate the rescue of European Jews to either a war aim or a humanitarian priority. In precis, no nation established — or permitted Jewish leaders to establish — either responses or structures appropriate for confronting a tragedy of such vast, continent-wide proportions. Despite this chronic, fearsome handicap, valuable results were achieved by Jewish organisations, often by groups (such as the ORRC) that recognised the futility of attempting to involve government agencies in meaningful rescue endeavours. The reality is, however, that the world only comprehended the enormity of the *Shoah* after the final German debacle.

To repeat: on the one hand, Himmler's lack of political sophistication towards the West, his tenuous grasp of the realities behind the Grand Alliance, and his almost obsessive focus on utilising his fallacious "trump card" (Hungary's Jews), well-nigh programmed his Istanbul overture for contemptuous Allied dismissal as yet another satanic Nazi ploy. On the other hand, the Allies' political considerations, divergent interests and absolute focus on military priorities — augmented by Stalin's Judeophobia, Arab antipathy to rescue, Allied Antisemitism, and the indifference or hostility of Western public opinion — ensured that Jews in Axis territory were caught in a classic lose-lose situation. We are left with the tragic paradox that, for the West, the prospect of successful negotiations probably negated the very possibility of negotiations. Quite simply, Europe's Jewish remnant remained, until the end, bound between the relentless German hammer and the impassive Allied anvil.

GLOSSARY

Aliya	Jewish emigration to Palestine or, subsequently, Israel.
Einsatzgruppen	Mobile death squads responsible for the mass murder of Jews and commissars in the USSR.
Endlösung	The Nazi plan to exterminate Jews; the Final Solution to the "Jewish Question".
Führer	Leader of the Nation.
Halutz	Hebrew for pioneer. In Hungary during 1944, the underground Zionist youth movement.
Halutzim	Plural of Halutz; members of a Halutz movement.
Hashomer Hatzair	The largest Zionist youth movement in Hungary.
Hauptsturmführer–SS	Captain in the German *SS*.
Histadrut	Jewish Labour Federation in Palestine, subsequently Israel.
Honved	Member of the Hungarian military forces.
Honvedseg	Hungarian army
Judenrat	Jewish Council appointed by Nazis or their collaborators.
Kehilah	Jewish Community or congregation.
Kibbutz	Collective agricultural settlement in Palestine, subsequently Israel.
Kulfoldieket Ellenorzo Orszagos Kozponti Hatosag (**KEOKH**)	National Authority for the Control of Foreigners.
Magyar Izraelita Egyetemi es Foiskolai Hallgotok Orszagos Egyesulete (**MIEFHOE**)	National Association of Hungarian Jewish Students.
Magyar Izraelitak Partfogo Irodaja (**MIPI**)	Hungarian Jewish Welfare Bureau.
Magyar Zsidok Lapja	Hungarian Jewish Journal (HJJ).
Mizrachi	Religious sector of the Zionist movement.
Munkaszolgalat	Jewish Labour Service (JLS).
Nyilas	Literally: archer. Member of the ultra-Right Arrow Cross Party.
Obersturmbannführer-SS	Lieutenant-Colonel in the German *SS*.
Orszagos Izraelita Irodak Hadviseltek Bizottsaga	National Bureau of Jewish War Veterans (NBJWV).
Orszagos Magyar Izraelita Kozmuvelodesi Egyesulet (**OMIKE**)	National Hungarian Jewish Cultural Society.
Orszagos Magyar Zsido Segito Akcio (**OMZSA**)	National Hungarian Jewish Assistance Campaign.
Pracovna Skupina	The Working Group. Underground Jewish resistance organisation in Bratislava.
Schutzpass	Protection or exemption document.
Schutzpässe	Plural of *Schutzpass*.
Sonderkommando	SS group implementing the *Endlösung* programme.
Swabe, Swabian	Ethnic German resident in Hungary.
Tiyul	Hebrew for trip. In Hungary during 1944, the illegal emigration of Jews — generally to Roumania.
Tiyulim	Plural of *Tiyul*.
ut	Hungarian for road.
utca	Hungarian for street.
Va'adat Ezra ve'Hazalah	Underground Jewish Relief and Rescue Committee.
Yeshiva	Orthodox Jewish school for religious study.
Yishuv	Jewish Community in Palestine during the British mandate.
Zsido Tanacs	Jewish Council during the German Occupation of Hungary.

BIBLIOGRAPHY

Ainsztein, Reuben
1974 *Jewish Resistance in Nazi-Occupied Europe*. London: Paul Elek.
Anger, Per
1981 *With Raoul Wallenberg in Budapest*. Translated by David Paul and Margareta Paul. New York: Holocaust Library.
Arad, Yitzhak, Yisrael Gutman and Abraham Margaliot
1987 (eds) *Documents on the Holocaust*. Jerusalem: Yad Vashem and Pergamon Press.
Arendt, Hannah
1963 *Eichmann in Jerusalem*. New York: The Viking Press.
Aronson, Shlomo
1997 "The 'Quadruple Trap' and the Holocaust in Hungary." In David Cesarani (ed.), *Genocide and Rescue*. Oxford: Berg, pp 93-121.
Balla, Erzsebet
1969 "The Jews of Hungary: A Cultural Overview." In Randolph L. Braham (ed.), *Hungarian-Jewish Studies*. New York: World Federation of Hungarian Jews, pp 85-136.
Barany, George
1990 "The Age of Royal Absolutism, 1790-1848." In Peter F. Sugar (general ed.), *A History of Hungary*. Bloomington and Indianapolis: Indiana University Press, pp 174-208.
Barta, Istvan
1973 "Toward Bourgeois Transformation, Revolution and War of Independence." In Ervin Pamlenyi (ed.), *A History of Hungary*. Budapest: Corvina, pp 207-284.
Bauer, Yehuda
1978 *The Holocaust in Historical Perspective*. Canberra: Australian National University Press.
1979 *The Jewish Emergence from Powerlessness*. Toronto: University of Toronto Press.
1981 *American Jewry and the Holocaust. The American Jewish Joint Distribution Committee, 1939-1945*. Detroit: Wayne State University Press.
1994 *Jews for Sale? Nazi-Jewish Negotiations, 1933-1945*. New Haven: Yale University Press.
Becher, Kurt
1946 "Affidavit." Document No. 438 in Randolph L. Braham, *The Destruction of Hungarian Jewry. A Documentary Account*. New York: Pro Arte for the World Federation of Hungarian Jews, 1963; pp 895-905.
Benoschofsky, Ilona
1987 "The History of the Museum." In Ilona Benoschofsky and Alexander Scheiber (eds), *The Jewish Museum of Budapest*. Budapest: Corvina, pp 7-26.
Benoschofsky, Ilona and Elek Karsai
1958 (eds) *Vadirat a nacizmus ellen. Dokumentumok a magyarorszagi zsidouldozes tortenetehez*. I. 1944 marcius 19–1944 majus 15. [Indictment of Nazism. Documentation of the History of Jewish Persecution in Hungary. Vol. I, 19 March 1944–15 May 1944.] Budapest: A Magyar Izraelitak Orszagos Kepviselete Kiadasa.
1960 (eds) *Vadirat a nacizmus ellen. Dokumentumok a magyarorszagi zsidouldozes tortenetehez*. II. 1944 majus 15–1944 junius 30. [Indictment of Nazism. Documentation of the History of Jewish Persecution in Hungary. Vol. II, 15 May 1944–30 June 1944.] Budapest: A Magyar Izraelitak Orszagos Kepviselete Kiadasa.
Ben-Tov, Arieh
1988 *Facing the Holocaust in Budapest. The International Committee of the Red Cross and the Jews in Hungary, 1943–1945*. Dordrecht: Martinus Nijhoff Publishers.
Berend, Ivan T.
1985 "The Road Toward the Holocaust: The Ideological and Political Background." In

Randolph L. Braham and Bela Vago (eds), *The Holocaust in Hungary: Forty Years Later.* USA: Social Science Monographs and Institute for Holocaust Studies of The City University of New York and Institute for Holocaust Studies of the University of Haifa. Distributed by Columbia University Press, pp vii-x.

Berend, Ivan T. and Gyorgy Ranki
1973 "The Horthy Regime (1919-1944)." In Ervin Pamlenyi (ed.), *A History of Hungary.* Budapest: Corvina, pp 451-534.

Biss, Andre
1973 *A Million Jews to Save. Check to the final solution.* London: Hutchinson.

Braham, Randolph L.
1963 (ed.) *The Destruction of Hungarian Jewry. A Documentary Account.* New York: Pro Arte for the World Federation of Hungarian Jews.
1966 (ed.) "Introduction." In *Hungarian-Jewish Studies.* New York: World Federation of Hungarian Jews, pp xi-xiii.
1966b "The Destruction of the Jews of Carpatho-Ruthenia." In *Hungarian-Jewish Studies.* New York: World Federation of Hungarian Jews, pp 223-35.
1969 (ed.) "Introduction." In *Hungarian-Jewish Studies.* New York: World Federation of Hungarian Jews, pp xi-xiv.
1973 (ed.) *Hungarian-Jewish Studies.* New York: World Federation of Hungarian Jews.
1971 "Zionism in Hungary." In Raphael Patai (ed.), *Encyclopedia of Zionism and Israel.* New York: Herzl Press/McGraw-Hill, pp 523-27.
1974 "The Rightists, Horthy and the Germans: Factors Underlying the Destruction of Hungarian Jewry." In Bela Vago and G.L. Mosse (eds), *Jews and Non Jews in eastern Europe, 1918-1945.* New York/Jerusalem: John Wiley and Sons/Israel Universities Press, pp 137-56.
1977 *The Hungarian Labor Service System, 1939-1945.* New York: East European Quarterly, Columbia University Press.
1977b "The Official Jewish Leadership of Wartime Hungary." In *Patterns of Jewish Leadership in Nazi Europe 1933-1945.* Proceedings of the Third Yad Vashem International Historical Conference. Jerusalem 1979: Yad Vashem, pp 267-85.
1981 *The Politics of Genocide: The Holocaust in Hungary*, Vols I and II. New York: Columbia University Press.
1985 "Preface." In Randolph L. Braham and Bela Vago (eds), *The Holocaust in Hungary: Forty Years Later.* USA: Social Science Monographs and Institute for Holocaust Studies of The City University of New York and Institute for Holocaust Studies of the University of Haifa. Distributed by Columbia University Press, pp vii-x.
1986 "Preface." In *The Tragedy of Hungarian Jewry. Essays, Documents, Depositions.* USA: Social Science Monographs and Institute for Holocaust Studies of The City University of New York. Distributed by Columbia University Press, pp v-viii.
1995 *The Wartime System of Labour Service in Hungary. Varieties of Experience.* Boulder, USA: Social Science Monographs.

Breitman, Richard
1992 *The Architect of Genocide. Himmler and the Final Solution.* London: Grafton.
1997 "Nazi Jewish Policy in 1944." In David Cesarani (ed.), *Genocide and Rescue.* Oxford: Berg, pp 77-92.
1998 *Official Secrets. What the Nazis Planned, What the British and Americans Knew.* Ringwood: Viking.

Browning, Christopher R.
1978 *The Final Solution and the German Foreign Office.* New York: Holmes and Meier Publishers, Inc.

Bullock, Alan
1956 "Introduction." In Walter Schellenberg, *The Schellenberg Memoirs. A Record of the Nazi Secret Service.* London: Andre Deutsch, pp 9-18.

Carsten, F. L.
1967 *The Rise of Fascism.* London: B.T. Batsford Ltd.
Cohen, Asher
1981 "He-Halutz Underground in Hungary: March-August 1944." In *Yad Vashem Studies XIV.* Jerusalem: Yad Vashem, pp 247-67.
1985 "The Halutz Resistance and the Anti-Nazi Movements in Hungary, 1944." In Randolph L. Braham and Bela Vago (eds), *The Holocaust in Hungary: Forty Years Later.* USA: Social Science Monographs and Institute for Holocaust Studies of The City University of New York and Institute for Holocaust Studies of the University of Haifa. Distributed by Columbia University Press, pp 139-46.
1986 *The Halutz Resistance in Hungary 1942–1944.* Translated by Carl Alpert. USA: Social Science Monographs and Institute for Holocaust Studies of The City University of New York.
1988 "The Comprehension of the Final Solution in France and Hungary: a Comparison." In Asher Cohen, Joav Gelber and Charlotte Wardi (eds), *Comprehending the Holocaust: Historical and Literary Research.* Frankfurt am Main: Verlag Peter Lang, pp 243-65.
1989 "German Hegemony and National Independence During the Second World War." In Franklin H. Littell *et al* (eds), *The Holocaust. In Answer...* West Chester, Pennsylvania: Sylvan Publishers Ltd, pp 161-80.
Conway, John S.
1986 "The Holocaust in Hungary: Recent Controversies and Considerations." In Randolph L. Braham (ed.), *The Tragedy of Hungarian Jewry. Essays, Documents, Depositions.* USA: Social Science Monographs, Boulder and Institute for Holocaust Studies of The City University of New York. Distributed by Columbia University Press, pp 1-48.
Crankshaw, Edward
1981 *The Fall of the House of Hapsburg.* London: Papermac.
Dagan, Avigdor
1984 (ed.) *The Jews of Czechoslovakia. Historical Studies and Surveys. Vol. III.* Philadelphia/New York: The Jewish Publication Society of America, Society for the History of Czechoslovak Jews.
Deak, Istvan
1985 "The Peculiarities of Hungarian Fascism." In Randolph L. Braham and Bela Vago (eds), *The Holocaust in Hungary: Forty Years Later.* USA: Social Science Monographs and Institute for Holocaust Studies of The City University of New York and Institute for Holocaust Studies of the University of Haifa. Distributed by Columbia University Press, pp 43-51.
1989 *Hungary From 1918 to 1945.* New York: Institute on East Central Europe, Columbia University Press.
1990 "The Revolution and the War of Independence, 1848-1849." In Peter F. Sugar (general ed.), *A History of Hungary.* Bloomington and Indianapolis: Indiana University Press, pp 209-34.
Dombrady, Lorand
1990 *A Legfelsobb hadur es hadserege.* [The Supreme Warlord and his Army.] Budapest: Zrinyi Kiado.
Don, Yehuda
1986b "Anti-Semitic Legislations in Hungary and Their Implementation in Budapest — An Economic Analysis." In Randolph L. Braham (ed.) *The Tragedy of Hungarian Jewry; Essays, Documents, Depositions.* USA: Social Science Monographs and Institute for Holocaust Studies of The City University of New York. Distributed by Columbia University Press, pp 49-72.
1990 "Patterns of Jewish Economic Behaviour in Central Europe in the Twentieth Century." In Yehuda Don and Victor Karady (eds), *A Social and Economic History of Central European Jewry.* New Brunswick, USA: Transaction Publishers, pp 121-54.

Eichler, Hava
"Zionism and Youth in Hungary Between the Two World Wars." Ph.D Thesis, Bar-Ilan University, Israel, 1982.
Encyclopaedia Judaica
Corrected Edition. Jerusalem: Keter Publishing House Jerusalem Ltd.
Eppler, Elizabeth
1946 *Protocol.* Testimony of Elizabeth Eppler, translated by Jacques Sarlos, *Dokumentacios Ugyosztaly* [Documentation Department] Jewish Agency for Palestine; Budapest, 27 February 1946. Typewritten, eight pages.
1977 "The Rescue Work of the World Jewish Congress During the Nazi Period." In Yisrael Gutman and Efraim Zuroff (eds), *Rescue Attempts During the Holocaust.* Jerusalem: Yad Vashem, pp 47-69.
Fabian, Bela
1927 *"Az egyenlo jog — legfobb nemzeti erdek."* [Equal rights — the prime national interest.] In Vilmos Kecskemeti (ed.), *Zsido Evkonyv 1927/28.* [Jewish Yearbook 1927/28.] Budapest: n.p., pp 141-42.
Farkas, T.
1971 "Hungarian Jews in Israel." In Raphael Patai (ed.), *Encyclopedia of Zionism and Israel.* New York: Herzl Press/McGraw-Hill, pp 522-23.
Fein, Helen
1979 *Accounting For Genocide. National Responses and Jewish Victimization During the Holocaust.* New York: The Free Press.
Feingold, Henry L.
1970 *The Politics of Rescue. The Roosevelt Administration and the Holocaust, 1938–1945.* New Brunswick, USA: Rutgers University Press.
Frank, Tibor
1990 "Hungary and the Dual Monarchy, 1867-1890". In Peter F. Sugar (general ed.), *A History of Hungary.* Bloomington and Indianapolis: Indiana University Press, pp 252-66.
Freudiger, Fulop
1944 "Letter From Fulop Freudiger to Rezso Kasztner." In Randolph L. Braham (ed.), *The Tragedy of Hungarian Jewry. Essays, Documents, Depositions.* USA: Social Science Monographs, Boulder and Institute for Holocaust Studies of The City University of New York (1986). Distributed by Columbia University Press, pp 289-94.
1972 "Five Months." In Randolph L. Braham (ed.) *The Tragedy of Hungarian Jewry. Essays, Documents, Depositions.* USA: Social Science Monographs, Boulder and Institute for Holocaust Studies of The City University of New York (1986). Distributed by Columbia University Press, pp 237-87.
Freudiger, Fulop *et al*
1944 "Report on Hungary: March 19–August 9, 1944." In Randolph L. Braham (ed.), *Hungarian-Jewish Studies* (1973). New York: World Federation of Hungarian Jews, pp 75-146.
Gergely, Gyorgy
1940 *Felhivas.* [Notice.] Budapest: July 1940. Typewritten, 7 pages, in Hungarian, GGA.
1941 *Faj vagy Vallas?* [Race or Religion?] Budapest: June 1941. Typewritten, 43 pages, in Hungarian, GGPA.
1941 *Zsido Sargakonyv.* [Jewish Yellow Book.] Budapest: September 1941. Typewritten, 19 pages, in Hungarian, GGA.
1943 *Jelentes es Kialtvany a magyar izraelita nagykozonseges.* [Report and Proclamation to Hungarian Jews.] Budapest: Orszagos Izraelita Irodak Hadviseltek Bizottsaga [NBJWV], December 1943. Typewritten, 36 pages, in Hungarian, GGA.
1944 Report to the President of the Pest Jewish Community. Budapest: 7 September 1944. Typewritten, 2 pages, in German, GGA.

1944 *Hidveres.* [Bridge Building.] Budapest: September 1944. Typewritten, 4 pages, in Hungarian, GGA.

1944 Report to Hans Weyermann. Budapest: 16 December 1944, Ref. DrG/D[?] No. 254. Typewritten, 4 pages, German text with French nomenclature, GGA.

1944 *Note.* [Draft of *Note* to the Portuguese Legation.] Budapest: 20 December 1944. Typewritten, 3 pages, in French with postwar annotations in English, GGA.

1944 *Bericht.* [Report, to Hans Weyermann.] Budapest: 28 December 1944. Typewritten, 7 pages, in German, GGA.

1945 *Jelentes a Nemzetkozi Voroskeresztbizottsag Magyarorszagi Delegacioja "A" Szekciojanak "Hazkezelosege" mukodeserol, 1944 11 Nov-tol 1945 13 Januar.* [Report on the Activities of the IRC Hungarian Delegation's Section "A", 11 November 1944 to 13 January 1945.] Budapest: 13 May 1945. Typewritten, 18 pages, in Hungarian, GGA.

1945 *Beszamolo a Magyarorszagi Zsidok Szovetsege ideiglenes Intezo Bizottsaga munkajarol.* [Report on the Activities of the Provisional Executive of the Association of the Jews of Hungary.] Budapest: *circa* (northern) Spring 1945. Typewritten, 39 pages, in Hungarian.

1958 Statement. "In the Matter of Herman Krumey, Otto Hunsche and the Activities of the s[o] c[alled] 'Eichmann Sondereinsatzkommando' in Hungary from the 19th March, 1944." Sydney: 12 April 1958. Typewritten, 9 pages, GGA. (Covering letter: 1958b)

1971 Statement. "The Attempt to Arm the Jewish Labour Service Brigades, September-October 1944." Sydney: 1971. Typewritten, 19 pages, GGA.

1987 Oral Memoir. Transcript of tapes, edited version. Transcribed and edited by Andrew Parle. Sydney: 1987. Typewritten, 150 pages, GGA.

n.d. (*circa* early 1940s) *A zsidosag es a szocialis kerdes. Tervezet.* [Jewry and the Social Question. Plans.] Budapest. Typewritten, 24 pages, in Hungarian, GGPA.

Gilbert, Martin

1984 *Auschwitz and The Allies.* London: Arrow Books Limited.

1985 *Jewish History Atlas.* London: Weidenfeld and Nicolson.

Goldfarb, Zvi

1973 "Hehalutz Resistance in Hungary." In Jacob Glatstein *et al* (eds), *Anthology of Holocaust Literature.* USA: The Jewish Publication Society, pp 314-18.

Grosz, Endre [subsequently David Gur]

1946 *Jegyzokonyv.* [Report] Testimony of Endre Grosz [David Gur]. Budapest: 21 June 1946. Typewritten, in Hungarian, 11 pages, MA.

Gutman, Yisrael and Shmuel Krakowski

1986 *Unequal Victims: Poles and Jews During World War Two.* New York: Holocaust Library.

Gyorgy, Istvan

1945 *Fegyvertelenul A Tuzvonalban.* [Unarmed in the Firing Line.] Budapest: Cserepfalvi Kiadas.

Hajdu, Tibor and Zsuzsa L. Nagy

1990 "Revolution, Counterrevolution, Consolidation." In Peter F. Sugar (general ed.), *A History of Hungary.* Bloomington and Indianapolis: Indiana University Press, pp 295-318.

Hanak, Peter

1973a "The Period of Neo-Absolutism (1849-1867)." In Ervin Pamlenyi (ed.), *A History of Hungary.* Budapest: Corvina, pp 285-320.

1973b "The Dual Monarchy (1867-1918)." In Ervin Pamlenyi (ed.), *A History of Hungary.* Budapest: Corvina, pp 321-418.

1988 "The Period of Absolutism and Dualism." In Peter Hanak (ed.), *One Thousand Years: A Concise History of Hungary.* Budapest: Corvina, pp 122-76.

Handler, Andrew

1980 *Blood Libel at Tiszaeszlar.* Boulder, USA: East European Monographs. Distributed by Columbia University Press, New York.

1982 (ed.) "Introduction: The Historical Framework". In Andrew Handler *The Holocaust in Hungary: An Anthology of Jewish Response*. Alabama: The University of Alabama Press, pp 1-29.

1985 *From the Ghetto to the Games: Jewish Athletes in Hungary*. Boulder, USA: East European Monographs. Distributed by Columbia University Press, New York.

1996 *A Man for All Connections. Raoul Wallenberg and the Hungarian State Apparatus, 1944-1945*. Westport, CT: Praeger.

Hasomer Hacair

1948 *A Hasomer Hacair. A Zsido Ellenallasi Mozgalomban, 1942-1944*. [Hashomer Hatzair and the Jewish Resistance Movement, 1942-1944] Budapest: Hasomer Hacair.

Hausner, Gideon

1977 *Justice in Jerusalem*. New York: Holocaust Publications, Inc.

Hilberg, Raul

1972 (ed. with commentary) *Documents of Destruction. Germany and Jewry 1933–1945*. London: W. H. Allen.

1985 *The Destruction of European Jews*, Vols I, II, III. New York: Holmes and Meier Publishers, Inc.

Hilberg, Raul, Stanislaw Staron and Josef Kermisz

1982 (eds) *The Warsaw Diary of Adam Czerniakow. Prelude to Doom*. Translated by Stanislaw Staron and the staff of Yad Vashem. New York: Stein and Day.

Hohne, Heinz

1972 *The Order of the Death's Head. The Story of Hitler's SS*. Translated from German by Richard Barry. London: Pan Books Ltd.

Horthy, Nicholas

1956 *Memoirs*. Translated from *Ein Leben Fur Ungarn* (Athenaum-Verlag, Bonn) London: Hutchinson.

Janos, Andrew C.

1982 *The Politics of Backwardness in Hungary, 1825-1945*. Princeton, New Jersey: Princeton University Press.

Jeszenszky, Geza

1990 "Hungary Through World War I and the End of the Dual Monarchy." In Peter F. Sugar (general ed.), *A History of Hungary*. Bloomington and Indianapolis: Indiana University Press, pp 267-94.

Juhasz, Gyula

1984 "Some Aspects of Relations Between Hungary and Germany During the Second World War." In Gyorgy Ranki (ed.), *Hungarian History — World History*. Budapest: Akademiai Kiado, pp 209-20.

Kallay, Nicholas

1954 *Hungarian Premier. A personal account of a nation's struggle in the second world war*. London: Oxford University Press.

Kann, Robert A.

1977 *The Multinational Empire: Nationalism and National Reform in the Habsburg Monarchy, 1848–1918*, Vols I and II. New York: Octagon Books.

Karady, Victor

1990 "Demography and Social Mobility: Historical Problem Areas in the Study of Contemporary Jewry in Central Europe." In Yehuda Don and Victor Karady (eds), *A Social and Economic History of Central European Jewry*. New Brunswick, USA: Transaction Publishers, pp 83-119.

1992 "Religious Divisions, Socio-Economic Stratification and the Modernization of Hungarian Jewry after the Emancipation." In Michael K. Silber (ed.), *Jews in the Hungarian Economy 1760-1945*. Jerusalem: The Magnes Press, pp 161-84.

Karsai, Elek
1967 (ed.) *Vadirat a nacizmus ellen. Dokumentumok a magyarorszagi zsidouldozes tortenetehez. III. 1944 majus 26–1944 oktober 15.* [Indictment of Nazism. Documentation of the History of Jewish Persecution in Hungary. Vol. III, 26 May 1944–15 October 1944.] Budapest: A Magyar Izraelitak Orszagos Kepviselete Kiadasa.

Karsai, Elek and Laszlo Karsai
1988 (eds) *A Szalasi Per.* [The Szalasi Trial.] Hungary: Reform.

Katz, Jacob
1978 *Out of the Ghetto: The Social Background of Jewish Emancipation 1770-1870.* New York: Schocken Books.

1980 *From Prejudice to Destruction: Anti-Semitism, 1700-1933.* Cambridge, USA: Harvard University Press.

1990 "The Identity of Post-Emancipatory Hungarian Jewry." In Yehuda Don and Victor Karady (eds), *A Social and Economic History of Central European Jewry.* New Brunswick, USA: Transaction Publishers, pp 13-31.

Katzburg, Nathaniel
1966 "Hungarian Jewry in Modern Times, Political and Social Aspects." In Randolph L. Braham (ed.), *Hungarian Jewish Studies.* New York: World Federation of Hungarian Jews, pp 137-170.

1969 "The Jewish Congress of Hungary, 1868–1869." In Randolph L. Braham (ed.), *Hungarian Jewish Studies.* New York: World Federation of Hungarian Jews, pp 1-33.

1974 "The Jewish Question in Hungary during the Inter-War Period — Jewish Attitudes." In Bela Vago and George L. Mosse (eds), *Jews and Non-Jews in eastern Europe 1918-1945.* Jerusalem: Israel Universities Press, Keter Publishing House, pp 113-24.

1981 *Hungary and the Jews: Policy and Legislation 1920-1943.* Ramat- Gan, Israel: Bar-Ilan University Press.

1984 "The History of the Jews in Hungary." In *The Story of the Jews in Hungary.* Tel Aviv: Beth Hatefutsoth, pp 5-17.

1984b "Zionist Reactions to Hungarian Anti-Jewish Legislation 1939-1942." In *Yad Vashem Studies XVI.* Jerusalem: Yad Vashem, pp 161-76.

1985 "The Tradition of Anti-Semitism in Hungary." In Randolph L. Braham and Bela Vago (eds), *The Holocaust in Hungary: Forty Years Later.* New York: Social Science Monographs and Institute for Holocaust Studies of The City University of New York and Institute for Holocaust Studies of the University of Haifa. Distributed by Columbia University Press, pp 3-12.

1988 "Problems of Organisation within the Hungarian-Jewish Community during the Inter-War Period." In Robert Dan (ed.), *Occident and Orient: A Tribute to the Memory of Alexander Scheiber.* Budapest: Academiai Kiado/Leiden: E.J. Brill, pp 261-72.

1988b "Hungarian Antisemitism: Ideology and Reality (1920-1943)." In Shmuel Almog (ed.), translated by Nathan H. Reisner, *Antisemitism Through the Ages.* UK: Vidal Sassoon International Center for the Study of Antisemitism, The Hebrew University of Jerusalem, Pergamon Press, pp 339-48.

1988c "The Destruction of Hungarian Jewry in Hungarian Historiography." In Yisrael Gutman and Gideon Greif (eds), *The Historiography of the Holocaust Period.* Jerusalem: Yad Vashem, pp 369-86.

1990 "Central European Jewry Between East and West." In Yehuda Don and Victor Karady (eds), *A Social and Economic History of Central European Jewry.* New Brunswick, USA: Transaction Publishers, pp 33-46.

Klein, Bernard
"Hungarian Jewry in the Nazi Period: A Story of Persecutions and Communal Reactions." M.A. Thesis, Columbia University, 1956 (*circa*).

Klibanski, Bronia
1983 "The Archives of the Swiss Consul General Charles Lutz." In *Yad Vashem Studies XV.* Jerusalem: Yad Vashem, pp 357-66.
Komoly, Otto
1942 *Cionista Eletszemlelet.* [Zionist View of Life] Budapest: *Magyar Cionista Szovetseg* [Hungarian Zionist Federation].
1944 "The Diary of Otto Komoly: August 21–September 16, 1944." In Randolph L. Braham (ed.), *Hungarian-Jewish Studies* (1973). New York: World Federation of Hungarian Jews, pp 147-250.
Kosary, Dominic (as "updated and re-evaluated by the Danubian Research Centre")
1969 "Part 1: 830-1919 A.D." In *History of the Hungarian Nation.* Astor Park, Florida: Danubian Press, Inc., pp 15-244.
Kovacs, Maria M.
1994 *Liberal Professions and Illiberal Politics. Hungary from the Habsburgs to the Holocaust.* New York: Oxford University Press.
Kramer, T. D.
"From Utility to Catastrophe." Ph.D Thesis, The University of Sydney, 1994.
Kulka, Erich
1984 "The Annihilation of Czechoslovak Jewry." In Avigdor Dagan (chief ed.), *The Jews of Czechoslovakia,* Vol. III. USA: The Jewish Publication Society of America (Philadelphia) and Society for the History of Czechoslovak Jews (New York), pp 262-328.
Lakatos, Geza
1993 *As I Saw It. The Tragedy of Hungary.* Englewood: Universe Publishing Company.
Laqueur, Walter
1985 *The Terrible Secret. Suppression of the Truth About Hitler's "Final Solution".* New York: Penguin.
1989 *A History of Zionism.* New York: Schocken Books.
Laszlo, Erno
1966 "Hungarian Jewry: Settlement and Demography, 1735-38 to 1910." In Randolph L. Braham (ed.), *Hungarian Jewish Studies.* New York: World Federation of Hungarian Jews, pp 61-136.
1969 "Hungary's Jewry: A Demographic Overview, 1918-1945." In Randolph L. Braham (ed.), *Hungarian Jewish Studies.* New York: World Federation of Hungarian Jews, pp 137-182.
Lederer, Sandor
1927 "A Magyar Zsido." [The Hungarian Jew.] In Vilmos Kecskemeti (ed.), *Zsido Evkonyv 1927/28.* [Jewish Yearbook 1927/28.] Budapest: n.p., pp 238-43.
Lendvai, Paul
1972 *Anti-Semitism in eastern Europe.* London: Macdonald.
Lengyel, Gyorgy
1990 "The Ethnic Composition of the Economic Elite in Hungary in the Interwar Period." In Yehuda Don and Victor Karady (eds), *A Social and Economic History of Central European Jewry.* New Brunswick, USA: Transaction Publishers, pp 229-47.
1992 "Hungarian Banking and Business Leaders Between the Wars: Education, Ethnicity and Career Patterns" In Michael K. Silber (ed.), *Jews in the Hungarian Economy 1760-1945.* Jerusalem: The Magnes Press, pp 227-36.
Lester, Elenore
1985 "Raoul Wallenberg: The Righteous Gentile From Sweden." In Randolph L. Braham and Bela Vago (eds), *The Holocaust in Hungary: Forty Years Later.* USA: Social Science Monographs and Institute for Holocaust Studies of The City University of New York and Institute for Holocaust Studies of the University of Haifa. Distributed by Columbia University Press, pp 147-60.

Levai, Jeno (Eugene)
1947 *A Pesti Getto*. [The Budapest Ghetto] Budapest: Officina.
1948 *Black Book on the Martyrdom of Hungarian Jewry*. Edited by Lawrence P. Davis. Zurich/Vienna: The Central European Times Publishing Co. Ltd., in conjunction with The Panorama Publishing Co.
1948a *Raoul Wallenberg. His Remarkable Life, Heroic Battles and The Secret of his Mysterious Disappearance*. Translated by Frank Vajda. Melbourne: WhiteAnt Occasional Publishing, 1988.
1948b *Zsidosors Magyarorszagon*. [Jewish Fate in Hungary.] Budapest: Magyar Teka.
1961 (ed.) *Eichmann In Hungary: Documents*. Budapest: Pannonia Press.
1966 "Research Facilities in Hungary Concerning The Catastrophe Period." In Randolph L. Braham (ed.), *Hungarian Jewish Studies*. New York: World Federation of Hungarian Jews, pp 261-93.
1973 "The War Crimes Trials Relating to Hungary: A Follow-Up." In Randolph L. Braham (ed.), *Hungarian Jewish Studies*. New York: World Federation of Hungarian Jews, pp 251-90.
Levin, Dov
1977 "The Attitude of the Soviet Union to the Rescue of Jews." In Yisrael Gutman and Efraim Zuroff (eds), *Rescue Attempts During the Holocaust*. Jerusalem: Yad Vashem, pp 225-36.
Levine, Paul A.
1996 *From Indifference to Activism. Swedish Diplomacy and the Holocaust, 1938-1944*. Uppsala: Acta Universitatis Upsaliensis.
Lipscher, Ladislav
1984 "The Jews of Slovakia: 1939–1945." In *The Jews of Czechoslovakia*, Vol. III. USA: The Jewish Publication Society of America (Philadelphia) and Society for the History of Czechoslovak Jews (New York), pp 165-261.
Littlejohn, David
1985 *Foreign Legions of the Third Reich, Vol. 3*. San Jose, USA: R. James Bender Publishing.
Lucas, John
1989 *Budapest 1900*. London: Weidenfeld and Nicolson.
Macartney, C. A.
1954 "Foreword." In Nicholas Kallay, *Hungarian Premier: a personal account of a nation's struggle in the second world war*. London: Oxford University Press, pp v-xxix.
1957 *October Fifteenth: A History of Modern Hungary 1929-1945*, Vols I and II. Edinburgh: Edinburgh University Press.
1971 *The Habsburg Empire 1790-1918*. London: Weidenfeld and Nicolson.
Macartney, C. A. and A. W. Palmer
1962 *Independent eastern Europe, A History*. London: Macmillan and Co.
Magyar Zsidok Naptara, 1942-5702
[Hungarian Jewish Diary, 1942-5702]. Budapest: OMIKE [National Hungarian Jewish Cultural Society].
Makkai, Laszlo
1973 "The Origins of the Hungarian People and State." In Ervin Pamlenyi (ed.), *A History of Hungary*. Budapest: Corvina, pp 1-27.
1990 "The Foundations of the Hungarian Christian State." In Peter F. Sugar (general ed.), *A History of Hungary*. Bloomington and Indianapolis: Indiana University Press, pp 15-22.
Manvell, Roger and Heinrich Fraenkel
1965 *Heinrich Himmler*. London: Heinmann.
Marrus, Michael R.
1988 *The Holocaust in History*. London: Weidenfeld and Nicolson.

Martin, B. and T. R. H. Havens
1989 "Peace Overtures." In Marcel Baudot *et al* (eds), *The Historical Encyclopedia of World War II*. New York: Facts on File, pp 372-85.
Marton, Ernest (Erno)
1966 "The Family Tree of Hungarian Jewry." In Randolph L. Braham (ed.), *Hungarian Jewish Studies*. New York: World Federation of Hungarian Jews, pp 1-60.
McCagg Jr, William O.
1972 *Jewish Nobles and Geniuses in Modern Hungary*. Boulder, USA: East European Quarterly.
1989a *A History of Habsburg Jews, 1670-1918*. Bloomington and Indianapolis: Indiana University Press.
1989b "Vienna and Budapest Around 1900: The Problem of Jewish Influence." In Gyorgy Ranki (ed.), *Hungary and European Civilization*. Budapest: Akademiai Kiado, pp 241-63.
1990 "The Jewish Position in Interwar Central Europe: A Structural Study of Jewry at Vienna, Budapest, and Prague." In Yehuda Don and Victor Karady (eds), *A Social and Economic History of Central European Jewry*. New Brunswick, USA: Transaction Publishers, pp 47-81.
McClelland, Roswell S.
1945 "Report on the Activities of the War Refugee Board Through its Representation at the American Legation in Bern, Switzerland: March 1944-July 1945." In John Mendelsohn and D. S. Detwiler (eds), *The Holocaust. Volume 16. Rescue to Switzerland: The Musy and Saly Mayer Affairs*. New York: Garland Publishing, Inc (1982), pp 27-87.
Mendelsohn, Ezra
1983 *The Jews of East Central Europe Between the World Wars*. Bloomington: Indiana University Press.
Mendelsohn, John and Donald S. Detwiler
1982 (eds) *The Holocaust. Volume 8. Deportation of the Jews to the East: Stettin, 1940, to Hungary, 1944*. New York: Garland Publishing, Inc.
1982a (eds) *The Holocaust. Volume 15. Relief in Hungary and the Failure of the Joel Brand Mission*. New York: Garland Publishing, Inc.
1982b (eds) *The Holocaust. Volume 16. Rescue to Switzerland: The Musy and Saly Mayer Affairs*. New York: Garland Publishing, Inc.
Mendes-Flohr, Paul R. and Jehuda Reinharz
1980 (ed.) *The Jew in The Modern World*. New York: Oxford University Press.
Miller, Francis Trevelyan
1945 *History of World War II*. Philadelphia: Universal Book and Bible House.
Morse, Arthur D.
1968 *While Six Million Died: A Chronicle of American Apathy*. New York: Ace Publishing Corporation.
Munkacsi, Erno
1947 *Hogyan Tortent? Adatok es okmanyok a magyar zsidosag tragediajahoz*. [How Did It Happen? Data and Documents on the Tragedy of Hungarian Jewry.] Budapest: Renaissance.
Nagy, Gyorgy
1995 "History of Labor Service Company 108/84 of Bor." In Randolph Braham (ed.), *The Wartime System of Labor Service in Hungary*. Boulder, USA: Social Science Monographs, pp 55-127.
Nagy, Zsuzsa L.
1973 "Revolution in Hungary (1918-1919)." In Ervin Pamlenyi (ed.), *A History of Hungary*. Budapest: Corvina, pp 419-49.
1988 "Our Modern History." In Peter Hanak (ed.), *One Thousand Years: A Concise History of Hungary*. Budapest: Corvina, pp 177-249.

Nagy-Talavera, Nicholas M.
1970 *The Green Shirts and the Others. A History of Fascism In Hungary and Rumania.* Stanford, California: Hoover Institution Press.

Nassi, Tzevi
"The Hungarian Jews and the Hungarian Revolution (1848-1849)." M.A. Thesis, Ben Gurion University of the Negev, 1986.

Ofer, Dalia
1977 "The Activities of the Jewish Agency Delegation in Istanbul in 1943." In Yisrael Gutman and Efraim Zuroff (eds), *Rescue Attempts During the Holocaust.* Jerusalem: Yad Vashem, pp 435-50.
1990 *Escaping the Holocaust. Illegal Immigration to the Land of Israel, 1939-1944.* New York: Oxford University Press.

Padfield, Peter
1990 *Himmler. Reichsführer-SS.* London: Papermac.

Pamlenyi, Ervin
1973 (ed.) *A History of Hungary.* Budapest: Corvina.

Pamlenyi, Ervin and Gyorgy Szekely
1967 (eds) *Magyarorszag Tortenete,* Vols I and II. [History of Hungary.] Budapest: Gondolat Konyvkiado.

Patai, Raphael
1985 "The Cultural Losses of Hungarian Jewry." In Randolph L. Braham and Bela Vago (eds), *The Holocaust in Hungary: Forty Years Later.* USA: Social Science Monographs and Institute for Holocaust Studies of The City University of New York and Institute for Holocaust Studies of the University of Haifa. Distributed by Columbia University Press, pp 161-74.

Peto, Erno
1956 "Statement." In Randolph L. Braham (ed.), *Hungarian-Jewish Studies* (Vol. III, 1973). New York: World Federation of Hungarian Jews, pp 49-74.

Pill, Mose
1946 *Protocol.* Testimony of Mose Pill, translated by Jacques Sarlos, *Dokumentacious Ogyosztaly* [Documentation Department] Jewish Agency for Palestine, Budapest 30 January 1946. Typewritten, four pages.

Pinkas Hakehillot
[*Encyclopedia of Jewish Communities — Hungary*]. [In Hebrew] Jerusalem: Yad Vashem, 1976.

Pinter, Istvan
1986 *Hungarian Anti-Fascism and Resistance 1941-1945.* Translated from *Magyar antifasizmus es ellenallas* (Kossuth Konyvkiado, Budapest) by Gyorgyi Jakobi, Peter Ipper and Vera Sarkany. Budapest: Institute of Party History of the Central Committee of the Hungarian Socialist Workers' Party/Akademiai Kiado.

Por, Deszo and Oszkar Zsadanyi
n.d. (*circa* early post-World War II) (eds) *Te Vagy A Tanu! Ukrajnatol Auschwitzig.* [You Are the Witness! From the Ukraine to Auschwitz.] Budapest: Kossuth.

Porat, Dina
1990 *The Blue and the Yellow Stars of David.* Cambridge, USA: Harvard University Press.

Rabinowicz, Oskar K.
1971 "Czechoslovak Zionism: Analecta to a History." In *The Jews of Czechoslovakia*, Vol. II. USA: The Jewish Publication Society of America (Philadelphia) and Society for the History of Czechoslovak Jews (New York), pp 19-137.

Ranki, Gyorgy
1984 "'Unwilling Satellite' or 'Last Satellite' — Some Problems of Hungarian-German Relations." In Gyorgy Ranki (ed.), *Hungarian History — World History.* Budapest: Akademiai Kiado, pp 261-88.

1990 "Hungary — General Survey." In Israel Gutman (general ed.), *Encyclopedia of the Holocaust*, Vol. 2. New York: Macmillan Publishing Company, pp 693-98.

1992 "The Occupational Structure of Hungarian Jews in the Interwar Period." In Michael K. Silber (ed.), *Jews in the Hungarian Economy 1760-1945*. Jerusalem: The Magnes Press, pp 274-86.

Rothkirchen, Livia

1968 "Development of Anti-Semitism and the Persecution of the Jews in Hungary, 1920-1945. A Survey." In Moshe Sandberg, *My Longest Year. In the Hungarian Labour Service and in the Nazi Camps*. Jerusalem: Yad Vashem, pp iv-xxxiii.

1968b "Hungary — An Asylum for the Refugees of Europe." In *Yad Vashem Studies VII*. Jerusalem: Yad Vashem, pp 127-42.

Rozett, Robert

"The Relationship Between Rescue and Revolt: Jewish Rescue and Revolt in Slovakia and Hungary During the Holocaust." Ph.D Thesis, The Hebrew University of Jerusalem, 1987.

1988 "Jewish and Hungarian Armed Resistance in Hungary." In *Yad Vashem Studies XIX*. Jerusalem: Yad Vashem, pp 269-88.

Sakmyster, Thomas

1984 "A Hungarian Diplomat in Nazi Berlin: Dome Sztojay." In Gyorgy Ranki (ed.), *Hungarian History — World History*. Budapest: Akademiai Kiado, pp 295-305.

1994 *Hungary's Admiral on Horseback. Miklos Horthy, 1918-1944*. Boulder: East European Monographs.

Sandberg, Moshe

1968 *My Longest Year. In the Hungarian Labour Service and in the Nazi Camps*. Jerusalem: Yad Vashem.

Sandor, Pal

1927 "Vazsonyi Vilmos." [Vilmos Vazsonyi.] In Vilmos Kecskemeti (ed.), *Zsido Evkonyv 1927/28*. [Jewish Yearbook 1927/28.] Budapest: n.p., pp 218-20.

Schapiro, J. Salwyn

1959 *Modern and Contemporary European History (1815-1952)*. Cambridge, USA: Houghton Mifflin Company.

Schellenberg, Walter

1956 *The Schellenberg Memoirs. A Record of the Nazi Secret Service*. Ed. and translated by Louis Hagen. London: Andre Deutsch.

Schindler, Pesach

1990 *Hasidic Responses to the Holocaust in the Light of Hasidic Thought*. Hoboken, New Jersey: Ktav Publishing House, Inc.

Schwartz, Zehava

"The Orthodox Jewish Community in Hungary 1939-1945." Thesis, Bar-Ilan University, Israel, 1989.

Seton-Watson, Hugh

1962 *eastern Europe Between the Wars, 1918-1941*. Hamden, Connecticut: Archon Books.

Silagi, Denis

1986 "A Foiled Jewish Political Venture in Hungary, 1939-1942." In Randolph L. Braham (ed.), *The Tragedy of Hungarian Jewry. Essays, Documents, Depositions*. Boulder, USA: Social Science Monographs and Institute for Holocaust Studies of The City University of New York, pp 191-235.

Singer, Zoltan (Csima)

1995 "History of Labor Service Company 110/34." In Randolph L. Braham (ed.), *The Wartime System of Labor Service in Hungary*. Boulder, USA: Social Science Monographs and Institute for Holocaust Studies of The City University of New York, pp 15-53.

Snyder, Louis L.

1989 *Encyclopedia of the Third Reich*. London: Blandford.

Somogyi, Eva
1990 "The Age of Neoabsolutism, 1849–1867." In Peter F. Sugar (general ed.), *A History of Hungary.* Bloomington and Indianapolis: Indiana University Press, pp 235-51.
Steinberg, Jonathan
1990 *All or Nothing: The Axis and the Holocaust 1941-1943.* London: Routledge.
Stern, Samuel (Samu)
1945 *Protocol.* Testimony of Samu Stern, translated by Jacques Sarlos, *Dokumentacios Ugyosztaly* [Documentation Department] Jewish Agency for Palestine, Budapest 28 December 1945. Typewritten, in Hungarian, 26 pages.
Stockler, Lajos
1946 "Deposition." In Randolph L. Braham (ed.), *The Tragedy of Hungarian Jewry. Essays, Documents, Depositions.* USA: Social Science Monographs and Institute for Holocaust Studies of The City University of New York. Distributed by Columbia University Press, 1986, pp 321-26.
Street, C. J. C.
1923 *Hungary and Democracy.* London: T. Fisher Unwin Ltd.
Szaraz, Gyorgy
1985 "The Jewish Question in Hungary: A Historical Perspective." In Randolph L. Braham and Bela Vago (eds), *The Holocaust in Hungary: Forty Years Later.* USA: Social Science Monographs and Institute for Holocaust Studies of The City University of New York and Institute for Holocaust Studies of the University of Haifa, pp 13-30.
Szenes, Sandor,
1990 " 'Saving People Was Our Main Task...' An Interview with Reverend Jozsef Elias." In Randolph L. Braham (ed.), *Studies on the Holocaust in Hungary.* USA: Social Science Monographs and Institute for Holocaust Studies of The City University of New York, pp 1-64.
Szinai, Miklos and Laszlo Szucs
1965 (eds) *The Confidential Papers of Admiral Horthy.* Budapest: Corvina Press.
1972 (eds) *Bethlen Istvan Titkos Iratai.* [The Confidential Papers of Istvan Bethlen.] Budapest: Kossuth Konyvkiado.
Taylor, A. J. P.
1988 *The Struggle for Mastery in Europe, 1848-1914.* UK: Oxford University Press.
Taylor, Edmond
1963 *The Fall of the Dynasties: The Collapse of the Old Order, 1905-1922.* London: Weidenfeld and Nicolson.
Tokes, Rudolf L.
1984 "The Unwilling Satellite: Questions of Evidence and Interpretation." In Gyorgy Ranki (ed.), *Hungarian History — World History.* Budapest: Akademiai Kiado, pp 289-93.
***Trial of Adolf Eichmann*, Volume III.**
1993 State of Israel, Ministry of Justice. Jerusalem.
Trunk, Isaiah
1972 *Judenrat. The Jewish Councils in eastern Europe Under Nazi Occupation.* New York: The Macmillan Company.
Tuchman, Barbara W.
1982 *Practicing History. Selected Essays.* London: Macmillan.
Ujvari, Peter
1929 (ed.) *Zsido Lexikon* [Jewish Lexicon]. Budapest: n.p. Repr. 1987.
Vago, Bela
1969 "Germany and the Jewish Policy of the Kallay Government." In Randolph L. Braham (ed.), *Hungarian Jewish Studies.* New York: World Federation of Hungarian Jews, pp 183-210.
1970 "Budapest Jewry in the Summer of 1944. Otto Komoly's Diaries." In *Yad Vashem Studies VIII.* Jerusalem: Yad Vashem, pp 81-105.

1974 "The Attitude Toward the Jews as a Criterion of the Left-Right Concept." In Bela Vago and George L. Mosse (eds), *Jews and Non-Jews in eastern Europe 1918-1945*. Jerusalem: Keter Publishing House/John Wiley and Sons, Inc., pp 21-49.

1974a "The Intelligence Aspects of the Joel Brand Mission." In *Yad Vashem Studies X.* Jerusalem: Yad Vashem, pp 111-28.

1977 "The British Government and the Fate of Hungarian Jewry in 1944." In Yisrael Gutman and Efraim Zuroff (eds), *Rescue Attempts During the Holocaust*. Jerusalem: Yad Vashem, pp 205-23.

1983 "The Horthy Offer. A Missed Opportunity for Rescuing Jews in 1944." In Randolph L. Braham (ed.), *Contemporary Views on the Holocaust*. Boston: Kluwer-Nijhoff Publishing, pp 23-45.

1989 "The Reaction to the Nazi Anti-Jewish Policy in East-Central Europe and in the Balkans." In Francois Furet (ed.), *Unanswered Questions. Nazi Germany and the Genocide of the Jews*. New York: Schocken Books, pp 199-234.

Vardy, Steven Bela
1969 "Part 2: 1919-1968 A.D." In *History of the Hungarian Nation*. Astor Park, Florida: Danubian Press, Inc., pp 247-381.

Vargha, Julius De
1911 *Hungary: A Sketch of the Country, Its People and Its Conditions*. Budapest: Printing-Office of the Athenaeum.

Varga, Laszlo
1990 "The Losses of Hungarian Jewry. A Contribution to the Statistical Overview." In Randolph L. Braham (ed.), *Studies on the Holocaust in Hungary*. USA: Social Science Monographs and the Institute for Holocaust Studies of the City University of New York, pp 256-65.

Veghazi, Istvan
1969 "The Role of Jewry in the Economic Life of Hungary." In Randolph L. Braham (ed.) *Hungarian-Jewish Studies*. New York: World Federation of Hungarian Jews, pp 35-84.

Venetianer, Lajos
1922 *A Magyar Zsidosag Tortenete*. [The History of Hungarian Jews.] Budapest: Fovarosi Nyomda RT. Repr. 1986: Budapest, Konyvertekesito Vallalat.

Vida, Marton
1939 (ed.) *ITELJETEK! Nehany Kiragadott Lap A Magyar-Zsido Eletkozosseg Konyvebol*. [JUDGE FOR YOURSELF! Scrapbook of Hungarian-Jewish Co-existence.] Budapest: n.p.

von Lang, Jochen and Claus Sibyll
1983 (eds) *Eichmann Interrogated. Transcripts from the Archives of the Israeli Police*. New York: Farrar, Straus & Giroux.

Wasserstein, Bernard
1988 *Britain and the Jews of Europe, 1939-1945*. Oxford: Institute of Jewish Affairs, London and Oxford University Press.

Weiss, Yehuda
1963 "In Budapest During the War." In *The Massacre of European Jewry: An Anthology*. Kibbutz Merchavia, Israel: World Hashomer Hatzair, pp 319-36.

Wisliceny, Dieter
1945 "Transcript of an Interrogation of Dieter Wisliceny." Pretrial Interrogation Series of the International Military Tribunal at Nuremberg, 15 November 1945. In John Mendelsohn and Donald S. Detwiler (eds), *The Holocaust. Volume 8. Deportation of the Jews to the East: Stettin, 1940, to Hungary, 1944*. New York: Garland Publishing, Inc. (1982), pp 71-101.

1947 "Affidavit by SS *Hauptsturmfuehrer* Dieter Wisliceny on Edmund Veesenmayer and the Deportation of Hungarian Jews." Nuremberg Document NG 1823. In John

Mendelsohn and Donald S. Detwiler (eds), *The Holocaust. Volume 8. Deportation of the Jews to the East: Stettin, 1940, to Hungary, 1944*. New York: Garland Publishing, Inc. (1982), pp 237-39.

Wistrich, Robert S.
1991 *Antisemitism: The Longest Hatred*. London: Thames Methuen.

World Jewish Congress (WJC). Publication no. 10, Statistical Department, WJC. *Hungarian Jewry Before and After the Persecution. IInd Part. Demography of the Israelite Population of Hungary*. Budapest: WJC, 1948.

Wyman, David S.
1985 *The Abandonment of the Jews. America and the Holocaust, 1941-45*. New York: Pantheon Books.
1990 (ed.) *America and the Holocaust. Volume 8: War Refugee Board, Hungary*. New York: Garland Publishing, Inc.

Zuccotti, Susan
1987 *The Italians and the Holocaust: Persecution, Rescue, Survival*. New York: Basic Books, Inc.

ARTICLES

Randolph L. Braham. "The Jewish Question in German-Hungarian Relations During the Kallay Era." *Jewish Social Studies*, Volume XXXIX (1977): 183-208.

Richard Breitman. "American Rescue Activities in Sweden." *Holocaust and Genocide Studies*, Volume 7, No. 2 (1993): 202-215.

Richard Breitman and Shlomo Aronson. "The End of the 'Final Solution?' Nazi Plans to Ransom Jews in 1944." *Central European History*, Volume 25, No. 2 (1993): 177-203.

Charlotte Carr-Gregg. "The Inaction of the Red Cross During the Holocaust: Some Comments on Jean-Claude Favez' Study 'Une Mission Impossible?' " *Menorah*, Volume 3, No. 2 (December 1989): 10-19.

Asher Cohen. "Continuity in Change: Hungary, 19 March 1944." *Jewish Social Studies*, Volume XLVI, No. 2 (Spring 1984): 131-44.

Israel Cohen. "The Jews in Hungary." *The Contemporary Review*, November 1939: 3-11. [CZA 26/441.]

Istvan Deak. "Fun City", review of *Budapest 1900: A Historical Portrait of a City and Its Culture*, by John Lucas. *The New York Review of Books*, 16 March 1989: 21-25.

Istvan Deak. "Survivors." *The New York Review of Books*, 5 March 1992: 43-51.

Istvan Deak. "Holocaust Heroes." *The New York Review of Books*, 5 November 1992: 22-26.

Yehuda Don. "The Economic Effect of Antisemitic Discrimination: Hungarian Anti-Jewish Legislation, 1938-1944." *Jewish Social Studies*, Volume XLVIII (1986): 63-82.

Stuart G. Erdheim. "Could the Allies Have Bombed Auschwitz-Birkenau?" *Holocaust and Genocide Studies*, Volume 11, No. 2 (1997): 129-70.

R. J. W. Evans. "Unwarlike Warriors", review of *Beyond Nationalism: A Social and Political History of the Habsburg Officer Corps 1848-1918*, by Istvan Deak. *The New York Review of Books*, 16 August 1990: 47-50.

Gila Fatran. "The 'Working Group'." (Translated by Naftali Greenwood) *Holocaust and Genocide Studies*, Volume 8, No. 2 (1994): 164-201.

Robert Edwin Herzstein. "Is It Time to Stop Asking Why the West Failed to Save More Jews?" *Holocaust and Genocide Studies*, Volume 12, No. 2 (1998): 326-38.

Meredith Hindley. "Negotiating the Boundary of Unconditional Surrender: The War Refugee Board in Sweden and Nazi Proposals to Ransom Jews, 1944-1945." *Holocaust and Genocide Studies*, Volume 10, No. 1 (1996): 52-77.

Elek Karsai. "Edmund Veesenmayer's Reports to Hitler on Hungary in 1943." *The New Hungarian Quarterly*, Volume V, No. 15 (Autumn 1964): 146-53.

Jacob Katz. "The Uniqueness of Hungarian Jewry." *Forum*, Number 2 (27), 1977, pp 45-53. Jerusalem: World Zionist Organisation, Organisation and Information Department.

Bernard Klein. "The Judenrat." *Jewish Social Studies*, Volume XXII, No. 1 (January 1960): 27-42.

Bernard Klein. "Hungarian Politics and the Jewish Question in the Inter-War Period." *Jewish Social Studies*, Volume XXVIII (1966): 79-98.

Bernard Klein. "Anti-Jewish Demonstrations in Hungarian Universities, 1932-1936: Istvan Bethlen vs Gyula Gombos." *Jewish Social Studies*, Volume XLIV, No. 2 (Spring 1982): 113-24.

Bogdan Krizman. "Austro-Hungarian Diplomacy Before the Collapse of the Empire." *Journal of Contemporary History*, Volume 4, No. 2 (April 1969): 97-115.

Sydney Leperer. "Historical Overview of Antisemitism." *L'Eylah* 31, March 1991: 12-13.

Richard H. Levy. "The Bombing of Auschwitz Revisited: A Critical Analysis." *Holocaust and Genocide Studies*, Volume 10, No. 3 (1996): 267-98.

Zsuzsa Nagy. "The Secret Papers of Istvan Bethlen." *The New Hungarian Quarterly*, Volume XIV, No. 49 (Spring 1973): 171-76.

Gyorgy Ranki. "The Road to German Occupation (Hungary in 1944)." *Acta Historica*, Tome 31 (3-4) (1985): 309-18.

Livia Rothkirchen. "The Slovak Enigma: A Reassessment of the Halt to the Deportations." *East Central Europe*, 10 (1983): 3-13.

Robert Rozett. "Aliya from Hungary and the Struggle for Certificates, 1943-1944." *Studies in Zionism*, Volume 8, No. 1 (1987): 83-98.

Laszlo Varadi. "The Hungarian Jewry in the Twentieth Century." *Acta Historica*, Tome 31 (3-4) (1985): 409-21.

INDEX

Page numbers in italics (e.g. *64*) refer to illustrations.
Page numbers in bold type (e.g. **66–70**) indicate the major discussion of a topic.
Notes which contain more than bibliographical references are indexed, in the following form:
    222n326 indicates Note 326 on page 222
    263(nn70, 71, 80, 88) indicates Notes 70, 71, 80 and 88 on page 263
    12 Ropirat (12 Tracts) (Antisemitic journal), 15, 17–18